INDIAN POLITICS
Constitutional Foundations and Institutional Functioning

THIRD EDITION

M.P. SINGH
Formerly Professor
Department of Political Science
University of Delhi

REKHA SAXENA
Professor
Department of Political Science
University of Delhi

PHI Learning Private Limited
Delhi-110092
2025

In fond memory of ***Shri Asoke K. Ghosh*** *(October 1942 – February 2024), Founder Chairman and Managing Director of PHI Learning, whose vision endlessly inspires.*

The Legacy Continues....

Published by Pushpita Ghosh, PHI Learning Private Limited, Rimjhim House, 111, Patparganj Industrial Estate, Delhi-110092 and Printed by Syndicate Binders, A-20, Hosiery Complex, Noida, Phase-II Extension, Noida-201305 (N.C.R. Delhi).

₹895.00

INDIAN POLITICS: Constitutional Foundations and Institutional Functioning
Third Edition
M.P. Singh and Rekha Saxena

ISBN-978-81-946851-2-8 (Print Book)
ISBN-978-81-946851-3-5 (e-Book)

Dedicated
to
Our Students

Contents

Preface

We are delighted to offer the third edition of our book on recurrent demand of readers and the publisher despite our current preoccupations. Since 2011, when the second edition was published, Indian Politics and Comparative Politics have witnessed very significant changes almost transforming the parameters of the political universe. Among these are the rise of Rightwing nationalism in India and practically all over the world, with the possible or at least partial exception of Canada and Australia. It has been caused by the rise of identity politics after the end of the Cold War and the global financial crisis in the citadels of metropolitan capitalism in 2008. These, especially the latter, have had impact in some degree globally, triggering 'slowbalisation' or de-globalisation, economic protectionism, trade war, anti-immigration backlash, and ethnic polarisation. These trends have caused the unravelling of liberal national as well as global political orders.

In India, the party system fragmentation evident since the 1989 general elections and unstable or dysfunctional federal coalition governments since then came to be contained by the rise of the Hindu Right Bharatiya Janata Party (BJP). This has been seen by some sections with alarm as heralding majoritarian and authoritarian turn in India's liberal democracy marked by communal polarisation, decline of institutions, neglect of or pressures on independent regulatory authorities, including the judiciary, economic downturn, etc. We do not deny; however, a deeper and objective assessment of the situation would appear to suggest that we cannot miss the tendencies and trends of greater degree of liberalisation and constitutionalisation of the BJP and the Rashtriya Swayamsevak Sangh (RSS) evident in the pronouncements and ideological reorientations of both since the late 1970s. In the early 1970s, the Bharatiya Jana Sangh joined the Jayaprakash Naryan anti-corruption and anti-authoritarian movement, and subsequently, merged with the Janata Party in 1977 to become a mainstream political force. After the premature fall of the

Janata party government in July 1979, the Jana Sangh constituent of the Janata Party like other constituents formed a separate party, BJP, with 'Gandhian Socialism' as its programme of action which incrementally tended to shift to a combination of business liberalism mixed with welfarism. This trend continued in the period of gradual electoral rise of BJP during the 1980s and 1990s. And this process of mainstreaming of the 'cultural nationalism' and inclusive 'Hindutva' of the BJP and RSS gathered a greater momentum when the BJP led by Narendra Modi won a single-party majority after a long gap of three decades in 2014 and was re-elected with greater majority in 2019. The reorientations in the BJP and the RSS evident during these more recent decades are yet to be objectively studied and analysed. A beginning is made in case of the RSS by Walter Anderson and Shridhar D. Damle (The RSS: A View to the Inside, New Delhi: Viking, 2018). Such a study of the New BJP is still awaited. This phenomenon is comparable to the liberalistation and constitutionalisation of the communist parties in the eras of Nehru and Indira Gandhi.

The third edition of Indian Politics is a thoroughly revised and updated version of our exceptionally comprehensive and popular standard text in Indian political studies, combining a study of political institutions, political sociology, and political economy.

We welcome comments and critiques by our readers.

M.P. Singh
Rekha Saxena

Preface to the First Edition

Traditional India of the 18th Century began to undergo the throes of neo-traditional, post-Mughal changes with the emergence of rebellious Maratha, Sikh, Jat, and Afghan states while the Rajput and Nababi riyasats became independent of Mughal overlordship even without raising banners of revolt. India in the 19th Century took a turn towards colonial modernity with paradigmatic shifts in politico-economic and socio-cultural spheres that accelerated in the 19th and 20th centuries and the onset of the 21st century. The changes traversed include transition from feudalism to colonialism, to nationalism, to post-colonialism, to post-modernism, in mixed and patchy ways.

Around the turn of the 20th Century, the major paradigms of the State and national and global civil societies were in for a new and qualitatively different transformation that is only partially visible at the beginning of the 21st Century. We are now witnessing the Indian Nation-State coming to terms with the triple challenges of what we call the 'double movements' of the emerging regimes of federalism and neoliberal as well as State capitalism. Federalization, supra-national regional integration, and globalization are the major facets of new politics in India. It is a fascinating scenario that we have been interpreting and explaining to the contemporary generation of Indian and overseas students, in the courses on Indian politics at the University of Delhi in the recent decades.

Writing of this book was prompted by a felt need of a comprehensive standard textbook in the field of Indian government and politics, taking into account the great transformation that has come about in the polity, civil society, and the political economy across the world in the new millennium. Most standard textbooks in this area are awefully dated. Some edited books of readings that came up in the meantime do not present a holistic and integrated account of the new developments.

In this book, we have tried to fill in a major gap in the existing systematic social-scientific analysis of India. The novelty of this book is not only in terms of an uptodate analysis of the themes discussed but also in bringing to bear new conceptual and theoretical sensitivities that are becoming part and parcel of contemporary political analysis. The major organizing analytical frameworks that we employ in this book are evident from three major parts dealing with the State and the Government, the civil society, and the political economy of development. In each of these parts, the contemporary trends and patterns straddle both the new and the old, the continuities and the changes. The theoretical perspectives of new institutionalism, with renewed emphasis on organization and good governance, civil society revival and generation, democratic developmental state adapting to neoliberal capitalism, are employed to offer explanation of the unfolding scenario of politics in India today and in the foreseeable future. Broadly speaking, we look at the new trends through the prisms of democratization, multicultural secularization, federalization, and globalization. The legacy of the democratic developmental State of India is called upon to come to terms with the panoply of post-modernist critiques as diverse as feminism, ecologism, *dalit-bahujan critique*, cultural nationalism, and new social movements.

The book is intended as a standard text for the undergraduate and postgraduate students of political science. Besides, it will also serve the purpose of those appearing for the civil services examinations.

We are thankful to the political scientists Douglas Verney, Bidyut Chakrabarty and Pralaya Kanungo for their encouragement and advice. The latter two took interest in reading the manuscript and also offered a few suggestions. We also wish to thank the editorial and production team of the Publishers, Prentice-Hall of India for their careful processing of the manuscript. Mohan Dayal Rijhwani and V.K. Ohri have been our standard references for legal queries and have been helpful in providing legal documentation when needed.

This work would not have been possible without the encouragement and support of our family members and friends. M.P. Singh would like to pay his tribute to his late wife Munni Singh and thank his scions Sunil and Sangeeta Singh, Rajesh Kumar and Vijaylaxmi Nanda, Neeraj and Seema Sinha, Dwarka and Neeta Rai, and Neeraj and Sunita Singh and their kids. Rekha Saxena would like to express her gratitude to late Prof. M.M. Sankhdher and Mrs. Mandakini Sankhdher for their kindness and help. She would also like to thank her uncle R.B. Saxena and his family, sister Renu and brother-in-law Shailesh Srivastava, brother Deepak and his late wife Anuradha, and nephews Abhishek, Shashank, and Rishabh for their affection and support. Further, she would like to pay homage to the memories of her late parents Ram Babu and Asha Saxena.

M.P. Singh
Rekha Saxena

List of Cases

A.K. Gopalan v. *State of Madras, 168*
Almitra Patel v. *Union of India, 176*
Ashoka Kumar Thakur v. *Union of India and others, 36*
Association of Unified Tele Services Providers & Others v. Union of India, SC, 2014, 109

BALCO Employees Union v. *Union of India, 175*
Blitz case, *Keshavram Reddy* v. *Nafisul Hasan and the State of UP, 121*

Center for Public Interest Litigation v. *Union of India, 176*
CITU v. *Union of India, 176*

D.C. Wadhwa v. *State of Bihar, 125*
Delhi Science Forum v. *Union of India, 176*

Election Commission of India v. *Union of India & others, 277*

Golak Nath v. *State of Punjab, 170, 173*

Hargovind Pant v. *Raghukul Tilak and others, 208*
HPCL-BPCL v. *Union of India, 176*

I.C. Golaknath v. State of Punjab, 3
Indira Gandhi v. *Raj Narain, 172, 173*

Chapter 1

Indian Model of Constitutionalism

Quasi-Federal, Federal to Quasi-Confederal?

INTRODUCTION

This book seeks to understand and explain the contemporary politics in India in terms of its constitutional design and developmental vision within the context of its evolving civil society. We set out to interpret politics *within* India leaving out non-political and external domains of politics *among* nations to experts in other sub-fields. We do not, however, abandon the agenda of reforms and transformation within the liberal democratic parameter subsuming the institutions of government, state, civil society, and political economy so far as they relate to the critical and creative enterprise of politics. The dominant running themes of this work are the paradigmatic shifts (a) from a quasi-federal parliamentary model of government to a federal denouement, (b) from the state to the civil society, and (c) from a socialistic, nationally protectionist economic policy regime to one of business liberalism or neo-liberal policy regime of privatization and globalism. Since much of this transformation is marked by a greater degree of continuity than in post-communist Eurasia and East Asia, contemporary India gives the impression of muddling through a landscape enveloped in winter fog. The changes in Indian politics and economy may, therefore, appear at first glance to be a slide from order to chaos or shifts without arrival at a new paradigm. We hope the analysis presented in this book will make the transformation somewhat more comprehensible and understandable. And since to know is to act, we can probably pretend to be in better control of our political destiny.

THE CONSTITUTIONAL GENEALOGY

Every political system is embedded in its own contemporary dilemmas and historical and cultural and geographical matrices. Simultaneously, it is also a part of a broader genealogy of models of comparative government and politics. In terms of models of contemporary comparative constitutionalism, India belongs to the genealogy of parliamentary–federal political system, the first examples of which go back to Canada (1867) and Australia (1901). These constitutional experiments that combined the classical British parliamentary system and the classical American federal system sought to formulate a framework of government for a country that valued the principle of unitary government by way of parliamentary supremacy, but at the same time, wished to federally accommodate a wide range of cultural and regional diversities. Douglas V. Verney has observed that the combination of parliamentarism and federalism in these countries has faced problems in their satisfactory conciliation, as the two principles are, in parts, contradictory—one premised on centralization and the other on decentralization, but "in practice, parliamentary federations have succeeded. This may be because the peoples involved have tended to be pragmatic".[1]

At another place, we can delineate two models of republican constitutionalism, namely, evolutionary and revolutionary. The Westminster and the White British Commonwealth—Canada, Australia, and New Zealand—belong to the former, while the United States and France belong to the latter. And, even the American Revolution and the French Revolution themselves legated two models of modern states—the former produced a federal national state and the latter a unitary monolingual nation state. The transformation from colony to nation in the White Commonwealth was entirely gradual and evolutionary so much so that even their Constitutions were products of the British Parliament, and the symbolic myth of the Crown connection is still nominally maintained.

In the revolutionary republican model, the Constitution and its structure leave little doubt about the source and locus of sovereignty in the system. For example, the Constitution of the United States begins with the ringing declaration of popular sovereignty in the Preamble: "We, the people of the United States ..." The basic structure of the Constitution then proceeds to set up a government based on the principle of horizontally separate and coequal organs of the federal government and vertically divided powers between federal and state governments. Power is so systematically checked by power that some say it is difficult to pinpoint the exact location of sovereignty in the US government, although the courts do end up having a final word of arbitration and adjudication. The US constitutional theory sought to chart out a course different from the British constitutional theory. The English Civil War between the army of the Crown and that of the Parliament resulted in the victory of the latter, and the doctrine of royal absolutism was simply exchanged for parliamentary sovereignty gradually tempered by rule of law and constitutional conventions, as classically explicated by Albert V. Dicey (1885). Thus, the US constitutional theory, with its system of institutional checks and balances, is contrary to the classical modern British system, where parliamentary sovereignty is neither subject to judicial review nor to royal veto. However, parliamentary federal systems in Canada and Australia do allow judicial review of parliamentary enactments and executive orders.

Moreover, revolutionary republican constitutionalism in France and Switzerland found expression in the power of the Parliament in the former and the direct democratic institutions of popular initiative and referendum in the latter. It was essentially an Assembly form of government in France until the Fourth Republic in which the National Assembly could make and unmake governments at whim. The Fifth Republic incorporated measures to curtail the powers of the Assembly by combining parliamentary system with an executive presidency, in which a Prime Minister elected by the Parliament is countervailed by a popularly elected President. In Switzerland, the people in constitutionally specified number can initiate law-making or reject government proposals in a referendum.

India does not exactly fit into either the evolutionary or revolutionary model of constitutionalism. For, even though the transfer of power in India in 1947 was through an Act of British Parliament, it was preceded by a long and ideologically deep and differentiated nationalist movement whose dominant stream since the 1920s used mainly extra-constitutional, though non-violent, methods of agitation. Thus, even though the transfer of power largely in India was a legal tender, the Constitution of India makes an affirmation of popular sovereignty in its Preamble: "We, the people of India…" Thus, the Indian model of constitutionalism is mixed in the sense of the continuity of transferred constitutional and legal authority as well as invocation of popular sovereignty.

THE INDIAN CONSTITUTIONAL THEORY

What are the contours of Indian constitutionalism or constitutional theory that independent India opted for and how has it developed in practice since the commencement of the Constitution? The answer to these questions may be explored at the levels of the laws and of institutions established under the Constitution. The Indian legal system comprises at least three kinds of laws. These are positive laws based on the Constitution and legislative statutes, customary laws flowing from tradition—tribal or religion-based personal and family laws, and case laws or constitutional laws as laid down by the judiciary. Article 13 (3)(a) of the Constitution of India defines 'law' as inclusive of 'any ordinance, order, bye-law, rule, regulation, notification, custom or usage having in the territory of India the force of law...' The 24th Amendment (1971) added to this Article a new clause [Article 13 (4)], which sought to explicitly exclude constitutional amendments from the definition of law in reaction to the Supreme Court judgement in *I.C. Golaknath v. State of Punjab* (1967), which had ruled that under Article 13, the Parliament could not pass any law (as well as any amendment) curtailing fundamental rights as the makers had intended such rights in an image of permanence akin to natural rights. Hence, the Indira

Gandhi government added to Article 13 the stipulation that 'Nothing in this Article shall apply to any amendment to this Constitution made under Article 368.' The Supreme Court in *Keshavananda Bharat v. State of Kerala* (1973) retreated to concede that the Parliament or aggregate legislature could amend any part of the Constitution including the fundamental rights, but in doing so, it cannot extend the amending power to alter or destroy 'the basic structure' or 'essential features' of the Constitution or rewrite the Constitution.

India belongs to the common law system prevalent in the Anglo-Saxon North America and British Commonwealth democracies of Canada, Australia, and New Zealand rather than the civil or Roman law system prevalent in continental European democracies and Latin American countries. The former is constitutional-court-centric system of law, while the latter is legislature-centric legal system. In other words, the former is predicated on judicial supremacy flowing from the American Revolution (1765–1783), the US federal Constitution (1787), *The Federalist* (1887), and the American constitutional law (e.g., *Marbury v. Madison*, 5 U.S. 137), while the latter is premised on parliamentary sovereignty flowing from the French Revolution (1789–1799) and social democratic movements and parties in Europe.

Rule of Law

The term rule of law, due process of law and constitutionalism are close kins. The first two connote equality of law in conception and application in a country. The third one refers to the political Constitution under which a government works and it also means that how a government is limited and regulated by a Constitution. Albert V. Dicey's classic formulation of rule of law is specific to the British legal tradition, and means in the words of Dicey as follows:

1. A person can be punished only for a clear breach of law;
2. No Briton is above law, and whatever one's rank or position, one is subject to the common law of the realm and amenable to ordinary courts (not to special administrative law courts where the officers of the state enjoy special sanction and protection as in continental Europe, especially France with its tradition of *droit administratif*); and
3. The general rules of constitutional law stem from ordinary law of the land instead of resulting from the Constitution as in continental Europe.[2]

In Dicey's interpretation, British constitutionalism is a harmonious construction based on an amalgamation of three constituent elements: parliamentary sovereignty, rule of law, and conventions of the Constitution regarding executive prerogatives and parliamentary privileges. The first two constitute the law of the unwritten Constitution enforceable by ordinary courts of law, and the third, forms part of the constitutional morality or understanding that is habitually followed and, in the United Kingdom, is beyond the courts of law. (We must hasten to add that this is not true of Canada and India, where the conventions of the Constitution are established precedents, which in case of dispute, the courts will uphold.) The three elements together represent a hierarchy of values making the will of the House of Commons, and ultimately the will of the people, supreme.[3]

This concept of the rule of law was inherited by India from the tradition of the British rule only in parts. For example, we do have equality before law and the system of common or regular courts. Yet the pre-British tradition of cumulative inequalities in caste- and community-divided Indian society prompted the makers of the Constitution to import the American system of constitutionally entrenched fundamental rights. Moreover, in the Indian Constitution parliamentary sovereignty was also federally divided between the national Parliament and the state legislatures. In fact, the charter of fundamental rights and a long written Constitution that sought to leave little scope for conventions of the Constitution. This put serious limitations on parliamentary supremacy within the institutional framework of the government. Beyond it, the Constitution made the will of "We, the people of India…" ultimately supreme.

Moreover, it is important to note different manifestations of the theory of separation of powers in comparative constitutional discourses. British constitutionalism is largely based on the fusion of apex legislative, executive, and judicial powers in the Parliament. The United States used separation of powers among the three governmental organs to promote checks and balances to checkmate the "tyranny of majority", whereas the Commonwealth parliamentary federations like Canada and India partly rely on fusion of powers (between Parliament and Cabinet) and partly on separation of powers (in making judiciary separate and independent). France, with its system of administrative law (*droit administratif*), denying ordinary court's jurisdiction over cases involving agents of the states, only pays a lip service to *separation des pouvoirs* and arms the government with the power to subordinate the judges.

The general tendency of commentators is to argue that a fuller growth of the culture of rule of law and constitutionalism in India is hampered by feudal and colonial history and the cumulative inequalities of the caste and community systems. However, N.R. Madhava Menon argues, though not in an entirely persuasive way, that for the Indian culture shaped in the philosophy of *dharma*, "rule of law" is not an alien concept. It is innate in the Indian ethos and tradition.[4] Menon's contention is open to dispute in view of the hierarchical unequal and exploitative aspects of the Indian tradition, yet the complexity and multilayered structure of this tradition also makes it possible to find at least some strands of thought in India's past that invoke universal humanistic ideas like Vedic idealism, Asoka's *dhamma, bhakti and sufi* saints, etc. A selective use of these aspects by modern reformers thus makes the Indian tradition pliable.

Indian Constitution as a document has generally been interpreted as a quintessential liberal document. Granville Austin, for example, is highly appreciative of India's choice of constitutional principles and values but also the method of making of the Constitution through liberal democratic consensus and accommodation. According to Austin, the Indian Constitution rejected the methods adopted by China and Russia and aimed at the tripartite goal of national unity, democracy and social revolution as three distinct strands interwoven into a "seamless web".[5] This line of interpretation would appear to facilitate the emergence of the modern culture of constitutionalism in India.

A somewhat different interpretative note on Indian constitutionalism is struck by Uday S. Mehta. To quote him:

> Democratic Constitutions like the Indian Constitution expressly eschew the absolutism that is featured in Hobbes' thought. However, that fact does not by itself settle the question of whether such Constitutions can—given their commitments to unity and social uplift—secure a principled and practical distinction with the form of power, Hobbes advocates. Notwithstanding the often-touted liberal credentials of figures such as Nehru and Rajendra Prasad, Hobbes may be the largely unacknowledged mentor of Indian constitutionalism.[6]

Mehta substantiates his contention by pointing to the preference for a strong central power in the Indian Constitution by the readiness to allow the state to impose 'reasonable restrictions' on the fundamental rights in the interest of public order, security and defence, national unity, public morality, public interest, etc. and limits the autonomy of the federating states for the sake of national development and defence. Besides, during three kinds of constitutionally contemplated emergencies, the federal structure is particularly transformed into a unitary set-up. In addition, the objective of social and economic transformation often also requires a strong state action. Mehta compares the Indian freedom struggle with the French and American revolutions as well to illustrate his point. The Indian approach to social revolution and constitution-making is contrasted from the American approach and is found somewhat closer, if not exactly identical with the French approach. Since the Indian freedom struggle never acquired the revolutionary proportions of the French Revolution, there were obviously no Jacobin absolutists in the Indian political experiment. However, in terms of their mindset, Indian nationalists appear to be more akin to the mindset of the writers of *The Federalist* (1787) in the USA.

The Constituent Assembly of India never displays the suspicion of *The Federalist* against absolute political power. Neither do we find the attempt in the Indian Constitution to systematically checkmate power by countervailing power by the application of the principles of separation of powers and checks and balances as in the American Constitution. Nevertheless, despite the brilliance of Mehta's argument, it is difficult not to feel that his argument is overstated. This is because the ideology of the Indian nationalist movement and its manifestation in the Constitution of India is characteristically one of moderation, balance, reconciliation and avoidance of extremes. This approach is not only ingrained in the Indian Constitution but also broadly informed its practice in the eight decades since its commencement.

The concept of the rule of law is fundamental to any discussion of a legal or constitutional system. In an interesting exploration of post-colonial legality, Upendra Baxi delves into colonial legal systems in the Third World and outlines three broad types represented by Mozambique on the one hand and India on the other with the middle space filled by "settler colonialism" in many parts of Africa. Mozambique represented a case of complete Portuguese metropolitan domination and determination of the legal system of Mozambique. At the other end of the spectrum, lay the subcontinent of India where "toleration and at times grudging indifference to civilizational and cultural traditions of the colonized, animated by the exigencies of empire-building, entailed recognition of indigenous legal traditions. The Hindu and the Muslim law as practiced for centuries in India required (so tied were these bodies of law to land, forms of property, religion, and culture) sustained recognition in law, policy, and administration. Colonial mediation, of course, results in hybrid formations now known as Anglo-Hindu and Anglo-Muslim law (Derrett). And protection of "personal" (religious/customary) law systems thereby became typical stratagems of "divide and rule" practices of communalization of governance and politics".[7]

In the middle zones between the two foregoing extremes, the colonial regimes operated with mixed legal systems comprising Western legal framework and the African customary law including the institution of chieftainship.

Analysing the distinctiveness of the rule of law in India, Upendra Baxi[8] argues that it provides significant revisions of the liberal conceptions of rights. In his opinion, the Indian rule of law normatively arms the citizens with a sword of fundamental rights against the state domination on the one hand as well as with a shield of directive principles of state policy that empowers progressive state intervention in civil society. Finally, Baxi highlights the constructive leadership of the Supreme Court in the development of new dimension of rule of law by way of social action litigation or public interest litigation. The most important contribution of this extension of the rule of law may be seen in

> the fashioning of new ways of judicial enunciation of human rights, a complex affair in which the Supreme Court especially brings back to life rights deliberatively excluded by the Constitution makers (such as the right to speedy trial), creates some component rights to those enunciated by the constitutional text (such as the right to livelihood, privacy, education and literacy, health and environment), re-writing the Constitution by way of invention of new rights (such as right to information, immunity from practices of corrupt governance, rights to constitutional secularism, right to compensation, rehabilitation, and resettlement for violated populations).[9]

Our exploration of the nature of Indian constitutionalism needs to be extended to the plane of governmental institutions established under the Constitution. A survey of the institutional terrain of governments in India presents a thick network of institutions pertaining to the federal, regional and local self-governments besides the set of public authorities created under parliamentary as well as legislative laws.

THE BROADER MODEL OF DEMOCRATIC GOVERNANCE

The implicit constitutional theory of India that underlies the analysis presented in this book may be shown (Figure 1.1) as follows:

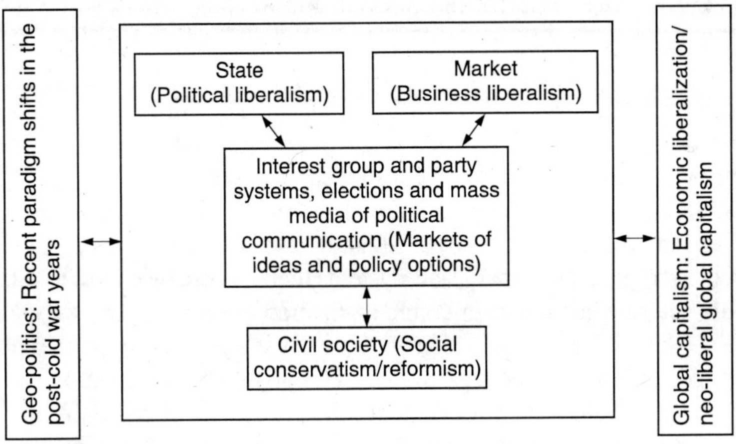

Figure 1.1 Paradigmatic shift to a structural adjustment: from State to market and civil society in India.

The three constituent structures of the Indian political system discussed here are the state, the market and the civil society. These three entities are marked by considerable structural differentiation and functional specialization within their own spheres. Each domain is mutually demarcated and endowed with a certain degree of autonomy, even though they are mutually interactional and interdependent. The State enjoys a certain degree of preeminence among them by virtue of its sovereign regulatory role over the market and the civil society. The interrelationships between the state, market and civil society are intermediated by three crucial infrastructures of the interest groups system, party system, and the media of mass communication. We would set out by sketching the ideal-type notions of state, market and civil society as well as infrastructural linkage mechanisms of interest groups, political parties, and media. The state is the expression of the sovereignty of the people and is democratically constituted through the process of elections.

In the arenas of party politics and mass media, ideas, interests, and identities compete with each other for wider acceptance by the society and the market. The economic market of capitalism is premised on the notion of consumers' sovereignty in the same way as the political market of democracy is based on voters' sovereignty and freedom to form associations and propagate competing interests and policies. Similarly, the media is an open market for competition of ideas and free flow of information. Political parties and the media are the most vital links between the State and the civil society. In liberal political theory, political parties and media are considered parts of the civil society, albeit subject to state regulation, whereas in Marxist theory they turn into parts of "ideological State apparatus."

Elections determine which party or group of parties will form the government and thus use the power of the state for regulating the civil society as well as the market. In contemporary liberal democracies, parties must win democratic legitimacy which includes electoral support as well as support of the non-state organized corporate sector. This paradox of capitalist democracy "manifests itself in the fact that if parties want to gain or retain the power of office, they have to secure the trust of private investors and of the masses simultaneously"[10].

Figure 1.1 depicts the interface between the state, market, and civil society in the Indian context. Indian federal national state occupies the space between the two polarities, namely, geopolitics on the left side and the neo-liberal global capitalism on the right side. The concerns of external relations and internal economic management of India must be manoeuvred between these two parameters of geo-politics and global capitalism.

This book is primarily concerned with politics *within* the Indian nation rather than politics *among* nations. Yet the importance of external dimension of the Indian political system cannot be gainsaid. Broadly speaking, India has had to deal with external affairs under varying kinds of geopolitical configurations. For four decades after independence, India tried to cope with a bipolar world order dominated by two superpowers—the capitalist USA and the socialist USSR—that emerged in the post--World War-II period through a policy of non-alignment and an inward-looking, import-substituting strategy of national economic development aimed at self-reliance and "socialistic pattern of society". Non-alignment was of no practical help in dealing with India's regional problems with Pakistan and China. India had wars with Pakistan over Jammu and Kashmir in 1947 and 1965. The first was ended by the UN intervention, and the latter by the Soviet intermediation. Yet the Kashmir dispute remains unsettled. India's intervention in the civil war in Pakistan between the eastern and western parts of the country in 1971 brought into existence the new state of independent Bangladesh. It was swift and decisive, and made India the dominant power in South Asia. The Sino-India war over border disputes occurred in 1962. In humiliating retreat in face of the Chinese aggression, India sought American help that promptly began to arrive. It raised the question whether India was really nonaligned. But then India had also maintained a very close relations with the USSR, and subsequently moved more close to the Soviets than the Americans. The pretence of non-alignment was still maintained.

With the collapse of the USSR and the disintegration of the socialist bloc by the end of the 1980s and the termination of the Cold War between the capitalist and the socialist blocs, non-alignment's self-evident relevance for the newly emergent states of Asia and Africa in quest of some autonomous space between the two major power blocs of the world came to be questioned. By around the same time, Indian socialist pattern of development with a dominant state sector of the economy vis-à-vis the private sector also ran into deep economic crisis. In the unipolar world dominated by the single hegemon, the USA and with the economic failure of the state sector at home, India made major paradigm shifts to adapt to the new brave world. These were signalled in the economic reforms with accent on liberalization, in 1991, and the Indo-US civilian nuclear deal signed in 2005 that made India and the USA strategic partners, if not exactly allies. The economically rising India rapidly became a major power regionally and globally in the fast emerging multipolar world from a brief moment of unipolarity.

LEVELS OF DEMOCRATIC ARCHITECTURE AND THE INDIAN PRAXIS

The working of a democratic system operates on at least four different levels: (a) ideology, (b) institutions, (c) civil society, and (d) culture.[11] Ideology is a framework of normative values and beliefs about democracy and its correlated market structures. Democracy preceded capitalism as a system. Paradoxically, democracy and capitalism may appear to be contradictory to each other, but in contemporary history it is also a fact that one is not found to exist without the other. Democracy so far has survived only in combination with a market economy. In a non-capitalist economy, democracy has not survived for long. Yet, it is also true that "liberalism has conspired with the imperatives of the capitalist economy to erode all collective bodies standing between the state and the individual save one: the capitalist corporation."[12] The contemporary liberal democracies and capitalist economies still continue to coexist, but their continuation is not entirely unproblematic for reasons inherent in both the structures of capitalism and state. The promise of "post-liberal democracy" is the affirmation of "the traditional democratic forms of representative democracy and individual liberty and proposes novel forms of social power independent of the State; namely, democratically accountable, chartered freedoms in community and work. These aspects of economic democracy, including the democratic control of investment and production, are not desirable in their own right, they are also an increasingly necessary condition for the viability of democratic control of governments."[13]

The level of institutions includes the framework of laws and Constitution, party system, and market structures. Institutions are less likely to change as compared to ideologies in response to changing political atmospherics. The Constitution of India is one of the very few post-World War-II Constitutions in the Afro-Asian world to survive until and beyond the turn of the century. Japan and Sri Lanka (with one major parametric alteration from parliamentarism to executive presidency) are probably the only other exceptions. Indian party system, of course, has made a transition from one-party dominance to a multi-party configuration since the 1989 Lok Sabha elections. But the Constitution has remained unchanged. The Indian print media is one of the most developed in this part of the world and electronic media has undergone a considerable expansion since the early 1990s.

The civil society represents the realms of secondary groups and associations separate from the state. These structures grow even more slowly than political institutions. The weakness of the civil society in India has been a recurrent theme in political analysis. Since the 1990s, there has been a conscious effort to promote civil society revival in India in the wake of the failings of the state, which was earlier considered the prime mover of India's modernization.

Political culture is the sum of values, attitudes and opinions that underlie the political institutions. "Just as democratic institutions rest on a healthy civil society, civil society in turn has precursors and pre-conditions at the level of culture. Culture can be defined as a rational, ethnical habit passed on through tradition; although it is malleable and can be affected by developments in the three upper levels, it tends to change the most slowly of all."[14] The contemporary political culture of India is a product of four "cultural revolutions" and acculturative evolutions: (a) Aryan–Dravidian (and we may add Mongoloid) racial aggregations and admixtures; (b) Vedic or Brahmanical foundational worldview and Jain, Buddhist, Bhakti, Sikh sects and a variety of neo-Hindu reform movements; (c) Hindu–Muslim encounter and co-existence; and (d) Indo-European contact and British colonial conquest of India, and the beginning of Indian modernity and national Independence.[15] This evolutionary historiography of Indian national culture underlines its composite pluralism, which, in more recent times, is usually referred to as multiculturalism.[16] This special version of Indian multiculturalism is the foundation of the contemporary plural and federal nationalism of India.

India witnessed the political and electoral rise of Hindutva nationalism (inspired by V.D. Savarkar's *Hindutva*, first published in 1923) during the 1980s and 1990s. It transpired in the wake of the joining of the anti-Congress Jayaprakash Narayan Movement by the Bharatiya Jana Sangha (BJS) and the Rashtriya Swayamsevak Sangh (RSS); the imposition of internal national emergency on June 25, 1975, by the Indira Gandhi government in the early 1970s; the merger of the BJS into the Janata Party in 1977; the exit of BJS elements from Janata Party in 1980 and formation of the Bharatiya Janata Party (BJP) after the premature collapse of its government in 1979; the Ram *Rath Yatra* from Somanath to Ayodhya led by L.K. Advani (September–October 1990) for construction of a Ram temple in Ayodhya on the site of the Babri mosque allegedly built on the original Ram temple there during the reign of the Mughal ruler Babar; and the demolition of the mosque by an irate Hindu mob on December 6, 1992. Parallel to this Hindu mobilisation and electoral rise of the BJP and its 'cultural wing RSS in major north and west Indian states and finally at the Center under the then Prime Minister, Atal Bihari Vajpayee, and later, the Prime Minister, Narendra Damodardas Modi, an interesting phenomenon of liberalization and constitutionalization of the BJP and RSS has occurred. It may not be out of place to hypothesize that just as the then Prime Minister, Nehru may be credited to have facilitated the liberalization and constitutionalization of the communist movement and parties in India, JP, Vajpayee, and Modi may well have played a similar role in bringing the Hindu Right wing parties and organizations into the mainstream democratic and constitutional politics in the country.

India's multicultural national identity and federal democracy are not only historically and contemporaneously constitutive of each other but also symbiotically sustaining and evolving. Indian civic nationalism can be better hermeneutically interpreted through multicultural rather than ethnic national lenses. Political and fiscal parliamentary federal arrangements are particularly appropriate for a country of India's subcontinental cultural diversities and socio-economic and regional disparities. India has found it easier to accommodate linguistic identities than religious communalism, particularly in the colonial and neo-colonial contexts. It is notable that the Indian approach to politics and religion is rather unique. For, the state in India is secular in terms of grant of religious freedoms, but the Constitution prompts the state to strive for a common civil code analogous to a common criminal code introduced since 1861 by the British Raj for all citizens irrespective of religious affiliation. Thus, Indian secular state, in the sense of equal treatment without abandoning the power of legislating positive reforms in religious communities in the country, is *evolutionary* in its developmental perspective rather than *revolutionary* like the secular states in the USA and France that put a wall of separation between the state and church/religion.

As in case of contemporary democracies in general, in India as well, it can be said that there is a workable consensus at the level of ideology and institutions. The challenges that Indian democracy faces are mainly at the level of civil society and culture. India's problem today is not of democratic initiation, nor of democratic restoration, but of democratic consolidation. Not that everything is well with India at the levels of ideologies and institutions. Religious fundamentalism is arguably the most serious threat to democracy, among others. And if India is not exactly a failed state in the ultimate analysis, failings of the institutions of the state and market are self-evident in the crisis of governability and service delivery, economic scams and market manipulation, corruption and criminalization of politics, malnutrition and starvation, if not outright famine, etc. Yet the challenge of building up a vibrant civil society and transforming the culture of inequality and caste/class/gender exploitation is a more formidable and long-term challenge before the contemporary Indian democracy. As Amartya Sen has often emphasized, India happens to be a country with the largest number of illiterates in the world today. And while Indian elite health services are of an international standard, attracting what is being called "medical tourism", from the West included, the elementary health care is not available to millions of masses, and even middle classes are finding the increasing health costs prohibitive and distressing.

Democracy is a Prometheus that was born free but finds itself bound in ever-growing fetters. It is only by the force of habit that we continue to call India a liberal democracy. Illiberal features of India's liberal democracy have been increasing. Conceptually self-conscious interpreters of Indian democracy, who call it an 'electoral democracy', seem to imply that India has, with a reasonable degree of promise, institutionalized free and fair elections, thanks to the Election Commission of India, the federal judiciary, and the national media. The unstated premise is that other more refined aspects of democracy would follow in due course.

India's tryst with democratic destiny began with falling "in love with the idea of concrete", symbolized by the construction of "massive dams like that at Hirakud on Orissa's Mahanadi river and at Bhakhara Nangal in Punjab."[17] That love affair continues, if now in the midst of contested social and ecological legitimacy, stirred up by Narmada Bachao Andolan over the Sardar Sarovar Dam. Ironically, India's democracy has, for reasons far beyond the showpiece dams, evolved into what may be called a "dammed democracy". One after another, issues have been taken out of the arena of party politics, if not formally, at least substantively. That is why an empirically inclined political scientist may like to call India a "limiting case" democracy, or a Weberian-minded social interpretor, an "ideal type" electoral democracy.

Foreign policy the world over is generally regarded as a bi- or multi-partisan affair. Changes in this domain are dictated more by geopolitical factors than national choice. If formal nonalignment in India turned into an informal alignment with the Soviet Union earlier, and has subsequently turned into an informal alignment with the United States of America and others, it was largely due to post-Cold War geopolitical changes since the 1990s. This strategic shift, which makes India less than an ally and more than a partner of the USA and some other great powers, was formalized by a ten-year defence agreement with the USA in the monsoon of 2005, fine-tuned into a nuclear deal in the spring of 2006 which is still being hotly contested between the government and the opposition over the change of the goalpost between the US Hyde Act and the 123 supplementary Indo-US agreement. This rapprochement with the USA has not prevented India from cultivating strategic alliances with other great powers of the contemporary multipolar world.

Even India's nuclearization in 1998 was not a regime-specific decision. It is also by now a commonplace that it cannot be exclusively attributed to the Bharatiya Jana Sangh as an idea; Prime Ministers of the past also belonging to the Indian National Congress also nurtured it.

There are other examples of multipartisan consensus on policies. Nehru's 'socialism' and Indira Gandhi's *garibi hatao* populism were superseded by what is commonly called LPG—liberalization, privatization, globalization—incrementally from 1980 to 1984, and in a package since 1991 after the severe balance of payments crisis. This was more due to the imperatives of global capitalism than national policy failings or democratic choice. Every Government of India since 1991, including the Government headed by P.V. Narasimha Rao that accelerated LPG (but excepting the Congress-led UPA), has been said to be a victim of the "incumbency factor" by psephologists (as if this factor invariably entails *negative* effects in electoral terms!). As a result, successive governments have grown warm and then quickly cold to what are called "economic reforms". The Rao-led Government was followed by the left-of-center Janata Dal-led United Front Government. The United Front Governments led by H.D. Devegowda and I.K. Gujral were followed by right-of-center Bharatiya Janata Party-led National Democratic Alliance (NDA). The NDA Governments led by Atal Bihari Vajpayee were followed by a left-of-center Congress-led United Progressive Alliance (UPA) Government, guided by Congress President Sonia Gandhi and headed by Prime Minister Dr. Manmohan Singh, the first technocrat-economist to be the Prime Minister. The pace of economic reforms has grown faster under right-of-center administrations and slower under left-of-center Governments. What has largely remained unchanged is the direction of economic reforms. Hence the puzzled dismay of India's leading psephologist, Yogendra Yadav:

> As the participatory upsurge leads to the downward spread of democracy, the political processes begin to disturb the inherited ritual social hierarchy and trouble the established elite with hitherto unknown anxieties. Since elections are associated with much of this upheaval, the spectacle of election has come to occupy an aura of *'samudra manthan'*, the grand ritual churning of the social sea by the small gods of democracy with the help of the modern instrument of a vote. But just as this churning seems poised to yield the proverbial 'amrita', it comes up against the rocky bed of economic inequality. The *maya* of collective action and the invisible *'rakshasa'* called ideology conspire against all the small gods. The churning does not stop, the spectacle goes on[18].

However, democratic upsurge itself has its own attendant problems. Alexis de Tocqueville in his classic work *Democracy in America* sagely drew pointed attention to the fact that unrestrained democratization undermines liberty and rule of law.[19] It is not for nothing that Albert V. Dicey in interpreting British constitutionalism in his path-breaking classic *An Introduction to the Study of the Law of the Constitution (1885)* did not stop at deciphering parliamentary supremacy as its foundational principle; he hastened to add to it the twin principles of the rule of law and conventions of the Constitution.[20] In the contemporary Indian context, this argument has, perhaps for the first time, aptly and forcefully made by Fareed Zakaria in his justly famous *The Future of Freedom: Illiberal Democracy at Home and Abroad:*

> India has a hallowed place in discussions of democracy. Despite being desperately poor it has had a functioning democracy since 1947. Whenever someone wants to prove that you do not need to develop economically to become democratic they use their one example—India. Much of this praise is warranted. India is a genuinely free and freewheeling society. But looking under the covers of Indian democracy one sees a more complex and troubling reality. In recent decades, India has become something quite different from the picture in the hearts of its admirers. Not that it is less democratic: in important ways it has become more democratic. But it has become less tolerant, less secular, less law-abiding, less liberal. And these two trends—democratization and illiberalism—are directly related.[21]

Moreover, democracy has a strange, though not estranged, bedfellow in capitalism, as mentioned above. The two have only survived in mutual symbiosis. Capitalism cannot outlive democracy. Capitalism needs democratic legitimacy to keep itself a going concern. Globalization can only stand on the twin pillars of democracy and capitalism. The political standard of globalization today is democracy rather than capitalism. Without democracy, capitalist globalization is as much doomed to disaster as communist Internationals. That is where democratic rule of law and constitutionalism comes in. Indian democracy is paralyzed and in intensive care unit (ICU) in parts of the country badly affected by extreme poverty, communal riots and caste and class killings, external terrorism and insurgencies.

Still, Indian democracy is a relatively successful example of the global idea of democracy.[22] To quote Atul Kohli: "After more than five decades of periodic elections in which all political offices are contested, and in which all adults are qualified to vote, there is little doubt that democracy in India has taken root. Moreover, India enjoys free and lively media, freedom of assembly and association, and considerable scope to express political dissent and protest." Kohli aptly credits Indian democracy less for its "substantial accomplishments" and more for its "procedural institutionalization".

In the chapters that follow, we try to unravel this rather exceptional Third World democratic success story in a critical yet constructive way. We begin with an analytical and empirical analysis of the post-colonial State that came into existence out of the immediate political legacies of the 19th and 20th centuries in Indian history to face the challenges of the second half of the last century and the onset of the 21st. The independent Indian State acquired the characteristics of a democratic developmental State. It sought to embrace democracy, even when the supposed socio-economic preconditions of such an experiment were lacking. India proceeded with the new experiment on the sheer strength of the democratic commitment of the founding constituent group at the historic midnight hour of independence when Nehru delivered his 'tryst with destiny' speech in the Constituent Assembly. However, the original 'socialistic' model ran into crisis by the late 1980s and the political class, with the cheering endorsement of the business class, made a cautious switch-over to business liberalism.

The parliamentary federal structure of the government started its career as a predominantly parliamentary system overshadowing the federal features on account of the one-party dominant system under the aegis of the Indian National Congress. However, with the gradual transformation of the one-party dominant system into a pluralist and regionalist multi-party system with federal coalition/minority governments, the predominantly parliamentary tenor of politics in India gradually slid into a more federalized system with some degree of regional segmentation and differentiated patches of religious, caste, and subaltern mobilizations. Besides, the emergence of larger middle classes, organized working classes of labour aristocracy, and women's groups, along with civil society organizations like non-governmental organizations (NGOs) and new social movements on quality of life and service delivery issues, prompted the growth of civic activities. These developments as also the expansion of electronic mass media created a new moment in democratic consolidation in India. Moreover, the decline of Parliament and executive efficacy prompted enormous expansion of judicial review and activism as a compensatory response in its search of systemic legitimacy. All these developments, particularly "judicialization" of politics via judicial review and activism and independent constitutional and statutory authorities like the Election Commission of India and a variety of semi-judicial autonomous regulatory authorities in various sectors of the national economy, have contributed to the development of a counter-majoritarian consensus system in the era of increasing federalization and globalization.

It is, however, important to remember, according to Maravall and Przeworski,[23] that "the conflict between the rule of majority and rule of law is just a conflict between actors who use votes and laws as their instruments. Whether legislatures or courts prevail in particular situations is a matter of politics." "The romance of democracy", opines Pratap Bhanu Mehta, "must be accompanied by *political* hard work, and politics in its highest form, is nothing if not hard."[24] No judicial rationalization can ever ultimately substitute and suffice without finally being itself politicized and undermined—for the political process. The critical and creative role of politics in what Rajni Kothari called the "Indian model of development" in his classic *Politics in India*[25] can hardly be exaggerated. The states, no doubt, have failed or been made to fail by ideological assault. But they continue to be (a) "critical organizational vehicles for modern political order," (b) civil societies are still, "more likely to work with rather than resist the exertions of the states" that "institutionally restrain the coercive power of government—through normative consensus and legal constitutional rules," and (c) rely more on sovereignty of interdependence rather than conventional outmoded notions of national and Westphalian sovereignty.[26]

REFERENCES

1. "Reframing Continuity," an Interview with Douglas V. Verney by Rekha Saxena, *The Pioneer*, New Delhi, 5 April 2001.
2. Albert Venn Dicey, *Introduction to the Study of the Law of the Constitution,* Foreword by Roger E. Michner, Indianapolis: Liberty Fund Inc., 1982, p. 110. A reprint of the 1885 classic as published in its 8th and the last edition in Dicey's life time by Macmillan, London, 1915 with a new Introduction written in 1914.
3. *Ibid.* The reference is to the argument made in the whole book.
4. N.R. Madhava Menon, "Constitutional Institutions and the Maintenance of Rule of Law", Chapter 5 in N.R. Madhava Menon (Ed.), *Rule of Law in a Free Society,* Oxford University Press, New Delhi, 2008, pp. 43–44.
5. Granville Austin, *The Indian Constitution: Cornerstone of a Nation,* Oxford University Press, New Delhi, 1966 and 1972, a Classic Reissue in 2001, Chapters 2 and 13.
6. Uday S. Mehta, "Constitutionalism" in N.G. Jayal and P.B. Mehta (Eds.) *The Oxford Companion to Indian Politics,* Oxford University Press, New Delhi, 2010, p. 19.
7. Upendra Baxi, "Post Colonial Legality" in Henry Schwarz and Sangeeta Ray (Eds.), *A Companion to Postcolonial Studies,* Blackwell, London, 2000, Chapter 28.
8. Upendra Baxi, "The Rule of Law in India", SUR—International Journal of Human Rights, No. 6, year 4, 2007, also available in digital format at www.surjournal.org.
9. *Ibid.*, p. 20.
10. Habermas, *The Theory of Communicative Action,* Volume 1: Reason and the Rationalisation of Society. Translated in Germany by Thomas A. MacCarthy, Cambridge: Polity Press, 1981.
11. Francis Fukuyama, "Democracy's Future; The Primacy of Culture", *Journal of Democracy*, Vol. 6, No. 1, January 1995, pp. 7–114.

12. Samuel Bowles and Herbert Gintis, *Democracy and Capitalism; Property, Community, and the Contradictions of Modern Social Thought,* Rautledge & Kegan Paul, London, 1987, p. 177.
13. *Ibid.*
14. Fukuyama, *op. cit.,* p. 8.
15. Dinkar, *Sanskriti Ke Char Adhyaya (*Patna: Udayachal, 1956, forward by Nehru).
16. Gurpreet Mahajan, *Multicultural Path: Issues of Diversity and Discrimination in Democracy*, New Delhi: Sage Publications, 2002. See especially Will Kymlicka, *Contemporary Political Philosophy: An Introduction,* Oxford University Press, New Delhi, 2002, 2nd ed., (Indian ed.), Chapter 8.
17. Sunil Khilnani, *The Idea of India*, Hamish Hamilton, London, 1997, Ch. 2.
18. Yogendra Yadav, "Electoral Politics in this Time of Change: India's Third Electoral System," 1989-99, *Economy and Political Weekly*, Vol. XXXIV, Nos. 34 & 35, 21 August, 3 September 1999, p. 2393.
19. Alexis de Tocqueville, *Democracy in America* (The Henry Reeve Text as revised by Francis Bowen now further corrected and edited with a historical essay, editorial notes, and bibliographies by Phillips Bradley), II Vols. (New York Vintage Books, A Division of Random House, 1945).
20. Albert V. Dicey, *An Introduction to the Study of the Law of the Constitution* (With Introduction by E.C.S. Wade), 10th ed., First Indian Reprint 1994, Macmillan, London/Universal Book Traders, Delhi, 1959.
21. Fareed Zakaria, *The Future of Freedom: Illiberal Democracy at Home and Abroad,* W.W. Norton & Company, New York & London, 2003, p. 106.
22. Atul Kohli (Ed.), *The Success of India's Democracy,* Cambridge University Press, Cambridge, 2001, p. 3.
23. Jose Maria Maravall and Adam Pzeworski (Eds.), *Democracy and the Rule of Law,* Cambridge University Press, Cambridge, UK, 2003, p. 15.
24. Pratap Bhanu Mehta, *The Burden of Democracy,* Penguin Books, New Delhi, 2003, pp. ix–x. Emphasis in the quote in the source itself.
25. Rajni Kothari, *Politics in India,* Orient Longman, New Delhi, 1970, Chapter IX.
26. G. John Ikenberry, "What states can do now?" in T.V. Paul, G. John Ikenberry, and John A. Hall (Eds.), *The Nation-State in Question,* Princeton University Press, Princeton & Oxford, 2003, "Conclusion".

Chapter

2

The Making of the Constitution and Its Operationalization

INTRODUCTION

The Constitution of India was the product of a greatly complex set of factors and forces, some of which originated from colonial rulers and others from the nationalists in India. The locales and sites at which the proposals and policies crystallized were also varied, e.g. the Central Legislative Assembly in the colony and the Parliament of the United Kingdom, nationalist elites and masses organized into various pressure groups/political parties/and movements, and dominant personalities and policy-makers in India and Great Britain. The imperial and colonial contexts in which the events unfolded gradually and accelerated to the denouement of the Great Indian Drama were also subject to overwhelming domestic and international transformations like the rise of mass nationalism, separatism, and globally unsettling events like the two World Wars and economic depression of the 1930s and the Bengal famine of 1943. The inter-related developments peaked in the "Quit India Movement" of 1942, the Independence of India Act of 1947 passed by the British Parliament, and the enactment and adoption of the Constitution by the Constituent Assembly of India in 1949–50.

We begin with the backdrop of the British Constitutional reforms in India in the twentieth century, i.e., Government of India Acts of 1909, 1919, and 1935 passed by the British Parliament. These were incremental constitutional reforms meant to respond and manage the growing tempo of nationalist demands in India that, by the turn of the century, were no longer satisfied by only growing participation of Indians in the bureaucratic apparatus of the British colonial State. The hallmark of the twentieth century constitutional reforms was the increasing political representation of Indians in the British Government of India in legislatures by a slowly expanding franchise. The Government of India Act, 1909, known as the Morley–Minto Reforms after the names of the Secretary of State for India and the Viceroy, changed the official majority that existed in the provinces under the Indian Councils Acts of 1861 and 1892. Election was also nominally introduced in the Central Legislative Council, but with official majority intact. An entirely new feature of this Act was the introduction of separate electorate for Muslims, the driving wedge of communalism that eventuated into the partition of the country. The next installment of constitutional reforms was brought in 1919 by Secretary of State Montague and Viceroy Chelmsford, which introduced a system of diarchy that combined administration by the bureaucratic as well as elected ministerial personnel in the provinces but not at the Centre. The third major constitutional advance was the Government of India Act, 1935, that innovated a measure of provincial autonomy within a type of federal Government with demarcation of jurisdictions in terms of central, provincial, and concurrent lists of subjects. It also proposed an Inter-Provincial Council and established a federal court for the first time. However, the reluctance of the Princely states to join the proposed federation, and the outbreak of the Second World War aborted the implementation of the central component of the new Constitution. The Central Government continued to be run under the Act of 1919, but elected provincial governments took office under the scheme of provincial autonomy. However, the Congress ministries resigned after the onset of the war and the fundamental differences between the Government and the Indian National Congress.

International and national political developments moved fast to transform the political scenario in India. The economic depression of the 1930s and the consequences of the War radically altered the political chessboard for both the Indian nationalists and the imperialist power. Great Britain could no longer hold on to its Indian Empire on account of the diminution of its international economic and military role. The changed international and national atmospherics also boosted the forces of nationalism in India. The Indian National Congress that had moved the resolution for complete independence at its Lahore session in December 1929, presided over by Jawaharlal Nehru, reinforced its institutional as well as agitational activities with increasing mass participation. Gandhi's civil disobedience movement of the early 1920s and the non-cooperation movement of the early 1930s were followed by the Quit India Movement launched by the Congress in 1942. The left wing in the Congress was led by Nehru himself but more radically by Subhash Chandra Bose (who later left the Congress to form the Forward Bloc) and Jayaprakash Narayan and his other eminent Congress Socialist Party cohorts. Though the Government arrested the top leadership of the Congress to crush the Quit India Movement, the movement spread like a prairie fire fuelled from the underground by leaders like Jayaprakash Narayan who then overnight joined the ranks of the top national leaders.

On the other hand, the All India Muslim League passed the Pakistan Resolution at its Lahore session in 1940 demanding a separate homeland for Muslims. This was, of course, an expression of the paranoia of the Muslim League at the possible advent of democracy based on universal adult franchise and the possible Hindu domination due to their numerical superiority. This was also related to the British imperial policy of 'divide and rule' by prompting Muslim communalism to undercut the broader nationalist platform of the Congress.

The idea of a Constituent Assembly for India had been in gestation for a long time both in the nationalist quarters and in the British ruling circles. As early as 1922, Mahatma Gandhi had published an article "Independence" in the *Young India* (5 January 1922) broaching the idea of a Constitution by Indians themselves. The Commonwealth of India Bill, 1925, sponsored by Mrs. Annie Beasant was introduced in the House of Commons in 1925 mooting the idea of a constituent assembly for India, but with the defeat of the Labour Government in England, it lapsed. In 1927, Motilal Nehru moved a resolution at the Bombay session of the Congress that called upon the Congress Working Committee to initiate the process of drafting a Constitution for India in consultation with the elected members of the central and provincial legislatures and the major political parties in the country.

However, the first concrete step in constitution making was taken in 1928 by an all parties conference attended, in addition to the Congress, by the All India Muslim League, the All India Hindu Mahasabha, the Central Khilafat Committee, the All India Conference of Indian Christians, the States' Peoples' Conference, and the All India Liberal Federation in Delhi. The outcome of this endeavour was the Motilal Nehru Committee Report, 1928. This was the first detailed Constitution drafted by Indians for India that bore the imprints of the Canada Constitution Act, 1867, and the Constitutions of Australia and New Zealand. It proposed Dominion Status for India under the British Empire. A new feature of this document that diverged from the tradition of Westminster-based parliamentary federalism was the inclusion of fundamental rights of citizens and minorities. The Nehru Committee Report could not be enacted into a statute by the British Parliament on account of subsequent differences among Indian political leaders and organizations, as well as the British government's own reservations against it which clarified that its idea of self-government for India was for the future and not for the then current time.

The demand for a Constituent Assembly continued to be made by the Indian nationalists including central and provincial legislatures. This demand received the first authoritative recognition by the British Government, albeit indirectly, in the August Offer of 1940 made by Viceroy Linlithgow. The Viceroy's statement included, among other things, the following: "There has been very strong insistence that the framing of that scheme should be primarily the responsibility of the Indians themselves and should originate from Indian conceptions of the social, economic and political structure of Indian life."[1]

In March–April 1942, the British Government dispatched Stafford Cripps, a member of the War Cabinet, to personally have consultation with Indian political leaders regarding a new Constitution for India. The Cripps offer outlined the process of making a new federal Constitution uniting the British

Indian provinces and the Indian princely States. The Constitution-making body would go into action after the end of the War and it would be elected by all the members of the lower houses of provincial legislatures by the system of proportional representation. The Constitution-making body thus elected would be about one-tenth of the number of its electoral college. Besides, Indian states would represent their total population as in the case of representatives of British India. These two components of the Constituent Assembly would be free agents, with the difference that the proposed union was intended to be obligatory for the British Indian provinces but volitional for the princely States. Moreover, a treaty would be signed between His Majesty's Government and the Constitution-making body to ensure "the protection of racial and religious minorities". The Congress rejected the Cripps proposals and proceeded to pass its historic Quit India Resolution on 8 August 1942 at its Bombay session.

In July 1945, the newly elected Labour Government in England prompted Viceroy Wavell to announce the Government's policy on September 19 to convene a constitution-making body for India "as soon as possible". A conference between the British Cabinet Mission and the representatives of the Congress and the Muslim League was held at Simla in April–May 1946. This was the first of a series of such roundtables to resolve the fundamental differences between the Congress, which stood for a united India, and the Muslim League, bent on an independent sovereign Pakistan. The Cabinet Mission put forward a proposal for a constitutional structure that would include a Union Government with jurisdiction over foreign affairs, defence and communications, and two groupings of provinces, one predominantly Hindu and the other predominantly Muslim, with jurisdiction over other subjects. Finally, the proposed union would also possibly include the Indian princely States. All these efforts led to the Cabinet Missions' Plan of 16 May 1946. It included the following cardinal points:

1. There should be a Union of India, embracing both British India and the States, which should deal with the following subjects: Foreign Affairs, Defense, and Communications; and should have the powers necessary to raise the finances required for the above subjects.
2. The Union should have an Executive and a Legislative constituted from British Indian and States representatives. Any question raising a major communal issue in the Legislature should require for its decision a majority of the representatives present and voting of each of the two major communities as well as a majority of all the members present and voting.
3. All subjects other than the Union subjects and all residuary powers should vest in the Provinces.
4. The States will retain all subjects and powers other than those ceded to the Union.

5. Provinces should be free to form Groups with executives and legislatures and each Group could determine the Provincial subjects to be taken in common.
6. The Constitutions of the Union and of the Groups should contain a provision whereby any Province could, by a majority vote of its Legislative Assembly, call for a reconsideration of the terms of the Constitution after an initial period of 10 years and at 10 yearly intervals thereafter.[2]

The Cabinet Mission Plan had included the provisions for the elections to the Constituent Assembly, as already mentioned above. The elections were held in July 1946, the provincial legislatures previously elected in 1936 acting as the electoral college. It may be added that the provincial legislatures themselves were elected on the basis of a franchise extended to about 25 per cent of the adult population on the basis of educational and property qualifications under the provisions of the Government of India Act, 1935. The Constituent Assembly thus elected included a total of 389 members to which nominees of the princely States were to be added later. Province-wise representation in the Constituent Assembly was as follows: Madras 49, Bombay 21, United Provinces (UP) 52, Bihar 36, Central Provinces (CP) 17, Orissa 9, Coorg 1, Delhi 1, Punjab 24, North West Frontier Province (NWFP) 3, Sind 4, Baluchistan 1, Bengal 59, Assam 10. Party-wise representation in the Constituent Assembly is given in Table 2.1.

The standing committee of the Chamber of Princes appointed a committee to negotiate the entry of the States into the Constituent Assembly. Likewise, the Constituent Assembly appointed a states committee to negotiate this matter with the committee set up by the Chamber of Princes. The princely state of Baroda opted for a direct dealing with the Constituent Assembly instead of through the Chamber of Princes. On the basis of these negotiations, 93 seats were settled for the representatives of the princely States in the constitutional convention. The first meeting of the Constituent Assembly was held on 9 December 1946. After the preliminaries, Jawaharlal Nehru moved the historic Objectives Resolution on 13 December. The text of the resolution is given below:

1. This Constituent Assembly declares its firm and solemn resolve to proclaim India as an Independent Sovereign Republic and to draw up for her future governance a Constitution;
2. wherein the territories that now comprise British India, the territories that now form the Indian States, and such other parts of India as are outside British India and the States, as well as such other territories as are willing to be constituted into the Independent Sovereign India, shall be a Union of them all; and
3. wherein the said territories, whether with their present boundaries or with such others as may be determined by the Constituent Assembly and thereafter according to the law of the Constitution, shall possess

TABLE 2.1 Election Analysis Showing the Relative Strength of Political Parties In the Union Constituent Assembly

	Strength	*Percentage of total seats*	*Percentage of seats for British India*
* *The Congress including:*			
(a) Congressmen General .... 171} Muslim .... 4}	175	44.98	59.12
(b) Congress Nominees other than Congressmen General .... 30} Muslim .... 0}	30	7.71	10.14
The Muslim League Unionists General .... 2} Muslim .... 1}	73 3	18.76 0.77	24.66 1.01
Communists General .... 1}	1	0.26	0.33
Scheduled Castes Federation General .... 1}	1	0.26	0.33
Backward Tribes General .... 2}	2	0.51	0.66
Landlords General .... 3}	3	0.77	1.01
Commerce & Industry (Independents) General .... 2}	2	0.51	0.66
Krishak Proja Muslim .... 1}	1	0.26	0.33
Shahid Jirga Muslim .... 1}	1	0.26	0.33
Vacant Sikh .... 4 States (Max) 93	4 93	1.03 23.90	1.35 ...
TOTAL	**389**	**99.98**	**99.93**

Source: B. Shiva Rao (Ed.), *Framing of India's Constitution: Select Documents,* Vol. I (New Delhi: IIPA, 1966, p. 292). *The total under this head comes to 205, percentages of total seats, 52.69; percentages of seats in British India, 69.26.

and retain the status of autonomous units, together with residuary powers, and exercise all powers and functions of Government and administration, save and except such powers and functions as are vested in or assigned to the Union, or as are inherent or implied in the Union or resulting therefrom; and

4. wherein all power and authority of the Sovereign Independent India, its constituent parts and organs of Government, are derived from the people; and
5. wherein shall be guaranteed and secured to all the people of India justice, social, economic and political; equality of status, of opportunity, and before the law; freedom of thought, expression, belief, faith, worship, vocation, association and action, subject to law and public morality; and
6. wherein adequate safeguards shall be provided for minorities, backward and tribal areas, and depressed and other backward classes; and
7. whereby shall be maintained the integrity of the territory of the Republic and its sovereign rights on land, sea, and air according to justice and the law of civilized nations, and
8. this ancient land attains its rightful and honoured place in the world and makes its full and willing contribution to the promotion of world peace and the welfare of mankind.[3]

Although the fate of the Cabinet Mission Plan was already hanging in the balance due to changing attitude towards it in the Indian National Congress, the Muslim League, and the Chambers of Princes, the Objectives Resolution was still moved within the parameters of the Cabinet Mission Plan, hoping that the Muslim League members then boycotting the meeting would perhaps finally join. This explains the imprint of the Cabinet Mission proposed in the Objectives Resolution in terms of a confederal union of British Indian provinces—predominantly Hindu and predominantly Muslim—and the princely States. As it happened, this turned out to be a belied hope. The Indian rump of the Constituent Assembly never formally repealed the Objectives Resolution, and the partition of India became a reality under the Mountbatten Plan. The British Parliament finally passed the Independence of India Act, 1947, creating two sovereign States of India and Pakistan, and granting the princely States the options of remaining independent or joining either of the two major successor States. The Indian National Congress, the dominant party in the Assembly, turned its back to the Cabinet Mission's confederal union and proceeded to draft a federal Constitution with a strong parliamentary centre. Before the Constitution was formally enacted and adopted by November 1949, the Government of India led by Jawaharlal Nehru and its Home Ministry under the stewardship of Sardar Ballabhbhai Patel had successfully negotiated the accession of the 500-odd princely States to the Union of India, barring the two largest ones—Hyderabad and Jammu and Kashmir. The last two fell in line following "police action" by India in Hyderabad and a veiled aggression (allegedly by 'tribals' of upper Kashmir, but really by army regulars along with them) by Pakistan in Jammu and Kashmir.

After due diligence and deliberation for about three years, the Constituent Assembly, which doubled as the constitutional convention as well as the provisional Parliament, produced the text of the Constitution that went into effect from 26 January 1950. The first Parliament of India in accordance with the new Constitution was elected on the basis of universal adult franchise in 1952. The Constitution, the longest written one in the world, incorporates the basic outlines of the Governments at the union, state, and local levels, in addition to a memorable Preamble and ringing declarations of fundamental rights (and duties, added by the 42nd Amendment) of citizens and directive principles of State policy as the essential and desirable goals of Government and governance. It envisages a single citizenship and a single constitutional text of India, with only one separate State Constitution for Jammu & Kashmir (1957) conforming to the principles and structures of the national Constitution. [In August 2019, the Narendra Modi government deoperationlized these features of Jammu and Kashmir's 'special status' by parliamentary action and President's Order.]

There are those who see the Constitution of India as ambivalent between colonial continuity and postcolonial discontinuity. But, some have taken a more nuanced view. Granville Austin (1966 and 1999) has conceptualized the Indian constitutional edifice as 'a seemless web' composed of three intertwined strands of triple revolutions, namely, a national revolution of independent pluralist nationalism, social revolution of socio-economic equality, and a political revolution of state formation.[4] Gautm Bhatia (2019) in a similar vein argues, 'The Constituent Assembly might have owed its legal existence to the colonial regime, but one of its first acts was to declare itself sovereign, and frame the Constitution on its own terms. In defending himself against the charge that '[it] had simply copied the 1935 Act into the Constitution, Babasaheb [Dr B.R. Ambedkar], the principal draftsman of the Indian Constitution, insisted that it was only the "details of administration" that had been borrowed....' Bhatia goes on to refer to Uday Meha, who avers despite all the surface similarities with the colonial past, there was much in the Constitution that was a radical departure: universal adult franchise in a predominantly illiterate country, criteria of citizenship detached from race, caste, religion or creed, a secularist state in a deeply religious society, abolition of untouchability and hierarchy and rank, a federal democracy where the immediate past experience had been with colonial, princely, and feudal order.[5] [Upendra Baxi (2008) writing more generally on 'postcolonial legality' formulates that postcolonial constitutionalism in the Third World deals with (i) structures, forms, and apparatus of governance and modes of legitimation of power; (ii) constitutionalism is the contested site for both ideas and practices;

and (iii) constitutionalism provides narratives of both rules and resistance. Thus, postcolonial constitutionalism is not only about providing rules but also about social transformation].[6]

FUNDAMENTAL CONSTITUTIONAL PRINCIPLES AND PHILOSOPHY

The Constitution of India reflects the confluence of a variety of ideological streams and constitutional norms and values. These features are a product of both the Indian cultural, philosophical, and historical traits and the post-War international predicaments and worldviews. At the outset, our Constitution seeks to combine apparently two contradictory principles of popular sovereignty and notional priority of the parliamentary and the legislative wing to the government. The opening words of the Preamble "We, the people of India" are an obeisance to the people as the source of all power. This is quite consistent with the freedom struggle against colonialism in which nonviolent direct action of *Satyagraha* was used during the Gandhian phase of the nationalist movement as a moral force. This strand of the Indian political heritage was further reiterated during the J.P. Movement in the early 1970s against authoritarianism and corruption. Prime Minister Indira Gandhi and Lok Nayak Jayaprakash Narayan both confronted each other in the movement, the former advocating the democratic legitimacy of the elected Parliament and State legislatures and their mandate for a full five-year term, and the latter asserting the right of the people to recall their representatives, as in the perception of the leaders of the movement, the Union and State Governments had lost the popular legitimacy. Another[7] attempt at reconciliation of seemingly contradictory principles of Government made by the Constitution of India is the combination of the Westminster tradition of parliamentary Government with the federal principle, first invented in modern times by the United States Constitution. In doing so, India was emulating this kind of combination attempted in the Constitution of Canada (1867) and Australia (1901). Yet, the Indian parliamentary federal system has tended to develop some distinctively Indian characteristics. This point would become clearer in the subsequent chapters, but it may suffice here to say that among the Commonwealth countries mentioned above, the Indian Constitution in practice has moved in significant ways towards the system of separation of powers, federal division of powers, and constitutionally entrenched fundamental rights of individuals and communities, and the resultant institutional checks and balances reminiscent of the American Constitution. In formal terms, a parliamentary system is based on the system of fusion of powers between the Parliament and the executive as the latter springs from the former itself and survives in office only so long as it enjoys the confidence of the popular chamber of the Parliament. However, the Indian case, in some ways, is different as the Supreme Court has in several judgements maintained that the legislative, executive and judicial powers and functions are distinct and should not grossly be intermingled.[8]

In the United Kingdom, the Parliament until 1999 was the depository of not only the legislative and executive powers but the ultimate judicial authority (the Law Lords in the House of Lords in the Judicial Committee of the Privy Council acted as the highest court of Appeal). Since 1999, a Supreme Court of the UK has been set up as the apex court of the land, but parliamentary sovereignty is still beyond its adjudicatory jurisdiction, but the executive and even the Prime Minister are not beyond its reach. The Indian federal experiment also significantly departs from the classic American federal system in as much as the Indian States neither enjoy the residual legislative power (which belongs to the Parliament) nor is there equal representation of federating States in the federal Second Chamber (as is the case in the US Senate). India also differs from parliamentary federal systems of the White Commonwealth, for it has a unique cadre of civil service in All-India Services as distinguished from the Central and State civil services. The contradiction between parliamentary centralization (sovereignty) and federal decentralization of powers is resolved in the Indian Constitution by giving the Parliament some overriding legislative and executive powers and Emergency powers on the one hand, and by making the Supreme Court the ultimate arbiter over disputes between the Union and the states and between the states and the citizens, on the other. This has ultimately culminated into the principle of the supremacy of the Constitution, as interpreted by the Supreme Court as the source of all powers that the different organs of the Government exercise.

A closely related feature to the foregoing that characterizes the Indian Constitution is the judicial precept of the rule of law. The Indian version of the rule of law is most strongly reflected in the fundamental rights of citizens, specially the right to equality, liberty and justice and the generic concept of "the procedure established by law" which is explicitly mentioned in Article 21 (right to life and liberty), but it actually underlies all rights. Comparable ideas similar to our rule of law can be found in the classic exposition of this principle by A.V. Dicey in the United Kingdom, the American idea of the "due process of law" and the status of the Constitution as a higher law, and the German concept of *Rechtsstaat* (a State based on law). In several recent judgements of the Indian Supreme Court, the concept of ''procedure established by law'' has been interpreted in a way indistinguishable from the "due process" of law in the USA (e.g. the Maneka Gandhi case 1978 that reflects acceptance of due process of law whereas in the Gopalan case 1950, the Supreme Court was satisfied with the procedure established by law formulation in Article 21)[9].

Another important contribution of the Indian Constitution to the theory and practice of rights and public policies of the State is reflected in its approach vis-à-vis (a) liberal individual rights and community or group rights, (b) fundamental rights and directive principles of State policy, and (c) fundamental rights and fundamental duties. It is remarkable that even though the Indian Constitution was made in the early post-World War II years (1949–1950) when the ideological orientation of the time basically emphasized liberal individual rights in the universalist mould [as reflected in the UN Universal Declaration of Human Rights (1948)], our Constitution also incorporated cultural and educational rights of linguistic and religious minorities. The major philosophical premise appears to be universalist individual rights, but the minor philosophical premise is minority rights. Over the years, as the ideological climate in the world at large and in India developed greater sensitivity to communitarian rights with social and cultural overtones, the rights discourse in Indian constitutional law has also moved in the same direction. In tune with this sensibility, Neera Chandhoke observes: "I suggest that cultures and communities are a good for the individual and that access to this good is of such overriding importance that we should secure this access through the grant of a right. The question that can logically follow is: if cultures are a good for the individual, why do we need only minority rights? Should not the right of each individual to culture and community be secured, irrespective of whether she/he belongs to the majority or the minority?"[10] This argument assumes greater relevance in a globalizing world where not only the language and culture of the minority but also of the majority are threatened.

As regards the fundamental rights and directive principles, the Constitution originally appears to have given the former an explicit primacy over the latter by making the former *legally* enforceable whereas making the latter only *desirable* goals of governance. However, the Congress governments of Nehru and Indira Gandhi preferred to give primacy to the directives in pursuit of progressive public policies in favour of the weaker sections of the society. The Courts, nonetheless, stood for rights without, of course, rejecting the directives. After a series of constitutional amendments (e.g. 24th, 25th and 26th Amendments, all in 1971) and judicial reviews, the constitutional law settled for the harmony between the two as one of the 'basic features' of the Constitution that cannot be amended.[11] Thus, ideally neither of the two can be sacrificed for the other and the conflict between the two must be reconciled as much as possible.

As in the Western theory of rights so also in the Constitution of India, originally only rights were emphasized rather than duties presumably because the discourse on rights originated in the context of fight against feudal and colonial privileges of the rulers and the elite. However, 42nd Amendment in 1976 added a new Part IV A and Article 51A, to the Constitution outlining the fundamental duties of citizens. Even though this Amendment was introduced by the authoritarian Emergency regime of Indira Gandhi, in principle there can hardly be any objection to the idea as every right must entail some duties. In case law, the courts have invoked this part of the Constitution in protection of environment and ecology as well as in validation of laws where their constitutionality is challenged. Duties have also been relied on by the courts in obliging the State as well as to observe them.[12]

Conventionally, Constitutions have generally dealt with only the structure of the Government. Our postcolonial Constitution also concerns itself with some aspects of a more desirably free and egalitarian civil society and economy.

Article 12 defines the State broadly to include "the Government and Parliament of India and the Government and the Legislature of each of the States and all local or other authorities within the territory of India or under the control of the Government of India." The self-image of the Indian State is stated clearly in the Preamble as a 'Sovereign, Socialist, Secular, Democratic, Republic'. The constitutional power map outlines in a fairly detailed manner the patterns of relationship among the three major organs of Governments at Union, State and local levels as well as among Governments at each of these levels. These structures at Union and State levels are invested with binding legality, whereas the structure of the local Government is in the form of a model Act that requires conforming State laws to give legal effect to them. The images of the constitutional visions of the ideal civil society and the economy are outlined in Parts III and IV of the Constitution dealing with Fundamental Rights and Directive Principles of State Policy. Rejecting feudal and caste hierarchy and privileges, the Fundamental Rights aim at creating a modern democratic and egalitarian society. The Directives exhort the State(s) in India to aim at creating and operating the economy wherein "the ownership and control of the material resources of the community are so distributed as best to sub-serve the common good," and work the system in a way that "does not result in the concentration of wealth and means of production to the common detriment" [Article 39(b) and (c)].

The State(s) is/are also directed to "strive to promote the welfare of the people by securing and protecting as effectively as it may a social order in which justice, social, economic and political shall inform all the institutions of the national life." To this directive is added another responsibility on the State(s) to reduce inequalities of income, status, facilities and opportunities among individuals and groups residing in different regions and different vocations (Article 38, Clause 1 and 2). Granville Austin appropriately regards the Indian Constitution first and foremost as a political document of "social revolution". In his interpretation, the Constitution and its working over the years reveals a 'seamless web' by integrating three foundational principles, namely, individual dignity and national unity, democracy, and a social revolution. The political system has faced grave and difficult challenges since its inception, but the Constitution has survived and at least so far the 'seamless web' continues to be its sheet anchor.[13]

EVALUATION

The foregoing discussion suggests that the vision of the future India projected in the Constitution of India can be broadly summed up as India's "tryst with destiny" by ensuring the fundamental rights to democracy, development and national culture in a world of peace and global order. To what extent has the Indian political system succeeded in achieving this Indian dream? Assessments vary, sometimes radically. While the international assessment of India's success is generally more optimistic, Indian intellectuals themselves often present an evaluation that betrays sneaking pessimism. The approach of foreign scholars is best illustrated by a recent book, *The Success of India's Democracy* (2001) edited by Atul Kohli. In the words of the editor of this volume:

> After more than five decades of periodic elections in which all political offices are contested, and in which all adults are qualified to vote, there is little doubt that democracy in India has taken root. Moreover, India enjoys free and lively media, freedom of assembly and association, and considerable scope, to express political dissent and protest.[14]

To illustrate the latter approach, see, for example, the following observation from Rajni Kothari's reflections in his most recent book, *Rethinking Democracy* (2005):

> Democracy has remained a dream and an aspiration. As a system it has not been realized in practice. But the aspiration is very much alive, both in the conscientious sections of the educated and thinking class and, in fact even more in the deprived and dispossessed sections of the population. The latter continue to face backlashes from the dominant State, and are often forced to join streams of militancy and violence. But the aspirations continue to challenge both the mass public and the visionary segments of the as yet unclear and ambivalent intelligentsia. Together the masses and the intelligentsia, could engage in a diversity of struggles.[15]

India's distinct characteristic in a comparative perspective has been that we have tried to simultaneously achieve the goals of democracy as well as development as against the erstwhile socialist/communist systems that sacrificed liberty for the sake of equality, and East Asian countries that prized economic development over democracy. In the Nehru era of "democratic Socialism" when the level of politicization was not all that high, the major achievements accomplished were laying down the foundations of the Constitution and heavy industrialization largely under the sponsorship of the state. Another major creditable work done was the passage of most progressive labour laws in the developing world and organized trade union movement at least in the industrial and salaried employment sectors. However, the major failings were the lopsided development in agriculture and the infrastructural sector excepting the railways. Another major casualty was lack of development in quality health care and education, especially at the mass scale. While it may be considered that the scarcity of resources did not allow an all-round development, there is no denying the fact that a more balanced growth in all these sectors could have had a greater multiplier effect in terms of a more comprehensive developmental spiral.

Besides, despite the huge expansion of the State sector of the economy, often negating the self-sustaining logic of the capitalist or market economy resulted in loss-making public enterprises. By the time of the fourth general elections in 1967, the economic as well as political crisis of the regime of Indian Socialism had deepened to the extent of almost a grinding halt. The new Congress regime under Prime Minister Indira Gandhi demanded radical remedies that took the form of populist economic and political measures to buy electoral support from the newly politicized sections of the society of the new generation of post-Independence Indians and lower middle classes. While a new lease of political survival of the Indira Gandhi regime could somehow be managed, but it was at great economic costs. Indira Gandhi's major achievements were the Green Revolution that became necessary in view of the stoppage of PL480 wheat imports from the USA and recurrent droughts in the mid and late 1960s. But the populist policy of *garibi hatao* and the 1971 Indo-Pakistan war over Bangladesh derailed the process of planned economic development and proved to be a great fiscal strain on revenue and nationalized banks. In a short-range, these policies made the electoral restoration of the Congress Party possible and transformed Indira Gandhi into a charismatic political leader. However, the democratically institutionalized structure of the Congress Party in the Nehru era was destroyed in the process and was replaced by a personalized political machine with a large mass following without the intermediation of political institutions. For, it was not only the Congress Party that became the casualty but also the federal features of the political system, which were undermined by over-centralization of power at the top. The two detrimental effects were the fiscal overload over the State and regional political alienation that erupted into State autonomy movements in Assam and Punjab, where, at least in the latter case, religious fundamentalism and separatism raised its ugly head even during the premiership of Indira Gandhi. Separatism in Jammu and Kashmir and Assam were somewhat slower in coming.

The deepening political and economic crisis of the 1970s and '80s were further underlined by a massive mass movement against growing corruption and authoritarianism in the political system that developed into the classic confrontation between the J.P. Movement and the Emergency regime. These tensions were relieved by federal trends of the 1980s, reflected in the restoration of democratically chastened Congress Governments of Indira Gandhi and Rajiv Gandhi and more effectively by the 1989 Lok Sabha elections which transformed the one-party dominant system into a multi-party system with coalition/minority Governments. The 1990s witnessed three fundamental reorientations in the political system in the form of the New Reservation Policy (1990), Neoliberal Economic Reforms (1991), and the rise of the Hindutva forces around the time of the demolition of the Babri Masjid in Ayodhya (1992). All the three developments unleashed unsettling political and economic trends that posed unprecedented challenges to the political consensus of the preceding decades. Uncertainties came to haunt secularism and upper-caste and middle-class accustomed ways of dealing with the political and social universe. While the aspects of secularism and liberalization/privatization/globalization are discussed in greater detail in the chapter on the State in India, a few additional comments may be offered here. Under the impact of the foregoing developments, the constitutional goals are facing tough times. Without any formal amendment to the Constitution and without adequate debate, recent developments have put question marks on the sovereign, socialist, secular and republican characteristics of the political system. The sovereignty and territorial integrity of the country is compromised. Socialist objectives have been abandoned and the role of the Planning Commission considerably watered down. The secular character of the State faced serious challenges in Gujarat and Jammu and Kashmir. The Sachar Committee, appointed by the Congress-led United Progressive Alliance Government (UPA), has drawn attention to the lags in the development of the Muslim minorities in more recent decades. Its report states that "community exhibits deficits and deprivation in practically all dimensions of development."[16] (Table 2.2.)

TABLE 2.2 Distribution of Socio-religious Categories by Income Groups (Income categories, per cent)

Hindus (General)		
• Low 8.9	• Middle 73.9	• High 17.2
Hindus (SC/ST)		
• Low 28.6	• Middle 65.1	• High 6.3
Hindus (OBC)		
• Low 25.9	• Middle 72.6	• High 1.5
Muslims		
• Low 30.8	• Middle 65.0	• High 4.2

Source: Sachar Committee estimate from National Sample Survey Organisation 2004–05, 61st Round, Schedule 10 as reported in the *Frontline*, 29 December 2006, p. 121.

The unending demand for the spoils of reservation seems to have gone beyond the limits of the principles of justice and equity. Poverty alleviation programmes have suffered under the imperatives of privatization and globalization. The data reported in the table show that so far as the middle income group is concerned, the disparities between Hindus and Muslims are not at all that alarming. The representation of Hindus (General), Hindus (SC/ST), and Hindus (OBC) in the middle income group ranges from 65.1 per cent to 74 per cent, whereas Muslim representation is at 65.0 per cent. A similar pattern is noticeable in the representation of Muslims (30.8 per cent), Hindu OBC (25.9 per cent), and Hindu SC/ST (28.6 per cent) in terms of their representation in the low income group. It is here that the contrast between the Hindus (general) (8.9 per cent) and the Muslims (30.8 per cent) is distressing. But so is the condition of Hindu SC/ST and OBCs. In other words, Hindus (general) are much better off in this category not only in comparison to Muslims but also Hindu SC/ST and OBCs. The distribution of various groups in the high income group is even more disturbing. This is because a disproportionately larger representation of Hindus (general) in the high income group (17.2 per cent) than the other three groups: Hindu SC/ST (6.3 per cent), and Muslims (4.2 per cent), and Hindu OBCs (1.5 per cent).

RESERVATION POLICY

The reservation policy, especially its new avatar as Mandal-I and Mandal-II of 1990 and 2006 vintage, is developing into a great dilemma of Indian politics. In the words of Myron Weiner: "There is a tension between, on the one hand, the goal of casteless society in which the individual is the unit of public policy and, on the other, the concept of reservations for scheduled castes and scheduled tribes with the group as the unit of public policy."[17]

The reservation policy for historically disadvantaged castes in various religious communities aimed at their adequate representation in educational institutions, Government jobs, and legislatures have by now created a new middle class and a powerful political lobby that must be reckoned with by all political parties, whether in Government or in opposition. The reservation of legislative seats was initially for ten years and only for SCs and STs outside of south India. (Reservation for educational and economic opportunities for SCs/STs were also *provisional* but they did not specify any time limit.)

However, latter reservation were continued indefinitely and extended to Other Backward Castes (OBCs) in almost all states, and finally at the Centre as well by the early 1990s. The policy has had a greater impact at the state-level, though even at the Centre it has not been inconsequential. The SC/ST reservations were set up with consensus by the Constitution (but riotous protest against them have begun to be witnessed, for example in Gujarat in the mid-1980s). The OBC reservations have always provoked more opposition, in fact, violent agitations, wherever they have been introduced in the North since the late 1970s (for example, in Bihar in 1978 and in UP in the 1990s). In the early 1990s, their introduction in Uttar Pradesh triggered the regional movement for separate state of Uttarakhand in the Indian Union at Himalayan foothills where the OBCs are practically non-existent but stand to benefit by a sizeable chunk of reserved government jobs in the backward region and in the state as a whole. The movement turned violent and was ruthlessly repressed by the UP Government headed by Mulayam Singh Yadav. The reservation policy has used caste as the criteria of backwardness for all practical purposes. In the Supreme Court judgement, as Sivaramayya observed:

> The majority opinion gave primacy to the caste test and justified it as social fact, while the minority emphasized the secular ideals of the Constitution and the need to eschew prohibited classifications like race, religion/caste. In rejecting the alternative modes of identifying OBCs like 'occupation-cum-social-cum-educational-cum-economic criteria', and in opting for caste test, the majority buttressed caste not only among Hindus but also among Muslims and Christians.[18]

We agree that while the caste test may be valid by and large for the top and bottom strata of caste-class nexus, the big middle band does not conform to it. Treating caste as class at this level, creates distortions. The growing political clout of the OBCs by the late 1950s in the South and by the mid-1960s in the North, and intermittently thereafter in the late 1970s and again in the late 1980s at the Centre, has "Mandalized" Indian politics. The crutches of OBC reservation in south India, in the telling metaphor of Andre Beteille,[19] have been used as sticks to beat and distort the system with; north India too has now followed suit. The abrasive rise to political power of Laloo Prasad Yadav and Mayawati–Kanshiram in the 1990s may well have happened in the subcontinent only in India. However, the reservation policy has now degenerated into a political mobilization gimmick with scant regard for equity, merit, and efficiency. Almost all political parties are now either asserting for OBC reservations or acquiescing to it for mobilizing the numerically dominant middle and lower strata of the society and are party to it. It is the Janata Party/Dal to which the paternity of the Mandal reservation at the Centre could be traced. The second Backward Classes Commission chaired by B.P. Mandal was appointed by the Janata Government in the late 1970s. By the time its Report was submitted in the early 1980s, the Janata Government was replaced with a Congress one. The Congress Government shelved the report for a decade. Except for occasional outbursts by the Janata leaders, no tears were shed. When the National Front Government led by the Janata Dal came to power in 1989, this long-standing controversial issue exploded into a bombshell, precipitated by a factional fight between Prime Minister V.P. Singh and Deputy Prime Minister Devi Lal. It resulted in the implementation of the Mandal recommendations for reservation of 27 per cent jobs in the Central Government Services (besides those for SCs/STs). The Left and regional parties too in the National Front coalition Government joined the Mandal bandwagon, despite the fact that the 1989 election manifestos of these parties had promised or said nothing on Mandal! The Mandal reservations were, as already mentioned, questioned in the Supreme Court. By the time the matter came into prominence in the judiciary, the United Front Government had fallen. The Congress minority Government headed by P.V. Narasimha Rao in its submission to the Court did not express any intention to withdraw it nor did it ever rescind it. The Supreme Court upheld the Mandal reservations but with the caveat that the OBC "creamy layer" be excluded while administering it. In Indian conditions the gap between intent and implementation may leave a wide margin. The Government in Kerala made no efforts to put into practice the Court's formulation about the creamy layer, with the Chief Secretary of the State testifying in a contempt of court proceeding that the Minister chose to sleep over the file put up!

The latest version of the new reservation policy is the Congress-led UPA Government's attempt to introduce the reservation for OBCs in admission to elite institutions of higher education such as IITs, IIMs and Central universities. The matter raised enough controversy to be taken to the Supreme Court. In *M. Nagaraj and others* v. *Union of India and others* (2006), the Court directed the Government to restrict the scope of reservation policy in admission as well as employment for OBCs and SCs/STs in general to the most backward sections of these groups and keep the resourceful "creamy layers" out from the benefits. The Nagaraj judgement in the Mandal-II case thus signaled a departure from its judgement nearly a decade and a half earlier (1993) in the *Mandal-I/Indira Sawhney* case. In the latter judgement, the Court by majority had gone out of the way to point out that the "creamy layer" formulation was "confined to Other Backward Classes only and has no relevance in the case of Scheduled Tribes and Scheduled Castes". The direction issued to the Government of India was "to specify the basis of exclusion, the extent of holding or otherwise of 'creamy layer'... as early as possible, but not exceeding four months."[20] This caveat is now removed in the Nagaraj judgement. In the opinion of a group of scholars, this judgement

> marks another significant moment in the long and stormy debate on reservation. The elaboration provided by the Constitution Bench on question of discrimination, backwardness, affirmative action, and 'creamy layer' is of critical reasons why this is so, three are worth mentioning here. One, the ruling explicitly recognises and addresses itself to the polarization of caste interests within our society rather than reiterating the worn-out slogan of a homogeneous society. Two, it draws upon a terminology that currently dominates discussions not only in the Courts but also among policy-makers, academics, and media persons. Three, it more clearly than ever before legitimises the grievances of the 'upper castes' even as it seeks to checkmate the pro-backward moves of Parliament.[21]

In the first major challenge to the Supreme Court in decades, the Manmohan Singh's government proceeded to enact the Mandal-II reservation for OBCs in admission to elite institutions of higher education without the exclusion of creamy layer. But the Supreme Court subsequently stayed it, pending a final judgement. In *Ashoka Kumar Thakur* v. *Union of India and Others* (2008), the Supreme Court by majority upheld the reservations but with several doubts and conditions, the crucial condition being that the move would be unconstitutional if the creamy layers among the OBCs are not excluded from among the beneficiaries of these reservations.[22]

POVERTY ALLEVIATION POLICY

After Indian "socialism" and "populism" came to grief and neoliberal policy regime was adopted in the 1990s, poverty alleviation policy is another welfare measure, in addition to reservation, that has continued. In a sense, this is inescapable. For, according to the World Bank data, 35 per cent of the Indian population in 1995–2003 lived in extreme poverty (defined as percentage of people living on less than one US $ a day) as compared to 17 per cent of the Chinese population. India is better off in this regard only than some sub-Saharan countries about whom data are available. India does not fare all that well in terms of some other more specific human development indicators as well. For example, 47 per cent of children under five years in the same time period as above were malnourished, and under-five mortality rate per 1000 children was 87 in 2002–2003. Among those who survived in 2000–2003, 81 per cent completed primary education. Gender parity index in 1998–2002 was 80 as compared to 71 in Pakistan and 97 in China, 100 in the USA and Canada, and 116 in the United Kingdom.[23]

In contemporary India, poverty is becoming more concentrated in developmentally lagging states and rural areas. In general, urban poverty is less crippling than rural poverty which explains the endemic migration to cities and metropolises and sprawling slums. More than half of India's poor now live in Bihar, Madhya Pradesh, Orissa, and Uttar Pradesh—and more than two-thirds in rural areas. In rural areas incidence of poverty is highest amongst agricultural workers, many of whom are casual workers and marginal peasants. Scheduled castes and scheduled tribes in the countryside are more likely to be poor than other social groups because low status and lack of resources still operate as social obstacles that block or exclude them from opportunities.

India's poor suffer from lower incomes and access to basic public services such as health, education, and infrastructure. Both the specifically designed services for the poor and universal services for all pass the poor by on account of pervasive corruption and degeneration of the representative institutions and processes. Arguably, in the context of India's poor it appears empirically more fruitful to talk about poverty still in terms of hunger and malnourishment than human development and capabilities—the concepts pioneered by Amartya Sen and Mahbub-ul Haque and the World Bank. The vicious circle of poverty conspires to reincarnate poverty even in supposedly developed regions. This is evident from the spate of suicides of farmers and peasants in states like Punjab, Maharashtra, and Andhra Pradesh, where the integration of farming with market and banking institutions has given rise to capitalist agriculture but the attendant economic problems overwhelm the agriculturalists who are driven to seek escape in debt and death. Is the need-based economy of India's poor poised to make a safe transition to want-based economy of neo-liberal and national and global capitalism? India's experience of dealing with poverty suggests that political and economic empowerment in tandem is equally important. This will lead to integral ability of the people to shape their own social, economic, and political lives. Individuals' ability to influence public policies that affect them in terms of basic needs, including public education and health and ability to build and protect their assets, is the precondition of such empowerment.

The State(s) in India have followed both indirect and direct policies having bearing on poverty alleviation. The direct policies include policies aimed at agricultural growth and food security, terms of trade between agriculture and industry, subsidies and investment in agriculture, building of infrastructures and institutions, industrial and employment policies, service sector, trade policies, etc. Direct poverty alleviation programmes include wage employment like public works, self-employment programmes like Integrated Rural Development Programmes (IRDP), Public Distribution System (PDS) of essential serials, and nutrition programmes like Integrated Child Development Services (ICDS), rural public works programmes like Employment Guarantee Scheme pioneered by Maharashtra and expanded by the Congress-led United Progressive Alliance Government at the Centre under a formal legislation National Rural Employment Guarantee Act (NREGA), Jawahar Rojgar Yojana (JRY), etc.[24]

Ashutosh Varshney implies that the pre-neoliberal reform regimes in India followed a direct strategy of attack on poverty. He says in explicit terms that the reforms are an indirect method of poverty alleviation without going into reasons for the failure of the state-directed strategy of development earlier. His argument is that democracies in the developing world in general have had a moderate success in reducing poverty. The reason, in part, according to him, is that while there has been an elective affinity between democracies and direct methods of poverty alleviation, direct methods are not as effective and lasting as indirect methods.[25]

In a more well-documented and India-focused study, S. Mahendra Deva concludes: (1) Long range trends demonstrate absence of any change in poverty ratios in the 1950s to the mid-1970s. But there is a marked decline in poverty in the late 1970s and the 1980s. In the post-neoliberal reform period, rural poverty remained static till 1993–94, but urban poverty significantly declined in the 1990s. Rural poverty reduction showed significant improvement between 1993–94 and 1999–2000. These trends relate to gross aggregate economic indicators. In terms of human development and quality of life indicators, India lags even behind the average of medium human development categories of the World Bank. (2) Trends of development in terms of employment in the 1990s record a decline. Non-farm employment initially declined in the post-reform period till 1993–94 but rose in 1999–2000. Security and quality of jobs deteriorated due to recourse to causal and contract jobs without dearness allowance, annual increment, and retirement benefits like gratuity, leave encashment, and pension. (3) Disturbing trend of inter-state disparities is noticeable. While poorer states in the Hindi-heartland and Orissa failed to reduce poverty, richer states in the South and the West and Punjab and West Bengal have succeeded in making a headway in poverty alleviation. (4) In the 1980s the following important factors were found to be more central to poverty reduction in terms of more pervasive results: agricultural growth, rural-urban differential in relative food prices, rural non-farm employment supplementing income from the farm, and increased public expenditure in development and wages. Besides, expenditure on roads and agricultural research are more strongly correlated with decrease in poverty ratio. (5) In the 1990s despite improved terms of trade for agriculture vis-à-vis industry and increased private investment in agriculture in the post-reform period, agricultural growth decelerated. (6) Domestic deregulation is more facilitative of agricultural growth than trade liberalization. And the incremental effect of growth in infrastructures, institutions and technology on agriculture cannot be overemphasized. (7) In the context of industrial employment growth the neoliberal reform enthusiasts have overstressed negative role of continuing rigidities in labour law regime. For rise in employment to the tune of around 4 per cent in the period of mid-1980s to mid-1990s flies in the face of the above flat assertion. (8) The impact of PDS on the poor in 1986–87 was found to be not significant but later evaluation of the scheme in Bihar and UP revealed that the poor look upon it as an important anti-poverty measure. (9) There is a rationale for greater involvement of non-governmental organizations and community organizations in the Government employment programmes. (10) Both in immediate and prospective terms the effective role of education and vocational skills with added emphasis on women groups must be expanded. He further adds, "The second generation of reforms should concentrate more on agricultural growth and rural infrastructure.[26]

The United Nations Multidimensional Poverty Index 2018 indicates that 271 million people moved out of poverty between 2005–06 and 2015–16 in India. The poverty rate has come down by half from 55 per cent to 28 per cent over the ten-year period. The Narendra Modi's government has launched several welfare schemes since 2014. These include schemes for the welfare of farmers, housewives, workers, students, small shopkeepers, etc. Among the prominent schemes are the Ujjwala, Jandhan, PM Kisans, Skill India, Make in India, Clean India, etc.

REFERENCES

1. B. Shiva Rao *et al.* (Eds.), *The Framing of India's Constitution: Select Documents,* Vol. 1, New Delhi, IIPA, 1966, p. 124.
2. *Ibid.*, p. 213.
3. *Ibid.*, Vol. 2, pp. 3–4.
4. Austin, *Indian Constitution: The Cornerstone of a Nation*; and *Working a Democratic Constitution: A History of The Indian Experience*, Oxford University Press, New Delhi, 1966 and 1999.

5. Bhatia, *The Transformative Constitution: Radical Biography in Nine Acts*, HarperCollins India, New Delhi, 2019.
6. Baxi, 'Postcolonial Legality,' in Henry Schwartz and Sangeeta Ray (Eds.), *A Companion to Postcolonial Studies*, Blackwell Publishing, London, 2008.
7. Bipan Chandra, *In the Name of the Democracy: JP Movement and the Emergency,* Penguin Books, New Delhi, 2003.
8. *Madhav Rao* v. *Union of India, All India Reporter*, 1971, Supreme Court, pp. 530... .
9. *A.K. Gopalan* v. *State of Madras, All India Reporter,* 1950, Supreme Court, p. 27 onwards and *Maneka Gandhi* v. *Union of India, AIR*, 1978, Supreme Court, p. 597... .
10. Neera Chandhoke, "Individual and Group Rights: A View from India", in *India's Living Constitution: Ideas, Practices, Controversies,* Zoya Hasan, E. Sridharan, R. Sudarshan (Eds.), Delhi: Permanent Block, 2002, p. 224.
11. *Keshavananda Bharati* v. *State of Kerala, AIR,* 1973, Supreme Court, pp. 1461 onwards and *Minerva Mills Ltd.* v. *Union of India, AIR,* 1980, p. 1789....
12. *Rural Litigation and Entitlement Kendra* v. *State of UP, AIR,* 1987, Supreme Court, p. 359... ; *Mohan* v. *Union of India,* 1992 Suppl. 1, *Supreme Court Cases,* p. 594... ; *Mumbai Kamgar Sabha* v. *Abdulbhai, AIR,* 1976, Supreme Court, p. 1455.
13. Granville Austin, *The Indian Constitution: Cornerstone of a Nation,* Oxford University Press, New Delhi, 1966, *Working a Democratic Constitution: The Indian Experience,* Oxford University Press, New Delhi, 1999 and "The Expected and the Unintended in Working a Democratic Constitution" in Zoya Hasan, E. Sridharan, R. Sudrashan (Eds.), *India's Living Constitution: Ideas, Practices, Controversies,* Permanent Block, New Delhi, 2002. See also, Shibanikinkar Chaube, *Constituent Assembly of India: Springboard of Revolution,* 2nd ed., Manohar, New Delhi, 2000.
14. Atul Kohli (Ed.), "Introduction", *The Success of India's Democracy,* Cambridge University Press, New Delhi, 2001, p. 3.
15. Rajni Kothari, "On Democracy: Emancipation and Democracy", *Rethinking Democracy,* Orient Longman Private Limited, New Delhi, 2005, p. 166.
16. *The Frontline*, 29 December 2006, p. 121.
17. Myron Weiner, "The Struggle for Equality: Caste in Indian Politics" in Atul Kohli (Ed.), *The Success of India's Democracy,* Cambridge University Press, New Delhi, 2001, p. 200.

18. Sivaramayya, "The Mandal Judgement: A Brief Description and Critique" in M.N. Srinivas (Ed.), *Caste: Its Twentieth Century Avatar,* Viking-Penguin India, New Delhi, 1996, pp. 237–238.

19. Andre Beteille, "The Problem" posed for a special issue on Reservation, *Seminar* (New Delhi), No. **268**, December 1981.

20. *The Frontline,* 17 November 2006, pp. 32–34.

21. Rekha Pappu, M. Madhava Prasad, K. Satyanarayana, & Susie Tharu, "Reservation or Affirmative Action?" *The Hindu,* New Delhi, 12 December 2006, p. 10.

22. The World Bank, *Miniatlas of Millennium Development Goals: Building a Better World,* Washington, DC, 2005, pp. 54–63.

23. S. Mahendra Dev, "Poverty in India: Trends, Macro-Policies, and Direct Programmes' in M. Govinda Rao (Ed.), *Development, Poverty, and Fiscal Policy: Decentralization of Institutions,* Oxford University Press, New Delhi, 2002, pp. 61–66.

24. Ashutosh Varshney, "Why Haven't Poor Democracies Eliminated Poverty"? In his edited anthology *India and the Politics of Developing Countries: Essays in Memory of Myron Weiner,* Sage, New Delhi, 2004.

25. https://indiakanoon.org/doc/63489929/.

26. S. Mahendra Dev, *op. cit.,* pp. 67–69.

Chapter

3

A Multicultural-Secularist and Democratic-Developmental State in a Globalizing-cum-Deglobalizing/'Slowbalising' World

INTRODUCTION

The terms state, government, and political system are not coterminous. They have partly overlapping meanings, but they have different nuances. To Giovanni Sartori, 'For quite a long time, English has preferred "government" to "state", and has indeed translated the French *etat* and German *Staat* into "government." Much of the continental European literature has taken the opposite course, thus considering "government" one of the partitions of the "state" (the general term).'[1] Like the state, political system is also conceptualized as an entity embedded in its society and endowed with authoritative powers of allocation and distribution of resources and power. But political system is a more society-centered concept than the state. The state is supposed to be the most concrete institutional embodiment of sovereignty within a territory and political community.

Ancient India is supposed to have no equivalent of the term government, it only had the term state.[2] Kautilya's *Arthashastra* outlines the theory of *saptang rajya* (postulating a seven-organ institution of state, including *swami* (king), *amatya* (minister), *janapada* (population and territory), *durga* (fort), *kosh* (treasury), *danda* (sceptre), and *mitra* (ally). Yet the Kautilyan ideal of a centralized bureaucratic monarchy was not always and easily approximated after the decline of the Mauryan state in Magadh with a sub-continental reach. S.N. Eisenstadt (with Harriet Hartman) remarks: "The major center of Indian civilization was not political but the religious-ritual one. In close relation to its other-worldly emphasis, its wide ecological spread, and its being strongly embedded in various ascriptive units, this center was not organized in a homogeneous, unified, organizational ritual subcenters—pilgrimage shrines and networks, temples, sects, schools—spread throughout the sub-continent, and often cutting across political boundaries."[3]

In pre-modern India, inclusive of the medieval period, the "micro-foundations of power lay in the structure of village communities" above which regional Kingdoms and sub-continental states "exercised a real and proximate political authority".[4] "Sovereignty in Indian history was partly crystallized and partly diffused. Strong states were appreciably centralized but not without some decentralizing features in parts. This pattern of sovereignty not only allowed appreciable autonomies to groups and regions within the state but also visualized a complex inter-state alliance system in the sub-continent in which the allies were the constituents of, and not external to, the states. This was true of even strong sub-continental states like the Mauryas, and the Mughals (only the British colonial state may be an exception in approximating the concept of Westphalian sovereignty). Feudal autonomies of the past as well as the earlier republican tradition of *ganasanghas* may be seen as precursors of the autonomy of state governments under the parliamentary-federal constitutional system in India today."[5]

The modern State in India was, at least in its immediate origins, the product of British capitalism in its imperialist phase. The British colonial state that emerged in this process undermined the traditions of the preceding feudal states and social and economic relations. It reconstructed itself in varying proportions in forms of modern bureaucratic organizations, colonial capitalism, and suzerain and subsidiary princely states under the paramountcy of the British Crown. The British Raj charted a course of development of a modern state that joined the tradition of, and yet was different from, strong sub-continental states of the Mauryas and Mughals with their ambitious *mahamatyas* and *mansabdars* ideally supposed to be manning the top agrarian bureaucracies under a monarchical rule.[6] The absence of a European model of absolutist state in Medieval India was at least partly made up by the British colonial state. It was this state under which centralized modern bureaucracies developed superseding patrimonial bureaucracies of the Maurayas and Mughals. It was this state, again, that helped India to break out of the mould of the feudal states that preceded it and laid down the foundations of capitalist economy.

The British colonial state also introduced limited representative institutions at various levels in a gradual way. By 1935, about 28 per cent of the adult population was enfranchised on the basis of educational and property qualifications to elect provincial and federal legislatures. The Government of India Act, 1935, enacted by the British Parliament was the first experiment in federal government, though it was partly aborted by the refusal of the princely states to join the proposed Union with the British Indian provinces. So, the Union only included the British Indian provinces; and the federal level was still governed under the Government of India Act, 1919. The only federal institution operationalized under the provisions of the 1935 Act was the Federal Court of India for adjudicating disputes between the Government of India and the provincial governments. In any case, the 1935 Constitution significantly contributed to the more perfect federal Union established under the 1950 Constitution after India's Independence.

The formation of the modern Indian state in some ways is unique in what was once called the Third World (between the First World of Western Liberalism and the Second World of Communism). The 'mixed' Indian modernity differs from the kind of crystallized post-Enlightenment modernity that produced European liberalism. The pre-modern hangovers in Indian modernity also differ from the revolutionary break with the past that had produced communism in some countries as the ruling political ideology. State formation in India has been a complex process whose history goes back to the medieval and ancient times. The formation of modern nation-state in India has been significantly influenced by (1) the British colonial state, (2) the nationalist movement for Indian independence, and (3) the pre-colonial state traditions in a remote and indirect way.

The state formation in modern India has thus occurred in the context of not only a colonial and feudal history but also in the background of the highly complex ancient civilization and a modern political culture. The Indian middle classes in contemporary India with the intellectuals and intelligentsia at the core, took the leading role in mobilizing the nationalist movement with a composite and inclusive nationalist ideological discourse. They also played the central role in establishing the post-colonial state with its commitment to political democracy and economic and social transformation towards a more equal and just society. But right from the early twentieth century, the masses and classes were also mobilized into political action and participation by the nationalist leadership. It must also be borne in mind that this state formation developed in the backdrop of India's hierarchical caste system and patriarchal tradition. Moreover, the process has also had to contend with considerable religious, linguistic and ethnic pluralism articulated along sectional as well as regional dimensions. All these diverse factors have had impact on the historical and contemporary state formation in India. Indian states in history, and particularly in modern and contemporary times, have felt normative and pragmatic compulsions to transform the existing socio-economic realities on the ground into a developmental and progressive mould as well as to transcend the myriad cultural and social cleavages in order to produce a pan-Indian and nationally integrated political framework.

The modern national state in India is expected to perform three major political functions which, though broadly related with each other, may not always be consistently complementary. Instead of moving in tandem, they may occasionally contradict one other. These three functional dimensions relate to (1) sovereign democratic republicanism, (2) multicultural pluralism or secularism, and (3) democratic developmentalism.

SOVEREIGN DEMOCRATIC REPUBLICANISM

The first function expects the state to symbolize sovereign democratic republicanism. Sovereignty in Indian history was mostly diffused; it was crystallized only at the core, if at all. It is reflected even in Kautilya's theories of *Saptang* state and *Rajmandala*, though his professed objective was to strengthen the monarch and bureaucratic component of the state. In the Kaultiyan theory, the allies were the seventh constituent of the state. The sharing of sovereignty between the monarch and the vassals in a feudal state, and limited sovereignty or suzereignty enjoyed by the princely states in colonial India under the sovereignty of the British Crown are other examples of our statement about the nature of sovereignty being diffused in Indian history. These ideas of shared sovereignty are very different from the theories of absolute sovereignty formulated by Jean Bodin in the sixteenth century France and Thomas Hobbes in the seventeenth century England. They theorized the rise of absolutist sovereign state in Europe with concentrated and crystallized sovereignty. Among the historical states in India, the Mauryan state in Magadh and the British colonial state were perhaps the ones that asserted sovereign powers most emphatically within the territories under their jurisdictions.

Sovereignty under the post-Independence Indian Constitution underwent a significant process of modernization in at least three senses. First, the post-colonial Indian state inherited the full sovereign powers of the British imperial state in a more crystallized absolute sense, but within the context of a modern nation-state. Second, the national sovereignty of India was reformulated in a democratic and republican way. Third, this sovereignty came to be divided and shared between the union and the state governments within a federal framework, though with clear legal preponderance of the Centre over the States.

The sovereign and republican nature of the Indian state is Janus-faced in the sense that it is a power that is coercive as well as legitimate and noble. Needless to say that the monopolistic claim of the state over the use of legitimate violence and coercion is derived from its sovereign and democratic character. Sovereignty within its national territorial limits does not brook any other superior sovereign power. Within its jurisdiction, the sovereign state is the supreme authority. However, this sovereignty is also supposed to be exercised within the framework of the Constitution and laws of India. It is this aspect that makes the claim to sovereignty legitimate. The state must maintain the delicate balance between its power of coercion and domination on the one hand, and its democratic legitimacy, on the other. Any imbalance between the two elements may lead to problems. Arbitrary and authoritarian exercise of coercive power leads to public discontents and popular protests which under the extreme conditions may undermine the security and survival of the state itself. What is less clear is the fact that excess of democracy may also create conditions of ungovernability and even anarchy. It is this threat that compels constitutions to contemplate emergency. The Indian Constitution is also alive to this threat in its emergency provisions—within a particular state or within the nation at large. The chapter on fundamental rights in the Constitution also combines the discourses on rights as well as duties. Besides, every right is subject to "reasonable restrictions" consistent with security of the state, public order, health and morality of the political community. Moreover, right against arrest and detention in certain cases is also coupled with the provision for preventive detention, which has kept the Indian state on the horns of dilemma right from the Nehru era.

The declaration of internal emergency by Prime Minister Indira Gandhi in 1975 stands out as a major divide when the coercive power of the Indian state caused a great anxiety as to its legitimacy and the survival of democracy in the country. The provision of national Emergency under Article 352 of the Constitution was invoked against the popular mass movement organized by the opposition parties and students and led by Jayaprakash Narayan. Not only the entire official Opposition but also the dissidents in the ruling Congress party were put behind the bars, press censorship was imposed, and the 42nd amendment undermined some basic democratic features of the Constitution. This was the first suspension of democracy in a significant way in post-Independence India. Besides undemocratic political excesses of the state, the police atrocities during the Emergency also assumed a menacing threat to the democratic governance. The emergency regime also undermined political neutrality of bureaucracy and independence of the judiciary by the call of "committed" pubic services and judges. The Shah Commission of Inquiry appointed by the post-Emergency Janata Party government has documented these excesses and atrocities. This misuse of the coercive power of the state against a popular democratic mass movement protesting against the growing authoritarianism and corruption in the Congress governments prompted the coming together of both Liberals and Marxists to call a convention in October 1976 that led to the formation of the All India People's Union for Civil Liberties and Democratic Rights (AIPUCLDR). This convention against the then proposed 42nd amendment to the Constitution was attended by the activists of various political hues in the country—Liberals, Gandhians, Royists, Socialists and Marxists, etc.[7]

Ironically, both the Movement and the State acted in the name of democracy. The Prime Minister claimed to be acting in defense of democracy from anarchy asserting the right of her party governments in New Delhi and States democratically elected in the preceding general election to rule until their mandates were over. The leaders of the Movement, on the other hand, invoked the idioms of legitimacy of democratic opposition and protest, right of the people to recall their representatives who had lost their trust, and Gandhian Satyagraha. The JP Movement went to the extent of giving a call to the Army and the police not to obey illegal orders of the government and incite the people to take their rebellion to the brink that might have led to uncontrollable violence, Prime Minister Indira Gandhi asserted.[8]

In the opinion of historian Bipan Chandra, what Indira Gandhi and JP respectively did had the potentiality of creating conditions for authoritarian intervention in the democratic process—either by the state or by the masses. So, both were on slippery slopes. As it happened, it led to the former to impose the Emergency rule by the decision of the government. Bipan Chandra thinks that rather than demanding Mrs. Gandhi's resignation, JP could have perhaps waited for law to take its course. For Mrs. Gandhi a more honourable course could have been to go for a snap election rather than impose an emergency.[9]

Another context in which the coercive power of the state has come into dispute is the rise of mass movements of protest degenerating into insurgencies and even separatism in Assam in the late 1970s to mid-1980s, Punjab in the 1980s, and Jammu and Kashmir in the 1990s. Insurgencies in some Northeastern States date back to even earlier periods. Separatism and insurgencies with terrorist overtones, often with foreign connections, are still continuing in Jammu and Kashmir and some Northeastern States, even though electoral processes and democratic governance have been restored in these states since the 1990s. If the Emergency in the late 1970s highlighted the misuse of police power, these insurgencies have brought into debate the governments' tendency of relying on the Armed Forces where democratic and federal political processes failed. The democratic and civil rights activists as well as academics are not easily and entirely persuaded by the argument of the State elites that the use of armed forces was the only option left. Arguably, the Central state elites are as much to be blamed in the first place for denial of democratic rights and federal autonomy to these peripheral border states as others. India's "crisis of governability" in fact began in the larger and the mainstream parts of the country first, where the decline of the once democratically dominant Congress party was not made up by the rise of viable democratic alternatives. "The result", according to Atul Kohli, "has been a growing crisis of governability that has manifested itself in unstable political coalitions, governmental policy ineffectiveness, and most important, the increasing use of force and violence in politics".[10]

The number of extraordinary laws in India ranges from the Preventive Detention Act (PDA) (1950) through the Terrorist and Disruptive Activities (Prevention) Act (TADA) (1985) to the Prevention of Terrorist Activities Act (POTA) (2001–2002), and the Unlawful Activities (Prevention) Act (UAPA), 2019. The last named confers upon the Central government the summary power to designate an individual as a terrorist; Section 35 of the Act does not specify detailed reasons based on which an individual can be so declared, one's property seized, and travels banned. Besides, similar laws are operating in different States such as the Armed Forces Special Powers Act (AFSPA) (1958) and the Public Safety Act (PSA) (1978). In a scathing critique of frequent recourse to such laws by governments in India, Ujjwal Kumar Singh laments:

> Two distinct and related trends may be identified in this process, each having important ramifications for institutional structures and norms

> of democratic governance: (a) a trend towards the 'executivization' of law leading to the use of law as a 'political instrument', eroding thereby the basic principles of the rule of law, and (b) their imbrication in center-state relations as an abrasive centralizing force, counterproductive in a polity that sees federalism as a manifestation of democratic decentralization and a means to preserve political/ ideological and cultural plurality.[11]

Anti-Terror laws in India have had the support of the executive, parliament and judiciary, by and large, as well as of the Law Commissions. No such law has been declared unconstitutional by the Supreme Court or a High court, though the apex Court has made occasional observations on their misuse, e.g. in relation to misuse of POTA. It was, in fact, a Law Commission that recommended in its 173rd Report a new anti-terror law when the notorious TADA enacted in 1985 was allowed to lapse in 1995. In pursuance of this recommendation, the government enacted a draft bill and submitted to the National Human Rights Commission (NHRC) for its consideration. The NHRC rejected the draft bill on considerations of threat to civil and human rights. However, the Government of India in the new climate generated by the terrorist attack on the twin World Trade Center Towers in New York and Pentagon in Washington and a terrorist attack on the Parliament of India on 13 December 2001 proceeded to promulgate an anti-terror ordinance which was subsequently enacted into a law called POTA. More recently the UAP Acct, 1967, was amended in 2019 to give the state the power to designate an individual a terrorist without giving the accused any effective way to defend himself.

MULTICULTURAL SECULARISM

The second important dimension of the democratic State in India is its multicultural secular nature. The important relationship between the State and the nation in India is constitutionally defined in 'secular', or better 'multicultural' and pluralist, terms. To some observers, the secular ideology of the Indian State appears as a paradox in view of the deeply religious orientation of the Indian society. This phenomenon must be understood in terms of the nature of Indian nationalism. The imagined Indian national community[12] came to be conceived in a way that both the nation and the State were closely intertwined. The civic-territorial conception of the nation in India was conceptualized in terms of aggregation of the various cultures and communities that had historically co-existed within the same territorial and social space. There was no lag between the projected national community and the projected State that the Indian nationalists in the latter half of the nineteenth century and early decades of the twentieth century envisioned, notwithstanding the cancerous growth of communalism between Muslims and Hindus from 1930 to 1940, largely due to colonial "divide-and-rule" policy. Both the nation and the State remained in the making in British India and were born together in 1947. Indian secularism/ multiculturalism/pluralism was a product of this imagined national community.

The modernizing elites of India evolved, during the freedom movement against the British Raj, a concept of multicultural secularism that was premised on the crystallization of: (i) a common focus of national allegiance to the nation in the making, and (ii) the development of rule of law and a common Indian citizenship. They did not visualize a State that would maintain a wall of separation between the State and religion as it happened in the USA and France in the wake of the American Revolution and the French Revolution. This was not only because Indian religions lacked the institution of an autonomous corporate church.[13] This was also because of the felt-need for reforms in Indian religious traditions, especially the rituals, behaviour patterns and family laws offensive to modern/rational sensibilities. But the nationalists were also sensitive to religious cleavages and their divisive potentialities in Indian society. The Indian National Congress, therefore, either abdicated the field of social reforms in favour of reformist organizations and movements within various religious communities themselves under their community leaders, or else it took up an issue of communal import only when it perceived a substantial concurrent consensus for it in society, including within the minority communities.

However, the nationalist leadership in colonial India encountered two formidable hurdles to national integration. Soon after the establishment of the British Raj on the ruins of tottering Mughal State, the British rulers adopted the policy of "divide and rule" that led to the politicization of communal and caste consciousness on an unprecedented scale. For, the communal segregation and splendid isolation of communities in the traditional society came to an end with the onset of the process of modernization. And the colonial rulers manipulated the emerging ethnic cleavages by playing one community against the other to their own advantage. Besides, a section of Indian Muslims perceived political change in India in an essentially historically rulers' mindset and "reverse majoritarian" mode of thought. To them, Hindu majority in the society automatically meant a Hindu majority in the polity. Intermediation by liberal political institutions between society and the polity whereby the Hindu majority—more categoric than real in any case—would be broken into cross-cutting political allegiances and alliances did not make much sense to them. From Sir Syed Ahmed Khan's exhortations to Muslims to keep away from the Congress to Mohammed Ali Jinnah's demand for a separate homeland for Muslims was a logical culmination of this counter-majoritarian but sectarian mode of thought. The more intimate familiarity of Indians with the majoritarian Westminster model of parliamentary government based on plurality or first-past-the-post system of electoral representation rather than the Western European political systems based on proportional representation and consensus or concurrent plural majorities was not very helpful in this context. And the communal safeguards and federal measures introduced by the British to modify the majoritarian model in India did not have much positive impact either. These measures only fanned the fires of paranoia of separatism among the Hindus and fuelled the embers of insecurity and communalism and secessionism among the Muslims. In the normal course of national evolution in India without a colonial intervention, these measures might have had more positive results in terms of classical Indian syncretic and coexistential cultural construction. And in India today, despite the bitter historical memories and paranoia about fissiparous tendencies, some institutional reforms towards federalizing India's predominantly parliamentary system appear to be necessary. In the process, we must combine a responsible parliamentary government with responsible federalism.

Nehru and Gandhi represented two major models of secularism in modern Indian political thought. Both stood for Indian national unity and a common legal basis for Indian citizenship. But, whereas Nehru emphasized the liberal-individualist foundation for Indian citizenship and national identity, Gandhi patronized an approach that sought to aggregate the primordial pluralities and communitarian-ethnic identities into a larger composite national communitarian consciousness. Thus, the Nehruvian stance came closer to the Western liberal-individualist view of secularism drawing sustenance from rationalism and scientific temper. The Gandhian approach, on the other hand, adhered to the traditional Indian ideal of *sarvodharma samabhava* (equal empathy for all religions). Nehru was quintessentially liberal while Gandhi was primarily communitarian but not communal or sectarian.

The concept of secularism adopted in the Indian Constitution combines both the Nehruvian and the Gandhian approaches to Indian citizenship. The Constitution first guarantees a series of Fundamental Rights—right to equality before law; right to political, civil, occupational, and religious freedoms and protection of life and personal liberty; right against exploitation, and right to constitutional remedies—to all Indian citizens irrespective of religion, race, caste, creed, sex, place of birth or any of them. It then extends some cultural and educational rights to religious and linguistic minorities to conserve their language, script or culture and establish and administer educational and religious institutions of their choice. However, no educational institutions maintained by the State or receiving aid out of State funds shall deny admission to any citizen on grounds only of religion, race, caste, language or any of them. Moreover, the constitutional granting of freedom of conscience and free profession and practice of religion under Article 25(1) does not prevent the State from legislating regulation or restriction of (a) economic, financial, political or other secular activities which may be associated with religious practice, and (b) provision for social welfare and reform or the throwing open of Hindu (Sikh, Jain or Buddhist) religious institutions of a public character to all classes and sections of these religions (Article 25, Clause 2(a) and (b) and Explanation 11). Furthermore, the freedom of a religious denomination or any sect thereof to manage its own affairs in matters of religion, including the establishment and maintenance of institutions for religious and charitable purposes is "subject to public order, morality and health" (Article 26). In addition, State-aided educational institutions shall not provide any religious instruction (Article 28, Clause 1). Thus, the secular State in India is essentially a "rule-of-law secular State", though it does not abjure an absolute jurisdiction over matters of religion. Indeed, it considers the securing of a uniform civil code for all its citizens so desirable as to incorporate it as one of the Directive Principles of State Policy (Article 44). Similarly, the overriding importance of promoting national integration is underlined by inclusion in the Constitution of Fundamental Duties of citizens, among others "to abide by the Constitution and respect its ideals and institutions, the National Flag and the National Anthem" (Article 51a).

In addition to economic and religious factors exacerbating communal conflicts and silent discrimination against Muslims by Hindus and against Hindus by Muslims, another major factor fomenting communalism in India is the political variable. And, besides secular parties, there are communitarian parties like the Bharatiya Janata Party, Shiromani Akali Dal, and Muslim League, sometimes verging on sectarian communalism. Even so-called secular parties degenerate into pseudo-secularism verging on sectarian communalism in pursuit of 'vote-bank' politics in appeasement of the minority voting blocks. All parties, including the communal ones, loudly profess their commitment to the constitutional values or travel some distance on the secularist path when it electorally suits them. If this is largely true of the secular parties like the Congress, Janata Dals, CPI (M) and CPI, this has also been true in some measure of communitarian parties like the BJP and Akali Dal, both of which underwent a perceptible process of de-communalization in the 1960s and 1970s[14] before being overtaken by a new phase of Hindu revivalism and Sikh fundamentalism. Nonetheless, even secular parties enter into electoral alliances with communal parties or hobnob with Rashtriya Swayamsevak Sangh (RSS) chief or go to the Imam of the Jama Masjid for an appeal to Muslim votes. From one point of view, a greater degree of commensality among secular and communal parties should be welcome. It must have at least some nationally integrating impact on the party system in general.[15]

Whether the steep rise of Hindu and Muslim and Sikh fundamentalism in the 1980s and 1990s was the driving wedges of fascism in India? Or does it mean that India has come of age as a secular State and hence can withstand the beginning of a more natural political expression of religious identities? Will the tumult of mighty disharmonies rocking the ship of the Indian multicultural State subside to the normal levels of electoral politics typical of multi-religious Western democracies? Or, will it lead to the excavation of its foundations? When the Hindu communal backlash gave the Congress in 1984 its unprecedented electoral landslide victory before it finally shifted to effect the mighty revival of BJP in 1989 and later in the decade, it was well within the bounds of parliamentary politics. In a perceptive interpretation of the Hindu vote in 1984, Kothari had remarked[16]:

> While everyone seems to sense this in one way or another, it is necessary to see how this happened and how it represents a basic reversal of India's political culture (as also of the core of Hindu identity). A long period of plural segmented existence was leading to a slow sense of uneasiness with mainstream politics to a sense of being cheated, a feeling that the very spirit of accommodation and tolerance on which the Hindus pride themselves was being misused, that the 'minorities'—from Muslims and Sikhs to Dalits and Adivasis—were being pampered. They had the reservations, they owned the arms, they got the benefits of State patronage, and here were we, the so-called majority, left high and dry.

This electoral realignment was preceded by long periods of Congress predominance based on an electoral winning coalition of Brahmins, Muslims, Sikhs, Harijans and Adivasis. The Hindus, then, were more an artifact of categorization than a homogeneously conscious religious community. This made possible the crosscutting electoral coalition of minorities and Dalits. This radically changed over the years to prepare the ground for the tremendous upsurge of BJP in 1989 in the Hindi heartland in general and in 1991 in Uttar Pradesh in particular. The Rudolphs attempted to explain the phenomenon in the following terms:

> Religious performance, celebrations, and demonstrations began to transcend localities and to acquire national dimensions. As they did so, they became more strident and militant. The agitations and yatras (pilgrimages) of the Hindu solidarity and unity movements, such as the Vishwa Hindu Parishad, were no longer the local phenomena they had been in the 1880s when Bal Gangadhar Tilak aroused Hindu political solidarity around the Ganesh festival at Poona. Aided by the proliferation of religious symbolism in the print and electronic media, Hindu themes and organizations crossed State boundaries and helped diverse sects, castes and classes to acquire the consciousness of a popular and more homogeneous Hinduism.[17]

The Hindutva ideology of the RSS–BJP combine has been dubbed by some as an Indian variant of fascism. This characterization is made on the supposed similarity of the *Hindutva* political forces with inter-War fascist parties and movements in Europe in terms of religious-ethnocentrism, stigmatization of minorities, authoritarian monolithic nationalism, and simultaneous emphasis on Hindu *sangathan* as well as plebiscitary mass appeal with religious nationalist motives and charismatic leadership. Yet Indian variants of so-called fascism are also supposed to have some specific indigenous features. For example, Ahmad opines:

> The striking feature of Hindutva fascism is that unlike the German or Italian or even the Irani variants, it speaks relatively rarely of

> the economic instance and fashions its ideological discourse along categories, of `nation' and `community'—through the methodical use of violence as a political instrumentality. That communal violence draws upon many other kinds of routine violence in our society is a central part of my argument; at the same time, however, it is this single-minded politicization of violence—even a certain rationalization of violence as a means for capturing State power—that distinguishes Hindutva fascism from other kinds of violence as well as from other forms of authoritarian populism.[18]

Ahmad[19] goes on to point out that Hindu fascism decries secular Indian nationalism as a failed nationalism and employs an upper-caste Hindu revivalism in a distinctly non-class mobilization strategy.

However, some degree of caution and circumspection is called for in blanket characterization of Indian religious communalism as downright fascist. For one thing, religious communitarianisms in India do not outrightly reject the Indian Constitution and the liberal-democratic regime. The BJP, for example, formally subscribes to what it calls "positive secularism", distinguishing it from what it decries as "pseudo-secularism", or "minorityism". Its "integral humanism"(*a la* Deen Dayal Upadhyay) privileges the claims of the collectivity over those of the individual, but it is society-centric rather than statist, and the protagonists of *Hindutva* or *Hindu Rashtra* (*a la* Vinayak Damodar Savarkar) have been at pains to clarify that this conception is coterminous with Indian territoriality inclusive of all religious communities residing here rather with only the Hindu religious group in any narrow sense. It must, however, be pointed out that the term Hindu Rashtra does alarm and frighten the minorities. However, compulsions of electoral politics in India's diverse society and polity have led to a palpable degree of moderation of the Hindu Right parties and organizations like BJP and RSS. The BJP leadership apparently realizes that to win power at the national level and to promote secular nationalism in Pakistan, it has to become a more liberal and pluralist political formation. Its departure from the ideology of revocation of the 1947 Partition of India (*Akhand* Bharat) is underlined by the visit of Prime Minister Vajpayee in 1999 to Minar-e-Pakistan in Lahore built to commemorate the passing of the Muslim League's Pakistan Resolution in 1940, and reference by former BJP president and leader of the Opposition L.K. Advani to Jinnah's secular vision in his inaugural speech in the Pakistan Constituent Assembly during the 2005 visit to Pakistan.

The Vajpayee-led National Democratic Alliance (NDA) government lost in the Lok Sabha elections in 2004 to the Congress-led United Progressive Alliance (UPA), which ruled for two terms from 2004 to 2009 and 2009 to 2014. Narendra Modi-led NDA was restored to power with a bang in 2014, marking a turning point in the politics of the nation in winning the first single-party majority for the BJP (and even a bigger majority for the NDA) after a long gap of three decades since 1989 when the phase of federal coalition governments began. The last such single-party majority was won in 1984 by the Rajiv Gandhi-led Congress party. In fact, the BJP was re-elected in 2014 with a larger majority both for itself and the NDA. The Prime Minister, Modi has followed a strategy of Hindutva nationalism and national security in combination with development and welfare for all (*sab kaa saath, sab kaa vikaas)*, both for electoral mobilization and governance. The RSS has also shown a remarkable accommodation of Indian multicultural fabric, including Muslims. The present RSS chief, Mohan Bhagwat has gone on record, moving away from a former RSS chief, Guru Golwalkar's harsh assessment of the Muslim community and showing that the organization now sees. Muslims as an important part of the Indian society, saying that Hindutva will cease to exist if it does not consider Muslims or any other set of people as parts of this country, as Hinduism does not discriminate against anyone on the basis of religions and other distinctions. He went on to say that Bharat is a Hindu *Rashtra* and all who consider Bharat as their motherland are Hindu by culture, if not religion.[20]

Indian nationalism was invented for integrating the multi-cultural pluralities of the society into a common nation-state as well as for containing the explosive potentialities of the imperial 'divide and rule' policy and the Muslim League's "two-nation" theory in British India. Indian secularism is different from Western versions of secularism of which two broad models are (a) the *de facto* British secularism where the State has become secular in spite of the conventional association of the Anglican Church of England with the State, and (b) *de jure* American and French models where the Constitution puts a formal wall of separation between the State and church/religion. What, then, are the basic features of the secular State in India? These may be summed up as follows: (a) freedom of religion to all citizens as a fundamental right, (b) certain specific rights to religious minorities relating to education and culture, (c) no formal State religion and a prohibition on taxation on religion, (d) no separation between State and religion evident in the grant in the of legislative and judicial jurisdictions of the State over religious matters such as reforms of family laws and practices and enabling legislation for management of religious shrines and estates. Besides, the State in India has formally and persistently endeavoured to free education and election from the use of denominational instruction and religious electoral campaigns. Even if there have been attempts on the part of some governments, e.g. the BJP-led NDA regime, these have been restrained by the political opposition, the press and universities, the Election Commission of India, and the judiciary.

What has been the successes or failures of the Indian secular State? Again, a clear-cut positive or negative answer is difficult to offer. Perhaps the most significant indicator of the success is that there is no political party in India that has formally rejected the constitutional ideal of secularism. Even the BJP which is often considered to be a challenge in divided India to the secular State says that it is not opposed to secularism per se, only to "pseudo-secularism" or "minorityism". It professes what it calls "positive secularism" and clarifies that for it, cultural nationalism or 'Hindu Rashtra' and 'Bhartiyata' of the Indian Constitution are not contradictory. Yet, the fact remains that the greatest Indian dilemma today is religious communalism and fundamentalism that led in the past to the partition of India. Practitioners of this brand of politics on both majority and minority sides strut the land with injured psyches of historical and imperial victimhood, demanding cultural autonomy, ethnic identity, and right to history and therefore to the future. Hindus, Sikhs and Muslims alike have critiqued the "pseudo-secularism" or "minorityism" (*a la* BJP) of the Congress regime (though no party can be fully absolved of indulging in covert or overt communalism), and have also been somewhat averse to the homogenizing and hegemonizing policies of the Indian aggregate State(s) and the attendant discriminations and disparities. Frequent communal riots, chain-bombings, and other kinds of sabotage, often carried out with foreign connivance, seemed to have become the standard machinations of the government, opposition, and terrorists alike at least until 1993 when the National Human Rights Commission, judicial activism and activities of civil rights groups made their presence felt. Punjab, in the latter half of 1980s, and Jammu and Kashmir, in the early 1990s, remained infested with terrorist violence and religious fundamentalism. Hindu fundamentalists worked up in the latter half of the 1980s a powerful mass movement for the restoration of a Ram temple in Ayodhya on the site of the Babri masjid to rectify a historical wrong by the Mughal invaders; and the medieval structure was demolished by a frenzied mob on 6 December 1992. Narsimha Rao-led Congress minority Government at the Center, which was having an informal rapprochement with the BJP in the preceding period, finally reacted by dismissing the BJP governments under Article 356 of the Constitution in Madhya Pradesh, Rajasthan and Himachal Pradesh, for the apprehended failure of the governments in these States to implement the ban on some Hindu (and Muslim) communal organizations imposed by the Rao government at the Centre. The BJP Government in UP had resigned on its own. The Supreme Court made judicial history by reviewing presidential proclamation of emergency in States for the first time in the *S.R. Bommai and Others* v. *Union of India and Others*[21] and upheld the dismissal of the BJP governments, MP, Rajasthan, and Himachal Pradesh. In the same judgement, the earlier dismissals of State governments in Karnataka in 1989 and Meghalaya in 1991 were found to be unconstitutional. The Court went so far as to observe that but for the fact that new elections had since been held in some of these States, it would have formally struck down the proclamations and directed the revival and restoration of the respective governments and legislative assemblies. The Supreme Court in the above judgement also appropriately declared that democratic form of governments, federal structure, unity and integrity of the nation, secularism, socialism, social justice and judicial review are "basic features" of the Constitution and hence beyond repeal by the amending power of the Parliament.

The challenges to the secular character of the Indian State strike at the very foundations of composite national culture and multicultural nature of the Indian nation-state. The nation in India was born with democracy and secularism as its integral constituents. BJP's advocacy of what it calls "cultural nationalism" implies that secular Indian nationalism is anti-cultural. This is untenable and strikes a deadly blow to multicultural State and nationalism born in the throes of the anti-colonial nationalist struggle and founded on the eve of Independence. Maybe the BJP itself does not reject what we are calling here multicultural Indian nationalism; for it has gone on record that it seeks to remove distortions of Indian secularism by putting in place what it calls "positive secularism". It augers well for the future of multicultural Indian nationalism. There is no doubt that despite the recent stresses and strains, India continues to be a secular state. Elucidating the nature of Indian secularism, Bhargava aptly observes:

> India was never intended to be either a hyper-substantive or an ultra-procedural secular state. It was never meant to exclude every religious practice or institution from the domain of politics. The dominant justification of the policies and practices of the Indian state was done by appealing to contextual secularism of the principled distance variety, exclude religion for some purposes and include it to achieve other objectives, but always out of non-sectarian considerations.[22]

Some observers have taken a serious alarmist view of the rise of Hindutva forces in the 1990s. To be sure, the destruction of the Babri Masjid in 1992 by a frenzied mob mobilized by Hindu communal organizations was most shocking. In its wake, a number of Hindu and Muslim communal organizations were rightly banned, but the BJP was not one of them. It "responded by appearing less militant and dissociating itself from the Vishwa Hindu Parishad (VHP), which had been weakened by the ban and ebbing of emotions after the demolition of the mosque, which it had previously portrayed as a symbol of Hindu humiliation."[23] In his study, Jaffrelot analyses the BJP in particular and the Hindu nationalist movement in general as oscillating between two partly contradictory and partly complementary strategies of mobilization, namely, the moderate and the militant. The former relied on electoral strategy and co-optation of social notables, while the latter employed the strategy of Hindutva identity formation by simultaneous stigmatization and emulation of the adversarial other. In a more recent piece, Jaffrelot (2010) has added, 'Whether the Hindu nationalist parties opted for the path of radicalization or that of moderation has chiefly depended on their relation with their mother organization, the RSS, the perception of the Muslims that prevails at a given time in India, or the attitude of other parties regarding secularism—in correlation with the variables mentioned above—of the most effective electoral tactic.' (Christophe Jaffrelot 2010),

This is an apt characterization. The BJP has indeed swung from militancy to moderation and the RSS has been an important but not the only factor. An earlier phase of moderation had culminated in the merger of the Bharatiya Jana Sangh, BJP's earlier incarnation, in the Janata Party in 1977. "(T)he real challenge before Janata", writes Rajni Kothari, "was to bring the Jana Sangh within the democratic framework just as the Communists had been under Nehru."[24]

As a result of religious fundamentalism, nonetheless, the secular State in India has come under tremendous strain. However, the future of secular state in this country should never be in doubt. This is so not only because of the millennial tradition of "high tolerance and low integration" in the Indian society[25] but also because both secular and religious nationalists have a stake in the multicultural secular state, which is the only viable framework for civilized well-being and national unity[26]. Again, the immense possibilities of pluralist and federal politics in India are unfolding in electoral politics and coalition/minority governments that tend to promote secular politics. Another point also needs emphasis. Despite their calls for Hindu and Sikh hegemonies (*dharma's* supremacy and *Khalsa's bolbala*),[27] neither the BJP nor the Akali Dal has ever demanded the abolition of the secular state in India. BJP leaders have ridiculed what they derisively call "minorityism" of the secular parties[28], but their call for "positive secularism"[29] does not jettison the secular ideal in toto. The increasing levels of conflict in the Indian society and polity, coupled with insufficient integration of regional sub-cultures with the mainstream, mean that the principle of supremacy of the Constitution would move to the center-stage in the years ahead. The principle of parliamentary supremacy was already modified in the Constitution on account of India's effort to combine it with federalism and judicial review. The processes of secularization and political reconciliation would be greatly helped if it becomes a constitutional convention that the Supreme Court verdict in religious matters would not be sought to be overridden by the executive and the Parliament (as it was done by the Rajiv Gandhi regime in the Shah Bano case) without an all-party consensus behind the parliamentary majority. This needs to be incorporated into the Republic's Constitution. And secularism needs to be reoriented as multiculturalism in view of multiple cultural cleavages in the Indian society like languages and ethnicity in addition to religion.

DEMOCRATIC DEVELOPMENTALISM

The third functional aspect of modern Indian state flows from its democratic developmental role. In the Indian model of constitutionalism, both democracy and development are closely combined. This is evident in the framework of fundamental rights and democratic governance, on the one hand, and the ideal of a socialistically-inclined welfare state outlined in the directive principles of state policy and provisional reservation policy for Scheduled

Castes (SCs), Scheduled Tribes (STs) and Other Backward Classes (OBCs) outlined in the Constitution, on the other. There was, however, a prioritization in the Constitution in the sense that while the former were made legally enforceable, the directives were declared to be non-justiciable yet "fundamental in the governance of the country". Nevertheless, the very fact that both these dimensions were constitutionally entrenched, it allowed the possibility of prioritizing the directive principles as the Nehru and Indira Gandhi Congress governments did. This kind of manoeuvrability was also feasible in judicial behaviour as the courts actually did, in emphasizing property rights initially but later in taking the initiative to clothe some of the directives with the status of the fundamental rights in their post-Emergency phase of judicial activism.

In comparative terms, if some East Asian economies gave primacy to economic development over democracy, India sought to reconcile the claims of both democracy and development. The East Asian economic miracle led to the formulation of the theory of developmental state that tried to explain how under certain conditions, capitalist development may be possible even under non-democratic regimes.[30]

But, it required certain facilitating conditions. These facilitating conditions were the introduction of distributive land reforms and universal education by the Japanese colonial rulers in case of Korea and American provisional occupation rulers in case of post-World War II Japan, and by the early national modernizers in case of non-colonies at a time when the society was still emerging out of pre-modern to precursive modern conditions. The modernizing national and post-colonial states subsequently formulated policies to promote commercial and industrial enterprise under some kind of state-private business partnership in which the government did not take upon itself the task of setting up public sector corporations. Rather, it followed mercantilist policies to facilitate the growth of private business enterprise. The successful capitalist development that emerged as a result of these policies led to formulation of the theory of developmental state by political economists such as Gordon White, Chalmers Johnson, Adrian Leftwitch, and others. The so-called East Asian economic miracle that came to pass in this way was mainly export-led economic development. This pattern of economic success subsequently came to be patronized, promoted and prescribed elsewhere by multi-lateral global financial institutions like the World Bank (WB), the International Monetary Fund (IMF) and later the World Trade Organization (WTO).

The theory of developmental state of this vintage has run into difficulties and has come to be criticized on account of various reasons. First, the East Asian economic success suffered a serious financial meltdown in 1997, bringing into focus the infirmities of export-led economies in the global market. Appearance of some problems in East Asian economies resulted in sudden and heavy withdrawal of finances by foreign investors, resulting in a crippling crash which turned millionaires into paupers. Moreover, conditionalities imposed by the IMF and the World Bank in lending money to the borrower countries and inequities of trade between the developed and developing economies also made this model unpopular in the underdeveloped parts of the world, which have become suspicious of neo-liberalism as a veiled neo-imperialism. Further, the growing integration of dependant economies with global capitalism caused not only growing economic disparities among nations but also increasing class and regional economic inequalities within nations. It is in this background that a new theory of developmental state has come to be formulated by a group of political economists that has come to be known as 'democratic-developmental state'.

The Indian model of development is a precursor to an alternative theorization that is more in line with the historical trajectory of Western liberal democracies. As Mark Robinson and Gordon White remark:

> Experience in industrialized societies suggests that there is scope for constructing regimes which fulfil the twin desiderates of broad-based and sustainable development on the one hand, and a legitimate and inclusive democracy on the other. The political and institutional basis for such regimes lies in a new form of developmental state, one which can simultaneously carry forward a development project founded on growth and equality, and which rests on democratic political formulations. This is our conception of the democratic developmental state.[31]

This theory presupposes that a successful democratic developmental state must operate on the assumption of compatibility between political democracy as well as economic development. Political democracy according to this theory must be pervasive and participatory and development must be distributive and inclusive. This theory assures that the two could be mutually reinforcing. Robinson and White go on to clarify the following point: "It is our contention that, if a 'model' of democracy is needed to guide the political evolution of developing societies, it should be social rather than liberal democracy."[32]

James Manor points out that there are at least six major dualities which a state must balance and reconcile if democratization is to be achieved as well as development is to be made possible: (a) order and conflict, (b) self-interested personalized politics and institutionalization, (c) informal and formal politics, (d) 'top down' and 'bottom up' initiatives, (e) continuity and innovation, and (f) confidentiality and transparency.[33] Manor remarks that the late 1970s and early 1980s demonstrated the futility of centralized and commandist governance after a period following the Second World War when this kind of approach had reached a great deal of acceptance. In the prevailing conditions in the world striking a balance between the six foregoing dualities may well receive a greater receptivity in the process of governance than in the past.[34]

Although Manor's discussion in this piece is done in the framework of comparative political analysis, it may not be entirely out of place to suggest that this prescribed approach to governance bears a striking resemblance to the strategy of governance and development that India broadly adopted. Manor indeed illustrates some of these points with Indian examples. It may also be suggested that India is arguably a very promising example of the model of democratic–developmental state here discussed. Nehru's India was generally considered a successful democracy but failed developmental state. Both democracy and development suffered serious challenges in the Indira Gandhi era. Post-Emergency India demonstrated an effective democratic recovery and post-Rajiv Gandhi India also demonstrated economic developmental recovery. India's rise as an economic power since 1991 when neo-liberal economic reforms were accelerated is the talk of the times today. During the decades of the 1980s and 1990s, India was a great success story with credible record in democratic consolidation as well as sustained economic development. All in all, India emerged as a credible example of a reasonably promising democratic developmental state in the world.

It must, however, be conceded that India does not fully conform to the theory of democratic developmental state referred to above. By universal consensus, India has become a reasonably successful functioning federal democracy. However, as a democracy the success of India is more procedural than substantive.[35]

So far as India's success in achieving economic development is concerned, its record has been fairly poor. India's reputation as a rising economic power is relatively recent. It cannot be dated earlier than the early 1990s when neo-liberal economic reforms were accelerated in a comprehensive way. Even this claim to success is disputed. Pranab Bardhan for example argues that despite its recent economic rise, India still has to overcome not only serious economic developmental inadequacies like extreme class and regional economic disparities, bedevilled by severe democratic accountability failures.[36]

Since the declaration of the Prime Minister, Narendra Modi's ill-conceived and adventurous demonetization policy in November 2016, India has also suffered considerable economic decline and stagnation as well as weakening of democratic institutions. Nevertheless, India still remained one of the fast growing economies of the world with the estimated growth rate of 6.5–7 per cent for some time. But soon the economy began to show the downturn due to the ill-effects of demonetisation on small and medium enterprises and the large informal sector of the economy. And on its heels came the crippling effects on the macro economy of the COVID-19 pandemic in early 2020.

Yet, the democratic and developmental prospects of India are not as bad and unpromising in the post-COVID-19 scenario as to write it off as a democratic-developmental state in the Global South.

Liberal Democratic Dimension

The liberal democratic perspective on the Indian State focuses on the frameworks of rights of citizens and obligations of the state, the governmental apparatus, and democratic construction of state power through elections. It is important to keep in mind that the transfer of power from the British rulers to the Indian state was, despite a prolonged freedom struggle in which extra-legal methods of agitations were used, through legal means finally, in as much as India attained freedom by the Independence of India Act, 1947, enacted by the British Parliament. Under this Act, sovereignty was transferred to the Constituent Assembly of India which, in turn, was elected by elected members of provincial legislatures in 1946, who were themselves elected in 1936 under the Government of India Act, 1935. After the lapse of the paramountcy of the British Crown under the 1947 Act, princely states became free to join either India or Pakistan or to remain independent. By the time of promulgation of the 1950 Constitution, all princely states on the Indian side of the Radcliffe Line had, either voluntarily in most cases or under compelling circumstances as in the cases of Hyderabad and Jammu and Kashmir, joined the Union of India.

The basic elements of the democratic state in India may be culled from the Constitution, supplementary parliamentary enactments, and the Election Commission orders. The Constitution outlines the Preamble, Fundamental Rights of Citizens and Directive Principles of State Policy, the structures of parliamentary federal government at the Center, and in the States, and local governments. The Representation of the People Acts, 1950 and 1951, lay down the electoral laws. The Election Commission, register and recognize political parties, prepare electoral rolls, conduct elections, and monitor the electoral code of conduct during the Union and State elections.

Liberal interpretations of the Indian state have highlighted its liberal democratic character. The two features that loom large in this analysis are the autonomy of the state from its social base, and its elective nature. The assumption underlying these writings is that the state is above the social divisions and a common political agency irrespective of which party happens to be in control. The interface between the state and the civil society is intermediated by the party systems—national and state, pressure groups, other organizations of the civil society, including non-governmental organizations (NGOs), and new social movements. The liberal perception of the Indian state has been generally regarded it as either a "soft state" (Gunnar Myrdal)[37] or a "weak-strong state" (the Rudolphs).[38] Myrdal's characterization stems from the fact that, in his assessment, the states in South Asia were not effective in implementing their plans for economic development. The Rudolph's contradictory characterization is influenced by the combination of the continuing legacy of strong states immediately preceding the post-colonial state as well as its weakness in the face of the great responsibilities it has undertaken and the challenges it faces after Independence.

In a more or less similar vein, Atul Kohli drew attention to the paradox of centralization of power in the state and its powerlessness at the same time. To quote Kohli: "'Powerlessness' refers to the repeated incapacity of rulers to fulfil their state objectives." This, he adds, is despite the fact that they concentrate enormous amount of power in the Central organs of the state. The examples he offers are those of "the incapacity of Indira Gandhi to follow through on her major commitments to alleviate poverty, and the political difficulties that Rajiv Gandhi ran into when he attempted to redirect India's import-substitution development model in a more 'liberal' direction."[39]

Other commentators like Rajni Kothari, who were also earlier impressed by the early promise of the Indian state, later gradually got disillusioned by the authoritarian trends in the Emergency regime that underlined what he called a "crisis of institutions". In Kothari's own words: "With the decline of the party as the basic institution of the system and its displacement by the bureaucracy, on one hand, and personal charisma on the other, the system has entered a period of crisis."[40]

Contrasting the Indian state from the Western liberal democratic states, the Rudolphs highlight three distinctive features of the Indian variant. First, the State in India emerges as an autonomous "third actor" between labour and capital. Second, as against pressure groups and lobbies using institutional channels in the West, the Indian political scene is marked by what they call the "demand groups" that easily take to the politics of the street mounting mass pressures. Third, like Kothari, the Rudolphs also refer to the phenomenon of what they call "deinstitutionalization" or "decline of political institutions."[41]

The theme of the crisis of institutions also recurs in the work of other political scientists. M.P. Singh, for example, draws attention to the need for a more balanced Constitutional functioning on the part of the institutions of the state. "It is not yet sufficiently realized", he laments, "that the Indian matrix of political and economic institutions involves a series of checks and balances: between the Parliament, Cabinet, and Supreme Court; between the federal and state governments; between the liberal Fundamental Rights and socialistically inclined Directive Principles of State Policy; between the Constitution and conventions and judicial interpretations; between the public and private sectors of the economy; between the political elites and civil, military, and state enterprise bureaucracies, and so on."[42]

In more recent writings, there is an attempt to understand these changes from two perspectives. The first of these emphasizes the growing democratization of the Indian State by the deepening of the process of electoral democracy that may, in the short term, appear to be somewhat unsettling for the ways in which the institutions had functioned so far. Yogendra Yadav, for example, regards the elections in the 1990s as the third "democratic upsurge after the earlier phases of democratization in the Nehru and Indira Gandhi eras."[43]

The second of these perspectives looks at the changes since the 1990s as the growing federalization of the political system which had earlier functioned predominantly in the parliamentary mode due to dominance of the Congress party under Nehru and Indira Gandhi.[44] The potential centralization of the Indian state was inbuilt in the text of the Indian Constitution, largely patterned on the Canada Constitution Act 1867, on which the Government of India Act,

1935, was modeled, and which, in turn, was incorporated, with modifications, in the Constitution of independent India by the Constituent Assembly of India. The lessons of India's history, marked by divisiveness and the contemporary trauma of the partition of the country in 1947, were used as justifications for a federal model with a strong parliamentary centre. These departures from the classical American model of federalism prompted K.C. Wheare to characterize both the Canadian and Indian Constitutional models as "quasi-federal"[45]. This textual centralization was further accentuated by a national "umbrella" party, the Indian National Congress that ruled in New Delhi as well as in all states, to begin with, and in almost all states until at least 1967. A similar effect emanated from the All India Services (AISs)—Indian Administrative Service, Indian Police Service, and Indian Forest Service—a unique feature of the Indian federal system. AISs are a federal service, as distinguished from the central and provincial services, and serve in highest rungs of Union as well as state governments. They are recruited by the Union Public Service Commission and are largely entrenched in the Constitution itself. They belong to various state cadres and occasionally go on deputation to work for the Union government. Moreover, the inauguration of centralized democratic planning for a "socialistic pattern of society" by the Nehru government in the early 1950s also reinforced the foregoing forces of centralization.

By the end of the 1980s, all these centralizing factors were either over or transformed and regionalized. The Congress Party dominance, and later majority, was gone. It was replaced by a multi-party system with strong regional parties and federal coalition and/or minority governments. This party system transformation altered the presence of a centralized federal government into veritable confederal coalitional Governments haunted by instability. Political regionalization and power-sharing on a wide horizontal and vertical plane also forced the AISs and the planning process to accommodate to the pressures for a more federalized mode of functioning from the predominantly parliamentary one. The political chessboard became diversified as well as regionally segmented. The two Houses of Parliament, the offices and the President and Vice-President of the Republic, various state Assemblies and governments came to be controlled by different parties or coalitions of parties. This chequered political matrix put a premium on consociational and federal consensus and coalition building on executive, legislative, and electoral levels. Political diversities and compulsions at different levels often conflicted and demanded cooperative response among same as well as different sets of parties at one plane and adversarial response on another. Federal coalition governments transformed prime ministerial or chief ministerial Cabinets into collegial Cabinets. The collective responsibility of the Union executive to the Parliament was diluted. The Cabinet became compartmentalized and ministries were parcelled out to various parties in a coalition. Powerful satraps of regional parties in states preferred to stay in states as Chief Ministers and sent their protégés as Union ministers and remote-controlled them. Under these conditions, the President and Governors acquired some discretionary manoeuvrability. Fragmented and conflicted executive and legislative branches of the government left the field wide open for enormous expansion of the power of the judiciary by ways of its interpretative, review, and activist roles. This process of federalization has diffused the condensed power of the national state in India and considerably democratized the executive-driven political system.

How has the Indian democratic state worked in over seven decades of its existence? It is difficult to answer this question in a straightforward positive or negative way. It is no mean achievement that the Constitution of India has survived the tumultuous decades after World War II until the second decade of the 21st century. In addition, India has successfully maintained its tradition of free and fair elections despite heavy odds. However, mere survival is not a big deal and elections are not all that only matter in a democratic system. The Preamble to the Constitution proclaims India to be a 'Sovereign, Socialist, and Secular Democratic Republic'. Without any formal amendment to the Constitution and without adequate open debate, recent developments have put question marks and undermined each of these cardinal Constitutional values. The sovereignty and territorial integrity of the country is compromised. Democratic and Republican values were undermined by the Emergency regime. The Indian democratic state was rescued by a massive mass movement against corruption and authoritarianism led by Morarji Desai and Jayaprakash Narayan and the 1977 Lok Sabha elections. These values have subsequently also appeared seriously undermined by the challenges to the democratic and secular foundations of the state. Unstable and divided governments have been a feature of governance in India in the decades since then. Corruption and criminalization of politics are far more alarming than in the 1970s. Yet, no democratic intervention by a mass movement that could rescue India from this morass has been in sight. Of course, a new pattern of social movements have appeared in recent decades wherein micro grassroots movements based on single issues (e.g. environment, ecology, gender, citizens interest groups etc.) predominate. But their efficacy and integrated political impact are yet to be seen. The Anna Hazare Jana Lokpal Movement started as a wave in 2011 but soon turned into a ripple by 2012. However, it left a legacy of the Lokpal and Lokayukta Act belatedly passed in 2013, which remained unenforced until January 2018. Its impact is yet to be seen.

Until some time back, politics in India was generally considered an area of relative success in comparison to the tardy rate of growth in the economy. India was given additional credit in relation to China whose faster rate of economic growth was seen to lose some of its sheen due to its authoritarian politics in comparison to democratic India. However, if India has remained democratic, the apparent democratic formalism of elections and legislative paraphernalia barely conceal substantial departure of the Indian political system from the substance of elections fully free from money and muscle power, of constitutionalism, parliamentarianism, and federalism. In the absence of the substance, Indian democracy has practically been reduced to a "quasi-democracy", in the words of Vir Chopra.[46] The politics of defection among legislators since the late 1960s for money and ministerial posts, not only in States but now also at the Center, has robbed the legislatures of public esteem and trust. Criminalization of politics has reached alarming proportions. A fairly common observation of commentators is that in the past criminals and musclemen were used by politicians; now the criminals themselves have joined the ranks of politicians. There is no political party today that does not harbour a number of criminals holding party and even legislative/ministerial posts, the figure in some running into double digits as revealed by press reports. A high-level Union Government administrative committee headed by Home Secretary N.N. Vohra in its Report in 1993 draw pointed attention to a nexus between politicians, criminals, police and bureaucrats in various parts of the country.[47] There is evidently little follow-up action on the Report either at the legislative or administrative levels.

An activist Election Commission in the 1990s brought about some cosmetic changes in the conduct of elections, but its efforts to bar criminals from the electoral-political processes have not yet been very successful. It may also be added that on the Supreme Court directive, the Election Commission of India has obliged since 1998 all candidates to submit an affidavit regarding criminal charges and conviction and financial assets and liabilities along with their nomination papers. The Commission took the initiative of convening an all-party meeting in November 1997 on this issue. In states like Bihar, citizens owning any property in rural and urban areas had to fend for themselves by forming private "armies" or vigilante groups. There has also developed in this state a parallel system of private coaching institutes with government-aided universities and colleges practically going defunct. In some states, even governments and private corporate companies have stooped to either sponsoring or colluding with mafia gangs and separatists to terrorize the Government and Opposition to buy reprieve. In economically stagnant Bihar since the corporate political funding is largely unavailable, Congress and Janata Dal Chief Ministers in the late 1980s and '90s and later maintain packs of personal followers and sycophants legislators virtually as private retainers, siphoning off huge amounts from the government treasury in innumerable scams, the flagship of which goes by the name of the Bihar Fodder Scam. That Bihar is not unique in this regard is clear from the *hawala* mega-scam involving huge illegal payments to a large group of top politicians in the Congress, the Janata Dal and the Bharatiya Janata Party (BJP). States like Bihar resorted to the device of Ordinance Raj with Ordinances being repeatedly renewed without ever being legislated!

For a long time, there has occurred subversion of federal provisions of the Constitution, misuse of Article 356, fiscal and administrative subordination of the States by the Center's overriding powers in these areas. Ironically, both the parliamentary and federal components of the constitutional system have been undermined. Responsible parliamentary government at the state level has remained an illusory ideal due to de-federalization of the constitutional office of the Governor, who until recently, and in some cases even now, has mostly and practically been treated as an errand boy of the Center. At the Center itself, the Cabinet system in practice degenerated into the prime ministerial system, marginalizing not only the Cabinet but also the Parliament. These trends have been to an extent reversed since the 1990s but the fragmentation of the party system has entailed endemic instability of coalition governments. While some federal features and instrumentalities of the Constitution have come into their own for the first time, paradoxically chronic governmental instability at the Center has caused grave anxieties as to the viability of forming and maintaining any parliamentary government at all.

The abuse of civil rights on whims and caprices of the agents of the State—litany of unconstitutional conducts of those in power—has been legion. In recent years, however, some improvement in federal as well as civil rights matters could be seen. These improvements may be largely attributed to a more federalized party system, judicial activism, growing self-consciousness of the President and some Governors regarding their constitutional role, the activities of the civil rights groups, and the setting up of a National Human Rights Commission under an Act of the Parliament in 1993.

Comparative political experience about modern and modernizing political system has revealed that multi-party elections and a viable party system are indispensable to representative democracy. The party system has been the catalytic factor in the growth and stabilization of a democratic state. As Klaus Von Beyme has observed, "political parties have been central to the growth not only of democratic politics but also of political science; ... it is no coincidence that it was on political parties that Lowell, Bryce, Ostrogorski and Michaels produced the first books that could be described as genuine political science."[48] From this perspective, the de-institutionalization of the major national and regional parties and authoritarian and dynastic domination of these democratic instruments of governability would appear to be a major symptom of the crisis of political institutions in India. India's one-party dominant system within a multi-party configuration was not initially and inherently undemocratic. However, over the years, by the 1970s, the formalism of one-party dominant system turned into an instrument of authoritarian rule that finally culminated in the first formal termination of constitutional rule under the Emergency regime. India's parliamentary federal system was replaced by a neo-patrimonial regime with ministers, MPs, Chief Ministers and MLAs practically being nominated and appointed by a "presidential" Prime Minister (presidential in the American sense). With the departure of internal democracy in political parties, democracy in political system remained a will-o'-the-wisp. But when decline of one-party dominance gave way to a multi-party system, federal potentialities of the system came into fruition. However, due to party system fragmentation, stability of parliamentary government itself became problematic. Paradoxically, federal regeneration was accompanied with parliamentary decay.

The crisis of political institutions of democratic state in contemporary India and the much lamented de-institutionalization may be seen from the perspective of the growing democratization and the attendant teething troubles. As Bhargava[49] remarks: "... [T]he current crisis of liberal democracy is in large part due to its own success. Civil liberties give voice to the mute and the democratic process creates the space to play it out. Those debarred from the public domain entered it with modes of speech and action different from ones to which the initiators of liberal democracy were accustomed to and in numbers that greatly exceeded the tiny upper crust that led the national movement." Observers like Yadav[50], taking off from disproportionate increase in electoral turnout in State Assembly elections, compared to the parliamentary ones, make out a case for the "second democratic upsurge" in the post-Congress phase: "as the politics got decentered in the 1990s, democratic urges found primary expression at the state level. The aggregate turnout of Assembly elections held between 1993 and 1996 (which covered all the states except Jammu and Kashmir and Punjab) represents a major jump which also enables us to read a weak trend in the same direction in the previous decade." These arguments undeniably sound plausible. It is difficult not to feel, however, that this is only a partial truth, for the democratic upsurge is not coupled with institutionalization of procedures and values as reflected in rampant abuse of democratic power for personal, partisan, and even corrupt and criminal ends. The decline and dysfunctionalities of the institutions of the state and the civil society has caused a great deal of alarm, but is mercifully compensated to an extent and countered by institutional responses such as judicial activism in area of constitutionalism and public accountability, public interest litigation for environmental protection and on behalf of the poor, as well as new social movements and what Kothari calls 'non-party political processes'[51] In a similar vein, Manor[52] argues: "The greater susceptibility of informal institutions to decay and the greater ease with which formal institutions undergo regeneration have brought about a dramatic change in the pattern that prevailed up to the late 1960s. In that earlier period, one informal institution, the Congress Party, predominated—and both protected and stunted the growth of formal institutions. And there is much more balance between formal and informal institutions with the former performing many important tasks which they had not (or had not fully) performed earlier—often taking the lead in regenerative and other activities."

Indeed, the current crisis of liberal democracy in India has generated a lively debate on the origins and nature of Indian liberalism itself. In his critique of Khilnani's book, *The idea of India*[53], Bhargava[54] cogently argues against the former's hypothesis that Indian liberalism was stillborn as it was produced by British utilitarianism, an ideology with relatively collectivist calculus (the greatest good of the greatest number) and the inherently collectivist ethos of the Indian tradition. Bhargava also disagrees with Khilnani's claim that in India, "Liberty was understood not as an individual right but as a nation's collective right to self-determination," and that liberal democracy in India was imposed on an unsuspecting mass uninitiated into liberalism by an elite lacking in self-confidence and unaware of the larger implications of its decision in a fit of absent-mindedness. Bhargava observes that neither utilitarianism nor Indian nation alone were completely lacking in their awareness and recognition of the worth of the individual and his inalienable rights. Besides, he also makes the point that collective struggle against absolute monarchical and colonial power is not any less liberal. The concern of the Indian nationalist elite for economic equality and justice is also considered to be a part of the 20th century liberalism, though it may be lacking in classical liberalism. Bhargava also contends that the Indian political elites, some of whom included most outstanding leaders of an entire millennium, were no more absent-minded than the British colonial masters, both sets of the elites were, after all, human historical agents representing the Hegelian 'cunning reason', who can at best be aware of the intended consequences of their actions and cannot fully preclude the inevitable unintended consequences. We may add that even Gandhi, the dominant figure of the nationalist struggle, who is generally interpreted with a collectivist bias did not only mobilize one of the greatest mass movements in Indian history, but also asserted that even if a single individual is convinced that he must offer conscientious objection to the State, it is not only his right but also duty to do so. In an interview in 1946, Gandhi articulated his political vision of the relationship between the individual, the state, and the world community by juxtaposing two contrasting metaphors of the Pyramid versus the Oceanic Circles; he emphatically preferred the latter.[55]

Coercive Aspect of State

We are witnessing today, in the post-9/11 world, the phenomenon of national security state, which enjoys extraordinary powers that are derived from the situation which Agamben describes as a "state of exception". Anti-terror laws come under the category of extraordinary laws because they have some provisions that are different from ordinary laws such as provisions related to detentions, trials, evidence and burden of proof. Such acts enacted from time to time by the Parliament of India include the Terrorist and Disruptive Activities (Prevention) Act (TADA), 1985, 1987; the Prevention of Terrorism Act (POTA), 2002; and the Unlawful Activities Prevention Act, 1967 (UAPA) as amended in 2004, 2008, 2012 and recently in 2019. The last amendment to UAPA was made in 2019. It is indeed updated.

Ujjwal Kumar Singh (2012) has argued that these three laws can be seen as "three distinct regimes for addressing terrorism in India". Such extraordinary laws far from being "temporary laws", have virtually become a new normal. "The experience with anti-terror laws in India has shown that the persistent lament of the existence of a pernicious internal enemy, and the fear of a legal system being unable to cope with it, have produced the context for the normalization of extraordinary laws" (Singh, 2012).[56]

CLASS OR SOCIAL BASES OF STATE

The class basis of the Indian State has received a great deal of attention in the neo-Marxist literature. The neo-Marxists have come a long way from the orthodox Marxists who regarded the Indian State as dominated by the capitalists and the landlords. In neo-Marxist assessment, neither the bourgeoisie nor the working class has been able to establish its hegemony on the State. This is because the post-Independence State as well as the colonial and pre-colonial States was overdeveloped in relation to the civil society. Anupam Sen argues that around the time of Independence, the leading industrial capitalists of India formulated the so called Bombay Plan (1944) as a fifteen-year perspective plan in which the State was envisaged to play a leading role in India's industrialization, especially in areas where the private capital was either weak or unwilling to invest on account of the long gestation period and the nature of industries that demanded State intervention in view of their relevance for the social sector and national defence. The leading role for the State in the strategy of planned economic development initiated by the Nehru Government was thus welcomed by the private sector itself.[57]

To neo-Marxists, the State could never be absolutely autonomous from its class base in the long run, but at least for the present, the Indian State enjoys a *relative autonomy* from its class base. Pranab Bardhan avoided the standard Marxist terms like the "ruling class" in his study of the Indian State and instead postulated a coalition of "dominant proprietary classes" of industrial capitalists, rich farmers, and professionals (civilian and military including white collar workers). Bardhan remarks: "The first thing that strikes one in this respect in the Indian scene is the plurality and heterogeneity of these classes, and the conflicts in their interests are sufficiently important not to make this comparable to the division of the bourgeoisie in industrially advanced countries into different, largely complementary, 'fractions', like industrial capital, finance capital and mercantile capital."[58]

In Bardhan's opinion, the "semi-feudal" agrarian class in India "has largely disappeared". "In most parts of the country", says he, "agrarian capitalism is sprouting and in the better irrigated regions, it may even be described as thriving."[59] Bardhan also notes a complex intermesh between the class and caste in the rural areas. He says that in order to channelize State subsidies and inputs in their favour "the farmers of one *jati* have to form alliances with other *jatis* of similar occupation". These relations are "more like uneasy political coalitions, held together more by pragmatic class interest than by homogeneity: two farmers… may not accept food from each other but will pull together for higher prices or lower taxes."[60]

Regarding the class of professionals, Bardhan says: "It is not customary to include them among proprietary classes but if physical capital can be the basis of class stratification so can be human capital in the form of education, skills and technical expertise."[61] This incidentally is a more open class category for upward mobility for the lower classes and castes who find in education and public employment "a passport to the prospect of a secured job in the bureaucracy and the professions". This explains why "some of the bitterest caste struggles in various parts of urban India have been over the issue of reservation of seats in medical and engineering schools and of jobs in the government for lower castes."[62]

Achin Vanaik's characterization of what he calls the "social character" of the Indian State is broadly similar to Bardhan's, but he differs with him on two points. First, among the various terms used in the literature in this context —"ruling oligarchy, power bloc, ruling-class alliances, dominant coalition/ruling coalition"— he considers the last one as "most appropriate because of the considerable tension among its various components, above all the tension between the industrial, and agricultural bourgeoisie. "'Coalition', rather than 'bloc', 'oligarchy', or 'alliance', better captures the looseness of this arrangement and the pivotal mediating role that its third component, the apex of the State bureaucracy, has played and continues to play." Second, he also thinks that it would be apt to include in the third component of the dominant coalition, not only the higher rungs of the non-State professional strata, the middle classes as a whole (ranking lawyers, journalists, establishment Professors and educationists, media stars, etc.) but also a smaller segment of the working class.[63]

Nation-State and Nationalities

The complex relationship between the state and the nation in India has been constructed along three dimensions: (a) the civic, (b) the developmental, and (c) the cultural. The civic dimension encapsulates the state and the nation and is signified by the phrase "We, the people of India..." in the Preamble to the Constitution of India. It is ideal-typically embodied in the Parliament of India, especially the Lok Sabha directly elected on the liberal-individual-based franchise. The developmental state first appeared in the garb of the national planning state under Nehru, wedded to the creation of an industrial economy in which the state would scale "the commanding heights of the economy" and secure the well-being of the teeming millions of the starving and naked people of India. By the early 1990s, when the state-led strategy of development ran into crisis, the state made a gradual shift to neo-liberal capitalist economy, without, however, entirely abandoning the public sector. The cultural dimension of the Indian nation-state was expressed in an attempt to reconcile the liberal framework of individual rights with the multicultural framework of linguistic and religious and tribal rights, recognized both on the *horizontal* parliamentary plane and *vertical* federal levels going down to states and tribal scheduled areas in the Fifth and Sixth schedules of the Constitution. The Fifth Schedule is administered directly by the Union through the Governor with the help of the Tribal Advisory Councils. The scheduled areas, under the

Sixth Schedule, in Assam, Meghalaya, Tripura, and Mizoram in particular are designated autonomous districts and regions. These areas enjoy wide-ranging self-governing powers exercised by District Councils and Regional Councils that are partly directly elected and partly nominated by the Government of the State concerned. Laws of the Parliament and State Legislatures do not automatically apply to these areas unless the district or regional councils so desire and direct within their jurisdictions.

The rise of Indian nationalism, a product of the 19th century (compare with the emergence of nationalism in Western Europe in the 18th century), was the catalytic force that began the transformation of dynastic and colonial States in India, into the nation-state.

Democracy and development, and, above all, culture have played the crucial role in this transformation. The rationalities and legitimacies of these three dimensions do not always go together. For, whereas democracy is premised on popular support for universal abstraction of the State, some public policies aimed at gross economic growth may not be popular, and ethnic communities in the larger national political community may at times be swayed by conflicting considerations. These contradictions may be particularly endemic in the case of Indian nationalism which is multicultural rather than monocultural. Like nationalisms elsewhere, Indian nationalism is also, in the well-known phrase of Benedict Anderson, an "imagined community", more an invention than a discovery, and a product of print capitalism that originated in British India and created and propagated the Indian nation in the large new reading public in English and vernacular languages. Writing about European nations, Anderson sums up his argument: "The convergence of capitalism and print technology on the fatal diversity of human language created the possibility of a new form of imagined community, which in its basic morphology set the stage for the modern nation." Underlying the cultural roots of nations of Europe, Anderson goes on to remark:

> What I am proposing is that nationalism has to be understood by aligning it, not with self-consciously held political ideologies but with the large cultural systems that preceded it, out of which—as well as against which—it came into being.[64]

Where Indian nationalism differs most from the typical pattern of European nationalism is that, language rather than religion provided the ethnic foundation of nation because nation-states in Europe emerged as the result of the weakening and break-up of the sway of the Papacy of Rome over the Christian world and the decline in hold of the classical Latin. The Indian subcontinent has developed three major nation-states. The largest, India, to borrow the terms of Anthony D. Smith[65], is an example of "polycentric nationalism" and Pakistan and Bangladesh are "ethnocentric" nations founded primarily on religion (Islam) and language (Bengali). All these three kinds of nation-states in our neighbourhood have their own problems in all the three dimensions of democracy, development, and culture—communal and national. India's track record in reconciling these problems and contradictions has not been spectacular, but it has been remarkable and promising, especially in the Afro-Asian world. Optimists hold out India as a great success story of a multicultural democratic developmental State.[66] The pessimists, on the other hand, paint a bleak future in which the contradictions between democracy, community, and capital would continue in this "grand narrative" in our part of the world. "This will mean a substantialization of cultural differences, necessarily excluding as `minorities' those who would not conform to the chosen marks of nationality. The struggle between `good' and `bad' nationalism will be played out all over again."[67] This pessimist historical speculation bears a trace of Orientalism and a strange diehard mix of colonial and Marxist historicist vision. Neither naïve optimism nor historicist pessimism would appear to be warranted.

We now proceed to analyze the relationship between the *ethnies* (as distinguished from smaller ethnic groups) in the sense of what the Marxists dub as nationalities. The relationship between the nation(s)-state and nationalities in India has not received much scholarly attention, presumably because after the partition of the country on Muslim League's 'two-nation theory' in 1947, the issue has largely become one on which new states have been formed within the framework of the Constitution of the Union of India. While the number of federating states have more than doubled over the years, no separatist movement has succeeded. Hence, the question of nationalities in the Indian political discourse has, by and large, been carried on within the framework of multiculturalism and federative nationalism. Although a variety of ethnic identities are active in democratic politics of India, only religion, language and tribe have served as the basis of state formation. Using the concept of 'national minorities' put forward by Will Kymlicka[68] and applying it to the Indian context, we can identify four such communities, namely, Muslims, Sikhs, Christians and some aboriginal tribes. Each of these national minorities has at least one or more states to represent them within the Union: Jammu and Kashmir (predominantly Muslim), Punjab (predominantly Sikh), Nagaland (predominantly tribal Christian), Mizoram (predominantly tribal Christian). Caste or caste-clusters have been relevant in electoral politics but they are not state-forming.

However, the language has proved to be the most important ethnic and regional identity that has proved to be State-forming in the largest number of cases. Out of the twenty-eight States (Jammu and Kashmir was reorganized into the union territories (UTs) of Jammu and Kashmir and Ladakh in August 2019, but the government has indicated the former may again be reorganized as a state), twelve are based on non-Hindi linguistic groups [one State to each: Andhra Pradesh (Telugu), Assam (Assamese), Gujarat (Gujarati), Kerala (Malayalam), Tamil Nadu (Tamil), Maharashtra (Marathi), Karnataka (Kannada), Odisha (Oriya), Punjab (Punjabi), West Bengal (Bengali), Jammu and Kashmir (Kashmiri but the State Government has declared Urdu as the official regional language), and Manipur (Manipuri)]. Ten states of the Union including the National Capital state of Delhi are Hindi-speaking. Significantly, Hindi has not led to the formation of one state, nor is there a common regional institutional forum of Hindi-speaking states separate from others. Thus, at least in the case of Hindi-speaking states, geographical or regional factor has been more important in state-formation than the linguistic identity. This may be because the standard Hindi (*khari boli*) is really not the mother tongue of any area, where Magahi, Bhojpuri, Maithili, Brajbhasha, Avadhi, Rajsthani, etc. are the dialects spoken in the Hindi heartland. What Amir Khushro in the fifteenth century called *Hindiavi* and is now called Hindi developed as a hybrid in the medieval army camps and markets in Delhi–Meerut and Hyderabad, where initially it was also called *Rekhta*. During the British Raj and after Independence, Hindi or what Gandhi called Hindustani was sought to be Sanskritized by the Hindus and Persianized by Muslims. Due to these tendencies, the two styles of Hindustani—Hindi and Urdu—got pulled in opposite directions, thus creating a political hiatus. As Selig S. Harrison observes, "These regional identities are old and persistent: literary tradition in most regional languages or their precursors can be traced without difficulty to the first centuries after Christ, and there are, in all of the regional languages, more or less unbroken literary traditions at least eight centuries old."[69] The history of linguistic states in India goes back to the pre-Independence period. The Simon Commission, appointed by the British Government in 1927 to consider constitutional reforms in British India, received a number of memoranda for the creation of linguistic provinces for the people speaking Oriya, Telugu, Tamil, Kannada, and for the transfer of Sylhet from the province of Assam to the Bengal presidency. The respective provincial legislatures had also moved resolutions and passed them in most of these cases. Besides, some tribal groups of Chhotanagpur, depressed classes and Momins (Muslim weavers) had also made submissions to the Simon Commission for formation of separate provinces for them.[70]

In the early 1920s when Mahatma Gandhi made his dramatic appearance on the national political horizon of India, he was instrumental in getting the Congress party organization reorganized on linguistic basis rather than on the basis of the then existing provincial boundaries. As a nationalist movement, the Congress supported the idea of linguistic states; however, when it formed the government after Independence, its approach radically changed. Prime Minister Nehru as well as committees appointed by the Congress party and the Constituent Assembly of India rejected the demands for unilingual states on the ground that such a move would be divisive of national unity. Multilingual states, on the other hand, would promote national integration. The States Reorganization Commission appointed by the Nehru Government in 1953 in the face of persistent linguistic agitations submitted its report in 1955, endorsing unilingual states already created under pressure but recommended in favour of retaining multilingual states elsewhere. The State Reorganization Act passed by the Parliament in 1956 accepted and implemented the recommendations of this Commission. Nonetheless, agitations for linguistic states continued to appear in the coming years and the Union Government was forced to concede their demands. Thus, unilingual states were created by bifurcating the Bombay state into Maharashtra and Gujarat in 1960 and trifurcating Punjab into Punjab and Haryana (and parts merged with the newly created Himachal Pradesh). Nagaland was the first northeastern state carved out of Assam in 1962. By the 1970s, Assam had been further divided into six other states. The states carved out of Assam—which itself had been separated from Bengal in the early 1870s—were mostly created on the basis of tribal identity. The latest four states of Jharkhand, Uttarakhand and Chhattisgarh were formed in 2000 in considerations of regional economic backwardness in the case of Uttarakhand and regional as well as tribal backwardness in the cases of Jharkhand and Chhattisgarh, and Telangana in 2013 bifurcating Andhra Pradesh, and also, in consideration of backwardness.

Despite all this internal political fragmentation, there are still some such pending demands, as many as 31 demands for States or sub-States.[71]

Gender and the State

The theory of State in India is perhaps most underdeveloped in relation to the women's question. This in fact may be true not only of India but the West as well. Everywhere half of the humanity, euphemistically "the better half", was last to be enfranchised in the march of modern democracy. Conventional wisdom both in biology and culture may explain, but not justify, this lag in women's development in relation to men. Biologically, the woman was supposed to be physically weak and unsuited to some areas of work, and more vulnerable to exploitation. This assumption was used to exclude them from some professions as well as to put them in *purdah.* Even Sigmund Freud appears to have built his theory of psychoanalysis on the assumption that anatomy is destiny. Not only classical biology and classical psychoanalysis of individual personality but also society and culture conditioned men and women differently for different social and cultural roles. These conventional sex stereotypes were subsequently questioned to theorize gender equality. Thus, now in social sciences the distinction between sex and gender has become a commonplace. While sex is a biological difference, gender is a socially constructed and conditioned role and identity. It can be resocialized to be free from anatomical differences to allow for social and cultural construction of gender to obliterate sex stereotypes. By now, practically all professions are open to women including those previously supposed to be a male domain.

The contemporary feminist political theory has challenged the difference commonly and unquestionably made in terms of the *private* sphere and *public* sphere. Almost all contemporary political ideologies and theory consider this a legitimate demarcation to build their arguments, as to what areas of life are open to State control and what areas are not. The role of the State, and even society, is supposed to intervene in public matters to the exclusion of private matters. The feminists argue that this apparently innocuous difference between public and private is still being used to sustain residual patriarchy to the disadvantage of women. Women still mostly work in the private sphere of the family where their contribution to the family or to the national economy is not even indexed and constructed into an economic indicator of the national or global economy. Even the working women generally end up having to work in the place of employment as well as do the conventional chores at home, metaphorically the perpetual 'double shift'. Even this disproportionately larger contribution to the family and the national economy goes unindexed and does not entitle them to enhanced share in the property. Indeed they are not only exploited economically and sexually in the private as well as public domain but also not accorded the usual difference and obligation that comes naturally to men. To quote Martha Nassbaum, "the participation of women in governance has long been hindered by the assumption that their proper sphere is the 'private' sphere and this same assumption has been an obstacle to good theoretical and practical work on the question of gender and governance."[72]

Gendering governance in India is now an 'in-thing' but it has come lately. Modern Western impact is supposed to have triggered this process and by now forward sections of society as well as the political class claim to be committed to this cause. However, to sample only two important social science publications, gender equality as an issue does not figure in Dharma Kumar's and Andre Beteille's well-known works on equality in India.[73]

Women in India got the voting right under the Government of India (GOI) Act of 1919. This Act enfranchised 3,15,000 adult women. The GOI, 1935 extended suffrage to more than six million women. When elections were held under this Act, eight women were elected from "general" constituencies and 42 from "reserved" constituencies. When provincial ministries were formed under this Act, six women were included as ministers.[74]

The contribution of the freedom struggle in involving women in social and political spheres in India is considered tremendous. What is even more remarkable is that this participation was forthcoming not only from upper class/caste/educated women but also from middle class/caste and rural women, especially in the Gandhi-Nehru era of mass nationalist mobilization. The record of women's development after Independence with formal or informal role in this sphere of the State and civil society would appear to be a mixture of success and failures. While women in modern sectors would appear to have gained significantly through steady increase in their representation in the educational and employment sectors, their lot in the share of ancestral property has been inadequate. Thus, modernity has opened up avenues of upward mobility for them, but traditions and conventions of the Indian society still continue to be largely dominated by patriarchical structures and values. The adoption of universal civil code would have been the most effective way of emancipation of women as it would have brought about gender equality both in modern and traditional sectors of society and culture in all religious communities. In the absence of this while women's education and literacy (50.4 per cent female literacy compared to 70.3 per cent male literacy) as well as their representation in structures of the polity and economy has gradually moved up, real gender equality continues to be a will-o' the-wisp. Despite several reforms in Hindu family law before and after Independence, women continue to be unequal in relation to men in property, succession, marriage and divorce. There are two systems of Hindu family law, namely *Dayabhaga* prevalent in eastern India and *Mitakshara* followed in the rest of the country. In the former, sons could claim right to property and partition only after the death of the father. In the latter, sons are entitled to these rights during father's lifetime itself.[75]

The Hindu family property rights today are regulated by the Hindu Succession Act (HSA) of 1956 applicable to 82.0 per cent of the Indian population in all States excepting Jammu and Kashmir. The Hindu personal law is commonly shared by Hindus, Sikhs, Jains and Buddhists. The objective of the Act is to make sons and daughters equal in inheritance right but some escape clauses still leave significant gender inequalities. To quote Bina Agarwal:

> The virtually unrestricted testamentary rights provided under the Act are gender-neutral in principle, but can be used (and often are used) in practice to disinherit potential female heirs. Some other inequalities, while explicit, are of a relatively minor character, such as not recognizing the children of a predeceased daughter of a predeceased daughter among the class I heirs, while recognizing the children of a predeceased son of a predeceased son.[76]

But there are also substantial gender inequalities stemming from two major sources: (i) the continued recognition of Mitakshara joint family property; and (ii) the special treatment given to agricultural land. In a few States, due to subsequent amendments of the HSA, some of the inequalities relating to joint family property have been reduced, or have changed in character, but in most States they persist unaltered.[77] The Supreme Court in a recent judgment (August 2020) has reiterated that daughters cannot be deprived of their right of equality conferred upon them by HSA. It recognises that in a coparcenary property, the daughters have an equal right.

In Muslim personal law in India, women are entitled to share in immovable property, albeit not equally. The 1937 Shariyat Act that remains valid after Independence is not iniquitous in some States, but it is so elsewhere. These inequities vary from State to State according to local customs, that are "over and above the basic ones embedded in the Shariyat (for example, a daughter's share being half that of a son)."[78] Goa Christians follow the Portugese Civil Code and Muslims from Cochin and Travancore in Kerala until recently the Christian Succession Acts for those areas of 1921 and 1916. Both these Acts entail notable gender inequalities. However, after a Supreme Court judgement in the Mary Roy case (1986), daughters and sons now have equal share in their father's property. Among all Indian communities, Parsis who are covered by the Indian Succession Act of 1925, subsequently amended twice, have the most equal succession practice.

> Paradoxically, neither the State nor the civil society, and the former because of the latter, can be said to be pro-actively inclined to bringing about gender equality. In the State, the judiciary is perhaps the most progressive in its approach to the gender question. Reservation, which has become the open sesame to social justice for the political class in India, is also withheld with serious reservations when it comes to women. If anything, there is greater resistance to reservations for women at State and national levels in political parties than in the general public. A survey conducted by *India Today* shows 75 per cent women and 79 per cent men supporting active female participation in politics and 75 per cent men and women are for reservations in legislatures. The opposition in the political class is both "gendered and caste based". The Janata Dal, Rashtriya Janata Dal, Samajwadi Janata Party and Bahujan Samaj Party were all opposed to women's reservation bill pending in the Parliament on the ground that there was no provision for reservation within reservation for backward classes' women. Among women MPs there was an overwhelming support for this legislation (which still has not become a law) (Amrita Basu).[79]

Given these formidable hurdles to gender equality, it would appear that as things are, women could expect more from political mobilization and women's movements than from the State or the civil society. A survey of women's movements in India concludes:

> The slogans that 'personal is political' determined this journey from beyond to within. While the earlier movements stifled the vitality that this analysis promises, the women's movement continues to explore this tool, for it holds an explanatory potential to comprehend gender-based subordination, domination and oppression that cut across class and caste.[80]

Ethnicity and State

In a multicultural and multiregional country like India in transition, all the factors discussed before are important determinants not only of electoral politics but also of public policies emanating from the federal and regional States. At some level, therefore, these factors enter into the generic concept of the Indian State in aggregate terms as vaguely defined in Article 12 of the Constitution. We use the term 'ethnicity' here as a rubric for such ascriptive categories as language, religion, caste and tribe. Any analysis at this level of abstraction must appear to be a bit nebulous. Yet, it is inescapable because we are operating at the all-India level and trying to make generalizations about the generic Indian State. In political science literature on electoral and legislative politics categories such as religious and linguistic minorities and tribes are treated almost like the category of 'caste'. For example, political scientists analyzing representation of various communities in legislatures and Council of Ministers treat groups such as religious, linguistic and tribal alongside caste groups. Obviously, these categories in society and politics mean different things for a sociologist and a political scientist.

Francine Frankel in the Introduction to the book *Dominance and State power in Modern India: Decline of a Social Order,* co-edited with M.S.A. Rao, has offered two interesting categories of 'Dominance' and 'Power' for analyzing the society-State relationships in Indian States. In this analytical framework, dominance refers to "the exercise of authority in *society* by groups who achieved politico-economic superiority, and claimed legitimacy for their commands in terms of superior ritual status, or through alliances, with those who control status distribution."[81] Conversely, power means "the exertion of secular authority by individuals appointed or elected to offices of the *State,* who claimed legitimacy under law, to make and implement decisions binding on the population within their territorial jurisdiction."[82] Frankel suggests the applicability of these concepts to the analysis of patterns of power and domination in India both historically and in contemporary or modern times. Her projected historical power structure in India can be diagrammatically put forward as follows (vertical arrows denote hierarchical relationship, whereas double-edged arrows stand for interaction):

Historical Power Structure (as suggested by Frankel)

The following pattern of power structure has been suggested by Frankel.

Maharaja

↕

Raja

↕

Intermediary Zamindars [Jagirdars]

↕

Zamindars

↕

Peasants

The patterns of power and domination in States in British Indian history ran from the Maharaja at the top and the peasants at the bottom. The intermediary power structures were the regional Raja, the intermediary zamindars [jagirdars], and the zamindars—in that order—linking the peasants at the base and the Maharaja at the apex. The whole power structure represented by the institutions of the State was built on a complex network of alliances of social domination at the middle level by the regional Raja and the intermediary zamindars and at the local level by the zamindars and the substantial peasants. The same analytical framework is applied with apt modifications to the post-Independence democratic structures of State power and of social domination by ethnic groups. Frankel's analysis shows the elements of continuities as well as dramatic changes between the colonial and post-colonial periods. During the colonial period, the overwhelming hold of religious and caste ideologies over the system of political and social legitimacy was gradually weakened and a new basis of legitimacy was created that was gradually made more and more universalist as distinguished from ascriptive criteria of birth and wealth. To quote her: "Under the conditions described above, a centralized State could emerge only when Governmental institutions were established whose authoritative basis was normatively independent of Brahmanical legitimation, and whose regulatory and coercive capabilities penetrated down to the localities. Such conditions appeared in India only from the colonial period, and even then, with great variations of degree across regions."[83]

The court system administering reformed civil and criminal law, access to English education and accumulation of wealth were the principal ways through which the traditional social status system was gradually transformed into a new political and economic status system based on class. These changes accelerated more rapidly and widely after Independence with an electoral system based on the universal adult franchise without any communal or weighted representation, excepting reservations for backward classes. Implicit in Frankel's analysis is a developmental model of interconnected networks of political power and social domination in electoral and institutional politics.

The elite-based social alliances between the British rulers, princely rulers under the paramountcy of the crown, zamindars and substantial peasants were subsequently replaced after Independence by a more complex alliance system involving established elites and newly emergent elites and democratically mobilized voting blocs in an ever expanding spiral of political participation. This pattern had already crystallized by the 1920s and 1930s during the freedom struggle itself as exemplified by "conflicts between *Brahmins* and non-Brahmins, `Dravidians' and `Aryans', Caste Hindus and untouchables, and between *zamindars* and peasants ..." "Even in the Hindi heartland," Frankel goes on to say, "which provided the fulcrum of the nationalist movement, escalating class struggles between peasants and *zamindars* led by socialists and communists active in provincial *Kisan Subhas* nearly caused a split in the national Congress organization."[84]

POLITICAL LIBERALISM AND THE STATE

Although the Indian National Congress, both during the period of freedom struggle and post-colonial reconstruction, was essentially a movement or party with middle-of-the road ideological orientation, it did have a small but influential left wing that included such towering leaders as Nehru, Subhash Chandra Bose and Jayaprakash Narayan. The developmental programme of the Congress was largely a product of this group of leaders who ranged in thinking from liberalism to Marxism. The most important pre-Independence landmarks of this ideological component of the Congress ideology were the Karachi Resolution (1931) of the Indian National Congress and the deliberations of the National Planning Committee (1938) appointed by the Congress President, Subhash Chandra Bose, with Nehru as Chairman after a conference of ministers of industries in provincial Congress Governments formed under the Government of India Act, 1935. It was a fifteen-member committee that included four leading merchants and industrialists, five scientists, two economists, one engineer who had just written a book on planning, and three political leaders including Nehru. The Karachi Resolution emphasized that the economic development policies of the future Indian State should include the objectives such as free primary education, a living wage, humane working conditions for the workers, old, sick and unemployed, abolition of bonded labour, protection of women workers, and maternity leave for them, prohibition against employment of children of school going age in factories, trade union rights for workers and suitable machinery for settlement of industrial disputes by arbitration, reduction in agricultural rent, and relief to small zamindars, protection of indigenous textile industry, control over exchange and currency policy to help Indian industries and provide relief to the masses, and State ownership of key industries and mineral resources.[85] The National Planning Committee's work was hampered by the outbreak of the Second World War, resignation of the Congress ministries and Nehru's arrest, but, as Partha Chatterjee aptly observes, it was "the first real experience of the emerging State leadership of the Congress, and of Nehru in particular, with working out the idea of 'National Planning'."[86]

At the time of Constitution-making, the Congress left wing was considerably weakened on account of Bose's split from the Congress and his tragic death and boycott of the Constituent Assembly by the Congress Socialists. That may have been one of the reasons, among others, why economic rights were delinked from political and legal rights and relegated to the non-justiciable Directive Principles of State Policy. Yet, Nehru did manage to make the strategy of planned economic development with socialistic objectives a centerpiece of economic ideology of the Indian State since 1950 onwards.

In a perceptive piece on development planning of the Indian State, Partha Chatterjee draws attention to the inner conflict between the development and democratic roles of the State. On the one hand, the developmental State would find its distinctive content in its developmental function, "something which the colonial State, because of its alien and extractive character, never possessed". On the other hand, planning would become a rational economic work of experts, "a bureaucratic function, to be operated at a level above the particular interest of civil society, and institutionalized as such as a domain of policy-making outside the normal processes of representative politics and of execution through a developmental administration."[87]

The Nehru–Mahalanobis strategy of economic development that was put in place by the time of the formulation of second five-year plan allowed the State to take a leading role in industrialization and scale the "commanding heights" of the economy. The principal components of this development strategy were (i) restructuring economic dependency on metropolitan capitalism into independent economic development; (ii) State capitalist and capitalist developments in the urban sector; and (iii) transition from semi-feudal agriculture to capitalist farming.

The strategy of economic and political restructuring under Nehru carved out an area of ideologically motivated State action autonomous from both international and domestic pressures. Nehru's major achievements were the laying of the foundations for self-reliant economic growth and for a parliamentary system morally surcharged with a political mission. Also, it was on account of his ideological commitment to democratic socialism and the presence of sizable socialist and communist movements that traditions of trade union bargaining were established and some protective legislation for the working classes, especially in the organized sector, were enacted. Policies initiated by Nehru also deepened India's commitment to the policy of nonalignment with military blocs in international relations and helped to diversify India's trade and defense supply links with Western as well as socialist countries. But Nehru's zeal for basic industries and "scaling the commanding heights of the economy" led to the neglect of industrial, defense, and urban infrastructures as well as to some measure of condescension and shabby implementation of agricultural development.

Dependence on foreign food supplies, humiliation in the war with China, and the chaotic urban life followed directly from these policies and trends. The growing State sector eventually did scale the commanding heights of the economy but it tended to grow inefficient by being sheltered from both domestic and international competition. It also concentrated enormous bureaucratic and political power and economic resources in the hands of the State elites and fettered the initiative and drive of the private sector. Simultaneously, the failure of the economy to perform well resulted in mass miseries and the practice of politics of populism by both the ruling party and the parliamentary opposition. Extra-parliamentary mass movements of protest in the North brought home the paradoxical spectacle of the Union and State Governments enjoying massive legislative majorities but no legitimacy. In the face of such mass protests, the ruling elites betrayed their inclination to take recourse to authoritarian intervention in the political process by proclaiming the Emergency. A part of the pattern was the repeated attempt by the ruling elites to curb the freedom of the press during and even after the Emergency. Such authoritarian measures were retraced in the face of the most determined protests and agitations in the press and the underground. Ever since the Emergency, the misuse of the Government-controlled electronic mass media continued, as has the tendency of the ruling parties to politicize the professional neutrality of the civil service and to undermine the independence of the judiciary. The elitist mentality and wasteful lifestyles have created an enormous elite-mass gap. Indeed, we notice a series of these gaps and chains of exploitative relationships in the State and civil society, in the rural and urban political economies, and among the privileged and the alienated, and deprived ethnic and regional groups.

However, correctives to these distortions have come from seven major sources and factors. First, food deficits, famines and starvation, and the drain on reserves of foreign exchange due to massive grain imports through the 1950s and 1960s propelled agricultural development to the front of the economic agenda, leading to initial spurts by the mid-1960s of a Green Revolution in some parts of the country. Second, the disastrous conduct of India–China war in 1962 resulted in a major reorientation in strategic and defense policies that led to the military hegemony of India in South Asia underlined by its successful intervention in the liberation of Bangladesh and, more recently though with less diplomatic finesse, in Sri Lanka. Third, inefficiencies of the State sector through the 1960s and 1970s forced the liberalization of the economy in 1980s and 90s—loosening the fetters of the "permit-quota-license raj" at home, and opening up the economy to international financial investment and technology. Fourth, the industrial bourgeoisie has grown in size and internal differentiation along both regional lines and those of the small-scale manufacturing sector. The national bourgeoisie has also tended to become increasingly intermeshed in joint ventures with multinational corporations as well as with the State sector controlled by Central or State Governments. Indian multinational corporations have also been expanding in Third World countries and elsewhere.

Fifth, a vibrant class of capitalist farmers and middle-level peasantry has emerged and has been growing increasingly more assertive in politics; legislators with farming backgrounds have surfaced as the largest category in State capitals and in New Delhi. Effective national organizations of farmers have proved abortive, but powerful organizations and movements of farmers in areas of agricultural modernization have heavily impacted the political process. Sixth, the spectre of inflation, particularly in the 1970s but continuing to a slightly attenuated degree even now, created a heightened awareness of minimizing deficit financing by the Central Government and overdrafts on the Reserve Bank of India by State Governments. Tardy tax receipts, especially with regard to direct taxes, liberal subsidies to farmers, staple food subsidies to urban consumers, and wasteful non-plan expenditures have led to increased dependence on borrowing and mounting interest payments. In the 1987–88 budget, these payments reached one-sixth of the total budgetary expenditure and 4.5 per cent of GNP[88], high but not alarming figures. They do, however, show that the plan objectives of zero net foreign aid and debt position are still will-o'-the wisp.

This relative manoeuvrability is matched by the resilience of the economy in tiding over the phenomenal increase in the price of petroleum in 1973, mainly by virtue of the emergence of new markets for Indian exports in the oil-exporting countries of West Asia and the Gulf. India's trade relations over the years have become increasingly diversified both in terms of trade partners (with the United States and European Union emerging as the largest trading partners) and trade components. The trade deficit reached a peak of 3.7 per cent of GDP in 1985–86, but "declined in 1986–87 to 3.2 per cent of GDP both on account of better export performance and deceleration in import growth and further declined to 2.8 per cent of GDP in 1987–88 mainly due to good growth in exports"[89]. Seventh, feeding on agrarian grievances (especially unfavorable terms of trade between rural and urban sectors and unremunerative prices for agricultural products), ethnic alienation and regional disparities, and authoritarianism of the Central Government, powerful State and regional autonomy movements as well as agitations for freedom of the press by the sophisticated and influential press corps increased in frequency in the 1980s and after.

BUSINESS LIBERALISM AND THE STATE

The year 1991 witnessed a major paradigm shift in India's economic policy. Ironically, earlier initiatives since the late 1970s as well as the acceleration in economic liberalization in 1991 may be, at least formally, attributed to the Congress Governments of Indira Gandhi (1980 onwards), Rajiv Gandhi (1984–89) and P.V. Narasimha Rao (1991–96), all claiming the heritage of 'Indian socialism' *a la* Jawaharlal Nehru by party and/or dynastic association. Alongside, the Janata Government (1977–79) was also an early initiator, of course, and the National Front and United Front Governments since 1989 did not reverse the policy. Moreover, when the Rao Government stepped up the policy, it was a minority one-party Government based on a larger legislative coalition that comprised Communist, BJP, and other national and regional parties. But, significantly, the Rao Government did not turn around even when it managed to fabricate a majority in the Parliament in the latter half of its mandate, though it slowed the pace of economic reforms due to a series of defeats in Assembly elections in the meantime, which were attributed by the party rank and file to the loss of the pro-poor image of the Congress on account of its association with the policy of economic liberalization. All in all, it can be said that despite opposition to the aspects and pace of economic reforms in sections of the Communist parties, BJP, and Janata Dal in ideological terms, the new policy initiatives and revisions have enjoyed a broad consensus in the entire spectrum of the party system, by and large.

While earlier, successive measures were described as 'reforms by stealth'[90] the economic liberalization package of the early 1990s is said to involve a more comprehensively radical transformation of the economy.[91] The package included sets of two complementary measures bearing on short-term stabilization of the economy and medium-run and long-run structural adjustments. As summarized by Byres,[92] stabilization included devaluation of Rupee by 20 per cent, curb of public expenditure (e.g. subsidies for farmers and consumers, restraint on fiscal deficit and free flow of foreign capital. Structural adjustment policies comprised freer trade and partial convertibility of Rupee, industrial decontrol, public sector disinvestment and dereservation in some areas where they were making losses, greater autonomy in price-fixing, freer banking sector both national and foreign, tax reforms in excise and customs duties, more foreign direct investment in non-debt form to allow access to technology and market.

Various factors are said to have contributed to the adoption of the policy of economic liberalization which involved some degree of shift from the State to the market in economic development. Marxists have probably exaggerated the role of external, neo-imperialist pressures on India emanating from the USA and West-dominated multilateral international financial instrumentalities like International Monetary Fund (IMF) and World Bank to liberalize and globalize its economy. Premising their argument on both nationalism and Marxism, they have bewailed the loss of India's economic and political sovereignty on account of this policy-shift and decried its anti-people and pro-rich bias. Baldev Raj Nayer,[93] argues that the real cause of the neoliberal economic reforms in 1991 was India's own failure with its state-led strategy of industrialization. If the IMF and the World Bank pressed for their preferred policy prescription, "they were pressing against an already open door." In the post-reform phase, India has, and retained its economic autonomy by remaining relatively insulated form world economy by choice. While not discounting such external pressures as 'negligible' or over, Baru[94] appears to be more realistic in observing:

> The picture that emerges is not a black and white one of national sovereignty either triumphing over or succumbing to imperialist bossism. There are shades of grey which illustrate a complex mix of dependence and independence where both internal and external interests mesh together to produce complicated policy outcomes.

The Indian economy being relatively protectionist of domestic industries against forces of globalization in the past, the main explanation for economic liberalization of the 1990s may be found in the declining rate of industrial growth since the mid-1960s, fall in public investment, insufficient and uneven pattern of agricultural development both in terms of regional and social indicators, and as a result of all these, the vicious circle of depression in demand and supply. To quote Roy[95]

> The growth rate of industrial production fell from 7 per cent between 1951 and 1965 to 3.3 per cent between 1965 and 1970; over 1970–77, it increased to 4.8 per cent, but again declined by 1.4 per cent between 1979 and 1980. Since the mid-'60s, however, the rate of growth of some industries has been negative. Some economists have questioned the basis of the increase in the rate of growth in the '80s.

At the same time when public investment for economic development was declining, predatory claims on public expenditure by populist politics of the Indira Gandhi brand of plebiscitary mass democracy and rural populism of the Janata phase of governance at the Center and their regional versions in various States since then were mounting. The public sector in the States as well as at the Center and the nationalized banks became particularly vulnerable to populist and organized trade union pressures. "Indian socialism" turned into a veritable rent-seeking semi-feudal, neo-patrimonial political economy.

Nevertheless, the phase of populist politics in the 1970s and 1980s at the Union and State levels respectively had at least one positive effect in terms of the decline of mass poverty. National Sample Survey (NSS) data reveal a marked dent in rural poverty between the mid-1970s to the end of the 1980s. This trend was not noticeable in earlier decades. Hence, arguably, there is some positive correlation between increase in social sector expenditure by Governments and decline in mass poverty.[96]

However, expansion in public expenditure in the 1970s and large borrowing from the market—national and international—in the 1980s, along with the loss of trade with the socialist block—the USSR and Eastern Europe—around the same time, precipitated an unprecedented fiscal crisis of the State and serious erosion of balance of payments in India's imports and exports by the end of the 1980s. This problem was especially aggravated by the spiraling cost of oil imports from West Asia that proved to be the proverbial straw on the camel's back triggering the major turnaround in economic policies in mid-1991. The new economic policies (NEP) or economic reforms included bureaucratic deregulation of the heavily controlled economy and structural adjustment programme (SAP) in terms of privatization and capitalist globalization.

These changes in India conformed to the neo-liberal assault on post-war Keynesian political liberalism and welfare State in the West, "which gathered strength in the 1970s and became hegemonic among orthodox, neo-classical economists by the 1980s."[97] Moreover, India's relative economic decline in comparison to the economic success of the marketized East and South-East Asian economies led to similar neo-liberal critique of the Nehru and Indira Gandhi strategies of development and the revisionism of economic liberalization.[98]

However, neither the neo-liberal critique of the welfare State in the West nor the collapse of communism in the erstwhile Soviet Union and Eastern Europe has swept India off its feet. Compared to many other economies that have recently liberalized themselves, political elites in India have been rather cautious in opening up the economy and the Indian electorate until before the 2010 and 2011 elections had been reluctant to kick out the Marxist State Governments lock, stock and barrel or to deny the communist parties the opportunity of being co-sharers in coalition Governments in New Delhi. A decisive break with the past is neither possible nor desirable for constitutional, sociological, and economic reasons. Constitutionally, India is not only an economy but also a polity. It is built on the Venn diagrammatic overlap of the political market of voters' sovereignty and the economic market of consumers' sovereignty. As Chatterjee writes:

> …in the specific context in which planning was taken up in India, accumulation had to be reconciled with legitimation. 'Adoption of a representative form of Government based on universal adult suffrage did have an effect on the exercise of political power, and so did the whole legacy of the national movement with its specifically articulated set of economic objectives'. These two objectives—accumulation and legitimation—produced two implications for planning in India. On the one hand, planning had to be `a way of avoiding the *unnecessary rigours* of an industrial transition in so far as it affected the masses resident in India's villages. On the other hand, planning was to become 'a positive instrument for resolving conflict in a large and heterogeneous subcontinent' (emphasis Chatterjee's)[99]

This dual imperative in some measure is indeed characteristic of any economic policy-making in any way in a liberal democratic regime. Commenting on the tension between capitalism and democracy, Jurgen Habermas[100] observes: "This paradox also manifests itself in the fact that if parties want to gain or retain the power of office, they have to secure the trust of private investors and of the masses simultaneously."

Sociologically, powerful classes in the Indian society may be opposed to a wholesale globalized economic liberalization. While the internal bureaucratic deregulation is welcome to all except Marxist political parties and the bureaucracy, globalization of the economy is generally opposed by the national bourgeoisie, the peasantry, and the working classes. Since the Indian State's economic policies must, in the long run, reflect the composite interests of all these politically relevant classes and groups, a mixed policy output may well be expected. Sections of regional bourgeoisie, rich farmers, and the labour aristocracy in MNCs may initially support globalization, as they have in fact done in good measures. Questioning the conventional characterization of FICCI as the representative of national bourgeoisie and ASSOCHAM as that of comprador bourgeoisie (for, both have been supportive of foreign investment and technology and import liberalization), Baru[101] perceptively observes:

> To suggest that this only proves the comprador nature of all business is begging the question and also goes counter to the actual historical

> experience of the last forty or fifty years. A possible explanation would hinge on the interest of big business in utilizing the opportunity provided by a process of liberalization, especially external liberalization, in order to restructure, rationalize, and rehabilitate its industrial enterprises.

He goes on to lament:

> The Government of India, unlike the Government of Japan or South Korea, has not pursued a vigorous policy of compelling Indian firms to be technologically dynamic. Consequently, Indian industry can catch the new technological bus only by becoming even more dependent and by utilizing the opportunity afforded by economic liberalization in order to upgrade its technological base. If it entails a compromise with foreign capital, so be it.[102]

So, it makes good economic sense in terms of *swaraj* and *swadeshi* that while the State should promote greater competitiveness in the economy both internally and externally, it should continue to play the role of the market-friendly facilitator of economic development and indicative planner of national priorities.[103]

The dilemma before India is to steer clear of the sick State of Nehruvian 'socialism' behind and a possible failed market ahead due to accumulating incremental monopolistic trends and iniquitous spin-off of social, economic and regional disparities. For the present, the worry may be the negative economic consequences of a pseudo-socialism and pseudo-democracy. The following comparative comment on China and India is worth considering: "China's revolutions have prepared the ground for democracy now to flower. India's democratic foliage blocks out the sunlight for anything under its shadow to grow on the ground. The grass roots need nurturing."[104]

Business liberalism at home and growing integration of the national economy with global capitalism offers challenges as well as opportunities. The overriding economic imperatives of profitability and sustained economic growth may entail heavy social and ecological costs. The social costs are evident in the decline in public expenditure by the Governments which affects the poorer and weaker sections of the society and backward regions more than the affluent classes and communities and advanced regions. Private investment prefers greener pastures and caters to the needs of the monied people. In its drive to power capital is less constrained by qualms of conscience for the people and the environmental protection. Limits, if any, begin to be recognized only when the problem reaches the point of crisis in terms of ecological disaster and human extinction.

The new economic policies impact the rural and urban areas, affluent urbanites and middle classes, and the marginalized urban and rural poor differentially. The following two quotes from Pamela Shurmer-Smith (2000) illustrate these points succinctly:

A. In a situation as poor as exists in India's rural areas, only the State can provide the investment needed and yet policies of liberalization require increasingly market-driven approaches. The market will not bring about the application of land reform which is so desperately needed; neither will it ensure that persons displaced by development schemes get adequate land in compensation. There is every indication that the emphasis on cash crops will cause greater landlessness, increased indebtedness and also competition for water.[105]

B. India's urban areas are growing at a pace of about 3.5 per cent per annum; about half of this growth is natural increase, the other half is rural-to-urban migration. Some of the fastest growth is in the smaller towns in the wealthier agricultural areas, such as the Punjab and Western Uttar Pradesh. This is particularly noticeable for those mofussil towns which are within easy reach of major metropolitan areas, for example, Muzaffarnagar, Ghaziabad and Meerut, where new industries have sprung up to take advantage of a combination of agricultural capital, feudal political and employment structure, and relaxed health and safety and pollution controls.[106]

In both these contexts, the absence of State intervention spells unabashed market Darwinism and enormous increase in crime and violence.

Yet with the record of State sickness in the immediate past in India and neo-liberal ideological thrust globally, bureaucratic deregulation and privatization are being seen as a fire exit, at least initially. The complex scenario and inherent dilemmas are graphically evident in a study in South India.[107] The authors in this study take a pragmatic approach in relation to State and market in the contemporary Indian context. The concluding remark of M.N. Srinivas and G.S. Aurora[108] is illustrative. They welcome the structural adjustment to downsize the State and streamline fiscal policies, but emphasize "the need for restructuring not only the economy but also political and civil society" and "objectives of humanistic development". Some other observers interpret the ongoing politico-economic transformation in terms of (a) the replacement of the bureaucratic State by a market-regulating State, and (b) the transition of a predominantly parliamentary system into a more federalized political system.[109]

GLOBALIZATION AND THE STATE

Globalization is fast becoming a catchword that encapsulates wide range of changes taking place on a world scale today. Like all such words, it lacks precision. It refers to the phenomenon of globalization of information, technology, and capital in particular, though other incidental changes are also included in its ambit. While it is not an entirely new phenomenon, the extent and pace of it today has reached a moment when some foundational assumptions and structures that had become the commonplace are beginning to be seriously questioned. Observe, for example, the two following statements made by two leading social scientists around the same time:

A. Sovereignty, as a socially constructed principle, has always been at odds to varying degrees with reality, and it has been both threatened and intensified in recent decades. Yet, it is the basis on which the interstate system exists and is defined.[110]

B. "Put simply, in terms of real flows of economic activity, nation States have already lost their role as meaningful units of participation in the global economy of today's borderless world."[111]

The reality must, however, lie somewhere in between these competing perceptions about the role and relevance of the nation-states in the contemporary world. Besides, the internal and external contexts of the Indian State must also be taken into account in investigating the impact of globalization. In the post-war Keynsian ideological ambiance of the time, India began its career as a democratic developmental State[112] in the early 1950s with the objectives of growth with justice built on national economic self-reliance. By the beginning of the 1970s, however, this strategy of development ran into crisis and India had to make a choice whether it gave priority to democracy or development. In the original Indian model of development, both democracy and development were given equal weightage but the compulsions of a backward economy and politics of scarcity did not allow the luxury of having both the objectives in equal measures. Unlike South Korea and some other east-Asian countries, as already alluded to before, India muddled through on the democratic path without, however, formally abandoning the developmental goals. Authoritarian interventions in east Asia proved to be more feasible than in India.[113]

Indira Gandhi's emergency regime was somewhat reminiscent of the East-Asian experience at least in the sense that in both of these development got priority over democracy, but the momentum of electoral democracy proved to be unstoppable in India. Nevertheless, economic constraints proved to be insurmountable by the beginning of the 1990s when a serious balance of payment crisis forced the Government of India to open up the economy to global capital and technology. The neo-liberal shift in the economic policy that had already taken place in the West in the 1980s became part of the Indian experience since 1990s.

However, the distinctive features of the Indian context must also be taken into account while examining the Indian State in relation to globalization. These features relate to the nature of the Indian State and the economy, India's relations with its neighbours and the world at large, as well as the geo-political context. To begin with, like the 'weak-strong' State of India, the Indian economy is also a weak-strong one. Parts of both the State and the economy have reasonably developed sophisticated institutions along with clusters of underdevelopment. In sheer size also, India has a huge market within which internal trade can serve as a cushion to mitigate the limitations of its regional and global linkages. This may explain the paradox of the Indian corporate companies that maintain a promising global presence coexisting with a large unorganized sector. Despite its deficiencies, the unorganized sector caters to the regional and the national markets.

For reasons of the Indo-Pakistan feud and general backwardness of South Asia, India is, if anything, more integrated globally than regionally in South Asia. The South Asian Association for Regional Cooperation (SAARC) is not only rather late in being formed in 1985, it also remains one of the weakest regional economic groupings in the world.

India can be treated as an interesting case study in the contemporary world that can demonstrate how the competing forces of nationalism, regionalism and globalism worked themselves out. As Kacowicz observes, these three forces are "relative to and overlapping with one another, sometimes antagonistic and sometimes cooperative towards each other but never harmonious."[114]

India continues to be weakly integrated with South Asia as a supranational region as well as with global capitalism. If anything, India's integration with the global economy is relatively more than with the regional economy in South Asia or the Afro-Asian world. There have been at least five reasons for this state of affairs. First, India initially acted upon economic nationalism of self-reliance with a mix of statist and protectionist economic policies. A development strategy long on statism and political liberalism and populism and short on business liberalism, coupled with a huge domestic market, also precluded an export-oriented economy. Second, India's pragmatic nonalignment with a Soviet tilt prompted trade relations with the Soviet and East European socialist/communist economies (that subsequently suffered setback after the collapse of communism in the West). Third, security concerns in South Asia conceived in Realist terms have overshadowed issues of regional economic integration. Even the integrated economy of undivided India was ruptured by the Partition and Realist geopolitical complications that have persisted ever since. India–Pakistan and India–China rivalries, especially the former, also stand in the way of a smooth move towards regional integration. India's South Asian neighbours, especially smaller ones, also apprehend that India may use its economic and military power to push regional integration to its advantage. Fourth, the Realist security atmospherics of the region have constantly put India under pressure to divert its scarce economic resources to the compulsions of defence. Right since its birth, India has been facing wars—in 1947, 1962, 1965 and 1999—with Pakistan or China. India's regional security concerns or huge influx of refugees also sucked it into the liberation and birth of Bangladesh in 1971 and into peace-keeping intervention on invitation in Sri Lanka in 1984. Fifth, the Realist security concerns of India and its major neighbours culminated into nuclear weaponization of India and Pakistan in tandem in 1998, draining scarce economic resources from development to defence. For all these reasons, India's regional economic integration is still far behind its global integration of whatever quantum.

It was in this rather uncongenial regional atmosphere that the South Asian Association for Regional Cooperation was launched and held its first biennial summit in 1985 in Dhaka. The SAARC's Articles of Association preclude contentious bilateral issues beyond the scope of its summits. This is both a source of its weakness and strength. Bypassing liberalization of trade at earlier summits, in fact in the Charter itself, the 1991 summit at Colombo resolved to forge a South Asia Free Trading Arrangement (SAFTA), but so far trade still is largely along bilateral channels. This is not for nothing. As an observer rightly remarks: "The smaller States fear that regional liberalization will allow India to dominate their economies and, in turn, India fears that the smaller States will be used as staging posts by transnational corporations and other States determined to gain access to India's large market."[115]

The 1993 Dhaka summit took another important step in promoting economic cooperation with the signing of South Asian Preferential Trading Arrangement (SAPTA). It aimed at mutual trade among member-countries on the basis of reciprocity and phase-wise reduction or removal of tariff barriers by selecting specific groups of commodities. Four least developed member-countries—Bangladesh, Bhutan, Maldives, and Nepal—were offered selected products for which relatively more developed member-countries—India, Sri Lanka, and Pakistan—would give them preferential trade treatment.

Table 3.1, which gives data regarding exports within major regional groupings in the world, shows that when SAPTA was signed, intra-regional trade in South Asia only amounted to 3.2 per cent; by 1999, it inched ahead to nearly 5 per cent. It is, however, still miniscule compared to 22.2 per cent for ASEAN, 54.6 per cent for NAFTA, and 62.6 per cent for the European Union.

TABLE 3.1 Export Among Major Regional Groups 1980–1999 (% per year)

Regions	1980	1990	1996	1999
SAARC	4.8	3.4	4.3	4.7
ASEAN	16.9	18.7	23.2	22.2
NAFTA	33.6	41.4	47.5	54.6
EU	61.0	68.0	61.5	62.6
MERCOSUR	11.6	8.9	22.8	20.5

Based on *World Bank Development Indicators*, 2001.

A comparison between regional cooperation groups nearer home—SAARC and ASEAN—would be more apt here. Both in percentage per year growth rates of merchandise exports and imports, ASEAN is expectedly ahead of SAARC, the averages for the two regions in 2002 is shown in Table 3.2.

TABLE 3.2 Growth Rates of Merchandise Exports and Imports in 2002 in SAARC and ASEAN (% per year)

Region	*Exports*	*Imports*
SAARC	0.27	3.56
ASEAN	5.56	5.67

For lack of data from World Bank sources Brunei, Darussalam and Myanmar are excluded from the computation.

Intra-regional growth rate in exports for ASEAN stood at 5.56 per cent and 0.27 per cent for SAARC. The corresponding figure for imports works out at 5.67 per cent for the former and 3.56 per cent for the latter. India–Pakistan peace process reached a new momentum in the spring of 2005 following the opening of the Srinagar–Muzaffarabad bus service across the line of control in the Indian State of Jammu and Kashmir and Pakistan-occupied Kashmir. The Manmohan Singh–Musharraf "cricket diplomacy" in New Delhi in April the same year seems to have cleared the way for a new moment not only in Indo-Pakistani relations but has also raised optimism regarding the settlement of the Kashmir dispute and lifting the SAARC to a level of high potential of cooperation. The event was preceded by a historic visit by the Chinese premier Wen Jiabao to New Delhi and a significant advance towards an understanding of the Sino-Indian border dispute. India–China trade has been expanding spectacularly, and from being an insignificant supplier until the early 1990s, China has moved ahead of the United States of America as India's top import partner. However, even if China and India joined ASEAN in a free trade agreement, or "an effective Asian bloc will not be signing an FTA agreement with each other."[116] After the Indo-US civilian nuclear deal still in process in August 2007, Sino-Indian relations have been cooling a bit.

Taking the tack of globalization, India's global integration is more in terms of information technology and open book printing, market, and brain-drain than in economic and fiscal terms. As of now, neo-colonial cultural and educational and information domination of the West is more threatening to Indian cultural mores and ways of life than neo-colonial economic domination. Through the more open communications policy—the open skies since the 1990s in the field of electronic mass media—globalization has simultaneously affected cultural identities in favour of global and local cultures and wakened the national culture with its centralizing overtones. Until the 1980s, the official electronic media played a strong centralizing role in India. Though their regional stations in the States catered to local languages, there was considerable national content in their news. Now the field is wide open to national as well as international private TV channels, as well as direct-to-home telecast (DTH). Book printing is open in India, though newspapers and magazines are excluded from foreign ownership by a 1955 Cabinet resolution of the Nehru

Government. The National Democratic Alliance Government, headed by Atal Bihari Vajpayee, since 2002 allowed 26 per cent foreign equity in this sector, with editorial and managerial incumbency remaining with Indian nationals.[117]

"Historically, as well as in her contemporary setting", writes Bendix,[118] "India presents a striking contrast to the European experience: the hiatus between her modernizing elite who at present exercise authority and the strength of `communal' ties in the population at large". This elite-mass gap in India has been deepened by the massive political mobilization of the countryside both during the nationalist movement and in the post-Independence electoral politics. As Varshney[119] remarks:

> The historical paradox of rural power ... [is that] although in the process of economic development the population of countryside loses power, the combination of a democratic polity and industrial economy later seems to empower it. India defies this historically derived paradox. It is a low income country with over 65 per cent of the population still dependent on agriculture, yet the rural sector has acquired substantial power in the polity. By now over 40 per cent of India's Parliament has a rural background, as opposed to about 20 per cent in the 1950s. Rural mobilization on prices, subsidies and loans flourished in the 1980s. All political parties support the rural demand for more 'remunerative' agricultural prices and for higher investment of public resources in the countryside. A considerable fraction of outstanding agricultural loans was waived in 1989–90. Finally, some of the key bureaucratic bodies involved in policy-making in Delhi are by now substantially rural in social origins (though for rural politicians that may still not be adequate).

Such massive mobilization of India's peasant population may bring tremendous pressures on the modernizing political elites to reduce the kind of elite autonomy that we have discussed above. Yet, contours of party politics in India do not decisively suggest such apprehended political polarization, despite the proclivity of the BJP and the JD and its successors like Rashtriya Janata Dal, Samajwadi Party, and Janata Dal (Secular) to use Hindutva and Mandal reservation as their main strategies of political mobilization of the Hindu and the OBC vote-banks, respectively. Ideally, religious communalism is as much undesirable as casteism. However, Kothari[120] makes a plea that caste politics is more "democratic" than religious politics, as the former counters the latter!

It is also notable that the process of moderation in the BJP seen during the years of the National Democratic Alliance (NDA) government led by the then Prime Minister, Atal Bihari Vajpayee (1999–2004) has not radically reversed this process of moderation during its political loss of power to the Congress-led United Progressive Alliance (UPA) for two terms (2004–2009 and 2009–2014). Following that, the two terms of return to federal power under the Prime Minister, Narendra Modi (2014–2019 and 2019–2024), with a single-party majority albeit in the NDA coalitional framework, along with its governments in a large number of states, have indeed made the BJP a dominant political force much like the Indian National Congress of the yore, displaying an accommodative political posture with a considerably liberalized Hindu cultural nationalism within the mantle of overarching constitutional Indian nationalism.

GLOBALIZATION AND MIDDLE CLASS

The middle class has for a long time been a part of Indian society, but new middle class has emerged after the economic liberalization since 1991. According to Leela Fernandes (2006), "... the rise of the new middle class represents the political construction of a social group that operates as a proponent of economic liberalization. This middle class is not 'new' in terms of its structural or social basis. Its newness does not refer to upwardly mobile segments of the population entering the middle class. Rather, its newness refers to a process of production of a distinctive social and political identity that represents and lays claim to the benefits of liberalization. At a structural level, this group largely encompasses English-speaking urban white-collar segments of the middle class who are benefiting from new employment opportunities (particularly in private-sector employment)".[121]

The new middle class is not entirely free from its pre-modern social position; rather it is embedded in its social and cultural context. The composition of middle class as well as new middle class which emerges after economic liberalization is partly affected by the social hierarchies that exist in India. Leela Fernandes and Patrick Heller (2006) have argued that the politics of new middle class is characterized by the production and reproduction of social hierarchies and distinctions. Middle class derives its power from its cultural and educational capital, it actively engages in holding and leveraging its accumulated privileges and in reproducing social distinctions. In the Indian context, this implies that caste and other cultural attributes become critical assets in the continued struggles that define class fractions. Hence, socio-cultural inequalities and identities (such as those based on caste) are an integral part of the process of middle-class formation. They further argue that even as the new middle class vociferously celebrates the status equality of a market society, its many fractions actively deploy caste, community and kinship to defend their social position. Hence, the new middle class, which claims to be free from its pre-modern and historical identities, itself produces social hierarchies.[122]

The composition of middle class in India is largely upper caste. So, even if the issue of development and economic growth claims to be free from identities, its origin in middle class discourse makes it identity-driven. Satish Deshpande (2013) in his article "Caste and Castelessness" has discussed that how the upper-caste identity is such that it can be completely overwritten by modern professional identities of choice, whereas lower-caste identity is so indelibly engraved that it overwrites all other identities and renders them illegible, along with the choices that they may represent. The upper caste can afford the language of castelessness because it has encased its traditional caste capital into modern forms of capital. Hence, only a few can afford the politics free from ethnic identities.[123]

According to Ruchira Ganguly-Scrase (2003), the lower middle class also perceives economic globalization as a beneficent force, even when it may find greater economic problems in its own life. Lower middle class has emerged as new aspirational class and it regards development and growth more important than identity in electoral politics. Rising expectations and aspirations have created a desire for higher economic incomes and consumption power, which certainly have impact on electoral arena too, and it pushes development as a primary issue in politics.[124]

According to Leela Fernandes and Patrick Heller (2006), the new middle class plays dominant role in creating "hegemonic consensus" that liberalism is beneficial for the people. Middle class is also not homogenous class, but a segmented class in which upper middle class creates "hegemonic aspirations". The lower middle class cannot afford the consumption pattern of upper middle class, but there is an aspiration for lower middle class that it can become like upper middle class.[122]

Gopal Guru (2012) has also analyzed how the rise of Dalits as millionaires is used as a spectacle. He argues that neo-liberal capitalism uses the spectacle of Dalit millionaire which is a low-intensity spectacle, but it continues to maintain cultural hegemony on Dalits and legitimizes the neoliberal capitalist development even among the lower castes. The low-intensity spectacle works much like hegemonic aspirations mentioned by Leela Fernandes.[125]

Whither Globalization?

Since the great financial recession in 2007–2008 in the USA and Western Europe, the golden age of globalization appears to have entered into a phase which in being described as de-globalization, or at any rate 'slowbalization', to adapt a term coined by a Dutch writer. As *The Economist* (London, January 26–February 1, 2019: 9) remarks: "The new world will work differently. Slowbalization will lead to deeper links within regional blocs. Supply chains in North America, Europe and Asia are sourcing more from closer to home. In Asia and Europe, more trade is already intra-regional, and the share has risen since 2011. Asian firms traded more foreign sales within Asia than in America in 2017. As global rules decay, a fluid patchwork of regional deals and spheres of influence is asserting control over trade and investment. The EU is stamping its authority on banking, tech and foreign investment. China hopes to agree on a regional trade deal this year, even as its tech firms expand across Asia. Companies have $30 trn of cross-border investment in the ground, some of which may need to be shifted, sold or shut." The world faces an uncertain future. In some ways, the whole world benefited from globalization but little was done to mitigate its costs. The Indian state must gear its policies to help mitigate the class and regional disparities within the nation aggravated by globalization as well as promote regional and global economic integration in mutually beneficial ways in quest of economic prosperity and international peace. The abrasive rise of China, China-Pakistan entente against India, and its increased military pressures on the LaC have posed formidable challenges to India both economic and strategic in negotiating its way ahead in the new environment—regional and global. It also needs to contribute to collective enterprises in addressing the problems of global warming and climate change.

REFERENCES

1. Giovanni Sartori, "Guidelines for Concept Analysis" in G. Sartori (Ed.), *Social Science Concepts,* Beverly Hills, California, Sage Publications, 1984, p. 19.
2. R.S. Sharma, *Origin of the State in India: D.D. Kosambi Memorial Lecture,* 1987, University of Bombay Publication, Bombay, 1989, p. 2.
3. S.N. Eisenstadt with Harriet Hartman, "Historical Experience, Cultural Traditions, State Formation and Political Dynamics in India and Europe" in Martin Doornbos and Sudipta Kaviraj (Eds.), *Dynamics of State Formation: India and Europe Compared,* Indo-Dutch Studies on Development Alternatives 19, Sage Publications, New Delhi, 1997, p. 39.
4. Sudipta Kaviraj, "The Modern State in India" in Kaviraj & Doornbos (Eds.), *op. cit.,* p. 227.
5. M.P. Singh, "Indian State: Historical Context and Change", *The Indian Historical Review,* Vol. XXI, No. **1–2**, July 1994 & January 1995, p. 52.
6. R.S. Sharma, *Aspects of Political Ideas and Institutions in Ancient India*, 3rd edition; Motilal Banarsidas, Delhi, 1991, Romila Thapar, *From Lineage to State: Social Formations in the mid-First Millennium B.C., in the Ganga Valley,* Oxford University Press, Delhi, 1984; Hermann Kulke and Dietmar Rothermund, *A History of India*, Rupa and Company, Delhi, 1991.
7. Kuldeep Mathur, "The State And the Use of Coercive Power in India", *Asian Survey*, 1992, p. 341.

8. Bipan Chandra, *In the name of Democracy: JP Movement and the Emergency*, Penguin Books, New Delhi, 2003.

9. *Ibid.*

10. Atul Kohli, *Democracy and Discontent: India's Growing Crisis of Governability*, Cambridge, Cambridge University Press, 1991, p. 393.

11. Ujjwal Kr. Singh, *The State, Democracy , and Anti-Terror Laws in India*, New Delhi, Sage, 2007, p.16. On this issue, we also benefitted from our discussion with V.K. Ohri, criminal lawyer in the Supreme Court of India.

12. Benedict Anderson, *op. cit,* theorizes the origins and evolution of nationalism as a modern phenomenon largely produced by print/ (media) capitalism and democracy. This theory—somewhat over-simplified—can also explain the Indian case.

13. Donald E. Smith, *India As A Secular State,* Princeton University Press, Princeton, 1966.

14. Rajni Kothari, "Towards a Politics of Intervention", in his *Politics and the People: In Search of a Humane India*, Ajanta, Delhi, 1990. Harish Puri, "The Akali Agitation: An Analysis of Socio-Economic Basis of Protest", *Economic and Political Weekly*, Vol. XVIII, No. **4**, 22 January, 1983.

15. M.P. Singh, "Whither Indian Pluralism", in Urmila Phadnis (Ed.), *Domestic Conflicts in South Asia, Vol. I, Political Dimensions,* South Asia Publishers, New Delhi, 1986.

16. Rajni Kothari, "The Problem", Special Issue on the 1984 General Elections, *Seminar*, No. **306**, February 1985.

17. Rudolph, Lloyd and Susanne Rudolph, "Confessional Politics, Secularism and Centrism in India", in J.W. Bjorkman (Ed.), *Fundamentalism, Revivalists and Violence in South Asia,* Manohar, New Delhi, 1988.

18. Aijaz Ahmad, "*Radicalism of the Right and Logics of Secularism*", in Praful Bidwai, Harbans Mukhia and Achin Vanaik (Eds.), *Religion, Religiosity and Communalism,* Manohar, New Delhi, 1996.

19. *Ibid.*

20. *India Today*, October 9, 1919, www.indiatoday.in

21. Supreme Court, *S.R. Bommai & others* v. *Union of India & others, Judgements Today*, Vol. 2, No. **8**, March 1994.

22. Rajeev Bhargava, "*The Secular Imperative*" in M.P. Singh & Rekha Saxena (guest-editor for this volume) in Political Science Annual 1997 edited by Subrata Mukherjee & Sushila Ramaswamy, Deep & Deep, New Delhi, 1998.

23. Jaffrelot Christophe, *The Hindu Nationalist Movement & Indian Politics 1925 to the 1990s* Viking-Penguin India, New Delhi, 1996, p. 529; 'Refining the Moderation Thesis regarding Two Religious Parties and Indian Democracy: the Jana Sangh and the BJP between Hindutva Radicalism and Coalition Politics, Abstract, Centre d'etudes et de recherches internationales Sciences Po, Paris, December 2010).
24. Rajni Kothari, "Towards Intervention", *Seminar*, New Delhi, No. **269**, January 1982, p. 23.
25. S.C. Dube and V.N. Basilov (Eds.), *Secularization in Multi-Religious Societies: Indo-Soviet Perspectives,* Concept Publishing Company for ICSSR, New Delhi, 1983.
26. Achin Vanaik, *The Painful Transition: Bourgeois Democracy in India,* Verso, London, 1990, pp. 171–172.
27. M.P. Singh, "Ideological Spectrum of Indian Party System: A Middling Pattern with Persisting Multipolarity" in M.P. Singh & Rekha Saxena (Eds.), *India's Political Agenda: Perspectives on the Party System,* Kalinga, Delhi, 1996.
28. L.K. Advani, "*Fallouts of Minoritysm*" in M.M. Shankhdher & K.K. Wadhwa (Eds.), *National Unity and Religious Minorities,* Gitanjali, New Delhi, 1991.
29. Bharatiya Janata Party (BJP): *Election Manifesto, Lok Sabha Elections 1989,* Central Office, New Delhi, 1989, p. 7.
30. Gordon White, *Development States in East Asia*, London: Palgrave Macmillan, 1988; Adrian Leftwitch, "Bringing Politics Back In: Towards a Model of the Developmental State", *Journal of Developmental Studies*, Vol. 31, No. 3, February 1995, pp. 400–427 and Chalmers Johnson, *MITI and the Japanese Miracle*, Stanford: Stanford University Press, 1982.
31. Mark Robinson and Gordon White (Eds.), *The Democratic Developmental State: Politics and Institutional Design,* New York: Oxford University Press, 1998.
32. *Ibid.*, pp. 150–186.
33. James Manor, "Democratization and the Developmental State: The Search for Balance" in Mark Robinson and Gordon White (Eds.), *op. cit.,* pp. 125–149.
34. *Ibid.*
35. Atul Kohli (Ed.), *The Success of India's Democracy*, Delhi, Cambridge University Press India, 2001.
36. Pranab Bardhan, Awakening Giants: Feet of Clay: Assessing the Economic Rise of China and India, New Delhi, OUP, 2010.

37. Gunnar Myrdal, *Asian Drama: An Inquiry into the Poverty of Nations* (Abridged by Seth S. King), Vintage Books, New York, 1972.

38. Lloyd and Susanne Rudolph, *In Pursuit of Lakshmi: The Political Economy of the Indian State,* Orient Longman, New Delhi, 1987, Ch. 1.

39. Atul Kohli, *Democracy and Discontent: India's Growing Crisis of Governability*, Cambridge University Press, Cambridge, UK, 1991.

40. Rajni Kothari, "The Crisis of the Moderate State and the Decline of Democracy", in Peter Lyon and James Manor (Eds.), *Transfer and Transformation: Political Institutions in the New Commonwealth;* Leicester University Press, Leicester, 1983.

41. Rudolphs, *In Pursuit of Lakshmi*, *op. cit.*, pp. 83–102 and Chapter 4.

42. M.P. Singh, "The Crisis of the Indian State: From Quiet Developmentalism to Noisy Democracy", *Asian Survey,* Vol. XXX, No. 8, August 1990. See also C.P. Bhambhri, *Indian State and Political Processes*, Shipra, Delhi, 2007.

43. Yogendra Yadav, "Understanding the Second Democractic Upsurge: Trends of Bahujan Participation in Electoral Politics in the 1990s", in Francine R. Frankel *et al.* (Eds.), *Transforming India: Social and Political Dynamics of Democracy,* OUP, Delhi, 2000.

44. B.D. Dua and M.P. Singh (Eds.), *Indian Federalism in the New Millennium,* Manohar, New Delhi, 2004; Ujjwal Kumar Singh, *The State, Democracy and Anti-Terror Laws in India,* Sage, New Delhi, 2007.

45. K.C. Wheare, *Federal Government,* 4th ed., Oxford University Press, New York, 1964.

46. Vir Chopra, "India's Quasi-Democracy", Keynote address to the National Seminar on the Golden Jubilee of India's Independence, Kurukshetra University, 22nd January, 1998.

47. Government of India, *Vohra Committee Report*, Ministry of Home Affairs, New Delhi, 1993.

48. Klaus Von Beyme, *Political Parties in Western Democracies,* Aldershot Hants, Gower, 1985, p. 1.

49. Rajeev Bhargava, "The Democratic Vision of a New Republic: India 1950", The International Seminar on Democracy and Social Transformation: India 50 years After Independence, University of Pennsylvania Institute for the Advanced Study of India (UPIASI), New Delhi, November 16–19, 1997.

50. Yogendra Yadav, "Understanding the Second Democratic Upsurge", The UPIASI Conference, November 16–19, 1997.

51. Rajni Kothari, *State Against Democracy*, Ajanta, Delhi, 1988.

52. Manor, James, "Political Institutions in India: Formal and Informal, Coercive and Non-Coercive", UPIASI Conference, November 16–19, 1997.

53. Sunil Khilnani, *The Ideal of India,* Hamish Hamilton, London, 1997.

54. Rajeev Bhargava, *op. cit.,* at note 48.

55. Anthony Parel*, Gandhi's Vision: the Pyramid vs the Oceanic Circle (1946),* Cambridge University Press, Cambridge, 2009.

56. Agamben, G., *State of Exception*, University of Chicago Press, Chicago, 2005. Also see (Singh, U.K., "Mapping anti-terror legal regimes in India", in Victor, V. Ramraj *et al.* (Eds.), *Global Anti-terrorism Law and Policy*, Cambridge University Press, Cambridge, 2012.)

57. Anupam Sen, *The State Industrialization And Class Formations in India: A Neo-Marxist Perspective in Colonialism, Under-development and Development,* Routledge and Kegan Paul, London, 1982.

58. Pranab Bardhan, *The Political Economy of Development in India,* OUP 1984, New Delhi, p. 40.

59. *Ibid.*, p. 48.

60. *Ibid.*, p. 50.

61. *Ibid.,* p. 51.

62. *Ibid.*, pp. 52–53.

63. Achin Vanaik, "The Social Character of the Indian State" in Zoya Hasan (Ed.), *Politics and the State in India*, *op. cit.*, pp. 90–91.

64. Benedict Anderson, *Imagined Community: Reflections on the Origin and Spread of Nationalism,* revised edition, Verso, London & New York, 1991, pp. 46 and 12, respectively.

65. Anthony D. Smith, *Theories of Nationalism,* second edition, Duckworth, London, 1983, pp. 158–160.

66. Atul Kohli (Ed.), *The Success of India's Democracy,* Cambridge University Press, New Delhi, 2001.

67. Partha Chatterjee, *The Nation and its Fragments: Colonial and Post-Colonial Histories,* Oxford University Press, New Delhi, 1995, p. 238.

68. Will Kymlicka, *Contemporary Political Philosophy An Introduction,* Oxford University Press, New Delhi, 2002, first Indian edition 2005, Ch. 8. Also see, his "Federalism and Nationalism in Canada: A Comparative Perspective" in Rekha Saxena (Ed.), *Mapping Canadian Federalism for India,* Konark, Delhi, 2002, Ch. 2.

69. Selig S. Harrison, *India: The Most Dangerous Decades*, Princeton University Press, Princeton, 1960, p. 15.

70. Suniti Kumar Ghosh, *India's Nationality Problem And Ruling Classes,* Calcutta, 1996, p. 17.

71. Ajay Kumar Singh, 'Federalism and State Formation: An Appraisal of Indian Practice' in B.D. Dua and M.P. Singh (Eds.), *Indian Federalism in the New Millennium*, Manohar, New Delhi, 2003, p. 94.

72. Matha Nussbaum *et al.* (Eds.), *Essays on Gender and Governance,* Macmillian India Limited for UNDP, New Delhi, 2005, p. 5.

73. Dharma Kumar, *Colonialism, Property and the State*, Oxford University Press, New Delhi, 1998; and Andre Beteille (Ed.), *Equality and Inequality: Theory and Practice*, OUP, New Delhi, 1983.

74. M.N. Srinivas, *The Changing Position of Indian Women,* Oxford University Press, Delhi, 1978, p. 27.

75. Fali S. Nariman, *India's Legal System: Can It Be Saved*? Penguin Books, New Delhi, 2006, p. 158.

76. Bina Agarwal, *Gender And Legal Rights in Landed Property in India,* Kali for women, New Delhi, 1999, p. 15.

77. *Ibid.*, p. 38.

78. *Ibid.*, pp. 43–46.

79. Amrita Basu "Gender and Governance: Concepts and Contexts" in Martha Nussbaum *et al.* (Eds.), *op. cit.*, p. 45.

80. Lakshmi Lingam, "Taking Stock: Women's Movement and the State" in Ghanshyam Shah (Ed.), *Social Movements and the State,* Sage Publications Pvt. Ltd., New Delhi, 2002, for a similar emphasis on the activist role of feminist movements, see Nivedita Menon, *Recovering Subversion: Feminist Politics Beyond the Law,* Permanent Black, Delhi, 2004.

81. Francine R. Frankel and M.S.A. Rao (Eds.), *Dominance and State Power in Modern India: Decline of a Social Order*, Vol. I, Oxford University Press, Delhi, 1989, p. 2.

82. *Ibid.*

83. *Ibid.,* p. 7.

84. *Ibid.,* p. 12.

85. Arjun Dev & others (Eds.) *Human Rights: A Source Book,* NCERT, New Delhi, 1996, pp. 16–18.

86. Partha Chatterjee, "*Development Planning and the Indian State*" in Zoya Hasan (Ed.), *Politics and the State in India, op. cit.*, p. 117.

87. Partha Chatterjee, *Ibid.*, pp. 122–123.

88. Figures are from A.M. Khusro, "Economic Party Initiatives: II-High Interest and Subsidy Regime", *Economic Times*, New Delhi, 9th Febraury, 1988.

89. Ministry of Finance (Economic Division), *Economic Survey 1989–90,* New Delhi, Government of India Press, 1990, p. 110.

90. Jagdish Bhagwati and T.N. Srinivasan, *India's Economic Reforms,* New Delhi, Ministry of Finance, Government of India, 1993, p. 9.

91. C.T. Kurien, Economic Reforms and The People, Madhyam Books, Delhi, 1996, pp. 3-4, 10 and Terrence J. Byres (Ed.), *The State, Development Planning and Liberalization in India,* Studies on South Asia (SOAS), OUP, Delhi, 1997, pp. 4–5.

92. Terrence J. Byres, *Ibid.*, pp. 5–6.

93. Baldev Raj Nayar, "Globalization and India's National Autonomy" in Baldev Raj Nayar (Ed.), *Globalization and Politics in India,* New Delhi: Oxford University Press, 2007, pp 346–383.

94. Sanjaya Baru, "Continuity and Change in Indian Industrial Policy" in T.V. Satyamurthy (Ed.), *Industry and Agriculture in India: Since Independence,* OUP, Delhi, 1995, p. 132.

95. Sumit Roy, "Liberalization and the Indian Economy: Myth and Reality", in T.V. Satyamurthi (Ed.), *op. cit.*, p. 136.

96. Rumki Basu, *Economic Liberalization And Poverty Alleviation: Social Sector Expenditures and Centre-State Relations,* Deep & Deep, New Delhi, 2000, p. xi.

97. Byres, *op. cit.*, p. 1.

98. Neeraj Kumar, *The Role of the State in Developmental Process: A Study of the South Korean Experience, Ph.D.,* Thesis in Political Science, University of Delhi, 2004.

99. Partha Chatterjee, "Development Planning and the Indian State", in Byres, *op. cit.,* p. 91.

100. Jurgen Habermas, *The Theory of Communicative Action, vol. II, Life World and System: A Critique of Functionalist Reason* (Trans. From the German by Thomas McCarthy), Cambridge, Polity Press, 1987, First Published in German in 1981, p. 346.

101. Sanjaya Baru, *op. cit.*, p. 130.

102. *Ibid.*

103. Neeraj Kumar, *op. cit.*

104. T.K. Arun, "Nurture the grass roots," *The Economic Times*, New Delhi, 14th April 2005, p. 12.

105. Pamela Shurmer-Smith, *India: Globalization And Change,* Arnold, London, 2000, p. 79.

106. *Ibid.*, pp. 57–58.

107. M.N. Srinivas and G.S. Aurora, "From Structural Poverty and Adjustment to Structural Change" in G.S. Aurora (Ed.), *Economic Reforms: The Social Concerns,* New Delhi, Academic Foundation in Association with Institute for Social and Economic Change, Bangalore, 2004.

108. *Ibid.*, p. 145.

109. Lloyd and Susanne Rudolph, "Iconization of Chandrababu: Sharing Sovereignty in India's Federal Market Economy", *Economic and Political Weekly,* Vol. XXXVI, No. **18**, 5–11 May 2001; M.P. Singh & Rekha Saxena, "India Independent: The First Half Century of Political Development and Decay", *The Indian Historical Review,* Vol. XXVI, July 1999. Also see the Introduction in Rekha Saxena, *Situating Federalism: Mechanisms of Intergovernmental Relations in Canada and India,* Manohar, New Delhi, 2006; B.D. Dua, M.P. Singh, and Rekha Saxena (Eds.), *Indian Federalism in the New Millennium*, New Delhi: Manohar, 2003; and Akhtar Majeed (Ed.), *Federalism within the Union*, Delhi: Manak, 2004.

110. Connie L., McNeely "The Determination of Statehood", in Frank J. Lechner and John Boli (Eds.), *The Globalization Reader,* Blackwell Publishers, Oxford UK, 2000.

111. Kenichi Ohmae, "The End of the Nation State" in Frank J. Lechner and John Boli (Eds.), *The Globalization: Reader*, Blakwell Publishers Ltd., USA, 2000.

112. For a theoretical and empirical discussion of Developmental State in Comparative Perspective, *see* Mark Robinson and Gordon White, *The Democratic Developmental State: Political And Institutional Design,* Oxford: Oxford University Press, 1998.

113. For a theoretical argument as well as empirical elaboration on this theme, see Rekha Saxena, "Democracy-Development Interface: Divergent Concerns", in M.P. Singh and Rekha Saxena (Eds.), *Ideologies and Institutions in Indian Politics,* Deep & Deep Publications, New Delhi, 1998.

114. Arie M.M. Kacowicz, "Regionalization, Globalization and Nationalism: Divergent or Overlapping?", *Alternatives*, Vol. 24, No. **4**, October–-December 1999, pp. 5–7.

115. Andrew Wyatt, "South Asia", in Anthony Payne (Ed.), *The New Regional Politics of Development,* Houndmills, Basingstoke, Hampshire, UK, Palgrave Macmillian, 2004, p. 158.

116. Arvind Panagariya, *The Economic Times*, 20 April, New Delhi, 2005, p. 14.

117. M.P. Singh, "Economic Liberalization and Political Federalization in India: Mutually Reinforcing Responses to Global Integration", in Harvey Lazar, Hamish Telford and Ronald L. Watts (Eds.), "*The Impact of Global and Regional Integration on Federal Systems: A Comparative Analysis*", Montreal McGill-Queen's University Press, 2003.

118. Reinhard Bendix, *Nation-Building and Citizenship: Studies of Our Changing Social Order,* University of California Press, Berkeley, 1964.

119. Ashutosh Varshney, *Democracy, Development, And the Countryside: Urban-Rural Struggles in India,* Cambridge University Press, Cambridge UK, 1995, p. 3.

120. Rajni Kothari, "Caste, Communalism and the Democratic Process" in Praful Bidwai *et al.* (Eds.), *Religion, Religiosity and Communalism,* Manohar, New Delhi, 1996.

121. L. Fernandes, *India's New Middle Class: Democratic Politics in an Era of Economic Reform*, University of Minnesota Press, Minneapolis, 2006.

122. L. Fernandes, and P. Heller, "Hegemonic Aspirations", *Critical Asian Studies*, Vol. 38, No. **4**, 2006, pp. 495–522.

123. S. Deshpande, "Caste and Castelessness: Towards a Biography of the 'General Category'", *Economic & Political Weekly*, Vol. 48, No. **15**, 2013, pp. 32–39.

124. R.G. Scrase, "Paradoxes of Globalization, Liberalization and Gender Equality: The Worldviews of the Lower Middle Class in West Bengal, India", *Gender and Society,* Vol.17, No. **4**, 2003, p. 545.

125. G. Guru, "Rise of the 'Dalit Millionaire: A Low Intensity Spectacle'", *Economic & Political Weekly*, Vol. 47, No. **50**,, 2012, pp. 41–49.

Chapter

4

Parliament

Gulliver in the Land of Lilliputs?*

INTRODUCTION

Of the three classical organs of the Government, if the executive is generally associated with the reason of the State, and the judiciary with the rule of law and guardianship of the Constitution, the Parliament is the ultimate custodian of the popular will. In the evolution of Government as the will of the people needed to be expressed beyond the direct popular action at the local level, the Parliament emerged as the supreme political institution of representation and legitimacy. Thus, the Parliament, more than any other organ of the Government, can claim to be the direct institutional expression of "We, the people of India...," who are proclaimed as the real source of all powers in the Preamble to the Indian Constitution.

Technically, the Parliament is called "the President-in-Parliament". The President and Vice-Presidents are an integral part of the Parliament as the heads of the federal state and latter as the chairperson of the Rajya Sabha. The President summons and prorogues each house of the Parliament from time to time, and may dissolve the Lok Sabha under certain conditions. He or she may also address either house of Parliament or both the houses in a joint session and may send messages to either house, "whether with respect to a Bill then pending in Parliament or otherwise". The President also addresses both houses of Parliament in joint session and "informs Parliament of the causes of its summons".

Rajya Sabha is house of regional representation and the Lok Sabha is a house of national representation. There is no equality of representation of states in Rajya Sabha qua states (numbers vary from 31 for U.P. and 1 for smaller

---

**Gulliver's Travels* (1726, amended 1735) is a novel by Jonathan Swift which narrates the foreign voyages of the protagonist Lemuel Gulliver. On his first voyage he was ship-wrecked and washed ashore and found himself a prisoner of a people one-twelfth his size. We use it as an allusion to the idea of the all-supreme powers of the British Parliament adopted in India but knotted in constraints.

states, say of the Northeast). Representation in both Rajya Sabha and Lok Sabha are in proportion to the size of the population of the state concerned. The range of variation of membership of states in the Lok Sabha is 80 from U.P. and 1 from smaller states.

The President also promulgates ordinances having the effect of an Act of Parliament for a specified period when the Parliament is not in session. An ordinance will lapse if not made into a parliamentary enactment within six months. It is notable that the Rajya Sabha is never dissolved and can be called to session any time at short notice. The powers of the two houses are notionally symmetrical under the Constitution in law making, except for money bills. In case of a deadlock between the two houses on a legislative bill, there is a provision for a joint session in the Constitution where the Lok Sabha would have preponderance of numbers. Yet, no government can work in a way to require joint session on every piece of legislation. Moreover, the government is collectively responsible only to the popularly elected chamber, Lok Sabha. Significantly, the Rajya Sabha enjoys veto on parliamentary approval of proclamation of constitutional emergencies in the nation, in a state, and financial emergency in India or a part thereof under Articles 352, 356, and 360 of the Constitution, and on a constitutional amendment, by virtue of a silence in the constitution vis-à-vis joint session of the two houses provided for in case of deadlock on a non-money bill, approval of President's rule in a state, approval of constitutional emergencies, and a constitutional amendment bill. These implied vetoes flow from the status and power of the Rajya Sabha on patently federal matters as the federal second chamber.

The Constitution takes pains to ensure the autonomy of the Parliament from the executive and any external powers. This is evident in provisions relating to the separation of powers between the three classical organs of government as well as in the provision debarring a person from the membership of the Parliament holding any office of profit under the executive or any external powers.

The structure of the Parliament of India is based on the triple notion of representation: (a) it represents the Nation/People, (b) it represents different interests/classes, and (c) it represents the federation/regional States qua States. In a famous lecture to his electors at Bristol, the British parliamentarian, Edmund Burke had said: "Parliament is not a *congress* of ambassadors from different and hostile interests; which interests each must maintain, as an agent and advocate, against other agents and advocates; but Parliament is a deliberative assembly of one nation, with one interest, that of the whole, where not local purposes, not local prejudices ought to guide, but the general good."[1]

This idealized Burkean notion of representation glorifies the role of the British Parliament in representing the British nation as one people to the eclipse of its role in representing diverse interests and classes constituting that nation. The British Parliament in reality fulfils at least two representative functions. It represents the 'Commons' and the 'Lords'. The Indian Parliament represents the people of India and those of the constituent States forming the federation via the federal Second Chamber, the Rajya Sabha.

Besides representation, the Parliament is also a deliberative body which in fact underlies all the rest of the functions it performs such as ventilating the grievances of the people, debating the major questions of the day, holding the Government accountable for its executive actions and expenditure, and exercising the constituent power of amendment to the Constitution.

The functions of Parliament revolve around the relationships between the people and the government and between the government and the opposition. Synoptically, the Parliament is thus the most crucial institution of government performing the cardinal functions of representation, making the government, making the government behave, making the laws, and legitimizing the government and the process of governance. Making peace and war or treaty-making power in the British Parliament and the Commonwealth Parliaments, unlike in the US Congress (where treaties require post facto approval by the Senate), is an executive act but since cabinet government is ultimately parliamentary government, here again the ultimate accountability amounts to be parliamentary and/or popular.[2] Under the Indian Constitution, treaties signed by the Union executive do not require prior or subsequent parliamentary approval, but in case a law is to be made for the whole or part of India for implementing a treaty for giving effect to a treaty, the Parliament comes into the picture (Article 253)[3]. So far, there has been no instance of Parliament rejecting such a treaty implementing bill, but in case of bicameral discordance such as that has prevailed since the 1989 general elections to date (1 November 2019), such an event cannot probably be ruled out. The Supreme Court in *T.K. Dhanashekhar* v. *Union of India* (2016) has ruled that Article 253 must be read in conjunction with entries 10 (foreign relations), 12 (UNO), 13 (participation in international conferences and organizations and decisions made thereat and their implementation), and 14 (treaties with foreign powers) of the Union List in the Seventh Schedule of the Constitution. But, this judgement mutes the powers of the states, as does Article 253 of the Constitution as well, in this matter, not of the Parliament's[4].

Parliamentary control of the executive is exercised through a series of weapons in the armoury of the Parliament, e.g. obligation of the government to keep the Parliament informed by making ministerial statements and, placing documents on the floor or library of the Parliament, the question hour, passing of a calling attention or adjournment motion, and defeating the government on a major issue of public policy which may result in the fall of the government. The ultimate instrument of parliamentary control is, of course, refusing to vote supplies or defeating the government on a financial measure or passing a substantive motion of no-confidence in the Council of Ministers. In the last two instances, the fall of the government is certain. But these are measures of last recourse. And time series data show a trend of lower frequency of trust votes over the years in the Indian Parliament (Figure 4.1). In the entire decade of 2000s there were only two trust votes as against seven in the 1960s, and 10 in the 1980s–90s.

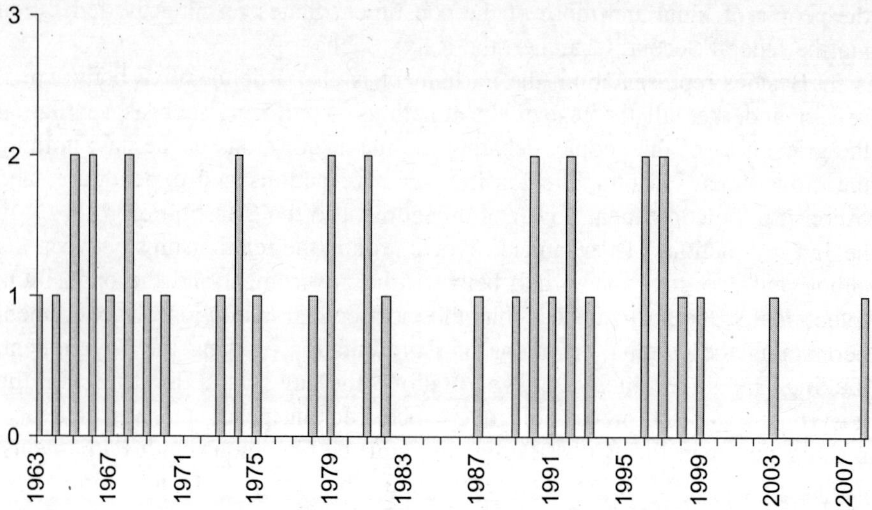

FIGURE 4.1 No confidence motion in Lok Sabha.

It is important to bear in mind that the task of parliamentary control of government and administration in India is complex, given the patterns of the evolution of Indian administration and economy since independence. Two features are particularly notable. First, since the 1950s until his demise in 1964 Prime Minister Jawaharlal Nehru launched a massive drive of planned economic development led by the public or state sector of the economy, a trend that continued until at least the 1970s under Prime Minister Indira Gandhi. Second, since the paradigm shift from state socialism to business liberalism in 1991 under Prime Minister P.V. Narasimha Rao and Finance Minister Manmohan Singh, a series of autonomous regulatory authorities have come to be established under various acts of Parliament in different sectors of national economy, e.g. electricity, telecom, insurance, company's affairs, real estate, so on and so forth. These regulatory agencies replaced the direct ministerial or bureaucratic control of these sectors, although their annual reports are to be placed in the Parliament. A study reports that both the contents and quality of these reports and extent and regularity of parliamentary oversight are inadequate[5]. Also, parliamentary control is more immediate and direct in the case of ministries and departments than the public sector undertakings and the corporate business sector regulation. Parliamentary control over public sector undertakings is exercised through its committee on these enterprises. However, when it comes to parliamentary control over planning and the new regulatory regime following economic liberalization, privatization, and globalization, is either tenuous or non-existent. There was no parliamentary scrutiny of five-year plans prepared by the Planning Commission (which itself in an extra-constitutional and extra-parliamentary body set up by a cabinet resolution of the Nehru government in the early 1950s, and stands abolished by the

Modi government since 2014). Appropriations for the plans were of course made by the Parliament, but the plans themselves were a *fait accompli* so far as the Parliament was concerned. The plans were approved by the National Development Council (NDC), a forum of "executive federalism" representing the executive heads of the Union and State governments. But the point is that the Parliament was kept out of the loop, which did not have a committee to consider the decisions of the intergovernmental bodies like the NDC and the Inter-State Council (ISC). The newly established independent regulatory authorities are kept inadequately under parliamentary scrutiny and control. Telecom licenses, are, for example, issued by the minister in the light of recommendations and rules of the Telecom Regulatory Authority of India (TRAI) which operates outside the purview of the Public Accounts Committee or even the Comptroller and Auditor General of India. TRAI's annual report is subject to submission to Parliament. A 2014 Supreme Court judgment has also made telecom private sector companies subject to audit by the Comptroller and Auditor General of India (Association of Unified Tele Services Providers & Others v. Union of India, SC, 2014). Thus private telecom service providers have also now brought under the government's scanner.

The first Parliament of India elected in 1952 was the unique democratic institution in the sense that it was the first such legislative organ of the federal State that was elected on the basis of the universal adult franchise (Lok Sabha) in Indian history, and its Upper Chamber (Rajya Sabha) was the first such elected federal Second Chamber ever constituted in India. Pre-independent representative political institutions introduced by the British rulers were based on the limited franchise and limited legislative powers and they were entirely lacking in federal pretensions before the Government of India Act, 1935. The largest extent of franchise introduced under the Government of India Act, 1935, amounted to nearly 25 per cent of Indian adult population predicated on educational qualifications and property ownership. British Indian legislatures were also legislatures only by courtesy, for they lacked full powers to discuss all matters of State and were subject to executive control and domination. Moreover, even though the Government of India Act, 1935, introduced a limited federal principle for the first time, the federal component of this Constitution was put in abeyance because the princely States who were supposed to be one category of federating units, along with the British Indian provinces, finally refused to join the proposed federation. The provincial legislatures were, of course, elected in 1936 and worked for some time and governed on the subjects transferred to elected ministers like elementary education, local government, and primary public health.

Bicameralism in the Indian Parliament is a reflection both of the principle of bicameral revision of legislation (the sobering effect of Philip Sober on Philip Drunk) and regional representation in the federal Second Chamber. Yet the criteria of federal representation was muted considerably by the principles of parliamentarism and nationalism. One of the bedrocks of parliamentary government is the supremacy of the First Chamber of the Parliament representing the nation qua nation over the Second Chamber representing federating States qua States. The principle of federal equality of States in the Second Chamber in India was generally discounted in the Constituent Assembly of India on account of great variations in size and population of provinces and princely States. The latter in particular were also enormously large in number and likely to unduly outnumber the provinces overwhelmingly. The Constituent Assembly also, on second thoughts, "reduced from thirty to fourteen days that the upper house could retard the passage of a money bill". In case of provincial Second Chambers, the popularly elected First Chamber was straightaway given supremacy over the Second Chamber elected from functional or professional non-territorial constituencies. In case of the federal Second Chamber, the provision of a joint sitting of the two houses was made to resolve the deadlock between the two Chambers. And Dr. Ambedkar explained that this was done due to "the federal character of the Central Legislature."[6]

The Lok Sabha is constituted on the basis of the direct election by the people in presently 545 electoral constituencies with a maximum of 250 throughout the nation. Its members are supposed to represent constituencies to be delimited on the basis of population by a Delimitation Commission after every decennial Census. The last such exercise was done in preparation for the 1967 Lok Sabha elections on the basis of the 1961 Census. The process was postponed on a piecemeal basis in subsequent elections until 2002 when it was frozen until 2025. This has resulted in an anomaly such that in the regions with higher fertility rates, the population of the frozen constituencies has expanded far out of proportion to the constituencies in the regions of slower population growth. According to one estimate recently done, if delimitation of Lok Sabha constituencies is done today, South Indian States may have to surrender over a dozen Lok Sabha seats to the North Indian States.[7] This representational imbalance has resulted in a distortion whereby MPs in some constituencies represent voters several times larger than those in less populous States. Unless it is timely resolved, it too can turn into an explosive federal question of great regional conflict.

Another representational anomaly regarding elections to the Lok Sabha relates to constituencies reserved for Scheduled Caste candidates. A case from such a constituency in Rajasthan is pending before the Supreme Court. The case argues that the general category voters in the constituency have been denied the right to contest since the first general elections because the constituency has continued to be reserved for Scheduled Castes.

By virtue of directly representing the popular will, the Lok Sabha enjoys a special position in the structure of the Government as the parliamentary chamber in which the trust or confidence of the Parliament as well as control of the string of the purse rests. The Council of Ministers is collectively responsible to this chamber and money bills can also only originate in it and cannot be ultimately vetoed by the Rajya Sabha. The Constituent Assembly

Debates reflect concerns of the founding fathers to make the Rajya Sabha a chamber of legislative revision, a federal Second Chamber, and a council of elders, the arguments, typical of the theory of constitutional politics relating to bicameralism.[8] However, the federal character of the Rajya Sabha was not incorporated to the extent of granting equal representation to States qua States and population was accepted as the criteria in this context. The rationale behind the constitutional "design of the Rajya Sabha" is summed up by the Sarkaria Commission in terms of the following four points:

(a) mature input in legislative and constituent process from more experienced persons represented there,

(b) representation to the viewpoints of the States represented there. The seats allotted to each State range from one to Arunachal Pradesh, Goa, Manipur, Meghalaya, Mizoram, Nagaland, Sikkim, Tripura, Pondicherry to 31 for UP,

(c) lending some degree of continuity to the parliamentary work in view of the fact the Rajya Sabha is a continuous chamber partially renewed at the rate of 1/3rd every six years, and

(d) working with the Lok Sabha in a coordinated way with speedy resolution of conflicts and deadlock at a joint session[9]. (So far only four joint sessions had to be convened, in 1961, 1978, 2002 and 2008.)

However, the Rajya Sabha is also endowed with a special position as the federal Second Chamber. In this role, it is the Rajya Sabha which can authorize the Parliament to legislate on a State subject by a 2nd/3rd majority under Article 249. Besides, All-India Services, to be shared by Union as well as the State Governments, can also be created by a Rajya Sabha resolution. Moreover, on parliamentary approval of constitutional emergencies and constitutional amendments, the Rajya Sabha enjoys a veto right. In all these areas of federal concern, the Rajya Sabha has some special powers as the federal Second Chamber. However, there are provisions in the Constitution that also dilute the federal credentials of the Rajya Sabha. For one thing, the Rajya Sabha is constituted on the basis of population in the same way as the Lok Sabha. As a federal Second Chamber, the Rajya Sabha could have represented the States of the Union on the principle of equality of representation as the American Senate does, with two Senators from each State. Representation by population in both the Chambers means that the larger or more populous States have larger number of members in the Lok Sabha as well as in the Rajya Sabha to the disadvantage of smaller States. This line of argument goes on to say that the Rajya Sabha is, by and large, a federal Second Chamber only in name; it is designed in the parliamentary mode rather than the federal.

In the early years of the Republic, the British political scientist, W.H. Morris-Jones, in his classic study also did not find any appreciable federal role or relevance for the Rajya Sabha: "The Upper House is a Council of States of the Union and its members are elected by the State Assemblies.

This, however, does not seem to have made the floor of the Council a battle-ground between Center and States; a defence of 'States-rights', an expression of regional demands, is just as likely to be heard in the other house."[10] Morris-Jones did not also find the Rajya Sabha performing the task of a Chamber of revision. In his view, similar in members' background as well as in rules of procedure, the Rajya Sabha "provided neither for technical revision nor for a wider or more leisurely debate."[11] The only relevance as a Second Chamber that Morris-Jones could find for the Rajya Sabha was: (a) as the site for first initiation of bills in conjunction with the Lok Sabha to reduce the burden of the Lok Sabha as the First Chamber of legislative initiation; and (b) the Rajya Sabha was "beginning to try its wings as a forum for grand and soaring debate."[12]

The situation depicted above has changed a bit in view of M.P. Singh, who argues that the regionalization of the party system in more recent decades has invested the Rajya Sabha with a greater potentiality as a federal Second Chamber. His arguments are: (a) the Rajya Sabha has equal power on general legislation (i.e., non-money bills), and veto power in the federally important matters of parliamentary approval of constitutional emergencies and constitutional amendments, deadlock on which between the two Houses is not specifically mentioned in the constitution for resolution at a joint sitting; (b) in a joint sitting of the two Houses in the cases of deadlock between the two sitting separately, the division may not always go in favour of the Lok Sabha simply by dint of larger numbers, as a complex coalitional inter-party configuration at the joint sitting may win the day for the Rajya Sabha; and (c) the Rajya Sabha can block the intentions of the Government to legislate on a State subject or to create an All-India Service. Singh concludes: "So it would appear that the essentially parliamentary interpretation of the powers of the Rajya Sabha was a by-product of the one-party dominant system in the early decades of the Indian republic. The federal relevance of the Rajya Sabha is likely to increasingly become more salient with the growing regionalization and federalization of the political system."[13]

An analysis of the membership composition of the Rajya Sabha from 1952–2002 indicates gradual increase in the number of members who do not really belong to the States from where they were elected. The domiciliary requirement was somehow fudged up on paper that was substantively fake.[14] This dilutes the federal character of the Rajya Sabha even more than what was originally designed by the Constitution. A more serious attack on its federal credentials was made by the NDA Government which abolished even the domiciliary requirement in 2003. A case filed by a former Rajya Sabha member, Kuldip Nayar, challenging this constitutional amendment on the plea of the federal character of the Rajya Sabha was not upheld by the Supreme Court.[15]

The changing profile of the members of the Parliament in terms of their socio-economic background is an interesting aspect of the Parliament's adaptation to the society which it represents. In the first Parliament elected in 1952, as much as 64.5 per cent of Lok Sabha members came from professional/

modern middle class occupations like lawyers (35.6 per cent), journalists and writers (10.4 per cent), teachers and educationists (9.9 per cent), medical practitioners (4.9 per cent), and civil and military professions (3.7 per cent). The percentage of agriculturists was 22.5 per cent and traders and industrialists 12.0 per cent. This pattern has been changing considerably over the years. The changes are particularly reflected in consistent increase in the percentage of representation of two professions/occupations, (a) agriculturists, and (b) political and social workers. A third notable change is the consistent decline in the number of those coming from the category of traders and industrialists. The increase in the category of social and political workers is indicative of what may be called the growing 'professionalization of politics', i.e., members who report their primary profession as "politics and social work".[16] The increase in the proportion of agriculturists may be indicative of what may be called the growing 'ruralization of the Parliament', i.e. members who report to be agriculturalists. It may also be added here that the category agriculturalists is a rather vague one as it may include substantial farmers, small peasants as well as agricultural workers. The source for this set of data reported here does not give any clue to the numbers of MPs with trade union background. It is our impression that the number of parliamentarians with trade union background is not negligible. Perhaps, the trade unionists are lumped in the category of political and social workers.

PARLIAMENT AND POLITICS OF COALITION

The evolution of working of the Parliament can be broadly divided into at least three phases: (a) Parliament under one-party majority governments, (b) under minority governments, (c) under coalition governments, and (d) under de facto one-party majority government still preferring to form a coalition government (i.e., the BJP-led National Democratic Alliance governments formed in 2014 and 2019). The role of the Parliament has, of course, varied in these phases. Under the one-party dominant system, parliamentary control of the executive was conditioned by a greater degree of party discipline, giving the executive a greater degree of control over the Parliament's functioning. This phase itself is divisible between the pattern in the Nehru era and that in the Indira Gandhi era in the heyday of her power. The Parliament functioned with greater role and efficacy during the Nehru era when the phenomenon of the decline of the Parliament was less frequently heard. The Committee system worked with greater diligence and effectiveness. Despite comfortable Congress majority, Nehru took the Parliament seriously. The standard of parliamentary debate was also impressive and the Parliament also had longer sessions. During the Indira Gandhi–Rajiv Gandhi years in the 1970s and 1980s, there was a perceptible decline in the role and relevance of the Parliament in the process of Government. There was an evident revival of the role and relevance of the Parliament during the Janata Party interlude (1977–79), when significant constitutional amendments superseding those made by the Emergency regime were passed and a series of legislations and policy reforms were debated and made, e.g. repeal and replacement of the forty-second Amendment by the forty fourth.

The Janata Government was a *de facto* coalition in the sense that the five constituent parties that had hurriedly merged on the eve of 1977 elections never carried the process of integration to its logical conclusion and continued to function as autonomous constituents under the formal name of the Janata Party. It was also an inter-party coalition with the Akali Dal. The greater autonomy of Parliament reached its apogee under the Congress minority government headed by P.V. Narasimha Rao as the government had to function under the control of an oppositional majority. It must, however, be noted that midway during its mandate, the Rao government managed to get a majority either through accretion of numbers through by-elections or defection from other parties to his party. All measures of the government had to be carried out with the consensus within the Parliament where the government did not enjoy the power of the party whip to line up the party faithful behind the policy of the government.

Although democracy and coalition-building are the two sides of the same currency bill, the term "coalition politics" in the comparative political theory discursively refers to the phenomenon of inter-party groupings of the Government and the Opposition in a legislative setting without a clear majority for any one political party. Congress-Muslim League abortive coalition Government, in idea or action in British India apart, coalitional governance in independent India is largely a phenomenon that occurred in the wake of the decline of the one-party dominant system with the Indian National Congress at its head, first at the provincial level by the late 1960s, and subsequently at the Union level, first in the late 1970s and then again since the late 1980s. Inter-party coalitions in India are caused by both the need for a "cultural synergy" in a fragmented society and a "political expediency" in a fragmented polity.[17] Coalition politics has indeed become a necessary mechanism to orchestrate governmental as well as oppositional activities. It is the growing trend of the emergence of "divided Government(s)"[18] in the sense of a political landscape where the President/PM, Cabinets, Lok Sabha and Rajya Sabha, and various State governments come from or are formed by different political parties or groups of parties.

Since the onset of coalition/minority Governments in New Delhi in 1989, the Parliament has seen three versions of such political formations. First, there were the Janata Party/Dal (JP/JD)-led National Front and United Front governments. This was an attempt to float a third front between those led by BJP and Indian National Congress (INC). However, the JP/JD that appeared poised to emerge as a historic alternative to the grand old INC in 1977 got soon so fragmented along caste and state lines by the late 1990s that it was easily overtaken by the BJP as the most serious contender for federal power vis-à-vis the INC. After the eclipse of the JP/JD, two of the subsequent coalition governments at two points in time came to be led by the BJP-dubbed National Democratic Alliance (NDA), and two consecutive coalition governments came to be led by INC called United Progressive Alliance (UPA). The two major pivot parties finally left in the field for federal coalitional power-brokering were mainly characterized by ideologies, which, for lack of better terms, may be loosely described as *liberal democracy* and *Hindutva democracy*, respectively. In 2014 and then again in 2018, the BJP led by Narendra Modi presented a subcategory of the NDA led by the BJP as a de facto single-party majority won by the BJP, but still preferring to continue federal coalitional government under the NDA.

The three versions of coalition governments, barring the Modi-led NDA and Sonia Gandhi-led UPA, have faced serious problems in both *electoral* and *policy* domains. On the electoral plane, the JP/JD version had faced acute problem in reconciling caste divisions, the BJP version in resolving the problems of religious nationalism. On the policy plane, the principal challenges to be faced concerned balancing the cultural and economic claims of various sections of society on state's developmental agenda and regulatory role.

Studies of coalition politics and government in India have generally hypothesized that this has been a positive development inasmuch as there has occurred a greater representativeness and responsiveness to a vast panoply of social, cultural, and regional demands to an extent to which it was not possible in dominant or majority party governments of the past. A wider federal power-sharing has promoted a greater degree of national integration. The main negative effects related to governmental instability, erosion of prime ministerial primacy and cabinet collegiality as coalition partners tended to treat ministries allotted to them as semi-feudal fiefdoms and cesspools of corruption, especially in the first decade, and delay and indecisiveness in the government. Here, the Union government can draw some lessons from the NDA led by the then Prime Minister, Atal Bihari Vajpayee and the UPA led by Congress President, Sonia Gandhi and Prime Minister Manmohan Singh, and more successful coalition experiments in West Bengal during 1977 to 2011 and Kerala since the 1980s.[19]

The Modi-led NDA has been free from the threats to prime ministerial primacy and cabinet collegiality, blackmail and corruption, but marked by the tendency of prime ministerial cabinet (or 'presidential'cabinet, in the US sense) and pressures mounted on the autonomous institutions, the independence of the judiciary in the government and the freedoms of the media and the civil society organizations.

During the era of federal coalition coinciding with the onset of multi-party systems since 1989 Lok Sabha elections, the autonomy of the Parliament may be presumed to have increased a great deal. Multi-party coalition governments lack a unified executive power that comes easily to one-party majority governments. For this reason, the function of consensus making is no longer largely limited to the Council of Ministers. The executive power becomes more diffused which gives greater opening to the coordination committee of the inter-party coalition governments and powerful Chief Ministers sharing power in federal coalition governments. However, this does not automatically increase the autonomy and efficacy of the multi-party parliamentary committees. There is some evidence that lesser number of bills were being referred to committees in the era of coalition governments than earlier.[20] The real parliamentary work actually gets done in the committees. This naturally gives greater opening to parliamentary interventions in the process of government.

However, this debatable increase in the autonomy of the Parliament during these phases has coincided with some other developments that have contributed to the decline of the Parliament as well. In recent decades, there has been an alarming increase in what has to come to be known as criminalization of politics. Almost all parties have legislators with criminal background. A Prime Minister is under pressure to include even such legislators in the Cabinet if the coalescing parties nominate them as Ministers. The United Progressive Alliance (UPA) Government in its early days filed an affidavit in the Supreme Court saying that the Constitution does not disqualify persons with criminal charges unless proved by the highest court to be elected to the Parliament and to be included in the Cabinet. Nevertheless, this lowers the Parliament and the Government in the public esteem. Moreover, the collective responsibility of the Cabinet to the Parliament is also diluted by coalition governments as coalitional allies like TDP, DMK, AIADMK and others retain their top leaders in State politics as Chief Ministers and nominate their second-rung leaders to the Union Cabinet. Such Union Ministers are remote-controlled by Chief Ministers from state capitals. This practice compromises the principle of collective responsibility of the government which the Constitution reposes in the Lok Sabha.

In addition, there has also been an increasing extension of judicial intervention pertaining to matters happening on the floor of the Houses, which was normally supposed to be a sovereign partisan and parliamentary domain. The controversial rulings of the Speaker under the anti-defection law enshrined in the Tenth Schedule of the Constitution have become subject to judicial review. Moreover, unruly behaviour on the floor of the Parliament and disruption of the entire parliamentary proceeding for months by the Opposition have tended to increase. In fact, the boundary between the politics of the street and political behaviour on the floor of the Parliament has got blurred. The Ninety-First constitutional amendment has made defection more difficult by limiting the size of the ministry at 15 per cent of the membership of the popular Chamber.

Further, the patterns of political recruitment have in recent decades became overly influenced by money and muscle power and what may be called 'celluloid politics'. Even Presidential nominations to the Rajya Sabha, which the Constitution expects to be on considerations of achievements attained by the nominee in the fields of social service, arts and science, are made on partisan considerations by the ruling party. Rajya Sabha seats are also known to be bought by industrialists on hefty donations to parties on whose ticket they manage to get elected by the Rajya Sabha electoral college, consisting of the elected members of the State Legislatures.

A member of Parliament got paid nearly rupees one lakh per month by way of salary, allowances and perks, to say nothing of pensions. This has been considerably raised in 2010. The Union Budget 2018 also proposed a law for an automatic revision of salaries for MPs every five years indexed to inflation. Yet, absenteeism from parliamentary work on the part of the members has reached alarming proportions. This often results in proceedings in empty Chambers and lack of quorum. An average Member of Parliament also makes personal money on the sly by selling public utilities which they are supposed to distribute to the public under their supervision, e.g. petrol pumps, telephone connections, gas connections, and other allotments. Legislators have turned into rent-seeking neo-feudal lords and white elephants.

The Rao-led Congress Government introduced the scheme of Local Area Development Fund allotted to an MP who, in turn, gets it administered under his supervision by District Administration. A sum of rupees one crore, subsequently doubled, is annually dished out to each MP under this scheme. In principle, this kind of scheme is ideally administered under the executive rather than the members of the legislatures. The Lok Sabha Speaker, Somanath Chatterjee had gone on record in newspaper reports suggesting the abolition of the scheme as ill-conceived in theory and problematic in practice. In reality, this public money is often known to be siphoned off for personal gratification or for party funding, as occasional newspaper reports reveal. A study has also found that in several cases, involving even a former Prime Minister, the allocation remained less than fully utilized.[21]

PARLIAMENTARY COMMITTEES

More than any other institution, parliamentary committees are the backbone of parliamentary power and autonomy. The Parliament being a large body is usually unwieldy and ill-organised for effective parliamentary work that goes beyond the power of lungs and filibustering. The real parliamentary work relating to scrutiny of legislative and Constitution amendment bills and control of the executive and administration gets done in parliamentary committees rather than in the whole House. Being all-parties bodies, committees are different from the Cabinet and Council of Ministers which are exclusively majority-party or ruling coalition bodies. In this sense, the Parliament elects two steering committees to work on its behalf: the Cabinet which in a way is the most important committee of the Parliament to conduct the work of the Government; and the all-party parliamentary committees which are elected to conduct the legislative work of the Parliament more closely. The effectiveness of parliamentary control of the executive depends on the quality of committee work.

Indeed, Parliament's power to make the executive accountable hinges on (a) its power to make laws, and (b) the efficiency and effectiveness of its committee system. In comparative terms, Continental European Parliaments and the US Congress pioneered in establishing a series of standing committees shadowing all major fields of governmental activities, say, agriculture, trade and commerce, foreign affairs, finance, and so on. These committees are not only specialized but also standing or permanent. The British and Commonwealth Parliaments preferred instead to operate with mostly ad hoc committees constituted for considering a particular bill from any ministry or department within a ministry. The only exceptions were the select or standing committees on Estimates and Public Accounts. The British and Commonwealth parliamentary institutions began with the paternalistic attitude that the government knew the best and the role of the Parliament was primarily as an instrument of Burkian representation and democratic legitimization of the actions of government. This tradition changed only slowly but surely as the British and Commonwealth Parliaments also gradually adopted ministry or department-based standing committees in good numbers: the United Kingdom in 1979, Canada in 1989 and India in 1993.

India began with seventeen such committees whose number has now (2010) increased to 24.[22] There is another helpful comparative contrast between the US Congressional committees and the committees in the Commonwealth Parliaments including India, and this contrast, that still remains unchanged, relates to legislative committees of inquiries into public affairs set up from time to time. In Commonwealth Parliaments no such inquiry committee can be set up unless the government acquiesces to the demand. Such Congressional or parliamentary committee of inquiry are set up in the USA and Europe despite government's reservation against them. This practice is rare in Britain and the Commonwealth. "It is more usual to appoint some outside body—a Royal Commission or a committee of inquiry—which might include members of Parliament among its membership but need not."[23]

The new committee system in the Indian parliament has now been in existence for more than one and a half decades. Their role is advisory but vitally important in terms of presenting an alternative thinking of the Parliament, which is independent of the thinking of the Cabinet. Good quality committee work can enrich the quality of governance by offering broader and better alternatives for the Government to emulate and incorporate. As Subhash Kashyap aptly remarks:

> Without weakening the parliamentary system, the concept of departmentally related standing select committees provides to Parliament sharper and more effective surveillance tools, restores the balance between parliament's legislative and deliberative functions and its role as a representational body, and above all, saves valuable parliamentary time to the mutual advantage of both Parliament and Government.[24]

A recent study of the new committee system of the Parliament suggests that the committees have mostly given attention on the demands for grants relating to the ministries they oversee. It also expresses concern at the poor attendance of members in committee meetings; the average ranges of only between 35 to 40 per cent. Since committee meetings are held during the months of recess after the budget presentation to the Parliament, the absence in committees is not attributable to attendance in the house.[25]

There is a deplorable trend of fewer bills being referred to the committees over the years. From 60 per cent of such bills in the 14th Lok Sabha (2004–2009), the figure appreciably rose to 71 per cent in the 15th Lok Sabha (2009–2014), but it lamentably dropped to 27 per cent in the 15th Lok Sabha (2014–onwords, inconclusive). There is also absenteeism of members from committee meetings, which is about 50 per cent around 2014–2016. In India, there is no rule found generally in older developed parliaments for a mandatory referral of bills to the committees; there is a convention that the ministry concerned piloting the bill recommends to the Speaker to refer a bill to the relevant standing committee. Presently, members are nominated to a committee for a year only for rotation and wider participation but hampering specialization and expertise. The Vice-President as the Chairman of the Rajya Sabha has stressed the need to extend the tenure of committee members. Another problem is that the reports of the committees are not discussed in the Parliament except for reference in certain debates on bills. Recommendations are neither discussed in detail nor implemented. The committees are also not backed by research support in their work. In India, strangely ministers do not appear before the committees; only other functionaries do. There is a crying need to strengthen the committee system to improve parliamentary functioning and quality of legislation.[26] In a comparative study of Parliaments in India, Sri Lanka and Bangladesh, Taiabur Rahman has presented an assessment of some committees of the Indian parliament in ensuring executive accountability (shown in Table 4.1).[27]

TABLE 4.1 Role of Parliamentary Committees in Control of Executive

Committees	*Implications of the committee in ensuring accountability at these levels*		
	Initiation	*Recommendation*	*Implementation*
Public Accounts Committee	Excellent	Excellent	Moderate
Estimates Committee	Well	Well	Moderate
Committee on Public Undertaking	Moderate	Moderate	Moderate
DRSC on Home Affairs	Well	Well	Well
DRSC on Agriculture	Moderate	Moderate	Moderate
DRSC on Defence	Good	Good	Good

Source: Rahman, *Parliamentary Control and Government Accountability in South Asia*, New York: Routledge, 2007.

Note: The author lamentably does not define the categories and criteria for evaluation in his study.

Assessment of some committees on the basis of ensuring executive accountability is presented here. The Public Accounts Committee emerges here as the star among the parliamentary committees.

PARLIAMENTARY PRIVILEGES

In essence, privileges of legislatures are the milestones of democracy in its struggle to free representative and responsible institutions from the burdens of (a) feudal privileges and/or (b) arbitrariness of an authoritarian executive. Instead of creating another chasm between the rulers and the ruled in post-feudal modern societies, parliamentary privileges are meant to enable people's representatives to perform their duty without fear or favour, pressures or intimidations. The history of the growth of these privileges in the 'Mother Parliament' (the UK) suggests that the privileges were fought for and won by the House of Commons from the royalty, aristocracy, and Courts. The privileges were consolidated by constitutional conventions rather than constitutional legislation by the Parliament. In the words of Thomas Erskine May: The privileges of the House of Commons are "the sum of fundamental rights of the House and its individual members as against the prerogatives of the Crown, the authority of the ordinary courts and special rights of the House of Lords". The privileges subsequently expanded into "peculiar rights enjoyed by each House collectively as a constituent of the High Court of Parliament and by members of each House individually, without which they could not discharge their functions, and which exceed those possessed by other bodies of individuals."[28]

Major parliamentary privileges in the UK include freedom from civil arrest, freedom of speech and debate, internal autonomy and the privilege of disciplinary power over members, ordering attendance of witnesses and punishment of non-members for disobedience, right to open or close door debate, general warrant for contempt of the House, privilege to summon persons and to demand the assistance of civil and military authorities, and the right of access to the Queen.[29]

The faint beginnings of the recognition of the right to free speech in the Governor General's Council by a fourth member who was not a servant of the East India Company can be traced in the Charter Act of 1833 and the subsequent Charter Act of 1853 and the Indian Councils Act of 1861. Larger Indian representation was allowed by minutes or executive letters, but none of these documents expressly provided for legislative privileges.

The Government of India Act, 1909, for the first time provided for indirect election of the Legislative Council. The idea of free speech was gaining ground to an extent, but the British Indian Government was not yet prepared for formal grant of legislative privileges. It could develop gradually only by convention and inclination for frank speech on the part of Indian members.

The first statutory recognition of privileges came in the Government of India Act, 1919: "Subject to the rules and standing orders affecting the council, there shall be freedom of speech in the Governor's Legislative Council. No person shall be liable to any proceeding in any court by reason of his speech or vote in any such council, or by reason of anything contained in any official report of the proceedings of any such council."[30] Privileges of legislators were reinforced by amendments to the Civil Procedure Code in 1925 exempting them from arrest or detention under civil process in course of meeting of the legislature or any of its committees. A similar amendment in the Criminal Procedure Code exempted members from serving as jurors or assessors. The Government of India Act, 1935, was another positive step in the same direction, but it did not grant the Indian legislatures the contempt power to punish alleged violators of its privileges.

The Constitution of independent India guarantees the usual liberal democratic "powers, privileges and immunities" to the members of Parliament and State legislatures and others who have right to speak in, and take part in, the proceedings of a House. These rights include exemption from liability to judicial prosecution "in respect of anything said or any vote given" in a House or any committee thereof and any publication by or under legislative authority. These rights are, of course, subject to the provisions of the Constitution and rules of business of the House. The Constitution originally stipulated that in "other respects", "the powers, privileges and immunities" of legislators and members of legislative committees would be those enjoyed by the members of the House of Commons of the United Kingdom at the time of the making, and commencement of the Constitution of India.[31] The forty-fourth amendment, 1978, formally changed the position to the effect that the privileges, etc. "shall be such as may from time to time be defined by Parliament by law, and until so defined, shall be those of that House and of its members and committees immediately before the coming into force of Section 15 of the Constitution (Forty-fourth Amendment) Act, 1978."[32]

So far neither the Parliament nor the Courts, despite several suits, have finally codified the immunities nor judicially determined them under its original jurisdiction, except for an advisory opinion of the Supreme Court in a presidential reference case in 1964, discussed below.

The *Blitz* case, *Keshavram Reddy* v. *Nafisul Hasan and the State of UP*,[33] was the first case in independent India regarding legislative privileges. The *Blitz* editor was arrested for breach of the privilege of the UP Assembly on the order of the Speaker. The Supreme Court ordered his release as the petitioner had been lodged in a hotel in UP, and not produced before a magistrate as per Article 22(2). H.M. Seervai contends the cases relating to the matter have laid down no law.about the privileges of legislatures generally.[34]

The *M.S.M. Sharma* v. *Sri Krishna Sinha and others*[35], case involved a Patna daily, *The Searchlight*. It published a portion of the speech by an MLA on the floor of the Assembly vehemently criticizing Chief Minister S.K.

Sinha which the Speaker had ordered to be expunged. A show cause notice to the editor was sent by the Assembly. The editor moved the Supreme Court, under Article 32 on the plea that legislative privileges did not control his individual right of speech and expression under Article 19(1)(a). The Court by a majority of 4 to 1 held that until Parliament or State Legislatures made a law under Articles 105(3) or 194(3) respectively, the privileges were not subject to Fundamental Rights. This position was reiterated in *Premchand* v. *Excise Commissioner*[36], where the Court held that Article 19(1)(a) was subject to Article 194(3). In *P.V. Narasimha Rao* v. *State*[37] the Court held that Article 19(1) was subject to Article 194(3). The five-judge bench of the Court agreed on the point that freedom of speech available to Members of Parliament under Article 105(1) is wider in amplitude than the right to freedom of speech and expression under Article 19(1)(a) since the freedom of speech in Parliament under Article 105(1) is not subject to the limitations contained in Article 19(2).

Another landmark case arose out of the conflict between UP Legislative Assembly and the Allahabad High Court in 1964. One, Keshav Singh, published a pamphlet against an MLA. The House adjudged him guilty of committing its contempt and sentenced him to be reprimanded by the Speaker in the House. On 14 March 1964, when the Speaker administered a reprimand, he misbehaved in the House to cause offense whereupon it directed his imprisonment for a week. Singh's advocate, one by name of Solomon, moved a petition at the Lucknow bench of the Allahabad High Court under Article 226 and obtained an interim bail for Keshav Singh until final disposal of the case. The Assembly took offense and ordered arrest of the judges of the bench granting bail and of Keshav Singh and his advocate for contempt of the House. The two judges moved the High Court under Article 226 of the Constitution impugning the resolution of the Assembly as unconstitutional whereupon a full bench of 28 judges of the Allahabad High Court ordered stay of the implementation of the order of the Assembly.

In the wake of this unprecedented constitutional crisis, the President of India on the advice of the Nehru government referred the matter to the Supreme Court under Article 143(1) for its advice. The Court by a majority of six to one opined that the two judges had not committed contempt of the Assembly and a citizen had the right to move the Court and an advocate was duly bound to assist the judicial process independent of Articles 105(3) and 194(3), the Parliament and Assemblies having never been conferred upon the status of a court of law. After this advisory opinion, the Allahabad High Court reconsidered the Keshav Singh case and recognized the Assembly's power and jurisdiction to commit for its contempt and sentence an offender, and ruled the courts could not go into the correctness, propriety or legality of the commitment. "This Court cannot in a petition under Article 226 of the Constitution act in appeal over the decision of the Legislative Assembly committing the petitioner of its contempt."[38]

The Supreme Court also held in *Tajkiram Jain* v. *N. Sanjiva Reddy*[39] that a speech made in the Parliament was immune from legal proceedings in the

Court. In India, the position of parliamentary privileges vis-à-vis fundamental rights and the Court remain fluid. This helped MPs to degrade themselves and obtain crores of rupees in bribe and vote for the Government of P.V. Narasimha Rao on 28 July 1993 and later go scot-free against the provisions of the IPC 1860 and Prevention of Corruption Act, 1988 by virtue of protection provided by Article 105(2) of the Constitution. The Supreme Court held by a majority of 3 to 2 in the P.V. Narasimha Rao case that MPs who allegedly accepted bribes and voted in favour of the Government were entitled to immunity under parliamentary privileges. This is absurd. Parliamentary privileges must yield to the basic principles of good Government, freedom, equality, justice—the bulwarks of the rule of law.

A more recent privilege case, as much bizarre as inconclusive, arose out of the resolution of the Tamil Nadu Assembly under the AIADMK Government headed by J. Jayalalitha towards the end of the year 2003, ordering arrest and two-week imprisonment of editors and senior journalists of *The Hindu* and the *Murasoli* for the breach of the privilege of the legislature by publishing and editorially commenting on some news regarding the Chief Minister, Speaker, and a Committee. The journalists moved the Supreme Court which stayed the arrests and referred the matter to a five-judge Constitution Bench, as, in the opinion of the Court, the case involved some important issues in constitutional law.[40] The case was subsequently withdrawn without a conclusive settlement of the matter.

A noted jurist opines: 'Our legislators have the power to be the sole judges to decide what their privileges are, what constitutes their breach, and what punishment is to be awarded in case of breach. Is this not too wide a power which clearly impinges on constitutionalism, i.e., the idea of (rule of law and) limited powers? The fault lies with the framers of the Constitution, who, while drafting the lengthiest Constitution of the world, left the vital area of legislative privileges undefined.'[41] The British doctrine of parliamentary sovereignty of Gulliver's gigantic proportions has already tied down in Lilliputian ropes of constitutionally entrenched fundamental rights and federal division of powers in the written Indian Constitution. This last anachronistic vestige of uncodified parliamentary privileges also needs to be adapted to the needs of Indian constitutional democracy and judicial review more formally and fully.

As stated above, parliamentary privileges in India are partly mentioned in the Constitution and partly left to the conventions of the British Parliament. Except for a few privileges specified in the Constitution, the rest remain still uncodified despite recommendations in favour of this idea by a number of Committees and Commissions. The problem is that the British conventions are neither crystal clear nor are they directly applicable to India. The precedents emanating from the Parliament and State legislatures cannot be elevated to the position of constitutional conventions in view of the fact that they suffer from internal contradictions.

The case law in this regard could have been a possible way of defining and legally settling the privileges and immunity of legislators. But this also has not happened. This is for the reason that the question so far has remained in the grey area between the legal and the political aspects of the problem. A brief review of the cases decided by Courts so far makes this point amply clear. A certain degree of ad hoc and provisional approach to the problem is reflected in the judgements.

Were the privileges meant to be used against executive or judicial encroachments only? Can they be used against individual rights guaranteed under Part III of the Constitution? This may be a difficult question, for there was no extensive discussion/deliberation on this issue in the Constituent Assembly. In any case, comparison with the British feudal monarchy now substantially democratized is not apt.

Several nagging questions crop up. Why are privileges not invoked these days even when the press, public, even politicians among themselves make wanton charges against Ministers/legislators and among themselves within the political class? Why does the opposition not invoke the privileges of the Lok Sabha when Chief Ministers in federal coalitions impose/withdraw Ministers on/from the PM and wanton demands are made on Prime Minister by regional satraps sharing power in the federal coalitions? Has politics of defection also been "sheltered" by parliamentary privileges?

WHITHER PARLIAMENT?

The decline of Parliament is a recurrent lament all over the democratic world. Even in the case of the so-called Mother Parliament in the United Kingdom, the argument appeared in the literature soon after the 19th century heyday of parliamentary supremacy was over by the early 20th century.[42] The growth of the party system, Cabinet Government, "presidentialization" of the office of the British Prime Minister (in the American sense), enormous expansion of the functions and areas of government between and after the two World Wars, etc. were the major factors responsible for this development. Even without the growth of a strong party system in the West European sense in India, the other foregoing factors in the years after the "Nehru-Patel duumvirate"[43] passed into history and prompted the growth of executive dominance and "prime ministerial" system in the Nehru and Indira Gandhi eras, and to a lesser extent in the Rajiv Gandhi years.

The foregoing constraints on the power of Parliament from the executive is part of the process of cabinet government in a single-party government with a modicum of party discipline. There are, however, indication of the decline of Parliament in other ways as well, e.g. the shortening sessions and decrease in time spent in scrutinizing budget, and the tendency to bypass the Parliament by legislating by ordinances. There has been a sharp reduction in the number of session days in the Lok Sabha from the high of over 160 in 1964 to around 40 in 2008. The 16th Lok Sabha worked for 1,615 hours in all, 20 per cent more than the 15th Lok Sabha. Yet, it is 40 per cent lower than the average of all full-term Lok Sabhas, which works out to be 2,689 hours. The trend of general decline in the number of sitting days continues. The 16th Lok Sabha sat for 331 days. It is lower than the average working days of 468 days of all the full-term Lok Sabhas. The 6th Lok Sabha lost 16 per cent of its scheduled time to disruptions, which is lower than the corresponding figure for the 15th Lok Sabha (37 per cent), but higher than that for the 14th Lok Sabha (13 per cent)[44]. A similar decline in time spent in discussing bills in the Lok Sabha is evident in Figure 4.2. The budgetary preoccupation of the Lok Sabha from over 140 units of time in the early 1950s dipped to over 80 in the late 2000s. Although the situation with regard to legislation by ordinance is not as bad at the state level where ordinance raj has incurred a good deal of stricture by the Supreme Court (e.g. *D.C. Wadhwa* v. *State of Bihar*)[45], yet the Government of India have often taken recourse to issuing ordinances where Parliament would have been feasibly used for the purpose under the given circumstances.

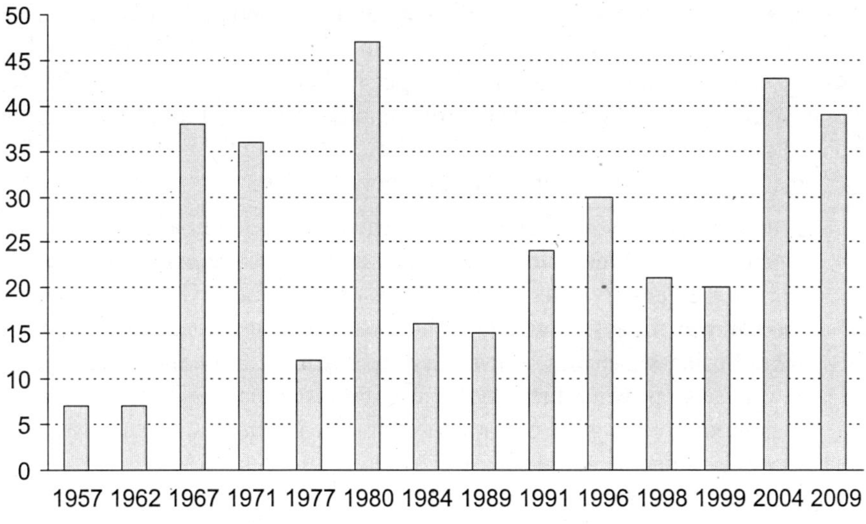

FIGURE 4.2 Time taken to discuss bills in Lok Sabha.

Since the late 1980s, the decline of the Parliament has further continued due to corruption and criminalization of electoral and party political processes on an unprecedented scale.[46] An alarming increase in political and bureaucratic corruption, social and political fragmentation and the weakening of the party system, crass commercialism, and tendency towards market fundamentalism, etc. have caused a comprehensive crisis of political institutions. An institutional response to this crisis has come forward in the increasing reliance of the political system on judicial power of interpretation and review of laws and the Constitution, going to the extent of judicial activism. The political system has often appeared to be judiciary-driven,[47] improvising for the degeneration and atrophy of the democratic political process. But this compensatory functional response is fraught with the dangers of continued dysfunctionalities of parliamentary and executive organs of the federal State and politicization and corruption of the judiciary. What is really needed is a balanced Constitution and all-round growth of in political institutionalization.

Nevertheless, the most telling pointer to the decline of the Parliament in India in relation to other competing institutions of government is that Parliament has lost to the judiciary as the locus of the constituent power. The Constitution has vested the power to amend the Constitution in the Parliament. Since *Keshavananda Bharati* v. *State of Kerala*[48], the Supreme Court has become a decisive co-sharer in this sovereign power.

PARLIAMENTARY REFORMS: NATIONAL COMMISSION FOR REVIEW OF THE WORKING OF THE CONSTITUTION (NCRWC) REPORT 2002

The NCRWC was appointed by the BJP-led National Democratic Alliance (NDA) Government in 2000 under the chairmanship of Justice M.N. Venkatachaliah with ten other commissioners with distinguished careers as jurists, journalists, administrators, and parliamentarians. Among other aspects of the working of the Constitution for half a century, the Commission also studied and recommended parliamentary/legislative reforms. This Report observed:

> If there is a cause of unease with the way the Parliament and the State legislatures are functioning, it may be due to a decline in recent years in both the quantity and quality of work done by them. Over the years the number of days on which the houses sit to transact legislative and other business has come down very significantly. Even the relatively fewer days on which the houses meet are often marked by unseemly incidents, including use of force to intimidate opponents, shouting and shutting of debate and discussion resulting in frequent adjournments. There is increasing concern about the decline of Parliament, falling standards of debate, erosion of the moral authority and prestige of the supreme tribunal of the people.[49]

The NCRWC Report has recommended a series of measures to make the parliamentary institutions more "representative, responsible and responsive". The proposed reforms may be grouped under four headings: (a) parliamentary procedures, (b) committee system, (c) in relation to the executive, and (d) in relation to the mass media and public.

Parliamentary Procedures

In view of the Commission, the time-honoured parliamentary procedures are sound, yet some "archaic and time-consuming procedures" may be reformed. The agenda of reforms could include reorganization of parliamentary time between

Government and opposition, better training, streamlining of the question-hour, the "zero hour", adjournment motions, absenteeism, budgetary procedures, reduction of time-consuming voting to the "barest minimum", etc. *The best way to deal with issue of procedural reforms in a professional (and not political) manner is to have them studied by a Study Group outside Parliament as was done in [the] UK*[50] (Emphasis in the original source). The Rules Committees of the Houses can then consider the recommendations thus made.

During the COVID-19 pandemics in 2019–2020, the Parliament and its committees at this writing (October 2020) Parliament has been virtually marginalised by the Union executive and the Union-state mechanism of 'executive federalism,' i.e. Prime minister-Chief ministers conferences and the National Disaster Management Authority, which are in primary charge of handling the pandemics.

Strengthening the Committee System

While the 1993 reforms establishing 17 departmental standing committees of Parliament are commended by the NCRWC as "a path-breaking innovation", it goes on to deepen these reforms by suggesting measures to make the working of these committees more focused and specialized and less marred by chronic absenteeism on the part of members (to the extent of excess of 50 per cent!). To this end, the commission recommends smaller committee membership (from the present 45 members each), reduction in the number of ministries shadowed by a committee, increasing the tenure of committees from the present tenure of one year, a more professional and specialized approach on the part of political parties while nominating members to these committees, provision of specialist advisers to the committees, etc.

Perhaps the most out-of-the-box restructuring in the existing parliamentary committee system that the NCRWC recommended was the establishment of three nodal standing committees, one each on national economy, legislation, and constitutional amendments, for continuous and specialized work on behalf of the Parliament but independent from the Government. These committees would work in coordination with, but not in duplication of, the Cabinet committees. Presently, the Parliament has only one, that is, the official line preferred by the Government to go by. These parliamentary committees can offer alternative policy frames to improve the final policy output. With these nodal standing parliamentary committees set up, "it may not be necessary to continue the existing committees on Estimates, Public Undertakings and Subordinate Legislation"[51] (Emphasis in the source).

Parliament's Relation with the Executive

The reformist agenda of the NCRWC with regard to the relationship between the Parliament and the executive are aimed at (a) tackling the problem of governmental instability, and (b) strengthening parliamentary control of the Government. As for the first problem, the commission recommended a complete ban on defection of MPs/MLAs to a party other than on whose tickets they are elected, and a "constructive vote of no-confidence" (i.e. a no-confidence vote to be allowed only when it is accompanied with a credible alternative ministry to take the place of the dislodged Government). As for ensuring parliamentary control of Government, the commission recommends the empowerment of the Public Accounts Committees in national and State legislatures as "the keystone of the arch of parliamentary control of public finances"[52]. Fiscal responsibility Acts at Union and State levels are also suggested to ensure parliamentary control over Government borrowing. The commission also opines that "public audit is a powerful instrument of good governance"[53]. In view of the fact that the constitutionally entrenched authority of the Comptroller and Auditor General of India set up for auditing the accounts of the Union as well as State Governments is rather excessively centralized, the Commission recommends an Audit Board in addition under parliamentary and State legislations "for better discharge of the vital function of public audit" "with a view to enhancing the efficiency and effectiveness of the office of the CAG"[54]. The Audit Board would be chaired by the Comptroller & Auditor General of India and comprise such other members with such qualification as the President may consider desirable.

Parliament's Relation with Mass Media and Public

The NCRWC considers it important to improve the image of the Parliament in the mass media and the public. Its recommendation is: "The Parliamentarians have to be like Ceasar's wife, above suspicion. They must voluntarily place themselves open to public scrutiny through parliamentary ombudsman. Supplemented by a code of ethics which has been under discussion for a long time, it would place Parliament on the high pedestal of people's affection and regard."[55] Along with the Parliament, the media is another important, if unofficial, forum of public debate. A triangular linkage between the Parliament, interest group and the media is an indispensable institutional framework for good governance.

CONCLUSION

To conclude, the Parliament has suffered a gradual and of late precipitous decline since the 1950s when it began its career in the Nehru era in a generally promising way. The Parliament must blame itself for this rather than the Constitution. For, the Constitution sets a great store by the Parliament as the moral and sovereign voice of the nation, as the custodian of the Constitution by virtue of its amending power, as the master of the executive and the finances of the nation. The Parliament has virtually lost the moral leadership of the nation and the legal custody of the Constitution to the judiciary.[56] This has happened due to the development of the institution of Public Interest Litigation (PIL) and the constitutional law of the unamendability of the 'basic structure of the Constitution.' Among the various organs of the federal State, the Parliament has probably sunk to the lowest levels in public esteem. It is, however, heartening that the Parliament of late seems to be waking up to the imperative of regaining its lost ground and glory by asserting autonomy from legal encroachment by Courts on what goes on within the Parliament itself by way of its legitimate proceedings. For example, early in 2006, both the Houses promptly expelled nearly a dozen members cutting across party lines who were caught in a sting operation by a TV channel accepting bribe for raising certain questions on the parliamentary floor. When some expelled members moved the Supreme Court on their summary expulsion without being given an opportunity to present their views to the Houses or their committees, the Supreme Court sent summons to the Speaker of the Lok Sabha and the Chairman of the Rajya Sabha. In reaction to it, a Speakers' conference convened by Lok Sabha Speaker Somnath Chatterjee decided that the presiding officers would refuse to answer the summons as the Constitution guarantees autonomy to parliamentary proceedings from any external interference. However, it must be plain that this belated attempt to assert its autonomy on the part of the Parliament would succeed only if the claim is fortified by scrupulous avoidance of any violation of legal and moral codes of conduct within the framework of the laws of the land and various parts of the Constitution are harmoniously constructed.

Incidentally, the autonomy of the Parliament from the executive got a shot in the arm in the spring of 2006 by a stricter enforcement of Article 102(1)(a) of the Constitution by the political system. Several members of the Parliament were constrained to resign their seats on the ground that they were holding "offices of profit" along with the parliamentary membership, which is a ground for disqualification from the seat under the above mentioned Article. The quasi-judicial recommendation of the Election Commission of India to the President of the Indian Union in the first test case involving Jaya Bachchan, a Samajvadi Party MP holding the chair of the Uttar Pradesh Film Development Council, cited a Supreme Court judgement laying down the following criteria for determining an "office of profit": whether a Government makes the appointment and removal, and offers any remuneration, and whether the holder of the office performs functions for the Government over which the Government exercises some control. A series of resignations and implied threats of removal hanged in the balance.[57]

On Jaya Bachchan's petition to the Supreme Court challenging the presidential order regarding her disqualification, the Supreme Court held that it was irrelevant whether a person holding an office of profit was actually receiving any payment or not. "What is relevant is the amount receivable in connection with the office one holds."[58]

REFERENCES

1. Quoted in Carl J. Friedrich, *Constitutional Government and Democracy,* 4th edition, Oxford and IBH Publishing Company, Calcutta, 1974, p. 277.
2. K.C. Wheare, *Legislatures,* London, Oxford University Press, 1968, Chapters 3–6. Also see, Parliamentary Accountability: Enforcing Responsibility in Ajay Mehra (Ed.) *The Indian Parliament and Democratic Transformation*, India, Routledge, 2017.
3. See also National Commission to Review the Working of the constitution, 'Treaty-Making Power Under Our Constitution: A Consultation Paper', *legalaffairs.gov.in>sites>files* PDF. Accessed 1.11.2019.
4. See A.G. Noorani, Governance: Treaties and States, *Frontline*, Volume 29, Issue 02, January 18-February 10, 2012, *frontline.thehindu.com.* Accessed 1.11.2019 and Rekha Saxena, ''Treaty Making Powers: A Case for 'Federalization' and 'Parliamentarisation', *Economic and Political Weekly*, Vol. XLII, No. 1, 6 January 2007.
5. N.K. Singh, a former IAS officer and a member of the Planning Commission and currently a Rajya Sabha member, in a conference on Effective Legislatures organized by PRS Legislative Research in New Delhi, 9 December 2009.
6. Granville Austin, *The Indian Constitution: Cornerstone of a Nation*, Oxford University Press, Delhi, 1966, Classic Reissue 1999, pp. 156–163; the quotes are from pages 161 and 162.
7. Ashish Bose, "North-South Divide in India's Demographic Scene", *Economic & Political Weekly*, Vol. XXXV, No. **20**, 13 to 19 May 2000, pp. 1698–1700.
8. *Constituent Assembly Debates (CAD)*, Vol. IV, p. 877, e.g. the speech by Gopalaswamy Ayyangar. See also Loknath Mishra's speech *CAD*, Vol. VII, p. 1208.
9. Commission on Centre-State Relations, *Report*, *Part-I*, Government of India Press, Nasik, 1987, p. 68. Chair: Justice R.S. Sarkaria.
10. W.H. Morris-Jones, *Parliament of India,* Longmans Green, London, 1957, p. 256.
11. *Ibid.*, p. 257.
12. *Ibid.*, p. 258.
13. Mahendra Prasad Singh, "The Parliament" in Mahendra Prasad Singh and Himanshu Roy (Eds.), *Indian Political System*, 3rd ed., Manak, Delhi, p. 117. See also Rekha Saxena, "The Rajya Sabha: A Federal

Second or Secondary Chamber," *Indian Journal of Federal Studies*, 1/2007.

14. Sandeep Shastri quoted in Ajay Mehra, "The Role of the Rajya Sabha", in Ajay K. Mehra, D.D Khanna, and Gert W. Kueck (Eds.), *The Indian Parliament: A Comparative Perspective,* Delhi: Konark, pp. 418–419.

15. Kuldip Nayar v. Union of India & Others, 2006.

16. Balveer Arora, "The Indian Parliament and Democracy" in A.K. Mehra *et. al.* (Eds.), *op. cit.,* pp. 26–27.

17. Bidyut Chakrabarty, *Forging Power: Coalition Politics in India,* Oxford University Press, New Delhi, 2006, Ch. 1.

18. For the concept of "Divided Government", see Robert Elgie (Ed.), *Divided Government in Comparative Perspective,* Oxford University Press, Oxford, UK, 2001.

19. See M.P. Singh and Anil Mishra (Eds.), *Coalition Politics in India: Problems and Prospects,* Manohar, under the auspices of the Rajendra Prasad Academy, New Delhi, 2004; Bidyut Chakrabarty, *op. cit.;* Katherine Adeney and Lawrence Saez (Eds.), *Coalition Politics and Hindu Nationalism,* Routledge, London, 2005.

20. Rajesh Jha's doctoral dissertation on *Legislation under Coalition Governments* in the University of Delhi, Department of Political Science, 2007.

21. Arun Agarwal, "The Indian Parliament" in Devesh Kapur and Pratap Bhanu Mehta (Eds.), *Public Institutions in India: Performance and Design,* Oxford University Press, New Delhi, 2005, Ch. 2.

22. K.C. Wheare, *Legislatures*, *op. cit.,* pp. 91–93.

23. *Ibid.,* p. 93.

24. Subhash C. Kashyap, "New Parliamentary Initiative: Subject-Based Standing Committees of Parliament", *Economic and Political Weekly*, Bombay, 6th October 1990, p. 2278.

25. Sandeep Shastri, "Parliamentary Committees in India and Legislative Control over Administration", A.K. Mehra *et. al.* (Eds.), *op. cit.,* p. 219.

26. PRS India, Parliamentary Logjam, Part 4, https://www.prsindia. org>media. Accessed 2.11.2019.

27. Taiabur Rahman, *Parliamentary Control and Government Accountability in South Asia: A Comparative Analysis of Bangladesh, India and Sri Lanka*, New York: Routledge, 2007, pp. 154–67.

28. Thomas Erskine May, *The Law, Privileges, Proceedings and Usages of Parliament,* Butterworth's Co. Ltd., London, 17th ed., 1964, p. 42.

29. *Ibid.*, pp. 42–189.

30. *Government of India Act,* 1919, Govt. of India, Central Publication Branch, Calcutta, 1924, Section 72-D, Sub-section 7.

31. *Constitution of India*, Articles 105 and 194.

32. *The Forty-fourth Amendment, 1978.*

33. *AIR* 1954, SC 636...

34. H.M. Seervai, *Constitutional Law of India: A critical commentary,* Vol. 2, New Delhi: Universal Law Publishing Co., 1993, 4th Ed., Chapter XX, Section II.

35. *AIR* 1959, SC 395 ....

36. Quoted/cited in *Kunj Behari Lal Aggarwal* v. *Union of India*, *AIR* 1963, SC 996....

37. *CBI/SPE, AIR* 1998, SC 2120... .

38. Special Petition No. 1 of 1964 by the President of India to the Supreme Court. The judgement accessed from Supreme Court's website: *www.supremecourtofindia.nic.in.*

39. *Taj Kiran Jain* v. *N. Sanjiva Reddy, AIR,* Supreme Court, 1970: 1573.

40. *Asian News Digest,* New Delhi, Vol. IV, 2003, pp. 3252–3317.

41. Faizan Mustafa, 'Comment: Bring the House up to date', *The Hindu*, 11 July 2017, www.the hindu.com. (Accessed 2.11.2019).

42. Philip Norton (Ed.), *Legislatures,* Oxford Readings in Politics and Government, Oxford University Press, New York, 1990, especially selections from Walter Bagehot and Lord Bryce, first published in 1867 and 1921, respectively. Also Louis Massicotte, "Parliament in the 1990s" in James Bickerton and Alain Gagnon (Eds.), *Canadian Politics,* 3rd ed., Broadview Press, Peterborough, Ontario, 1999).

43. The term is Michael Brecher's from his *Political Succession in India,* Oxford University Press, New Delhi, 1966.

44. PRS India, 'Functioning of 16th Lok Sabha (2014–2019)' www.prsindia.org.) Accessed 2.11.2019.

45. *D.C. Wadhwa v. State of Bihar, All India Reporter,* 1987, SC 579.

46. See A. Surya Prakash, *What Ails Indian Parliament? An Exhaustive Diagnosis* Indus, New Delhi, 1995, and Chandan Mitra, *The Corrupt Society: The Criminalization of India from Independence to the 1990s* Viking: Penguin Books India, New Delhi, 1998, especially "Election, Defection, Corruption" and "Anatomy of the Scam Trinity".

47. Rajeev Dhavan, "Governance by Judiciary: Into the Next Millennium" in B.D. Dua, M.P. Singh and Rekha Saxena (Eds.), *Judiciary and Politics in India: The Changing Landscape,* Manohar, New Delhi, 2007.

48. *Keshavananda Bharati* v. *State of Kerala, All India Reporter,* 1973, SC 1461.

49. *National Commission for the Review of the Working of the Constitution (NCRWC)*, 2002; Ch. 5, para 5.2.

50. *Ibid.*, para 5.21.5.

51. *Ibid.*, para 5.9.1.

52. *Ibid.*, para 5.13.

53. *Ibid.*, para 5.16.1.

54. *Ibid.*, para 5.15.2.

55. *Ibid.*, para 5.11.1.

56. See Granville Austin, "The Supreme Court and the Struggle for Custody of the Constitution" in B.N. Kripal *et al.* (Eds.), *Supreme But Not Infallible: Essays in Honour of the Supreme Court of India,* Oxford University Press, New Delhi, 2000.

57. *The Hindu,* New Delhi, 26 March 2006, p. 10.

58. *Ibid.*, 9 May 2006, p. 1.

Chapter

5

Union Executive
Between a Prime Ministerial Cabinet or Cabal

INTRODUCTION

This chapter dwells on the Union Executive and its role in parliamentary and federal government and governance in India. A modern executive consists of its political and bureaucratic arms. Since the Indian Constitution seeks to combine parliamentary as well as federal principles of government, the executive here has roles both in parliamentary and federal components of the government.

Under the Indian Constitution, the political executive is legally and democratically constituted and is subject to legislative control and judicial review. It would be largely untenable to sustain any argument of executive prerogative or privilege in the monarchical tradition in independent India. For the legal transfer of power in India notwithstanding, the sovereign Constituent Assembly to which the British Parliament bequeathed ultimate authority resolved to begin the Preamble with the ringing declaration of popular sovereignty with the words "We the people of India ..." as the source of political power. According to Article 53 of the Constitution, executive power is "vested in the President and shall be exercised by him either directly or through officers subordinate to him in accordance with this Constitution." Dr. Rajendra Prasad, the first two-term President, on the one hand, and the Attorney General and incumbent Prime Minister, Jawaharlal Nehru, on the other, thought differently.[1]

The then Presidents Radhakrishnan, Fakhruddin Ali Ahmed (even in declaration of the national emergency with no questions asked in 1975 by Indira Gandhi) and R. Venkataraman, who succeeded Zail Singh, also acted out a strictly nominal or constitutional role, although both Venkataraman and Zail Singh thought that the then President could act in his discretion in dealing with the allegation of corruption in l'affaire Bofors gun deal for arms purchase; none finally acted upon their intentions. Venkataraman left an ambiguous opinion in his autobiography, saying both sides of opinions were not entirely immune to assailing or dissenting interpretations. The then President, Radhakrishnan was never in doubt about the nature of President's executive authority. He always showed his formal addresses to the Prime Ministers, except on one occasion when Lal Bahadur Shastri was not easily at hand. Shastri subsequently murmured about it.[2] Radhakrishnan was quite forthright in his informal public comments on the policies or performance of the Nehru Government, particularly after India's debacle in the China War. "Radhakrishnan's reading of the Constitution was that there should never be a vacancy in the office of Prime Minister, with the corollary that the president should never directly exercise executive authority."[3]

The President of India is the head of the federal state in the parliamentary mode, i.e., he acts as a parliamentary federal functionary on the Union cabinet's advice. However, in certain situations he/she may initially act in personal discretion, i.e., when the party system fails to yield a majority party government after an election or later midstream due to unforeseen contingencies. The written text of the Constitution (Article 75) provides that the prime Minister shall be appointed by the President and other Ministers shall be appointed by the President on the advice of the Prime Minister. The Council of Ministers shall be collectively responsible to the Lok Sabha. A Prime Minister has in practice been appointed from either the Lok Sabha or the Rajya Sabha or even one who at the time of appointment is not a member of any of the two houses of the Parliament. But he must be elected to the Parliament within six months of such appointment or bow out of the office. This rule also applies to the appointment of a minister.

In the event of death of three Prime Ministers in harness—Nehru's in 1964, Shastri's in 1966, and Indira Gandhi's in 1984—Presidents Radhakrishnan and Zail Singh conducted the prime ministerial succession in different manners. On the two former occasions, Radhakrishnan immediately sworn in the senior-most cabinet colleagues of the deceased Prime Ministers pending the election of the regular leader of the Congress parliamentary party. The interim Prime Minister on both these occasions was Gulzarilal Nanda, while the party's final choices were Lal Bahadur Shastri and Indira Gandhi, respectively. In these instances, the President had no Prime Minister to advise him and had to decide on his own; he immediately appointed a caretaker Prime Minister, creating a constitutional precedent.[4]

However, these precedents could not develop into a convention. In the event of Indira Gandhi's assassination, the then President, Zail Singh, ignored the senior-most cabinet minister, Pranab Mukherji and sworn in Rajiv Gandhi in deference to his loyalty for the Nehru-Gandhi dynasty. Critics saw it as the anointing of dynasty's heir apparent. Zail Singh remarks in his autobiography: "My first thought about Mrs. Gandhi's successor was riveted on Rajiv Gandhi. Apart from that I had great respect for Pandit Jawaharlal Nehru and affectionate feelings for Mrs. Gandhi, I wanted to appoint someone, who would be acceptable to the majority party in the Lok Sabha. One who could properly lead the country at that particular juncture."[5] Arun Nehru's remembrance of the fateful day from close quarters is: "There was no controversy on the 'succession' or 'swearing-in' issue. Few leaders were available in the initial hours when crucial decisions were to be taken. I did not discuss the issue of leadership with anyone in particular. Remember we had no cell phones in 1984 and nor was there any time to consult the CWC [Congress Working Committee] members. Rajiv Gandhi was the natural and correct choice and everyone endorsed this as time went by and to my knowledge there was no dissension. There was discussion on the 'modalities' to be adopted and these were later used to settle scores and the person to suffer in particular was Pranab Mukherjee".[6]

The fact remains that the precedents set by Radhakrishnan were more consistent with constitutional propriety than the one set by Zail Singh. Radhakrishnan's foregoing precedents were not followed by Zail Singh, but the idea of a caretaker government caught on and has become a constitutional procedure and practice after the announcement of the election schedule for a fresh poll by the Election Commission of India. During this period, while pending the formation of the post-poll government, the transitional government is expected to carry on only day-to-day decisions and desist from making policy decisions or announcing any new schemes of expenditure. However, the Bharatiya Janata Party-led coalition Government headed by Atal Bihari Vajpayee was faced with the contingency of the Kargil war in 1999 during its caretaking period in the run-up to the Lok Sabha election later that year. It had to take vital policy decisions going beyond routine day-to-day administration. Some suggested that Vajpayee must call the Rajya Sabha (which is never dissolved) into a session; he instead called a Chief Minister's Conference during the period as a fig leaf of his government's accountability. Incidentally, the idea of a caretaker government has also been adopted in Bangladesh, following the Indian practice. It might be considered one of the few constitutional conventions evolved in independent India, at least in the context of the period following the announcement of election schedule by the Election Commission of India. The same may be said for the period when after an election, a hung house emerges without a party or coalition with a clear majority; in such a situation, the President or a governor requests the incumbent government to continue as a caretaker until a new government with majority comes to be formed.

In terms of Indian constitutional law, executive power is the residue of governmental functions that are neither legislative nor judicial.[7] In certain exigencies, it can be used prior to legislative sanction subject to the Constitution.[8] The Constitution, in broad terms, includes at least three limitations on the Union executive power: separation of powers between the three classic organs of government, albeit within the parliamentary crucible which in practice fuses legislative and executive powers; federal division of powers between the Union and States; and fundamental rights of citizens. All these limitations flow from the Constitution, case laws, and conventions of the Constitution.

The Federal Executive in India is partly elected and partly appointed. It comprises the President, the Prime Minister and his Cabinet, and the bureaucracy. The relation between the President and the Prime Minister was, until the 44th Amendment in 1978, largely governed by convention (rather than the codified constitutional text), according to which the former is nominal head of the State, while the latter is the real head of the government. The 44th Amendment changed this convention into an explicit provision in the written text of the Constitution, whereby the President must ultimately go by Cabinet advice, subject to only one request for reconsideration. This development largely rendered infructuous the argument of Rajendra Prasad, the first two-term President, that the Indian head of the State was not analogous to the British Crown. For, he/she was elected, impeachable, and a federal functionary, neither of which was true of the British monarch.[9] The advice rendered by M.C. Setalvad, the first Attorney General of India, to Rajendra Prasad regarding the scope of his powers remains as valid today as when it was offered in the 1950s:

> In this interview which I had with him I pointed out to him what I thought was the constitutional position of the President. He could, like the British monarch, try and persuade his Ministers, and persuasion coming from so high a quarter would undoubtedly carry great influence as it had done many a time in British Constitutional history. But if such persuasion failed, I told him that he was bound to act according to the advice of his Ministers.[10]

By writing this conventional law into the text of the Constitution by the 44th Amendment, India joined the company of the Irish Republic, whose Constitution has a similar provision, though the Irish Constitution is otherwise patterned after the Westminster model in which this matter is governed by an unwritten constitutional convention.

This precaution did not, however, settle all matters of relations between the President and the Prime Minister. Fresh questions cropped up during the presidencies of Zail Singh and his successor R. Venkataraman. Zail Singh complained of denial of power and opportunities to be briefed by Prime Minister Rajiv Gandhi in person as well as to be provided with the Thakkar Commission Report on Indira Gandhi's assassination that he had requisitioned. Singh contended that he was entitled to these courtesies/rights under Article 78 which enjoins upon the Prime Minister to keep the President informed about the affairs of the State.[11]

Later, when the Bofors arms deal scandal involving the Rajiv Gandhi Government surfaced, Singh and his successor Venkataraman were consecutively approached to dismiss or sanction prosecution against the Prime Minister on corruption charges.[12] Neither actually took this drastic step which, to our mind, was correct. For, going by strictly legal and constitutional norms, the President should in such cases neither short-circuit judicial procedure nor circumvent a parliamentary majority. However, writing about his dealing with this question, Venkataraman in his memoirs records that the Attorney General veered to the position that the Supreme Court's ruling in *Karunanidhi's* case would suggest that the Chief Minister (and therefore a Prime Minister) might be deemed to be a public servant under the Prevention of Corruption Act, 1988, and the Governor (and therefore the President) could remove a Chief Minister (and therefore a Prime Minister) for proven charges of corruption.[13] Besides, he also argued that in terms of the *R.S. Naik* case, the President or the Governor should decide independently of the Council of Ministers in sanctioning such prosecution. However, both the President and the Attorney General thought that both "these positions could be assailed in appropriate proceedings."[14]

The post-Independence Constitution of India (1950), embodying the discursive decision in the Constituent Assembly in favour of parliamentary Cabinet system, provided for "a Council of Ministers with the Prime Minister at its head to aid and advise the President," whom the 44th Amendment obliged to go by his Council's advice subject to one and only one presidential request for reconsideration (Article 74, Clause 1). In view of the constitutionally sensitive relationship between the President and the Council of Ministers, the Constitution also stipulates: "The question whether any, and if so what, advice was tendered by Ministers to the President shall not be inquired into in any Court" (Article 74, Clause 2). As in another context where the Constitution-makers preferred to use the term "Union" to federation, in this context too the term "Council of Ministers" was preferred to Cabinet. This presumably reflected a desire to make a new beginning in India without being unduly encumbered by the deadwoods of histories of other nations, even though the debates and committee papers of the Constituent Assembly leave no one in doubt that the constitutional systems of Westminster and the early Commonwealth parliamentary systems were in reference. The term Cabinet occurs in the Rules of Business of the Council framed under Article 77(3) of the Constitution. The Council as a body never meets. The Cabinet caucus and its committees frequently meet and decide in the name of the Council.

An idea about the dimly defined ways of the role of the Prime Minister and his ministerial colleagues can be found in the exchange of classic notes between Jawaharlal Nehru and Vallabhbhai Patel through Mahatma Gandhi at a time of grave misunderstanding in the relations between the first Prime Minister (Nehru) and the Deputy Prime Minister (Patel). Nehru's note in part read:

> As I conceive it, the Prime Minister's role is, and should be, an important role. He is not only figurehead but a person who should be more responsible than anyone else for the general trend of policy and for the co-ordination of the work of various Government departments. The final authority necessarily is the Cabinet itself. But in the type of democratic set-up we have adopted, the Prime Minister is supposed

> to play an outstanding role....Otherwise there will be no cohesion in the Cabinet and the Government and disruptive tendencies will be at work.... If this view is correct, then the PM should have full freedom to act when and how he chooses, though of course such an action must not be an undue interference with local authorities who are immediately responsible.[15]

In reply, Patel's note in part read:

> The Prime Minister's position, according to my conception, is certainly pre-eminent: he is first among equals. But he has no overriding powers over his colleagues; if he had any, a Cabinet and Cabinet responsibility would be superfluous. In my view the Prime Minister, as the leader of the party and the head of the whole administration is inevitably concerned that Cabinet decisions are effective and that there is no conflict between one Ministry and another. But the entire responsibility for implementing the policy of Government rests upon the Ministers and Ministries under them which are concerned with the subject matter of the Cabinet decisions. He had accordingly the right to ask for information from Ministers concerned as well as the right to consult and advise on the lines of policy to be adopted and even the manner in which the policy is to be implemented. But the responsibility for the implementation of the policy must be that of the Ministry concerned and the Minister in charge, and the Prime Minister should influence action by way of consultation with and advice to the Minister.[16]

Both Nehru and Patel were to see Gandhi on this matter, but before the meeting could take place, Gandhi was assassinated. But the two stalwarts did sink their differences in the trail of the tragic event and worked jointly to guide the destiny of the stunned nation. In any event, what this exchange of notes makes suggestively clear is that the relations between the Prime Minister and powerful Cabinet colleagues cannot be precisely laid down in simple formulas for all times and personalities. This is so for the simple reason that the nature of these equations is contingent on such objective conditions as the factional balance of forces in the ruling party or coalition and such subjective factors as personalities of the principal actors involved.

Except for the bare outlines of the institutions of the Prime Minister and his Cabinet provided in the written text of the Constitution, the major aspects of the political executive in India are still left to the conventions or rules of business to be framed for its smooth functioning. The category of ministers, the practice of caretaker government, the office of Deputy Prime Minister, if at all, are also matters of precedents or conventions. Arguably, these conventions can be reconstructed on the basis of the Constituent Assembly debates, precedents and conventions of India and those of the old Commonwealth federations applicable to India. In case of doubt, the matter is finally determinable by the judiciary. Conventions, amendments, and judicial interpretations are the principal ways through which the Constitution has grown and grows.

The connecting link between the constitutional text and convention can be found in Article 75(2) and (3) that provides, with apparent contradiction, that "Ministers shall hold office during the pleasure of the President" and "The Council of Ministers shall be collectively responsible to the House of the People." The apparent contradiction can be removed by the obvious inference that the President can only appoint a person as the Prime Minister who can command a majority support in the popular Chamber of the Parliament. The Ministers appointed on the recommendations of the Prime Minister by the President must be members of either House of the Parliament or must become one within six months of their appointment (Article 75, Clauses 1 & 5). So far, all Prime Ministers, except P.V. Narasimha Rao and H.D. Deve Gowda, have been members of either the Lok Sabha or the Rajya Sabha, mostly of the former. Rao and Deve Gowda subsequently got elected to the Lok Sabha from Andhra Pradesh and Karnataka, respectively, within the stipulated period.

An unwritten rule of the Cabinet system in India that has become more or less well-established is the principle of regional and ethnic representation in the formation of the Council of Ministers. It has come to be expected and politically advisable for any Prime Minister to include in the government representatives of India's major States and regions and castes and communities, sometimes even at the cost of talent and efficiency outside the vital ministries of finance, home, external affairs, and defence. Regional or community representatives in the ministries are even expected to an extent to draw the attention of the Cabinet to the legitimate expectations of their clientele. In Canada the regional representation in the Cabinet has developed into a veritable convention of the Constitution such that the Prime Ministers go to the extent of appointing Senators from important provinces and regions and elevate them to ministerial status if the party in power does not electorally win any representatives from those areas in the House of Commons.

Because the Rajya Sabha is a relatively weak federal second chamber, and the Canadian Senate is even weaker, the federal Cabinets in both the countries have emerged as a far more effective instrument of regional representation than the upper chamber despite its declared federal character. This is inevitable in a parliamentary federal system where the Cabinet is collectively responsible to the popular parliamentary House. This tendency of regionalization of the Council of Ministers has become even more marked with the onset of federal coalition governments in India since 1989. Incidentally, Canadians are committed practitioners of party governments. If a hung Commons emerges from the hustings, Canadians prefer to form minority governments instead of coalition governments. Canadians generally prefer party governments, even a minority party government, to coalition governments.

One can, it seems to us, delineate at least three patterns of executive leadership in India's constitutional history.[17] These are (a) predominantly *parliamentary/quasi-federal* premiership during the Nehru-Patel duumvirate that eventuated into the *prime ministerial Cabinet* system under Nehru following Patel's death in December 1950 (1946–1971); (b) *quasi-parliamentary/quasi-federal/patrimonial prime ministerial* system under Indira Gandhi through the bulk of the 1970s, when due to overcentralization of powers in the Congress Party and the government in New Delhi even Chief Ministers were named by the Prime Ministers and subsequently endorsed by Congress Legislature parties in States; and (c) precursive phase of *federal* premiership of Morarji Desai, Indira Gandhi, and Rajiv Gandhi (1977–1989), and (d) *federal* premiership of the era of coalition/minority Governments (since 1989 to date) when the federal features of the Indian political system demanded a reconfiguration of supremacy of prime ministerial authority and of the principle of collective responsibility of the Cabinet in practice, if not in theory.

Nehru's "fine art of government" is characterized in the following words by his biographer Sarvepalli Gopal:

> To Nehru democratic government was a fine art, the achievement of a cooperation within a series of widening circles which gave a sense of participation to everyone involved. He exploited his personal dominance to secure, as he hoped, its own destruction. It was a magnificent effort which did not quite come off.[18]

This metaphorical invocation of Gandhi's imagery of "oceanic circles" is more poetic than valid of Nehru's prime ministership. It was in fact neither an exercise in dualistic federal power-sharing nor in Gandhian notion of radical decentralization. Nehru's towering personality and Congress dominance at Union as well as State levels of power could not have made any such thing possible. Sure, the power structure in the Nehru era was more pluralistic than during the Indira Gandhi Government in the 1970s, but neither of the two periods was truly federal. Some Chief Ministers were given greater consideration than others, but their respectful relations were mutual. Nehru wrote regular, and long letters to the Chief Ministers, but these were monologues rather than interactions concerning Union-State demarcated jurisdictions. As the editorial note to one of the volumes compiling these letters remarks:

> In these letters Nehru touches on every problem, large and small, and all the efforts being made to deal with these problems. The progress of planning, community development projects, land reforms, administrative issues and the development of the north-east frontier areas are but some of the matters he considers; but he always sets them in the wider context of the right objectives and proper directions towards those objectives. So too, in foreign policy, he explains repeatedly the true nature and significance of non-alignment and puts in their proper setting the immediate issues such as the negotiations on Korea, relations with Pakistan.[19]

The first Union Cabinet was virtually a diarchy between Prime Minister Nehru and Deputy Prime Minister and Home Minister, Vallabhbhai Patel. The two stalwarts exchanged notes on their divergent views about the role of the Prime Minister and the Cabinet system through Gandhi, as discussed above. Gandhi's assassination "reunited Nehru and Patel. Their reconciliation not only saved Congress and India's Central Government from collapse, but it kept Nehru in power. Without the Sardar's strength and support Nehru might have broken down or been forced out of high office. Vallabhbhai ran India's administration for the next two years while Nehru indulged mostly in foreign affairs and high Himalayan adventures."[20] After Patel's death in December 1950, Nehru exercised unchallenged power in the Cabinet virtually until his death in May 1964. Even though Nehru is often likened with a Grand Moghal sitting over a highly centralized political pyramid,[21] Michael Brecher observed that the "magnitude of his responsibilities compels him to rely on others". Brecher goes on to remark:

> The Congress elite has changed little since the death of Patel in 1950. The key group in the Congress Working Committee is of about twenty members. But of these only a half-dozen were and are involved in making important decisions. Other than Nehru and Azad, the dominant figures have been Pant, Morarji Desai and Dr. B.C. Roy. Approaching the inner group is Lal Bahadur Shastri of the UP. In central Cabinet...it is much the same group. Following the Prime Minister, the unofficial ranking is Pant, Morarji Desai and Shastri, with Krishna Menon occupying a special status in foreign affairs.[22]

During this phase, it was essentially a prime ministerial Cabinet under Nehru's tutelege. The Shastri and the early Indira Gandhi Cabinets as well as the Desai Cabinet were more collegial. However, Indira Gandhi's Cabinets in the 1970s and the 1980s were predominantly prime ministerial. The Government under Rajiv Gandhi was in our view also more or less similar, though somewhat more collegial and collective in its working.

With the advent of multi-party federal coalition governments, the internal equation of the cabinet system of one-party governments has undergone a sea change. In theory, the Prime Minister still continues to be keystone of the cabinet arch but his/her position has radically changed in practice. Serious limitation on the choice of cabinet colleagues and the power to coordinate and control come into operation. These extraneous political manoeuvers are either directly manipulated by the various parties joining the coalition governments or through some coordination committee of parliamentary parties that are partners in the *executive* cabinet coalition of the government or only extend support from the parliamentary floor without joining the government. Such coordination committees were formed in practically all coalition governments at least formally but in practice they played some notable roles only in the Janata Dal-led National Front and United Front governments led alternately by V.P. Singh or H.D. Deve Gowda or I.K. Gujral, and the Congress-led United Progressive Alliance (UPA) governments headed by Manmohan Singh. Some observers occasionally complained that the National Advisory Council (NAC) of the UPA headed by the Congress president Sonia Gandhi seemed at times to eclipse the Prime Minister and the cabinet.[23] However, the fact remains that the NAC acted as a clearinghouse of policy options and presented alternative perspectives to the government to choose from. Its role in innovative democratic experiments like the Right to Information and social sector and welfare measures like Mahatma Gandhi National Rural Employment Guarantee, forest rights, tribal welfare, food security, etc. were particularly notable.

The 2014 Lok Sabha elections marked a turning point inasmuch as the Narendra Modi-led BJP won a single-party majority after three decades since the Rajiv Gandhi-led Congress had last got such a majority in 1984. This virtually ended the compulsions of federal coalition governments that began in 1989 and continued until 2014, even though BJP has continued its coalitional government with its partners in the National Democratic Alliance. The BJP and NDA under Modi were re-elected in May 2019 general elections with even larger majority for the BJP alone as well as in unison with NDA. Modi has run a prime ministerial cabinet dominating over both the BJP and NDA cabinet colleagues and coalescing parties. With the Prime Minister's Office and handpicked civil servants in various ministries and even supposedly autonomous agencies in vigilance, information, statistics, and in various sectors of national economy, the Prime Minister has considerably reversed the trend of federalization and rampant regionalization. Soon after coming to power, the government abolished the Planning Commission, the 64-year mechanism of centralized planning and a regular body of experts well-entrenched in economic decision-making since the early Nehru era. It has been replaced with a similar body of experts called National Institution for Transforming India (NITI) Aayog (Commission), but acting as a think tank on request or on its own, but without being a regular wheel of the vehicle of the government unlike the Planning Commission. NITI Aayog's Governing Council replaced the National Development Council (NDC), which used to give guidelines for formulations of five-year plans and accord approval to the plan documents. The compositions of the NDC and the NITI Aayog's Governing Council are similar inasmuch as both comprise the executive heads of the Union, State, and UT governments. But, the functional role and relevance of the old and new bodies differ radically; this centralizes powers and decision-making in the Union Finance Ministry and other Union ministries in the overall federal policies and structure. Also, early on, the Modi Government, with the overall support of all political parties proceeded to replace the judicial collegium by the National Judicial Appointments Commission in 2014. The former had been playing a decisive role with a primacy in appointments of the Supreme Court and High Court judges since 1993. The latter sought to give primacy to the Union Executive in judicial appointments. However, the Supreme Court declared the constitutional amendment and the conforming parliamentary statute introducing this change unconstitutional in 2015. The Reserve Bank of India has also considerably lost its formal powers and functional autonomy under the Modi governments in the domain of monetary policy and its fuller control over the banking sector. The media and the NGOs have also felt the informal or formal control of the government tightening on them.

The political capital of the Modi Government has been high on account of the personal honesty and integrity of the Prime Minister, his ardent nationalism with Hindutva tinge exposing pseudo-secularism, crusade against political and administrative corruption, and tough action against terrorism at home and from Pakistan. Recent legislative changes in the party financing have also enormously increased the corporate donations to the BJP's party and campaign funds.

FEDERAL PREMIERSHIP STYLE

During the era of coalition/minority Governments, the prime ministerial Cabinets that had operated under Nehru after Patel's death in December 1950, under Indira Gandhi in the 1970s (excepting the Janata Party rule), and under Indira Gandhi and Rajiv Gandhi during the 1980s became a thing of the past. Instead, a more collective Cabinet system came into existence. The difference between the 1970s and the 1980s only was that the Congress Prime Ministers had to contend with more autonomous non-Congress state governments, especially in the non-Hindi speaking rim-lands. During the latter half of the 1980s, more differentiated party systems at the State level dotted by non-Congress governments was also combined with a differentiated configuration of party representation in the Lok Sabha and the Rajya Sabha. The Congress governments could manage to muster a parliamentary majority but with considerably reduced margins. By the 1990s Congress and non-Congress coalition governments managed to somehow muster majority in the Lok Sabha, but the Rajya Sabha was invariably controlled by the parties or coalitions in opposition.

The formation of the first minority-cum-coalition government formed by the Janata Dal-led National Front (NF) under the leadership of V.P. Singh brought about a sea change in the role of the Prime Minister and the working of the Cabinet system. This was for the reason that although it was a coalition government presaged by the *de facto* coalition government, like that formed by the Janata Party in the late 1970s, but unlike the latter it was not a majority coalition government. A minority coalition government was also presaged by the Rao Congress Government during 1991–96, but it was a minority government, not a coalition government. It faced an oppositional majority in the Lok Sabha. The United Front was a minority as well as coalition government. The task for the V.P. Singh government was thus more complicated. To outsiders, V.P. Singh appeared inexperienced and temperamentally unsuitable for this doubly difficult situation. For example, he failed to reconcile his differences with his deputy Prime Minister, Devi Lal. A factional feud between the two turned out to be irreconcilable. The Prime Minister took an apparently impulsive and precipitate action in dismissing his powerful deputy. Soon thereafter, he proceeded to hurriedly implement the Mandal Commission Report (1978) that was shelved for nearly more than a decade by the Indira Gandhi and Rajiv Gandhi Congress governments during the 1980s. By available indicators, he consulted neither the full Cabinet nor the National Front (NF) coordination committee and took the plea that the item was included in the National Front election manifesto.

However, an insider's account provided by the leading journalist, Prem Shankar Jha who served as Information Advisor to the Prime Minister, differs from this public perception. Jha[24] opines that V.P. Singh was acutely aware of "the smallness of his party and its dependence on two disparate allies" and "evolved a style of political management that minimized these disadvantages."[25] Jha proceeds to write: "At the center, V.P. Singh sought to build the consensus through an elaborate, multi-tier process of consultation: with all political parties; then with his own 'friendly' parties, the Bharatiya Janata Party (BJP) and the Left, and lastly within the National Front (NF). In all these ways he attempted to build a consensus, as far as that was possible, on key issues facing the country, as a prelude to taking the necessary legislative or executive action."[26]

Jha does, however, give some instances where these exercises at consensus building were not "equally successful."[27] The intractable examples related to Punjab where initial hopes for a consensual solution could not bear fruits. However, an all-party meeting "achieved a consensus of sorts on a few peripheral issues", e.g. the repeal of the Fifty-Ninth Amendment which had temporarily suspended enforcement of Fundamental Rights by Courts during an Emergency in Punjab.[28] All-party delegation to Kashmir as well as on electoral reform also by and large failed to produce consensus that could facilitate decisive action on the part of the government.[29]

With the transformation of the party system and the advent of coalition governments, the presidential power had acquired a new dimension. As James Manor hypothetically explores:

> The President has become more important since 1989 because he is the referee in the game of government formation, and he decides whether to grant a Prime Minister's request for dissolution of Parliament. In this era of hung Parliaments, the former task has become more complex and difficult, and the latter is a potential problem. This makes it much more likely that the presidency will be engulfed in heated disputes which may occur even if presidents seek to avoid controversy—as they usually do.[30]

Manor's apprehension has not happened, at least to any crisis proportions. A few other episodes may be cited here to illustrate what we have called the federal premiership style. Two of these relate to the K.R. Narayanan—I.K. Gujral period, and two to the presidency of A.P.J. Abdul Kalam in his relationship with Atal Bihari Vajpayee and subsequently Manmohan Singh. The Gujral Government recommended the dismissal of the RJD government in Bihar for its inability to maintain law and order but President Narayanan requested the Union government to reconsider its proposal. As it happened, the proposal was not presented to the President again. On another occasion, the UP Governor Romesh Bhandari dismissed a BJP government and replaced it by an all-defector government headed by a Congressman, Jagdambika Pal. The Janata Dal–led United Front government in New Delhi headed by Gujral adopted an ostrich policy and left President Narayanan without any advice in the midst of repeated representation to the Union government for intervention in the matter. Narayanan on his own faxed an advice of disapproval—not any specific directive—to the Governor. Finally, the matter reached the Supreme Court which ordered the restoration of the dismissed government.

During the presidency of Kalam, the Vajpayee government sent a bill to him annulling the Election Commission (EC) directive requiring candidates to file an affidavit along with nomination paper regarding their financial assets, educational qualifications and involvement, if any, in criminal activities. The EC directive was in pursuit of a Supreme Court judgement. Kalam returned the bill for reconsideration. The Cabinet reiterated its proposal whereupon the President granted his assent to the bill. The 2005 elections in Bihar returned a hung assembly, resulting in an impasse in formation of a government for months together. Governor Buta Singh recommended to the Centre that the Assembly be dismissed just when a NDA–led coalition government appeared to be on the cards, alleging horse trading in legislators. The Congress–led United Progressive Alliance (UPA) government at the Centre headed by Manmohan Singh sent a proposal to the President endorsing the Governor's report. President Kalam signed on the dotted lines, but later the Supreme Court declared the dissolution of the Assembly unconstitutional.

Kalam was succeeded by Pratibha Patil, the first woman to be appointed to the highest constitutional position, but she was in controversy regarding her excessive foreign trips, over her plans to build a retirement home for her on land owned by defence ministry in Pune and came under sharp criticism for clemency spree.

Pranab Mukherjee served as the President during the second term of the then Prime Minister, Manmohan Singh, and the part of the first term of the Prime Minister, Modi. Mukherjee was the most dynamic minister in the first-term Congress/UPA cabinet of Singh and was often considered a possible successor to Singh if the UPA got re-elected. But, he was probably 'pushed upwards' to the presidency to make room for the heir apparent of the Nehru-Gandhi dynasty, Rahul Gandhi, in the same way as he had been passed over by the then President, Zail Singh in favour of Rahul's father, Rajiv Gandhi, in 1984 after Indira Gandhi's assassination, as already narrated above. His role as

President in relation to the Modi government marks silent and shrewd exercise of the President's discretion. Despite difference in his party affiliation with the Prime Minister, the two appear to have maintained a 'balanced' relationship. There were no open differences between the two. He apparently went along with signing in quick sequence the three ordinances relating to amendments in the Land Acquisition Act, 2013, proposed by the Modi government, thus making it easier to acquire land from farmers and peasants for industrial and infrastructural developments. But, the government failed in enacting any of these ordinances into legislations within the constitutionally specified period on account of the Opposition majority in the Rajya sabha. However, the then President, Mukherjee apparently persuaded the Prime Minister, Modi not to take the route of a joint session of the two Houses of the Parliament to outvote the recalcitrant federal second chamber by the superior numbers or the government majority in the Lok Sabha.

Ram Nath Kovid is currently serving as the fourteenth President of India. He declared the abrogation of Article 370 that gave special status to Jammu and Kashmir on 07 August 2019.

During the federal premiership phase, the supreme political power of the Prime Minister in practice has become subject to multi-party coalitional power-sharing. Besides, collective responsibility of the Cabinet to the Parliament (Lok Sabha, to be more specific), must take into account powerful regional and national parties in the coalition. The top leaders of these regional parties often prefer to stay back as Chief Ministers and nominate their junior partners to the Union Cabinet and remote-control them. This results in the fragmentation of the collegial nature of the Cabinet system and debilitation of prime ministerial control and coordination as well as initiation of significant policies of reform.

To be sure, the Indian Cabinet system cannot be a duplication of the British model. This is for the obvious reasons that (a) India is not only a parliamentary system but also a federal system, (b) we also have had for long to deal with the imperatives of coalition/minority governments in New Delhi (and in some States), and (c) our Constitution not only incorporates rights of federating States but also fundamental rights of citizens that make the judiciary the ultimate arbiter in the political system. Parliamentary supremacy in the United Kingdom does not have to contend with any of these limitations. If anything, a comparison between India and Canada in this connection would be more apt. For, the two political systems are congenital twins due to coincidence of common British colonial history. The British Parliament enacted the Government of India Act, 1935, largely patterned after the British North America Act, 1867, also a product of the Parliament in London, and now renamed as the Canada Constitution Act, 1867.

Yet, the fact remains that the weakening of the prime ministerial authority and the 'cabalization' of the Cabinet system that we have witnessed since the 1990s can hardly qualify as a wholesome exercise in good governance. We have witnessed the tendency of 'empire-building' among coalition partners in the ministries parceled out to them, endless roll-backs of Cabinet decisions under external pressures from the constituents of the ruling coalition, patronage to the special interests, undemocratic pressures from corrupt and criminal parties and individuals, and massacres of Dalits and upper castes in Bihar, and of Muslims and Christians in Gujarat at the connivance of the State governments or the Union government or both. To compound all these problems, or perhaps mercifully, most governments in New Delhi were also unstable, until at least the late 1990s, when the NDA and UPA governments managed to bring about some degree of governmental stability.

And, since 2014, the BJP/NDA majority under the Prime Minister, Modi has transformed the political scene for even greater governmental stability and effectiveness free from coalitional blackmails and rampant regionalism.

THE EXECUTIVE UNDER COALITION GOVERNMENTS

The advent of coalition governments on the Indian political scene altered the pattern of executive functioning in a significant way. Multi-party coalition Governments have meant a departure from or at least modifications in the pattern of executive functioning influenced by the classical Westminster parliamentary tradition, which is now changing. In fact, it is a second step away from the British parliamentary principle and practice. The first step away was the combination in the Indian Constitution between parliamentarism and federalism, as in Canada. The second step away became evident under the imperative of federal coalition governments between 1989 and 2014.

The working of federal coalition Cabinets resulted in larger Cabinets and, in turn, greater federalization (in the sense of regionalization) of the Cabinet system in India. Coalition Governments in New Delhi made possible a greater degree of State or regional autonomy. There had also been a wider power sharing between the national and regional parties which had promoted national unity and integration. However, coalition Cabinets were also characterized by instability of Union Governments until the late 1990s, though States became more autonomous and stronger. Coalition Governments were also bedevilled by policy incoherence and at times even policy paralysis or atrophy.

In retrospect, looking at the executive government at Union as well as in States, we can delineate at least three phases of coalition governments in India. First, there were the post-1967 catch-all coalition governments in north Indian States spanning from Punjab to Bengal. These coalition governments were formed under the spell of "non-Congressism", the arch priest of which ideology was Dr. Ram Manohar Lohia. Dr. Lohia forged the strategy of non-Congress catch-all coalitions inclusive of all non-Congress parties ranging from the right to the left: Bharatiya Jana Sangh, Swatantra Party, Ganatantra Parishad, a number of Jana-Congress parties that had split from the Congress on the right, and Samyukt Socialist Party, Communist Party of India (Marxist) on the left. On account of their ideological diversity, these coalition governments turned out to be very unstable, except for a Ganatantra Parishad-led right-wing coalition government in Orissa. This coalitional phase in north-Indian-State politics was superseded by the restoration of Congress dominance under the leadership of Indira Gandhi after the 1969 Congress split.

Second, the post-1977 coalition governments of like-minded parties in West Bengal [CPI(M)-led Left Front], Kerala [CPI(M)-led Left Democratic Front and Congress-led United Democratic Front], and in Tripura [CPI(M)-led Left Front]. These ideologically compatible coalition governments had been effectively more stable.

Third, there had been the post-1989 coalition governments at the Union level of three muted heraldic hues: (a) the Janata Dal-led National/United Fronts; (b) the BJP-led National Democratic Alliance; (c) the Congress-led United Progressive Alliance governments in 2004 and 2009; and (d) the single-party-majority BJP-led NDA coalition governments since 2014 to this writing (October 2020).

From the point of view of executive government, the moral of the working of these coalition governments in New Delhi can be summed up in terms of the following 'dos' and 'don'ts'. For stable executive government, there is need for programmatic coherence among coalescing parties, genuine power sharing and mechanisms for reconciliation of differences, e.g. coordination committee, etc. The things to be avoided in the interest of governmental stability are hidden agendas by partners, 'outside' support (from the legislative floor without joining the Cabinet), overstraining the collective responsibility of the Cabinet to centers of power outside the Parliament and thus reducing the prime ministerial power to a vanishing point. Or else, a recipe for stability is a de facto majority party like BJP leading the NDA coalition.

Coalition governments become more probable in the following two conditions:

(a) if the party system gets too fragmented to prompt a seasoned observer to wonder if the Indian political system has transited from "quasi-federation" to "quasi-confederacy"[31]; and
(b) if there is a patent lack of class polarization or communal polarization.

As for reforms in coalitional governance typical of the federal-level Indian scenario during the 1990s, the problem can be addressed at three levels: (a) electoral system, (b) the party system, and (c) rules of business of Parliament. The stability of coalition governments is closely linked with the system of representation and the party system. The expectation that plurality representation or first-past-the-post electoral system generally leads to a two-party system has not been fulfilled in India largely because of the exceptional social and regional diversities in the country. However, proportional representation is likely to lead to even greater fragmentation of the party system. Hence, the alternative that remains is to introduce the majority electoral system which requires a party or a candidate to win at least 50 per cent plus votes in an election. This system may necessitate more than one balloting if no party secures more than 50 per cent vote in the first instance. The second voting with only two candidates with largest number of votes remaining in the field will produce the desired result. If more than one balloting is considered expensive and cumbersome, then the system of preferential voting in terms of first, second and third preference with votes of the least successful candidate being transferred to most successful ones may be tried.

At the level of the party system, a comprehensive legislation on parties with incentives for formation of federal parties combining the regional ones would reduce the number of parties. This would be conducive to a stable cabinet government. Moreover, the system of national convention of federal parties for electing their leaders as in Canada would also set in motion a federal aggregation of political forces in the country into fewer numbers of parties.

At the level of rules of legislative business, the recommendation of the National Commission for Review of the Working of the Constitution (NCRWC) in favour of electing the Prime Minister or Chief Ministers on the floor of the House and "constructive vote of confidence" (allowance of a non-confidence motion only when it is accompanied by a proposal for an alternative government) is worth considering, as in Germany.

THREE BASIC PROBLEMS OF EXECUTIVE GOVERNANCE

Since the 1990s to 2014, a greater degree of federalization produced by coalition/minority governments also brought to the fore at least three basic problems that seriously weakened the effectiveness of federal executive governance. First, increased federalization reduced parliamentary supremacy and gave federal features of the Constitution a freer play. The combination of parliamentary and federal principles of government in the Constitution and the resultant contradictions between the two was supposed to be primarily reconciled by giving the Parliament or the Union executive supremacy at the cost of State autonomy. Parliamentary and federal principles of government are inherently contradictory as the former is premised on supremacy of the Parliament and the latter is predicated on decentralization of powers. The Indian Constitution seeks to reconcile this contradiction by giving the Parliament and Union executive certain overriding powers over State Legislatures and State governments. Between 1989 and 2014, parliamentary supremacy came to be seriously compromised by federal coalition Cabinets with regional/State parties. Such regional parties were also in power at the State level having a decisive balancing role in federal coalition governments. When parliamentary supremacy came to be undermined by such federal coalition governments, it produced judiciary-driven governance in place of executive-driven governance of the past. Moreover, with the growing social mobilization and political participation, federalization and the fragmentation of the party system of the national level, the ways and means of reconciliation must also be found at the levels of multi-party system and intergovernmental forums of Inter-State Council and National Development Council [Governing Council of NITI Aayog].[32] All these developments require a different style of prime ministerial leadership and Cabinet system that, as mentioned above, we have called a federal prime ministership and a federalized collective Cabinet system.

The second problem that has often stared the Indian political system in its face with its growing federalization is even more fundamental and complex. The kind of Union executive intervention for protection of minority rights that could be possible in the past became difficult later. For example, the situation in Jammu and Kashmir in the 1990s, Punjab, Assam, and Bihar in the 1980s, and Gujarat in 2002 have raised a complex question: How can the rights of minorities or weaker sections be adequately protected in a federal system of divided authorities and responsibilities? This problem became more acute in States demographically dominated by communities that are national majorities but regional minorities. The plight of Kashmiri Pandits in Jammu and Kashmir, Hindus in Punjab, Dalits and upper castes in Bihar, and linguistic minorities in any State are the cases in point. In the era of one-party Congress dominance, the Union government was looked upon as a more trusted protector of minority rights everywhere.

During those days, the Union government could effectively intervene by the use of its executive power under Article 356 which allows President's rule in States under constitutional emergencies. With greater federalization of the system and increase in State autonomy, such interventions have become difficult due to the regionalization of the party system and judicial interpretation of the Constitution ensuring federal autonomy of State governments since the Supreme Court judgement in *S.R. Bommai* v. *Union of india* (1994) [33], which made President's rule open to judicial scrutiny with attendant uncertainties. The majority for the opposition parties in the Rajya Sabha, which has generally been the case since the 1990s also creates political uncertainties. For example, after the massacre of Dalits in the Narayanpur village in Bihar, the Rashtriya Janata Dal (RJD) Government in the State was dismissed by the National Democratic Alliance (NDA) Government at the Center. The Presidential order was passed by the Lok Sabha but rejected by the Rajya Sabha, resulting in the restoration of the dismissed State government. In the Gujarat riots in 2002, the NDA Government at the Center did not even go through the motions of seeking to invoke the constitutional emergency in the State against the BJP Government led by Narendra Modi despite evident complicity of the Gujarat police and complacency of the State government in the communal conflict.

The third problem that beset federal executive governance especially between 1989 and 1999 is governmental instability due to social and political fragmentation and politics of defection and corruption. In 14 years, since the 1989 Lok Sabha elections, we have witnessed as many as nine federal governments with varying terms and uncertainties. Six elections had to be held where a maximum of three would have normally sufficed. However, since 1999, the NDA and UPA coalition governments have proved to be stable. And the BJP/NDA governments since 2014 have been even more securely stable.

ALL INDIA SERVICES

An analysis of the Indian federal executive will be incomplete without a discussion of the civil services and the party system. Of these two factors, bureaucracies are internal to the Union and State governments, while parties are a vital link that connect the civil society and the state. Both these structures have had significant functional roles in the emergence and working of the Indian federal political system. A synoptic view of the evolution of Indian federalism suggests that the colonial design was conceived as a bureaucratically driven system. In fact, the Central government under the Government of India Act, 1935, continued to be a bureaucratic regime, as the federative union of British Indian provinces and princely States could not come into existence due to the reluctance of the latter to join it. Ministerial regimes with limited powers in areas of "transferred" (as distinguished from "reserved") subjects briefly emerged in the provinces. However, Congress provincial ministries formed in 1937 resigned in 1939 when the British government involved India in the Second World War without consulting the Indian National Congress.

As mentioned earlier, besides the elected political part, the Union executive also has an appointed bureaucratic part. This comprises the central services that are exclusively used by the Union government. Then, there are the unique All India Services (AISs), originally two—Indian Administrative Service (IAS) and Indian Police Service (IPS) and presently three, since 1966, with a third added on to the list—Indian Forest Service. Their immediate antecedents go back to the British Indian Civil Service (ICS) and Indian Police (IP). The Constituent Assembly decided to reinstitute them on the basis of a consensus decision at a provincial Premiers' conference in July 1946, convened and chaired by the Home Minister of India Sardar Vallabhbhai Patel. Patel persuaded Prime Minister Jawaharlal Nehru not to leave these highest cadre services (to be commonly used by federal as well as provincial governments) to the legislatures of the two orders of governments. As it turned out, they are regulated by the Constitution itself and supplementary legislations. They are recruited by an independent constitutional commission, the Union Public Service Commission (UPSC), and are trained in central academies and in field administration in States to whose cadres they belong. They mostly serve under State governments and are occasionally loaned to the federal government on deputation. The two levels of Governments have, of course, their own Central and State civil services recruited by Union Public Service Commission (UPSC) and similar constitutionally entrenched Public Service Commissions of respective States.

The AISs lend a certain degree of centralization and coordination in the working of the federal system without, however, unduly standing in the way of decentralization if the party system and the civil society so desire. This is amply borne out by the experience of the Janata Party government in New Delhi in 1977–1979 and after the transformation of the party system from Congress dominance to multiparty system since 1989 for decades. The AISs have weathered the test of working under different political regimes in New Delhi as well as in States. Also, under one political party or coalitional regime in New Delhi and governments of other political persuasions in States. The demand for abolishing these services is no longer made today which was quite recurrent during the 1980s. They have also worked under one-party majority governments as well as coalition governments. The initial suspicion about their loyalty in the minds of non-Congress governments after a long spell of Congress dominance has by now disappeared. By the "merciless use of the power of transfer" by the newly emergent non-Congress governments was enough to get over their initial suspicion.[34]

PARTY SYSTEM

The impact of the party system on the Indian federal executive has been tremendous. The three systems of prime ministerial leadership outlined above are, as a matter of fact, more related to the variations of the nature of the party system than the personalities of the incumbents. To be sure, personalities of the incumbents have varied considerably from Nehru to Narendra Modi. However, personalities were partly helped or hindered by the varying political atmospherics shaped by the prevailing party system. A strong personality (e.g. Nehru, Indira Gandhi, or Narendra Modi) would emerge as a stronger prime ministerial leader in a one-party government sans factional feuds than a modest personality (e.g. Shastri). However, even a strong personality would be hamstrung in a factionalized and fragmented party government (e.g. Desai in the Janata Party government during 1977–79). Minority and/or coalition governments in a multiparty system are, of course, an entirely different proposition; they require moderate personalities with reconciliatory skills, i.e. leaders who creatively lead by following. What we have earlier called the *federal* prime ministerial leadership style is typically the product of the post-1989 multiparty system. This phase has witnessed coalition governments with the number of parties ranging from eight to 24, some of them "national" or all–India parties and some others, "State" or regional parties.

Three different coalitional assortments of these parties have rallied round three "pivot" national parties at various points in time since 1989: Janata Dal, Bharatiya Janata Party, and Indian National Congress. A fourth national party, Communist Party of India (Marxist), was once offered the leadership of one of the Janata Dal-led United Front Governments with Jyoti Basu, the West Bengal Left Front Chief Minister, as the Prime Minister. While Basu was inclined to accept the offer, his party rejected it on the consideration that it would not join, let alone lead, a coalition government in which it was not in a dominant position. Basu later described this decision of his party as a "historical blunder".

These four real or potential pivot national parties have been of special importance to the working of federal executive governance in India. It must be noted, however, that by 1998–99 the Janata Dal disintegrated into nearly half a dozen state splinters and was reduced to the status of regional parties. Moreover, by 2009–2010 the CPI(M) suffered heavy electoral reverses nationally as well as in West Bengal and Kerala. The net effect was that national political party system was, for all practical purposes, transformed into a bi-coalitional configuration led respectively by the INC and the BJP. They were more likely than regional parties to head a federal coalition governments, although the latter often played a crucial balancing role in deciding which of the two major national parties was to form the government. By 2014, and then again in 2019, the BJP turned into a majority party almost rivalling or promising to become what Rajni Kothari called the "Congress System" in the Nehru era.

In a country of multicultural and federal proportions like India, coalition politics in the legislative arena may find expression at two planes: intra-party and inter-party. The Indian National Congress in its dominant phase was the *locus classicus* for intra-party coalitions on a grand scale. The Janata Party of the late 1970s was at least formally such an intra-party coalitional formation, although one can also argue that it would be more appropriate to regard this party as a *de facto* inter-party coalition of Congress (Organization), Bharatiya Lok Dal, Socialists, Bharatiya Jan Sangh, and Congress for Democracy. For, these pre-merger constituent parties of the Janata Party never fully merged their separate organizational elements into a truly single party and kept working as veritable parties (rather than factions) under the makeshift canopy of the hurriedly formed Janata Party.

The inter-party coalitions since 1989 provided a fecund breeding ground for mushrooming and growth of regional parties—new and old—and fragmentation and dwarfing of national parties. One can delineate at least two types of national parties that have led the various inter-party coalitions since 1990s: federal and confederal. A federal party may be defined as one with a more regularized pattern of articulation between the central and State units of the party organization with reasonable degrees of central direction and branch autonomy for State units. A confederal party is an amalgamation of fairly strong State branches with nominal central control. The Indian National Congress, BJP, and CPI(M) illustrate the category of federal parties, while the Janata Party/Dal exemplified a confederal party.

CONCLUSION

In sum, we may briefly highlight the relational aspects of the constituent elements of the Union .Executive. The President is primarily a nominal parliamentary functionary with some nominal federal roles to play. He must act on the advice of the Cabinet. The Vice-President chairs the meetings of the federal Second Chamber of the Parliament. The Prime Minister is elected from a Lok Sabha constituency, but ultimately he ends up having a nationwide audience and influence. The Union Cabinet usually represents all the regions and States of the Union and is a more effective forum of federal representation than the Rajya Sabha. The All India Services are a unique bureaucracy in the universe of federal political systems in the sense that they alternately serve both the federal and the provincial States. By virtue of this experience, they build interpersonal bridges between the Union and State governments under the respective political executives of both orders of governments in India.

The relational aspects of the political component of the Union Executive have a different beat under a majority party or under a minority party coalitional or multi-partisan configuration. These two different parliamentary situations do not make much of a difference so far as the role of the President is concerned. However, a minority party Prime Minister must contend with an oppositional parliamentary majority as the opposition. A Prime Minister under a coalitional dispensation finds himself under the compulsion of a bi- or multi-partisan Cabinet control which is a different proposition than a single party Whip. Even in a majority party government, the prime ministerial authority is subject to the factional balance of forces in the Cabinet (e.g. period of the Nehru-Patel duumvirate). In case of a Prime Minister with an undisputed supremacy in the Cabinet, his authority may transform the collective Cabinet system into virtually a prime ministerial (or 'presidential', in the US American sense) Cabinet system (e.g. the Cabinets under Nehru, Indira Gandhi, Rajiv Gandhi, and Narendra Modi). In such a situation, if the Parliament turns into a meek assembly, the parliamentary checks and balances may give way to a potentially authoritarian situation (e.g. the Emergency regime, 1975–77). In such a situation, only civil society checks and balances and the mass electoral intervention remain as devices of the last recourse.

Since the 1990s, what we have called the collective-collegial and federal prime ministerial style and cabinet system began with a vengeance, and it only changed under the Modi Government since 2014. If anything, the collective responsibility of a weak coalitional cabinet to the parliament has often appeared dispersed beyond the parliament to other centers of power in the federal domain and cabinet cohesion has become fragmented. With weakened prime ministerial role and power, inter-party as well as intra-party differences in the working of coalition governments had become the order of the day under unbridled coalition governments before 2014. Ministries were practically parceled out to coalescing parties sans prime ministerial or cabinet control. Even ministers of the leading party in the coalition government tended to get a longer leash in conducting a ministry by default than is typical in a cabinet government. The roles of Suresh Prabhu (Power), Arun Shourie (Ministry of Disinvestment), Murali Manohar Joshi (Human Resource Development), Yashwant Sinha

(Finance), Jaswant Singh (Foreign Affairs) in the NDA government (1999–2004) and Mani Shankar Aiyar (Petroleum, later Panchayat Raj), Murali Deora (Petroleum), Kapil Sibal (Human Resource Development), Jairam Ramesh (Environment) in the UPA government I and II (2004–2009 and 2009 and onwards) were the cases in point. The role of the coordination committee of the coalition governments, which was important and boisterous in Janata Dal-led coalition governments between 1989 and 1998, subsequently declined and practically disappeared. In the UPA governments, a significant role was played by the National Advisory Council (NAC) consisting of experts, opinion leaders, and social activists, and chaired by the Congress president Sonia Gandhi. It offered policy inputs with alternative perspectives to the cabinet led by the then Prime Minister, Manmohan Singh. Freer play to imaginative and competent ministers in the coalitional governance had led to healthy policy discourses in the government and media. But policy and good governance become a casualty to ministries parcelled out to unscrupulous and corrupt regional satraps.

REFERENCES

1. Granville Austin, *Indian Constitution: Cornerstone of a Nation,* Oxford University Press, Delhi, 1966. A classic reprint recently reissued by the OUP.
2. Survepalli Gopal, *Radhakrishnan: A Biography,* Oxford University Press, Delhi, 1989, Chapter 12.
3. *Ibid.*, p. 394.
4. *Ibid.*, p. 331.
5. Giani Zail Singh, *Memoirs of Giani Zail Singh: The Seventh President of India,* Har-Anand Publications Pvt. Ltd., New Delhi, 1997, pp. 203–204. As narrated to Manohar Singh Batra.
6. Arun Nehru, "Seats of Power: What I remember of Oct. 31, 1984," *The Asian Age*, New Delhi, 5 September 2004, p. 13.
7. *Madhav Rao* v. *Union of India*, *AIR* 1971, SC 530, paragraphs 94 & 96.
8. *Maganbhai Ishwarbhai Patel* v. *Union of India* (1970), 3, *Supreme Court Cases*: 400, *AIR* 1969, SC 783 ....
9. Austin, *op. cit.,* pp. 142–143.
10. Motilal C. Setalvad, *My Life: Law and Other Things,* N.M. Tripathi Pvt. Ltd., Bombay, 1970. Excerpted in M.P. Singh and Ravi Bhatia, *An ICHR Project Report on Indian Constitutional Documents,* 2002, p. 83.

11. Singh, *op. cit.,* Chapters 35–36.

12. Singh, *op. cit.,* pp. 188–190.

13. R. Venkataraman, *My Presidential Years,* Indus, New Delhi, 1994.

14. *Ibid.*, pp. 278–279.

15. Durga Das (Ed.), *Sardar Patel's Correspondence, 1945–50*, Vol. 6, Navajivan Press, Ahmedabad, 1973, pp. 18–19.

16. *Ibid.*, p. 24.

17. For an early conceptualization of this idea, see M.P. Singh and Rajesh Singh, "Three Modalities of Electoral Politics & Landmarks of Premiership and Party System Evolution" in M.P. Singh (Ed.), *Lok Sabha Elections 1989: Indian Politics in 1990s*, Kalinga Publications, Delhi, 1992.

18. Gopal, *op. cit.,* 1989, p. 196.

19. G. Parthasarathi, editorial note to *Jawaharlal Nehru: Letters to Chief Ministers 1947–1964,* Vol. 3, 1952–1954, Jawaharlal Nehru Memorial Fund, Teen Murti House, New Delhi, 1987, distributed by OUP, Delhi.

20. Stanley Wolpert, *Nehru: A Tryst with Destiny,* Oxford University Press, New York and London, 1996, p. 433.

21. Wells Hangen, *After Nehru Who?* Rupert Hart Davis, London, 1963.

22. Michael Brecher, *Nehru: A Political Biography,* Jaico, Bombay, 1969, p. 296.

23. Joya Hasan, *Congress After Indira: Policy, Power, Political Change (1984–2009)*, Oxford University Press, New Delhi, 2012; Sanjaya Baru, *The Accidental Prime Minister: The Making and Unmaking of Manmohan Singh*, Penguin Books, New Delhi, 2014.

24. Prem Shankar Jha, *In the Eye of the Cyclone: The Crisis in Indian Democracy*, Viking Penguin Books, New Delhi, 1993, Chapter 5.

25. *Ibid.*, p. 92.

26. *Ibid.*, pp. 92–93.

27. *Ibid.*, p. 93.

28. *Ibid.*

29. *Ibid.*, pp. 93–94.

30. James Manor, "The Presidency", in Devash Kapur and Pratap Bhanu Mehta (Eds.), *Public Institutions in India: Performance and Design*, Oxford University Press, New Delhi, 2005, p. 106

31. Douglas V. Verney, 'From Quasi-Federation' to 'Quasi-Confederacy'? The Transformation of India's Party System'; *Publius: The Journal of Federalism,* Vol. 33(4), Fall 2003, p. 171.

32. For a detailed study of intergovernmental mechanism, see Rekha Saxena, "Strengthening Federal Dialogue: Role of NDC and ISC", *Contemporary India,* Vol. 1(**3**), July–September 2002; Swenden, Wilfried and Rekha Saxena, "Rethinking Central Planning: A Federal Critique of the Planning Commission", *India Review*, Vol. 16, Issue 1: Continuity and Change in Contemporary Indian Federalism, 2017, pp. 42–65.

33. *S.R. Bommai & others* v. *Union of India, AIR* 1994, SC 1918... .

34. M.P. Singh's Interview in New Delhi with B.P. Singh, IAS, who served under the Assam Government as well as the Union Government, as Home Secretary and Secretary, Culture, Delhi, 4th June 2004.

Chapter

6

Judiciary
The Battle of the Books and Beyond*

CRUCIBLE OF CONSTITUTIONAL DEMOCRACY

The Indian Constitution is founded on two sources of political power: (a) the principle of popular sovereignty embodied in the opening line of the Preamble that begins with the ringing declaration of "We the People of India ...." as the ultimate source of sovereignty, and (b) evolutionary continuity underlined by the legal transfer of power from the British Parliament to the Constituent Assembly of India by terms of the Indian Independence Act, 1947. These dual legacies are naturally open to alternative and alternating notions of ultimate popular sovereignty and periodical parliamentary sovereignty, depending on the pendency of parliamentary polls and the ideological temperament of the times.

So, the question is often raised: is Indian constitutionalism founded on popular sovereignty or parliamentary sovereignty? A straightforward, categorical answer to this question is not possible. Indian constitutionalism, in our view, is a mixed case of contextual interpretation; we may also add that our Constitution is predicated on shared sovereignty among and the institutions of governments, subject to the binding interpretation by the Supreme Court of India. Yet, arguably, there is a contingent infinality; sovereignty, at least in the last resort, must belong to the people. However, a distinction must be maintained between electoral mandate and constitutional mandate. A transient electoral verdict is neither intended to nor can it justifiably undo the constitutional mandate given by the people of India in the historic moment of political Independence and the making of the Constitution. That power can only be exercised by a new Constituent Assembly, not by a periodic parliament.

* The title of a satire by Jonathan Swift written in the early 18th century depicting a fictive war of wits between the King's Library for supremacy, used here as a symbol of judicial wrangling.

The Constituent Assembly bequeathed the constituent power to amend the Constitution under Article 368 to the Parliament alone in some cases, i.e., Fundamental Rights and Duties and Directive Principles of State Policies, the Fifth and Sixth Schedules relating to tribal areas in some States or tribal States (Part D, clause 7 of the Fifth Schedule, and Part III, clause 21 of the Sixth Schedule), or to the Parliament and State Legislatures in aggregate legislative capacity in case of other federal features of the Constitution. However, in the competing claims over representing "stateness"[1], the Parliament has gradually lost the "custody" over the Constitution to the judiciary[2], thanks to the ingenious judicial doctrine of the "basic structure of the Constitution" invented by the judiciary in the *Keshavananda Bharati* v. *State of Kerala* (1973) and subsequent related cases. In the dynamics of institutional interaction among the Parliament, executive and judiciary, the latter has thus ended up having the last word on the Constitution and what it means and to what extent it can be amended. It is also clarified in case law that in the event of conflict between an electoral mandate and the constitutional mandate, the latter has the primacy by virtue of the fact that the constitutional consensus and mandate not only predates an electoral mandate but also sets the legal and constitutional parameters within which a periodic mandate can have any validity.[3] Nevertheless, this putative argument for judicial supremacy has not gone unquestioned, as the opening paragraph of this chapter suggests. Pratap Bhanu Mehta also opines:

> The reality of constitutionalism has been that the legislature and the judiciary are likely to remain *Competitors* when it comes to interpreting the Constitution. It is by no means settled who has the final word. The decisions of each are more like one link in a long chain of events that can be played out any number of times. Parliament can pass legislation, the courts can determine its constitutionality, Parliament can try to circumvent the courts by amending the Constitution, the courts can pronounce that Parliament has limited powers of amendment, Parliament can … and so on and on.[4]

Since Mehta's perceptive comment, the Supreme Court suffered external pressures from the executive soon after the return of the single-party majority under Prime Minister Narendra Modi-led Bharatiya Janata Party (albeit in a still coalitional National Democratic Alliance), supported by all the parties in the Parliament, with the solitary abstention of the All India Dravida Munnetra Kazhagam. It brought about and enacted the 99th Constitutional Amendment Act and the National Judicial Appointments Commission (NJAC) Act, both in 2014, abolishing the system of appointment of Supreme Court and High Court judges and transfer of the latter by the judicial collegium introduced under the case law laid down under the *Supreme Court Advocates on Record Association* v. *Union of India* (1993) and *Presidential Reference to Supreme Court under Article 143(1)* (1998/1999), deoperationalizing the process of these judicial appointments provided for the executive in consultation with the

Chief Justice of India and some other senior-most judges. The amendment and the conforming statute were supported by all parties in the Parliament, with the solitary abstention from voting by the All India Dravida Munnetra Kazhagam. [The impugned collegium system had amounted to virtually reversing the process such that it gave primacy to the judiciary which made proposals to the executive in consultation with it, which the executive could return to the collegium for reconsideration, but once the latter finalized it with or without executive suggestions, it (the executive) was to forward it to the President with binding effect. In the backdrop of unprecedented assault on the Constitution and the Courts by the Indira Gandhi Emergency regime during the 1970s, the Courts were basking in the sunshine of glory and legitimacy and were conceded this extraordinary primacy by the public and other organs of the state.] The Supreme Court on a public interest petition in *Supreme Court Advocates on Record Association* v. *Union of India* (2015) declared both the amendment and the legislation unconstitutional for their violation of the independence of the judiciary, which had been declared as a part of the 'basic structure of the Constitution', and therefore, unamendable in *Keshavananda Bharati* v. *State of Kerala* (Supreme Court, 1973) and *Minerva Mills Ltd. and Others* v. *Union of India* (Supreme Court, 1980). Moreover, the higher courts have more recently also witnessed a series of allegations of corruption against High Court judges and removal or resignation of some of them, and an Opposition parties' unsuccessful move to impeach/remove Chief Justice of India, Dipak Misra for alleged misdemeanour—an unprecedented press conference was called by his (Misra's) four senior-most colleagues charging him of apparently biased allocation of cases to junior judges ignoring senior judges. The executive has, of late also been delaying action on implementing the recommendations of the judicial collegium on appointment and promotion of judges and transfer of High Court judges and appointment of Chief Justices of High Courts, and filling of a large numbers of vacancies in the courts.

- Madhav Khosla and Ananth Padmanabhan have recently added: "...the Court is no longer in the position that it was two or three decades ago. Over the past decade, it has lost much of the competitive institutional legitimacy that it once enjoyed. Unless it can look inward, tackling both doctrinal incoherence and administrative mismanagement, not to mention major concerns regarding corruption and accountability, its time in the sun is unlikely to last".[5]
- Yet, it is difficult not to feel that the scenario outlined above by Khosla and Padmanabhan is more political and relates to electoral and institutional balance of forces than to strictly jurisprudential.

HISTORICAL BACKGROUND

For understanding the legal and constitutional theory underlying the structure of the judicial branch of the Indian state, we should refer back to the British rule in India, and the tradition of constitutional engineering of the British Commonwealth which India was the first Republican nation to join. The British Raj transformed the legal foundations of India, especially in relation to constitutional and criminal law. Laws in these areas were universalized in the sense of making them common for all Indians; although in matters of civil or family laws pre-existing social and religious customs were continued. Despite the ideal of a common civil code set forth in the Directive Principles of State Policy (Article 44 of the Constitution), this goal has not yet been achieved as even the independent Indian State is inclined to move liberally, rather illiberally, in this direction, hoping that the reforms should by and large come from the communities concerned.

During the British rule, the civil and criminal laws were administered by judges-cum-magistrates, with the Judicial Committee of the Privy Council (JCPC) in England acting as the final court of appeal. The separation between the executive and the judiciary was made gradually, and by the Government of India Act of 1935, the highest court in India was established in the form of the Federal Court which, however, was subordinate only to the JCPC. The British colonial period also witnessed the emergence of a corporate legal profession that provided pleaders and advocates for presenting the cases of clients to the judges or magistrates.

The Supreme Court of India, the first fully independent Court for the country, was first set up under the 1950 Constitution. The Constitution also set up an integrated hierarchy of courts for a more parliamentary federal system compared to the Government of India Act, 1935. The 1935 Act was neither a fully parliamentary system (as the Governor General of India retained independent executive powers uncontrolled by the Central Legislature) nor fully a federal system (as provincial autonomy was considerably less than the autonomy of States under the present Constitution). The Governor General had independent executive powers in budgetary and security matters and the Central Government had important executive powers over the provincial Governments.

STRUCTURE

The hierarchy of courts runs from the Supreme Court at the federal level, High Courts at the State level, and District Courts at the sub-state levels. In the appointment of judges at all the levels, the President of India (in case of Supreme Court and High Courts) and the Governor of the State concerned (in case of subordinate Courts) are involved. Courts at all the levels act under the jurisdiction of the immediate superior level of the judiciary. Appointments are formally made by the executive at the appropriate level in consultation with judges. The Union executive appoints the judges of the Supreme Court and High Courts "after consultation with such of the judges of the Supreme Court and of the High Courts in the States as the President may deem necessary for the purpose". It is also provided by the Constitution that in appointment of a judge, "the Chief Justice of India shall always be consulted" (Article 124, Clause 1). These constitutional provisions have, however, changed under case law, as we will see in what follows. Since 1993 and later, the Supreme Court has introduced under case law a system of collegium of judges who in consultation with the executive render binding advice to the government for appointment of judges in the Supreme court and High Courts.

Only the Supreme Court and High Courts enjoy, under the Constitution, the status of constitutional courts in the sense that cases relating to fundamental rights, center-state and inter-state conflicts can be adjudicated only by these courts. In fact, in certain respects, the High Courts have been given more extensive powers than the Supreme Court. For example, while both the apex court and High Courts are constitutionally empowered to issue certain writs under Articles 32 and 226 respectively for the protection and enforcement of fundamental rights, the High Court under the Constitution has this power "for any other purpose" in addition to fundamental rights. To exercise any such additional power, the Supreme Court needs special conferment by a parliamentary enactment.

The appointment of Supreme Court judges has been a matter of some controversy and a body of case laws has grown over the years. In *S.P.Gupta* v. *Union of India* (1982)[6] and *Union of India* v. *Sankalchand Seth* (1977),[7] the Supreme Court ruled that this "consultation" does not imply "concurrence" though there must be exchange of views as to the merits of the appointees. The *Supreme Court Advocates on Record* v. *Union of India* (1993)[8] has changed the procedure. Now the advice of the collegium of judges routed through the cabinet has become binding on the President of India. In *re Presidential Reference* (1998/99), the Supreme Court held that a recommendation from the Chief Justice of India bereft of the "norms and requirements of the consultation process" is not binding on the union executive[9]. It is an advisory opinion of the court under Article 143 of the Constitution.

The Superior Courts thus have virtually become a self-appointed institution causing some disquiet to the executive which feels that its powers have been unduly constrained by the case law. The National Commission for Review of the Working of the Constitution (NCRWC) appointed by the Union Government in 2000 in its Report submitted in 2002 has recommended the appointment of a National Judicial Commission consisting of the Chief Justice of India (CJI) as the chairman and two senior most judges of the Supreme Court, the Union Minister of Law and Justice and "one eminent person nominated by the President of India after consulting" the CJI as members.[10]

The BJP-led National Democratic Alliance (NDA) government brought an Amendment Bill in the Parliament for establishing this Commission but had to withdraw it in face of stiff opposition in the Parliament, public and the media. The Congress-led United Progressive Alliance (UPA) government that followed in 2004 and was re-elected in 2009 did not make any attempt to implement this proposal. Yet, the then Prime Minister, Manmohan Singh addressing a conference of Chief Justices in India made reference to "judicial overreach" and hoped for self-correcting moves. Recent years have witnessed a series of instances of judicial corruption and misdemeanour and growing demand for judicial accountability. There has also been a spate of judges recusing themselves from hearing a case either in face of opposition from the bar or on a voluntary basis on account of conflict of interest in the case involved. The Union law ministry has been saying for long that it contemplated law to institute a greater degree of judicial accountability than what there already is, mostly measures of last recourse of parliamentary/presidential removal of a judge. It is widely felt that this ultimate measure comes too late in the day and it is ineffective too, as the cases of the attempted removal of Justice V. Ramaswamy of the Supreme Court in 1993 illustrates. The move failed due to discordance between the Lok Sabha and the Rajya Sabha majorities divided along party and regional lines. The crisis in the process of judicial appointments by a collegiums of senior-most judges has also shown cracks and opposition, as already narrated in the opening section of this chapter. After a decade and a half, since this process began in 1993, for the first time, the union law ministry has rejected selectively two nominations for elevation of judges to the Supreme Court and returned them to the collegiums of judges for reconsideration. The cases in point are Justice P.D. Dinakaran, the Chief Justice of the Karnataka High Court and Justice C.K. Prasad, the Chief Justice of Allahabad High Court. The ministry thought that the Supreme Court collegium made the proposals without proper verification of credentials of the judges concerned as there were allegations of corruption against them. A Supreme Court Bar Committee on Judicial Accountability expressed concern at the turn of events and demanded that the collegium should consult the Bar before making its recommendations to the government. (The process of removal of Justice Dinakaran was subsequently initiated in the Parliament in 2010, he resigned before process could reach its conclusion and closure).

The UPA-II government sent a proposal to the Chief Justice of India suggesting changes in the memorandum of procedure of appointment of judges to give greater say to the executive in the appointments and to ensure more transparency. In the opinion of Chief Justice K.G. Balakrishnan just before his retirement in May 2010 in a special interview to *The Hindu*[11], the change will require a review petition in the Supreme Court as the collegium's method is the result of two judgements of the apex court, namely, the *Supreme Court Advocate on Record Association* v. *Union of India* (1993) and an advisory opinion in a presidential reference case in 1998/1999.

As already discussed in the opening section of this Chapter, it was left for the Modi Government to take on the collegium system of judicial appointments and promotions in the Supreme Court and High Courts and transfer of High Court judges frontally and replace it by a National Judicial Appointments Commission (NJAC) by the 99th Constitutional Amendment and a conforming parliamentary statute (both in 2014). However, both the amendment and the legislation were declared unconstitutional by the Supreme Court in *SC Advocates on Record Association* v. *Union of India* (2015) for their violation of the 'basic structure of the Constitution', as already narrated above. The judgement was open to renegotiation of the Memorandum of Appointments between the executive and the Court. But, the executive has been rather uncooperative and dilatory in the process, and it has not yet reached finalization and closure since 2015 at this writing (August 2020).

Jurists have of late become increasingly conscious of the great overload on the Supreme Court resulting in huge backlogs as well as distance of the courts' headquarters in New Delhi to the Southern States. A senior Supreme Court Advocate, K.K. Venugopal[12] has made a thoughtful and well-documented plea for the creation of four regional courts of appeal in the country as final appellate courts, while restricting the Supreme Court of India to act as an exclusive constitutional court. This will leave the apex court dealing essentially with the following matters: (1) substantial questions of law concerning the interpretation of the Constitution or matters of national or public importance; (2) settling differences between High Courts and regional courts of appeal; (3) validity of central and state laws; (4) judicial review of constitutional amendments; (5) inter-state or center-state jurisdictional conflicts, and (6) presidential references under Article 143 of the Constitution. Notably, the original jurisdiction of the Supreme Court under Article 32 relating to fundamental rights is in this proposal basically left to be decided by the regional courts of appeal, subject to final appeal to the Supreme Court only in the cases involving questions that will have general relevance beyond the particular case in point.

JURISDICTION AND JUDICIAL REVIEW

The Constitution has given the Supreme Court original, appellate and advisory jurisdictions (Supreme Court) under Articles 131 and 131(A),/132/133/134/134(A), and 143. Article 142 provides that the Supreme Court in the exercise of its jurisdiction may pass such decree or make such order as it is necessary for doing *'complete justice'* in any case or matter pending before it. It is a very wide and reserve power, but it is subject to the provisions of the Constitution and relevant statutes. Article 143 gives the President of India, in effect the Union executive, to consult the Supreme Court on a question of law or fact for its advisory opinion 'and the Court may, after such hearing as it thinks fit, report to the President its opinion thereon'. Article 144 provides that all civil and judicial authorities in India "shall act in aid of the Supreme Court". The term "civil" here obviously includes all legislative and executive authorities. And since the military authority in India is subject to civilian control, it includes all the coercive arms of the State as well.

The Supreme Court's original jurisdiction includes Union-State and inter-State disputes regarding the federal division of powers, separation of powers among the Parliament, executive, and judiciary, and fundamental rights of citizens. These matters can be directly raised in the Supreme Court itself (Article 131). A case law arising out of *T.N. Cauvery Sangam* v. *Union of India* (1990)[13] has extended the original jurisdiction to include inter-State river water disputes as well, although courts can be barred from this matter under Article 262 and have been barred under the Inter-State River Water Dispute Act, 1956, enacted under this Article. The appellate jurisdiction of the Supreme Court includes appeals from High Courts in certain cases in civil, criminal, and other proceedings, if the High Court certifies that the dispute raises substantial question of law regarding the interpretation of the Constitution (Article 134). In other instances, the Supreme Court may grant "special leave to appeal" to itself in "any cause or matter passed or made by any court or tribunal in the territory of India" (Article 136, Clause 1). The Parliament can further enlarge the jurisdiction of the Supreme Court by law with regard to the Union List, and in relation to the State List and Concurrent List as well, if the Union and State Governments so agreed (Article 138, Clauses 1 and 2).

The original and appellate jurisdiction of a High Court is limited to the territorial extent of the State for which that court is set up. Under Article 226, High Courts have power to issue writs in the nature of *habeus corpus*, *mandamus*, prohibition, *quo warranto*, and *certiorari*, or any of them, for the enforcement of any of the fundamental rights conferred by Part III of the Constitution (just as the Supreme Court), '*and for any other matter*'. It is notable that this addition of the proviso 'and for any other matter' is not there in Article 32 conferring the power of the Supreme Court to issue writs for enforcement of fundamental rights. Thus, the writ power of the High Courts is wider than that of even the Supreme Court.

The Supreme Court and High Courts, like all courts, including those in classical parliamentary systems like England, have the power to interpret laws in cases of ambiguity and dispute. In England, the courts do not go beyond this power of interpretation because of the constitutional doctrine of parliamentary supremacy. There neither the Crown nor the judges can sit in judgement over the wisdom of parliamentary enactments. That also included executive orders until 1977 because of the explicit or implied parliamentary sanction for them. Since 1977 the courts have been allowed the limited power of review over mere executive orders. Courts in India can go beyond interpretation of laws and executive orders for making the legislative intentions clear and subject them to judicial scrutiny and review them as to their constitutional or legal validity.

The Constituent Assembly debates reveal some degree of ambiguity regarding the power of the judiciary vis-à-vis the Parliament. There were members like P.S. Deshmukh (Maharashtra), Brajeshwar Prasad (Bihar), H.V. Kamath (Maharashtra), Mahavir Tyagi (UP) who preferred a flexible amendment process typical of the British parliamentary system. Jawaharlal Nehru (UP) also had expressed similar views on the parliamentary power over amendment elsewhere in the debates, but an amendment to this effect in the course of the debate on the issue of amendment standing in his name was finally not moved in favour of the drafting committee's preference for a more complex and mixed process whereby some provisions of the Constitution could be amended by a simple parliamentary majority, some by two-thirds majority, and some others (i.e. federal features) by the additional requirement of ratification by at least 50 per cent of State legislatures. The last point, in particular, necessarily implies judicial review. The views of some other members like K.K. Sidhva (Punjab) and Naziruddin Ahmad (Bombay) were also opposed to amendment by simple parliamentary majority. Ultimately, the view of the drafting committee as articulated by its chairman Dr. Ambedkar won the day.[14] The federal perspective with implied judicial review was also reflected in the speeches of Ambedkar (Chairman of the Drafting Committee) and Rajendra Prasad (President of the Constituent Assembly).[15]

It was initially not as clear as today that the federal judiciary in India would develop into perhaps the most powerful court system in the world. For, the courts in other federal systems review only legislations and executive orders, but the Indian Supreme Court today reviews constitutional amendments as well.[16]

Even astute legal experts in the initial decades of the Republic either descriptively or prescriptively emphasized the role of the judiciary in interpreting laws. It is interesting that Jagdish Swarup primarily dwells on an interpretative role of the courts in India. In a book of nearly seven hundred pages, the terms 'judicial review' and 'activism' are neither found in the contents nor in the index. The term 'right to review' is found in the contents but the discussion in the relevant passages of the book is in the legislative rather than in the constitutional context; it refers to legislatures' power to review its own earlier statutes.[17]

Judicial review in India inevitably follows from at least three features of the Constitution: (1) the chapter on fundamental rights of citizens that are guaranteed against any legislative Act or executive order, (2) the Seventh Schedule of the Constitution demarcating legislative and taxing jurisdictions of the Union and State legislatures in the Union List, State List and Concurrent List, and (3) the declaration that all laws previous to the 1950 Constitution would be void to the extent of their conflict with it.

A large corpus of case laws has grown over the years as a result of review powers of the superior courts. Most of the reviews center on right to property, liberty and equality. Until right to property was deleted from Part III of the Constitution on fundamental rights and transferred to Article 300-A as a legal right, it was the major cause of continuous confrontation between the judiciary and the Parliament. The Government claimed to be implementing its progressive agenda of land reforms or directive principles of state policy giving them primacy over fundamental rights. The courts, however, declared these legislations unconstitutional on the ground of unreasonable restrictions on right to property and adequate compensation for private property taken over by the state and other rights such as freedom of occupation and legal equality.

The case laws on right to life and liberty generally concern preventive detention and denials of this right guaranteed by Article 21 of the Constitution. To preventive detention in the interest of public order and security, more recently terrorist activities have been added from time to time to these series of Acts, for example, the Maintenance of Internal Security Act (MISA), the Terrorist and Disruptive Activities Act (TADA), the Prevention of Terrorism Act (POTA), the Unlawful Activities Prevention Act (UAPA)(still on the statute book), etc. In the context of Article 21 that provides that life and liberty of an individual shall not be taken away by the State except through "procedure established by law", the Constituent Assembly had deliberately avoided the American constitutional doctrine of the "due process of law". For, the latter had been a source of too much litigation in the United States due to the ambiguity and undefined nature of the "due process of law". The formulation "procedure established by law" would, it was hoped, bind the judicial flight of imagination to a given law made by the legislature.[18] However, Indian constitutional law on this matter has undergone a sea change from *A.K. Gopalan* v. *State of Madras* (Supreme Court, 1950) to *Maneka Gandhi* v. *Union of India* (Supreme Court, 1978), such that the court went by the Indian constitutional proviso of 'procedure established by law' in the former, but came to virtually subscribe to something akin to the American constitutional doctrine of 'due process of law' by requiring that the procedure established by law must not be arbitrary and against the principles of natural justice in upholding the protection of life and personal liberty under Article 21, right to freedom of speech and right to freedom of movement under Article 19.

A significant body of case laws has grown around the power of judicial review centering on the issue of constitutional amendments. This direction of the extension of judicial power was not clear to the makers of the Constitution who had apparently granted the decisive and final power of amending different parts of the Constitution to the Parliament and, in case of some federal concerns, to the aggregate legislatures (Parliament plus State legislatures).

This discursive body of constitutional law with profound jurisprudential reasoning has developed over seven decades since the late 1960s. This zig-zag evolutionary course may be divided into at least four broad phases: (a) 1950 to 1966 that broadly coincides with the tenures of the first and the second Prime Ministers, Jawaharlal Nehru and Lal Bahadur Shastri; (b) 1967 to 1972 that marks the decline in the electoral fortune of the Congress and early years of Prime Minister Indira Gandhi in office that heralded a new phase of the post-Nehru generation of Congressmen in office; (c) 1973 to 1979 which were the years of political ascendance as well as turbulence of Indira Gandhi's rule during the major part of the 1970s; and (d) the Janata Party's brief stint in power towards the late 1970s and later. The decade of the 1980s witnessed the return of a chastened Indira Gandhi from opposition to Government and Rajiv Gandhi's succession after her assassination in 1984. Since 1989 India has moved from Congress dominance to a period of multi-party system with coalition or minority Governments, often both, in New Delhi. In 2014, the Narendra Modi-led Bharatiya Janata Party won a single-party majority in the Lok Sabha and got re-elected in 2019, but continued the tradition of federal coalition governments with the National Democratic Alliance.

This periodization may appear to be primarily political but it is also significantly associated with the changing patterns of judicial behaviour in the country. This would become clearer as we proceed in our discussion.

First Phase of Evolution (1950–1966)

The first phase was characterized by relatively harmonious relations between the executive and the Parliament, on the one hand, and the judiciary, on the other. Not that differences did not crop up, but they were settled by compromise and accommodation.

Two characteristic cases decided by the Supreme Court during this phase were *Sankari Prasad* v. *Union of India* (1951)[19] and *Sajjan Singh* v. *State of Rajasthan* (1965)[20]. The first case arose on the question of the First Amendment to the Constitution (1951), which was validated. This Amendment had added the Ninth Schedule to the Constitution to protect certain progressive laws of land reforms and nationalization of private bus transportation operation, etc. from judicial review, as laws put in there were declared to be immune from judicial scrutiny. The Court had earlier declared these measures unconstitutional on their violation of property rights and freedom of occupation, etc. The Court, deterred by the First Amendment, now ruled that Article 368 granted the Parliament the power to amend the Constitution, including Part-III on Fundamental rights. The Court held that the term "law" in Article 13(2) did not cover constitutional amendments. For, laws are made by virtue of *legislative* power of the Parliament, whereas amendments emanate from its special *constituent* power.

In the years that immediately followed, several new amendments were made, of which the Fourth and the Seventh concerned the Fundamental rights. The Seventeenth Amendment (1964) added several new legislations to the Ninth Schedule. A case brought to the Supreme Court, *Sajjan Singh* v. *State of Rajasthan* (1965), challenged this. In the judgement on this case, three of the five judges of the Bench chaired by Chief Justice Gajendra Gadakar, agreed with the Supreme Court's earlier judgement in the *Sankari Prasad Singh Deo* v. *Union of India* (1951) that the Parliament was competent to amend the Constitution, Part-III included. Two judges (Hidayatullah and Mudholkar) in their minority but finally concurring judgement expressed some misgivings whether fundamental rights should also be amended without any limitations.

Second Phase of Evolution (1967–1972)

The second phase began with the Supreme Court's judgement in *Golak Nath* v. *State of Punjab* (1967)[21]. The judgement was delivered only a few days before the results of the Fourth General Elections (1967) were announced in which the dominant Congress Party lost half of the States of the Indian Union, though it retained New Delhi with a reduced dominance. In the early 1970s, there also appeared a mass movement of public protest on the issue of growing authoritarianism and corruption in the Congress regime. It ultimately drew the socialist-turned-Gandhian Jayaprakash Narayan from virtual political retirement into the vortex of an extra-parliamentary mass movement against the growing authoritarianism and corruption in the Congress governments. This period also witnessed a sharp conflict between the executive and the Parliament, on the one hand, and the judiciary, on the other.

This phase opened with the *Golak Nath* case which challenged the addition of the Punjab Security of Land Tenures Act, 1953, to the Ninth Schedule. The case argued that the Seventeenth Amendment as well as the First and the Fourth, by which new laws were added to the Ninth Schedule, were violative of the Fundamental Rights, mainly to property ownership. Two other petitions grouped with *Golak Nath* case challenged the inclusion of Mysore Land Reforms Act, 1962, as amended in 1969 in the Ninth Schedule on similar reasons. The Supreme Court by a majority of six to five reversed its earlier decisions and came to the conclusion that the amending power of the Parliament stopped short of Part-III on the Fundamental Rights. The ruling, however, was to have only prospective effect, saving the First, Fourth, and Seventeenth Amendments. The Bench chaired by Chief Justice Subba Rao, by majority, reasoned that in intents and purposes and constitutional scheme fundamental rights emerge as endowed with a certain permanence. The Court also ruled that Article 368 did not contain the *power* to amend; it only outlined the *process* of amendment. The power of amendment was contained in Articles 245, 246, and 248 dealing with the extent of legislative powers of the Union and States and the residuary powers of the Parliament respectively as also entry 97 in the Union List in the Seventh Schedule. The constituent power of the Parliament arises specially from its residuary power. However, amendment is a "law" within the meaning of Article 13(2) and, to the extent it abridges rights, it can be declared void by judicial review.

Third Phase of Evolution (1973–1979)

The Supreme Court judgement in *Keshavananda Bharati* v. *State of Kerala* (1973)[22] heralded a third phase in the Indian judicial behaviour. The case arose out of Kerala Land Reforms Act (1963) as amended in 1969 and 1971, when during the pendency of the case it was placed in the Ninth Schedule by the 29th Amendment. The petitioner challenged the validity of the 24th, 25th, and 29th

Amendments to the Constitution. By a 13-judge Bench chaired by Chief Justice S.M. Sikri all the judges came to the conclusion, reversing the *Golak Nath* judgement, that the Parliament had power to amend the entire Constitution, including Part-III, but seven judges (Chief Justice Sikri and justices, Shelat, Hegde, Grover, Jaganmohan Reddy, H.R. Khanna, and Mukherji) added a significant rider that amending power was subject to certain implied limitations such that "basic structure" or "essential features" of the Constitution were unamendable. Thus, the Court upheld the 24th Amendment and ruled that the Parliament's amending power could reach any or all parts of the Constitution, but it could not alter or destroy its basic structure. The majority view of the judgement is summarized as follows:

1. Golak Nath [judgement] is overruled;
2. Article 368 does not enable the Parliament to alter the basic structure or framework of the Constitution;
3. The Constitution (Twenty-Fourth Amendment) Act, 1971, is valid;
4. Sections 2(a) and 2(b) of the Constitution (Twenty-Fifth Amendment) Act, 1971, is valid;
5. The first part of Section 3 of the Constitution (Twenty-Fifth Amendment) Act, 1971, is valid. The second part, namely 'and no law containing a declaration that it is for giving effect to such policy [Directive Principles of State Policy] shall be called in question in any court on the ground that it does not give effect to such policy' is invalid;
6. The Constitution (Twenty-Ninth Amendment) Act, 1971, is valid;
7. The Constitution Bench will determine the validity of the Constitution (Twenty-Sixth Amendment) Act, 1971, in accordance with law.

Illustrative enumeration of the basic features of the Constitution varied from judge to judge with some overlaps as follows:

Chief Justice Sikri: (a) supremacy of the Constitution, (b) republican and democratic form of Government, (c) secular character of the Constitution, and (d) separation of powers and federal division of powers.

Shelat and Grover: (a) the mandate to build a welfare State contained in Part-IV of the Constitution, and (b) unity and integrity of the nation.

Hegde and Mukherjea: (a) sovereignty of India, (b) democratic character of the polity, (c) unity of the country, (d) essential features of individual freedoms of citizens, and (e) mandate to build a welfare State.

Jaganmohan Reddy: the preamble and its elaboration in the rest of the Constitution. The judgement was criticized by some as vague and confusing and as a product of a sharply divided Court.

It is, however, unfair to expect from a Court judgement, which arises from the specific context of a case or a bunch of cases in a particular time period, to have a Constitution-like precision and yet timeless and transcendent applicability. A Court judgement in the common law tradition is, in fact, meant to be paradigmatic whose application is gradually extended to new situations. The Constitution, too, has a similar paradigmatic applicability to changing times, only in more amplitude and lesser liability to paradigmatic shifts that we find in case laws. The case of *Indira Gandhi* v. *Raj Narain* (Supreme Court, 1975)[23] illustrates the kind of extensibility of a case law to new principles we alluded above. This judgement declared free and fair elections as part of the basic structure of the Constitution, in addition to those enumerated above.

Right to property, which had been the bone of contention between the Parliament and the Judiciary that initially gave rise to the basic structure debate right from the First Amendment (1951) to the late 1970s, was deleted from the Constitution by the Janata Party Government in 1978 by the 44th Amendment. Property was deleted from the status of a Fundamental Right and made into a legal right in Article 300A. The legal protection that "No person shall be deprived of his property save by authority of law" is still constitutionally available. The immediate access to the Supreme Court in case of Fundamental Rights is unavailable to law suits. The case must now move sluggishly up from the lower courts. This change did not, however, wind up the legal discourse on the basic structure of the Constitution.

Fourth Phase of Evolution (1977–to date)

The fourth phase may be said to have begun with *Minerva Mills Ltd* v. *Union of India*[24] (Supreme Court, 1980). The case arose on the issue of nationalization of a mill, which is a property matter, but Nani A. Palkhiwala argued the case on the issue of Parliament's power to amend the Constitution.

The Minerva Mills Bench, chaired by Chief Justice Chandrachud, declared Sections 4 and 55 of the Constitution 42nd Amendment Act (1976) beyond the amending power of the Parliament and unconstitutional. The former because of "a total exclusion of challenge" to any law on the ground that it was justified for implementing Directive Principles of State Policy. The Court found it violative of Article 14 (equality before law) and Article 19 (freedom of occupation, trade or business). Section 55 of the 42nd Amendment was also declared void because "it removes all limitations on the power of the Parliament to amend the Constitution so as to damage or destroy its basic or essential features or its basic structure" by prohibiting judicial review. Article 31C added to the Constitution by the 25th Amendment (1971) saving laws giving effect to Directive Principles from any judicial scrutiny, already declared unconstitutional by the *Keshavananda* case judgement, was again legally and metaphorically assailed for removing the two sides of the "golden triangle" of Articles 14, 19, and 21 (protection of life and personal liberty). "Three Articles of our Constitution, and only three, stand between the heaven of freedom into which Tagore wanted his country to awake and the abyss of unrestrained power." It is this "golden triangle which affords to the people of this country an assurance that the promise held forth by the preamble will be performed by ushering in an egalitarian era through the discipline of Fundamental rights, that is, without emasculation of the rights to liberty and equality which alone can help preserve the dignity of the individual."

Throughout the 1980s, '90s and later, case laws have brought numerous constitutional values threatened by the heat and fire of political conflicts and encroached upon by the State and industry under the protection of the basic structure of the Constitution. In the tenth revised edition of V.N. Shukla's legal treatise on the *Constitution of India* (2001, first published in 1950), Mahendra Pal Singh[25], citing a large body of case laws, observed: "With these pronouncements the existence of the doctrine of basic structure in our constitutional law is no more a matter of dispute. The only dispute remains about its contents. Some of the contents seem to have settled while others are in the process of settling and still some others will settle in course of time. From *Keshavananda Bharati* till *Sambharmurthy* judicial review clearly emerged as one of the aspects of the basic structure of the Constitution."

The theory of Basic Structure of the Constitution, in a nutshell, has evolved from case to case. The main contours of this evolution are chartered by so many cases but to mention only the most important ones by *Golaknath, Keshavananda, Minerva Mills, Wamon Rao, Indira Gandhi, Maneka Gandhi and S.R. Bommai, I.R. Coelho* v. *State of Tamil Nadu and Others* (2007) judgements of the Supreme Court. Shorn of details, the Supreme Court first stumbled upon the basic structure theory in *Golak Nath* and tried to immunize the fundamental rights from any amendment challenged by the government by a constitutional amendment rejecting this contention, the court retreated from this position conceding that the amending power of Parliament extended to all parts of the Constitution in *Keshavananda* but added the caveat that in doing so the basic structure and principles of the Constitution cannot be destroyed. The rest of the judgements mentioned above only emphasize illustrations or features of the Constitution considered unamendable. In *Golaknath,* the court had taken the position that amending power was part of the residuary legislative power of the Parliament and therefore subject to the express limitation of Article 13 providing that legislatures can make no law curtailing fundamental right beyond reasonable restrictions. Abandoning this position, the court admitted that amendment was part of the constituent power rather than residuary power yet subject to the limitation of inviolability of the basic structure of the Constitution.

JUDICIAL ACTIVISM

Besides, judicial review carried forward to the level of activism, another instrument of courts' empowerment is what has come to be regarded as Public Interest Litigation (PIL) or Social Action Litigation(SAL). In the opinion of some observers, it has indeed become "the most important vehicle for the expansion of its powers".[26]

Judicial Activism has been in the forefront of the discourse on the role of the judiciary in the Indian constitutional law and politics since at least the early/late-1970s. Despite contending views on the period when it may be regarded to have started and on arguments for and against it, there is a wide measure of support and approval for it, at least for the time being and at least as an emergency measure to alleviate the crisis of governance and dysfunctionalities of parliamentary and executive institutions. Competent observers of institutions of government are inclined to argue that the process of government in India that was largely executive-driven has now become judiciary-driven.[27]

The term judicial activism is often used in much of the literature without any attempt at precise conceptualization. Those who use it with a certain degree of conceptual clarity mean by it at least two things. First, a kind of assertiveness on the part of the judiciary in defence of its review power that was not there in the Nehru era or the early years of the Indira Gandhi rule. For example, right in the First Amendment, the Nehru Government created the Ninth Schedule in the Constitution as a kind of strong room in which Union and State laws were put, which the executive wanted to keep out of bounds for the judiciary to scrutinize. The Courts demurred but somehow tried to accommodate the views of the executive/state legislatures. The Supreme Court beginning with the *Golak Nath* (1967) and *Keshavananda* (1973) cases tried to cling to its power of judicial review of even constitutional amendments through which this power was sought to be taken away. The enlargement of this extent of judicial power may obviously be regarded as an instance of activism on the part of the Courts. In a similar vein, expansion of review powers to such areas as what happens inside the Parliament and State legislatures, e.g. Speakers' or Presiding Officers' rulings and obliquely to parliamentary/legislative privileges may also be considered indicators of judicial activism.

Secondly, the most glaring examples that came to be subsumed under the concept of judicial activism were the Public Interest Litigation (PIL) or Social Action Litigation (SAL). This extension of judicial power was made by the Supreme Court under the influence of some progressive judges like V.R. Krishna Iyer, P.N. Bhagwati and others who prevailed upon their colleagues to change the rules of business of the court. By this change the conventional rule of *locus standi* to allow the Supreme Court and High Courts to take cognizance of denial of fundamental and legal rights brought to the Court by third parties (other than those directly involved in the dispute) or even by a postal letter was made permissible. This has also come to be known as the "epistolary jurisdiction" of the Court in addition to the original, appellate and advisory jurisdictions mentioned in the Constitution.

This category of cases began with the right of the poor, construction workers, pavement dwellers, undertrials (who had been languishing in jails without being produced before a Magistrate or a Court for periods far in excess of the period of punishment for their offences under the law) etc. Besides these, the Public or Social Interest Litigation of the Court has been amplified to include rights of children, women, environment and ecology, historical monuments, and so on and so forth.

There seems to be a tremendous public support and approval for judicial activism today. A national probability sample survey has found that the judicial branch now happens to be the most legitimate organ of the Indian State in the public estimation and esteem.[28] Moreover, the challenges to the judiciary from the executive and legislative branches have also practically disappeared compared to the late 1970s and 1980s when such challenges were most formidable. During the Emergency, despite some lingering resistance to such onslaughts by some High Courts, the Supreme Court had more or less caved in under political pressures. However, in the wake of the post-Emergency election and the dismantling of the authoritarian 42nd Amendment, the Courts reasserted their review power with a vengeance. It was also in the post-Emergency era that judicial activism emerged in a most spectacular way and reached its apogee in the era of multi-party system and federal coalition governments. Thus, it has been so far so good.

In a perceptive study of judicial activism from sociological and psychological perspectives, Upendra Baxi locates this phenomenon in contemporary India where globalizing upper and middle classes have no qualms in practicing "*violent* social exclusion" of the poor, where politics tends to merge on callous dehumanization, and where the Constitution "stands *informally but comprehensively amended in an era of heedless and headlong globalization*", where rhetoric of justice and human rights are "increasingly harvested by the forces of comprador and global corporate capitalism", and where the judicial profession is wont to promote "the structural adjustment of judicial activism".[29] Baxi's impression is that even more than the psychology of Indian judges it is the growing constituencies of social and human rights activists who goad the judges into judicial activism. His enumeration of this supportive field of judicial activism includes: civil rights/people rights activists, consumer rights groups, anti-bonded labour groups, ecologists, child rights groups, custodial rights groups, poverty rights groups, indigenous peoples' rights groups, women's rights groups, Bar-based groups, media autonomy groups, assorted lawyers-based groups, assorted individual petitioners, etc.[30]

Since the onset of neo-liberal reforms and globalization in the early 1990s, there appears to be a perceptible change in judicial behaviour. While public interest litigation as an institution continues, there is a palpable shift to business liberalism (as distinguished from political liberalism) in some recent court decisions. For example, in *BALCO Employees Union* v. *Union of India* (2000), the employees of the Government Company had petitioned against the decision of the Government of India to disinvest on arguments, among others, that the process was arbitrary and lacking in transparency in fixing the reserve price for disinvestment. The Supreme Court dismissed the petition, observing: "The decision to disinvest and the implementation thereof is purely an administrative decision relating to the economic policy of the State and challenge to the same at the instance of a busybody cannot fall within the parameters of public interest litigation."[31]

Commenting on the judgement, Prashant Bhushan, a Supreme Court advocate and activist, wrote that this "effectively meant that a citizen could not challenge the loot of the public exchequer by way of PIL unless he was personally affected". Bhushan discusses some other cases like *CITU* v. *Union of India* (1997), *State of Karnataka* v. *Arun Kumar Agarwal* (2000), *Center for Public Interest Litigation* v. *Union of India* (2000), *Delhi Science Forum* v. *Union of India* (1996), *Union of India* v. *Azadi Bachao Andolan* (2003), *HPCL-BPCL* v. *Union of India* (2000), *Narmada Bachao Andolan* v. *Union of India* (2000), *N.D. Jayal* v. *Union of India* (2003), *Tata Housing Development Company* v. *Goa Foundation* (2003), *Almitra Patel* v. *Union of India* (2000), and *T.N. Rangarajan* v. *State of Tamil Nadu* (2003), and concludes:

> The above cases provide more than anecdotal evidence for the propositions that: (a) the Supreme Court as an institution has frowned upon challenges to any action of the executive taken in the purported furtherance of `economic reforms', even when such challenges were based on violations of statute and evidence of corruption; and (b) the court appears to have diluted its interpretation of Article 21, in the recent past. At the very least, it has often not acted to enforce the rights that it had declared earlier in favour of the poor and the weak.[32]

The CPI (M) ideologue and general secretary, Prakash Karat has also recently lamented that the judiciary was getting attuned to neo-liberal capitalism and globalism which are against the spirit of the Constitution of India. Referring to the Kerala High Court order putting ban on campus politics, he goes on to say that this is against the values of the freedom struggle and there was "nothing in the Constitution that prevents students from forming their associations".[33]

In 2007 two judges of the Supreme Court—Justice A.K. Mathur and Justice Markandey Katju—made *obiter dictum* while deciding a case that received a great deal of media attention: "Recently, the courts have apparently, if not clearly, strayed into the executive domain or in matters of policy.... In our opinion these were matters pertaining exclusively to the executive or legislative domain. If there is a law, judges can certainly enforce it, but judges cannot create a law and seek to enforce it."[34] In the debate that followed the view of Justices Mathur and Katju was generally adversely commented on with the counter-argument that in face of parliamentary and executive inaction and callousness, the judiciary must intervene to enforce the rule of law.[35] However, the Supreme Court continues to maintain that the court must be cautious against the overuse of judicial activism, which beyond a point is "against the rule of law" (Chief Justice of India S.H. Kapadia).[36] Similarly, a 3-judge Supreme Court Bench held that launching investigations into corruption charges against politicians is an executive domain, not that of courts'. The courts have used writ jurisdictions in the past at most monitor the progress of investigations or to transfer investigations from one agency to another.[37]

It would, indeed, be a naïve assumption that judicial activism is an unmixed blessing or a panacea for all problems of governance. For one thing, the judiciary may be the least dangerous branch and also the weakest branch. It neither controls the purse nor the sword. The former belongs to the Parliament and the latter to the executive. The power of the judiciary lies in its adherence to the rule of law. But the judiciary cannot ensure constitutionalism alone without a balanced constitutional government in which each branch performs its functions and duties within the framework of the Constitution. Hence, the guarantee of good governance can be found only within the framework of a balanced constitutional regime.

From this point of view, it would appear to be a welcome development that the Parliament and the State legislatures demonstrated to assert their control over parliamentary and legislative proceedings in the wake of Supreme Court directive to the Jharkhand legislature to meet and elect the leader of the House in the early months of 2005. Moreover, in the initial months of 2006 the Parliament summarily expelled some members after the sting operation by a TV channel which caught some of them accepting bribe for raising questions in the Parliament. The Supreme Court on being approached by some expelled members, issued directives to the Presiding officers. In response, the Lok Sabha Speaker, Somnath Chatterjee convened a Speaker's conference which decided that the Court's summons would not be accepted. The legislatures are thus belatedly seeking to reclaim the lost ground from the court at least in the matter of legislative proceedings which, under the Constitution, are beyond judicial intervention. But the legislatures to regain their legitimacy must adhere to ethics, law, and Constitution without the judicial and popular pressures.[38] For another thing, judicial activism in its overuse can degenerate into politicization and corruption of the judiciary. The lower judiciary in India is already not only hopelessly dilatory (with 270 lakh cases in arrears) but also extremely corrupt. Instances of corruption in higher judiciary have also been becoming rather frequent. And the access to higher courts is excessively expensive and prohibitive. For these reasons, the remedy of judicial activism may be cosmetic and it may eventually backfire and lead to constitutional crises. It may serve best as an Emergency light and beep to signal some grave wrong or imbalance in the system and offer an opportunity for restoring a constitutional equilibrium and good governance.

As already mentioned at the outset in the opening section of this Chapter, the return of a single-party majority under the Modi-led BJP/NDA in 2014 after a gap of three decades (since 1984 when the Congress won a last such mandate), the judiciary has faced attempts to clip its wings, though not without resistance from the Supreme Court. Nevertheless, of late, the higher judiciary itself has been becoming vulnerable to creeping corruption, internal differences, and inclination on part of some of the judges to compromise with the government of the day. Notwithstanding these unfortunate and disturbing tendencies, it is still possible to maintain that the higher judiciary in India is the least corrupt organ of the government. It is hoped that it will recover from setbacks and continue to be the best bet for constitutionalism and the rule of law in India.

REFERENCES

1. Llyod and Susanne Rudolph, *In Pursuit of Lakshmi: Political Economy of the Indian State,* Orient Longman, New Delhi, 1987, Chapter 3.
2. Granville Austin, "The Supreme Court and the Struggle for Custody of the Constitution" in B.N. Kripal *et al.* (Eds.) *Supreme but not Infallible: Essays in Honour of the Supreme Court of India,* Oxford University Press, New Delhi, 2000, Chapter 1.
3. V. Venkateshan, 'Tamil Nadu: Exit Jayalalitha,' *Frontline*, Vol. 18, No. **20**, September 29-October 12, 2001, frontline.thehindu.com.
4. Pratap Bhanu Mehta, "India's Judiciary: The Promise of Uncertainty" in Devesh Kapur and Pratap Bhanu Mehta (Eds.), *Public Institutions in India: Performance And Design,* Oxford University Press, New Delhi, 2005, p. 169. Also see Rajeev Dhavan and Rekha Saxena, "Republic of India", *A Global Dialogue on Federalism: Legislative, Executive, and Judicial Governance in Federal Countries,* Vol. 3, Katy Le Roy and Cheryl Saunders (Eds.), McGill-Queen's University Press, Quebec, 2006.

   This line of argument was most elaborately made with a great legal acumen by T.R. Andhyarujuna, *Judicial Activism and Constitutional Democracy in India*, (foreword by Professor Sir William Wade, q, c), Justice B.D. Bal Memorial Lecture, 1990, Bombay, M.N. Tripathi Private Ltd., 1992. Commenting on the theory of the basic structure of the Constitution, Andhyarujuna writes: "For one thing, the theory is too esoteric and its impact on the people is negligible. Barring politicians and lawyers, a few persons know of its existence. Secondly, the fractured state of the Indian polity with minority governments unlike the Nehru era has prevented a strong and determined response to judicial expansionism at the expense of other political branches.... Further, the Courts' claim has no solid foundations of either constitutional text or history or precedent to support it. The formulation of the theory has been rhetorical, inconsistent and unstable and its application necessarily political."(p. 24).
5. Madhav Khosla and Ananth Padmanabhan, "The Supreme Court", in Devesh Kapur, Pratap Bhanu Mehta, and Milan Vaishnav, (Eds.),

Rethinking Public Institutions in India, Oxford University Press, New Delhi, 2017, chapter 3, p. 114. Also see Manish Tewari and Rekha Saxena,"The Rise of Judicial Power and The Protection Of Federalism", *The Supreme Court Of India: Courts In Federal Countries: Federalists Or Unitarists*?, Nicholas Aroney and John Kincaid (Eds.), University Of Toronto Press, Toronto, 2017; Rekha Saxena and Wilfried Swenden, "The Indian Supreme Court and Federalism", *Federalism and Regionalism,* 2018.

6. *S.P. Gupta* v. *Union of India*, *AIR*, SC, 1982, p. 149.

7. *Union of India* v. *Sankalchand Seth*, *AIR,* SC, 1977, p. 2328.

8. *SC Advocates on Record Association* v. *Union of India*, 1993.

9. re Presidential Reference, *AIR*, 1999 SC, p. 1.

10. National Commission for Review of the Working of the Constitution, *Report of the NCRWC,* Universal Law Publishing Co. Pvt. Ltd., Delhi, 2002, Paragraph 7.3.7.

11. *The Hindu*, New Delhi, 9 May 2010, p. 1.

12. *The Hindu*, New Delhi, 30 April-1 May 2010, pp. 10 and 8.

13. *T.N. Cauvery Sangam* v. *Union of India*, 1990, *Supreme Court Judgements,* 2:547... .

14. *Constituent Assembly Debates* (CAD), Book No. 4, Lok Sabha Secretariat, New Delhi, 1999, 3rd reprint, pp. 1644–1671.

15. See Ambedkar's speech presenting the draft Constitution for debate and his reply to the debate at the deliberations running into about three years, and Prasad's valedictory address at the end. CAD, Book No. 2, pp. 31–44; and Book No. 5, pp. 972–981 and pp. 984–995.

Moreover, speaking in the Constituent Assembly, Nehru had observed: "Within limits no judge and no Supreme Court case make itself a third chamber. No Supreme Court and judiciary can stand in judgement over sovereign will of the Parliament representing the will of the entire community. If we go wrong here or there, it can point it out but in the ultimate analysis where the future of the community is concerned no judiciary can come in the way. And if it comes in the way ultimately the whole Constitution is a creature of Parliament. (*CAD*, Vol. 7, pp. 1195–96) quoted in T.R. Andhyarjuna, *op. cit.*, p. 5.

16. Upendra Baxi, *Courage, Craft, and Contention: The Indian Supreme Court in the Eighties,* N.M. Tripathi Private Ltd., Bombay, 1985, Chapter 3.

17. Jagdish Swarup, *Legislation and Interpretation*, Dandewal Publishing House, Allahabad, 1968.

18. Granville Austin, *The Indian Constitution: Cornerstone of a Nation*, OUP, Delhi, 1966, pp. 101–112.

19. *Sankari Prasad* v. *Union of India,* 1951.

20. *Sajjan Singh* v. *State of Rajasthan, AIR*, SC 1965.

21. *Golak Nath* v. *State of Punjab, AIR*, SC 1967.

22. *Keshavananda Bharati* v. *State of Kerala, AIR*, SC 1973.

23. *Indira Nehru Gandhi* v. *Raj Narain, AIR*, SC 1975.

24. *Minerva Mills Ltd.* v. *Union of India, AIR,* SC 1980.

25. *V.N. Shukla's Constitution of India,* Revised by Mahendra Pal Singh, 10th ed. first published 1950, Eastern Book Company, Lucknow, 2001.

26. Pratap Bhanu Mehta, "The Rise of Judicial Sovereignty", Journal of Democracy, April 2007, Vol. 18, No. 2, p. 71.

27. Rajeev Dhavan, "Governance by Judiciary: Into the Next Millennium" in B.D. Dua, M.P. Singh, and Rekha Saxena (Eds.), *Indian Judiciary and Politics: The Changing Landscape*, Manohar Publications, New Delhi, 2006.

28. S.K. Mitra and V.B. Singh, *Democracy and Social Change in India: A Cross Sectional Analysis of the National Electorate,* Sage, New Delhi, 1999.

29. Upendra Baxi, "The Avatars of Indian Judicial Activism: Explorations in Geographics of [In]Justice" in S.K. Verma and Kusum (Eds.), *Fifty years of the Supreme Court of India: Its Grasp and Reach,* Indian Law Institute/Oxford University Press, New Delhi, 2000, pp. 172–173.

30. *Ibid.*, pp. 173–176.

31. Prashant Bhushan, "Public Interest Litigation: Supreme Court in the Era of Liberalization" in B.D. Dua *et al.* (Eds.), *Indian Judiciary And Politics: The Changing Landscape*, Manohar, New Delhi, 2007, Chapter 6.

32. *Ibid.*

33. *The Hindu,* 24 January 2007, New Delhi, p. 14.

34. Quoted in Siddarth Sharma, "Myth of Judicial Overreach", *Economic and Political Weekly*, 8–14 March, 2008, p. 15.

35. *Ibid.*, pp. 15–18.

36. *The Hindu*, New Delhi, 3 May, 2010, p. 11.

37. *The Hindu,* New Delhi, 29 March, 2010, p. 10.

38. *The Hindu,* New Delhi, 1 August, 2010, p. 13.

Chapter 7

Towards Greater Federalization?

INTRODUCTION

Federalism, along with parliamentarism, is an axial principle of government in the Constitution of India. These two principles are contradictory in the sense that parliamentary government is premised on political centralization or legislative supremacy, while federalism is predicated on decentralization of political power.[1] Their combination in the Indian Constitution was considered necessary in view of the vast size and considerable regional and cultural diversity in the country, even after the Partition in 1947. Yet, drawing lessons from the historical divisiveness and partition at the birth of the Indian nation-state, the framers of the Indian Constitution considered it expedient to draft a Constitution with a strong parliamentary center. The inherent conflict between parliamentary supremacy and federal decentralization was sought to be reconciled by mechanisms of giving the Union government some overriding powers over the State governments in normal, and especially in emergency, situations, and by creating a federal Supreme Court with an integrated hierarchy of courts down to the district level. Besides, the Constitution also envisaged an Inter-State Council for coordinating Union-State relations.

Indian federalism is not a static entity. It has been evolving over the years from a predominantly parliamentary system during the era of the dominance of the Indian National Congress to a considerably federalized system under a multi-party system with federal coalition governments since 1989, although we have a de facto Bharatiya Janata Party majority government at the head of the National Democratic Alliance since 2014, re-elected in 2019. Increasing regional pressures, party system transformation, and changing judicial behaviour in a complex web of causation are accountable for this political denouement.

HISTORICAL BACKGROUND

During the British rule of nearly 200 years, conflicts among regional kingdoms on the subcontinent were contained by a strong colonial authority at the Center. The federal system was considered necessary around the time of the transfer of power in 1947 by the British rulers to the Indian political elites. Even before the 1950 Constitution was made, the British Raj had already attempted a federal experiment under the Government of India Act, 1935. In the early part of the British rule, administrative centralization was carried out, while in the latter part the process of devolution of powers to provinces was started. This move culminated into the 1935 experiment that remained abortive at the federal level due to the reluctance of the princely States to join the proposed Union. Thus, only the provincial component of the 1935 Act was implemented, while the Central government still worked under the Government of India Act, 1919.

The pre-1935 British Raj was a unitary system of administration. Thus, the Center preceded the units in case of the British Indian provinces. But then there were notionally independent princely States under the paramountcy of the British Crown that preceded the Indian federation. At the time of Independence, the princely States were given the right to self-determination whereby they could opt to remain independent or join one of the two newly created States of India and Pakistan. By and large, institutions established at the Center influenced the institutions established in the States.

The choice of a parliamentary federal Constitution for India is thus determined by the historical experience of the country. It is frequently said that India suffered from foreign aggression and colonization due to the weakness of the central authority. Hence, a strong parliamentary center was considered necessary. But then, India's unity in diversity also demanded a reasonable allowance for federal mode of integration of States with regional autonomy.

FEDERAL DESIGN

Both the Indian Constitution and the political system were traditionally described as 'quasi-federal'[2] and centralized to the extent of withering away of federalism. This interpretation was based on the federal design in the Constitution which provided for: (a) single citizenship; (b) an extensive Union and Concurrent Lists and smaller State List; (c) power of the Parliament to virtually unilaterally reorganize State boundaries—in consultation with and not concurrence of States; (d) a common integrated hierarchy of Union, State, and District courts; (e) a unique cadres of All-India Services filling the top administrative echelons in the Union as well as State governments; (f) a federal Second Chamber formed on the basis of States' population rather than equality of States qua States; (g) a Centrally appointed erstwhile Planning Commission as a creature of the Union executive (now, since 2015, replaced by a similarly appointed NITI Aayog); and (h) the early predominance of the Indian National Congress both at the Union and State levels for the first four decades, by and large (and now again moving towards a more or less similar dominance by the Bharatiya Janata Party since 2014, reinforced in 2019). However, over the years, especially since the 1990s to 2014, the Indian political system significantly moved towards greater federalization as first highlighted by the authors of the present book.[3] Indeed, Douglas Verney had gone to the extent of pointing out that transformation of the Indian party system to a regionalized multi-partisan configuration had encouraged the transition of the Indian political system from 'quasi-federation' to 'quasi-confederacy'.[4]

The Government of India today cannot be imagined without recognition of the federal principle. Understanding the federal system in India requires sensitivity to its unique historical and sociological contexts. This approach should not be diluted by a comparative perspective that is not informed of rigorous examination of equivalences and contrasts among the major federal systems of the world. The federal structure of India is sensitive to the country's culture, history, and geography as well as it has drawn from appropriate models of federalism around the world, especially the Commonwealth parliamentary-federal models of Canada (1867) and Australia (1901) more from Canada than Australia (1991).

The phenomenon of federalism in India has historically evolved and it is still in the process of evolution. Its historical trajectory has traversed from the imperial 'revenue and law and order model' to a 'planned development model' to a 'cooperative federalism' model to a federal 'bargaining model' to a 'collaborative model'. It may possibly develop into a 'popular democracy' model founded on decentralization and empowerment of local governments. Article 3 of the Indian Constitution empowering the Parliament of India to reorganize the States of the Union by the process of legislation (as distinguished from constitutional amendment) has often been considered to be a patently unfederal feature.[5] For, it only requires the Union to 'consult' the State(s) concerned and proceed with the reorganization irrespective of its/their wishes. However, if it is recalled that the pre-independence boundaries of States were products of accidents of history rather than natural socio-cultural territorial configurations, it becomes clear why the founding fathers of the Indian Republic decided to give the Parliament this unilateral power. Inter-State boundaries since 1950 have continuously been reorganized along linguistic, tribal, and regional-developmental lines, and the process is not yet complete. Given this fact, flexibility was an imperative.[6]

The 1950s witnessed the reorganization of South India, followed by reorganization of States in western and northern India in the 1960s, and of the north-east in the 1970s. In the year 2000, three new States—Uttrakhand carved out of UP, Chattisgarh out of MP, and Jharkhand out of Bihar—were created .Telengana became the 29th state in 2014 carved out of Andhra Pradesh. In 2019, the state of Jammu and Kashmir (J&K) was bifurcated into two independent union territories, Ladakh and J&K. The Home Minister of the Modi government stated in the Parliament that the UT of Jammu & Kashmir would be elevated to statehood later at an appropriate time. There are still outstanding demands for creating new States (e.g. Vidharbha in Maharashtra, etc.). What the internal boundaries of India will be is still an issue in debate.[7]

For a list of present States and Union territories, see Table 7.1.

TABLE 7.1 The Union of India (2019)

(i) List of States

1. Andhra Pradesh (1953, 1956, 1959)
2. Assam (1951, 1962, 1971)
3. Bihar (1950, 1956, 1968, 2000)
4. Gujarat (1960)
5. Kerala (1956)
6. Madhya Pradesh (1950, 1956, 2000)
7. Tamil Nadu (1950, 1953, 1959)
8. Maharashtra (1950, 1960)
9. Karnataka (1950, 1956, 1968)
10. Orissa (1950, 1960)
11. Punjab (1950, 1956, 1960, 1966)
12. Rajasthan (1950, 1956, 1959)
13. Uttar Pradesh (1950, 1968, 1979, 2000)
14. West Bengal (1950, 1954, 1956)
15. Nagaland (1962)
16. Haryana (1966, 1979)
17. Himachal Pradesh (1966)
18. Manipur (1971)
19. Tripura (1950)
20. Meghalaya (1971)
21. Sikkim (1975)
22. Mizoram (1971)
23. Arunachal Pradesh (1971)
24. Goa (1987)
25. Uttarakhand (2000)
26. Jharkhand (2000)
27. Chhattisgarh (2000)
28. Telengana (2014)

(ii) List of Union Territories

1. Delhi (1950, 1956)
2. Andaman and Nicobar Islands (1950, 1956)
3. Lakshadweep (1956)
4. Dadra & Nagar Haveli (1961)

5. Daman and Diu (1987)
6. Pondicherry (1962)
7. Chandigarh (1966)
8. Jammu and Kashmir (2019)
9. Ladakh (2019)

Note: Years in parentheses refer to the year of creation and/or reorganization.
Source: Adapted and updated from Rajeev Dhavan, "Indian Federalism and its Discontents: A Review", Typescript, 1996.

AN ASYMMETRICAL FEDERALISM?

Like any other federation, India has some *de facto* asymmetrical federal features in terms of differences of size, population, wealth, influence among the federating units. *Prima facie*, India also features some *de jure* or constitutional asymmetries in terms of special position, powers, and protection enjoyed by the states of Jammu and Kashmir (Article 370 of the Indian Constitution, deoperationalized in August 2019), Nagaland (Article 371A), Sikkim (Article 371F), and Mizoram (Article 371G). Moreover, the Fifth and the Sixth Schedules of the Constitution include some special provisions for administration and protection of scheduled areas and scheduled tribes in any state (Fifth Schedule) and in the states of Assam, Meghalaya, Tripura, and Mizoram (Sixth Schedule). The Acts of the Parliament of India applicable to other states of India do not automatically apply to the states of Nagaland and Mizoram in certain matters unless endorsed by the Legislatures of these states. These exceptional matters concern the religious and social practices of Nagas and Mizos, their customary law, and ownership and transfer of land resources. In the case of Sikkim, the Legislative Assembly of the state has a constitutionally guaranteed size of not less than 30 members, and pre-accession treaties are excluded from the jurisdiction of the Supreme Court or any other courts. The Governor of Sikkim, under the direction of the President of India, has some "special responsibility for peace and for an equitable arrangement for ensuring the social and economic advancement of different sections of the population" of the state. Similar "special responsibilities" are enjoined on the Governors of the concerned states in tribal affairs and welfare to which the Fifth and Sixth Schedules of the Constitution apply. These schedules also establish advisory or law-making institutions of governance for tribal communities and tribal areas.

There can be a debate in federal theory as well as in the context of its application to India regarding its impact on the working of federal systems in practice. Tarlton believes that asymmetrical federal arrangements are fraught with separatist and secessionist potential, whereas Barry is critical of them due to the creation of two classes of citizenships, one for nationality-based units and the other for merely regional units. On the other hand, Kymlicka, Taylor, Requejo, Gagnon and Gibb argue that constitutional asymmetrical status is equitous and necessary for countries that are not merely multicultural but are multinational for protection of community or minority rights in the context of identity politics of recognition.[8] Stepan contrasts India's "demos-enabling" (e.g. Article 3 of the Constitution empowering Parliament to reorganize states) federal model from the "demos-constraining" (e.g. separation of powers and checks and balances) model of federalism, and credits the former for its tackling of the multiple linguistic nationalism, especially Tamil separatism.[9] However, Tillin correctly argues that India's linguistic reorganization, including the Tamil case, was an exercise in symmetrical arrangement on closer examination. Nevertheless, Tillin's argument is valid only in relation to the regional languages (including Hindi, the regional language in 10 out of 28 states) that were accorded equal status in regional or state governments. But Hindi and English were/are still accorded a special status as co-official languages of the Union government as India's lingua franca, even if it was a climb down for Hindi that was to become the sole "official language" of the Union of India from 1965 under the original Constitution fifteen years after its commencement in 1950. Moreover, Tillin goes on to argue that Article 370 regarding Jammu and Kashmir was included in the Constitution in Part XXI under the caption "Temporary, Transitional and Special Provisions". More importantly, it was neither included in recognition to the states "distinct", Muslim-majority status to embed corresponding group rights nor intended as a challenge to India's composite and equal vision of territorial nationhood inclusive of all religions, languages, and ethnic groups. To Tillin, India's northeastern states come closest to *de jure* asymmetrical federalism. Yet, she turns around and tries to show that these states "are perhaps better seen as 'peripheral' units within India" and approvingly quotes Watts who says "these relationships are quite distinct from those of the main body of constituent units within the major political entity."[10] In our opinion, these arguments do not make sense in constitutional law at least. And about Jammu and Kashmir, whatever the intent and theory of the Indian Constitution, Article 370 survived until 5 August 2019, and could have been the basis of a final settlement with modifications, taking "the Indian federation into new constitutional waters."[11] However, with the deoperationalization of Article 370, this prospect is not ruled out, and asymmetry of Jammu and Kashmir in the Indian federation is rendered symmetrical. Subnational constitutionalism in operation in this state is now deoperationalised using Article 370(3) itself.

UNION-STATE RELATIONS

Legislative Relations

Constitutional demarcation of jurisdictions of Union and State governments is carried out in three lists in the Seventh Schedule of the Constitution, namely,

Union, State, and Concurrent. Broadly speaking, the division is based on the principles of exclusivity and concurrency. By exclusivity it is meant that whichever level of government can handle a particular subject more effectively is granted that subject. By concurrency, it is meant that the subjects in the twilight zone are allocated to both orders of governments, with the laws made by the Parliament prevailing over those made by State legislatures in case of conflict. The original Constitution had 97 items in the Union List, 66 in the State List and 47 in the Concurrent List. In the last seventy years or so, the State List has lost some items to the Concurrent or the Union List. Between 1950 and 2001, a total of 27 changes have been brought about by constitutional amendments: 9 in the Union List, 11 in the State List and 7 in the Concurrent List. Four out of 9 changes in the Union List have enlarged the executive, cultural and coercive powers of the Union vis-à-vis States (e.g. Sixth Amendment 1956 added a new tax to the Union List, namely, on sale and purchase of goods other than newspapers of the scope of inter-state trade and commerce). The above changes are mirrored in the other lists as the items gained by other lists were lost by the State List. Another major change in the Seventh Schedule was produced by the 101st Amendment (2016) to the Constitution in the run up to the landmark taxation reforms relating to the goods and services tax (GST) that was enforced from 2017. This Amendment affected 4 entries in the Union List and 4 entries in the State List by way of deletions or substitutions. No change took place in the Concurrent List.

The Concurrent List, thus, has not lost any item; it has only gained (e.g. 42nd Amendment, 1976 added four new items to this list, namely, administration of justice in a State and formation of lower courts, forests, education, and population control and family planning). In terms of different regimes, of the 27 amendments mentioned above, thirteen were made in the Nehru era, fourteen during the Indira Gandhi era and a few in the post-1989 multi-party coalition Government phase.[12]

Article 200 of the Constitution grants the Union an executive power to intervene in the legislative process of States. A bill presented to the Governor for his assent may be reserved for consideration by the Union executive with its power to either approve it or disallow it. There is exactly a similar provision in the Canadian Constitution, which over the years has become obsolescent under conventions of the Constitution. However, in India this has been a major irritant in Union-State relations as is amply documented by the Sarkaria Commission Report (1988). The Report shows that out of fifteen State legislations so reserved between 10.11.1969 and 7.6.1984, the Union government withheld its assent in nine cases. In six cases, decision was taken after one and a half years, in five cases after three years, in three cases after six years and in one case after twelve years. The Commission recommended that normally the Governor must abide by the advice of the Council of Ministers. In its views, the discretion of reservation of a State legislation by the Governor should be exercised in "rare and exceptional cases" when such a legislation is "patently unconstitutional". The Commission also recommended that a State bill so reserved should be disposed off within four months from the date of its receipt.[13] This practice of reservation of State bills has continued to the present time with occasional controversies when divergent parties are in power in New Delhi and the concerned state. The Justice M.M. Punchhi Commission on Center-State Relations (2010) has recommended the disposal of a bill so reserved within six months.

Administrative Relations

Executive powers of the Union and State Governments are coterminous with their legislative jurisdictions. The Constitution of India envisages what may be called "cooperative federalism" inasmuch as Article 256 stipulates that the executive power of the State "shall be so exercised as to ensure compliance with the laws made by Parliament". This Article goes on to say that "the executive power of the Union shall extend to the giving of such directions to a State as may appear to the Government of India to be necessary for that purpose".

Power to enter into any international treaties or conventions is a power of the Union executive. However, Article 253 of the Constitution requires a parliamentary legislation for giving effect to these agreements, if necessary. This provision of the Constitution has acquired a somewhat controversial dimension in the context of globalization. For example, the Union of India signed the WTO treaty in 1995 which entailed obligations for the federating States in subjects in their exclusive jurisdictions, e.g. agriculture. The States of Punjab, Rajasthan, Orissa and Tamil Nadu in fact filed cases in the Supreme Court precisely on this issue, which subsequently were withdrawn presumably after suitable assurances from the Union government for such occasions in the future. Article 253 was also in the eye of a political storm in 2007 in the context of Indo-US nuclear civilian deal in the Parliament where the opposition, especially the Communist party allies of the Congress-led coalition government in New Delhi and state units of left parties were up in arms for parliamentary approval of the treaty. In all probability, the Union of India would be more cautious in the exercise of its executive treaty making power in view of possible responses and reactions from the Parliament as well as from State governments.[14]

The Governor of a State in India has a delicate dual role—as the constitutional head of the provincial State and as the representative of the Union in the State government. In his first role, he has to act as the custodian of the Constitution to ensure a State ministry responsible to the legislature. In his second role, he is the eyes and ears of the President of the Indian Union to ensure that the government of the State is carried on in accordance with the broader provisions of the Constitution of India.

The office of the Governor has become perhaps the most contentious issue in Union-State relations. Controversies have arisen on the question of partisan appointment of the Governor by the party in power at the Center and patently political role of the incumbent to appease the powers that be, in New Delhi. Governorship has been often offered by the ruling parties to political loyalists and pliable bureaucrats as a kind of post-retirement patronage. In recent times, some political parties and State governments went to the extent of demanding the abolition of the office in their memorandums to the Sarkaria Commission and all insisted that the Chief Minister of the State concerned must be extended the courtesy of prior consultation before appointing a person as a Governor. The Commission did not agree to the idea of abolition but recommended the practice of appointing persons who have not been recently active in the politics of the State concerned and consulting the Chief Minister in the matter. The Commission further recommended that the Governors should generally allow the test of a majority claim of a prospective or incumbent government on the floor of the Assembly and restrain his discretion to the minimum and assess the situation as objectively as possible.

The emergency power of the Union to take over the government of a State under Article 356 on the recommendation of the Governor or otherwise is a unique and frequently criticized provision of the Indian Constitution with far-reaching implications for federalism. The Union executive can exercise this power in the event of the breakdown of the constitutional machinery in a State on the report of the Governor or otherwise. This power has been one of the most grossly misused emergency powers for partisan considerations by all parties in power in New Delhi in the past. A classic example of this abuse was the dismissal of nine Congress State governments and dissolution of their respective Assemblies by the Janata Party Government at the Center in 1977, and the dissolution of exactly nine State governments led by the Janata Party and other opposition parties by Prime Minister Indira Gandhi when she returned to power in 1980. In 1983, Indira Gandhi, under pressure of the Opposition, appointed the Sarkaria Commission on Center-State Relations. Several political parties and State governments in their submissions to this Commission demanded repeal of this provision or at least bringing it under greater constitutional limitations.

The Commission in its Report did not recommend the abolition of Article 356 but strongly urged the federal functionaries to exercise this power with due restraint expected by the framers of the Constitution. It also laid down some guidelines for the Governor, and by implication for the President and the Union Cabinet. However, not much has really changed until the one-party dominant system was transformed into a multi-party system. But the Supreme Court departed from tradition and made President's rule subject to judicial review in *S.R. Bommai & others* v. *Union of India* (1994).[15] A meeting of the Inter-State Council at Srinagar a couple of years back reached a consensus to incorporate the rules laid down in this case law into the Constitution by an amendment. This is yet to be done. It is, however, a good idea, for if it becomes a part of the Constitution in case law anyway.

FISCAL AND ECONOMIC FEDERALISM

Union-State relations and intergovernmental relations in India have largely conformed to the model of cooperative federalism by and large, some irritants and tension areas notwithstanding. Using its larger resources and spending powers, the Union had initiated centrally sponsored schemes (CSS) with the consent of State governments in all major policy areas, even in matters under exclusive jurisdiction of State governments. Some State governments have, however, been complaining about fiscal domination of the Center over the States and demanding redistribution of powers and revenue resources between the two orders of governments. But neither the Sarkaria Commission on Center-State Relations nor the National Commission for Review of the Working of the Constitution (NCRWC) nor the M.M. Punchhi Commission on Center-State Relations has recommended any substantial review in this arrangement. The Sarkaria panel had suggested the setting up of another Commission to study and report on the taxation system. This has not yet been done, though taxation system has been altered in significant ways to introduce value added tax (VAT) in 2005 and goods and services tax (GST) in 2017.

A paradigm shifts in economic policies and Union-State relations on account of growing federalization of the Indian polity and economic liberalization/privatization/globalization have occurred since the 1990s. Economic liberalization has augmented the autonomy of the private sector as well as of State governments. Federalization has accentuated the tendency towards political as well as economic regionalism. While a formal process of five-year plans is dispensed with since the abolition of the Planning Commission by the BJP government led by Narendra Modi in 2014, the public investment in the economy has considerably gone down. This has opened up opportunities for economically more developed States to chart out their own strategies of development in collaboration with the private sector, but backward States have been put to disadvantage on account of lack of their own resources and declining public investment on the part of the federal government. Private capital has been reluctant to invest in backward states and regions. Since the early 1990s, when economic liberalization and globalization accelerated, there has been a tremendous increase in regional economic disparities among states. Even newspaper reports project a visible parallel development of two contrasting corridors of growth, on the one hand, and poverty and destitution, on the other: "Blue Corridor" spanning Delhi-Gurgaon/Mumbai-Pune/Bangalore-Chennai on the western side and the "Red Corridor" of Maoist violence stretching across the hinterland tribal belt from the Indo-Nepalese border to the central and eastern side. Scholarly studies also reveal that during August 1991 to March 2000 the states of Andhra Pradesh, Gujarat, Haryana, Karnataka, Kerala, Punjab, and Tamil Nadu got proposals of private capital investment to the tune of 66.7 per cent as against only 27.4 per cent received by the states of Assam, Bihar, Madhya Pradesh, Orissa, Rajasthan, Uttar Pradesh, and West

Bengal. Differences in regard to foreign direct investment (FDI) are even more glaring. In the phase of globalization, only five states—Andhra Pradesh, Gujarat, Karnataka, Maharashtra, and Tamil Nadu—got a disproportionately large 75 per cent of FDI invested in India.

The Twelfth Finance Commission Report submitted in 2005 recommended increase in the share of States in the total divisible pool of federal resources from the existing 29.5 per cent to 30.5 per cent. However, this slight gain to the States may be cancelled out because of the neo-liberal economic policies that have put a strain on Union as well as State finances. In a view from the perspective of States on the *Twelfth Finance Commission (TFC) Report,* V. Sridhar has commented: Although the Constitution prescribed that the main task of the Finance Commission is to perform its role as an agency for setting the modalities for the transfer of resources from the Center to the States, the terms of reference of the Commission were expanded by asking it to suggest "a plan by which the (State) Governments, collectively and severally, may bring about a restructuring of the public finances, restoring budgetary balance, achieving macro-economic stability and debt reduction along with equitable growth''. In specific terms, there were fears that this was, apart from being a violation of the principles of federalism, an attempt by the Center to straitjacket the States in the liberal reform mode with all its harsh implications for the already financially beleaguered States.[16] The basic fiscal approach of the Thirteenth Finance Commission remained unchanged, within the broad objective of federal fiscal finance everywhere "to ensure that the states and local bodies have the fiscal potential to provide comparable levels of public services, at reasonably comparable levels of taxation".[17] In view of the fact, among others, that buoyancy of central taxes has been higher than that of state taxes, the Thirteenth Finance Commission recommended that raising the share of states in the net proceeds of sharable central taxes from 30.5 per cent to 32 per cent. The Commission thought that it would not pose an undue burden on the Center, and could be easily managed by reduction of its expenditure, subsidies, and centrally sponsored schemes.[18] As to the criteria and weights for revenue share of states and financial devolution, the Commission recommended the following: population (1971 Census), 25 percent, geographical area 10 per cent, fiscal capacity distance 47.5 per cent, fiscal capacity distance 47.5 per cent, fiscal discipline 17.5 per cent.[19] Beginning with the Tenth Finance Commission Report the weightage of population and size of states has been generally reduced in favour of their better resource generation and fiscal management. Taking into account the differences in per capita income, revenue, and expenditure as well as poverty levels among the states of India, the various finance commissions of India have divided them into "general category" and "special category" states (in the Thirteenth Finance Commission Report 11 states fell in the latter category: Nagaland, Manipur, Arunachal Pradesh, Mizoram, Meghalaya, Tripura, Assam, Himachal Pradesh, Sikkim, Jammu and Kashmir, and Uttarakhand, all sub-Himalayan states from the northwest to the northeast)[20]. In 2000–2001 the percentage of own revenue states was 52.5 per cent. The corresponding figure in the case of special category states was 20.1 per cent. The revenue gap was met by horizontal sharing of the national wealth among states by way of federal devolution.[21] Yet, issue of vertical and horizontal fiscal imbalances has been a cause of concern. In 2000–2001, Center's share in tax revenue account was 44.76 per cent, and that of the states 53.11 per cent after central transfer of resources to states. In non-tax revenue in the same year the shares of the Center and the states stood at 73.57 per cent and 26.43 per cent, respectively.[22] As to horizontal imbalance, *inter se* shares of states during the award period of the Thirteenth Finance Commission would vary from 19.677 per cent for Uttar Pradesh to 0.239 per cent for Sikkim.[23]

The Fourteenth Finance Commission Report (2015–2020) has surpassed any previous Finance Commission in recommending a considerable increase in the quantum of States' share vis-a-vis the Union's in the divisible pool of the national revenue: from 32 per cent under the previous dispensation to 42 per cent for the next five years. Grants-in-aid to be appropriated by the Parliament for additional budgetary needs of the States is recommended to be ₹ 1,94,821 crore. The weights of indicators for calculating inter se share of States in taxes have been fixed as: (i) 1971 Census population 17.5 per cent, 2011 Census population 10 per cent; (ii) Geographical area 2 per cent for smaller States, 15 per cent for general weight; (iii) Forest cover 7.5 per cent; and (iv) Income distance (distance of State's income from the State having the highest income 50 per cent. The Commission recommended that the deficit of states should be targeted at 3 per cent of the gross State domestic product (GSDP) during 2015–2020, with a flexibility of 0.25 per cent of their GSDP, if their interest payments are less than or equal to 25 per cent over this limit, this eligibility being dependent on their debt-GSDP ratio being less than or equal to 25 per cent in the previous year. States will have an option of borrowing of 0.25 per cent of their GSDP, if their interest payments are less than or equal to 10 per cent of their revenue receipts in the previous year. The Commission has also recommended compensation to States for losses if any suffered on account of transition to the forthcoming GST reforms by an autonomous GST Commission Fund for five years: 100 per cent in the first three years, 75 per cent for the fourth year, and 50 per cent for the fifth year. Federal fiscal transfers are also recommended for local governments in the States: ₹ 2,78,436 crore, of which ₹ 2,00,292 crore are meant for panchayats, and ₹ 87,144 crore for municipal councils. The overall grants to the rural and urban councils are to be disbursed in two parts, namely, basic grant and performance grant. For panchayats, 90 per cent grant should be basic and 10 per cent based on performance. For municipalities, the ratio should be 80:20 per cents. An amendment to the FRBM Act, 2003 is also recommended to remove the definition of effective revenue (difference between revenue deficit and grants for creation of capital assets. Moreover, an independent fiscal council is recommended to be created for evaluation of fiscal policy implications of budget proposals before the budget is announced. States are advised to amend their FRBM Acts in a similar way. Alternatively, the FRBM Act may be replaced with a Debt Ceiling and Fiscal Responsibility Legislation to lend greater legitimacy to fiscal management. (Fourteenth Finance Commission Report htprs://www.prs.india.org Accessed on 12 November 2019). The Modi government announced the acceptance of the key recommendations of the Fourteenth Finance Commission.[24]

Intergovernmental relations in India have been significantly facilitated by two specific aspects of the Indian political system: (1) an unusually detailed provision in the Constitution itself, especially in matters of fiscal federalism, to harmonize Union-State relations, and (2) the legacy of an established administrative procedure for Center-State relations emanating from the British Raj as well as from the earlier decades of one-party dominant system after the Independence. The Constitution has taken special care to meticulously provide for allocation, collection and sharing of tax revenue between the Union and the States. Besides, five yearly periodic review of this arrangement by an autonomous Finance Commission, largely composed of experts, is made in the Constitution itself under Article 280. These matters are subject to detailed negotiations by Ministers or officials of the Union and the States in other federations such as in Canada.

In addition to constitutionally mandated federal transfers to the States on the recommendations of the Finance Commission, there are discretionary Union transfers of funds to the States. A non-statutory Planning Commission had been in existence from 1950 to 2015, for advising the Center in these matters. The Finance Commission is unilaterally appointed by the Union government and is constitutionally entrenched, whereas the Planning Commission was unilaterally appointed by the Union government and was a creation of the Union Cabinet, even though largely a body of experts. So is the NITI Aayog, which has replaced the Planning Commission since 2015. Presumably for this reason, the Finance Commission recommendations are more impartial and objective, and carry greater legitimacy than those of the Planning Commission, though the latter also conducts detailed discussion with Ministers and officials of the State governments. It had brought about some degree of rule-based equity and justice in discretionary federal fiscal transfers by evolving the Gadgil formula named after a former deputy chairman of the Planning Commission of India. Last revised in 1991, the Gadgil formula was predicated on the following criteria of weightage: population (1971 Census) 61 per cent, per capita income 25 per cent, performance 7.5 per cent, special problems 7.5 per cent. The Sarkaria Commission on Center-State Relations in its Report (1987–88) recommended that the Finance Commission be made a permanent constitutional body (presently, it is appointed every five years provisionally and the Planning Commission be given a constitutional status. This is also reiterated by the M.M. Punchhi Commission Report on Center-State Relations (2010). The latter has indeed recommended a comprehensive review of financial transfers to states with a view to minimizing the component of discretionary transfers, particularly those channelled through centrally sponsored schemes (CSS).

When development planning was initiated in a significant way by the Nehru Government, an apex intergovernmental forum called the National Development Council (NDC) was set up in 1952 by a Cabinet resolution for the approval of plans by State governments prepared by the centrally appointed Planning Commission. With the abolition of the Planning Commission, NDC also stands abolished. The NDC consisted of the Prime Minister, some key Union Ministers heading economic ministries and Chief Ministers of all States and executive heads of the Union Territories. Chaired by the Prime Minister, the NDC decided by consensus as determined by the chair rather than by the majority rule. Even though State investment in development has declined with growing privatization of the economy, the NDC and the Planning Commission, which served as its secretariat, were still active as public investment in development continues to be considerable. The Planning Commission had also proved to be a useful 'think tank' for Union and State Governments for advising on the transition of the economy from socialistic to business liberalism.

In the recent decades, the architecture of fiscal federalism and policy paradigm in India have undergone a significant transformation. In 2005, the existing general sales tax laws were replaced with value added taxes (VAT) under the VAT Act, 2005 and rules and regulations thereunder. The typically applicable VAT rate was between 12.5 to 14.5 per cent and service tax and cess at the rate of six per cent (i.e., 15 per cent on 40 per cent abated value of food). The goods and services tax (GST), pending for long for lack of consensus among the Union and States, finally got instituted in 2017. It came to be hailed as the most significant indirect taxation reform since India's Independence. All the VATs and cesses came to be subsumed under the comprehensive GST regime, comprising the Central GST, State GST, and integrated GST. The total amount of indirect tax in the form of GST for any sale/manufacture of goods and rendering of services is proportionally distributed in both Central and State exchequers. The GST Council has included over 1300 goods and 500 services under four tax slabs of 5 per cent, 12 per cent, 18 per cent, and 28 per cent under GST.

A GST Council is formed under Article 279A of the Constitution by the President of India consisting of the Union Finance Minister as the chair and the Union Minister of State in charge of revenue or finance and the Minister in charge of finance or taxation or any other Minister nominated by each State government as members. The quorum for its meetings is fixed at one-half of the total number of members. Its decisions must be backed by a majority of not less than three-fourths of weighted votes of the members present and voting in accordance with the following principles:

1. the vote of the Central government shall count for the weightage of one-third of the total votes cast, and
2. the votes of all the State governments taken together shall have a weightage of the two-thirds of the total votes cast (Article 279A,

clause 9). Thus, any block with 25 per cent plus (say, 26 per cent) votes can block a proposal. The Center alone has one-third voting strength. It virtually amounts to a veto power.

INTERGOVERNMENTAL RELATIONS

The past tradition of informal intergovernmental forums set up by the initiative of the Union government has also stood India in good stead. Such national councils and advisory boards have existed in almost all major sectors of policy areas from the past. To cite just one such non-statutory body, there has been a Central Advisory Board for Education (CABE) chaired by the Union HRD Minister and comprising State Education Ministers, Union and State education secretaries, as well as leading educationists, media and cultural personalities, and so on. This arrangement was discontinued by the BJP-led National Democratic Alliance government led by the then Prime Minister, Atal Bihari Vajpayee that created unprecedented intergovernmental tensions and conflicts in the field of educational policies. The Congress-led United Progressive Alliance government on coming to power in May 2004 revived this defunct body. Besides the CABE, there are other agencies in the field of education set up under statutes for harmonizing intergovernmental policies. For example, there is the All India Council of Technical Education (AICTE) established in 1948 as an advisory body to assist the Central government in the field of technical education at the post-secondary level. This body was made a statutory one under an Act of Parliament in 1988. This is obviously a Central agency, but it has significant implications for States as well. A new development in the last two decades or so has been the emergence of 'self-financing' institutions in the private sector. Some of these institutions started as commercial ventures charging hefty capitation fees. The AICTE has been a source of advice to Union and State governments who have introduced legislative measures to regulate these 'self-financing institutions' in common public interest. Disputes in this policy area have often gone to the Supreme Court which has directed that governments and its agencies should lay down principles for the levy of fees, openness to merit, etc. for these educational institutions. Such national councils and advisory boards exist in almost all policy areas, e.g. health, urban development, local self-government, population, industries, agriculture, etc.

The foregoing discussion may help in explaining why Article 263 providing for an Inter-State Council (ISC) was left unused until 1990. This was partly because there were functional substitutes for the ISC as mentioned above and partly because the Union government thought that the foregoing forums would be more flexible than a formal constitutional forum of ISC. When it was first set up in 1990 at the beginning of the era of coalition governments in New Delhi, it was in response to an electoral promise of the Janata Dal-led National Front to activate federal provisions of the Constitution and in the process appoint the ISC. As already mentioned, the V.P. Singh government did so in 1990. Incidentally, its composition exactly overlaps with the NDC, discussed above.

Ironically, however, as Rekha Saxena observes, the expected activation of the ISC could never materialize. This was mainly for two reasons. First, coalition governments that came to be formed in this era tended to be unusually large assortment of parties, some of them heading State governments. Since many State governments found direct regional representation in the federal Cabinet itself, most of the intergovernmental matters could be negotiated at the level of the Union Cabinet itself. ISC was only needed for those State governments who were not represented in the federal government. Secondly, the NDC continued to be the forum for approval of economic plans, until 2014/2015 when the Planning Commission and NDC were abolished.[25] Had the NDC been merged with the ISC, then the ISC could have acquired some added significance. This was not done. The Sarkaria Commission Report had advised keeping them separate for the consideration of not politicizing economic policies. As it happened, the NDC continued to retain some importance as an apex forum for economic policy making, while the ISC was marginalized as an 'apex' political body. However, the National Commission to Review the Working of the Constitution (NCRWC) Report (2002) and the Common Minimum Programme (CMP) of the Congress-led UPA government underlined the importance of the ISC as the key intergovernmental forum and stressed the need to activate it in order to promote a true federal spirit. But, these ideas remained at the level of rhetoric.

Following the abolition of the Planning Commission and the NDC in 2014/2015, the Modi government replaced them with the NITI Aayog and its Governing Council with similar compositions—a body of experts and PM and some key Union Ministers and PM and CMs and executive heads of the Union Territories, respectively—but less regular and reduced roles in economic and political policy making. This has resulted in greater centralization of decision-making powers in the Union Finance Ministry and other Union ministries without recurrent consultation with a body of experts and State governments.

Yet, the reality of Indian intergovernmental relations suggests that informality is still the norm. The bulk of the nitty-gritty of intergovernmental negotiations and decisions are carried out by occasional informal conferences of officials, Ministers and finally Prime/Chief Ministers from the two orders of the governments. These conferences are far more frequent than the meetings of NDC and ISC. Another set of statutory intergovernmental forums, Zonal Councils, are, by and large, defunct, except for the North-Eastern Zonal Council (NEZC). This is presumably because the NEZC is embedded in an area that is perhaps the only political region in the country in geographical isolation and economic interdependence, at least more so than any other macro-region, e.g. Northwest, Hindi-heartland, South India, etc.

The foregoing are all examples of settlement of intergovernmental disputes by political means, though with important inputs from expert bodies like the Finance Commission and Planning Commission. Political resolution of conflicts was much easier when there was dominance of the Indian National Congress in New Delhi as well as in all or most States. Many a time, disputes were amicably settled in the top party forums themselves like the Congress Parliamentary Board and the Congress Working Committee representing most powerful leaders of the party at the Union and State levels. With the decline of this dominance, particularly since emergence of the multi-party system, this pattern of intergovernmental relations is not available. Nehru's fortnightly letters to Chief Ministers obviously would have been more effective within a dominant party framework than such letters from a Prime Minister later within a multi-party systemic configuration and federal coalition governments.

Inter-State River Water disputes have been another major area of Inter-State tension. The Parliament passed the Inter-State River Disputes Act (1956) which provides for referral of such disputes to a tribunal on the application of a State government and the satisfaction of the Union government that the dispute in question cannot be settled by administrative or political negotiation. So far, five such tribunals have been established for Narmada, Krishna, Godawari, Kaveri and Sutluj-Jamuna. Tribunals have also often referred the matter to a commission chaired by a retired Supreme Court judge. If both the tribunal and the commission fail, the matter finally goes to the Supreme Court. Water disputes have so far been more or less amicably settled excepting the disputes involving Punjab, Haryana and Rajasthan, and Tamil Nadu and Karnataka. In the last few years, the Kaveri dispute has often found the States of Tamil Nadu and Karnataka at loggerheads especially in drought years. Failing all political negotiations, the matter has often been provisionally settled by the Supreme Court's intervention. The Punjab Congress government has recently turned the heat on the sharing of water from Ravi-Beas-Sutluj and Yamuna by terminating Inter-State agreements between riparian States signed in 1981, 1985 and 1994 by a unanimous resolution of the State Legislature. The matter is still hanging fire. Kaveri tribunal award was submitted in 2007 but both Karnataka and Tamil Nadu continued expressing discontent, the former more than the latter. The Supreme Court delivered its verdict on Kaveri water dispute on 16 February 2018, allocating more water to the State of Karnataka. The final allocation for a total of 740 TMC is: Karnataka 284.75 TMC and Tamil Nadu 404.25 TMC.

In the proposal of interlinking all major rivers of India, mooted by the NDA government of the then Prime Minister, Atal Bihari Vajpayee was carried on by the UPA regime of the then Prime Minister, Manmohan Singh. The protagonists of the project, including NDA Prime Minister, Narendra Modi, argue that it will avoid the paradoxical occurrence of flood and drought simultaneously in various parts of the country by a rational apportionment of water resources of the country. The ecologists, however, argue that it will disturb the ecological balance and bring natural calamities in its trail as well as intensify Inter-State disputes and societal conflicts.

The final mode of federal dispute settlement under the Constitution is, of course, the Supreme Court of India under its original jurisdiction (Article 131) and advisory jurisdiction (Article 143). The ruling of the Court has often put greater emphasis on public investment, distributive justice and the planning process, even though the new liberal economic reforms are not likely to be reversed by available indications.

On the submission of the Eleventh Finance Commission Report in 2000, richer States led by Andhra Pradesh Chief Minister N. Chandrababu Naidu (TDP) met the Prime Minister and expressed some dissatisfaction with its recommendations. Finance Commission reports have consistently given greater weightage to backwardness and population in deciding federal fiscal transfers to States, beginning with the Seventh Finance Commission. Although the weightage of economic performance has been increased in recent Finance Commission reports, poorer States still get proportionately more than richer States. Any drastic change in the pattern of transfer is likely to increase regional economic disparities.

Intergovernmental relations have been a somewhat weak aspect of Indian federalism in absolute as well as comparative terms. Most observers have found the forms of intergovernmental relations to be either infrequently used or overly dominated by the Center. In comparison to intergovernmental relations in Canada, the Indian scene appears to be rather quiescent and ineffective.

In India, as already mentioned above, there are both formal and informal—mostly latter—relations between the executives of the various jurisdictions that comprise the federation. The most formal agency in this context is the Inter-State Council (ISC) that was set up belatedly under Article 263 of the Constitution in 1990. It consists of the executive heads of the two orders of the governments, namely, the Prime Minister and relevant Union Ministers on the one hand, and the Chief Ministers and the relevant Ministers in States, on the other. A lesser degree of formality can be attributed to the National Development Council (NDC) set up by a Cabinet resolution in 1952 and operational until 2015. The NITI Aayog and its Governing Council that replaced the Planning Commission and the NDC are not as regularly integrated with the economic and administrative and political policy making, implementing, and monitoring processes as the bodies that existed earlier. More formal bodies are the Zonal Councils consisting of the Home Minister of India and Chief Ministers of States in concerned regions set up under an Act of the Parliament (1956). But they are not regularly operational. The most informal forums are the ad hoc conferences attended by the Prime Minister and Chief Ministers, and ministers from the two levels of governments. These bodies are most operational and primarily serve the purpose of intergovernmental negotiations, policy-making and policy harmonization.

There is no formal cooperation between legislatures. The only informal inter-legislative forum is occasional conferences of Speakers or Presiding Officers of the legislatures to discuss the problems confronting these institutions and exchange their experiences in search of solutions. There are, of course, informal conferences of the Secretaries of the government of India and State governments. These are the most frequent events where the real nitty-gritty of intergovernmental relations are worked out for approval by Ministers and first Ministers.

However, the Common Minimum Programme (CMP) of the UPA Government framed in 2004 committed itself to make the NDC "a more effective instrument of cooperative federalism" and promised that the ISC would also be "activated".[26] These promises remained empty rhetoric.

REGIONAL PRESSURES

The federalizing process has in fact been long in the making. The over-centralization of the political system in the turbulent 1970s culminating in the internal emergency (1975–77) produced a political reaction, especially in Punjab and Assam in the 1980s and Jammu and Kashmir in the 1990s. It was under mounting regional pressures that Prime Minister Indira Gandhi, in 1983, appointed a Constitutional Commission on Center-State Relations, chaired by Justice R.S. Sarkaria. In 1987-88, the Commission submitted its monumental two-volume report[27], which has become the most frequently invoked document in federal discourse by all concerned.

In contrast to Indira Gandhi's generally rigid centralist orientation, Rajiv Gandhi adopted a more contextually specific accommodative approach to regional ethnic demands and movements. In quick succession, the Center reached regional accords with ethnic movements and parties in Punjab and Assam in 1985, Mizoram in 1986, and Tripura in 1988.[28] The Punjab Accord with the Akali Dal sought to resolve the territorial and Inter-State river water disputes between Punjab, Haryana and Rajasthan; it promised an all-India Gurdwara Act by the Parliament; it referred the Anandpur Sahib Resolution of the Akali Dal for 'redefining' Center-State relations for consideration to the Sarkaria Commission, and it assured a judicial inquiry into the massacre of Sikhs in Delhi in 1984.[29] Except for some debatable success on the last two points, the rest of the issues still largely remain unresolved.

The Assam Accord signed in August 1985 between the Home Secretary R.D. Pradhan and the Assam agitation leaders provided for detection and deletion of the names of Bangladeshi illegal migrants entering Assam prior to 1 January 1966; the disenfranchisement for ten years of the migrants entering between 1 January 1966 and 24 March 1971; and the detection and deportation of those coming on or after 25 March 1971. The implementation of the Assam Accord remained lackadaisical on account of the Congress government in New Delhi blinded by vote-bank politics in relation to the illegal migrants from Bangladesh. Even the Congress and non-Congress governments in Assam were hamstrung due to the federal tangles and the sheer complexity of the process of detection and deportation of foreigners. The matter was taken to the Supreme Court by some Assam leaders who joined the Hindu nationalist BJP. In *Sarbananda Sonobal* v. *Union of India* (2005), the apex court declared the Illegal Migrants (Determination by Tribunal) Act, 1983, got passed by the Indira Gandhi Congress government, illegal, invoking Article 355 of the Indian Constitution. The said Act placed the burden on the state to detect the foreigners, whereas under the Constitution, requirement would lie on the individual to rebut the allegation that one was a foreigner. In *Sarbananda Sonobal-II* v. *Union of India* (2006), the Supreme Court struck down the Foreigners (Tribunals) Amendment Order, 2006, as unnecessary and unreasonable. The court held that there was a lack of political will in ensuring that illegal migrants were sent out of the country. The court ordered a Supreme Court supervised process of updating of the National Register of Citizens (NRC) in Assam. The updated Assam NRC list 2019 when released included the names of 3.11 crore applicants and those of 19.07 lakh were found invalid. Those excluded have been given time for appeal for administrative redressal. However, the Supreme Court has also been faced with a spate of petitions challenging the final list. Both the Union and State governments of Assam have also moved the apex court seeking re-verification of 20 per cent of draft NRC data.

The Mizoram and Tripura Accords severally sought to restore normalcy by cessation of insurgency and rehabilitation of the armed underground elements. Normalcy has practically replaced the cycle of insurgencies and democratic processes of elections and federal governance have been restored in these States.

After nearly a decade of insurgency and repeated spells of Central rule, elections were held in Jammu and Kashmir in 1996. The major regional party, the Jammu and Kashmir National Conference, boycotted the parliamentary elections of that year as its demand that New Delhi issue an order under Article 370 of the Indian Constitution to restore the autonomy of the State in terms of the Delhi Agreement of 1952 was not conceded by the NDA government of the then Prime Minister, Atal Bihari Vajpayee. By the 1952 Delhi Accord, Sheikh Abdullah had endorsed the Instrument of Accession with India signed by the Maharaja in 1947 to avert forcible annexation by Pakistan. It implied a search for autonomy within India. The Sheikh subsequently wavered and toyed with the idea of an independent Kashmir and was deposed and put under house arrest by the then Prime Minister, Nehru. The Kashmir Accord between the then Prime Minister, Indira Gandhi and Sheikh Abdullah in 1974 signalled the latter's return to power in the State as the Chief Minister replacing a Congress government in the State.The demand of the Sheikh's son and political successor Farooq Abdullah for reversion to 1952, meant reversing the trend of greater integration of the State with the Indian Union. On New Delhi's offer of ''maximum autonomy'', Farooq Abdullah participated in the Assembly elections held in 1996 and won hands down. Panchayat elections held in 2000 witnessed enthusiastic popular participation. Terrorist outfits had given a call for the boycott of all these polls. The Jammu and Kashmir Assembly passed, on 26 June 2000, an autonomy resolution based on the Report of the State Autonomy Committee appointed by the National Conference government in the State. If implemented, Jammu and Kashmir would only remain a confederate State within the Indian Union, with the Center's role limited to defence, external affairs, and communication. This arrangement is reminiscent of the British Cabinet Mission scheme on the eve of India's Independence that was overtaken by the Mountbatten scheme of India's Partition on the pretext of Congress–Muslim League divide. The existing asymmetry in federal relations with this State in contrast to others would be so stretched that the Center would neither appoint a Governor there nor intervene in an emergency under Section 92 of the Constitution of Jammu & Kashmir corresponding to Article 356 of the Indian Constitution. The Governor would be replaced by *Sadr-e-Riyasat,* Head of State, to be elected by the State legislature. The report calls for the repeal of all orders subsequent to the Constitution Application to Jammu and Kashmir Order, 1950. It proposes a new accord between Jammu and Kashmir and the Indian Union "to restore the unconstitutionally eroded autonomy of the State and to remove the debris of the unhappy past and build a new relationship reflecting mutual trust and respect."[30] This Autonomy Resolution was rejected by the NDA government of the then Prime Minister, Vajpayee, on 4 July 2000 as it would "set the clock back and reverse the natural process of harmonizing the aspirations of the people of Jammu and Kashmir with the integrity of the nation".[31] The years since then have witnessed the global anti-terror war in Afghanistan and campaign in the world.

The Election Commission of India conducted a free and fair election to the J&K Assembly under the shadow of continuing cross-border terror strikes from Pakistan and presence of foreign diplomatic and media observers in the autumn of 2002. The ruling J&K National Conference and its ally Bharatiya Janata Party heading the National Democratic Alliance government in New Delhi heavily lost in the State, while the Congress, a new party called Progressive Democratic Party, and Panthers' Party gained ground. A Congress–PDP coalition government headed by the latter took over in October 2002, and by prior agreement Congress took over the chief ministership mid-way through the five-year mandate subsequently.

Following the Lok Sabha elections 2004 and the formation of the Congress-led United Progressive Alliance (UPA) government in New Delhi, the governments of India and Jammu and Kashmir initiated a dialogue with the moderates in the All-Party Hurriyat Conference, and for the first time allowed the Hurriyat leaders to visit Pakistan-occupied Jammu and Kashmir and Pakistan. This could have been a step forward in the then Indo-Pakistan peace process as well as the settlement of the Kashmir dispute. However, the governments of India and Pakistan continued to reiterate their known diplomatic positions, namely, India firmly stating that any more partition of the country is not negotiable, and Pakistan saying that the Line of Control (LoC) in Jammu and

Kashmir would not be acceptable to it as the international border. Nevertheless, a new development in that scenario was the opening of the LoC for bus services between the two parts of Jammu and Kashmir and the process of consultation between the Kashmir separatists and the Governments of India and Pakistan.

In the 2014 general elections, BJP-led NDA led by the Prime Minister, Narendra Modi came to power in New Delhi. In simultaneous Assembly elections in Jammu and Kashmir, there resulted a hung House with the following party position: People's Democratic Party (PDP) 28, BJP 25, National Conference 15, and INC 12, out of a total of 87 seats. An unlikely PDP-BJP coalition government was formed, which prematurely fell in June 2018 after the BJP withdrew its support, complaining lukewarm attitude of its partner in combating terrorism in the State. During the President's/Governor's rule in the State, the Union government, on 5 August 2019, deoperationalized the 'temporary' provision of Article 370 relating to the special status of the State and extended the whole of the Constitution of India to it, so far partly extended, using Clause (3) of the same Article of the Constitution of India that allows the President of India 'by notification' to 'declare that this article shall cease to be operative or shall be operative only with such exceptions and modifications and from such date as he may specify...', with recommendation of the Legislative Assembly of the State. As the powers and functions of the Assembly pass on to the Parliament during President's/Governor's rule, parliamentary approval was also simultaneously obtained. Under Article 3 of the Constitution, the Parliament also reorganized the State into two Union Territories—Jammu and Kashmir, and Ladakh, again Parliament doubling as the surrogate State Assembly and 'consenting' to the change. [Article 3 obliges the Government of India to 'consult' the Assembly; concurrence is not constitutionally mandated.] The critics allege that the move may not be construed to be illegal, but is against constitutional morality and spirit of federalism. A series of petitions are filed in the Supreme Court against the move of the Government of India. Most democratic governments of the world have considered it an internal matter of the Government of India. However, there have been some concerns expressed for complete lockdown of channels of communications and large-scale preventive detention of political leaders and activists that have continued for over 100 days. At this writing (October 2020), communications networks have been freed as also some prominent leaders. The petitions against abrogation of Article 370 are still subjudice in the Supreme court.

LOCAL GOVERNMENT: THE THIRD TIER OF THE FEDERAL STRUCTURE?

The third tier of the multilevel government is the local self-governing institutions in urban and rural areas. Local government is under the jurisdiction of State governments who legislate them into existence. They do not have any direct structural link with the Union government. Any link between the top and the bottom levels of the government are informal. Uneven and in some cases irregular state of affairs at this level prompted the 73rd and 74th constitutional amendments in 1992 for rural and urban areas, respectively. By virtue of these amendments, the Constitution now has a model local government legislation and distribution of responsibilities which the State Legislatures are prompted to adopt and enact (the 11th and 12th Schedules in the Constitution).

Initially, the 73rd amendment did not apply to the Scheduled Tribes Areas in the States of Andhra Pradesh, Madhya Pradesh, Rajasthan, Gujarat, Maharashtra, Himachal Pradesh, Orissa and Bihar. Subsequently, the Parliament legislated in 1996, the Panchayats (Extension to the Scheduled Areas) Act, or the PESA Act, without affecting or contradicting the Fifth Schedule constitutional provisions for the tribal areas in these States. By virtue of the PESA Act, tribal local bodies have been granted considerably vast powers for self-government.

There is generally three-tier structure of local government in rural areas at the village, mandal and district levels. In urban areas, there are municipalities in smaller towns Municipal Corporations in cities. These local bodies are directly elected. In rural areas, Panchayats at the village level are directly elected whereas Mandal Panchayats and Zilla Parishads are composed of the heads of the Panchayat Raj bodies at the next lower level. The structure of local government reflects population diversity in practice. Reserved representation is available for Scheduled Castes and Schedule Tribes proportionate to their population and for women to the extent of 33 per cent by the 73rd Constitutional Amendment Act, 1992. Bihar raised this reserved representation to women in local bodies to 50 per cent, followed by Andhra Pradesh, Chhattisgarh, Jharkhand, Kerala, Maharashtra, Odisha, Rajasthan, Tripura, and Uttarakhand. The Union government also proposed doing it by amending the Constitution, but it is not yet done. The Eleventh Finance Commission for the first time devoted a full chapter on the finances of the local self-governing institutions. Subsequent finance commissions have continued the practice. A new ministry of Panchayat Raj—earlier this department was in the Ministry of Rural Development—has been set up by the UPA Government since 27 May 2004.

Panchayat Raj institutions in their traditional form can be traced back to India's hoary past and in all phases of history. From vedic *Sabhas* and *Samitis* through medieval Panchayats/Sabhas/Urs/ Nagarams as parts of early states in evolution to the statutory local bodies set up in rural and princely India down to the post-Independence period, local political systems have had a chequered history in India. They reappeared in romantic and idealized visions of the village communities in British Indian conservatives like Charles Metcalf and nationalists like Mahatma Gandhi and Jayaprakash Narayan. The Panchayat Raj Institutions in the making of the Constitution and establishing the structure of post-Independence political system did not get a commensurate importance. The statutory Panchayat Raj Institutions set up by various State governments were a far cry from Gandhi's dream of 'Gram Swaraj' and JP's plea for 'Swaraj for the

People.' Even the 73rd and 74th constitutional amendments that have put the local self-governing institutions on the constitutional advisory footing have not substantially lifted them to a stage of functioning to justify such sentiments that extol the Panchayat Raj having graduated "from Legislation to Movement".[32] These dreams and sentiments would materialize only after India's full transition to a bourgeois democratic revolution. In the interim period, a more vigorous plebiscitary political mobilization of the heads of the local councils by the State level and central political elites was witnessed only in the period of over-centralization by the Indira Gandhi and Rajiv Gandhi regimes in the 1970s and 1980s. Notable among these episodes of local assertion of political power were witnessed in the periods of the Janata Party's electoral victory in 1977, the 1987 Panchayat elections in Karnataka during the chief ministership of Ram Krishna Hegde, elections to the local bodies in Orissa in 1992 held by Chief Minister Biju Patnaik, and Panchayat polls in West Bengal in 1993.[33]

ADMINISTRATION

Corresponding with the federal division of legislative and executive responsibilities, there are three broad categories of administration in India. The Union and State governments have their own respective administrative personnel called Central Services and State Services. In addition, Indian Union has a unique cadre of administrative personnel called All-India Services which are recruited by an autonomous constitutional Commission, Union Public Service Commission, trained in central academies of administration and in the field in State governments to which they are permanently allocated with provision for occasional deputations to the Union government.

In fact, senior-most administrative positions in the State as well as Union governments are held by these officers. They work under the disciplinary jurisdiction of whichever level of government they may be serving for at a particular time. In case of ultimate disciplinary measure of suspension and dismissal, a reference to the President, in effect to the Union Home Ministry, is mandatory. The All India Services are a unique feature of the Indian federation not found in any other federal political system in the world.

Administration in both orders of the governments is subject to the political control of the executive. Civil services can offer whatever advice they consider appropriate, but once a policy decision is made by the political executive, administration is duty-bound to carry it out. The relationship between the administration and legislature is not direct. It is intermediated through Ministers.

PARTY SYSTEM AND COALITION GOVERNMENTS

Besides the structure of the Constitution, the working of the legislative and executive government in the Indian federation is significantly influenced by the nature of the electoral system, party system, and judicial behaviour.

Contrary to the Duverger–Riker hypothesis about the plurality electoral system giving rise to two-party systems,[34] the Indian experience suggests that this kind of electoral law in a socially and regionally diverse federal system leads to fragmentation of the party system, ultimately leading to a multi-partisan configuration. The Duverger–Riker hypothesis is valid only for countries that are endowed with a relatively homogeneous political culture, e.g. the United Kingdom and Australia among parliamentary federal systems and the United States as a presidential federal system. Besides India, Canada occasionally emerges as another counter example of the Duverger-Riker hypothesis. Canada and India both historically developed phases of one-party dominant systems at the national level but subsequently turned into two-party plus a third minor party system and occasionally a multi-party system with increasing politicization and assertion of regional and ethnic identities. Thus, in these two cases, the effects of proportional representation are seen even under plurality electoral system due to the complicating 'third' factor of social and regional diversities, in the bivariate relationship between the system of representation and the party system. It is widely accepted that proportional representation leads to a multi-party system as in most continental European countries and Israel and belatedly New Zealand.

Party system is perhaps the most important intervening variable that significantly influences the working of a federal political system. As mentioned earlier, India began with a one-party dominant system, and since 1989 it has been a multi-party system. The centralized phase of Indian federation that spanned the Nehru and Indira Gandhi phases, by and large, was associated with one-party Congress dominance. This feature of the party system was clearly reflected in the working of all organs of the government. After an initial dispute about the interpretation of the powers of the President raised by Dr. Rajendra Prasad, the first President of India, the question was settled in favour of a nominal head of the State in the British parliamentary tradition. The Cabinet during this phase started with Nehru–Patel duumvirate but after Patel's death in December 1950, the Cabinet system virtually turned into a 'prime ministerial' system under Nehru. One-party control of the Parliament facilitated the emergence of a strong prime ministerial Cabinet. Autonomy of the federating States was somewhat overshadowed by the rule of the same party in New Delhi as well as in practically all States, yet State governments were not as powerless as they were to become later under Indira Gandhi. During the Indira Gandhi regime that followed after a brief interlude under Prime Minister Lal Bahadur Shastri, the political system became considerably less democratic and more centralized than in the past. The one-party control of the Parliament, Prime Ministerial domination of the Cabinet system, and Central hegemony over Congress-ruled State governments in particular, and Opposition-ruled State governments in general became further accentuated during this phase. Central intervention in State governments under Article 356 was frequently resorted to topple Opposition governments in States.

This overly centralized Union government was challenged by an extra-parliamentary mass movement, popularly called the Jayaprakash Narayan (JP) Movement, on the issues of authoritarianism and corruption in the Congress governments. This confrontation led directly to the imposition of internal Emergency by the then Prime Minister, Indira Gandhi and a wholesale arrest of the Opposition leaders. The 1977 elections routed the Emergency regime and voted the newly formed Janata Party to power in New Delhi and major North-Indian States. The Janata Party interlude of nearly two-and-a-half years was followed by the restoration of the Congress Party led by Indira Gandhi in 1980. After her assassination in 1984, she was succeeded by her son, Rajiv Gandhi. During this phase, the functioning of institutions came again to be marked by centralization, though somewhat lesser in degree than in the 1970s. For, several State governments during this phase were controlled by non-Congress parties. Indira Gandhi too was somewhat chastened by the Emergency imbroglio. The Rajiv Gandhi government in particular, brought a somewhat fresh approach to the problems, especially in relation to non-Congress States that were marked by agitational movements. He signed a series of peace accords with major regional parties in Punjab, Assam, Mizoram, and Tripura. Rajiv Gandhi also built bridges of understanding with the National Conference leader, and subsequently Chief Minister, Farooq Abdullah of Jammu and Kashmir.

A qualitatively new phase in Indian politics was ushered in with the advent of the multi-party system in 1989 elections which has continued ever since until Prime Minister Narendra Modi-led BJP/NDA coalition government since 2014, re-elected in 2019. With no clear majority for any one party during this phase, the coalition and minority Governments have been the rule, with decisive role played by some major regional parties. This complex set of changes has brought about a sea change in the political system. The prime ministerial system has dissolved into a kind of Cabinet system that has gone beyond recognition in comparison to the classical Westminster system based on collective responsibility of the Cabinet to the popular Chamber of the Parliament. The Indian Cabinet system today is in reality fragmented into segments nominated and controlled by participating parties, some of which led by powerful Chief Ministers. Legally, the Prime Minister is still the king-pin of the system in the sense that the ultimate power rests in his/her hands. But the Ministers are imposed upon him by coalition partners and withdrawn from his Cabinet sometimes against his will. Thus, the principle of collective responsibility is considerably strained which goes beyond the Parliament to the party bosses and the Chief Ministers. This is perhaps inevitable in a federal coalition Cabinet, but it is something alien to the Westminster system.

With the decline of prime ministerial power in coalition governments, the Presidential role has acquired some more elbow room, though this does not really amount to an independent role for the President. However, the recent Presidents have shown greater initiative and drive under coalition situations, particularly in formation of Governments and dissolution of the Lok Sabha in cases of uncertain majorities, than in the past. The phase of coalition and minority Governments have also increased the autonomy of the Parliament as well as that of State Governments than was ever the case under one-party majority Governments. It must be noted that under Prime Minister Modi, prime-minister-dominated cabinets are back, ending the vagaries of chaotic federal coalition governments.

RAJYA SABHA

The role of the Rajya Sabha as a federal Second Chamber was not found to be particularly notable by Morris-Jones in his classic study of the Indian Parliament in the 1950s. In his assessment, it was no more likely to be a forum for articulation of States' rights any more than the Lok Sabha. Both the Houses were more or less similar in terms of party affiliation and socio-economic background of members as well as in terms of style and standard of debate. However, with the transformation of the party system by the 1990s, the Rajya Sabha has emerged as a *federal* Second Chamber as it reflects a different party configuration than that of the Lok Sabha. The differential oppositional majority in the Rajya Sabha is attributable to a different party system configuration in the States whose legislatures form the electoral college for the federal Second Chamber. Thus, the governmental majority in the Lok Sabha now must make inter-house legislative understandings with the Rajya Sabha to facilitate passage of legislations and constitutional amendments.

A deadlock between the two Houses of Parliament is resolved only at a joint session. In a joint session, the Lok Sabha with its larger number is more likely than not to emerge successful. But no Government would like to make the joint session a regular feature of the parliamentary process. This is evident by the fact that joint sessions have so far been convened only four times (the latest being on Women Reservation Bill, 2008). Only three such Bills were passed, barring the fourth one mentioned here. A constitutional amendment in any case can be effectively blocked by the Rajya Sabha. Because the Constitution is silent on calling a joint session for this purpose. Federal representative character of the Rajya Sabha is clearly reflected in the fact that among the elected Rajya Sabha members between 1952and 2002, 59 per cent of the incumbents before their election to the House were active in State politics.

Since the 1989 general elections to date (mid-October 2020), none of the ruling coalition governments, including the Modi-led NDA coalition government with BJP de fact majority in the Lok Sabha between 2014 and 2019 and re-elected in 2019 with more sizeable majority both for the BJP and the NDA, has enjoyed a majority in the federal second chamber, the Rajya Sabha. This has enhanced the federal role and relevance of the Rajya Sabha, to the chagrin of the ruling coalitions led alternately by the Janata Dal, INC, and BJP alike.

JUDICIAL INTERPRETATION

In addition to the electoral and party systems, judicial behaviour is another important factor that affects the working of the legislative and executive governance in the Indian federation. Despite its common integrated structure, courts have generally been protective of the federal structure of the Constitution, especially in more recent decades. The courts have done this at least in four ways. First, as early as in *Hargovind Pant* v. *Raghukul Tilak and others* (1979)[35], the Supreme Court gave an essentially federal, as distinguished from central, interpretation of the role of the Governor. It observed, the Governor's "is an independent constitutional office which is not subject to the control of the Government of India". Second, in *S.R. Bommai and others* v. *Union of India and others* (1994), the Supreme Court reversed its earlier decisions in a number of cases previously decided wherein it had consistently maintained that the determination under Article 356 of the Constitution whether a constitutional machinery in a State had broken down or not was a "political thicket" best left in the hands of the Union executive. The Court now maintained that the satisfaction of the President in the matter was "subjective" but "not entirely absolute" and must be exercised on some palpable material or evidence in the public domain. The Court thus made this power of the Union executive subject to judicial review for the first time. This considerably reduced the greatest threat to the autonomy of State Governments from the arbitrary exercise of the executive power of the Union. Third, in the foregoing judgement as well as in *Keshavananda Bharti* v. *Union of India* (1973)[36] and *Minerva Mills* v. *Union of India* (1980),[37] the Supreme Court established the doctrine of the unamendability of the 'basic structure' of the Constitution, of which federalism is illustratively declared to be a part. Fourth, the Supreme Court in settling union-state legislative jurisdictional disputes over the years has acted in even-handed way, never leaning evidently this way or that way. Typical of the court's adjudication in this regard is its judgement in the *State of West Bengal* v. *Kesoram Industries Ltd.* (2004).[38] This case was related to constitutional allocation of legislative and taxation powers between the union and the states as regards coal, tea, brick-field, and minor minerals in which entries in the State List are subject to Union's power to regulation and development in public or national interest. The court prescribed the norm of accommodation of competing legislative and taxing claims of both orders of governments as far as possible. It ruled that "the Union's power to regulate and control does not result in depriving the states of their power to levy tax or fee within their legislative competence without trenching upon the field of regulation and control."[39]

During the Modi-led BJP-NDA coalition government since 2014, the Supreme Court twice declared Central interventions in 2016 in Congress-ruled Uttarakhand and Congress-ruled Arunachal Pradesh as unconstitutional and restored the dismissed governments to office in both the States.

PROSPECTS

The trend of greater federalization of the political system has continued at the turn of the century. The 2004 Lok Sabha elections again produced a hung Parliament. The National Democratic Alliance (NDA) lost power to the United Progressive Alliance (UPA). Left-of-center coalition thus replaced the erstwhile right-of-center coalition. More recent experience suggested that coalition politics was coming of age. This was reflected in greater stability of NDA Government that managed to complete its full mandate, and so did the UPA Government that was in fact re-elected in 2009. This was incidentally the first incumbent Union government to be voted back to power.

In 2014 general elections, Narendra Modi-led BJP-NDA marked a turning point in the sense that it won a single-party majority for the BJP after a gap of three long decades after the 1984 general elections in which the Congress under Rajiv Gandhi had last won such an electoral success. BJP still decided to continue the tradition of federal coalition governments since 1989 via the NDA. The BJP led by Modi was re-elected in the 2019 general elections with even a greater margin of victory both for itself as well as its NDA coalition. During Modi's two terms, a trend towards centralization has been witnessed. However, regional parties in Tamil Nadu, Andhra Pradesh, Kerala, West Bengal, and Odisha have continued to hold their forts. Moreover, more recent assembly elections in Punjab, Rajasthan, Madhya Pradesh, and Chhattisgarh have seen the Congress bounce back to power. In the 2019 assembly elections in Maharashtra and Haryana too, the regional parties have gained some ground. So, the trend of greater federalization, even though a bit under pressure, continues.

Neo-liberal economic reforms stepped up in 1991 have brought about a somewhat new feature in autonomous regulatory agencies set up under parliamentary Acts, some with semi-judicial powers. This is not an entirely new phenomenon, in fact, such agencies have existed in limited numbers even in the past. What is new is that their number has multiplied. This may be called the accentuated phenomenon of "sectoral federalism".[40] The examples of such agencies are Central Telecom Regulatory Authority, Central Electricity Regulatory Authority, Central Insurance Regulatory Authority, Competition Commission, SEBI etc. Despite being set up under parliamentary Acts, their activities vitally affect the working of the federal as well as State Governments.

In addition, supra-national regional economic integration in South Asia has gathered new momentum since the SAARC Islamabad Summit in January 2004. There is some progress in free trade agreements, there is also some talk at unofficial levels about South Asian currency. Although political integration at this stage appears to be far-fetched, if the progress at the economic level is substantial, in due course, political federalization in South Asia beyond the nation-States could also become a reality. However, with the abrasive rise of China more recently and its efforts to encircle India by bringing countries contiguous to India in its economic and political networks, the prospects of South Asian regional integration have suffered a serious setback.

REFORMIST DISCOURSE FOR A BETTER FEDERAL POLITICAL EQUILIBRIUM

Since the 1980s, three major constitutional commissions have reviewed the federal structure and its functioning, two exclusively dealing with Center-State relations and one broadly with the working of the Constitution in general: the Sarkaria Commission (1987–88), NCRWC (2002) and Punchhi Commission (2010). In this discussion, we will focus on the major recommendations of these three panels in relation to the political-institutional architecture and their normative operative norms only, as their recommendations relating to the other aspects have already been mentioned here and there in the foregoing parts of this chapter and in other chapters.

The basic approach of the Sarkaria Commission was to go for limited constitutional amendments for institutional restructuring of any magnitude and rely primarily on attitudinal and behavioural reorientation and changes on the part of the federal functionaries. It aimed at the transformation of elite political culture such that the Union Government and the governors would be respectful of norms of the Constitution and develop constitutional conventions consistent with these federal constitutional values. It laid down certain guidelines with suggested priorities to be followed by governors in formation of the government in case of a hung assembly and in recommendation to the Center for dismissal of a State Government and dissolution of an assembly. The crux of this idea was to go by the floor test in the House rather than backroom dealings. The Commission intended to enable the Rajya Sabha to play a stronger role as a federal second chamber in exercising the special powers such as allowing the Parliament to provisionally legislate on a state subject or in legislating the creation of a new All India Service but in doing so, it rejected the idea of giving equal representation to the states in the Rajya Sabha so as to give weightage to the smaller states. It hoped that the Rajya Sabha can empower itself as a federal second chamber in the use of its special powers by changing the rules of business of the House such that the smaller and concerned states in such matters would be given a special voice by a consensus in the House. Some minor constitutional changes that the Sarkaria Commission recommended, related to establishing the Inter State Council (ISC) under Article 263 of the Constitution, entrenching the Planning Commission as a constitutional body and making the Finance Commission a permanent constitutional agency. In doing so, the Commission apparently hoped that along with some pre-existing federal constitutional instrumentalities like Public Service Commissions, the CAG, the Attorney General of India etc., the Finance Commission and Planning Commission would act as a series of points of federal autonomy in the system. None of these constitutional amendments excepting the establishment of the ISC has been implemented by the government. But all Prime Ministers continue to use the ISC sparingly and in fact leave it neglected.

The NCRWC went for more far-reaching institutional restructuring than the Sarkaria panel. After reiterating the points made by the Sarkaria Commission, regarding activating the ISC and suggesting constitutionally consistent role of the Center and the State Governments, the NCRWC recommended two major political institutional reforms. The first was the idea of amending the Constitution to establish a National Judicial Commission for the empanelment of nominees for appointment as judges to the Supreme Court and High Courts and for the oversight of their conduct. The Commission would comprise the Chief Justice of the Supreme Court as its Chairperson along with two other senior most judges, the Union Minister of Law and Justice and one eminent person to be nominated by the President of India. Another major institutional reforms recommended by the NCRWC is enactment of a comprehensive law regulating the structure and functioning of political parties in a democratic way with transparent and publicly audited accounts. Besides, this Commission also prompts political parties to adopt on their own the system of national convention of party delegates to elect the leaders to lead them in elections and the parliament/state legislatures as in Canada.

The Punchhi Commission (2010) again reiterates the points made earlier by the previous two commissions such as two minor constitutional amendments and development of federally consistent conventions constitutional amendments and development of federally consistent conventions. It also makes clear that the existing constitutional provisions like Entry II A in the union list inserted by the 42nd constitutional amendment in 1976 making the deployment of the armed forces and police forces in a state in aid of civil power in a state allows the resort of "local emergency" without the invocation of constitutional emergency in a state under Article 356. The two major constitutional amendments relate to the federal second chamber and the dealing with terrorism. In an "out-of-box" thinking, it recommends equal representation to states in the Rajya Sabha to bring about a federal balance in favour of smaller states who are doubly handicapped in both the houses of Parliament on account of population-size of a state used to give them representation. The Commission is also highly critical of the constitutional amendment abolishing the domiciliary requirement for Rajya Sabha members in the states from which they are elected. It is predictably equally critical of the Supreme Court judgement validating this amendment in the Kuldip Nayar case decided by the Supreme Court in 2006 validating the domiciliary requirement for the candidates seeking election to the Rajya Sabha from a state. Another major institutional innovation recommended by this Commission is the establishment of a National Counter Terrorism Center (NCTC) in the union ministry of Home Affairs subsuming existing intelligence and investigative agencies including the newly established National Investigative Agency (NIA) to deal with all kinds of crimes including terrorist violence.

This review of the reformist discourse for a better federal equilibrium is constrained to conclude on a note of lament on account of a serious gap between the intention of the government to set up constitutional review commissions and their intention to implement the recommendations made by such commissions. Rare is a recommendation of these Constitutional

Commissions ever implemented by any government of India of any party or coalition of parties. Reforms, any, have mostly come by judicial interventions or under pressure of extra-parliamentary movements.

REFERENCES

1. M.P. Singh, "From Hegemony to Multi-Level Federalism? India's Parliamentary-Federal System", *The Indian Journal of Social Science*, Vol. 5, No. **3**, July–September 1992, Rekha Saxena, "Reframing Continuity" (Conversation with Douglas Verney), *The Pioneer,* New Delhi, 5 April 2001.
2. K.C. Wheare, *Federal Government,* Oxford University Press, New York, 1964, Fourth edition.
3. M.P. Singh, "From Hegemony to Multi-Level Federatism? India's Parliamentary Federal System," *Indian Journal of Social Science,* Vol. 5, No. **3**, July–September, 1992 and M.P. Singh and Rekha Saxena, *India at the Polls: Parliamentary Elections in the Federal Phase,* Orient Longman, Delhi, 2003. Also see Rajeev Dhavan and Rekha Saxena, "Republic of India", *A Global Dialogue on Federalism: Legislative, Executive, and Judicial Governance in Federal Countries,* Katy Le Roy and Cheryl Saunders (Eds.), Vol. 3, McGill–Queen's University Press, Quebec, 2006; Balveer Arora, K. K. Kailash, Rekha Saxena and H. K. Suan, "Indian Federalism" in K.C Suri (Ed.), *Indian Democracy*, ICSSR Survey Research, OUP, New Delhi, 2013.
4. Douglas Verney, 'From Quasi-Federation to Quasi-Confederacy? The Transformation of India's Party System," *Publius,* Vol. 33, No. **4**, Fall 2003, p. 171. Also see Lawrence Saez, *Federations Without a Centre*: *The Impact of Political And Economic Reform on India's Federal System,* Sage, New Delhi, 2002.
5. Wheare, *op. cit.,* pp. 26–28.
6. M.P. Singh, "*Borderless Internal Federal Space? Reorganization of States in India*", India Review, Vol. 6, No.**4**, October–December 2007, pp. 233–250; Rekha Saxena, "The Problems of Statehood in Indian Federalism: A Case for Territorial Pluralism", in Harihar Bhattacharyya and Lion Koenig (Eds.), *Globalization and Governance in India: New Challenges to Society and Institution*, Routledge, London and New York London and New York, 2015.
7. Ajay Kumar Singh, "Federalism and State Formation: An Appraisal of Indian Practice" in B.D. Dua and M.P. Singh (Eds.), *Indian Federalism in the New Millenium,* Manohar, New Delhi, 2003. See also

A.S. Narang, *Ethnic Identities and Federalism,* Indian Institute of Advanced Studies, Shimla, 1995.

8. For a review of this debate in comparative federal theory, see Louise Tillin, "*Unity in Diversity? Asymmetry in Indian Federalism*", Publius: The Journal of Federalism, Vol. 37,No. **1**, winter 2007, pp. 1–25; Rekha Saxena,"Is India A Case of Asymmetrical Federalism*?", Economic and Political Weekly,* January 14, 2012 and Rekha Saxena, "Asymmetrical Federalism in India: Promoting Secession or Accommodating Diversity?" in *Revisiting Unity and Diversity in Federal Countries: Changing Concepts, Reform Proposals and New Institutional Realities*, Alain-G. Gagnon and Michael Burgess Brill Nijhoff (Eds.), 2018.

9. Louise Tillin, *Ibid.* pp. 58-61.

10. *Ibid.*, pp. 52–58.

11. *Ibid.*, p. 62.

12. M.P. Singh, "Federal Division of Responsibilities in India", *Indian Journal of Federal Studies,* Vol. 1, January 2004, pp. 109–11. See also Akhtar Majeed (Ed.), *Federalism Within the Union: Distribution of Responsibilities in the Indian System,* Manak, New Delhi, 2004.

13. Commission on Centre-State Relations *Report*, Part I, Government of India Press, Nasik, 1988, Chapter 5. Chair: Justice R.S. Sarkaria.

14. See Rekha Saxena, "Supranational Intergovernmental Relations and Role of Judiciary" in B.D. Dua, M.P. Singh and Rekha Saxena (Eds.). *Judiciary and Politics: The Changing Landscape,* Manohar, New Delhi, 2007. On the treaty-making power of the Union Government, see also Rekha Saxena, "Treaty-Making Power: A Case for Federalization and Parliamentarization, *Economic and Political Weekly,* Vol. XLII, No. **1**, January 6, 2007.

15. *S.R. Bommai & others* v. *Union of India*, Supreme Court Cases, *Judgements Today,* 1994.

16. V. Sridhar, "Short-Changing the States", *Frontline*, 8 April 2005, pp. 34–35. For more details on fiscal federalism, see M. Govinda Rao and Nirvikar Singh, *Political Economy of Federalism in India*, Oxford University Press, New Delhi, 2005.

17. India (Republic), *Report of the Thirteenth Finance Commission*, 2010–2015. New Delhi: Akalank Publications, March 2010, p. 27.

18. *Ibid.,* p. 117.

19. *Ibid.,* p. 122.

20. *Ibid.,* p. 93.

21. M. Govinda Rao and Nirvikar Singh, Political Economy of Federalism in India, New Delhi: Oxford University Press, 2005, pp. 173–75.

22. Hemlata Rao, Fiscal Federalism: Issues and Policies, New Delhi: New Century Publications, 2006, pp. 34–35.

23. Government of India (Republic), Report of the Thirteenth Finance Commission, 2010–2015, *op. cit.*, p. 122.

24. Fourteenth Finance Commission Report htprs://www.prs.india.org Accessed on 12 November 2019.

25. Rekha Saxena, *Situating Federalism: Mechanisms of Intergovernmental Relations in Canada and India*, Manohar, New Delhi, 2006. Much of this section draws on this first book-length work on intergovernmental relations in India. Also see, Rekha Saxena, "Intergovernmental Relations in India", in Meghna Sabharwal and Evan M. Berman (Eds.), *Public Administration in South Asia: India, Bangladesh, and Pakistan,* CRC Press, Taylor and Francis Group, New York and London, 2013; M.P Singh and Rekha Saxena "Intergovernmental Relations in India" in Johanne Poirier, Cheryl Saunders, and John Kincaid (Eds.), *Intergovernmental Relations in Federal Systems,* OUP, Toronto, 2015; and Swenden, Wilfried and Rekha Saxena, "Rethinking Central Planning: A Federal Critique of the Planning Commission", *India Review*, Vol. 16, Issue **1**: Continuity and Change in Contemporary Indian Federalism, 2017, pp. 42–65.

26. UPA, *Common Minimum Programme of the United Progressive Alliance,* 27 May, New Delhi, 2004, p. 14.

27. Commission on Centre-State Relations, *The Report,* pts. I and II, Vol. I. Government of India Press, Nasik, 1987–88. Chair: Justice R.S. Sarkaria.

28. The texts of these accords are compiled in P.S. Datta, *Ethnic Peace Accords in India,* Vikas, Delhi, 1995. In a related development, substate regional movements led to the creation of three new States in 2000: Chhattisgarh, Jharkhand and Uttarakhand.

29. For the political situation in Punjab preceding this accord, see Robin Jeffrey, *What's Happening to India? Punjab, Ethnic Conflict, Mrs. Gandhi's Death and the Test for Federalism,* Holmes & Meir, New York, 1986, Chapters 2 and 3.

30. *Asian News Digest,* No. 1, 8–14 July 2000, pp. 435–36.

31. *Ibid.*, pp. 450–51.

32. George Mathew, *Panchayati Raj: From Legislation to Movement*, Concept Publishing Company, New Delhi, 1994 and "From Culture to Constitution" in Manoj Rai, *et al.* (Eds.), *The State of Panchayats: A Participatory Perspective,* Sanskriti, New Delhi, 2001.

33. *Ibid.*

34. Bernard Grofman and Arendt Leijphart (Eds.), *Electoral Laws and their Political Consequences,* Agathon Press, New York, 1986.

35. *Hargovind Pant* v. *Raghukul Tilak*, *AIR*, 1979, Supreme Court.

36. *Keshavananda Bharati* v. *State of Kerala*, *AIR,* 1973, Supreme Court.

37. *Minerva Mills Ltd.* v. *Union of India*, *AIR*, 1980, Supreme Court.

38. *Kesoram Industries* v. *State of West Bengal*, 2004.

39. For a detailed discussion on this theme see Rekha Saxena and M.P. Singh, "Role of Judiciary in Federalization of the Indian Polity", Jan Erk and Wilfried Swenden (Eds.), *New Directions in Federation Studies*, Routledge, London, 2010, Chapter 4; Manish Tewari and Rekha Saxena, "The Rise of Judicial Power and The Protection of Federalism", in Nicholas Aroney and John Kincaid (Eds.), *The Supreme Court Of India: Courts In Federal Countries: Federalists Or Unitarists?* University Of Toronto Press, Toronto, 2017; and Rekha Saxena and Wilfried Swenden, "The Indian Supreme Court and Federalism", *Federalism and Regionalism,*Vol. 17, 2017.

40. M.P. Singh, "The Impact of Global and Regional Integration on Indian Parliamentary Federal System". B.D. Dua and M.P. Singh (Eds.), *Indian Federalism in the New Millennium,* Manohar, New Delhi, 2003, pp. 379–435; and M.P. Singh and Rekha Saxena, *Federalizing Indian Politics in the Era of Globalization,* Primus Books, Delhi, 2013.

Chapter 8

State Governments and Regional Politics

INTRODUCTION

India is a Union of 28 States, eight Union Territories (UTs), including one of these UTs serving as the national capital territory of Delhi . Unlike the United States of America where federal and State Constitutions and citizenships are dual, the Republic of India is founded on a single Constitution and a unitary citizenship. One exception to this general pattern of symmetrical federalism was the State of Jammu and Kashmir, which until August 2019 had a subnational Constitution of its own largely conforming to the Constitution of India with a "Temporary Special Status" under Article 370, which now stands deoperationalized. It has also been reorganized into two UTs of Jammu and Kashmir and Ladakh. Some asymmetrical federal features relating to some other tribally predominant states in the Northeast and inlands, including the States of Nagaland and Mizoram, under the Fifth and Sixth Schedules of the Constitution are still there in the federal Constitution. By and large, both the Union and State governments function under a uniform Constitution that envisages representative and responsible governments at Union and State levels, and now, since the 73rd and 74th constitutional amendments (1992), at the local level as model Acts prompting state legislatures to adopt them as local government is a State List subject.

The structures of governments at Union and State levels are basically based on the parliamentary principle of government within a federal pattern of relationship among governments at various levels. The governance at the local rural and urban levels is also informed by parliamentary principle of responsible government, but this level is related to the State government on the principle of devolution rather than federalism.

Myron Weiner has aptly pointed out that since the Indian States are generally so large as to be comparable with several European nation-states, and since all work under the same constitutional provisions with varying patterns of politics, they offer a rare opportunity of comparisons in terms of their political and economic performance almost like a quasi-experimental research design.[1] Thus, if some States are politically more stable and others unstable or more vulnerable to central intervention, or if some States economically perform better and others fair badly, these differentials cannot be attributed to different systems of laws and Constitutions. They must be explained in terms of sociological and political factors or good or bad leaderships.

Social Science research on India after Independence initially tended to be almost entirely focused on national or federal politics. The studies of State politics were a late starter. The first notable works on politics in Indian States appeared in the late 1960s.[2] This initial spurt was subsequently dampened by the trend of over-centralization of politics in India during the heyday of Prime Minister Indira Gandhi in the 1970s in the first post-Nehru decade. The decentralizing tendencies unleashed in the wake of the demise of Jawaharlal Nehru in 1964 and by the Fourth General Elections were impeded by the 1969 Congress split and the rise of Indira Gandhi to political supremacy in the newly elected Congress party and government in 1971.[3] A survey of literature would show a sharp decline in scholarly interest in federalism as well as in State politics thereafter. Unprecedented "nationalization" of politics and concentration of political power in the Parliament and ultimately the Prime Minister were obviously the reasons. A concomitant centralizing political factor appeared in the form of a massive extra-parliamentary protest movement led by Morarji Desai in Gujarat and Jayaprakash Narayan (JP) all over north India. Indira Gandhi and JP were suddenly thrown up as the new charismatic mass leaders whose popularity transcended State boundaries. The tendency of regionalization and localization of State politics was thus checkmated. All that really mattered was national politics rather than State politics.

The second major spurt in the rise of politics of regionalism and emergence of States as more autonomous domains of politics followed in the wake of the post-Emergency Lok Sabha and Assembly elections in 1977 and in the decade that followed. In State after State, non-Congress governments came to be formed confronting the Congress government at the Centre; some of these were formed by resurgent old regional parties, for example,the Tamil parties such as Dravida Munnetra Kazhagam (DMK) and All India Anna Dravida Munnetra Kazhagam (AIADMK), J&K National Conference, and Shiromani Akali Dal (SAD), and others by new regional parties such as the Telugu Desam Party (TDP), Asom Gana Parishad (AGP), and others. State politics since then has never looked back. If anything, by the 1990s the formation of minority and/or coalition governments in New Delhi by fragmented and diminished national parties and reinvigorated regional parties "captured" Delhi, in a manner of saying. The new political scenario and the rise of State politics to an unprecedented level is suggested by titles of some studies of the period like *Federalism without a Centre* (Lawrence Saez) and "India from Quasi-Federation to Quasi-Confederation" (Douglas Verney).[4]

A sort of turning point came in the general elections of 2014 when the Narendra Modi-led Bharatiya Janata Party (BJP) and the National Democratic Alliance (NDA) won the first single-party majority for BJP after three decades since 1984, even though the tradition of federal coalition governments since 1989 was continued. It was re-elected with a larger such majority for BJP and its allies in the NDA in 2019. The BJP tended to acquire an aura reminiscent of the Congress party's predominance of the past decades. However, regional parties in the South and the East continued to hold their grounds in the face of expanding BJP across the board to an extent.

GEOGRAPHICAL, CULTURAL, AND POLITICAL REGIONS

Geographers divide India into four major physical regions: the Himalayas, the Northern Plains, the Deccan peninsula, and Oceanic islands.[5] In the opinion of a geographer, sub-regions and States are nestled into the first-order physical regions identified above on the basis of their "mutual dependence" and constitutional recognition. "Rising regional consciousness and cultural revival act as centrifugal forces, while economic forces in the form of railways, roads and now airways, industrial expansion, irrigation, power projects and population migration movements induce centripetal tendencies. Both these forces need a thorough understanding for the purposes of the right-ordering of regional as well as national loyalties. For, the cultural unity of the nation cannot be taken for granted politically."[6]

Political scientist Rajendra Vora and humanist Anne Feldhaus[7] trace the evolution of regionalism in India since Independence through three phases: (1) from 1947 to the early 1970s, (2) from the early 1970s to the early 1990s, and (3) from the early 1990s to the present. In the first phase, both the nationalist and the regionalist elites were tempered by the partition of the country. The former resisted all regionalist demands for creation of new regional States within the federal Constitution of India and the latter desisted from separatism (barring briefly Dravidian, rather Tamil, separatism).

The second phase coinciding with the Congress regimes of Indira and Rajiv Gandhi, especially the former in the 1970s, sought to impose national unity from above by over-centralization of power in a prime ministerial system (as distinguished from the collective Cabinet system). This centralizing drive provoked regional autonomy movements by the end of the seventies and the early 1980s in Assam and Punjab, fuelled also by local linguistic and religious tensions and conflicts. In the first half of the 1980s, Indira Gandhi made peace with some regional parties by offering them freer hand in State politics in bargain for their political support at the Centre and using police and military forces against separatism in some other States. In the second half of the 1980s, Rajiv Gandhi accommodated moderate regional parties by signing ethnic/regional accords in Assam, Mizoram, Tripura, and Punjab.

In the third phase since the 1990s, Indian national politics has itself become considerably regionalized by the formation of federal coalition governments with direct representation of powerful regional parties. As a result, "the militancy of regionalism has died down".[8] As the Vora–Feldhaus volume suggests, linguistic, religious, other ethnic factors as well as urban identities and interests are the major ingredients of regionalism in Indian politics.

In much of the literature on Indian politics, the term "regional politics" is often used synonymously with State politics. This is probably for the reason that most Indian States by the end of the 1970s were reorganized along linguistic lines, some along tribal lines as well, mainly in the North-East. Neither physical geography nor linguistic homogeneity are, however, determinants of political macro-regions in India. For example, geographically demarcated Zonal Councils set up since the mid-1950s have been practically defunct. Moreover, there are no regular political forums of either four South Indian States or 10 Hindi-speaking States, respectively. In the political sense, therefore, the North-East appears to be the only institutionalized region in the country formalized through the regularly meeting North-Eastern Council, representing the executive heads of all seven/eight federating units. In other instances, Chief Ministers of non-Congress States of South in the 1980s and Congress or BJP-ruled States in the 2000s occasionally met in conclaves convened by their central party leaders. But these meetings are held only occasionally and are basically motivated by party rather than regional identifications. This trend more or less continues until this writing (October 2020).

A recurrent refrain of writings on Indian politics since the 1990s is that politics has now become regionalized as against the nationalist temper and tenor of earlier decades of the predominance of the Congress party. In an attempt to explicate the meaning of the term "regionalization", also called "federalization" by others (notably and firstly the authors of this book), Suhas Palshikar refers to five referents of this concept: (i) political issues becoming region-specific; (ii) leadership becoming regionally structured or ratified; (iii) State or region specific political support base of some or most political parties; and (iv) political choices of the voters becoming limited to State or regional political theatres from the previously all-India political theatre. He also goes on to say that the term may refer "to a wide range of territorial configurations: a locality, a sub-region, a State, a supra-State region, etc."[9]

STATE GOVERNMENT STRUCTURES AND POLITICAL PARTIES

Constitutionally, the structure of the State governments is broadly similar to that at the Union level. Thus, all the three organs of government—legislature, executive and judiciary—are replicated in the States. In functional terms also, the principle of representative and responsible government umpired by the judiciary is supposed to operate on parliamentary lines along with federal linkages between the two orders of governments under the Constitution. There are some differences as well, however. For one thing, the parliamentary principle of government at the State level is carried on under a centrally appointed Governor who has an important supervisory role as a national observer in normal times, and who becomes the chief executive during the period of constitutional emergency under Article 356 of the Constitution.

The Constituent Assembly debates suggested a choice between three models of the head of the provincial State, namely, a Governor directly elected by the people of the State; a Governor elected by the State legislature; and a Governor appointed by the Union government. The first two models were rejected on the ground that a directly elected Governor would be incompatible with the parliamentary principle of government inasmuch as such a functionary would become an independent centre of power vis-a-vis the Chief Minister. A legislatively elected Governor was also ruled out because this would be incompatible with the federal principle inasmuch as such an incumbent could not serve as a viable link between the Union and State governments.[10] Finally, the Constituent Assembly settled for the idea of a centrally-appointed Governor who, in normal circumstances, would be bound by the advice of the Chief Minister and his Cabinet collectively enjoying the confidence of the majority party or coalition in the State Assembly. Thus, the Chief Minister and the Cabinet were constitutionally mandated to be the chief executive of the State government except during periods of constitutional emergency. The Constitution thus visualizes a double-headed executive in the Governor and the Chief Minister, formally similar to that at the Centre with the President and the Prime Minister. In normal times, the real executive power of the State government is exercised by the Chief Minister and his Cabinet who are supposed to work under the "pleasure" of the Governor, but this pleasure is dependent on the confidence of the House. Normally, when the confidence of the legislative Assembly is lost by the Chief Minister and the Cabinet, the pleasure of the Governor could be withdrawn. Only during constitutionally contemplated emergency in a State, the pleasure of the Governor is not bound by the confidence of the non-existent House, which, during an emergency, may be either dissolved or kept in suspended animation. In such an eventuality, the Governor becomes directly answerable to the Union government. It is in this way that the Governor is supposed to serve both as the agent of the Centre and the agent of the State government. This aspect of the State government has already been discussed in Chapter 7 on federalism in this book. (For more details, both the chapters should be read together.)

The political executive at the State level has undergone significant changes since the commencement of the Constitution. During the period of one-party dominance at Union as well as State levels, there were at least two phases typical of the Nehru era and the Indira Gandhi era (during her ascendancy in the 1970s only). In the Nehru era, the structure of power in the political system was at least pluralist, if not entirely federal in substance due to one-party

Congress predominance, though it was in a formal way. Emerging from the freedom struggle, both the national and State government leaders of the Indian National Congress had a good measure of autonomy from each other for two reasons. Firstly, they had fought shoulder to shoulder during the nationalist movement and had mutual respect for each other as well as some autonomous basis of power at their respective levels. The stalwart Chief Ministers like B.C. Roy (West Bengal), C. Rajagopalachari (Madras), S.K. Sinha (Bihar), Bhim Sen Sachar (Punjab), Ravi Shankar Shukla (Madhya Pradesh), and some others enjoyed some degree of autonomy in State governments. Secondly, their autonomous power base was reinforced through the process of intra-party democracy and regular organizational elections in the ruling party at all levels.

This pattern significantly changed during the Indira Gandhi era when after the 1969 Congress split, internal organizational elections in the Congress led by Indira Gandhi was dispensed with and the political system became overly centralized. It turned into a prime ministerial regime when Chief Ministers began to be nominated by the Prime Minister herself who were subsequently dutifully endorsed by the Congress legislature parties. The same pattern more or less continued under the then Prime Minister, Rajiv Gandhi, who succeeded her after her assassination in early June 1984, with the exception of the States of the Northwest and the Northeast.

During the brief Janata Party governments at the Centre and in most north Indian States, the situation became more pluralist and to an extent federalist. The major constituents of the ruling Janata Party—Congress (O), Bharatiya Jan Sangh, Lok Dal and Socialists—divided their spheres of influence both in Union ministries and in respective State governments where a particular Janata constituent had greater political presence and electoral strength.

During the 1980s and after the restoration of the Congress led by Indira Gandhi and after her assassination in 1984 her successor Rajiv Gandhi, the political situation presented a mixed scenario. In Congress-ruled States under Indira Gandhi, the Centre's dominance continued but federal autonomy gained some ground in non-Congress-ruled States where Chief Ministers like Ramakrishna Hegde, N.T. Rama Rao, Sharad Pawar emerged as effective Chief Ministers in their own rights. In the Rajiv Gandhi years, federal autonomy was allowed in some measure even in some Congress-ruled States where State autonomy movements had asserted themselves to the extent that the Prime Minister signed regional or ethnic accords with the Akali Dal in Punjab, the Asom Gana Parishad in Assam, the Mizo National Front in Mizoram and the Tripura National Volunteers in Tripura. However, in the Hindi-speaking States and the contiguous States of Maharashtra and Andhra Pradesh where the Congress remained in power, the Chief Ministers continued to be under New Delhi's domination.

In the 1980s and the 1990s, the State governments and their political executives became more widely characterized by federal autonomy on account of a number of new developments. Firstly, the Congress party continued to lose one state after another throughout the 1980s—Assam, Punjab, Andhra Pradesh, Karnataka, etc. Secondly, there was the onset of coalition governments at the Centre and the advent of non-Congress parties in major north Indian States originating from the Janata Party/Dal, for example, Rashtriya Janata Dal (RJD) in Bihar, Samajwadi Party in UP, Biju Janata Dal in Orissa, Janata Dal (Secular) in Karnataka. Thirdly, neo-liberal economic policy shift since 1991 has expanded the autonomy of not only the private sector but also of the State governments. Besides, with the resources of the national/federal State declining, the ability of the Centre to finance State budgets remained no longer what it was. State governments came to be increasingly advised to mobilize their own resources as far as possible. The net effect of all these developments contributed to the emergence of the Chief Ministers as effective chief executives as never before. They have to not only run their own governments with far greater autonomy from New Delhi but also to create economic climate that would attract private investment from the national as well as the global markets. An index of this unprecedented rise of the Chief Ministerial position in the Indian federal system is the annual public opinion sample survey conducted by the *India Today* on the best Chief Minister in the country in the public estimate in 2006[11] (see Table 8.1).

TABLE 8.1 Ranking of CMs by Public in 2006

	State	*Chief Minister*	*Ranking*
1.	Gujarat	Narendra Modi (BJP)	1
2.	Bihar	Nitish Kumar (JDU–NDA)	2
3.	Karnataka	H.D. Kumaraswamy (JD Secular–BJP)	3
4.	Assam	Tarun Gogoi (Congress)	3
5.	Maharashtra	V. Deshmukh (Congress)	5

Source: India Today, February 12, 2007, p. 22. Party/coalitional affiliations added by the authors of this book.

Note: The poll sample covered 12,386 voters of 98 parliamentary constituencies in 19 States, spread across urban, rural, male, female and different age groups. Apart from asking voters across the country their opinion on who they thought was the best Chief Minister in the country, voters were also asked to rate the performance of the Chief Ministers of their respective States. It is only natural that on the national level, the voters mostly responded positively of their own Chief Ministers, though in case of some, their popularities cut across State borders. Aggregate index of polls conducted in January and August 2006.

More recent data in Table 8.2 about the most popular Chief Ministers in January 2020 show Naveen Patnaik, the BJD CM of Odisha at No. 1, followed in descending order of popularity by Arvind Krjriwal of Aam Aadmi Party in the Delhi National Capital Territory, Yogi Adityanath of BJP in Uttar Pradesh, Uddhav Thackeray of Shiv Sena heading the Shiv Sena-Nationalist Congress Party—Indian National Congress (INC) coalition government in Maharashtra,

TABLE 8.2 Most Popular CMs

	State	*Chief Minister*	*Ranking*
1.	Odisha	Naveen Patnaik (BJD)	1
2.	Delhi	Arvind Kejriwal (AAP)	2
3.	Uttar Pradesh	Yogi Adityanath (BJP)	3
4.	Maharashtra	Uddhav Thackeray (Shiv Sena-NCP-INC)	4
5.	Telangana	K. Chandrashekhar Rao (TRS)	5

Source: India Today, January 24,2021, "Mood of the Nation Survey", Retrieved From: https://www.indiatoday.in/mood-of-the-nation/story/naveen-patnaik-most-popular-cm-at-state-level-motn-poll-1762239-2021-01-24

and K. Chandrashekhar Reddy of Telangana Rashtra Samithi in Telangana. We don't have data here of all the states of the Union, but at least in this set of states, the two major national parties—BJP and INC—do not appear in the best of the conditions. BJP, although pretty strong in India's largest state in the Hindi heartland, is trailing the three regional parties in the three states known to be their strongholds for some time. INC is the third partner in the Maharashtra coalition government trailing behind two regional parties in that state. This Table cannot be said to be revealing a new trend of growing regionalisation of the party systems–national plus states'–beyond what we already knew otherwise. The Table only indicates that the strongholds of these regional parties are not under any expansionist threat that the Modi-Shah team have been working hard to mount since the back-to-back electoral success of the BJP/NDA in 2014 and 2019 Lok Sabha elections.

It may be added here that there was often remarkable divergence in the public opinion and the intelligentsia in the media and the academia. For example, the opinion makers in universities and media generally rated Narendra Modi negatively for his hardcore Hindutva postures. However, the public rating, inclusive of the intelligentsia, reported by *India Today* was generally quite positive.

To understand the politics in Indian States in more recent decades, it may be instructive to look at the state of the State party systems in a comparative perspective with the national party system in 2014, when the rise of the BJP under Narendra Modi acquired some degree of semblance with the Congress predominance of the yore. As an article in the *India Today* (25 December 2014) noted: "The BJP will now have eight chief ministers from Haryana to Maharashtra, capturing the vast expanses of northern, central and western India. It has allies ruling in Punjab and Andhra Pradesh."[12] However, it must be noted that political and electoral volatility in Indian States has considerably increased in the post-Congress dominance phase in Indian politics. At this writing (9 December 2019), about five years later than the *India Today* report quoted above, the political map of Indian States has changed considerably. The BJP-ruled States at present happen to be Arunachal Pradesh, Assam, Goa, Gujarat,

Himachal Pradesh, Jharkhand, Karnataka, Manipur, Tripura, Uttar Pradesh, and Uttarakhand. It rules Bihar and Haryana in alliance with coalition partners—Janata Dal (United) and Jana Nayak Janata Party, respectively. Congress party rules in Madhya Pradesh, Punjab, Rajasthan, and the UT of Puducherry; a Shiv Sena (an erstwhile coalition partner of BJP of long standing)–Nationalist Congress Party-Indian National Congress has just taken over in Maharashtra. Communist Party of India (Marxist)-led Left Front is in power in Kerala. And, regional parties rule in the rest of States and UTs: YSR Congress Party in Andhra Pradesh, Telangana Rashtra Samithi in Telangana, Aam Aadmi Party in the National Capital Territory of Delhi, National People's Party in Meghalaya, Mizo National Front in Mizoram, Nationalist Democratic Progressive Party in Nagaland, Biju Janata Dal in Odisha, Sikkim Krantikari Morcha in Sikkim, AIADMK in Tamil Nadu, and All India Trinamool Congress in West Bengal.

The State legislature can be either bicameral or unicameral. Five States—Andhra Pradesh, Bihar, Maharashtra, Karnataka, and Uttar Pradesh—have bicameral legislatures, whose popular chamber is directly elected by the people in single-member constituencies by plurality or first-past-the-post voting system. The rest of the States have preferred to have only a popularly elected Assembly. The Second Chamber, Legislative Council, is indirectly elected in territorial constituencies formed on functional lines and elected by the system of proportional representation by means of the single transferable vote. The Constitution requires the members of the Council to be elected or nominated as follows: (a) one-third of the members are to be elected by an electoral college consisting of members of municipalities, district boards and other local authorities in the State; (b) one-twelfth to be elected by an electoral college consisting of university graduates; (c) one-twelfth to be elected by an electoral college consisting of teachers in universities, colleges and secondary schools; (d) one-third to be elected by members of the Legislative Assembly from amongst persons who are not members of the Assembly; and (e) the remainder are to be nominated by the Governor from amongst people having "special knowledge or practical experience" in the fields of "literature, science, art, cooperative movement and social service."

The Assembly is elected for five years, unless dissolved earlier and the Council is not subject to dissolution, but one-third of its members retire phase-wise on the expiry of every second year. The sessions of the State Legislatures are summoned, prorogued and dissolved by the Governor on the advice of the Speaker and/or the Chief Minister, except during constitutional emergencies when the Governor can exercise his own discretion, usually on the directive of the Union government. One important constitutional requirement is that there must not be a gap of six months or more between one session of the State Legislature and another during its five-year term, unless it is dissolved earlier.

The political neutrality of the presiding officers of the Houses of the legislatures is an essential factor for ensuring smooth deliberative and legislative process. However, the Indian tradition diverges in this respect from the tradition of the House of Commons in the United Kingdom where the Speaker belonging to a political party distances himself from his party and is extended the courtesy of uncontested return to the House in the next election. Specially since the Anti-Defection Act that has become the Tenth Schedule in the Constitution since 1985, the partisan role of the Speaker has become even more aggravated as the Speaker is required to give his ruling on defection, splits and mergers of parties, whose rulings smack of partisan considerations. Most Speakers have tended to act in blatantly political way necessitating intervention by courts. This unfortunate trend needs to be corrected in the interest of constitutional functioning of the legislatures.

In the autumn of 2019, the Speaker of the Karnataka Legislative Assembly, in the context of the crisis of survival faced by the Janata Dal (Secular)-Congress coalition government headed by the Chief Minister, H.D. Kumaraswamy, disqualified 17 rebel MLAs hobnobbing with the opposition BJP trying to topple the government. The Supreme Court upheld the order of the Speaker, K.R. Ramesh Kumar, disqualifying the Congress and JD(S) MLAs, but struck down the term of the disqualification which was till the end of the then current Assembly until 2023. The three-judge bench ruled that the Speaker acts as a "quasi-judicial authority," but under the Constitution, his inquiry is limited to examine whether the MLA's resignation from their parties was voluntary or not to determine if their action amounted to defection under the anti-defection law of the Constitution.[13]

The Constitution takes special care to keep legislative and judicial powers separate. The legislature is debarred to discuss the conduct of judges in the normal exercise of their judicial function. Similarly, the validity of legislative proceedings cannot be called in question by courts on ground of alleged irregularity (Articles 211 and 212). However, under case law it is clarified that the courts can look into a matter where the jurisdictional competence of a State Legislature is in dispute.[14] Recent case laws are, however, beginning to question both Article 212 of the Constitution and earlier case law upholding this Article.[15] For example, in early 2005 in a case relating to the Jharkhand State, the irregularity of a questionable legislative majority with the connivance of the Governor was not only entertained by the Court but it also directed the Speaker to convene a regular Assembly session by a certain date to undo the mischief done by the infirm majority and biased gubernatorial sanction. By out of court manoeuvres, the matter was settled in a round-about way to circumvent the stricture of the Court.

The structure of the judiciary at the State level from the High Court down to the district courts is such that the number of judges required and the fiscal and infrastructural requirements of the courts are determined and provided by the State Government, but the appointment of judges is autonomous from the political control of the State Government. High Court judges are appointed by the President of India as advised by a collegium of Supreme Court and High Court senior judges, and district judges are appointed by the Governor of the State as advised by the senior High Court judges. The attempted change of the collegium system of appointments in higher courts by the government in 2014 and its invalidation by the Supreme Court in 2015 are discussed in Chapter 6 on the judiciary in this book. Control over subordinate courts in a State is vested in the High Court (Article 235). It is clarified in the case law laid down in a number of cases decided by the Supreme Court that the term 'control' by High Court in Article 235 is meant to serve as a mechanism of ensuring independence of the subordinate judiciary from the State executive rather than one of putting undue pressure on them.[16]

The performance of State governments in India has been less relatively successful than that of the Union government, at least by and large. The only area of government in which at least some State governments seem to have gone ahead of the Union government is the management of coalition governments. Such governments became stabilized and institutionalized in the States of West Bengal and Kerala even earlier than at the Union level. In other areas, organization and working of State governments appear to be generally less developed, either due to socio-economic backwardness or migration of State-level leaders to the Centre from some States with strong national parties. For example, more successful leaders from Hindi-speaking States, especially UP, have historically been drawn to the national level politics leaving the State governments to the care of less enterprising and successful leaders. Even after the emergence of strong regional parties, top leaders in State politics in non-Hindi rimland-states like Punjab (Prakash Singh Badal and Amarinder Singh), Tamil Nadu (Jayalalitha and Karunanidhi), Andhra Pradesh (NTR and Chandrababu Naidu), etc. preferred to head the State governments instead of moving to the Centre.

So far as the bureaucratic executive is concerned, the State governments are generally not so much starved of talent. This is because the All India Services primarily belong to State cadres and occupy the highest rungs in State governments and alternately at the Centre on deputation.

Most State governments are executive-dominated, with State Legislatures and local self-governments being weak links in the whole structure. The Chief Ministers and their powerful colleagues and the chief secretaries and other senior civilians run the politico-administrative show with evidently weak legislative control and oversight. More recently, this process of executive dominance has been overtaken by a judiciary-driven government. High Courts and the Supreme Court have acquired enormous authority due to their power of judicial review and public interest litigation. However, this judicial aggrandizement is attributable more to the acts of omission and commission on the part of the executive and legislature than due to political ambition on the part of the judges. In addition to this development, the imperatives of protecting human rights and reviving civil society institutions have led to the enactments of Human Rights Commissions and Right to Information Commissions at both Union and State levels. The impact of judicial activism and National Human Rights Commission (which is more vigorous than State Human Rights Commissions) has contributed to greater "parliamentarization" of the political system than its "federalization" (in the sense of regionalization). Only the revival of civil society institutions and regionally dispersed nature of peasants, and workers' movements as well as new social movements concerned with the quality of life and ecological protection tilt the balance of political forces towards regionalization.

Historically, the process of government in Indian States was overshadowed by the imperatives of electoral and political mobilization. In more recent times, excessive politicization has been, to an extent, restrained by two factors. One such factor is what may be called 'judicialization of polities,' and the other is the shift of emphasis to economic development and better performance by State governments in initiating and implementing neo-liberal economic reforms in the backdrop of State failure on the front of economic development.[17] In the new ambience, the emphasis has shifted from the bureaucratic *government* to what has come to be known as the process of *governance* jointly shared by the government, the corporate economic sector, and the civil society organizations and institutions.

With growing accent on privatization and globalization, the fiscal capacity of the Union government to come to the rescue of State governments has been on the decline. The latter are generally reluctant to either mobilize their own resources, or make more optimum use of State taxes or improve their administrative and fiscal efficiency. Administrative decay, even though less alarming than the clogging of the political processes by corruption and criminalization and deepening fiscal crisis of the provincial States, is further compounded by the breakdown of social and legal order. There is a more comprehensive provincial State failure than the federal State failure. Whether we examine the State of public corporations, or transport infrastructures, social sector infrastructure (public education and health services), politico-bureaucratic rent-seeking, breakdown of law and order, relief from crime and tort, everywhere the provincial State cuts a sorrier figure than the federal State, barring rare exceptions.

Under economic compulsions, State governments are now seeking to attract investment, both national and foreign, in their economies by offering attractive terms and concessions within their jurisdictions. But in the new atmosphere of economic Darwinism, the backward regions and States lag behind the developed States and the national sectors of economy.

The considerable political federalization brought about by the rise of powerful regional parties and diminution or stunting of national parties is stumped by two major factors: (a) the limits to fiscal buoyancy of the provincial State, and (b) the formidable challenges faced by the small-scale industries and nascent regional bourgeoisie in economically vibrant States due to globalization. This argument can be illustrated with the fact that the most significant tax reforms as well as regional industrialization are being initiated by the federal State. The recent replacement of State sales tax by value-added tax (VAT) and the Special Economic Zones (SEZ) under the SEZ Act passed by the Parliament, facilitating regional industrialization with sponsorship in economic development by the State Governments and private Indian industrialists, are cases in point. So is the introduction of goods and services tax (GST) in 2017 hailed as the most important indirect tax reform in India since its Independence. In these instances, reluctance or opposition to these moves has mostly come from powerful political forces and economic classes entrenched in the political economy and politics at the State level. The traders allied with the BJP–ruled States and the peasants mobilized by the Trinamool Congress in West Bengal have delayed or partly stymied these reforms. However, it is difficult not to feel that peasants are being short-changed as well as displaced from their land by the collusion of capitalists and State governments. The worst peasant resistance to this move has ironically come to be seen in the Communist-ruled West Bengal, where Nandigram has become a glaring symbol of peasant exploitation by the entrenched CPM-led Left Front continuously in power in West Bengal since 1977 to 2011. The episode forced an amendment to the SEZ law/rules to the effect that industrialists must purchase land themselves rather than the State governments acquiring it for them. A cap on the size of the SEZ lands to be acquired and obligation to settle the displaced peasants must also be taken care of either by the industry or the state.

The BJP-ruled States, despite substantial fiscal cover of the costs of transition to VAT offered by the Union government, were the last to fall in line in embracing the State VAT. This was due to the pressure of opposition of the trading classes aligned with the BJP. Now, the way is cleared for introducing Central VAT and goods and services tax (GST), which is expected to considerably improve the public finances of both the States and the Union. Ultimately, of course, with the Congress-led Union government of the United Progressive Alliance all set, despite opposition from the Left, to allow the global retail giant Wal-Mart to enter the Indian market, the run-of-the mill Indian traders are likely to be wiped out by the builders of big Indian shopping malls in metropolitan cities and eventually by the global business. The Wal-Mart move was subsequently halted.

The Union Government was also taking the lead to connect all tax departments at the Centre, State, and local government levels as a prelude to link income tax, VAT, property registration and other indirect tax departments. Union Finance Minister P. Chidambaram was already in communication with the empowered committee of State Finance Ministers on GST, to prepare the ground for Union–State consultations and negotiations. The Union Finance Ministry had been considering alternatives of (a) levying GST at the Union level, (b) levying it at the State level, or (c) having dual tax structure. These changes would require constitutional amendment. The prevalent GST models in federal Canada and Brazil and confederal European Union were also being examined. The Centre's proposal was to pass on total revenue collection from 33 services to States and prompting the States to bring 44 new services under their tax net.[18] GST still remained forestalled for lack of consensus between the Union and the States.

Finally, the GST was introduced by the 101st Constitutional Amendment Act, 2016, enacted by the BJP-led National Democratic Alliance government headed by Narendra Modi. It went into effect on 1 July 2017. The event was marked by a historic midnight session of the two houses of Parliament. The conforming law under the Constitution of India replaced many indirect tax laws that previously existed in India and its States. GST is one indirect tax for the whole country. In intra-State sales, Central and State GST are charged. More about GST may be found in Chapter 7 on Federalism in this book.

PATTERNS AND TRENDS IN STATE POLITICS

The federal structure of the Indian Constitution makes a clear demarcation between Central and State political arenas. In a perceptive piece on political culture in India, Myron Weiner made a suggestive distinction between elite and mass political cultures in India. He argued that whereas elite perspectives on politics, planning and administration are to be found in national institutions like the Parliament, Council of Ministers, Planning Commission, etc. in New Delhi, mass political culture is more likely to be evident in political institutions and politics of Indian States and localities, especially closer to the rural society. Thus, the impact of caste, community and tribe is more evident in smaller and regional political parties, factions and State legislatures and local councils.[19] Decades after Weiner, M.P. Singh postulated that elite and mass political cultures had come closer to each other through the electoral, party-political and legislative processes via interactional and dialectical relationships between the elites and the masses.[20] In addition to institutional politics, regional and sons-of-the soil-movements have been another mechanism through which the process of social mobilization and politicization of the masses have expanded incrementally over the years into concentric "oceanic circles" of participatory democracy. The first expression of the regional movement was felt in the agitations for the creation of linguistic States soon after Independence. While provincial boundaries in parts of eastern India had already been reorganized along linguistic lines during the British Raj itself (creation of provinces of Assam, Bihar and Orissa out of the Bengal Presidency), linguistic reorganization of western and southern India had to await until after Independence. Linguistic agitations were triggered off by a mass movement for the creation of a separate Andhra Pradesh out of the Madras Presidency in the early 1950s. By the end of the 1950s and '60s, the Madras Presidency had been divided into Andhra Pradesh, Karnataka, Kerala, and Tamil Nadu; and the Bombay Presidency had been bifurcated into Gujarat and Maharashtra. In the 1960s again, a new State of Nagaland had been created out of Assam, and Punjab had been trifurcated into Punjab, Haryana, and Himachal Pradesh in 1966. By the end of the 1970s, Assam had been further divided into six more units, mostly the small tribal States of the North-East. State autonomy movements also gathered momentum by the 1980s, especially in Assam, Punjab, and Jammu and Kashmir. In all these three instances, the autonomy movements also spilled over in forms of politics of separatism and terrorism, often from support and promptings from across the international borders.

Three new States of Uttarakhand, Jharkhand and Chhattisgarh were carved out in November 2000 out of Uttar Pradesh, Bihar and Madhya Pradesh, respectively. A new State of Telangana was bifurcated from Andhra Pradesh in June 2014. These new States differed from the earlier newly formed States in that these are based on the considerations of regional and economic backwardness rather than on linguistic basis. Barring Telangana, the rest of the three are parts of the Hindi-speaking regions and do not differ from the parent States in this regard. Although the tribal factor was present to some extent in Jharkhand and Chhattisgarh, the tribal movement in Bihar became transformed into a demand based on regional economic backwardness as the non-tribal migrations into the Chottanagpur region of Bihar had practically outnumbered the tribal population in urban areas. And in Chhattisgarh, there never was a tribal movement for a separate statehood except perhaps in the 1960s when the chief of the erstwhile tribal State of Baster, Praveen Chandra Bhanjdev, had spearheaded some kind of rebellion and had lost his life in the political turmoil. These three States are richer in terms of mineral/forest resources than their parent States but had been socially and educationally backward and had received step-motherly treatment in allocation of revenues and developmental funds. A Regional Tribal Development Council had been briefly experimented with only in Jharkhand as a region of Bihar, but it had failed to satisfy the Jharkhandis. Telangana too was carved out of Andhra Pradesh on considerations of backwardness; both Andhra and Telangana are linguistically Telugu-speaking.

In a comprehensive study of regional movements in India, Sajal Basu has classified these movements in terms of their territorial and ethnic bases, the primary motivational factors, and the forms and objectives[21] (see Basu 1992, p. 2). Sajal Basu's typology of movements is interesting but somewhat confounding as the categories of classification appear to be jointly exhaustive of all kinds of movements, but they are not mutually exclusive. For example, the Dravidian movement is found both in categories 1 and 2, and the Jharkhand movement in categories 2, 3, 4 and 5. Similarly, Punjabi Suba occurs in categories 2 and 4. Category 7 is particularly incoherent and confusing. Yet, this typology is informative as to the causes and forms of articulation behind the various movements, in a realistically gross way.

Myron Weiner has put forward another classification of regional movements in India in terms of what he calls "ethnic" and "nativist" movements. To quote him: "Nativism is that form of ethnic identity that seeks to *exclude* those who are not members of the local and indigenous ethnic group from residing and/or working in a territory because they are not native to the country or region: nativism is antimigrant." The DMK, Akali Dal, Andhra Mahasabha, and Samyukta Maharashtra Samiti are dubbed as anti-migrant rather than nativist, whereas Jharkhand Party and Telangana Praja Samithi are regarded as nativist. The Shiv Sena founded in Bombay in 1966 showed its hostility towards the Tamil migrants occupying middle class jobs in the city and demanded their replacement by Marathi-speaking people. This nativist movement gradually became a force to reckon with in the Bombay Municipal Corporation and finally in the State Assembly as well. Its objective was originally "to convert Bombay from a cosmopolitan multiethnic centre to a Marathi city."[22]

Increased migration of middle-class job seekers from Hindi-speaking states to Mumbai and to north-eastern states in more recent years since the turn of the century has caused some nativist reactions against the migrants. In Mumbai in particular, the Maharashtra Navnirman Sena (MNS), a splinter of the Shiv Sena under the leadership of Raj Thackeray, nephew of Bal Thackeray, has spearheaded this violent campaign in the name of the 'marathi manush'. The issue has got entangled with inter-party competition in the state, though the move has roundly been condemned by civic-minded institutions, organizations and citizens.

Creation of Smaller States in India

The recent political events in early 2010 for or against state of Telangana out of Andhra Pradesh has again raised the debate whether the smaller states in a federal union are better. On a purely conceptual plane, the case for a smaller set of states may be premised on at least two considerations: convenience and benefits of participatory democracy for the people, and advantages of manageability of size in good government and governance (where the term "government" refers to the structure and function of the state and "governance" to the process involving the government, civil society, and the market institutions). However, in the context of our discourse, the matter would better be discussed on practical and pragmatic considerations. Each case would better be considered on its own merits yet in a wider framework as to how the reorganization affects the nation.

In any case, the political flare-up over Telangana preceding its creation, that first erupted in 1969 with 400 deaths in the agitation but was then settled by a promise of regional concessions and autonomy by the State Government and the Centre, has already fuelled similar demands backed by agitational politics by Gurkhas in Darjeeling hill districts of West Bengal and Bodos in Assam. The BSP Chief Minister of UP Mayawati, has also revived the idea, first put forward by B.R. Ambedkar, in a critique of the States Reorganization Act, 1956, for division of UP into three states broadly along Western, Central and Eastern regions. She went to the extent of formally dashing letters to the Prime Minister in this connection. The background of the demand for separate states of Harit Pradesh in Western UP and Bundelkhand in central-southern UP is already there.

The problem of creating new provinces and States is not an entirely new question confronting us. Historically provinces were created largely by military conquests and imperial purposes. This is true of ancient and medieval as well as modern periods of Indian history. The Mauryan Empire had, in addition to its core territory in Magadha with its capital in Pataliputra, three major provinces—the western, eastern, and southern with capitals in Taxila, Toshali, and Suvarnagiri, respectively. The Mughal Empire had, besides its three central provinces, 12 other Subahs (provinces). There were three categories of provinces in British India, namely, Presidencies, Governors' provinces, and Chief Commissioner's provinces. They were mainly dictated by administrative and military considerations. Yet even in British India, the provincial boundaries were redrawn on account of popular or democratic demands and agitations, e.g. annulling of Lord Curzon's partition of Bengal in the first decade of the twentieth century in the wake of the Swadeshi movement in Bengali-speaking parts of Bengal Presidency, creation of a separate province of Bihar and Orissa in 1911, and bifurcation of this province into those of Bihar and Orissa in 1936.

Independent India began with four categories of states: A, B, C, and D, which were legacies of British Indian provinces and integrated princely states and islands. These were altered by the States' Reorganization Commission Report commissioned by the Nehru Congress government. This Commission conceded the principle of linguistic reorganization of states of the Indian Union where there were strong political demands for them. For the rest, it suggested the retention of multilingual states as means of promoting multicultural coexistence and national integration. But sure enough, creation of some linguistic states fuelled similar demands and agitations elsewhere, including religion-based demands as in Punjab by the Akali Dal and tribal-identity-based demands as in Assam that then comprised the whole of tribal north-east. The 1960s witnessed the trifurcation of the state of Punjab into Punjab, Haryana, and Himachal Pradesh, and the separation of Nagaland from Assam. The rest of Assam was divided into six more states through the 1970s, all excepting the rump of Assam, along the lines of tribal identities, by and large.

As a result of the foregoing changes synoptically overviewed, India today consists of 28 states and eight Union Territories, including the National Capital Region of Delhi. In August 2019, the Constitution of India, already substantially extended by Presidential Orders since the Nehru era under Article 370, was wholly extended to the State of Jammu and Kashmir by the Modi government, thus deoperationalizing Article 370 in so far as the State's 'temporary provision, relating to its 'Special Status' as a feature of asymmetrical federalism. The Parliament also reorganized the State into two Union Territories of Jammu and Kashmir and Ladakh. (More about this controversial move may be found in Chapter 7 on Federalism in this book.)

What has been India's experience with smaller states? Are smaller states more successful in ensuring participatory and inclusive democracy, transparent and accountable administration, corruption-free and efficient governance? Are smaller states more likely to cause better economic development in material as well as human terms? Are smaller states better able to pursue the goal of sustainable development when global warming and climate change have become a major challenge to be addressed globally, nationally, and locally?

No simplistic answer to these posers is possible because of the complexity of the problem as well as insufficiency of data, to say nothing of constraints of time and space here. Yet some hypotheses may be offered for further explorations and probing.

Prima facie, creation of new states in British India until the 1960s at least resulted in backward regions of larger states to come into the limelight of democratic and developmental endeavour and achievements earlier not possible. The cases of Bihar and Orissa after their creation in the first half of the twentieth century bear this point out. Both were backward regions of their respective parent states but turned into new regions to experience better socio-economic and political development. The Madras and Bombay Presidencies were to repeat this experience following India's independence. So were the composite Indian state of Punjab, Andhra Pradesh, Gujarat, and Haryana/ Himachal Pradesh in their respective parent states of Madras, Bombay, and Punjab. All subsequently became more developed, economically as well as politically, problematic nature of democracy and development in new states as well as in whole of India notwithstanding. The new state of Goa also falls into this pattern.

The experience of new and far smaller states in the northeast is less clear, particularly due to the incidence of insurgencies and suspension of democratic and developmental processes over long periods intermittently. Yet despite all hurdles, including the anti-foreigners movement and United Liberation Front of Assam insurgency in the state of Assam and the unresolved problems of federalism within and illegal migration of Bangladeshi Muslims amounting to a demographic aggression, democracy and development are not exactly dead in the region. Indeed, it must be put on record that in a way the north-east is the only region with a well-functioning regional political institution in the Northeastern Council under an Act of Parliament. There are no such functioning political institution at the regional level in any other region of the country evidence by the largely dysfunctional Zonal Councils set up under the State's Reorganization Act, 1956.

The experience of most recently created new States of Uttarakhand, Jharkhand, and Chhattisgarh is again somewhat mixed. *Prima facie*, Uttarakhand presents a picture of creditable developmental and democratic performance, whereas the two other States have registered notable economic development but more than average incidence of Maoist political violence as well as alarming corruption in the political and administrative classes. The counter-Maoist measure of arming the private tribal militia called *Salwa Judum* by the Chhattisgarh government and violation of human rights in dealing with extremist political violence in the two predominantly tribal States (plus in the neighbouring Andhra Pradesh and West Bengal) have also been subjects of liberal critique by civil rights groups at home and abroad. In economic development the story of the three new states is more promising. All three have had higher average rates of annual growth at 9.31 per cent in Uttarakhand, 8.45 per cent in Jharkhand, and 7.35 in Chhattisgarh compared to the national Indian average at around 7 per cent since around 2003–2004 to 2007–2008. Despite the advantage of a new base-line and central concessions and tax holidays in states to attract private investment that may have artificially stepped up growth initially, this is an impressive start.

It must, however, be added that beyond a certain point any case for smaller States must become counter-productive. At least some States in India have managed to come into existence that are arguably too small for statehood for financial viability and administrative rationality. In fact all the 10 Himalayan States of India spanning the erstwhile State of Jammu and Kashmir in the northwest to the northeastern States are "special category states" in terms of fiscal federal dispensation created by the Finance Commission of India. All these States are dependent on federal transfers to the tune of 80 per cent of their revenue budgetary requirements. More States are already clamouring for this "special category" status! Needless to add, that any future States Reorganization Commission which the Government of India appoints would be acutely conscious of their constraint on the further creation of smaller States in the country. Indeed, instead of creating any new State in an *ad hoc* manner, the Government of India would do well to get the problem examined by an autonomous Commission in a wider perspective and make a well-considered report and recommendation.

STATE-SOCIETY INTERFACE IN STATE POLITICS

Patterns and trends of politics in the various States of the Indian Union are too variant and complex to be reduced to any neat classification or typology of models that is empirically grounded as well as theoretically fruitful. In the most comprehensive study of politics across Indian States published in 1989 and 1990, Francine R. Frankel and M.S.A. Rao made a significant systematic contribution to theorize the interaction between social dominance and State power in contemporary India.[23] "The traditional pattern of super-ordinate and subordinate relations in society", observes Rao, "underwent significant changes in colonial India, a process which was accelerated after Independence. The articulation of changing relationships between social dominance and political power, as new social formations seek to capture control of the State, and seize for themselves the power of those who dominate them form the main theme of these volumes".[24] Francine Frankel projects a trajectory of political transformation in modern India in terms of three broad stages marked by (a) the old elite-based political alliances among the dominant contenders for political power within the British Raj and the Brahmanical social order of the Hindu society; (b) newly emergent elite-based alliances of the period of the Congress dominance over the 1950s to the 1970s; and (c) the voters' alliances at the mass level with the deepening of electoral democracy since the late 1970s with the advent of the Janata Party on the political scene in the post-Emergency period.[25] To quote her: "As Brahmanical legitimacy weakened, the potentialities for conflict *within* society greatly expanded. Simultaneously, the forms which these conflicts assumed became more varied according to the situational context and the regional pattern of social organization."[26]

In the 'Aryan' heartland in North, the Congress Party could electorally count on the vote of the "twice-born" (*dwija*) castes of the Brahmanical social order but was also marked by inter-caste and/or multi-caste factional rivalries among the upper castes themselves for local political dominance and control over the Government. This provided the opening for the mobilized "vote banks" of minorities and subaltern castes whose leaders could be co-opted in an effort to build up political bridges spanning the Forward and Backward castes/classes.[27]

Down West and South, especially the linguistic States created after 1956 that were dominated by sub-regional or State-wide agriculturist middle castes, the mainstay of the Congress, was these castes in alliance with urban upper caste and middle classes as also scheduled castes-tribes and Muslims. "Thus, the Congress party consolidated its power in Andhra Pradesh with the support of *Reddys;* in Karnataka, with the *Lingayats* and *Vokkaligas;* in Maharashtra with the *Marathas;* and in Gujarat, with the *pattidars.*"[28]

In the deep South and the East, where there were no equivalents of the dominant cultivating castes, the situation was different from the foregoing. In Madras, later Tamil Nadu, the Congress leaned on the *brahmans* and the *vellalas* in the hinterland of Madras/Chennai city and on the notables of localized cultivating castes. In West Bengal, the urban *bhadralok* Congress leaders roped in village-level *jotedars* and intermediaries. In Orissa, the *Brahman-karna* middle-class leadership of the Congress built electoral linkages with the rich peasant *khandayats* and scheduled castes/tribes. In Rajasthan, the Congress mobilized the voters against the residual legitimacy of ex-maharajas and *jagirdars* with the help of urban educated middle classes and *jat* and *Rajput* peasants. In Punjab, it contended against the Akali Dal factions agitating for a Sikh-majority Punjabi *suba* and the Hindu-based opposition parties.[29]

The political scenario in the late 1980s and since changed fast and was marked by the rise and fall of the post-Nehru Congress Party under Indira Gandhi and Rajiv Gandhi, rise of Backward classes/castes under Janata Party/Dal and its fragmentation, the emergence of the Hindu Right Bharatiya Janata Party, and of a number of new regional parties in addition to the old ones of the Northwest and the South. The new political metaphors of the period since the 1990s are Mandal I & II, Mandir, and the Market, in addition to the phenomenon of Marxists holding forts in West Bengal without a break since 1977, and intermittently in Kerala, and Tripura. Politics in India in this phase has become regionalized and State-based more than before and extremely fragmented in terms of parties, castes, and tribes. Local self-governing institutions and grassroots politics are also coming into greater importance than ever, especially since the constitutional entrenchment of Panchayat/Nagar Raj by the 73rd and 74th constitutional amendments (1993). As State party systems have become differentiated from the national party system, hung Parliaments—both in the sense of lack of single-party majority in the Lok Sabha and divergent parties' majorities in the Lok Sabha and the Rajya Sabha—have become the stocks in the political trade. In addition, the

President and the Prime Minister too invariably come from different political parties and are chosen by coalitional consensus, often cutting across the Government and the Opposition. The same goes for the presiding officers of the two Houses of the Parliament. Add to this, the chequered political chessboard of Governors and Chief Ministers of varied political configurations. The inevitable consequences are coalition and/or minority Governments and the spectre of governmental instability. The functional responses to this political situation are judicial activism, greater role for independent regulatory authorities, and Government-civil society interface and participation in governance. Wider power-sharing among the Union and States, ideological and sociological strands, including the marginal ones, may at times result in delays and instability of Governments. Yet, the gain in terms of stability of the political system or the State system by virtue of national integration and citizenship allegiance is unmistakable.

NEW FRONTIERS OF STATE POLITICS

In a relatively recent study of regional and State politics in India, edited by Rob Jenkins,[30] the contributors have broken new methodological and intra-national comparative theoretical ground of great empirical and systematic import. In the introduction to this study, Jenkins has compared four aspects of democratic practice—economic policy making, subaltern politicization, civic engagement, and political leadership. The politics of neo-liberal economic policy making is examined in paired comparative studies of Andhra Pradesh and Tamil Nadu by Loraine Kennedy and of West Bengal and Gujarat by Aseema Sinha. While ruling parties both in Andhra Pradesh and Tamil Nadu have been implementing the new policy with considerable success, there is a notable difference in the political posturing towards and packaging of the new policy in the two States. The Telugu Desam Party (TDP) has gone out with a great deal of fanfare in projecting itself as an enthusiastic pioneer of reforms. But the All India Anna Dravida Munnetra Kazhagam (AIADMK) and Dravida Munnetra Kazhagam (DMK) have implemented the new policy with a public posturing of distancing themselves from the reforms. Why this difference? Kennedy explains it by referring to two factors: (a) the extent of fragmentation of the party system in the two States, and (b) variations in political mobilization among Dalits and other backward communities. On both these dimensions, Andhra Pradesh is found to be less fragmented in its party system and comparatively less marked by politicization of the lower castes. Thus, because of greater fragmentation of its parties as well as greater politicization of lower castes, Tamil Nadu leaders resort to neo-liberal policy reforms by stealth due to intense political competitiveness and adverse electoral reappraisals of the weaker sections of the society.[31]

In the comparative study of Gujarat and West Bengal, Aseema Sinha finds that even though West Bengal has since the late 1970s been politically very stable and Gujarat has been afflicted by social turmoil and political instability, yet the latter has received twelve times more investment than the former. The explanation for this divergence is offered in terms of the social democratic ideology of communism being dominant in West Bengal as against the prevalence of the centrist or right-wing political ideology in Gujarat. In addition, the politically relevant classes and interests in West Bengal are sharply divided such that the Communist Party of India Marxist (CPI-M) political leadership is now moving to adopt neo-liberal economic reforms, yet their employees' and workers' Unions are strongly opposed to such policies. Gujarat obviously is different. Moreover, industrialization in Gujarat is more widely dispersed whereas it is highly concentrated in West Bengal in and around Kolkata. For this reason, neo-liberal reforms have a wider social support in the western State than in the eastern.[32]

On the dimension of subaltern politicization, paired comparisons of four States are again presented: Bihar and Orissa by Sanjay Kumar and Uttar Pradesh and Madhya Pradesh by Christophe Jaffrelot and Jasmine Zerinini-Brotel. In Bihar, the rise to political dominance of OBCs transformed the party system of the State from the Congress dominance to the Rashtriya Janata Dal (RJD) preponderance with marginal coalitional support from some other parties. In Orissa, a similar transition took place replacing the Congress by Biju Janata Dal (BJD), but not as decisively as in Bihar. Sanjay Kumar points out that there is still a great deal of difference between the social bases of RJD and the BJD, both regional descendents of the Janata Party/Dal. Survey data show that RJD largely depends on the OBCs like Yadavs, whereas the mainstay of the BJD is upper castes like *karnas* and Brahmins. The reasons, according to Kumar, are that there is no dominant OBC caste in Orissa and the Scheduled Tribes of the State, even though sizeable, lack politicization and power. And the *khandayats* have an ambiguous caste status and are thus ambivalent between the upper and lower castes.[33] The studies of UP and Madhya Pradesh suggest that subaltern political participation has made notable strides indicated by the emergence of the Samajwadi Party (SP) and Bahujan Samaj Party (BSP) led respectively by Mulayam Singh Yadav and Mayawati in Uttar Pradesh. These parties have ended the dominance of the Congress and precluded the attempt of the BJP to occupy the space vacated by the Congress. However, the new party system in the State is quite fragmented and is endemically plagued by unstable coalition Governments. In Madhya Pradesh, on the other hand, neither the OBCs nor the Scheduled Castes have been able to project political parties of their own. Both the BJP and the Congress seek to follow the electoral strategy of forging "coalitions of the extremes", meaning thereby alliances of upper and scheduled castes. To quote Jaffrelot and Zerinini-Brotel: "Today's Uttar Pradesh has inherited much from an old socialist tradition of lower-caste mobilization that is clearly missing in Madhya Pradesh, a State where the numerous princely States exerted a strong conservative influence."[34]

The aspect of civic engagement is highlighted by studies of Hindu-Muslim riots in Kerala and Uttar Pradesh by Ashutosh Varshney and of anti-corruption movements in Maharashtra and Rajasthan by Rob Jenkins. The authors have argued that this dimension is better explored at a level of analysis lower than the State, i.e. cities or regions in the selected States. The greater proneness to riots in some UP cities stands out in contrast to greater communal harmony in the Kerala cities. Varshney explains this difference by the explanatory factor of presence or absence of civic engagements defined as inter-community relations and reconciliations. In his words, "Riot-prone cities have primarily *intra*-Hindu or *intra*-Muslim civic engagement which undermines peace and transforms rumours and tensions into violence and riots."[35] Jenkins sheds light on the activities of *Bhrashtachar Virodhi Jan Andolan* (BVJA) in the Ahmednagar district of Maharashtra and the *Mazdoor Kisan Shakti Sangathan* (MKSS) in the Rajsamand district in Rajasthan. The former is demographically Maratha-dominance area and the latter is predominantly Rawat in terms of caste. Uniquely, these two districts have been characteristic sites of anti-corruption movements targeted at the implementation of employment-generating public works in these two areas. What could be the possible explanations for the occurrence of these movements particularly in these areas? Jenkins suggests that the explanation could be found in the cohesive community structure of one particular caste that maintains social norms as well as does not let the political clash degenerate into inter-caste conflicts. In a socially fragmented setting, the clash could easily be given the colour of one caste against another. Another explanation is offered in terms of split personality of both Marathas and Rawats. Marathas are internally divided by class in the sense that the more prosperous sections claim and get away with kshatriya status whereas the less resourceful sections are treated as parts of the *Kunbi* peasantry. The Rawats also display a similar high-low status ambiguity, some calling themselves Rajputs and others claiming to belong to the OBC category for political and economic reasons. The author goes on to explain: "The reason why this point of similarity is important from the perspective of building and sustaining an anti-corruption movement is that poor and disadvantaged people from such hybrid-status communities are often less reluctant to engage in political activity than are people from castes that are almost universally regarded as of inferior status. They are also less likely to be viewed by economic elites as a threat to the established socio-political order."[36]

On the dimension of political leadership, James Manor offers contrasting illustrations from Andhra Pradesh and Karnataka and Mukulika Banerjee from West Bengal and Tamil Nadu. The political leadership in Andhra has found it more difficult to sustain political parties and at times to govern the State. This is due to a high level of social tension and conflict in the State indicated by the armed insurgency and separatist movement in Telengana, social tension in Rayalaseema, and thuggery in coastal Andhra. Karnataka has been relatively free from such tensions and conflicts. This contrasting pattern may explain why the two main parties in each of these two States have found themselves differentially successful in their efforts "to embed themselves in society by establishing transactional links between their organizations and major social groups."[37] Thus, Karnataka parties have been more embedded than the Andhra parties. On account of this difference, Andhra Pradesh has been more open to interventions by national-level parties and leaders than Karnataka. Banerjee presents an interesting comparison between Jayalalithaa of AIADMK of Tamil Nadu and Mamata Banerjee of Trinamool Congress in West Bengal.[38]

While neither is mainly a women's leader, the political persona of Jayalalitha is more glamorous while that of Mamata is more grassroots-oriented. The former may be regarded as an example of elitist and motherly (the *amma*) populism, the latter's populism is more commonplace and sisterly (the *didi*). To quote Banerjee, "as a result, both parties have found it necessary to bypass institutions altogether and attempt to reach voters directly through the forceful personalities of their leaders."[39] Their leadership styles are also rooted in the regional political cultures, to an extent, of West Bengal and Tamil Nadu.

CONCLUSION

The study of State politics gathered momentum in the 1960s and by now it has become established as a field of studies. However, there are still some less than fully explored areas such as neo-liberal economic reforms at the State level and the impact of globalization on politics in Indian States,[40] working of governmental institutions at the State level, and urban and rural local self-government (especially the former). New ground in this area of study can also be broken in more intensive studies of State party systems and the working of coalition governments in States. So far, more scholarly attention has gone into studying electoral and social movement politics at the State level. This is perhaps a reflection on the State of democratic development in India, specially at the State level, which has become a more or less fairly successful *electoral* democracy. For democratic consolidation, it is equally important for India to become an *institutionalized* parliamentary federal system at both the Union and State levels and a *constitutional* democracy where electoral majoritarianism is countervailed by liberalism and federalism, the rule of law and social and economic justice.

REFERENCES

1. Myron Weiner (Ed.), *State Politics in India,* Princeton University Press, Princeton, 1966, 'Introduction'.
2. Myron Weiner, *Ibid;* and Iqbal Narain (Ed.), *State Politics in India,* Meenakshi Prakashan, Meerut, 1967.
3. M.P. Singh, *Split in a Predominant Party: The Indian National Congress in 1969,* Abhinav Publications, New Delhi, 1981. Also accessible online as a Google Book.

4. Lawrence Saez, *Federalism Without a Centre: The Impact of Political and Economic Reform on India's Federal System*, Sage Publications, New Delhi, 2002; and Douglas V. Verney, "From Quasi-Federation to Quasi-Confederacy? The Transformation of India's Party System", *Publius: The Journal of Federalism,* Vol. 33, No. 4, Fall 2003, pp. 153–171.
5. C.D. Deshpande, *India: A Regional Interpretation,* Indian Council of Social Science Research & Northern Book Centre, New Delhi, 1992, Chapter 2.
6. *Ibid.*, p. 10.
7. Rajendra Vora and Anne Feldhaus, *Region, Culture, and Politics in India,* Manohar, New Delhi, 2006, 'Introduction', pp. 10–11.
8. *Ibid.*, p. 11.
9. Suhas Palshikar, "Caste Politics through the Prism of Region" in Rajendra Vora and Anne Feldhaus (Eds.) *Region, Culture and Politics in India*, Manohar, New Delhi, 2006, p. 272.
10. *Constituent Assembly Debates*, Book 3, Vol. 8, Lok Sabha Secretariat, New Delhi, 1999, 3rd printing, pp. 424–444.
11. "Mood of the Nation Poll: Best Chief Ministers", *India Today*, New Delhi, 12 February 2007, pp. 22–23.
12. *India Today*, "Majority of states now ruled by BJP or its allies", www.indiatoday.in.
13. *India Today*, New Delhi, 13 November 2019, https://www.indiatoday.in Accessed 9.12.2019.
14. *MSM Sharma* v. *Srikrishna Sinha*, *AIR*, 1960, Supreme Court, 1186, and *State of Kerala* v. *Sudarsan*, *AIR*, 1984, Kerala High Court, 1.
15. *Kihota* v. *Zachilhu*, *AIR,* 1993, Supreme Court, p. 412.
16. P.M. Bakshi, *op. cit.,* 2006, pp. 198–199.
17. Stephen Howes, Ashok Lahiri and Nicholas Stern, *State-Level Reforms: Towards more Effective Government*, Macmillan, New Delhi, 2003.
18. *The Economic Times*, New Delhi, 5 April 2007, p. 14.
19. Myron Weiner, "India's Two Political Cultures" in Lucian Pye and Sidney Verba (Eds.), *Political Culture and Political Development,* Princeton University Press, Princeton, 1965.
20. M.P. Singh, "Interview Response(s) on India's Political Culture" in R.A. Sharma and Sushma Yadav (Eds.), *Political Culture in Post-Independent India,* Krishi Kunj, New Delhi, 1989, pp. 183–209.
21. Sajal Basu, *Regional Movements: Politics of Language, Ethnicity, Identity,* Manohar Publications, New Delhi, 1992, p. 21.

22. Myron Weiner, *Sons of the Soil: Migrations and Ethnic Conflict in India,* Oxford University Press, Delhi, 1988, the quotes from p. 296 and p. 266.
23. Francine Frankel and M.S.A. Rao (Eds.) *Dominance and State Power in Modern India: Decline of a Social Order,* 2 Volumes, Oxford University Press, New Delhi, 1989 & 1990.
24. M.S.A. Rao, "Some Conceptual Issues in the Study of Caste, Class, Ethnicity and Dominance", *Ibid.,* Vol. I, p. 41.
25. Francine Frankel, "Introduction", in Frankel & Rao (Eds.), *op. cit.*
26. *Ibid.,* p. 12.
27. Francine Frankel, *Ibid.*, "Conclusion", p. 503.
28. *Ibid.*
29. *Ibid.,* pp. 503–4.
30. Rob Jenkins (Ed.), *Regional Reflections: Comparing Politics Across India's States,* Oxford University Press, New Delhi, 2004.
31. Loraine Kennedy, "The Political Determinants of Reform Packaging: Competing Responses to Economic Liberalization in Andhra Pradesh and Tamil Nadu," in Jenkins (Ed.), *op. cit.,* pp. 29–65.
32. Aseema Sinha, "Ideas, Interests and Institutions in Policy Change: A Comparison of West Bengal and Gujarat," Jenkins (Ed.), *op. cit.,* pp. 66–108.
33. Sanjay Kumar, "Janata Regionalized: Contrasting Bases of Electoral Support in Bihar and Orissa", Jenkins (Ed.), *op. cit.,* pp. 111–138.
34. Christopher Jaffrelot and Jasmine Zerinini-Brotel, "Post-Mandal' Politics in Uttar Pradesh and Madhya Pradesh" Jenkins (Ed.), *op. cit.,* pp. 139–174.
35. Ashutosh Varshney, "States of Cities? Studying Hindu-Muslim Riots", Chapter 6, pp. 177–218; and Rob Jenkins, "In Varying States of Decay Anti-Corruption Politics in Maharashtra and Rajasthan" *Ibid.*,pp. 219–252. Both in Jenkins (Ed.), *op. cit.*
36. Rob Jenkins, *Ibid.*,p. 237. See also Ashutosh Varshney, Ethnic Conflict and Civic Life: IIindua and Muslims in India, Oxford University Press, New Delhi, 2002.
37. James Manor, "Explaining Political Trajectories in Andhra Pradesh and Karnataka", Jenkins (Ed.), *op. cit.,* pp. 255–284.
38. Mukulika Banerjee, "Populist Leadership in West Bengal and Tamil Nadu: Mamta and Jayalalitha Compared", Jenkins (Ed.), *op. cit.,* pp. 285–308.
39. *Ibid.,* p. 304.
40. Arvind Panagariya, Pinaki Chakrborty, and M. Govinda Rao, *State Level Reforms, Growth, and Development in Indian States,* Oxford University Press, New York, 2014.

Chapter

9

Local Self-Government—The Third Tier of Multi-Level Governance
An Unexplored Internal Frontier?

INTRODUCTION

A local self-government is common to both parliamentary and federal constitutions. What differentiates the two constitutions is the fact that the parliamentary framework of a local self-government is devolutionary, whereas in a truly federal system, it could be federative. In the real world of federalism, however, Switzerland is probably the only country where one could talk of a federative structure of all the three levels of the governments, which derive their powers from the Constitution itself. Another recent example is the new Constitution of Nepal (2015). In other federations, only the federal and State governments are constitutional entities, whereas local self-government derives its structure and powers from the state legislations. In India, the 73rd and 74th constitutional amendments entrench the local self-government in the Constitution, but in reality they are prescriptive model Acts for the states which are constitutionally empowered to legislate them within their respective jurisdictions. Thus, the status of these amendments is more or less comparable to the Directive Principles of State Policy in the Constitution which are not "enforceable by any court, but … nevertheless fundamental in the governance of the country…" (Article 37).

HISTORY

The history of local political institutions in India goes back to the ancient and medieval times. In ancient India, literary and historical sources mention *sabhas, samitis*, and *vidatha* in the vedic period and *gramas, janapadas,* and *mahajanapadas* in the post-vedic period in north India and *sabhas, urs,* and *nagarams* in early medieval south India.[1] These institutions generally flourished with greater autonomy under the regional kingdoms but suffered a decline under the sub-continental states.[2] In the medieval India, the sub-continental states were largely minimalist in the sense that they left the local social and political institutions with considerable autonomy so long as the revenue flow was uninterrupted. In British India, the earliest municipalities were established in Madras, in 1688, and in Bombay and Calcutta in 1762. Lord Mayo's Resolutions of 1870 postulated the introduction of an elected President in the municipalities. Lord Ripon's Resolution on local self-government in 1882 established the rudimentary structure of municipal bodies that has continued in its essentials till today with incidental elaborations and modifications. After these executive-in-council resolutions, there followed statutory provisions under law, e.g. the Bombay Municipal Corporation Act, 1888, the City of Nagpur Corporation Act, 1957. These were all Central Acts in British India. The subsequent Acts that followed are all of the post-Independence period legislated by State governments under federal set-up, e.g. the Bombay Provincial Municipal Corporations Act, 1949, the Gujarat Municipalities Act, 1964, etc.

URBAN-RURAL VARIATIONS

The municipal management patterns vary between small towns and cities and in big and metropolitan cities, and between these two categories of urban areas. In towns and cities, the council and the chairman are assisted by (a) locally recruited municipal personnel, or (b) state cadre officials, or (c) by a mixed group of All-India and state services. In big cities and metros there are two management patterns. These are (a) the Commissioner system, and (b) the Mayor-in-Council system. The latter is found in municipal corporations in West Bengal, while the former system is typical of the rest of India. The Mayor-in-Council system is more democratic in which the elected functionaries constitute the executive and deliberative bodies and the Commissioner and other officials work under their directive and control. In the other system, the Commissioner and his staff exercise the real executive power and the Mayor and the Council function in deliberative and advisory capacity.[3]

In the rural domain, the beginnings were made by Ripon's Resolution of 1882 under which district boards and local/*Taluka* boards were set up with the nominated members to manage health, roads and education at the regional level. An executive resolution of 1918 stressed that the objective of these bodies was to train the people in the management of their regional or local affairs. The District Board Act, 1922, reconstituted these Boards to synchronize them with the scheme of Diarchy under the Government of India Act, 1919, that transferred some administrative subjects in education, public health, road maintenance, and drainage to the elected ministers at the provincial level.

The state of affairs of the urban governments in India have remained, even after Independence, largely under bureaucratic domination of the State governments. Besides this bureaucratic domination of municipal institutions, city councils are also elbowed out from their legitimate local self-government concerns by a large number of State government agencies dealing with urban development and utilities and services. The undemocratic nature of urban governance is well-attested by the 74th constitutional amendment bill itself as follows: "In many states local bodies have become weak and ineffective on account of a variety of reasons, including prolonged supersessions and inadequate devolution of powers and functions. As a result, urban local bodies are not able to perform effectively as vibrant democratic units of self-government".[4]

Between the German practice of *general competence* (any power not reserved for higher levels) and the British practice of *delegated* power of municipal bodies, India for obvious reasons belongs to the latter tradition. Various state laws give long and sometimes variable functions to urban local bodies. Yet the major functions actually performed by them are typically the following: (i) public health and sanitation, (ii) drinking water supply and drainage, (iii) public works and municipal roads, (iv) elementary education, and (v) health clinics and maternity homes. The 12th Schedule to the Constitution added by the 74th constitutional amendment has expanded municipal functions into new areas like economic and social planning, welfare of the weaker sections, and poverty alleviation. In practice, municipal governments now derive items not only from the State List but also from the Concurrent List in the 7th Schedule of the Constitution.[5] This is a point of federal significance whose implications are yet to be fully worked out and tested.

The process of downward political federalization in India has reached the state level where a minimal institutional, functional, and financial wherewithal has become operative with a certain degree of popular representation and accountability. In urban governance, bureaucratic and technocratic rationality with slant towards the centre and the state still prevails over the multipurpose representative town/city/metropolitan self-governing institutions. The half-hearted institutional scaffoldings that have been in existence or the exploratory ventures that have been made are riddled with territorial, institutional, public versus private partnership, and fiscal ambiguities. The scenario is still largely authoritarian with a bureaucratic bias. The issues of democratization and federalization are still far cries in the emerging concrete jungles, the shanty towns, and the suburbia. The questions of equitable services across the board on the basis of fair and equitable taxation cannot even begin to be addressed without democratization and federalization of these "areas of darkness" at the proclaimed dawn of neoliberal capitalist growth miracle in India today. An observer of the scene of urban governance in India bemoans: "The existing state of knowledge is barely sufficient to describe the institutional base at the level of cities. Virtually, nothing is known about the process of governing the urban areas; even less is known as to what distinguishes the governance of larger cities from the smaller ones."[6]

TWO PERSPECTIVES ON PEOPLE'S POWER

The state of urban local government finances are in a bad shape. In 2000/01 municipal finances were a mere 0.63 per cent of the GDP. In 2001/02 relative shares of own-source revenue in percentage terms were very skewed: 3.07 for municipalities, 39.5 for State Governments, and 57.5 for the Union government.[7]

Following the Independence, a major restructuring of the local self-government was attempted by the Union and State governments. There were, broadly speaking, two perspectives on this question. The Gandhian view presented a scheme of radical decentralization which would make the grassroots democracy the mainspring of political power in the polity. This was the 'bottoms-up' approach or power of the people scheme consistent with the principle of popular sovereignty advocated by the thinker like Jean Jaques Rousseau in his political thought. The approach actually adopted by a Congress-dominated Constituent Assembly was sharply different from this, which actually amounted to 'top-down' approach or power-to-the people approach as devolved from above. A version of the first approach was also developed by M.N. Roy in his Radical Humanist phase in the 1950s (genuinely powerful local communes or soviets within the larger framework of parliamentary democracy). Yet another alternative version was offered by Jayaprakash Narayan in the early 1960s during his Gandhian socialist phase in which the parliamentary federal structure would be replaced by a structure of panchayat democracy with directly elected bodies only at the local level, and the state panchayats and the national panchayats would be constructed indirectly by co-opting the executive heads of the lower panchayats.

POST-INDEPENDENCE TRAJECTORY

The post-Independence India first began with the structure of local self-government bequeathed by the British Raj and supplemented it with launching of a multi-purpose Community Development Programme (CDP) in rural areas as part of the planning process of the Nehru government. The CDP instituted a new administrative unit called *Block* intermediate between the sub-district unit called subdivision and the villages. The Block Development Officers (BDOs), Extension Officers (EOs) and Village Level Workers (VLWs) were pressed into service as the agents of change and development. In 1957, the Planning Commission of India appointed the Balwantrai Mehta Committee to review the working of the CDP and suggest measures to generate popular enthusiasm and participation in the process of planned economic development and local self-government. The Committee recommended a scheme of democratic decentralization with a three-tier structure of rural local self-governments at village, block, and district levels with transfer of resources and responsibilities. Prime Minister Jawaharlal Nehru in Nagaur district in Rajasthan inaugurated the restructured Panchayat Raj system under various State legislations in 1959. In the restructured Panchayati Raj Institutions (PRIs), some States introduced Block planning (Andhra Pradesh and Tamil Nadu) and some other initiated District Planning (Maharashtra and Gujarat).

By the late 1970s, the first inter-party transfer of power from the Centre to the States took place when the Congress lost to the Janata Party at the national level and practically all States in the north. The rise of the Janata Party symbolized a reaction against centralization of political power during the Congress regime of Indira Gandhi. Ideologically, the Janata Party was motivated by democracy and sociologically it was predominantly a peasant party led by middle-class intellectuals. The Janata Party government appointed the Ashok Mehta Committee to review the working of the PRIs. The Committee found fault with the policy of the previous governments in channelizing the development programmes through the bureaucracy, and devolving limited powers and finances to the PRIs. It also lamented the domination of these bodies by the socio-economically dominant sections of the society at the local level. It recommended a two-tier structure at the Block and the District level, presumably aiming at consolidation of villages to transform their scattered existence into *mandals or* blocks. It also suggested a departure from the Gandhian preference for a non-party political processes at the local level by allowing participation of political parties in panchayat elections. Moreover, it proposed reservation of seats for both women and weaker sections of the society.

The fall of the Janata Party governments at the Centre in 1979 and in most States in the north soon thereafter created an uncongenial atmosphere for the implementation of the Ashok Mehta Committee Report. However, the Janata Party government in Karnataka, the Left Front governments in West Bengal and Kerala, and the Telugu Desam Party government in Andhra Pradesh did restructure their PRIs following some of the recommendations of the Mehta panel. The Congress Party governments at the Centre under Indira Gandhi in 1980 and Rajiv Gandhi in 1984 appointed a series of committees to study and report on PRI reforms. Yet it is difficult to escape the conclusion that the official thought in the realm of rural self-government over all these years was to move away from the village, to the Block or to the District in the triangular relationship among democracy, development, and decentralization. The trend appears to be towards centralization, by and large. The Rajiv Gandhi Congress government in its swan-song action moved a constitutional amendment bill in 1989 that sought to bypass the states in significant ways and establish direct link of the centre with the Panchayat Raj by transferring local self-government from the State List to the Concurrent List. The bill was passed by the Lok Sabha with the government majority, but fell in the Rajya Sabha where non-Congress parties coming to power in various states throughout the 1980s had dented the Congress majority as the State Legislatures constitute the electoral college for the federal second chamber.[8]

POST-CONSTITUTIONAL AMENDMENTS SCENARIO

So far, the most notable development not only in the field of rural democratic decentralization but local self-governing institutions (LSCIs) *per se* transpired during the period of the P.V. Narasimha Rao Congress minority government (1991–1996). The 73rd and 74th constitutional amendments passed in 1992 and gazetted in 1993 have now put the local-level political systems on a sort of constitutional footing with a detailed uniform framework. The Acts were preceded by detailed Union-State consultations and accompanied by a broad government-opposition consensus in the Parliament. Going beyond Article 12 (defining the state) and Article 40 (organization of village panchayats), the Constitution incorporated a new Article 243 and the new schedules—11th and the 12th schedule—providing for the structures, functions and subjects of panchayats and municipalities. The "model Acts" in the Constitution prompted the States to establish under State statutes, a three-tier vertical structure of PRIs at village, intermediate, and district levels and a horizontal pattern of three kinds of city governments—Nagar Panchayats for transitional "suburban" areas, Municipal Councils for smaller urban areas, and Municipal Corporations for larger urban areas. For the first time the autonomous State Election Commissions were to be established for ensuring regularity of free and fair local elections and equitable and viable finances from the State governments to the local bodies.

The LSGIs were also made socially more inclusive by making it mandatory to reserve 1/3rd seats for women and proportional representation to SCs and STs in relation to their population in an area.[9]

The 73rd and 74th amendments have brought about the hope for a paradigm shift in grassroots democracy in the country. The conforming State Acts are in place all over the country and the State Election Commissions and the State Finance Commissions have also been formed in almost all States. This, in itself, combined with the mandatory representation of formerly excluded sections from the rural and urban power structures, must be regarded as a significant step forward.

Peter Ronald deSouza highlights the paradox of the new phase of decentralized democracy that begins with 73rd Constitutional amendment. The paradox lies in the fact that a constitutional amendment, which is a centralized instrument, has been deployed to empower panchayati raj, which is a dencentralized activity. He argues that the new PRIs create a new "opportunity space" for citizens and groups whereby they can compete for social resources. Since after Independence, there has been growth in the demands placed on the political system, new PRIs can be viewed as a response to meet demand overload. Moreover, the entry of new political leaders into the political system at the local level exerts pressure on state level leaders to improve service delivery, thus posing a threat of replacing state level leaders.[10]

In the restructured PRIs, an institution of crucial importance is the District Planning Committee (DPC) charged with the responsibility of preparing the draft development plan taking into account matters of common interest between the panchayats and the municipalities in the district including spatial planning, sharing of water and other physical and natural resources, and integrated infrastructural development and environmental conservation. The output of this exercise is to be forwarded to the State government. However, at this writing (October 2020), in some states, District Planning Committees are not yet constituted, while in most states where they are set up, they are formed not as envisaged in the advisory constitutional amendments. In states like Chhattisgarh, Gujarat, Madhya Pradesh, Odisha, Maharashtra, and Himachal Pradesh, ministers are chairpersons, making them centralised at the state level.

The massive political mobilization and equitable representational effect of the first round of PRIs' elections in the country is evident from the fact that 31,98,554 representatives were elected to the village panchayats throughout the country. The 5736 intermediate panchayats were put in place with 1,51,412 members. The 467 zila or district panchayats comprised of 17,935 members. The decentralization of powers and funds, of course, left much to be desired.[11] Yet neither the present scenario nor the prospects are considered pessimistic by competent observers. Developments such as Union Finance Commission's cognizance of the local bodies, the Right to Information Act (2002), National Rural Employment Guarantee Act (2005), a law granting semi-judicial powers to panchayats, etc., are expected to reduce the gap between their *de jure* and *de facto* status and empower them with the three requisite "Fs": functions, finances and functionaries.[12]

In the urban areas where Municipal Corporations barring those in metropolitan cities were practically superseded and placed under bureaucrats. This has now changed. In the rural areas, there is a great democratic ferment. For the first time, LSGIs have acquired a country-wide presence and recognition. The major success stories in PRIs have come from the states of Kerala and West Bengal where the Communist Party of India (CPI)(M) utilized the panchayats as the basis of popular mobilization against the bourgeois parties in the States and against the federal power structure. The ideological line in favour of such mobilization is attributed to E.M.S. Namboodiripad and Jyoti Basu. A similar grassroots mobilization but on non-left lines was initiated in Karnataka by the Janata Dal Chief Minister, Ramkrishna Hegde, by the Telugu Desam Party Chief Minister N.T. Rama Rao in Andhra Pradesh, and in Madhya Pradesh by the Congress Chief Minister Digvijay Singh. These earlier initiatives have created a new political momentum in these States and may perhaps have impacts in the rest of the country. In other States, the provincial governments have been rather reluctant to share power with PRIs. In Left Front-ruled West Bengal, the PRIs, were given an important role in the implementation of the Operation Barga aimed at identifying the real tillers of the soil and registering them as tenants. In Kerala, a powerful movement for decentralized development through local level participatory planning was launched. The initiatives of the communist parties presented a more consensual picture of local democracy and development in Kerala where the CPM-led Left Democratic Front (LDF) and the Congress-led United Democratic Front (UDF) have shared power alternatively on regular basis in recent decades. In West Bengal where the CPM-led Left Front ruled continuously since 1977 to 2011, there emerged a trend of the party cadres virtually monopolizing the PRIs. This trend of party in power at the state level and local government becoming indistinguishable, was challenged both electorally and through violent confrontation by the Trinamool Congress led by Mamata Banerjee, who finally dislodged the Communist Party of India (Marxist)-led Left Front after its nearly three and a half decades of back-to-back electoral majority and political power. This impression is supported by a close observation in the field that underlines "The partisan, character of distribution of resources at the local level by the GPs [Gram Panchayats], combined with centralized party control of inter-regional allocation of development funds".[13] In Madhya Pradesh, the PRIs played an important part in implementing the Education Guarantee Scheme of the State Government where more than 20 per cent increase in literacy was registered in the 1990s.[14] In Karnataka and Maharashtra, gram panchayats took steps to undertake collection of house taxes, which contributed to an increase of over 200 per cent on an average in the own-source revenues as contrasted with transferred finances from higher levels of government. The city corporation of Bangalore has pioneered in making its budget and working voluntarily transparent.[15] The Surat municipality in Gujarat after the pandemic plagues in the early 1990s, stirred itself into action. Surat today, responding to this crisis is among the well-functioning city governments and is one of the cleanest cities in India.[16]

Satyajt Singh in his book *The Local in Governance* attempts to shift the focus from a centralized state to self-rule at the local level. The book provides a political perspective on decentralization and emphasizes the significance of the "political" with regard to administrative reforms towards local governance. He argues that when diverse decentralized institution interacts with local politics, it leads to divergent outcomes. Thus, local governance is not only a result of institutions but also is determined by local politics. He views decentralization as an ongoing process and argues that by analyzing the working of local institutions, future administrative reforms can be directed. He emphasizes the role of institutions in transforming society and bringing changes in societal power relations leading to diverse outcomes from reordering of society and distribution of resources. He argues that the design and form of decentralization at the state level is contested and is a consequence of political engagement. The different models of decentralization in states are product of diversity of institution and political context. The move towards a democratic and decentralized state necessitates understanding of local political context and the architecture of intuitions.[17]

A notable development of the late 1990s has been the passage of the Panchayats (Extension to Scheduled Areas) Act (PESA), 1996, by the Parliament of India. It extends the provisions of the 73rd Amendment in the Constitution to the Fifth Schedule Areas in these 10 States: Andhra Pradesh, Chhattisgarh, Gujarat, Himachal Pradesh, Jharkhand, Madhya Pradesh, Maharashtra, Odisha, Rajasthan, and Telangana, with certain modifications and exemptions. These areas in these States have preponderance of tribal population. The objective of the PESA is to make the benefits of Panchayat available to the tribal inhabitants of the Fifth Schedule areas in a way that does not erode the federal autonomies and protection constitutionally guaranteed to them under the Fifth Schedule in a special way, under the discretionary power of the governor not subject to ministerial advice of the State government. This is a feature of what is called "asymmetrical federalism" in federal theory (See Chapter 7). The Union Ministry of Panchayati Raj is the nodal ministry for the implementation of the PESA in conformity with the Fifth Schedule provisions.

A LONG WAY TO GO

Yet there is still a long way to go. None of the State Acts has transferred all the 29 subjects to the Panchayats and the 18 subjects to the urban councils in the 11th and 12th Schedules of the Constitution. To quote two close observers of the working of LSGIs in India: "The involvement of the lSGIs in planning has undergone little change over the past. Recent evidence suggests that even elections have remained problematical in many states."[18] In India the share of local government expenditure in the total public expenditure is only 5 per cent as compared to 30 per cent in member countries of OECD. Similarly, the share of local government expenditure in India's GDP is only 2 per cent compared to around 14 per cent in OECD countries[19]. The LSGIs have yet to go a long way to be properly called the *third tier of the Indian federal structure*. The decentralization within the Constitution and State legislations continues to be *devolutionary*. They are not strictly federal in the strict sense of term. Only a radical mass movement for Gandhian decentralization can bring about a paradigmatic shift from devolutionary decentralization to federal decentralization in India. Another possible route to this denouement may be a judicial intervention and consequent change in constitutional law. Any change in this direction by the political leadership has turned out to be elusive.

REFERENCES

1. Romila Thapar, *A History of India,* Middlesex, Penguin Books, 1996.
2. Romila Thapar, *Ibid.*, and Burton Stein, *Peasant, State and Society in Medieval South India*, Delhi: Oxford University Press, 1980.
3. Asok Mukhopadhyay, "Politics and Bureaucracy in Urban Governance: The Indian Experience" in Om Prakash Mathur (Ed.), *India: The*

Challenge of Urban Governance, New Delhi: National Institute of Public Finance & Policy in Collaboration with Centre for Urban and Community Studies, University of Toronto, 1999, pp. 109–128.

4. Abhijit Datta, "Institutional Aspects of Urban Governance" in Om Prakash Mathur (Ed.), *Ibid.,* 89.

5. *Ibid.,* pp. 96–97.

6. Om Prakash Mathur, "Governing Cities: Facing up to the Challenge of Poverty and Globalization" in O.P. Mathur (Ed.), *Ibid.,* p. 43.

7. Om Prakash Mathur, "Local Government Organization and Finance: Urban India," in Anwar Shah (Ed.), *Local Governance in Developing Countries,* Public Sector Governance and Accountability Series, Washington, D.C., The World Bank, 2006, p. 196.

8. See for larger issues involved, M.P. Singh, "a Double-Edged Sword," *Seminar,* No. 360, August 1989, pp. 41–43, among others, in a special issue on "The Panchayati Renewal".

9. Scheduled Areas in Eight states—Andhra Pradesh, Madhya Pradesh, Rajasthan, Gujarat, Maharashtra, Himachal Pradesh, Orissa and Bihar under the Fifth Schedule of the Constitution had their own traditional tribal panchayats so the statutory panchayats were not applicable there. This state of affairs has now changed following the 73rd constitutional amendment by the panchayats (Extension) to the Schedule Areas Act, 1996.

10. Peter Ronald deSouza, Decentralization and Local Government: The 'Second wind' of Democracy in India, *India's Living Constitution.* Zoya Hasan, Eswaran Sridharan, and R. Sudarshan (Eds.), New Delhi, Orient Blackswan, 2004.

11. Nirja Gopal Jayal, Amit Prakash, Pradeep K. Sharma (Eds.), *Local Governance in India: Decentralization and Beyond,* New Delhi, Oxford University Press, 2006, p. 8.

12. V.N. Alok, "Local Government Organization and Finance: Rural India" in Anwar Shah (Ed.), *Local Governance in Developing Countries,* Public Sector Governance and Accountability Series, Washington, D.C., The World Bank, 2006, pp. 228–229.

13. Pranab Bardhan and Dilip Mookherjee, "Decentralization in West Bengal: Origins, Functioning and Impact" in Pranab Bardhan and Dilip Mokherjee (Eds.), *Decentralization and Local Governance in Developing Countries: A Comparative Perspective,* Cambridge, Massachusetts: The MIT Press, 2006, p. 221.

14. Vinod Vyasulu, "The Functioning of Local Government in Federal Systems: Perspectives from India" is John Kincaid and Rupak Chattopadhyay (Eds.), *Local Government in Federal Systems,*

Vol. 4 in the Series Unity in Diversity; Learning From Each Other, New Delhi, Viva Books, 2008, pp. 68–69.

15. *Ibid.*, p. 69.

16. *Ibid.*

17. Satyajit Singh, *The Local in Governance: Politics, Decentralization and Environment*, Oxford University Press, New Delhi, 2016.

18. T.M. Thomas Issac and Richard W. Franke, *Local Democracy and Development; People's Campaign for Decentralized Planning in Kerala,* New Delhi, Left World, 2000, p. 7.

19. *The Economic Times*, New Delhi, 13 July 2011, p. 2.

Chapter 10

Bureaucracy
The Permanent Government?

HISTORY

Bureaucracy, a regular feature of the executive organ of the Government, is among the earlier institutions correlated with State-formation, along with monarchy. It is also a ubiquitous feature of a modern democratic State as also of a modern authoritarian State. Authoritarian States, in fact, are primarily a bureaucratic entity through and through. Liberal democratic States typically began with rather limited bureaucracies, developed enormous bureaucratic organizations as the State increasingly took on the responsibilities of a Welfare State and/or intervened in the economy in the post-World War II era. By the late 1970s onwards, as the neo-liberal economic policies supplanted the Keynesian and socialistic policy frameworks, debureaucratization and downsizing the State have come to the forefront of the agenda of economic and political reforms worldwide.

Comparative political theorists have often been ambivalent towards bureaucracy. There have been those who consider it an essential condition of establishing a State or a capitalist system.[1] There have also been those who argue that in initial stages of democracy, if bureaucracy is too powerful in relation to political parties, it can damage the prospects of democracy.[2] In addition, there have also been reform movements in the past and neo-liberal crusades in recent years advocating the downsizing or gradual dismantling of bureaucracy. However, Ezra Suleiman cautions against celebrating the impending demise of bureaucracy and argues that bureaucracy plays an important role in building and preserving democratic political systems and its absence may endanger the survival of democracy itself. To quote him, "the historical development of the US, Britain, France, Japan, Prussia, and, in recent times, Korea, Taiwan, and India indicates that the development of bureaucratic authority accompanied and facilitated the development of the State and the subsequent development of democracy. Why, then, suggest a path of development to emerging democracies that no consolidated democracy has followed?"[3]

In a similar view, contributors to a volume on bureaucracy edited by Paul Du Gay underline the theme that distinctively bureaucratic forms of organization continue to serve values of good governance if this form of authority is adapted to the new emphasis on "public management" and the growth of the civil society. They argue that though the `end of bureaucracy' has been anticipated many a time in modern, social and political theory, bureaucracy would continue to have relevance in ordering our political, social, economic and cultural existence.[4]

India was one of the earliest countries to have developed an extensive bureaucracy as early as the 4th/3rd centuries B.C. under the aegis of the Mauryan State in Magadh. Founded by Chandragupta and carried forward to its apogee by Ashoka, the established historical interpretation of the nature of this State is that it was a vast centralized bureaucratic monarchy with a large officialdom on the payrolls of the State. When the Mauryan State declined in the early common era, the practice of land grants to State officials and Brahmans by post-Mauryan States transformed the bureaucratic nature of the monarchies into feudal States that were served by grantees of landed estates called *samantas* and later, in medieval India, the *iqtadars* and *jagirdars*. The Mughal State, especially under Akbar, tried to transform *jagirdars* into *mansabdars* (salaried State officials), but the move was largely unsuccessful.[5] These agrarian bureaucracies under bureaucratic as well as feudal monarchies were what Max Weber called traditional or patrimonial bureaucracies, in the sense of being treated as the extension of the royal household or the patrimony of the King.

The beginning of a modern Weberian bureaucracy in India, in the sense of achievement-(rather than ascription)-based recruitment and institutionalized autonomy, may be attributed to the British Raj in India. But this credit must be moderated in view of the two facts: (a) the establishment of the Indian Civil Service (ICS) around the mid-19th century was preceded by the existence of the venal bureaucracy of the East India Company, and (b) even after the replacement of the Company by the Crown in 1858, the British left the feudal structure intact in Indian princely states under the British paramountcy, as distinguished from the British Indian provinces directly administered under the Parliament and the Crown of the United Kingdom. Territorially, the British Indian provinces and the princely Indian states accounted for almost half each of the total extent of the British Indian empire. Indeed, more specifically, the princely states covered 52 per cent of the total territory. Moreover, the British abolished the *jagirdar* grandees, but retained/created a class of small and local *zamindars* in the Bengal Presidency, the earliest seat of British power in India. Thus, this system allowed a class of feudal or semi-feudal intermediaries between the State and the real tillers of the land. Other areas were subsequently brought under *ryotbari* and *mahalbari* systems in the rest of India where intermediaries did not exist.

POSTCOLONIAL TRADITION

The top-ranking bureaucratic apparatus of the postcolonial State in India was designed by the Government of India, dominated by Jawaharlal Nehru and Sardar Vallabhbhai Patel, the first Prime Minister and Deputy Prime Minister in charge of the Home Ministry respectively, acting through the representative institutions of the Constituent Assembly (doubling as the provisional Parliament) and the provincial premiers' conference chaired by the Union Home Minister. Even though Nehru, fancying himself as one of the "Children of the Indian revolution", was initially critical of the imperial British ICS and the Indian Police, he was subsequently persuaded by Patel to endorse the collective wisdom in the Constituent Assembly to adapt these bureaucratic structures to the needs of independent Indian developmental State to ward off "chaos" in the wake of the partition and religious communal holocaust.[6]

The Constituent Assembly finally resolved to institute the All-India Services (AISs), Central Services, and State Services with constitutional entrenchment and protection followed by a conforming parliamentary enactment. In other federal political systems, there are only two cadres—federal and provincial—and set up only under parliamentary statutes sans constitutional entrenchment. The AISs are a unique federal bureaucratic structure. So far, they comprise civil, police, and forest service officers. The Constitution has provision for creation of more such services by the Union executive if backed by a Rajya Sabha resolution backed by two-thirds majority. They are recruited by an independent Union Public Service Commission (UPSC) set up under the Constitution, trained in federal training academies, provided in-service field training under State Governments, and allocated to specific State cadres, accommodating, as far as possible, the preferences of the recruits.

Typically, about 50 per cent of IAS officers get empanelled by the Union Government on the basis of their confidential reports (CRs) and their performance in the State Governments, for their deputation to the Central Government. The performance rating is very rigorous. Through this channel, an IAS officer commonly may spend about 15/16 years (in piecemeal instalments) of their 30-odd years of service in their career, half of it in their allocated cadre and half at the centre on deputation.

These officials occupy the top echelons of administrative, police, and forest services both in the State and the Union Governments. When serving the Union, they are loaned on deputation from their parent State cadres to the Government of India temporarily. They are under the disciplinary jurisdictions of the specific Government under which they happen to be serving for the moment, though the ultimate disciplinary action against them is subject to the approval of the President of India acting on the advice of the Personnel Department of the Union Home Ministry.

The IAS is the paramount civil service in the country sitting over the pyramid of the labyrinthine bureaucratic apparatus of the various orders of

Governments in India. "Today the IAS is the core of the country's administrative structure, sharing its tasks with a number of All-India, Central, and State services and providing strong administrative links for the country."[7]

An astute observer of the "Public Services", the term used for bureaucracy in the Indian Constitution, remarked in 1971:

> The system of bureaucracy as it exists in India has a *continuous* history of more than one hundred years. While these hundred years have been revolutionary from the point of view of the country's social, economic and political life, the organization of bureaucracy and the assumption on which it is based have remained unaltered even unquestioned. The legacy has been accepted.[8]

A British observer, of what he calls "India's political administrators", writing in the first half of the 1990s, by and large, concurs with the above assessment: "Broadly speaking, I have tried in this book to describe central features of the ICS tradition of administration and to explain their persistence through time."[9] This bureaucratic legacy of the Raj put premium on a hierarchical, almost caste-like, bureaucratic structure and values and behaviour patterns consistent with it. The political administrators of the Raj had "allocated scarce resources with an eye to their political support" as district collectors and were "centrally involved in the formulation of policy both at the centre and in the provinces" as secretaries.[10] "Persons who shared that collective identity shared a particular location in society and a particular mode of thought and valuation attached to that location. It was that location and that mode that carried on as the ICS tradition, not the persons who came and went."[11]

The 1950s and '60s witnessed a great expansion in the size of the AISs due to (a) shift from revenue and law and order administration to development administration, and (b) the development of the mixed economy with a dominant state or public sector in the process of industrialization. Besides this horizontal expansion of the process of administration and public management, the governments in India also expanded vertically down to the district, subdistrict, and block levels. This diversification of the political economy and the political system put a special premium on political communication, public administration and public management. Since the 1990s, the shift to business liberalism demanded a new orientation in providing greater space and opening to market forces and civil society organizations of non-governmental type. The omnipresent AISs, especially the IAS officers, have been expected to smoothen these transitions as well as work them out. We have some data on the posting of IAS officers in 1983 that give us a glimpse of their strategic position and manoeuvrability. In 1983, 40 per cent of these officers were serving in the State Government secretariats, 27 per cent in district administration, 13 per cent in state or central public sector enterprises, 14 per cent in the Union Government secretariat, and 6 per cent accounted for the residual "Other" category.[12]

Potter's crystal gazing in this context is worth-quoting:

> In the intense struggle currently going on within the bureaucracy at the end of the twentieth century between the IAS and rival services from below demanding greater equality and an enhanced role for specialist expertise, one senses that the IAS and its tradition are becoming increasingly isolated, that more vigorous forces are closing in. The end of the essential political support may not be far behind. Once each IAS person is required to opt for a particular career pattern, a proposal being seriously considered in 1993 (even within the IAS), then the rationale for generalist collectors, secretaries, the tenure system, and all the rest is weakened.[13]

The bureaucratic hangover from the British Raj did not sit comfortably with the central features of the Constitution of independent India, such as parliamentary federal principles of Government emphasizing parliamentary control and federal autonomy, fundamental rights of citizens and directive principles of State policy and the strategy of planned economic development.[14]

In the wake of the first and subsequent phases of formation of non-Congress governments in states, critiques were mounted of the AISs and their relevance and place "in the context of India's developing multi-party system and federal structure" by political commentators, State Governments, Administrative Reforms Commission (1968–70) appointed by the Government of India led by the then Prime Minister, Lal Bhadur Shastri (Congress party) in 1966, the Rajamannar Commission on Centre-State Relations (1971) appointed by the first DMK government in Tamil Nadu, and the Sarkaria Commission on Centre-State Relations (1988) appointed by the Government of India led by the then Prime Minister, Indira Gandhi (Congress Party) in 1983. The memorandums submitted to the Sarkaria panel showed that five states would like to opt out of the AISs and rely exclusively on the state civil services, four others wished to have greater formal control over them, but a good majority of states expressed their support for the AISs.[15]

CLASS BIAS

Despite being open to talent in principle, the top bureaucracy in India, as elsewhere, has had a definite class-bias, in addition to having an internal stratification of its own. In the words of S.C. Dube, "on the whole it symbolized achievement rather than ascription. Over time, it came to have distinct vested interests, and was sensitive to all threats to its position and privilege which it guarded jealously against encroachment from any quarter".[16] A study of socio-economic background of IAS recruits in 1966–67 and 1968–69 showed that 27 out of 126 officers in the first group and 26 out of 111 officers in the second group came from rural background.

The corresponding figures for the two groups coming from urban background were 85 in both. Data about father's occupation of officers is given in Table 10.1. It is evident that there was a strong middle class or upper class bias in the recruitment to elite bureaucratic cadre. The service was, for all practical purposes, open to only the urban and rural middle and upper classes. There was none from the working class background. There is no strong reason to believe that this may have changed, except very marginally, mainly through the SC/ST reservation route. Data about the representation of Other Backward Classes/Scheduled Castes/Scheduled Tribes in the Service of Central Government in 1979 provide some evidence for the plausibility of the above inference (Table 10.2).

TABLE 10.1 Father's Occupation of IAS Recruits in 1966–67 and 1968–69

Father's Occupation	1966–1967	1968–1969
Agriculture	21	29
Middle Class Liberal Professions	31	20
Business	9	13
IAS & Other Govt. Officers	53	43
Others and M.D.	12	6

Source: Abstracted from C.P. Bhambhri, *Bureaucracy and Politics in India* (Vikas Publications, Delhi, 1971, p. 65).

TABLE 10.2 Representation of OBCs/SCs/STs in the Service of the Central Government in 1979, Classes I & II (Percentages)

Class I (*Total N* = 174021)		*Class II* (*Total N* = 912925)	
SCs/STs	OBCs	SCs/STs	OBCs
18.33	12.27	50.56	25.63

Source: Abstracted from the *Report of the Backward Classes Commission,* (Government of India), New Delhi, 1980, Part I, p. 88.

The upper class/caste bias in the compositions of both the bureaucratic and political elites of the early post-Independence decades that had created a more or less one-class ensemble in administration and politics has been gradually changing over time. Yet, since bureaucratic and political recruitments have been open to reservations and larger status reversals in the society and economy, a sharp class confrontation between the bureaucratic and political classes has been staved off.

PARLIAMENTARY/MINISTERIAL CONTROL OF BUREAUCRACY

The question of bureaucratic accountability in a democracy is a complex one. The conventional democratic wisdom is "to think of the bureaucracy as an instrumental apparatus for the execution of policies established through `political', non-bureaucratic institutions".[17] As the aphorism goes, the political executive, with legislative approval, lays down the policy, and the bureaucratic executive implements it. Bureaucrats are, of course, supposed to offer free and frank advice, and in the process may differ from their Ministers, but once a policy is politically determined within the framework of the law of the Constitution, officials must faithfully execute them.

In new democracies especially, this assumption may not always be taken for granted, even in countries like India and the Philippines with relatively developed parliamentary institutions. "The relative weakness of political organs means that political function tends to be appropriated, in considerable measure, by bureaucrats. Intra-bureaucratic struggles become a primary form of politics."[18] For this reason, Riggs differs from the view of Carl J. Friedrich offered in the latter's monumental work on democracy and constitutionalism. The latter argues that the emergence of constitutionalism in the West was preceded by a substantial development of bureaucratic arm of the State that was subsequently brought under control. The former, however, argues that in new democracies in the Third World "premature or too rapid expansion of the bureaucracy when the political system lags behind tends to inhibit the development of effective politics." Riggs goes on to deduce the corollary thesis that "separate political institutions have a better chance to grow if bureaucratic institutions are weak."[19]

The British theory and practice about the relation between Ministers and civil servants was outlined by Sir David Maxwell Fyfe (later Lord Kilmuir) in the House of Commons on 20 July 1954:

> The position of the civil servants is that he is wholly and directly responsible to his Minister. It is worth stating again that he holds his office at pleasure, and can be dismissed at any time by the Minister; and that power is nonetheless real because it is seldom used. The only exception relates to a small number of senior posts, like permanent secretary, deputy secretary, and principal financial officer, where since 1920, it has been necessary for the Minister to consult the Prime Minister, as he does on appointment.[20]

Sir David went on to elaborate four different categories of situations where different principles operate. First, where a clear order of the Minister has been carried out by the civil servant in accordance of the policy laid down, the former must politically defend the latter. Second, where the civil servant acts strictly within the parameters of the policy laid down, the civil servant is entitled to ministerial protection. Third, "where an official makes a mistake, or causes some delay, but not on an important issue of policy, and not where a claim to individual rights is seriously involved, the Minister acknowledges the mistake, and he accepts the responsibility, although he is not personally involved. He states that he will take corrective action in the department ... he would not in these circumstances, expose the official to public criticism." However, in the fourth contingency where a "reprehensible action of the civil servant is taken without a "prior knowledge" and which the Minister "disapproves", "then there is no obligation on the part of the Minister to endorse what he believes to be wrong, or to defend what are clearly shown to be errors of his officers". Sir David sums up by remarking that "it is part of a Minister's responsibility to Parliament to take necessary action to secure efficiency and the proper discharge of the duties of his department."[21]

The classic case of the relationship between the Union Finance Minister T.T. Krishnamachari and the Principal Finance Secretary H.M. Patel in the Nehru era gives a glimpse into the evolving constitutional practice in India regarding the foregoing. The case arose out of a decision by the Government to invest the government-controlled Life Insurance Corporation's ₹ 1,26,86,100 in private companies controlled by H.D. Mundhra in 1956. This episode throws light on Minister-civil servant relations, the Parliament and the Press, party financing, etc. The issue that surfaced in newspapers created a furore in the Parliament. An inquiry was ordered by the one-judge inquiry commission chaired by Justice M.C. Chagla of the Bombay High Court. Subsequently inquiries were also conducted by a Board of Inquiry under the All-India Services (Discipline and Appeal) Rules, 1955, and the Union Public Service Commission. The crucial testimonies of the Finance Minister and the Finance Secretary before the Commission contradicted each other. The Chagla Commission observed:

> ...whether the Minister was aware of what Mr. Patel had done on 24 June or not, when he did come to know of these transactions, he never *repudiated* the action of Mr. Patel. Therefore clearly there is *acquiescence* on the part of the Minister in the part played by Mr. Patel in bringing about the transaction of 24 June.[22]

In general terms, the Chagla Commission laid down the rule of the thumb:

> The doctrine of ministerial responsibility has two facets. The Minister has complete autonomy within his own sphere of authority. As a necessary corollary he must take full responsibility for the actions of his servants. It is true that this may throw a very great burden on the Minister because it is impossible to expect that in a highly complicated system of administration which we have evolved the Minister could possibly know, every action taken by his subordinates, let alone give his consent to them. But it is assumed that once the policy is laid down by the Minister, his subordinates must reflect that policy and loyally carry it out. If any subordinate fails to do

> so, he may be punished or dismissed but, however, vicariously, the responsibility of his action must be assumed by the Minister....[23]

As it happened, the drama ended in the denouement of the resignations by both the Minister and the Principal Finance Secretary. An important additional dimension of the episode is highlighted by the political scientist C.P. Bhambhri: "The driving force seems to be Mundhra's financial contributions to the [Congress] party funds. The Government helped him when he was in financial difficulties by using LIC as a 'milch cow'. For a businessman contributions to party funds constitute an investment for the return of favours from the Government."[24]

All this theory and practice from the Nehru era in India today appears abstract and distant. Impression, observation, experience—whatever is there to go by, all suggest a wide-spread politician-bureaucrat nexus, with corrupt brokers and criminal elements often forming part of it, for neo-feudal rent-seeking from government and society for private purposes and amoral familism. These trends have become evident at all levels from the district through the state to the centre in variable degrees, the rot at the top level being relatively less pervasive. In the opinion of an IAS insider with clean reputation, civil servants today have turned into "English-speaking politicians—corrupt, with short-term targets, narrow horizons, a feudal outlook, disrespect for norms, contributing nothing to the welfare of the nation, empty promises, and no action"[25]. He goes on to say, "Most IAS officers thus end up as deadwood within a few years of joining the service and their genius lies only in manipulation and jockeying for positions within the government"[26]. Another IAS insider narrates what a former Chief Minister of Uttar Pradesh, Mulayam Singh Yadav (Samajwadi Party) said about the IAS officers of the state while addressing an annual gathering of IAS officers of the state as the chief guest:

> You have such excellent minds and education; some of you are scholars; some of you have Nobel-prize minds; you will all succeed in any walk of life, whatever you turn your attention to; you have good jobs; you can educate your children well; and are respected by society;... why do you come and touch my feet? Why do you come and lick my shoes? Why do you come to me for personal favours? When you do so, I will do as you desire and then extract my price from you.[27]

CHANGING ROLE OF ADMINISTRATION: CHALLENGES SINCE 1947 AND THE 1990s

Bureaucracy in independent India was called upon to outgrow two of its historical legacies, namely, the law-and-order/revenue-oriented role in colonial India, and its feudalistic and patrimonial role in princely States integrated with the Indian Union. The post-Independence objectives of the Indian political system were conceptualized in terms of State-led strategy of industrialization and the goals of civic community development in rural and urban India. It was in this context that public administration in India tried to address, in its own way, the objective of building up a new structure of administration with a thrust on "development administration" conceptualized by Edward Weidner as "an action-oriented and goal-oriented administrative system".[28] Much of this discussion about development administration was made in the context of the new task of socio-economic change and national integration, though the concomitant development of the early decades after Independence was also the establishment of a bureaucratic apparatus for controlling the expanding scope of the public sector enterprises. Along with public enterprises, however, about 500 Bloc Development Officers in each newly created lowest level of administrative unit of the State were appointed and panchayati raj bodies of elected representatives were also set up. As decades rolled by, newer challenges of draught and growing mass poverty prompted additional strategies of development like the Green Revolution since the mid-1960s and Poverty Alleviation Programmes since the 1970s. Poverty alleviation measures like Antyodaya, Integrated Rural Development Programme (IRDP), White Revolution (dairy and poultry farming), etc. were initiated with assistance from nationalized banks. Thus, in the Nehru and Indira Gandhi eras, the goals pursued in terms of "socialistic" development (conceived mainly as an interventionist State with a predominant public sector) on the one hand, and populist slogan of *garibi hatao* given by Indira Gandhi (understood mainly in terms of endeavour by the State to reduce the number of the population below the poverty line) were actively undertaken.

By the end of the 1980s, both these components of development administration ran into a deep crisis. For one thing, public sector undertakings fell prey to overstaffing and irrational use of resources and incurred huge losses, while the private sector, despite heavy and often predatory regulations verging on corruption, performed much better. Besides, agriculture under private family cultivation also showed promising results in spite of inadequate investment by the State. These factors coupled with a severe balance of payment crisis—imbalance between import and export—necessitated remedial action on the part of the Indian State. Neo-liberal economic policies with accent on bureaucratic deregulation, privatization and globalization were introduced since 1991. To quote Kuldeep Mathur: "This paradigmatic shift now introduces a fresh challenge to public administration. It tends to reduce the scope of intervention, but at the same time expects a change in the quality of intervention in chosen sectors. The implication is that bureaucratic machinery is not the only instrument of policy implementation; there are alternatives in the civil society in which cooperative endeavours or community based organizations can develop their own capability of resource management and use.... The withdrawal of the State makes way for the voluntary sector. Indeed, the Eighth Plan makes a plea for a greater role of the voluntary sector as well as the market forces. In this new dispensation, then, the buzz words are bureaucratic accountability, decentralization, participation, and community-based organizations or NGOs."[29]

The new ambience has created an opening for a number of new ideas regarding New Public Management (NPM), alternative development, sustainable development, good governance, etc. New Public Management signals a shift from conventional public policy to norms of private managements in terms of cost-effectiveness. It also believes in matrix or clusters rather than pyramids of organizations for its structural framework. In addition, it emphasizes flexible and adaptive operational systems rather than rigid planning and conventional bureaucratic hierarchy.[30]

In face of increasing demand from political class and citizenry that Government should be run like a business enterprise, administrators and academic experts of public administration are under pressure to practise and theorize State administration differently from the ways and means of conventional wisdom. The new thrust has at least two major prongs: cost-effectiveness and autonomy from democratic pressure and oversight. To quote Richard C. Box:

> New Public Management seeks to separate politics (in the sense of decision making by the people or their representatives) from administration, allowing (or making) managers to manage according to cost-benefit economic rationality, largely free from day-to-day democratic oversight ... Such a separation resembles the old politics-administration dichotomy and Herbert Simon's (1945–1997) description of administrative decisions that are largely `factual'. In this reformed management setting, the public-private distinction is essentially obsolete and management is generic across sectors...[31]

However, while there is no gainsaying the imperatives of reforming a deficit-wrecked State and unprofitable public sector of the economy in India, it would be plain stupidity to roll back the State, to significantly reduce or not to extend further the role of the State in the social sector (e.g. education, health, public infrastructure, etc.) in India. The "Government in business" has largely failed in this country; Government in the social sector, where the private sector would be an unmitigated disaster from the points of view of public interest and social/national integration. Government spending in these sectors is shockingly and scandalously as low as between one to two per cent of the GDP. Private sector stepping in these areas only caters to the needs of the super-rich. This will create an explosive social and political upheaval and destroy the framework of social harmony and national integration.

Alternative development and sustainable development paradigms stress the importance of newer developmental concerns such as equity, quality of life, human development, gender and child justice, protection of environment and ecological balance, etc.[32]

The recent World Bank concern with management of development in the Third World countries has given rise to a growing literature on what is being called "governance" or "good governance". The Government is conventionally a *structure* while governance is a *process* in which agencies other than Government are roped in. A recent World Bank publication has identified the following governance indicators: (1) accountability, (2) political stability, (3) Government effectiveness, (4) regulatory quality, (5) rule of law, (6) control of corruption. The first two indicators operationalize "the process by which those in authority are selected and replaced". The next two indicators operationalize the quality, competence and independence of the civil service from political pressures and the credibility of Government's commitment to policies. The last two indicators summarize "the respect of citizens and the State for the institutions which govern their interactions."[33]

The 1990s witnessed a paradigm shift in Indian political economy, the two major dimensions of which are capsuled in the terms (a) neo-liberal economic policies with accent on privatization and globalization, and (b) political federalization with stress on decentralization of power and resources from the Centre to the States to the local political systems. A third dimension must also be lamentably mentioned here that points to unprecedented levels of corruption and criminalization of the political system.

The shift of emphasis from welfare liberalism to business liberalism requires adjustments on the part of the administration earlier attuned to the needs of a national administrative State to the new role of the State as the regulator of the emerging market economy nationally, regionally, and globally. Direct bureaucratic control by Government departments must be replaced by facilitatory regulation by independent, often semi-judicial, regulatory authorities in various sectors of national and provincial economies, e.g. Central or State Electricity Regulatory Authorities, Telecom Regulatory Authority, Security and Exchange Board of India (SEBI), Competition Commission, Central Insurance Regulatory Authority (CIRA) etc., all of which have been created under parliamentary or State legislative statutes since 1991.[34] Moreover, there is a growing emphasis on the need that in the changed context of marketization, public administration must be run like a business. "Evidence of the expansion of market concepts in the public sector may be found in the literature and practice of public administration in an emphasis on a constellation of cost-cutting and production management concepts from the private sector, currently drawn together as new public management. These concepts include, among others, privatization, downsizing, rightsizing, entrepreneurism, reinvention, enterprise operation, quality management, and customer service." New public management seeks to put venetian blinds against decision making by the people or their representatives in terms of political rationality to give a freer play to economic rationality, considers public-private distinction obsolete in a bid to make management uniform across sectors.[35] Furthermore, the growing integration of the Indian economy with global capitalism, puts premium on new skills in international political economy and law and on tough negotiations at global economic forums like World Trade Organization (WTO), regional trading blocks, climate change global summits, etc.

The federal trends in Indian politics have also placed imperatives on the All-India Services, in particular, and State public services, in general, to come to terms with decentralization of political power to States and local bodies. Since the All-India Services are designed to have a centralist mindset and a provincialist cadre allocation, they were naturally suspected by non-Congress State Governments when they were initially formed while the Congress still continued to hold the fort at the Centre. There were demands before the Sarkaria Commission on Centre-State Relations for the abolition of All-India Services, which the Commission did not concede.[36] It is a measure of successful adaptation of these services to deepening democratization and federalization of the political system that such demands are no longer heard. As a matter of fact, the All-India Services, having moved to and fro and worked for both orders of Government at different periods, proved to be well-informed intermediaries with a feel for the respective needs and problems of the Union as well as States. They turned out to be a factor for the smoothening of Centre-State relations at a time when divergent political perspectives of the two levels or orders of Governments could have increased the prospects of misunderstanding and conflicts. Both All-India Services and State services are yet to fully adjust to the prospects of grassroots democracy heralded by the 73rd and 74th Constitutional Amendments (1993), relating to the Panchayat Raj and Nagarpalika Raj.

ADMINISTRATIVE REFORMS

The post-Independence reformist thought in India, as expressed in various commissions and committees, reflects a trajectory of shift of concern from administrative problems to economic, political, and bureaucratic corruption. For example, the Paul Appleby Report and the A.D. Gorwala Reports in early 1950s–60s were exclusively targeted at administrative reforms. The Vohra Committee Report in the early 1990s gave an alarming glimpse of the growing nexus between politics, business, and crime syndicates.

In the perception of P.S. Appu, who served in the IAS from 1951 to 1982 in Bihar as well as at the Centre, in two instalments each, reminisces that the AISs functioned well for some two decades after Independence. The "decline" and "debasement" started in the late 1960s in Bihar and from around 1973–74 at the Centre.[37] Notably, bureaucratic degeneration here seemingly (not causally) coincides with rising temperature of the increasing intensity of inter-party competition and extra-parliamentary mass movement in the politics of independent India. We may here add that the most serious decline in administrative morale occurred during the national Emergency imposed by Prime Minister Indira Gandhi in 1975–1977 when she made a call for "committed bureaucracy"—to the ideology of the party in power which under the circumstances seemed to undermine bureaucratic neutrality and commitment to constitutional values. In the states like UP and Bihar especially, a practice has developed that whenever a new party comes to the power it orders wholesale transfer of secretariat-level and district-level officers to bring in officers loyal to the chief minister and party/parties that form(s) the new government. Loyalty in this context is measured by caste to which the CM/ministers belong or by pliability or corruptibility of the officers. A further dimension to this problem was thus added in the 1990s when politico-bureaucratic corruption and criminalization of the political process reached an alarming proportion. To quote Appu:

> "All over the country Chief Ministers became prisoners in the hands of conflicting political parties and groups. To survive in office they were obliged to placate numerous petty politicians. The new breed of ministers with tenuous tenures was ever on the lookout for pliable bureaucrats. There was no shortage of unprincipled opportunists in the bureaucracy. Before long a large number of civil servants aligned themselves with particular Ministers and became active collaborators leading to disastrous consequences."[38]

Nevertheless, Appu makes out a case for the retention and rejuvenation of AISs at least for three reasons. First, "even in their weakened State the All-India Services do offer some resistance to the arbitrary actions of cynical politicians." Second, he cites the experience of the Gujarat Riots of 2002 where "all over the State, the police acquiesced in the criminal activities of the Sangh Parivar, the superintendents of police in Kutch, Bhavnagar, Banaskantha, and Bharuch took firm action against the Hindu fanatics and gangsters." Third, the President and the Supreme Court being distant authorities, the civil and police administration, abiding by the Constitution, "will enable millions of citizens to enjoy the rights guaranteed under the Constitution".[39]

The problem of corruption by now has become so pervasive and the failure of administrative vigilance and legislations so patently persistent that only judicial activism on this front appears to be cutting some ice. In July 1993, the Government of India established a committee at the administrative level headed by the then Home Secretary N.N. Vohra "to take stock of all available information about the activities of crime Syndicate/Mafia organizations which had developed links with and were being protected by Government functionaries and political personalities." The Report, submitted in October 1993, made the following sinister submission, among others:

> CBI has reported that all over India crime syndicates have become a law unto themselves. Even in the smaller towns and rural areas, musclemen have become the order of the day. Hired assassins

> have become a part of these organizations. The nexus between the criminal gangs, police, bureaucracy and politicians has come out clearly in various parts of the country. The existing criminal justice system, which was essentially designed to deal with the individual offences/crimes, is unable to deal with the activities of the Mafia: the provisions of law in regard to economic offences are weak; there are insurmountable legal difficulties in attaching/confiscating the property acquired through Mafia activities.[40]

The Corruption Perception Index 2002 of Transparency International, Berlin, ranked India at the 73rd position among 102 countries with Finland as least corrupt and Bangladesh the most corrupt.[41] To quote, N. Vittal, a former Central Vigilance Commissioner:

> "There is a close relationship between the bureaucracy, the political leadership, the citizens, the business community and perhaps even the criminals, ... Trying to eliminate corruption in one sector of bureaucracy alone is not going to be effective. After all, tackling corruption is like tackling an epidemic. It is not possible to quarantine one section alone."[42]

Yet the process of reforms must begin from the centres of political and bureaucratic power. The socialist-turned Gandhian Jayaprakash Narayan, who led a massive anti-corruption and anti-authoritarian extra-parliamentary mass movement in the first half of the 1970s, described politics as the *gangotri* of corruption in India. The Herculean cleansing of the Augean stables of politics must take place at the source. A neo-feudal rent-seeking political and administrative class in India for transfers and postings still survives the dismantling, to a great extent, of the Permit-Licence-Quota Raj at the turn of the new millennium. It is an anachronism that must go.

There has been a distressing decline in the public image of bureaucracy. The National Election Study (NES) 1996 conducted by the Centre for the Study of Developing Societies has shown that the civil and police bureaucracy ranked at the lowest two positions in an index of popular trust in institutions. Out of a maximum score of 100, bureaucracy secured 27 and police 28, trailing far behind the Election Commission of India and the judiciary.[43]

The National Commission to Review the Working of the Constitution (NCRWC) in its Report (2002) has made a number of recommendations for administrative reforms. First, it recommends autonomous Personnel Boards under a parliamentary legislation within the framework of Article 309 of the Constitution for advising the political executive in matters of placement, promotion, transfers, and fast track advancements in conformity with advanced career management policies and techniques. Second, it suggests the establishment of a National Science and Technology Commission "as an umbrella organization for policy making, planning, promoting and funding of higher scientific and technological research" headed by the Prime Minister.

Third, it recommends legally instituted accountability of public servants for their *mala fide* acts of omission and commission and their liability to pay damages. Fourth, it suggests plugging the loopholes in anti-corruption laws like Benami Transactions (Prohibition) Act, 1988, and the Prevention of Corruption Act, 1988. Fifth, it proposes the establishment of Lok Pals/Lokayuktas under the Constitution and State legislations, respectively. Sixth, it suggests that the process of facilitating the conduct of inquiries and actions taken on them within the framework of the Commissions of Enquiry Act, 1952, by Union and State Governments. Seventh, to promote the values of transparency in administration, it recommends the passing of Right to Information Act. [This has been implemented. The Right to Information Act, it may be noted here, was enacted in 2005.] Under this law, Governments "must assume a major responsibility and mobilize skills to ensure flow of information to citizens".[44] We fondly hope the Governments in India would act upon these recommendations for the sake of good governance and in public interest. It has already passed the Right to Information Act, 2005.

The Administrative Reforms Commission-II (2005) is of the view that alongside accountability and transparency, there is need for separation of policy-making function from execution. Ministry/ department should be responsible for policy making, whereas implementation should be handed over to executive agencies.[45] It refers to the trend towards the proliferation of cabinet berths, especially due to the existence of regional parties based on local identities in the era of multiparty coalition governments. The commission underlines the need for reduction of cabinet size based on the strength of 10–15 per cent of state legislative assembly. A national consensus on this matter ought to be developed by deliberations between the Union and State Governments at the forum of Inter-State Council.[46] In the context of organizational structure of the Government of India, this Commission also emphasized the need to ensure the existing coordination mechanisms like group of ministers (GoMs) and committee of secretaries (CoSs) functions effectively and help in early resolution of issues. The unresolved issues concerning states which require inter-ministerial coordination in Government of India should be placed before CoSs and then referred to the Union cabinet for resolution.[47]

The Prime Minister, Narendra Modi, early in his first term (2014–2019), lent his support to the idea called 'lateral entry' of outside experts into the bureaucracy, long followed in miniscule number of cases by previous governments, and recommended by several ad hoc committees, including the second Administrative Reforms Commission in its Report in the recent past. The idea of lateral entry into the elite IAS faced a lot of opposition from the civil services as undue virtual privatization of the public services that might be a source of entry of vested interests into the government. However, the Department of Personnel and Training issued an advertisement in 2018 inviting applications for 10 positions of Joint Secretaries across various departments and ministries in the Government of India for which more than 6000 applications were received, putting the Union Public Commission and the Cabinet Secretariat in a fix how to take the process further.

Gulzar Natarajan, an IAS officer of the 1999 batch and a graduate student at the Harvard Kennedy School, USA, and D. Subba Rao, a former RBI Governor and a retired IAS officer, have supported the idea of lateral entry, but in an elaborately institutionalized way. Their support for the scheme is based on the following considerations:

Firstly, the IAS was designed for a statist era, whereas now since 1991, the state must open the way to the private sector and civil society organizations to make a transition from government to governance. Secondly, compared to potentially good young recruits who in some cases do not measure up to the expectations, mid-career lateral entrants with proven capabilities would be worthwhile. Thirdly, career progression in IAS is almost automatic which often endangers complacency. Lateral entrants would offer competitiveness and creative tension. To maximize these gains, they propose a suitably modified system of competitive recruitment by the Union Public commission for lateral entrants as well. Following the recruitment, the absorption of the lateral entrants should also include field training and 'district immersion'. And their inter-se seniority should be determined in such a dovetailed way that the interests of regular as well as lateral recruits are evenly balanced.[48]

A FULLER LOOK AT TWO MAJOR ADMINISTRATIVE DISCOURSES IN POST-NEHRU DECADES

We must take a broad view of two Administrative Reforms Commissions (ARCs) appointed in 1966 and 2005 by the then Prime Ministers, Lal Bahadur Shastri and Manmohan Singh, respectively. The former was chaired by Morarji Desai, later K. Hanumanthaiya, and the latter by M. Veerappa Moiley, respectively. The 20-volume Report of ARC-I was submitted in the years spread over the late 1960s to mid-1970s. The 15-volume ARC-II Report was submitted in the years between 2006 and 2009. The ARC-I recommendations focusing mainly on Union and State administrations may be summarized as follows:

ARC–I

Secretariat—Union and State: Both the Central and State Secretariats have become overstaffed and bounded with blurred responsibilities. Suitable reforms are needed (no formal layoff, but casualization of new appointments may be done) (being practised.) The Central Secretariat has become burdened with work that falls within the jurisdiction of States under the Constitution. Devolution is consistent with the Constitutional division of powers and the needs of economic development (done to a great extent). The following three staff offices should be created in each ministry: (i) a planning unit, (ii) a personnel unit, and

(iii) a finance unit. A Central personnel agency is to be placed directly under the Prime Minister with overall personnel concerns involving all categories of civil services and administrative tasks for implementation (implemented). The road to the top administrative ranks should be open to all categories of civil services—All India Services, Central Services, and State Services—such that the present practice of monopolizing such positions by the generalist All India Services to the blockage of specialized Central Services must be done away with. (The special interest group of the IAS officers has largely manoeuvred to forestall it.) Routine six-level movement of files from the bottom-level clerk to the Secretary at the top is to be reduced to only two levels of officials (happening to a great extent). Secretariat should shed functions of executive nature and concentrate on policy formulation and making, and leave the implementation to the executive agencies (being practised with certain exceptions).

State Administration: Replacement of the Board of Revenue by the Secretariat itself for its administrative and advisory functions and transfer of its appellate functions to a revenue tribunal consisting of a judicial officer of the status of a judge and a senior revenue officer from the administrative side (not implemented).

Abolition of the position of a Divisional Commissioner intermediate between the District Collector/Magistrate and the Secretariat. (Practice still varies among the States.) The omnibus or multifunctional District Magistrate is to be left exclusively with regulatory functions, law and order, and collection of land revenue and other taxes. The DM's judicial functions are to be transferred to a judicial magistrate and developmental functions to a district Development Officer (Implemented; in practice now).

Redress of Citizen's Grievances and Cases of Corruption: Responsible government and administrative accountability is to be supplemented by instituting Lokpal (Ombudsman) at the Centre and Lokayuktas (State Ombudsmen) in the states. (For nearly half a century, bills for this purpose were half-heartedly introduced in the Parliament, but were never carried to the logical conclusion, until an Act to this effect was finally passed in 2013, after ten failed attempts in the past. Justice Pinaki Chandra Ghose, a retired Supreme Court judge, joined as the first Lokpal of India in 2019.

ARC–II

To streamline the personnel administration in the Union and State governments, the ARC-II recommends that the governments at both the levels enact a comprehensive civil services law and set up a civil services authority at each level. This authority, with suitable autonomy and neutrality, should deal with matters concerning appointments/postings and tenure of senior officers of all ranks and in all ministries and departments.

In the context of the proliferation of statutory independent regulatory agencies in India since the initiation of the process of economic liberalization from the early 1990s, the ARC-II implied that such agencies created under the Union List subjects lack both the requisite autonomy and power. This defeats the purpose of having them in the first place, for they ought to 'differ from the conventional (bureaucratic) regulating system as they are separated from the executive wing of the government and enjoy a certain degree of autonomy'. The Central Electricity Regulatory Commission of India, established in 1998 by a parliamentary Act under entry 38 of the Concurrent List in the Seventh Schedule of the Constitution with semi-judicial powers and chaired by a serving or retired judge of the Supreme court and whose members can be removed for specified reasons only after an inquiry conducted by the apex court on reference received from the Union government, is a model of an independent regulatory authority that should be replicated in other policy areas or sectors of the economy where the agencies are less autonomous at present. Their accountability should be ensured through the respective departmentally related parliamentary standing committees, which should restrict their oversight to their major decisions rather than their day-to-day functioning. Periodic evaluation of their work by a panel of outside experts is also advisable to supplement the parliamentary scrutiny.[49]

As for the need to ensure the existing coordination mechanisms among various ministries at the Centre and between the Centre and the States, the Commission felt that the present instrumentalities of group of minsters (GOMs) and committees of secretaries (COSs) functioned effectively and helped in early resolution of problems. The unresolved issues concerning States require inter-ministerial coordination in the Government of India to be placed before the COSs and then the union Cabinet.[50] The Commission emphasised the importance of the Inter-State Council in creating Union-state consensus on issues of administrative and political reforms throughout the various volumes of its Report.

The Commission concurred with the view of ARC-I that it was no longer necessary to have an intermediate level of administration in the form of the commissioner between the state capital and the districts, both in view of the emergence of the district as the key unit of field administration and compression of time and space with the advancement in physical and electronic connectivity.[51]

The ARC-II reiterated the recommendation of the ARC-I that the district officers should be encouraged to specialize in their respective developmental/technical fields and that the administrative head of the district, district magistrate or collector should concentrate on the core functions such as land and revenue administration, maintenance of law and order, disaster management public distribution and civil supplies, excise, elections, transport, census, protocol, general administration, treasury management, and coordination with various departments/agencies. The district administration also needs reorientation to new political and administrative concerns such as technological and functional modernization and responsiveness to the Right to Information Act, civil society groups, media, and public grievances.[52]

The ARC-II also recommended that the activities and functions transferred by State government to Panchayat Raj institutions and urban local government councils need not remain with the district administration. Line departments such as those of water resources, public works, or health engaged in statewide projects should maintain their separate offices at district and subdistrict levels. They should provide technical support and guidance to district councils in planning and monitoring implementation.[53]

Moreover, the ARC-II recommended an entirely new concept of 'district Government' operationalized through an integrated governing structure in the district council, with representation from both urban and rural areas. The district officer (magistrate/collector) should have a dual role in it. On one hand, s/he should be fully accountable to the district council on all local matters, and on the other hand, s/he would also be fully accountable to the state government on all regulatory/other matters not delegated to the district government.[54]

Finally, as anti-corruption measures, the ARC-II recommends the streamlining of the existing vigilance commissions and the Lokpal and Lokayuktas at the Union and State levels first recommended by the ARC–I.[55] The Lokpal and Lokayuktas Act was passed in 2013 and put into effect in 2019 belatedly.

REFERENCES

1. Max Weber, *From Max Weber: Essays in Sociology,* Translated & edited with an Introduction by H.H. Gerth and C. Wright Mills, Oxford University Press, New York, 1946.
2. Fred Riggs, "Bureaucracy and Political Development: A Paradoxical View" in Joseph Lapalombara (Ed.), *Bureaucracy and Political Development,* Princeton University Press, Princeton, 1963.
3. Ezra Suleiman, *Dismantling Democratic States,* Princeton University Press, Princeton and Oxford, 2003, p. 316.
4. Paul Du Gay (Ed.), *The Values of Bureaucracy,* Oxford University Press, 2005, p. 2.
5. M.P. Singh, "Indian State: Historical Context and Change", *The Indian Historical Review*, Vol. XXI, Nos. 1–2, July 1994 & January 1995, is a critical review of works of historians R.S. Sharma, Romila Thapar, I.H. Qureshi, Doglas Strusand, etc.
6. Bidyut Chakrabarty and Mohit Bhattacharya (Eds.), *Public Administration: A Reader,* Oxford University Press, New Delhi, 2003, pp. 31–33.

7. O.P. Dwivedi and R.B. Jain, *India's Administrative State,* Gitanjali Publishing House, New Delhi, 1985, p. 35.

8. C.P. Bhambhri, *Bureaucracy and Politics in India,* Vikas, New Delhi, 1971, p. 57.

9. David C. Potter, *India's Political Administrators: From ICS to IAS,* Oxford University Press, Delhi, 1996, p. 257.

10. *Ibid.,* p. 80.

11. *Ibid.,* p. 81.

12. *Ibid.,* p. 213.

13. *Ibid.,* p. 263.

14. Granville Austin, *The Indian Constitution: Cornerstone of a Nation,* Oxford University Press, Delhi, 1966, Chs. 2, 3, 4, 8 and 9; and Potter, *op. cit.*, Ch. 1.

15. Balveer Arora and Beryl Radin (Eds.), *The Changing Role of the All India Services*, New Delhi: University of Pennsylvania Institute of Advanced Study of India and Centre of Policy Research, 2000: XIII.

16. S.C. Dube, "Bureaucracy and Nation Building in Transitional Societies", Jason L. Finkle and Richard W. Gable (Eds.), *Political Development & Social Change,* 2nd ed., John Wiley & Sons, INC., New York, 1971, p. 327.

17. Fred W. Riggs, "Bureaucrats and Political Development: A Paradoxical View" in Finkle and Gable (Eds.), *op. cit.,* p. 331.

18. *Ibid.,* p. 331.

19. FWR, *Ibid.,* pp. 331–335.

20. Quoted in C.P. Bhambhri, *op. cit.,* p. 80.

21. C.P. Bhambhri, *Ibid.,* pp. 80–81.

22. Quoted in *Ibid.,* p. 134.

23. Quoted in *Ibid.,* p. 135.

24. *Ibid.,* p. 171.

25. N.C. Saxena, "The IAS Officer—Predator or Victim?" *Journal of Commonwealth & Comparative Politics*, Vol. 48(4), November 2010: 448.

26. *Ibid.*, p. 449.

27. T.S.R. Subramanian, *Journeys through Babudom and Netaland: Governance in India*, Delhi: Rupa, 2004, quoted in Subrata Mitra, "Symbiosis, Re-use and Evolution: Administrators, Politicians, Citizens, and Governance in Post-Colonial India", Commonwealth & Comparative Politics, Vol. 48, No. 4, November 2010, p. 459.

28. Edward Weidner quoted in Mohit Bhattacharya, *Social Theory and Development Administration,* 3rd edition, Jawahar Publishers & Distributors, New Delhi, 2002, p. 4.

29. Kuldeep Mathur (Ed.), "Introduction: The Emerging Concerns in Public Administration" in *Development Policy and Administration,* Sage, New Delhi, 1998, p. 18.

30. Mohit Bhattacharya, *op. cit.,* pp. 129–130.

31. Richard C. Box, "Running Government Like a Business: Implications for Public Administration Theory and Practice" in Bidyut Chakrabarty & Mohit Bhattacharya (Eds.), *Public Administration: A Reader,* Oxford University Press, New Delhi, 2003, p. 234.

32. See Ashish Kothari, "Environment, Equity, Sustainability: The Essential Links" in M.P. Singh and Rekha Saxena (Eds.), *Ideologies and Institutions in Indian Politics*, Deep & Deep, Delhi, 1998, Ch. 14.

33. World Bank, "World Bank Policy Research Working Paper 3630" by Daniel Kaufmann, Aart Kraay & Massimo Mastruzzi, *Government Matters IV: Governance Indicators for 1996–2004,* Washington World Bank, June 2005.

34. M.P. Singh, "Economic Liberalization and Political Federalization in India: Mutually Reinforcing Responses to Global Integration" in Harvey Lazar, Hamish Telford and Ronald L. Watts (Eds.), *The Impact of Global and Regional Integration on Federal Systems: A Comparative Analysis,* McGill-Queens University Press, Montreal, 2003.

35. Richard C. Box, *op. cit.,* 2003, p. 234.

36. Government of India, *Commission on Centre-State Relations Report,* Part-I, (Chair: Justice R.S. Sarkaria), 1988, Ch. 8.

37. P.S. Appu, "The All-India Services: Deline, Debasement and Destruction" *Economic and Political Weekly,* Vol. XL, No. 9, 26 February–4 March, 2005, pp. 826–832.

38. *Ibid.,* p. 829.

39. *Ibid.,* p. 831.

40. Government of India, Ministry of Home Affairs, *Vohra Committee Report,* 1993, p. 1.

41. N. Vittal, *Corruption in India,* Academic Foundation, New Delhi, 2003, p. 33.

42. *Ibid.,* pp. 155–156.

43. P.K. Aggarwal, "A Survey of Bureaucracy in India" in P.K. Aggarwal and N. Vittal (Eds.), *I am Sorry: Indian Bureaucracy at Crossroads,* Manas, Delhi, 2005, p. 15.

44. Government of India, "National Commission to Review the Working of the Constitution", *NCRWC Report,* Vol. 1, Ch. 6, 2002. Chair: Justice M.N. Venkatachaliah.

45. Government of India, *Administrative Reforms Commission Report,* Vol. 15, New Delhi, 2009, pp. 18–19.

46. *Ibid.*, pp. 22 & 25.

47. Government of India, *Second Administrative Reforms Commission, Thirteenth Report, Organizational Structure of Government of India,* New Delhi, April 2009, p. 140, para 5.12.

48. Gulzar Natarajan and Duvvuri Subbarao, "The Case for Lateral Entry", *The Indian Express*, August 9, 2017, https://indianexpress.com/article/opinion/columns/...4788115 (Accessed October 2, 2019.)

49. Government of India, *Second Administrative Reforms Commission, Tenth Report Refurbishing of Personnel Administration: Scaling New Heights*, New Delhi, 2009, p. 2; and Government of India, *Second ARC, Fifteenth Report, State and District Administration*, New Delhi, 2009, pp. 39–42.

50. Government of India, *Second ARC Report, Fifteenth Report, State and District Administration, op.cit.*

51. *Ibid.* p. 45.

52. *Ibid.* pp. 80–86.

53. *Ibid.* p. 92.

54. *Ibid.* p.90.

55. Government of India, *Second Administrative Reforms Commission, Fourth Report, Ethics in Governance*, New Delhi, 2007. For a more comprehensive analysis of the reformist discourse in India since Independence, see Mahendra Prasad Singh, "Administrative Reforms in South Asia: India", in Meghna Sabharwal and Evan M. Berman (Eds.), *Public Administration in South Asia: India, Bangladesh, and Pakistan,* CRC Press: Taylor and Francis Group, New York, 2017, Chapter 7, pp. 135–253.

Chapter

11

Elections

An Area of Relative Success?

CONSTITUTIONAL AND LEGAL FRAMEWORK OF ELECTIONS

Free and fair elections are fundamental to the success of representative democracy. The idea of popular sovereignty envisioned in the Constitution is operationalised by parliamentary and legislative elections. Article 326 of the Constitution provides that elections to the House of the People and Legislative Assemblies of States are to be held on the basis of universal adult suffrage. The system of elections is outlined in Part XV of the Constitution and the Representation of the People Acts (RPA), 1950 and 1951 passed by the Parliament in pursuance of Article 327 of the Constitution. Article 325 stipulates that there shall be a common electoral roll for all Indian citizens irrespective of differences of religion, race, caste, or sex.

Article 324 of the Constitution vests the power of "superintendence, direction and control" of elections to the Parliament, State legislatures, to the offices of the President and Vice-President in the Election Commission of India. Beginning as one-member body, the Commission has three members now, including the Chief Election Commissioner. The Commission works through the rule of unanimity or majority. Appointed by the Union executive, the Chief Election Commissioner (CEC) shall not be removed from his office except in like manner and on the like grounds as a judge of the Supreme Court and the conditions of service of the CJI shall not be varied to his disadvantage after his appointment. Moreover, any other Election Commissioner or a regional Election Commissioner shall not be removed from office except on the recommendation of the CEC. This means that the CEC cannot be removed from office except by an order of the President passed after resolutions in each House of the Parliament supported by a majority of total membership and majority of not less than two-thirds of the members present and voting.

The RPA 1950 provides for the allocation of seats in, and determination of constituencies for the purpose of elections to, the House of the People and legislatures of States, including qualifications of voters and preparation of electoral rolls. The RPA 1951 lays down provisions for the actual conduct of elections, qualifications for members of the Parliament and State legislatives, eligibility for membership of these Houses, electoral malpractices and offences and decisions of electoral disputes. Under these constitutional and legal arrangements, the Election Commission of India has been guaranteed autonomy from the two orders of Governments in India. The Election Commission has its own Secretariat in New Delhi. Chief Electoral Officers and District Election Officers in States are to be designated or nominated by the Election Commission in consultation with State governments. They are deemed to be on deputation to the Election Commission under whose control, superintendence and discipline they work.

It would appear that the Constitution, read along with the debates of the Constituent Assembly, has taken great pains to institute an "independent" Election Commission. In more recent decades in the actual conduct of elections, the extent of autonomy of the Election Commission from the executive has appeared to hinge on the question of who, between the two, decides the date for an election, administrative arrangements for it and the stages of its completion. The matter has even gone to the Supreme Court which in the case *Election Commission of India* v. *Union of India & others* (1993) ruled: "...one thing seems clear. The jurisdiction of courts would not extend to issuing directions to the Election Commission for the conduct of particular polls on particular dates independently of the perception by the Commission as to their feasibility and practicability consistent with what may be needed to ensure the purity of the electoral process."[1]

All political parties are required to be registered with the Election Commission under Section 29A of the RPA 1951. Delimitation of constituencies and determination for constituencies reserved for SCs and STs is done by the Election Commission assisted by a Delimitation Commission. Delimitation is to be done after each decennial census. The last delimitation, however, took place after the 1971 Census. Postponed thereafter until 2003, it was further frozen till 2026. This has resulted in representational distortion on account of varying rate of population growth in various States. The postponement was rationalised in terms of the argument that the States who have successfully implemented family welfare programmes by curbing population growth should not be penalised. According to one estimate, the southern States would be required to surrender over a dozen seats in the Lok Sabha, which would go to the north Indian States. This may lead to an explosive federal dispute with increasing representational imbalance among States by 2026.

POLITICAL CONSEQUENCES OF ELECTORAL LAWS AND FORMS OF PARTY SYSTEMS AND GOVERNMENT

Different electoral and governmental systems have different political consequences in terms of number of parties in general and the party system in particular. Plurality or the first-past-the-post-pole electoral system is hypothesised to produce a two-party system, while proportional representation, a multi-party system. This is so because, unlike the proportional representation system, the plurality system tends to unduly punish smaller parties and reward larger parties. The net effect is said to promote a bipartisan division between the Government and the Opposition. Maurice Duverger and William Riker have independently produced some evidence on the basis of their studies of mostly Anglo-American and old Commonwealth democracies. They found the evidence so compelling that they were inclined to suggest the above proposition as an "iron law".[2] The Indian experience does not, however, conform to this supposed iron law, even though India follows the plurality electoral law. This is because from 1952 to 1984 Lok Sabha elections, the plurality law in India engendered a one-party dominant system, whereas from 1989 to date, we have had a multi-party system without any change in the electoral system.

How do we explain these "deviant" patterns in India? The one-party dominance in the earlier decades in India may be explained in terms of the homogenising effects of the anti-colonial nationalist movement and its hangover after the Independence. When the impact of this factor diminished with increasing political competitiveness, India transited to a multi-party system. Thus, increasing politicisation of social and regional diversities could not be reduced to a bipartisan pattern. It would therefore appear that the political consequence of the plurality electoral system for the party system is intermediated by the intervening third variable of social homogeneity or diversity. In homogeneous countries, it would be able to produce a two-party system (as in the Anglo-American and the White Commonwealth democracies studied by Duverger and Riker), but in a heterogeneous settings like India, it could result in a multi-party system. New Zealand is an interesting test case. When it operated under plurality system it had a two-party system. In 1996 it adopted a mixed-member proportional system after a referendum in 1993, and thereafter a multi-party system has developed there.

As mentioned earlier, the form of government also has some effect on the nature of the party system that emerges in a country. India has adopted a parliamentary-federal form of government. The Constitution seeks to reconcile the parliamentary principle with the federal principle of government. Parliamentarism by subscribing to the principle of supremacy of the Parliament in the system tends to reduce the number of parties by prompting them to divide between the Government and the Opposition. On the other hand, federalism by emphasising decentralisation of power to the States tends to create conditions in which parties may multiply, especially due to the effect of regional diversities.

Thus, in India one aspect of the government (parliamentarism) encourages political parties to configure into two blocs, while another component of the government (federalism) creates conditions for their multiplication. The effect of one factor is thus likely to be cancelled out by the other and there may be no consistent causation. Nevertheless, the effect of federalism, combined with regional and cultural diversities, has prevailed over that of parliamentarism in India on the balance, and produced a multiparty system at the regional as well as national level, with several regional parties in the States and some even making their presence felt at the national level, especially during the phase of federal coalition governments.

Yet, it is worth pointing out that within the multi-party system framework since 1989, there is some trend towards bi–coalitional pattern at the national level. In the initial years during this phase, there was a tri-coalitional pattern evident in the United Front that included the "third" force parties between the Congress and the BJP. Since the late 1990s, however, two major coalitional blocs have come to be formed—the Congress-led United Progressive Alliance (UPA) and the BJP-led National Democratic Alliance (NDA)—and the third front has disintegrated. This pattern has continued since 2014 BJP majority under the Prime Minister, Modi with increased dominance of the BJP in the NDA and considerable debilitation of the Congress and the UPA.

The effect of federalism on the growth of the multi-party system is evident in the trend of fragmentation of almost all national parties, especially the Janata Dals, but excepting the BJP. More importantly, not only have the old regional parties like National Conference, Akali Dal, and Tamil parties persisted but also a number of new regional parties have mushroomed, e.g. People's Democratic Party in Jammu and Kashmir, Telugu Desam Party in Andhra Pradesh, MDMK and PMK in Tamil Nadu, All India Trinamool Congress in West Bengal, Asom Gana Parishad in Assam, Janata Dal (United) and Rashtriya Janata Dal in Bihar, Biju Janata Dal in Orissa, Janata Dal (Secular) in Karnataka, Samajwadi Party and Bahujan Samaj Party in UP, Jananayak Janata Party in Haryana, etc.

PHASES/MODELS OF ELECTORAL MOBILISATION

In any election on the epic scale—Indian general elections are always a veritable Mahabharata—there are issues galore. Instead of enumerating them, however, let us for a moment pause and explore whether we can formulate some models of elections and patterns of party system and prime ministerial styles, basing our analysis on the elections held since 1947. Theorisations on electoral politics and party system in Western democracies emphasise the formative impact of some crucial historical experiences and the salient social cleavages in certain epochs that leave more or less lasting residues of influence on voter realignments and stages of party system formation.[3] Theories of political modernisation in the West and the Third World also seek to delineate the sequential occurrence of some political crises—mainly those of 'legitimacy', 'identity', 'participation', and 'distribution'—that mark out discernible phases through which a political system traverses the path from Tradition to Modernity.[4] But what these theories tend to overlook is the fact that due to the British colonial intervention in India, there is a peculiar telescoping of these political crises and historical evolution of the party system in this country; what is spread over several centuries in the West, India is destined to experience in less than a century, indeed most of it in the crucial seven decades of its post-colonial existence. So we find here a simultaneous politicisation of multiple social and cultural cleavages, some of which are cumulative and mutually reinforcing and some crosscutting in their structural configuration. That the scope of this chapter is limited to the over seventy years of post-Independence democratic politics does not detract from the fact that British and even pre-British Indian history are organically linked in the evolution of the Indian state and party system formation.

Looking back, we can try to discern some patterns and trends in electoral politics in the country since democratic elections began in British India on limited franchise that was made universal by the Constitution (1950) and laws in independent India. We first do this exercise in terms of phases of overall politicisation as it has unfolded in modern India. Having done this, we then proceed to delineate three models of electoral politics in the seventeen Lok Sabha elections held after Independence so far and identify particular patterns of party system and styles of prime ministerial leadership that configure with them, though not necessarily in the strict causal sense.

PHASES OF POLITICISATION

It seems plausible to argue that the process of politicisation in India has so far passed through at least seven roughly identifiable phases[5]: (1) the precursive phase broadly covering the last quarter of the 19th century and the first two decades of the 20th century; (2) the phase of mass nationalist movement since the 1920s to the early post-Independence decades; (3) the phase of "ruralising elections" in the 1960s (*a la* Huntington, 1968, Ch. 7)[6]; (4) the phase of the "deinstitutionalisation" of political processes and structures in the 1970s, especially during the authoritarian internal emergency declared by the then Prime Minister, Indira Gandhi of the Indian National Congress, under participatory pressures from below[7], (5) the post-emergency revival of democracy during the Janata Party government phase (1977–1979), followed by the restoration of the Indian National Congress under Indira Gandhi and Rajiv Gandhi during the 1980s, in the trail of the premature fall of the Janata Party government due to intense factionalism in July 1979, (6) the phase of minority federal government under P. V. Narasimha Rao (Congress) (1991–1996) or coalition governments led by minority national parties alternately—Janata Dal, BJP, and Congress (1996–2014), and (7) federal coalition governments led by the majority BJP under Narendra Modi (2014–to date).

Precursive Phase: Modern politics and party system in India originated in the context of a traditional colonial society in initial stages of modernisation. Social and religious activities preceded political awakening. Initially, with the relative blockade of political outlets, the renascent spirit expressed itself with amazing vitality in an outburst of creativity in the realms of social and religious reforms, literature and art, science and technology, education and administration, and trade and commerce. All these developments prepared the ground for the emergence of the Moderate and the short-lived Extremist currents of Indian nationalism before they were overtaken by the Gandhian mass nonviolent agitational political campaigns. The social forces behind this multi-petalled florescence were the English-educated urban and urbanised middle class and upper caste elements, who pioneered in creating various political associational groups in different coastal regions, subsequently federating into the Indian National Congress in 1885.[8]

The political stratification system during this phase was almost a mirror image of the social stratification system. In other words, leadership of political organisations and composition of nominated Indian components of legislative councils introduced under the Indian Councils Acts of 1861 and 1892, were entirely representative of the Westernised upper strata of society—urban or rural-urban middle in class terms and upper or "entrenched"[9] in caste terms. The near convergence of social and political stratification systems meant that politics during this phase was an affair of what may be called the *natural* leaders of the society who came to combine it with the new advantages of access to English education and opportunities of social mobility opened up by the process of modernisation. This process of *lateral mobility* from upper reaches of the social structure into politics also ensured continuing broad congruence, and slower disengagement, between the social and political stratification systems (data on early Congress leadership in Gopal Krishna, as well as those on the members of the Constituent Assembly in Granville Austin, illustrate this point).[10] This congruence would get increasingly strained during later phases of electoral mobilisation. Moreover, the predominantly lateral political recruitment indicated above also determined the kind of political issues that mainly held the stage during this phase of essentially pressure-group politics. Issues of participation first in colonial and dominion administration and subsequently in vaguely defined *swarajya*—were accorded priority over issues of national Independence and economic redistribution. Thus, focusing on the political competition and collaboration in India in the last quarter of the 19th century, historian Anil Seal observes that for political associations and Indian National Congress of the period "a conceptual system based on elites, rather than on classes, would seem more promising."[11]

Mass National Movement and Early Post-Independence Phase: Various streams of mass national movement (Extremism, Swadeshi, Home Rule and Gandhian) and limited constitutional reforms by the British rulers

(1909, 1919 and 1935)[12] represent the two broad strands of politicisation in the second phase, to which the 1950 Constitution added a third—elections based on universal adult franchise. In the colonial period, mass agitational politics had assumed greater estimation and value in the nationalist perception and strategy, while electoral and legislative politics based on limited franchise and effeminate legislatures was relegated to a secondary role. The hegemonic imbalance between the parliamentary framework and mass movements was, of course, to reverse in the post-colonial period. In the words of historian Bipan Chandra:[13]

> The Indian national movement is the only movement where the broadly Gramscian theoretical perspective of a war of position was successfully practised; where State power was not seized in a single historical moment of revolution, but through prolonged popular struggle on a moral, political and ideological level; where reserves of counter-hegemony were built up over the years through progressive stages; where the phases of struggle alternated with 'passive' phases.

During the long span of the national movement, the foundations of the Indian party system were firmly laid down, and, in ideological as well as structural terms, the continuities between the colonial party system and the post-Independence party system are in some ways more impressive than the changes. The changes that have undoubtedly occurred appear as extensions of the ideological spectrum and as sproutings from structural roots earlier struck rather than root-and-branch restructuring of the system. A look at the nationalist coalition put together under the Congress umbrella and the later disaggregation of political organisations allied with it in the process of its transformation from a national movement to a political party following Independence, illustrate this point.

In this phase of politicisation, the politically divisive and explosive potentialities of the multi-ethnic and economically stratified Indian social structure were restrained, on the one hand, by a lower level of social and political participation, and, on the other, by the fact that this early mobilisation took place under the overarching canopy of the national movement against colonialism. The Congress had, however, to contend with some viciously communal and caste-based organisations that by and large never accepted its hegemony and its claim to speak for all Indian communities, castes, and regions, e.g. the Muslim League, and Justice Party/Dravida Kazhagam. On the whole, however, the horizontal articulation of conflicts among communal and regional groups were moderated by nationalism, while the vertical articulation of class conflicts within the various ethnic and regional communities were dampened by feudal legacies or semi-feudalism, communalism, regionalism, and overlaying all, nationalism.[14]

Following Independence, especially since the inauguration of competitive elections, based on universal adult franchise, politicisation of the countryside made a rapid headway. The *zamindars* as a class, constituting the upper strata of the village, had until now generally kept off the Congress and remained allegiant to the British.[15] They now hurried to ride the ruling party bandwagon, which, in turn, welcomed these elements with open arms as a shortcut to electoral success. Since these upper strata of the rural society were groups with rural roots but urban orientations, often maintaining a *ghar* (home) in the village and a *dera* (residence) in the town, their entry into the predominant Congress party did not, by and large, produce sharp discontinuities between the early urban elements in the party leadership and the newer rural elements.

Ruralising Elections Phase: Taking the cue from changes in the socio-economic background of the State Chief Ministers under the impact of elections that significantly increased politicisation and representation of rural social groups in politics, we can date this phase roughly from the mid-1950s in the southern and western States and from the mid-1960s in the north.[16] The abolition of *zamindari* system following Independence removed the predominantly upper caste landlords from the top of the rural stratification system. This structural change led to the rise of the reasonably prosperous class of medium and small farmers and upper peasantry. These owner cultivators as a social force are a veritable tapestry consisting of both upper and middle castes. Its middle caste peasant component is the numerically dominant element and is officially designated as the Other Backward Classes (OBCs). It is notable, however, that this category constitutes a class only in the economic sense of convergence of interests of its diverse caste clusters and regional segments. The psychological dimension of a common class consciousness is bedevilled by caste divisions and regional dispersal characteristic of this group. The divergent political lines of Akali Dals in Punjab, Lok Dal component or the Janata Dal in UP, Haryana, and Bihar, and other peasant organizations such as Shetkari Sangathan led by Sharad Joshi in Maharashtra, Bharatiya Kisan Union led by Mahendra Singh Tikait in Western UP, and Karnataka Rajya Ryet Sangh led by M.D. Nanjundaswamy in Karnataka and those in Tamil Nadu, illustrate this point. Even Charan Singh's boast about creating an electoral commotion from Chandigarh to Patna following the mammoth *kisan* (peasant) rally in Delhi on his birthday anniversary in 1978 retrospectively tells the same story.

The political mobilization of the sizeable middle band of the Backward caste peasantry had, in fact, already started during the national independence movement, typically under the tutelage of upper caste and urban party elites. What was new during the ruralizing elections phase was that in the context of electoral politics their politicization accelerated and deepened and acquired an autonomous participatory momentum of its own.

The gradual rise of this class came to manifest itself on economic as well as *political* planes. First, they had good start inasmuch as the size of their landholdings, although apparently small and fragmented, was not too small, by Indian standards, to provide a basis for a slow transition from a subsistent farming to a surplus one, howsoever meager. Second, this trend came to be matched with and aided by the Government-initiated plans of agricultural development involving, among other things, improved agricultural inputs, institutional credits, and governmental subsidies. The problems earlier faced by development administrators and extension workers in motivating farmers to adopt agricultural modernization soon turned into the problem of meeting, with the limited resources available, the steadily increasing demands for these agricultural inputs. Third, there was a sub-cultural factor contributing to the economic rise of this class. One can observe in this class a tradition of a sort of protestant *ethic* emphasizing hard work and austere living as opposed to the lifestyle of extravagance and conspicuous consumption typical of upper caste village landlords—absentee or not. This applies to the upper caste as well as middle caste components of this class. The large middle caste component, especially in Western UP and Haryana, is for example, even less affected by status-based avoidance of manual work on the family farm by male members of the family in general and especially by women. This ethic of austerity and hard work in this class, originally rooted in its economic situation, was also reinforced by social reform movement like the Arya Samaj. Although the Arya Samaj was far from a purely backward caste and peasant-based social reform movement, it was, compared to the Brahmo Samaj and Theosophical Society, a much more tradition-oriented movement with a deeper mass and even rural roots. More recently, some movements emphasizing traditional millenarian orientations among these sections have emerged. One such movement, rooted in even more traditional and socially lower strata than the Arya Samaj, is the Jai Gurudev Dharma Pracharak Sanstha founded in 1964 in Mathura with its following spreading through almost the entire Hindi belt.[17]

The economic rise of the owner cultivators has generally characterized both its upper caste and middle caste components, but its political rise is more characteristic of the latter, who are, in terms of Kothari's model of politicization of castes, "ascendant castes".[18] In fact, the upper castes, who earlier occupied, in terms of legislative seat share, the centre of the political stage in all States and regions, have now been sizeably displaced by the middle castes. Of the three caste clusters—the upper, middle, and Scheduled (Dalit or Harijan)—the intermediate one happens to be numerically preponderant. This, along with their increasing agriculture-based prosperity, has greatly contributed to their political ascendancy. Their rise has been more rapid in politics than in education, administration and urban economy, but having emerged as the politically dominant social force, they have hopped into the frontlines of the areas of their lag from the areas of their lead and are thrusting forward. This has been done through middle-caste-dominated State Government's policy of extension of job reservation quotas, earlier available only to Scheduled Castes and Tribes (SCs and STs), to the middle castes dubiously listing them as the OBCs in several States, including Bihar and UP in the late 1970s and later. They have also been cornering public institutional credits and incentives for setting up small-scale industries and have thus begun to pack the ranks of new entrepreneurs.

The national movement was dominated mainly by upper caste clusters who remained in a position of dominance in the early post-Independence period. The ascendant middle castes, who, naturally, also felt inclined to join the Congress bandwagon, usually found their way blocked by the entrenched upper castes within the party. If at all admitted, they could enter the party only as apprentices or lieutenants of the upper caste party elites in the latter's bid to mobilize wider mass base as a result of intra-elite conflicts. This had the effect of factionalizing and weakening the emergent middle castes as a force in politics. This relative blockade turned the ascendant middle castes towards the various opposition parties which were more receptive to them, some even founded by them. After having made their political impact felt by having fast growing opposition parties, they later found the electoral success-oriented predominant Congress party more willing to open up and accommodate them, thereby replenishing its own declining predominance by draining the strength of the opposition.[19]

The political ascendancy of the backward middle castes was more rapid as well as phenomenal in States and regions where they happened to be the "dominant castes" (*a la* Srinivas)[20] in terms of major ownership of arable land as well as numerical strength. Through expanding politicization, the initial political preponderance of the entrenched upper castes came gradually to be undercut by dominant middle castes in State politics.

The impact of these ascendant castes has also been felt at the national level in various parties, including the Congress; but the Janata Party that briefly ruled in New Delhi and major northern States in the late 1970s, and the Janata Dal that emerged as one of the major centrist parties in 1989, are particularly a political expression of this change. However, national level politics generally continued to be more composite and often provided refuge to entrenched rural upper castes, especially Brahmins, eased out of political dominance in State politics. The response to this challenge has basically taken four forms: (a) holding on to the coat-tails of a national leader with a wide and even charismatic mass appeal; (b) forging a coalition of the top and the bottom against the broad middle band of the Hindu caste system and also roping in the minorities—religious, linguistic, and tribal; (c) seeking to factionalize the backward middle castes phalanx by co-opting and raising to power politicians from lower backward middle castes; and (d) playing the national unity and/or the Hindu card in seeking to make capital out of public reaction to secessionism and terrorism in Punjab and of the majority community's susceptibilities about living dog's existence in its own country. It is the cracks in these strategies of mobilization and coalition followed by the Congress party that have given the opposition parties their breaks.

"Deinstitutionalization" and Elite, Class and Mass Pressures during the 1970s and Beyond: The 1970s witnessed the great confrontation between the Gandhian Navanirman Movement led by Morarji Desai against the then Congress Prime Minister, Indira Gandhi in Gujarat, which spread to the anti-corruption and anti-authoritarian Jayaprakash Narayan (JP) Movement in Bihar that quickly conflagrated like a prairie fire throughout north India down to Bangalore/Karnataka. It forced the Congress government at the Centre to proclaim an internal emergency under Article 352, order arrest of the entire leadership of the Movement, the Opposition parties, and even Congress dissidents, and also, to impose press censorship. Mrs. Gandhi also brought about the 42nd Constitutional Amendment (1976) riddled with undemocratic and authoritarian features into the Constitution.

The 1977 general elections in March routed the Emergency regime of the Congress party and brought back to power a hurriedly forged coalition of non-Congress and non-communist opposition parties into the Janata Party. The Janata Party government came to be afflicted by serious factional feuds and prematurely fell in July 1979. However, during its brief term in office, it repealed the authoritarian 42nd Constitutional Amendment by enacting the 44th Constitutional Amendment, which severally fortified future abuse of power in trampling upon the fundamental right to life and personal liberty and freedom of expression under Articles 19 and 21 as well as of the power to proclaim internal national emergency under Article 352.

There is an almost universal agreement among analysts that, beginning with the 1969 split in the Congress party, a general trend of deinstitutionalization became evident in Indian politics. The most radical statements of this thesis are to be found in the writings of Kothari.[21] The symptoms of deinstitutionalization are diagnosed in an all-round decline of the Congress party and other parties and of parliamentary and federal institutions of the republic. Other symptoms of deinstitutionalization are found in the mounting levels of demands backed by violence among ethnic groups and against the State and the nation that the party system and political institutions of the republic were unable to contain or accommodate and channelise through their institutionalised performance.[22] Adhering to the liberal-pluralist or neo-conservative paradigms, these studies seek to explain deinstitutionalization in terms of the concomitant processes of rapid social mobilisation and change and the emergence of self-serving political elite misappropriating the political institutions of the republic. The neo-Marxists, with their theory of the relative autonomy of the Indian State from its class-base, generally concur with the liberal-pluralist diagnosis about the declining autonomy and capability of the Indian State in the post-Nehru era generally. But they appear more apprehensive of the machinations and evil designs of the industrial and agricultural capitalists than their liberal counterparts who pin high hopes on gradual economic and political reforms.[23] A pluralist-Marxist analysis of the crisis of political institutions in India is offered in Kaviraj. In Kaviraj's[24] view, the deepening crisis of political institutions is attributable to the convergence of social and political crises with state-sponsored capaitalism and to political centralisation attempted by Indira

Gandhi which, in effect, actually meant "a centralisation of difficulties". What he seems to be overlooking is that the decentralised Janata phase in the late 1970s was also partly disastrous. Besides, he does not clearly specify whether the crisis of political institutions was accentuated by the state of affairs in the public or private sector of the economy. Moreover, it would not be out of place here to point out that the crisis of political institutions would not automatically disappear with a full-fledged growth of either capitalism or socialism (as the terms mean in contemporary comparative politics), with the collapse of capitalism in the inter-war period and that of socialism in the *anus mirablis* of 1989 forming its backdrop. The solution, if at all, lies with a normative quest for a more perfect union of political democracy with true socialist freedoms.

The classical Marxist scholarship, adhering to the "two-stage theory of revolution", has been ambivalent between "socialist" and "democratic" revolutions and has focused attention on the extent of existence and weight of feudal, semi-feudal, compradore capitalist elements backed and dominated by imperialist advanced countries pursuing neo-capitalist devices to keep the formally liberated countries not merely 'dependent' but also 'underdeveloped'.[25]

From the perspective of grassroots violence, the most notable characteristic of politicisation in this phase is the rise of Dalit political consciousness to a critical level and moment, i.e. the transformation of Harijans into *dalits*—through party-political processes, if possible, through violence and extra-institutional means, if necessary. The political mobilisation of these deprived groups—landless agricultural workers in class terms and predominantly SCs in caste terms—is by no means an entirely new phenomenon; they have indeed formed part of the electoral political arithmetic right from the beginning. However, whereas these groups had earlier formed the manipulated parts in the hierarchical patron-client political networks presided over and controlled by the economically dominant upper and middle caste patrons, the clients have now tended to assume autonomous political postures. This has tended to disjoint the erstwhile, an almost overlapping, structures of the *jajmani* system and the economic and political patron-client systems. Earlier, fissions in the overall patron-client network in the village were caused by factionalism among the patrons themselves; the more serious challenges to their dominance are now increasingly coming from below. In fact, this increasing "verticial" articulation of political conflicts has tended to promote some measure of "horizontal" unity among the patrons.[26]

Roughly, the Harijans seem to have passed through three stages in their political mobilisation. First, they began at the receiving end of the patron-client networks. Second, moving out of the political tutelage of the locally dominant castes, they became available for political mobilisation by populist national leaders. Third, gradually becoming disillusioned with all leaders and parties, including the Left parties, and coming to realise that they were just going through the motions of ritualistic electoral politics, the Harijans and Adivasis took to the warpath—violent class conflicts under the leadership of

Dalit Panthers and Indian Peoples' Front and other Naxalite organisations or agitations and *bandhs* led by militant leaders like Shibu Soren and militant organizstions like Jharkhand Mukti Morcha, All Bodo Students' Union, etc.[27]

This growing irrelevance of institutional politics for the Harijans should not be surprising. Compared to other caste clusters which are quite uneven internally in economic terms, Harijans are more or less structurally unique in that they constitute the bottom of the social stratification defined either in terms of caste or class. In other words, in their case *caste* and *class* tend to overlap. This deepens the cultural incongruity between them and other caste clusters above them. This has, since time immemorial, helped stereotype Harijans in certain roles; the common element in all of which happens to be their structural dependence on, and psychological deference to, those above them.

In recent times, education, public employment, cottage and small-scale industries and business, and above all, politics—generally with incentives from governments—have opened up opportunities, with varying degrees of viability, for Dalits to move up in social and political stratification systems. But these are mostly urban phenomena that have, in addition, tended to drive a wedge between the newly emergent middle class Dalit elites and the Dalit masses.[28]

Spurred on by religious revitalisation and revivalist movements, modern political ideologies, competitive party politics, and Naxalite organisations, the Dalits have of late also begun to assert themselves within the local village communities. All these departures from the stereotyped images of Dalits create intense cognitive dissonance for the upper and middle caste clusters who almost impulsively resist mobility aspirations and strivings of Dalits by strategies ranging from subtle discrimination to atrocious reprisals. The cases of atrocities against Dalits have become legion, particularly since the late 1970s; a *prima facie* scrutiny of some of these cases shows: (a) that conflicts are both fierce and frequent between the backward middle castes and Dalits rather than between the top and bottom strata; (b) that earlier limited to the time and arena of electoral politics, the conflicts have now tended to spill over the entire social space and time-cycle; and (c) that conflicts are more endemic in traditional occupational structures than in modern, in rural settings than in urban, and at the local level of the political system than at State or national.[29]

Phase of Congress Minority Government of Prime Minister P.V. Narasimha Rao and Federal Coalition Governments led by Minority National Parties: The latter half of the 1980s and the early 1990s have witnessed two aggressive strategies of political mobilisation in the form of the Ayodhya Ram *mandir* agitation of the BJP and the *Sangh Parivar* and the *Mandalisation* of the OBC vote bloc by the Janata Dal-led National Front government and the parties of the Janata Parivar. The former led to the demolition of the Babri *masjid* in Ayodhya by a mob of Hindu *kar sevaks* on 6 December 1992. The Mandal campaign was triggered by the implementation of the recommendation of the Mandal Commission Report for 27 per cent reservation for OBCs by the V.P. Singh minority coalition government in the monsoon of 1990, that led to instant violent reaction by anti-Mandal students all across the north Indian campuses and urban centres. Challenged in the Supreme Court, the OBC reservation was subsequently re-implemented by the successor Congress (I) minority government headed by P.V. Narasimha Rao in a modified form incorporating the Supreme Court's stipulation about excluding the *'creamy layer'* of the OBCs from the benefits of reservation.

However, given the political and economic clout of the *creamy layer* of the OBCs, it is difficult to implement a just and equitable OBC reservation policy. In mid-1995 in Kerala, for example, the Congress-led United Democratic Front (UDF) government was dithering on implementing the *creamy layer* stipulation. In face of the continued delaying tactics of the government, the Supreme Court threatened the chief secretary and the Cabinet with contempt of Court on the issue. The chief secretary reportedly pleaded with the Court that he had put up the matter innumerable times before the Cabinet but in vain. The Court granted a two-month reprieve. The dilemma of the government was that the OBC castes of Ezhavas and those belonging to Muslim and Latin Catholic communities, who comprise 50 per cent of the State's 30 million population, had warned against the implementation of the *creamy layer* stipulations.

However, speaking in general terms, the BJP and the Janata Dal could reap only short-term and dubious electoral harvests from the *Mandir* and *Mandal* agitations. In December 1992, BJP held the reigns of government in UP, MP, Himachal Pradesh and Rajasthan. In the wake of the demolition of the Babri masjid, the BJP government in UP resigned and the other three BJP governments were dismissed by the Centre under Article 356 of the Constitution. In subsequent elections, the party managed to somehow form the government only in Rajasthan, with the addition of Delhi, though it was voted in subsequent elections in 1995 to power in some other States (Maharashtra and Gujarat). In the 1993 and 1995 Assembly elections, the Janata Dal suffered a humiliating defeat in the North, though face-saving success of sorts came its way in Karnataka and Bihar. The Samajvadi Party (SP)–Bahujan Samaj Party (BSP) alliance in UP reaped the electoral benefits of Mandalisation, though by the summer of 1995, their government fell, giving way to the BSP government headed by Mayawati with the legislative backing of the BJP and tacit approval of the Congress government at the Centre. The bang of the *dalit* rhetorics of Kanshi Ram's BSP was to end in the whimper of the compromise with the neo-traditional Hindu BJP and subsequently with the Congress.

Besides, the 1980s revived the threat of national disintegration in Punjab and Jammu & Kashmir from ethnic fundamentalism. As indicated above, a related development in the late 1980s and the early '90s was the rise of Hindu and Muslim communalism in large parts of north India. Even the Congress party, the architect of the secular state in India at the dawn of Independence, seriously compromised its secular credentials by taking recourse to covert communalism by pandering to Hindu revivalism, and only belatedly tried to extricate itself from the temptations of communal politics, but only after having been beaten in the game by the BJP in the 1989 elections. Writing in the early 1970s, Kothari[30] had opined that India had turned the corner, so far as the question of national unification was concerned. M.P. Singh had also optimistically observed that compared to a party system fragmented by deep ideological divisions of Hindu traditionalism, revolutionary communism and secessionist regionalism in the early days of the republic, the Indian political system by the early 1980s had come to be characterised by an appreciable degree of "party system integration."[31] These were valid conclusions in the background of the evident liberalisation of the Jana Sangh and Akali Dal (Sant Fateh Singh group), "nationalisation" of the DMK and National Conference, and the revival of party politics in a number of north-eastern States after decades of insurgency and military action. But some of these positive trends of the earlier decades suffered serious erosion in the 1980s, 1990s and thereafter.

In the wake of the breakdown of the Congress system consensus, opine Yogendra Yadav and Suhas Palshikar[32]: "Mandir, Mandal and Market should be seen on three projects to recreate the national community." They elaborate that the Mandir targeted at establishing the national community based on *Hindutva* or majoritarian secularism as its central pillar, while Mandal aimed at making the OBCs as the core element of the national community. Market viewed the middle class as the sheet anchor of the reinvented national community. The net design and the affect was "to project a meta-cleavage around which competitive politics would be conducted."

Federal Coalition Governments Led by the Majority BJP under Prime Minister Modi: The phase of unstable or blackmailed coalition governments between 1989 to 2014 came to an end after the 2014 general elections when the BJP under Narendra Modi won a majority in the Lok Sabha for the first time since 1984, but still decided to continue the trend of federal coalition government under the BJP-led National Democratic Alliance (NDA). The BJP was re-elected in 2019 with a still larger majority for itself as well as the NDA. In 2019, for example, the BJP won 303 seats in the Lok Sabha, which accounted for 55.90 per cent of the total seats in the house. The runner-up, the Indian National Congress, trailed far behind with 52 seats and 9.59 per cent of the total seats in the house. The percentage of the national vote registered by the former was 37.36 and the BJP's and NDA's combined 45 per cent. In contrast, the Congress share of the national vote remained the same as in 2014, i.e., 19.5. The next three parties ranking after the BJP and the Congress were regional parties—DMK from Tamil Nadu, YSR Congress Party from Andhra Pradesh, All India Trinamool Congress from West Bengal—scoring 24, 22, and 22 seats and 4.43, 4.06, and4.06 per cent of votes, respectively. The next five parties ranking after these—Shiv Sena from Maharashtra, Janata Dal (United) from Bihar, Biju Janata Dal from Odisha, Bahujan Samaj Party from Uttar Pradesh, and Telangana Rashtra Samithi from Telangana—were again all regional parties accounting for 18 seats (3.32 per cent), 15 seats (2.77 per cent), 12 seats (2.21 per cent), 10 seats (1.85 per cent), and 9 seats (1.66 per cent), respectively. The rest of all the parties—all regional parties—registered seats ranging from 6 to 1 and percentages of seats all zero with varying fractions. In terms of relative presence in the Lok Sabha, the BJP appeared to be virtually reminiscent of the Jonathan Swift's popular English fiction of Gulliver in the Land of Lilliputs!

This phase of Modi's premiership came to mark not only the most stable coalition governments but also ended the blackmail by the regional parties in the coalition governments, which the leading minority national parties like the Janata Party/Dal or the Congress party or even the BJP under the then Prime Minister, Atal Bihari Vajpayee in the preceding phase of coalition governments found difficult to resist for the sake of survival on the shaky saddle. The Prime Minister, Modi, restored the pre-eminence of the PM in the cabinet and effectively checked the tendency of the coalition partners to treat the ministries allocated to them as semi-feudal fiefdoms and be more beholden to their party supremos in the States than to the PM. The position of the BJP in the party system came to be somewhat akin to the 'Congress System' of the yore and some observers have also begun to use the epithet of the 'BJP System' now. However, there still remain some powerful regional parties ruling in some States or Union Territories, especially in the South (YSR Congress Party in Andhra Pradesh, Telangana Rashtra Samithi in Andhra Pradesh, DMK in Tamil Nadu (aligned with NDA), Left Democratic Front in Kerala, Indian National Congress in Puducherry), and in the East (All India Trinamul Congress in West Bengal, Biju Janata Dal in Odisha (generally friendly with NDA), Jharkhand Mukti Morcha (aligned with UPA) in Jharkhand, and the Sikkim Democratic Front in Sikkim (weakened by defections to BJP). The BJP/NDA has recently also lost power to the Indian National Congress in Assembly elections in Rajasthan, Chhattisgarh[33], and Madhya Pradesh where the congress government is on the edge of a fall due to the defection of Jyotiraditya Scindia to the BJP at this writing (mid-March 2020). In the northwest, Punjab is under the rule of the Indian National Congress under Captain Amrinder Singh. In the western State of Madhya Pradesh, the BJP has suffered by defection of its longest ally—the Shiv Sena, which has formed a coalition government with Nationalist Congress Party led by Sharad Pawar and the Indian National Congress. BJP is gradually gaining ground in West Bengal and Sikkim. Moreover, the Rajya Sabha continues to have an opposition majority, which has been a recurrent feature of the bicameral federal scenario since the 1989 general elections. In the heyday of the 'Congress System', the Indian National Congress ruled at the Centre as well as in all or most of the States; it was dubbed as the 'party of concensus' flanked by the marginal 'parties of pressure' with little near prospect of coming to power but democratically interacting with like-minded factions within the ruling Congress party[34]. Moreover, the Congress those days had had a bicameral majority in the national popular chamber as well as the federal second chamber.

MODELS OF ELECTIONEERING AND CONCOMITANT PARTY SYSTEMS AND PRIME MINISTERIAL STYLES

Different patterns of electioneering and party systems and premiership styles can be discerned in different periods and phases of Indian politics. Three such models are: (1) the locality-oriented pluralist network model; (2) the nationally-oriented personalised mass appeal model; and (3) the regionally and, to some extent, ethnically segmented model in which neither the locality nor the nation but the region is the most relevant arena of political and electoral activity.[35]

The locality-oriented pluralist network model was marked by a complex multi-layered factional and party-political structures that were locally articulated along caste, community, and factional lines in villages and districts and aggregated at the State level by reasonably autonomous sets of party elites in various States. These intermediary power structures were overlaid with a nationally aggregating supra-regional coalitions of national leadership headed by Jawaharlal Nehru during his long 'Pluralistic Premiership'.[36] This was the period of 'Consociational' Dominance by the Congress party ruling with overwhelming majorities in the Parliament and almost all State Legislatures. At frosty Himalayan heights of the Congress power structures sat Nehru, ingeniously redesigning the structures of the new, mixed economy with a dominant public sector, and tilting at the windmills of the semi-feudal society through his land reforms and rural development measures. The lower levers of power were dominated by the conservative urban middle class and rural middle class and caste leadership well versed in mobilising the masses and deradicalising the Nehruvian reforms and rhetorics in State Legislature and administrative implementation. In electoral campaigns during this phase, Nehru treaded the land like a colossus, but only occasionally and partly digging into the multi-layered village and district factional alliances; a more pervasive reach to the grassroots was yet to come. He was deputised in his endeavours by largely autonomous but deferential sets of Congress leadership in the States. Towards the fag end of his consociational premiership, there developed in the party a Syndicate of powerful State and regional leaders that played a crucial role in influencing the succession to Nehru in 1964 and the succession to Lal Bahadur Shastri in 1966.[37]

Our hypothesis is that the three General Elections held in 1952, 1957, and 1962—all "maintaining" elections—and, to some extent even the 1967 one, which was the first election (and "critical"[38] one) held after Nehru's demise, broadly conform to this model.

Our second model is the one we have called the nationally-oriented personalized mass appeal in which the national content of the preceding model becomes more pervasive; in addition, two of the preceding model's crucial features—the autonomous State Congress leadership and locality orientation of the electorate—come to be seriously undermined by a personalised mass appeal of the national leader, bypassing the intermediary structures of power and seeking to 'nationalise' political issues. This was the period of centralised dominance by the Congress Party under Mrs. Indira Gandhi who evolved a new style of executive leadership, which, for want of a better term, may be called patrimonial[39] premiership; Mrs. Gandhi developed it bit by bit by giving the call for a "committed" civil service and judiciary, dispensing with internal democracy within her party and federal autonomy of State governments, and making a direct mass appeal to the electorate without the intermediation of middle-level elites. Her drive to personal power and appropriation of the State also pitched her in a running battle with big business, princes, and landed interests and traders producing and marketing the surplus grain. However, she rode roughshod over these elements of opposition by the use of the state power by strong hand.

However, Mrs. Gandhi soon came under the pressure of a mass movement led by Jayaprakash Narayan outside the space of the party system, even though her party continued to command massive majorities in the Parliament and many State Legislatures. The mass movement and the internal Emergency imposed to arrest it by Mrs. Gandhi brought about a massive realignment in the party system, begetting the Janata Party voted to power in 1977 and 1978 in New Delhi and in most of the north Indian States. Factionalism in the Janata Party and the fall of its government in New Delhi in 1979 was again followed by a major voter realignment in the 1980 parliamentary elections bringing back to power a chastened Mrs. Gandhi; this, in turn, was followed by a vigorous reinforcement of this realignment in favour of Mrs. Gandhi's elder son, on her assassination, in the 1984 parliamentary elections. By all accounts, all these elections were 'wave elections' or 'plebiscitary elections' in which some overriding national issues overlaid the pale blighted presence of the local issues: *garibi hatao* in 1971, democracy versus authoritarianism in 1977, non-functioning of the Janata gvernment in 1980, and the threat to national unity and the sympathy vote for an orphaned political offspring in 1984.[40]

Our third model of electoral mobilisation is the regionally and ethnically segmented model in which overriding national issues do not predominate. Instead, it is the region and the locality that become the level or unit of prime political importance. Beginning with the 1980s, this model became prevalent on an unprecedented scale. What was earlier limited to a few States like Tamil Nadu, Jammu and Kashmir, etc. began to multiply in State after State. This phase has seen the heyday of regional parties, including some new ones like TDP, AGP, PDP, TRS, BJD, RJD, MDMK, PMK, JD(S), JD(U). The mushrooming of a large assortment of regional or nominally national parties gave rise to hung Parliaments without clear majority for any one party.

At the electoral level as well as legislative levels, this triggered the onset of coalition politics. In the initial years, legislative coalitions were generally formed after an election was over. This arena of electoral politics was dominated by provisional electoral adjustments among like-minded parties to avoid mutual contests and splitting of votes. Gradually, there was crystallisation of pre-poll coalitions. In time, two such broad coalitions remained in the field—Congress-led United Progressive Alliance (UPA) and BJP-led National Democratic Alliance (NDA). The JD-led United Front practically dissipated by the late 1990s. The two competing coalitions were congregations of a national party and an assortment of mainly regional parties. The NDA, which ruled for six years since 1998, was an assortment of earlier 18 and subsequently 24 parties. The UPA in 2004 included fifteen parties, and electorally survived with a varying number of parties in 2009. Such large numbers in each coalition are indicative of the emergence of States and localities as the hub of largely autonomous units of political mobilisation and participation.

The Congress-led UPA was re-elected in 2009 parliamentary election that turned out to be exceptional in the sense that for the first time since 1984, the leading ruling party did not suffer from anti-incumbency vote. Congress' position was doubly improved both in relation to parties in the UPA as well as major opposition parties, namely, the BJP and the Left wing. This has prompted the inference on the part of the observers that the trend suggested that the party system was back to the centrist ground where the Congress generally excelled. Yet it was perhaps be too hasty a conclusion that the party system was renationalised and the trend of regionalization was definitely halted.[41]

A new pattern of electoral mobilisation and prime ministerial style can be delineated under the Prime Minster, Narendra Modi of BJP/NDA since the 2014 general elections replicated with greater vigour in the 2019 general elections. The rise of the BJP under Modi is reminiscent of the Congress hegemony under Nehru and Indira Gandhi in some ways and to some extent. Modi has also revived the Prime Ministerial system of government prevalent in the phase of Congress hegemony. However, as already mentioned above, the BJP dominance presently has to contend with some powerful regional parties in the South, especially in Andhra Pradesh (YSR Congress Party) and Telangana (Telangana Rashtriya Samithi) and in Kerala where the CPI(M)-led Left Democratic Front and the Congress-led United Democratic Front regularly alternate in power; this is also the case in some eastern States like West Bengal (Trinamool Congress) and Odisha (Biju Janata Dal), although the BJP is gradually gaining ground in the former and has a friendly relationship with the ruling party in the latter. In the National Capital Region of Delhi, the Aam Aadmi Party has also continued to hold the ground very firmly. In more recent years, the BJP has also suffered some reverses in Punjab, Rajasthan, Chhattisgarh, Maharashtra, and Jharkhand. The State-level power structures are reflected in the federal second chamber, Rajya Sabha, where no government since 1989 has been able to gain a majority control, which the Congress in its heyday of power always did.

DETERMINANTS OF VOTING BEHAVIOUR

Broadly speaking, we hypothesise that three sets of factors influence voting behaviour in India. There are social factors like patron-client networks, caste and class, tribe, language, and religion, etc. There are also political factors like party identification, leadership image, issues and government performance, inter-party alliances and seat adjustments, candidate, etc. Besides, there are the three Ms—Media, Money, and Muscle power. It is difficult to determine conclusively which of these factors are more decisive. Presumably, their influence is a function of varying contexts and complex and intermeshed determination by all these factors. Their influence may also vary from place to place and election to election.

It seems reasonable to assume that patron-client networks and some ascriptive factors like caste and tribe generally influence voting locally, while class clusters and broader identities such as language and religion may impact voting over a larger area. It is also possible that religious and linguistic communities may get divided along caste and class lines. Moreover, economic classes like professionals, peasants and industrial and agricultural workers seldom vote in terms of uniform party choices all over the nation. Class factors like most other social factors are often confounded with a regional clustering effect in their impact on voting behaviour. These are the complex panoply of social forces on which the political factors operate again in a complex web of causation.

Voting decision is both a group and an individual choice. The two aspects may in fact be so inextricably intermeshed that it would be a great methodological challenge for psephologists to separate them. The legal fact of voting is an individual act *par excellence*. But its sociological and political nuances and causes may have group influences operating on them. Parties, personalities, issues and inter-party alliances are all basic political ingredients that shape electoral politics and voting behaviour in India. The party factor is important but it may be confounded with caste and other factors. Moreover, party factor is also often intermixed with the leadership image. In case of prime ministerial candidates, the impact of leadership image is generally greater than that of the party. Two other dimensions of the party factor are the incumbency effect (critical evaluation of the performance of the party in power) and inter-party alliance or seat adjustments.

In early post-Independence decades, the role of media, money and muscle power was not as important and as pervasive as it has become in more recent decades. Elections have now become a gigantic enterprise involving enormous amount of money on the part of parties and candidates. Table 11.1 shows, parliamentary and state assembly elections have been becoming increasingly more expensive since the first general election in 1952 to the one held in 1991, as the information offered by a veteran MP from Bihar.

What has come to be known as criminalisation of politics has assumed alarming proportions. Information culled from affidavits regarding criminal allegations filed by candidates in the 2004 Lok Sabha elections shows that there is hardly any party that does not harbour leaders with criminal taint (see Table 11.2). The Nationalist Congress Party (NCP) topped the list in this matter

TABLE 11.1 Election Expenses of Bihar, MP, 1952–1991

1952: Assembly Constituency	Spent ₹ 1900	Elected
1957: Assembly Constituency	Spent ₹ 2700	Elected
1962: Assembly Constituency	Spent ₹ 5200	Elected
1977: Lok Sabha Constituency	Spent ₹ 7.5 lakh	Defeated
1980: Lok Sabha Constituency	Spent ₹ 7 to 8 lakh	Elected
1984: Lok Sabha Constituency	Spent ₹ 7 lakh	Elected
1989: Lok Sabha Constituency	Spent ₹ 8 lakh	Elected
1991: Assembly Constituency	Spent ₹ 3 to 4 lakh	Elected

Source: A Surya Prakash, *What Ails Indian Parliament? An Exhaustive Diagnosis*, Indus, New Delhi., 1995, p. 280.

TABLE 11.2 Percentage of MPs with Criminal Charges in 2004 Lok Sabha Elections

BJP	19% (16/138)	NCP	56% (5/9)
Congress	10% (15/145)	RJD	40% (10/25)
BSP	37% (7/19)	DMK	13% (2/15)
CPI(M)	12% (5/43)	SS	33% (4/12)

Source: *Outlook*, New Delhi, 21 June 2004, p. 35.

with 56 per cent such candidates, followed by Rashtriya Janata Dal (RJD) (40 per cent), BSP (37 per cent), Shiv Sena (33 per cent), BJP (19 per cent), DMK (13 per cent), CPI(M) (12 per cent), and Congress (10 per cent).

The situation remained largely unchanged by the 2019 general elections. The Delhi-based Association of Democratic Reforms reported citing signed affidavits by candidates submitted to the Election Commission of India that about 19 per cent of contestants faced criminal charges, including rape, murder, and kidnapping. The law prohibits persons convicted of any offence and sentenced to imprisonment of two years or more from seeking elections. The tardy administration of criminal judicial system indirectly allows charge-sheeted persons to run in elections unless finally convicted. Percentage of such candidates was 17 per cent in 2014 elections, up from 15 per cent in 2009. In 2019, BJP fielded 40 per cent of candidates with criminal cases against them, followed by the Congress party with 39 per cent of such candidates. In some other parties, the proportion of such candidates mounts to more than 50 per cent[42].

To sum up our discussion of the determinants of voting behaviour in India, we reiterate our initial methodological skepticism that it is well-nigh impossible to neatly delineate the various determinants of voting behaviour in a country of India's diversities and assign precise and coherent causal weights to them. However, as members of the community of social scientists we let a leading psephologist in India today, Yogendra Yadav, to have a final word here. Interpreting the 2004 Lok Sabha polls, Yadav observed:[43] "There are no pristine intentions lying hidden somewhere, waiting to be recovered, the act of reading is never free of construction, the meaning of the text depends on the questions that are posed to it."

Let us examine, for example, the effect of caste and community factor on the outcome of the 2004 Lok Sabha elections. Survey data[44] show that caste is one among the several other factors that influence voting. At the all-India level, we have data about the voting intentions of three major caste/community clusters—Dalits, Adivasis and Muslims. The Dalit voters were more likely to vote for the Congress than the BJP and allies in almost all States excepting West Bengal, Assam and Uttar Pradesh. Of course, the extent of their likely support for the Congress ranged between 57 per cent in Haryana, 44 per cent in Gujarat, and 8 per cent each in Madhya Pradesh and Jharkhand. The non-Congress inclination of Dalits in West Bengal, Assam and Uttar Pradesh are understandable in terms of the regional strength of the Left Front in West Bengal, the Asom Gana Parishad in Assam, and the Bahujan Samaj Party in Uttar Pradesh. The Adivasi voters tended to support the Congress in disproportionately larger numbers in Maharashtra (34 per cent), Jharkhand (28 per cent), Andhra Pradesh (19 per cent), Orissa (18 per cent), Chhattisgarh (13 per cent), Meghalaya (13 per cent), Rajasthan (12 per cent) and Madhya Pradesh (8 per cent). However, the preferred choice of Adivasis in Arunachal Pradesh, Assam, West Bengal, and Gujarat happened to be the BJP and its allies, rather than the Congress. The Muslims who had, since the 1990s, moved away from the Congress, registered a comeback to the Congress fold. As many as 47 per cent Muslims intended to vote for Congress against only 11 per cent for the BJP and its allies. Significantly, 42 per cent of Muslims stayed away from both the major all-India parties and voted for other political formations, presumably regional parties. At the State level, the degree of Muslim support for the Congress ranged between 94 per cent in Delhi and 15 per cent in Uttar Pradesh. The BJP and its allies were the more preferred party of Muslims in Andhra Pradesh (34 per cent), Karnataka (21 per cent), Gujarat and West Bengal (20 per cent each), Maharashtra and Tamil Nadu (14 per cent each), and Rajasthan (13 per cent). More solid Muslim support than the foregoing went to major regional parties in Uttar Pradesh (82 per cent) and Jammu and Kashmir (75 per cent). Appreciable levels of Muslim support for parties other than the Congress and BJP-led alliances are evident in West Bengal (54 per cent), Kerala (40 per cent), Assam (28 per cent), Karnataka (25 per cent), Bihar (17 per cent), Gujarat and Maharashtra (14 per cent each), and Tamil Nadu (11 per cent).

We have survey data bearing on relationship between caste/community and party choice from at least eleven States. In Andhra Pradesh, the OBCs were more or less divided between the Congress and its allies and TDP–BJP alliance with a slight edge of the former over the latter. 45 per cent of peasant OBCs and 47 per cent of lower OBCs preferred the Congress, whereas 48 per cent of peasant OBCs and 45 per cent of lower OBCs were inclined to vote for TDP–BJP alliance. The TDP–BJP alliance had a disproportionately larger support among farmers (49 per cent) than the Congress (41 per cent). This pattern of relationship was reversed among agricultural workers. 51 per cent of them supported the Congress as against 41 per cent preferring the TDP–BJP alliance.

In Kerala, Hindu upper castes, Nairs, Ezhavas, OBCs and dalits were more often than not inclined to vote for the CPM-led LDF whereas Muslims and Christians, by and large, supported the Congress-led UDF. Some measure of support registered by the BJP in Kerala was spread over all Hindu castes, whereas minorities were only marginally inclined to vote for it.

Survey data from Karnataka show that Congress support is more or less evenly spread among the middle castes of Vokkaligas, OBCs and Lingayats. The Congress was preferred in larger proportions by dalits and Muslims. BJP and its allies scored highest measures of support among the upper caste and Lingayats. Adivasis were also more likely to support these parties than the Congress. The Janata Dal (Secular) was predominantly a party of Vokkaligas and Lingayats.

In Tamil Nadu, barring the upper castes who largely supported the AIADMK-led alliance, all other castes tended to join the bandwagon of DMK-led alliance that included the Congress. The latter's lead was somewhat reduced among the female and very poor voters.

Moving to the north, in Uttar Pradesh we find that BJP was predominantly an upper-caste party. Predictably, the BSP was a dalit-dominated political formation whereas the Samajwadi Party and Rashtriya Lok Dal were largely parties of Yadavs and other cultivating castes and Muslims.

The patterns of party preference by castes in Bihar suggest that RJD-led alliance that included the Congress was preponderantly supported by Yadavs, Muslims and dalits, whereas the mainstay of BJP support was among upper castes, Kurmis and Koeris.

In Jharkhand, the Congress support was disproportionately larger among adivasis and OBCs. Whereas the BJP support largely drew upon the upper castes, with dalits evenly distributed between the two alliances led by these two major national parties.

In Assam, the Congress had strongest support among Muslims whereas the BJP support was somewhat evenly distributed among Dalits, Adivasis, OBCs and upper castes. The regional outfit, AGP, was again mainly a party of upper castes and OBCs.

Survey data from Haryana demonstrate that the INLD, the erstwhile ruling party in the State, yielded ground to the Congress among all major castes and communities except Jats. The BJP support in Haryana was disproportionately larger among the Sikhs.

In the West, the pattern in Gujarat saw the BJP scoring better among upper castes, Patinas and adivasis, while the Congress was found scoring higher among dalits, Muslims and OBCs. In Maharashtra, the Congress was likely to get more votes among Muslims, Dalits and Adivasis; BJP among upper castes, Shiv Sena among Maratha-Kunbis. NCP support is more or less similar to Congress support with one difference that it registered a greater measure of support among Maratha-Kunbis, though lesser than the Shiv Sena.

A post-poll study of the 2019 Lok Sabha elections conducted by India Today-Axis My India based on a sample survey of more than seven lakh respondents across every parliamentary constituency revealed that at the all-India level, the BJP-led NDA was popular across all sections of population and the support for Modi cut across all sections. The Congress-led UPA generally lagged markedly behind, and others remained at the tail-end. Interestingly, the voters' preferences for NDA and UPA did not vary much across various income and age groups. Support for Modi was over-arching cutting across all sections. What were the factors that mattered most for the voters? The most important factor was the prime ministerial candidate (for 37 per cent of voters), followed by the local candidate (25 per cent), and the party and its manifesto (3 per cent). This clearly indicates the 'presidential' nature of the 2019 campaign (in the American sense of the term). Voting preferences by demographics also revealed the BJP far ahead of the other national party, the INC, and the remainder category, the others; BJP was preferred by 44 per cent males and 46 per cent females as against INC, which was supported by 27 per cent males and 27 per cent females. BJP was the choice of 44 per cent rural voters and 49 per cent urban voters, while INC secured 27 per cent rural votes and 26 per cent urban votes. In terms of caste and community, BJP scored the highest percentage of votes among the Scheduled Tribes (49 per cent), followed by the Scheduled Castes (41 per cent), and lowest among the Muslims (10 per cent). The corresponding figures for INC were Scheduled Tribes (30 per cent), Scheduled Castes (28 per cent), and Muslims (51 per cent)[45].

ELECTORAL REFORMS

Since the 1990s, the Election Commission has displayed an unprecedented activism. Even in the absence of parliamentary enactment of reforms recommended by the Commission itself and some other bodies, it has brought about a sea change on the electoral scene by stricter enforcement of the existing laws and by laws of political parties themselves, and of the moral code of conduct formulated by it in consultation with political parties.

The Rudolphs[46] aptly observe: "the strengthening of [Election Commission's] regulatory role has coincided with the period during which confidence in cabinet and the Parliament, the instruments of developmental, interventionist state has eroded."

In a national probability sample survey conducted during the 1996 general election by the Centre for the Study of Developing Societies (CSDS), Delhi, it was found that the public trust in the Election Commission of India exceeded the trust reposed by the people in the judiciary, State government, local self government etc.[47]

One serious problem which the Election Commission has recently been seized with is the difficulty to define a criminal and to prevent his or her entry in politics: The commission is conscious of the fact in the eye of law a person is presumed to be innocent unless proved guilty. In the Commission's considered opinion, a person who is facing trial in a serious offence, if kept out of the electoral fray till he is exonerated of the charge, should not have a legitimate grievance, as such restriction on his right to contest election would be reasonable restriction in the greater public interest and for bringing sanctity to the august Houses which are the supreme law-making bodies of the country.[48] Pending parliamentary enactment to this effect, the Election Commission took steps under the order of the Supreme Court in the elections held in 2003 and 2004 and required the filing of an affidavit regarding a candidate's non-involvement or otherwise in criminal activities and charge sheet on that account along with their nomination papers.

In 1998, two committees chaired, respectively, by Justice B.P. Jeevan Reddy and Indrajit Gupta (a CPI-MP and Union Minister) made contradictory recommendations for electoral reforms. The former opposed State funding of elections and the latter supported it. The Reddy Committee, which was adopted by the Law Commission, argued that the idea behind State funding of elections is to eliminate the undue influence of corporate funding and black money. State funding would be ill-advised without the precondition of ensuring internal organisational democracy and audited accounts by the Election Commission.[49]

The Law Commission, in a comprehensive review of election-related laws, recommended in 1999 a 25 per cent increase in the Lok Sabha and Vidhan Sabha seats, with the new Lok Sabha seats (138 in numbers) to be filled through the list system on the panels of prospective legislators furnished to the Election Commission by political parties. In apportioning these seats, parties with less than five per cent votes should be eliminated. Old territorial constituencies should also continue, but their number should stand frozen at 550 until the year 2025. If thus reconstituted, the Lok Sabha would have a total of 688 seats. This reform, in the view of the Law Commission, is necessary to rectify the anomaly arising out of the freezing of the Lok Sabha seats since the 1971 Census. Moreover, the Law Commission also recommended that political parties be brought within the purview of the law by amending the Representation of the People Act, 1951, which requires parties to constitute executive committees every three years, with specific powers to local party units in decision making and elections by secret ballot within the party, and regular maintenance of accounts.[50]

The National Commission for Review of the Working of the Constitution (NCRWC) chaired by Justice M.N. Venkatachalliah in its Report, 2002, has considered the issue of electoral reforms at some length. The Commission specifically identifies the following major problem areas to be addressed: (a) increasing cost of elections and corruption and criminalisation of politics; (b) the mismatch between the vote share and seat share among parties resulting from the first-past-the-post-electoral system and multiplicity of parties; (c) politics of defection; (d) inaccurate electoral rolls; (e) booth-capturing and bogus voting; (f) use of muscle power and intimidation of voters; (g) subversion of electoral process by officials and local administration; (h) miscounting of votes; (i) increasing number of candidates with criminal background; (j) misuse of religion and caste in elections; (k) judicial delays in disposal of election disputes; (l) fake and non-serious candidates; (m) representational distortion due to incongruities in delimitation of constituencies, and (n) "loss of systemic legitimacy due to decay in the standards of political morality and decline in the spirit of service and sacrifice in public life".[51]

The major recommendations made by the NCRWC include (a) the appointment of Election Commissioners on the recommendation of a committee comprising the Prime Minister, leaders of the Opposition in the Lok Sabha and the Rajya Sabha, the Speaker of the Lok Sabha and the Deputy Chairman of the Rajya Sabha. A similar procedure is suggested for the appointment of the State Election Commissioners; (b) a foolproof method for preparation of electoral rolls at the Panchayat level supplemented by a foolproof voter ID card/citizenship card for all adults; (c) nationwide use of electronic voting machines to prevent large-scale rigging; (d) legal authorisation of the Election Commission under Section 58A of the RPA 1951 to take decision on the report of the returning officers, observers or citizen groups in cases of booth-capturing; (e) a more effective implementation of laws against campaigns exacerbating tension on the basis of caste, community, religion, race or language; (f) amendment in the RPA to bar candidature of persons charged with offences punishable with imprisonment for a maximum term of five years or more; (g) determination of the period of disqualification under Section 8A of the RPA 1951 on grounds of corrupt practices; (h) fixation of the ceiling on election expenses by the Election Commission from time to time taking into account the expenses incurred by the candidate as well as his political party and friends; (i) declaration of assets and liabilities by candidates and their close relatives along with their nomination papers; (j) considerable reduction in the campaign period; (k) nomination of candidature for the same seat from only one constituency; (l) legal status to the code of conduct with cognizable penal action for its violation; (m) replacement of plurality system by majority electoral system; and (n) legal disqualification from membership of the House in case of defection on the recommendation of the Election Commission instead of the Chairman or the Speaker of the House concerned.[52]

So far, the Parliament has implemented only the suggested anti-defection reform. As already mentioned earlier, the Election Commission has obliged candidates in recent elections to declare their assets and liabilities and conviction for criminal activity on the order of the Supreme Court.

The latest bid of electoral reform has been introduced by the Modi government through the 2017–18 budget speech of the former Finance Minister, Arun Jaitley aiming at what he called 'Transparency in Electoral Funding', including capping cash donations at ₹ 2,000/- A key measure that is most novel as well as most controversial is the 'electoral bonds'. These are interest-free banking instruments, which can be bought from specified branches of State Bank of India (SBI) in multiples of ₹ 1,000, ₹ 1 lakh, ₹ 10 lakh, or ₹ 1 crore by individuals and companies who have to disclose their identity through 'Know Your Customers' (KYC) norms to SBI, while political parties, getting 1 per cent of votes polled in the last Lok Sabha or Vidhan sabha elections, can encash these bonds within 15 days only in their specified bank accounts. Critics say that the system is amenable to misuse by the government as the donors do not remain anonymous to the political establishment. The Union government reportedly ignored the warnings of the Reserve bank of India and the Election Commission of India against this move[53]. The matter was taken to the Supreme Court, but it refused to annul the scheme and directed the political parties to submit receipts of amounts received and identity of donors to in a sealed cover to the Election commission by May 30, 2019. The Court said it was an interim arrangement to prevent the tilting of balance in favour of one political party[54]. The Association of Democratic Rights (ADR) reported that the Electoral Bonds are skewed heavily towards the national parties, with the BJP being the biggest beneficiary garnering 94.5 per cent of the amount, leaving other national and regional parties high and dry. Moreover, a new amendment to the Foreign Contribution Regulation Act, 2010, has opened the entry of foreign funds into electoral financing that poses a mortal threat to national autonomy of elections in India. Petitions to the Supreme Court drew an interim approval with a rider in favour of a report to the Election Commission by political parties in a sealed cover mentioned above and refusal to pass an interim stay[55]. No final order from the Court has been there to this date (October 22, 2020)!

REFERENCES

1. *Election Commission of India* v. *Union of India & others* (1993), *Landmark Judgements on Election Law,* Vol. III, Election Commission of India, New Delhi, 2000, p. 39.
2. Maurice Duverger, *Political Parties: Their Organization and Activity in the Modern State,* John Wiley, New York, 1963; William Riker,

"The Two-Party System and Duverger's Law: An Essay in the History of Political Science", *American Political Science Review*, Vol. 76, pp. 753–766; "Duverger's Law Revisited in Bernard Gofman and Arendt Leijphart (Eds.), *Electoral Laws and Their Political Consequences,* Agathon Press, New York, 1986.

3. S.M. Lipset and Stein Rokkan (Eds.), *Party Systems and Voter Alignments: Cross-National Perspectives,* Free Press, New York, 1967.

4. Leonard Binder *et. al.*, *Crisis and Sequences in Political Development,* Princeton University Press, Princeton, 1971.

5. For an earlier version of this argument, see M.P. Singh, "Electoral Politics and Phases of Politicisation in India", *Trends in Social Science Research*, Vol. 3, No. 2, December 1996.

6. Samuel Huntington, *Political Order in Changing Societies* (1968: Ch. 7), uses the term "ruralizing elections" in the specific sense of the process through which the party system in a modernizing country adapts itself with the largely rural society by accommodating mass rural participation and political recruitment of rural voters and elites.

7. Rudolph Lloyd and Susanne Rudolph, *In Pursuit of Lakshmi: The Political Economy of the Indian State*, Orient Longman, Delhi, 1987, obviously use the term "deinstitutionalization" in the reverse sense of Huntington's (1968, p. 12) celebrated concept of "institutionalization" defined as "the process by which organizations and procedures acquire value and stability".

8. The best historical studies on these aspects of the Indian development are Amiya P. Sen (2003), *Social and Religious Reform: The Hindus of British India,* OUP, New York; and B.B. Misra (1961), *The Indian Middle Classes: Their Growth in Modern Times,* OUP, London, and B.B. Misra (1976), *The Indian Political Parties: An Historial Analysis of Political Behaviour upto 1947,* OUP, Delhi.

9. The term is Kothari's, used in his "Introduction" to his edited book, *Caste in Indian Politics,* Orient Longman, New Delhi, 1970 and occurs in his abstracted, indeed a historical, but extremely imaginative and plausible model of interactional politicization of castes in modern Indian democratic politics. For an elitist Indological perspective on Brahman-Kshatriya polarity of power in Indian tradition, see J.C. Heesterman, *The Inner Conflict of Tradition,* OUP, 1985.

10. Gopal Krishna, "The Development of the Indian National Congress as a Mass Organization", *Journal of Asian Studies,* Vol. 25, No. 3, May 1966; and Granville Austin, *The Indian Constitution: The Cornerstone of a Nation*, New Delhi, OUP, 1966.

11. Anil Seal, *The Emergence of Indian Nationalism: Competition and Collaboration in the Later Nineteenth Century,* Cambridge University Press, Indian reprint (1982), S. Chand & Co., New Delhi, p. 341.

12. The historiography of the national movement has immensely burgeoned and got differentiated in terms of the nationalist, colonial/imperialist, Marxist, Gramscian Subaltern perspectives. For major, but less than comprehensively exhaustive, discussions, see Bipan Chandra *et al.*, *India's Freedom Struggle for Independence,* Penguin Books, New Delhi, 1989; and *Subaltern Studies,* Foreword by E.W. Said, New York, OUP, etc. For the evolution of legislative institutions, see Sneh Mahajan (1983), *Imperialist Strategy and Moderate Politics: Indian Legislature at Work, 1909–1920,* Chanakya Publications, Delhi.

13. Bipan Chandra *et al., India's Struggle for Independence,* Penguin Books, New Delhi, 1989, p. 13.

14. M.P. Singh (1981b), *Split in a Predominant Party: The Indian National Congress in 1969,* Abhinav Publications, New Delhi.

15. Bipan Chandra, *Nationalism and Colonism in India,* Orient Longman, New Delhi, 1979, p. 331, has noted "a sharp differentiation within the class of zamindars and landlords" in the colonial period; he goes on to say that a "majority of rent receivers were in their incomes and even lifestyles not distinguishable from the rich or even middle peasants. They were impoverished and even getting further impoverished. They were becoming quite hostile to colonialism and as men born to education and status and used to political and administrative leadership they could and did begin to play an active role in the anti-imperialist struggle and to provide the latter with elements of mass support, especially in elections under a restricted franchise after 1919. They played an important role in the `massization' of the national movement". As one born in a medium size *zamindar* family in Gaya district of Bihar and familiar with their "upward" and "downward" class relationships, M.P. Singh is inclined to question Chandra's strong, but flat, assertion of the lower *zamindars'* numerically large and active role in the national movement. Singh's father, two of his maternal uncles, and a cousin's father-in-law were the only arm chair Congressmen in his extended family and large number of relations spread over several districts of central and north and south Bihar.

16. Information on these Chief Ministerial successions may be gleaned from the following volumes of studies in State politics in India: M. Weiner (Ed.) (1968), *State Politics in India,* Princeton University Press, Princeton, I. Narain (Eds.) (1967), *State Politics in India,* Meenakshi Prakashan, Meerut, I. Narain (1976), *State Politics in India,* Meenakshi Prakashan, Meerut, and B.L. Fadia (1984), *State Politics in India,* 2 Vols. Radiant Publishers, New Delhi.

17. The founder of the *Jai Gurdev* movement is a sadhu of unknown but controversial antecedents who commands considerable following in Uttar Pradesh, Delhi and neighbouring States, especially among the backward castes. Arrested under the Maintenance of Internal Security Act (MISA) during the Emergency, the Gurudev actively campaigned against Indira Gandhi and in favour of the Lok Dal and Janata Party during the 1980 Lok Sabha elections. His electoral blessings and his followers' support were later solicited for their parties by various political leaders, including Mrs. Gandhi, Jagjivan Ram, Atal Behari Vajpayee and others by paying him personal visits. This sect seems to have especially appealed to the ascendant lower castes and classes. In view of the non-millenarian character of Hinduism, a notable feature of the religious ideology of *Jai Gurdev* is the transposition of the *satayuga* from the past into the future. This millenarian faith promises that when the *satayuga* comes, India would become the greatest nation of the world ruled by a religiously oriented king, agricultural production would leap to a maund per *bigha* of land, women who have so far remained deprived of comforts and good clothing would wear expensive jewelry, a rich treasure trove would be discovered at the foothills of Himalayas, Hinduism would spread throughout the world, vegetarianism and abstention from alcoholic drinks would become universal, and there would be an amazing change in the educational system following which boys educated only up to class X would be employed on highest ranking jobs. *India Today* (New Delhi), January 16–31, 1980, p. 116.

18. Rajni Kothari, "Voting in India–1: The political change of 1967", *Economic and Political Weekly,* January 1971.

19. For illustrations of these processes at work in some States, see M. Weiner (1967), *Party Building in a New Nation: The Indian National Congress,* University of Chicago Press, Chicago; Angela Burger, *Opposition in a Dominant Party System: A Study of the Jan Sangh, the Praja Socialist Party, and the Socialist Party in Uttar Pradesh, India* (1969), University of California Press, Berkeley & Los Angeles; and M.P. Singh (1975), *Cohesion in a Predominant Party: The Pradesh Congress and Party Politics in Bihar,* S. Chand & Co. New Delhi, p. 6.

20. M.N. Srinivas (1966), *Social Change in Modern India*, University of California Press, Barkeley & Los Angeles.

21. Rajni Kothari (1988a), *State against Democracy: In Search of Humane Governance,* Ajanta Publications, Delhi, Rajni Kothari (1988b): "Integration and Exclusion in Indian Politics," *Economic and Political Weekly*, 23(43), 22 October.

22. James Manor (1988), "Collective Conflict in India, Conflict Studies", 212, The Centre for Security and Conflict Studies, London; M.P. Singh

(1980a), "[Violence] At the village," *Seminar*, 25 June; M.P. Singh (1990a) "From predominance to polarized pluralism: The Indian Party System," *Think India, 2(2),* April–June.

23. Pranab Bardhan (1984), *The Political Economy of Development in India,* OUP, Delhi, Anupam Sen (1982), *The State, Industrialization, and Class Formations in India,* Routledge & Keegan Paul, London.

24. Sudipta Kaviraj (1988), "On the crisis of political institutions in India," *Contributions to Indian Sociology,* New Series, 18(2).

25. A.R. Desai (1984), *India's Path of Development: A Marxist Approach,* Popular Prakashan, Bombay.

26. O. Lynch (1969), *The Politics of Untouchability: Social Change in a City of India,* Columbia University Press, New York, Janet Benson (1978), "Political activity in a parliamentary constituency of Andhra Pradesh in the 1977 General Election: Why Congress won," *Asian Survey,* 18(8), August, Ghanshyam Shah (1972), "Voting behaviour of Adivasi and Harijan leaders: A study of the 1971 elections, *Indian Journal of Political Science,* 33(4), October–December.

27. National and regional newspapers in the 1980s have published copious accounts of these agitations and incidents of violent conflicts. Gail Omvedt (Ed.) (1983), *Land, Caste and Politics in India,* South Asia Books, "Introduction" pp. 30–31, in an interesting theoretical and strategic formulation, observes: "Among the rural poor toilers, the continued existence of caste divisions and the continued, if varying, forms of the special oppression of dalit labourers means that a struggle against social cultural oppression and an anti-caste struggle is a crucial part of their general battle for liberation. But this is no longer a simple anti-feudal struggle as before. For one thing, the main enemies now are the rich farmers, including capitalist farmers, and the bourgeois State as such; for another, the dalits can no longer find their allies as the ex-sudra peasantry fighting against the "twice-born". Now the question has become one of uniting the dalits—and breaking the false, cross-class "caste unity" of the middle castes in order to bring the middle caste toilers into alliance with dalits; it is now a question of a dalit liberation movement along with the formation of a broader militant class unity among the rural poor under the slogan of 'dalit-shramik unity' (emphasis in the original)."

28. Sachhidananda (1977), *The Harijan Elite*, Thomas Press, Faridabad.

29. M.P. Singh (1980a), "[Violence] At the village", *Seminar*, No. 250, June; M.P. Singh (1980b), "Social Structure, Electoral Processes & Party System in India", *Indian Political Science Review,* 14(2) July.

30. Rajni Kothari, "The Congress System Revisited", *Asian Survey,* Vol. 12, No. 12, 1974.

31. M.P. Singh (1986), "Whither Indian Party System? A Crisis in Indian Pluralism," in Urmila Phadnis *et al.* (Eds.), *Domestic Conflicts in South Asia*, Vol. I, South Asian Publishers, New Delhi.

32. Yogendra Yadav and Suhas Palshikar, "Party System and Electoral Politics in the Indian States, 1952–2002: From Hegemory to Convergence" in Peter Ronald de Souza and E. Sridharan (Eds.), *Indian's Political Parties*, N. Delhi, Sage, 2006, p. 101.

33. Ramchandra Guha, *India After Gandhi: The History of the World's Largest Democracy*, 2nd ed., New Delhi: HarperCollins Publishers, 2011.

34. Rajni Kothari, *Politics in India*, Boston, Little, Brown & Co., 1970, Chapter 5.

35. For an earlier version of this idea, see M.P. Singh and Rajesh K. Singh (1992), "Three Models of Electoral Mobilization" in M.P. Singh (Ed.), *Lok Sabha Elections 1989: Indian Politics in 1990s*, Kalinga Publications.

36. In our opinion, Nehru's premiership style was in substance more pluralist and parliamentary than federal. This was, of course, facilitated by the towering personality of the first Prime Minister, predominance of the Congress Party at the national as well as State level, the quasi-federal nature of the Constitution and relatively limited extent of politicization of regional and ethnic identities in the early decades of Independence. It is revealing that two authoritative studies in the first decade of the Nehru Premiership, one by a British and the other by a Canadian political scientist, are both couched in the Parliamentary discourse, with little recourse to the federal idom. See Morris-Jones, W.H., *Parliament the India*, Longmans, Green & Co., London, 1957, and Brecher, Michael, *Nehru: A Political Biography*, Oxford University Press, London, 1959 (An abridged edition issued by Jaico of Bombay). It may have been, at least in part, a conceptual artifact of a paramount Parliament in constitutional design and actuality and the towering national presence of Nehru. One wishes these authors had given more attention to the question of Nehru's relationship with his Chief Ministers: one is surprised by the fact that even in discussing the patently federal issues like the reorganization of States and official languages of the Union, it is the Cabinet colleagues of Nehru that often figure in Brecher's account. The Chief Ministers of the affected States and their roles in resolving conflicts remain out of bounds in the narrative. Perhaps a new look and exploration of hitherto unexplored data with a widened conceptual aperture is called for. Some fresh light is shed on this theme by G. Parthasarathi's edited volumes of *Nehru's letter to the Chief Ministers*, 1947–1954, Oxford University Press, Delhi, 1987. But these letters are monologues rather than dialogues.

37. For an authoritative study of the 1964 and 1966 Prime Minister successions, see Brecher, Michael, *Political Succession in India,* Oxford University Press, Delhi, 1966.

38. See Campwell, Angus *et al.* (Eds.), *Elections and Political Order,* John Wiley, New York, 1966.

39. The concept of 'Patrimonialism' is borrowed from Max Weber, who used it to refer to any form of Government which is organized on the assumption that the Government is more or less an extension of the ruler's household with officials remaining as the personal dependents of the ruler (see Bendix, Reinhard, *Max Weber: An Intellectual Portrait* (with a new Introduction by Guenther Roth), University of California Press, Berkely, 1977, pp. 100–103. Weber apparently wished to contrast patrimonialism with feudalism, on the one hand, and democracy, on the other. Democracy is, of course, associated with the rational-legal system of bureaucracy, while the Government under feudalism is organized on fealty relation between the ruler and his vassal, the latter maintaining their own armies and exercising more or less autonomous power within the land granted to them by the State on a hereditary basis. The use of the adjective in our composite term 'Patrimonial Premiership' to designate the zenith of Indira Gandhi's power is thus rather figurative. For, she asserted or exercised patrimonial power demanding absolute personal loyalty within her party and Government (even 'appointing' Chief Ministers who were subsequently ritualistically elected by Congress legislature parties in States) within the frameworks of a bureaucracy recruited on legal-rational basis and legislatures democratically elected by the people. So here was essentially a version of political authoritarianism in a modern context and reflected a lag between structural modernization and cultural backwardness.

40. See articles or reports on these elections close on the heels of the events in the *Asian Survey, Seminar,* and *Economic & Political Weekly.*

41. Christophe Jaffrelot and Gilles Verniers, "India's 2009 Elections: Resilience Regionalism and Ethnicity", Internet: http:// mail.google. com/mail/? ui= 2 & view= bsp & ver= ohh 14 rw8mbn4 accessed on 13/5/2010.

42. *The Economic Times*, May 14, 2019, https://m.economictimes... Accessed on March 19, 2020.

43. Yogendra Yadav, "The Elusive Mandate of 2004," *Economic and Political Weekly*, Vol. XXXIX, No. 51, 18–24 December 2004, pp. 5383 at 5397. Yadav modestly concluded that the mandate's elusiveness is better seen as [its] constitutive feature" and that "A mandate is often earned, and learnt, retrospectively." (*Ibid.,* 5398).

44. "How India Voted: Verdict 2004", Supplement to *The Hindu,* New Delhi, 20 May 2004. For a more detailed analysis of 2004 Lok Sabha elections, see M.P. Singh and Rekha Saxena, "Lok Sabha Elections 2004: Change with Continuity", *Think India,* Vol. 8, No. 1, January–March 2005 and Lawrence Saez and Rekha Saxena, "Mandate 2004", *Mainstream,* Annual No., January 2005. For an account of preceding three Lok Sabha elections in 1996, 1998 and 1999, see M.P. Singh and Rekha Saxena, *India at the Polls: Parliamentary Elections in the Federal Phase,* Orient Longman, New Delhi, 2003.

45. Samarth Bansal, *India Today*, May 31, 2019, https://www.indiatoday.in..., Accessed on March 19, 2020.

46. Rudolph, Susanne Hoeber and Lloyd Rudolph, "Redoing the Constitutional Design: From an Interventionist to a Regulatory State" in Atul Kohli (Ed.), *The Success of India's Democracy*, Cambridge University Press, Cambridge, 2001, p. 161.

47. Manjari Katju, "The Election Commission and Functioning of Democracy", *Economic and Political Weekly*, April 29, 2006., p. 1636. Also see Ujjwal Kr. Singh, "Institutions and Democratic Governance: A Study of the Election Commission and Electoral Governance in India", NMML Monograph, No. 9, Nehru Memorial Museum and Library, Delhi, 2004.

48. Election Commission of India, n.d. but apparently 1998, *Electoral Reforms: Views and Proposals,* ECI, Nirvachan Sadan, New Delhi.

49. Report of both these committees excerpted in M.P. Singh and Ravi Bhatia, *Evolution of the Indian Constitution Since 1950: An Anthology of Documentary Sources,* 2006, Typescript. See also Ujjwal Kumar Singh (2004), *Institutions and Democratic Governance: A Study of the Election Commissioin and Electoral Governance in India,* Nehru MM & Library Monograph, No. 9.

50. *IIPA Newsletter*, Indian Institute of Public Administration, New Delhi, Vol. XLIII, No. 9, September 1992, p. 6.

51. Report of the National Commission to Review the Working of the Constitution (NCRWC), 2002.

52. *Ibid.*

53. *LiveMint*, December 4, 2019, https://www.livemint.com..., Accessed on March 19, 2020.

54. *India Today*, April 12, 2019, https://www.indiatoday.in..., Accessed on March 19, 2020.

55. *Business Standard*, April 5, 2019, https://www.business-standard.com..., Accessed on March 19, 2020.

Chapter

12

Whither Indian Party System?

INTRODUCTION

Political parties, Joseph La Palombara and Myron Weiner aptly remark, are a feature of "modern and modernizing societies."[1] They would appear to be indispensable to representative democracy. Local political institutions of direct democracy can presumably work without parties. However, wherever and whenever democracy is practised in larger aggregates, it must rely on representational devices through elected officials. For this, political parties cannot be dispensed with. That has at least been the experience of modern democracies in the contemporary world. In Western liberal democracies across the board, parties, the leftwing included, are in decline, but no competent observer of comparative politics has diagnosed it as the terminal phase in the life and times of political parties.[2]

Conservatives and liberals and founding fathers of nation-states or mass movements are inclined to express anti-party sentiments, e.g. George Washington, Lord Bolingbroke, Mahatma Gandhi, Jayaprakash Narayan in his Gandhian phase, and M.N. Roy in his Radical Humanist phase.[3] This is for the reason that parties are supposed to be inherently divisive of the organic unity of the national community. However, these initial reservations about political parties did not forestall their onward march to becoming one of the two major pillars of the nation-state along with bureaucracy. This is because parties are the vital link between the civil society and the state. As organizations, parties are amphibious creatures equally at home in the civil society and the state.

The importance of political parties has grown proportionately in accordance with the growing extension of franchise as it typically happened in Western liberal democracies. As political suffrage gradually became universal, parties emerged as agencies through which parliamentary cliques or factions needed them to acquire mass electoral support.[4]

In the Indian context, the earliest political parties emerged in local self-governing institutions introduced in British India by the Liberal Viceroy Lord Ripon after 1883. Subsequently, parties acquired more concrete form and functions in the councils and assemblies under the various Councils Acts after 1861 and the various Government of India Acts, 1909, 1919 and 1935.[5]

In India, however, the more significant context of emergence of mass movements and political parties was the freedom struggle against British colonial rule, particularly beginning with the twentieth century. In fact, the nationalist leaders gave greater importance to agitational politics than to institutional politics for the obvious reason that the representative institutions with limited franchise and power did not satisfy the nationalist leadership which increasingly moved towards the goal of complete Independence and fuller democracy.

PHASES OF PARTY SYSTEM EVOLUTION

India's "tryst with destiny"—democratic and developmental—may be divided and discussed into five waves of democratization the country has undergone since the faint beginnings of modern institutional politics in the latter half of the nineteenth century and vigorous advent of mass politics in the 1920s. The present discussion is here concerned more with the development of the party system than with other aspects of democracy and development. The six phases of party system development here suggested are: (a) the "Movement" party system (1920–1947); (b) the "Congress System" *a la* Rajni Kothari (1952–1969)[6]; (c) the phase of confrontation between the Indira Gandhi Congress and the J.P. Movement (1971–1977)[7]; (d) the phase that witnessed the growing differentiation between the national party system and party systems in States (1980s)[8]; (e) the deepening of the trends towards a regionalized multi-party system with federal coalition/minority Governments (1989 to 2014); and (f) a centralizing multi-party system under a *de facto* single-party majority under BJP's Narendra Modi in a federal coalition National Democratic Alliance since 2014 and re-elected in 2019 faced by a fragmented set of parties like the Indian National Congress and a congeries of regional parties.[9]

The significance of the first phase for the party system is that almost all political parties or their antecedent organizations can be traced back to the freedom movement in India. The Indian National Congress (INC) founded in 1885 was, of course, the aggregation of the crucible for practically all political parties that came to be formed since the last quarter of the nineteenth century to the middle of the twentieth century. The Congress was, in fact, first formed in 1885 as a pressure group for lobbying support for participation of Indians in British Indian administration and governance. It gradually acquired the role of a mass movement beginning with the partition of Bengal in 1905 and the Swadeshi movement to annul it and especially since the 1920s with the advent of Gandhi on the Indian national scene from South Africa and in the wake of the Jallianwala Bagh massacre in Amritsar. The Congress in reality was a national platform with which all other political organizations of the period had cooperative or conflictual relationships at various points in time. Even the Muslim League and the Scheduled Castes Federation had periods of reconciliation and pacts with this organization of central importance in British India, to say nothing of the Communists, Socialists, Hindu Mahasabha and Akali Dal, all of whom had variously more of cooperative interaction with Congress than conflictual during the freedom struggle. It is for these reasons that this phase of party system growth in India may be appropriately characterized as the "Movement Party System."[10]

The "Congress System", as conceptualized by Rajni Kothari, comprised what he called the "party of consensus" (namely, the Indian National Congress) and the "parties of pressure" (i.e. the non-Congress parties on the margins of the system). Buttressed by its institutional charisma as the party of Indian Independence and the personal charisma of its leaders, combined with the divided opposition, the Congress appeared invincible. Non-Congress parties did not appear to have a chance of forming government in the foreseeable future. The Congress combined within its fold the role of the Government as well as of the Opposition. The more effective opposition came from the Congress dissidents than from the formally Opposition parties. The non-Congress parties had a closer understanding and interaction with the like-minded Congress factions. It was through these mechanisms that the "dissident" Congressmen were able to dislodge the "ministerialists" and come to power and vice versa.[11]

The third phase may be said to have started with the 1971 snap parliamentary elections called by the Congress minority government of Indira Gandhi after the Congress debacle in 1967 and the great split in the party in 1969, between the Indira Gandhi faction and her rightwing opponents often called the 'Syndicate' of regional satraps, partly for personal and partly programmatic reasons. Reversing the decline of the party in the late 1960s, Indira Gandhi forced her rightwing senior colleagues out of the party and remoulded it into a more progressive party using the slogan of Remove Poverty or *garibi hatao*. This strategy paid her a good dividend in the form of restoration of the Congress to power in New Delhi in 1971 as well as in most States in subsequent years. This electoral success was, however, gained at a great cost to democratic as well as the developmental dimensions of the Indian state. Bypassing the intermediary structures of power in the Congress party and State governments, Indira Gandhi established a direct and personalized and plebiscitary mass contact with the people, but in this process, the democratically institutionalized party organization of the Nehru era was lost. It turned into a pack of personal and dynastic loyalists and followers. This populist turn in politics also hurt the development process as economic resources had to be diverted to mobilize mass electoral support at the cost of rational economic decisions in pursuit of planned economic development initiated in the Nehru era.[12] The Congress regime under Indira Gandhi in the 1970s turned into a political pyramid marked by extreme centralization of power at the top and populist mass mobilization of the electorate through personal and dynastic political charisma rather than a democratically constructed pluralist and federal Congress party. How did Mrs. Gandhi succeed in doing this despite a considerably institutionalized Congress regime that preceded it? Stanley A. Kochanek offers a persuasive explanation: "Since the formal structure of power outlined in both the Indian Constitution and the constitution of the Congress party was federal with strong unitary and centralizing features, the initiation of this new process did not require major structural change."[13]

This centralized political pyramid provoked the building up of a strong extra-parliamentary mass movement that first surfaced in the Navanirman Movement in Gujarat led by Morarji Desai and subsequently spread to Bihar and all across north India down to Karnataka that finally drew Jayaprakash Narayan (J.P.), the Socialist-turned Gandhian living in political retirement in Patna, to offer an overarching all-India leadership. Gradually, massive Congress majorities in the Parliament and State legislatures came to be confronted by the J.P. Movement and all-India railway workers strike led by the Socialist leader, George Fernandes in 1974 that paralysed the largest railway network in the world.[14] All these developments culminated into the proclamation of internal Emergency on 25 June 1975, after the Allahabad Bench of the Lucknow High Court unseated the then Prime Minister, Indira Gandhi on the charge of electoral malpractices in the 1971 elections. The entire leadership of the movement and the opposition parties, including Congress dissidents, were put behind the bars and the press censorship was imposed. The Emergency excesses and the rise of her younger son Sanjay Gandhi to extra-constitutional power made the Congress regime extremely unpopular, despite the initial sigh of relief by the public by restoration of law and order in place of the chaos disrupting normal working and civic life in the country due to continuous political agitations for years.[15] She only had to centralize the previously pluralist and federal structure of the party system and political system.

The early 1977 Lok Sabha elections offered a provisional escape from this politics of confrontation between the J.P. Movement and Indira Gandhi's government and party by bringing into power the Janata Party formed on the eve of elections by the merger of major non-Congress and non-Communist parties into it. This new centrist party could not, however, complete its mandate of power for five years and fell prematurely in mid-1979 due to internal factional fights and ego clashes between its top leadership—Desai, Charan Singh, Jagjivan Ram, and pre-merger Bharatiya Jana Sangh, Congress (Organization or Syndicate), Lok Dal, and Socialist constituents.[16] In the 1980 mid-term elections, Indira Gandhi's Congress was restored to power on the electoral slogan of promising a 'Government that works'.

From the point of view of party system evolution in India, the two notable developments of this phase were the rise and fall of the Janata Party and the restoration of the Congress party after its earlier defeat. The 1977 elections that formalized the ascendancy of the Janata Party to power heralded a brief period during which India was closest to a two-party system model inasmuch as only two parties—Janata Party and Congress party—accounted for nearly three-fourths of the Lok Sabha seats. The newly emergent party was the product of the shared experience of the parties that merged (to form the Janata Party in the eve of elections) during the J.P. Movement and during the jail terms of their leaders after the proclamation of Emergency. The Congress (Organization) led by Desai, the Bharatiya Lok Dal (BLD) led by Charan Singh, the Bharatiya Jana Sangh (BJS) led by Atal Bihari Vajpayee and Lal Krishna Advani, and Socialists led by George Fernandes and Raj Narain that hurriedly formed a common platform that facilitated their merger to face the common challenge. The Congress for Democracy led by Jagjivan Ram joined the band wagon a little later but prior to the election. However, the rise of the Janata Party was as spectacular as its premature fall midway through its mandate of five years due to factionalism among its pre-merger constituents.

As an organization, the Janata Party suffered from three major debilitating factors that incapacitated it to transform itself from a movement to a party, despite its large constituency. First, its 'big three' leaders—Morarji Desai of Congress (O), Charan Singh of BLD, and Jagjivan Ram of Congress for Democracy—had their enormous ego-clashes that could not be contained. All three wanted the top position in the government and it was only the intervention and persuasion of Jayaprakash Narayan and J.B. Kripalani that could clinch the issue in favour of Desai. Even though the Bharatiya Jana Sangh constituent of the Janata Party had the largest number of MPs, its top leaders Vajpayee and Advani appeared to be more understanding and reconciliatory in the internal bickerings of the party. This was probably for the reason that they were relatively younger at that point in time and the stigma of Hindu communalism was a heavy cross they carried around their necks. The Janata experience for them was their first opportunity to join the national mainstream of Indian politics.

Second, the five constituents of Janata Party, despite their formal merger into one party, in fact continued to function as separate units. The formal merger could never reach the level of real integration into one party. Despite its *ad hoc* common organization, the party could never complete the mass membership enrolment drive and hold full-fledged organizational elections within the party at the grassroots.

Third, the vast rural leadership and mass support for the Janata Party could be mobilized into a mass movement that helped it win the 1977 elections, but party cohesion and discipline could not be consolidated. Different castes in the rural society could not submerge their conflicting identities and interests and the party became a victim of factionalism and feuds, which is a characteristic of the Indian rural society. The ego clashes among leaders and previous party legacies of the constituent pre-merger parties merging into a single Janata Party aggravated this tendency towards fatal factionalism. In this light, it is possible to understand and explain why the party could not even complete its first mandate to rule and disintegrated between 1979 and 1980. The process of disintegration started on the issue of "double" membership of the BJS constituents in the Rashtriya Swayamsevak Sangh (RSS) raked up by the BLD elements. BJS elements refused to budge arguing that the RSS was a cultural rather than a political organization. The Janata Party split on the issue. By the beginning of the new decade, all the major constituents had deserted the parent party and formed new political formations along their previous party lines, e.g. the BLD resurfaced as the Lok Dal, and the BJS as the Bharatiya Janata Party. In fact, the tendency to fragment continued and by the end of the 1980s, the Janata Party, which was transformed into the Janata Dal in 1988 with the merger into it of a group of Congressmen led by V.P. Singh who left the Rajiv Gandhi government in 1987, split into the Rashtriya Janata Dal and the Samata Party in Bihar, the Biju Janata Dal in Orissa (now Odisha), the Samajwadi Party in UP, and the Janata Dal (Secular) in Karnataka.

The fourth phase in the evolution of Indian party system marked the restoration of the Congress party in 1980 under Indira Gandhi's leadership which came to be subsequently led by Rajiv Gandhi after her assassination in 1984. However, this opportunity of renewal of the party was lost for rebuilding it as a democratically constituted pluralist and federal Congress party. The Congress party organization that had suffered decline after the 1969 split and came to be transformed into a personalized pack following Mrs. Gandhi could never be rebuilt into a democratic institution comparable to what it was in the Nehru era. Internal organizational elections were practically dispensed with from 1971 to 1992, when the then Prime Minister, P.V. Narasimha Rao revived them in his own interest to free the party from the hold of the Indira Gandhi dynasty and acquire some degree of autonomy for his action and control in the party.

For these reasons, neither the Congress nor the Janata Party, the two major centrist national parties of Indian politics, could restore the institutionalized character of the party system that was evident in the Nehru era. Since these centrist parties dominated the system, their organizational traits (e.g. lack of democratically constituted organization) influenced or determined the dominant features of the whole party system.

In the fourth phase in the 1980s there occurred the growing differentiation and distance between the party system at the Union level and State party systems. Beginning with the Assembly elections in Andhra Pradesh and Karnataka in 1983 and continuing with elections in Assam, Punjab, Kashmir and the North-East through the rest of the decade, the Congress lost one State after another to Opposition parties, even though it continued to rule in New Delhi until 1989, under Indira Gandhi until 1984 and after her assassination under Rajiv Gandhi. Besides these electoral changes, mass movements verging on separatism surfaced in Assam, Punjab and Kashmir. Under pressure from these developments, underscored by the emergence of new regional parties like Asom Gana Parishad and Telugu Desam, in addition to the old ones in

Jammu & Kashmir (National Conference), Punjab (Akali Dal), and Tamil Nadu (DMK, AIADMK, etc.), under whose pressures Indira Gandhi appointed the Justice R.S. Sarkaria Commission on Center-State Relations in 1983, which submitted its two-volume monumental Report in 1987–88. These subterranean tectonic shifts altered the parameters of politics during the decade of the 1980s in spite of the apparent continuation of the Congress party at the Center. After Indira Gandhi's demise, Prime Minister Rajiv Gandhi signed a series of peace accords with dominant regional parties in Assam, Punjab, Mizoram and Tripura. Through the decade, the Congress party lost power in half of the States of the Union, and by 1989 it also lost control at the Center.

The fifth phase in the growth of the Indian party system started in 1989 and continued until 2014. It brought about a multi-party system with federal coalition/minority Government at the federal level. The trend of regionalization of politics that began in the previous decade (1980s) impacted New Delhi by the 1990s where a broad power sharing with stronger regional parties became necessary on the part of three major national parties— Janata Dal (JD), Bhartiya Janata Party (BJP) and Indian National Congress (INC)—that ruled alternately at the head of the United Front (UF), National Democratic Alliance (NDA), and United Progressive Alliance (UPA), respectively.

This phase of party system development came to be marked by the phenomenal growth of the BJP from the third position among national parties after the Congress and the Janata Dal to the first. The BJP's rise to power heading the NDA coalition is linked with the assertion of Hindu identity through the Ayodhya Ram Mandir Movement, backed by electoral mobilization. Oliver Heath has categorized the States where the BJP held some ground in terms of "primary", "secondary" and "tertiary" States. Primary States were those where the Jana Sangh had emerged as a viable opposition party in the 1950s and 60s (e.g., Rajasthan, Gujarat, Madhya Pradesh, Delhi, UP and Himachal Pradesh). Secondary States were the States where the Jana Sangh and subsequently the BJP made their presence felt before the 1989 boom (e.g., Karnataka, Bihar, Goa, Maharashtra, Andhra Pradesh, Orissa, Assam, Punjab, and Haryana). In the tertiary States, BJP expanded in the post-1989 period (e.g., Kerala, Tamil Nadu, West Bengal, and North-Eastern States).

To quote Heath:

> In each successive step that the BJP makes away from its homeland of the primary States, the groups that have expanded the most also move a step down the ladder of the party's traditional support base. Thus in the primary States, which represent the core of the party's stronghold, its core source of social support, that of the upper castes, has remained intact. The only other community that has been significantly mobilized in this region is that of the Scheduled Tribes.[17]

The 2004 Lok Sabha elections brought back to power a new coalition at the Center. At the core of this coalition was the Indian National Congress, and the largest partner extending support from the parliamentary floor were the Left parties led by CPI(M). This left-of-center coalition reflects an alliance between the left parties and the Congress. On economic issues, the Congress had moved right since the Rao Congress government accelerated the neo-liberal economic reforms in 1991. Throughout the NDA regime, the left parties tried to build bridges with the Congress and the latter had largely remained lukewarm. Following the debacle of the rise and power of the BJP-led NDA, the Congress had joined hands with the Left, which was elected with the largest ever contingent of leftwing MPs in the Lok Sabha numbering 63. In fact, the voters' realignment that turned the tide in favour of Congress and its pre-election allies also indicated a strategic electoral shift in favour of the Congress in the rural sector and among Muslims, and Scheduled Castes who had in previous elections drifted away from the Congress.[18] The post-election Common Minimum Programme of the United Progressive Alliance led by the Congress interpreted the poll verdict in terms of the people voting for "secular, progressive forces, for parties wedded to the welfare of farmers, agricultural labour, weavers, workers, and weaker sections of society, for parties irrevocably committed to the well-being of the common man across the country".[19]

Reporting on a national probability sample survey of the 2004 Lok Sabha polls, Yogendra Yadav observed:

> Some distinctive patterns of caste and community support are evident for various coalitions and parties. For example, the NDA registered a marked lead of more than twenty percentage points over the UPA among the upper Hindu castes. In lower caste clusters, there was a gradual decline in support for the NDA, though it continued to have an edge over the UPA. On the other hand, the UPA decisively scored over the NDA among dalits, adivasis, Muslims and Christians. The UPA's lead amounted to more than forty percentage points among the Muslims and Christians followed by fifteen per cent among the dalits and slightly less than ten per cent among the adivasis. The Left support was more concentrated in a few States than in most others. The BSP (Bahujan Samaj Party of the 'reservation aristocracy' of the Scheduled Castes) got about one-fifth of the dalit vote nationwide as compared to Samajwadi Party which secured about one-sixth of the Muslim vote. The Samajwadi Party also had strong support among yadavs.[20]

The foregoing pattern of party fragmentation more or less continued in the 2009 elections, although the situation slightly improved for the Congress-led UPA coalition which again formed the government. It consolidated itself considerably as its strength jumped from 215 seats in 2004 to 261 in 2009. The Congress improved its position from 145 seats to 201, thus making itself less vulnerable to internal blackmail by coalition partners. BJP-led NDA went into further reverses, its representation going down from 186 seats to 159. BJP's own tally went down from 138 seats to 121. Parties outside the framework of these two major coalitions got their own seats reduced from 136 in 2004 to 124 in 2009. The left parties suffered a precipitous fall from 59 seats to 24. Attempts to consolidate the third force parties outside the UPA and NDA into a new, third front turned out to be a mirage. Third front parties comprising the left and some regional parties like BSP, Biju Janata Dal, AIADMK, Telugu Desam, Janata Dal(S), etc. won 79 seats. Indeed a fourth front consisting of nine parties but mainly Samajwadi Party (UP) and Rashtriya Janata Dal (Bihar), also surfaced bagging 27 seats. The combined vote share of UPA (37.22 per cent) and NDA (24.63 per cent) stood at 61.85 per cent). The vote share of the two national parties leading these alliances were 28.55 per cent for the Congress and 18.80 per cent for the BJP.

In addition to the ups and downs in the fortune of political parties in the 2009 election briefly summed up above, the factors that contributed to the success of the Congress-led UPA in 2009 were the following: stable and secular government provided by UPA–I elected in 2004, the good team work maintained by the then Prime Minister, Manmohan Singh and the Congress President and UPA Chairperson, Sonia Gandhi, Rahul Gandhi's bold initiative to revive Congress in UP and Bihar, government's social sector initiatives like Mahatama Gandhi National Rural Guarantee Act, Bank loan waivers to farmers, Sixth Pay Commission salary revisions of Central government employees and Central university and college teachers. Besides, other positive factors were Right to Information Act, 2005, and the Forest Rights Act, 2006, recognizing traditional rights of tribal communities and other traditional forest dwellers to the use of forest resources for their livelihood. Another important factor was the shift of Muslim voters towards the Congress, deserting RJD in Bihar, SP and BSP in UP and in the Hindi heartland in general.

Going by the policies and performance of the UPA–I and UPA–II (e.g., Right to Secondary Education Act, 2010, Food Safety and Security Act, 2006, etc.), it is possible to surmise that the Congress leadership has tried to strike a balance between India's growing integration with global capitalism, on the one hand, and promotion of welfare measures with an eye to electoral politics, on the other. To quote M.K. Venu: "Both Sonia Gandhi and Nextgen Congress leadership led by Rahul Gandhi have a strong bias for redistributive intervention even while letting the government pursue its market-based economic reforms agenda. Now, there is bound to be creative tension between these two opposing ideological strains and that is part of a new dialectic that Indian politics is currently witnessing."[21]

The post-UPA- I and II phases of Indian politics started with the historic performance of BJP in 2014 general elections. The NES survey which was conducted by the Center for Study of Developing Societies (CSDS) suggested that as compared to the previous NDA electoral victories, the religion-based polarization played even sharper role than before.[22] In the 2014 elections, the BJP-led National Democratic Alliance (NDA) had won 336 seats, and the BJP alone secured 282 out of 428 Lok Sabha seats. It emerged as the tallest party in 2014 election. In comparison to the Congress which shrunk to 44 seats, it was a new low. Interestingly, other national parties such as Bahujan Samaj Party had secured not a single seat, and left parties such as Communist Party of India and Communist Party of India (Marxist) had secured 1 and 9 seats, respectively. The BJP registered the highest vote polled percentage, i.e., 31.34 per cent. The NDA aggregate vote percentage stood at 38.3. The UPA polled a total of 23 per cent votes in which Congress percentage of votes was 19.3. Furthermore, the NDA on 137 seats secured more than 50 percentage of votes, and on 132 seats, it secured almost 40 per cent of votes. The impact of 'New BJP' (in terms of Modi factor and new electoral strategy) wave has not only gained massive support in its traditional north-Indian cadre but also it gained comparatively increased support in non-traditional cadre states such as Jammu and Kashmir, Assam, Jharkand and West Bengal. In two-party competition states such as Himachal Pradesh, Uttrakhand, Madhaya Pradesh, Rajasthan, Gujarat and Chhattisgarh, it secured 50 per cent of the total vote share. The 2014 election results implied that BJP had added a new chapter to Indian politics, which presages the re-emergence of Dominant Party System, in which opposition appeared on the verge of decimation.

In the 2019 general elections, the BJP further improved upon its 2014 electoral victory. With a tally of 303 Lok Sabha seats, it superseded its own electoral record of 2014 election. With 52 seats, Indian National Congress remained on the margins of electoral performance. All India Trinamool Congress emerged on the third place with its 22 seats out of total 62 seats it had contested. The Bahujan Samaj Party emerged from nil in 2014 to 10 seats in 2019. The performance of the Left political parties—Communist Party of India and Communist Party of India (Marxist)—remained almost similar to their 2014 electoral performance with two and three seats, respectively, in 2019. In the 2019 elections, the Congress party was completely wiped out from 18 states. In 13 States and Union Territories, the vote share of BJP has hiked to 50 per cent.

In March 2020, the state party systems were also dominated by the the BJP and NDA: BJP happened to be in power in 12 states, and BJP-led NDA in 6 additional states. The tally of Congress was as follows: in power in 4 states and Congress-led UPA in 2 additional states. Regional parties in power in their respective states included Aam Aadmi Party in Delhi state, Trinammol Congress in West Bengal, BJD in Odisha, Telangana Rashtra Samithi in Telangana, YSR Congress Party in Andhra Pradesh, and CPM-led Left United Front in Kerala.

PARTIES AND PARTY FAMILIES

Despite proliferation of parties in the process of electoral deepening of democracy since 1951–1952 when the first general elections in India were held after Independence (the present number of parties registered with the Election Commission of India being 2,598: National parties 8, State parties 52, and Registered but unrecognised parties 2,538), it is possible to delineate nearly half a dozen of what may be called "party families" and associated networks of organizations. If we count parties and organizations in a particular party family as 'one', the number of individual parties is considerably reduced. Moreover, despite internal differences among them, and occasionally open conflicts, organizations in such a party family are more like-minded than others and they are also more likely to coalesce with each other than is the case with organizations outside such a party family. We sketch below the major party families operative in party politics in India today.

Congress Family

The Indian National Congress is the party family, the party patriarch of India so to say. It was the *locus classicus of* the nationalist movement, a platform holding practically all parties within its fold in conflict-cooperation relationships. The only parties that largely remained outside its umbrella were the Justice Party/ Dravida Kazhagam. Even the Muslim League, the vehicle of the dubious "two-nation" theory in British colonial India, had periods of warmth with the Indian National Congress during the Khilafat movement and the Lucknow Congress–League Pact during and immediately after the First World War.

The Congress, that started as a pressure group of English–educated middle classes in British India and turned into a mass political movement during the inter-war period, had to undergo a gradual process of transformation into a political party after Independence. One by one, Congress Socialists, Praja Socialists, Socialists, Gandhians, etc. had to depart from the broader Congress platform. The departure of these ideologues made the Congress a more pragmatic and electoral success-oriented party. A difficult period of transition began from a national movement to a political party after India's Independence.

In the post-Nehru era, the Congress is said to have come under the spell of the Nehru–Indira Gandhi dynasty. The dynasty has been a divisive factor, yet also a symbol of unity, loyalty, and allegiance. The party has been a witness to Nehruvian 'socialism', Indira Gandhi's populism, and Sanjay Gandhi's cronyism, Rajiv's Doon School boys' techno-managerial temperament, and Sonia Gandhi's graduated apprenticeship in politics, understanding and adaptation, ambivalence between power and renunciation, and Rahul Gandhi's truancy from politics, engagement, and withdrawal.

The Congress Party has also seen over the years several splinters of family resemblance: Jan Congress parties, Bangla Congress, Kerala Congress, Loktantric Congress, Indian National Congress (Requisitionists/Organization), Congress for Democracy, Congress (Swaran/Urs), Congress (Pawar), Jan Morcha, All India Indira Congress (Tiwary/Arjun Singh), Trinamool Congress,

Tamil Maanila Congress, Nationalist Congress Party, etc. These splits appear to be caused more due to politics of ambition and power—personal and regional—than programmatic or ideological differences. Only those with some prominent all-India or regional leaders of following have had some chance of survival or effectiveness. Most tend to merge back with the Congress or some opposition party. Greater chance of survival of such splinters has come to pass in the era of coalition governments.

A new organizational tendency is palpable in the Indian National Congress of late. We have seen a greater tolerance of somewhat autonomous State units in the 1990s and after, especially under Sonia Gandhi. The examples are Madhya Pradesh (Digvijay Singh), Rajasthan (Ashok Gehlot), Punjab (Amrinder Singh), Delhi (Sheila Dikshit), Manipur (Ibobi Singh), Kamal Nath (Madhya Pradesh), Rajasthan (Ashok Gehlot), Chhattisgarh (Bhupesh Baghel), Haryana (Bhupendra Singh Huda), who have in the more recent decades (2000s) been allowed long innings in State politics and greater regional autonomy by the central party leadership than under Indira Gandhi and Rajiv Gandhi. In the decades preceding, Congress Chief Ministers were frequently changed mid-term to undercut their independent personal or regional following and deny them autonomy.

In a perceptive recent piece on the INC, Harish Khare[23] begins with the argument that in a developing polity such as India's, the evolution of the party system has closely moved in relation to the evolving state order. He divides the growth of the Congress party broadly into three phases. The first was from 1947–1971 when the post-colonial state formation in India took place and the Congress played the role of a mid-wife *as the party for the state* .The second phase is dated back from 1971 to 1991 which was the period of the Indian state consolidation in which the Congress played the role of *the party of the State.* Khare highlights that the two central political dilemmas since the 1990s that the Congress has faced is (a) the tension between democracy and market, and (b) the socio-cultural tensions engendered by *mandir-masjid* conflict and the assertion of Mandal/OBC and Dalit rise to power and its backlash from the upper castes/new middle class sections turning from state-centered to market-centered solutions. These two tensions have produced for the Congress what Subrata K. Mitra has called the dilemma between "winning and governing".[24]

The Congress Party has since the early 1990s been ambivalent between neo-liberalism and electoral compulsions (*Congress ka hath aam admi ke sath*, 2004). Also, there was some slowing of the pace of economic reforms in the second half of the then Prime Minister, Narasimha Rao's mandate (1991–96) in response to electoral reprisals in State assembly elections, and there was the phase of cooperation and conflict between the Manmohan Singh government and the Left parties between 2004–2009 UPA–I government. Congress and communists were in coalition at the federal level but were main adversaries in West Bengal, Kerala, and Tripura.

The Congress in UPA–I parted company with the left parties in 2008 on the issue of Indo-US Civilian Nuclear Deal but survived with the last minute support from the Samajwadi Party. In the 2009 elections that followed, the Congress-led UPA was returned to power without any electoral alliance or post-election coalition government with the Communist parties that suffered heavy electoral decline.

The UPA-II government (2009–2014), which was as adrift and marked by endemic corruption as the UPA-I, yet the latter was relatively more purposive and reformist experimental with a series of rights-based legislations like the Right to Information Act, 2005, the Forest Rights Act, 2006, the Right to Education Act, 2009, innovative moves like the National Advisory Council (NAC) with civil society activists and public intellectuals with Congress President Sonia Gandhi as the chair, appointment of the Second Commission on Center-State Relations (chair Justice M.M. Punchhi) in 2007, appointment of the Second Administrative Reforms Commission (chair Veerappa Moiley) in 2005, etc. A few good initiatives like the Right to Food Act, 2013, and the Land Acquisition Act, 2013 during the UPA-II were eclipsed by the spate of scams and policy paralysis. The party is passing through a crisis in its top leadership due to Rahul Gandhi's resignation as the party president on 3 July 2019, in the wake of the party's debacle in the previous general elections[25]. Sonia Gandhi has stepped in as a stop gap incumbent.

Sangh Parivar

The central plank of the ideological mainspring of the Sangh Parivar is the concept of Indian nationalism primarily based on what V.D. Savarkar called *Hindutva*.[26] His 1923 text, *Hindutva* stipulated India as the land from the Himalayas to the oceans on the eastern side of the river Indus or Sindhu and called all communities living in this area as the 'Hindus', provided they regarded India as their *pitri bhumi* (fatherland) as well as *punya bhumi* (holyland). The author is evidently raising Hindutva from an ethnicity to cultural nationalism. It is in interesting contrast to Islam which excludes a number of Muslim communities like Ahmedia, Vohras, Bhais, etc. whom orthodox Muslims regard as un-Islamic! Pratap Bhanu Mehta's comment on this is: "many well-meaning citizens were attracted to it, and in some ways, the book provides politically most potent articulation of Hindu anxieties to dominate the Indian political scene".[27]

This party family is divided among five broad streams: (a) RSS: the *sangathan* core, the Maharashtrian Brahmans were its founders and Sarsanghachalaks until Rajendra Singh (Rajju Bhaiya) in the 1990s. There have been bands of dedicated *pracharaks* for Jan Sangh/BJP in the Hindi belt, tribal belts in the hinterland, and elsewhere. *Pracharaks* were planted from outside areas beyond RSS's initial strongholds; (b) Then there are the parliamentary and Assembly wings of BJP; (c) Vishwa Hindu Parishad was later founded in the 1980s by resident or non-resident Indians of the Hindu diaspora; (d) The new political recruits subsequently followed since the period of electoral ascendance, including the lumpen riotous elements and election workers in the Bajrang Dal; (e) The Shiv Sena in Maharashtra, a nativistic movement in Bombay/Mumbai/Maharashtra since the 1960s is now spreading its tentacles elsewhere. The Shiv Sena–BJP alliance formed a government in Maharashtra in the late 1990s. A long-time ally of the BJP, the Shiv Sena jointly contested the 2019 Assembly elections with the BJP, and the duo as parts of the National Democratic Alliance won a majority in the newly elected House, the BJP winning the lion' share but short of majority. With the Shiv Sena haggling to get to lead the government, the two fell apart; the Shiv Sena opened negotiations with the Nationalist Congress Party of Sharad Pawar and the Indian National Congress and formed a government.

The BJP has tended to develop beyond the Hindi-speaking States and its Brahman–Bania syndrome has also become somewhat more inclusive of OBCs/Dalits/Muslims under the tutelage of the "true believers". There have been BJP's areas of direct influence and those where it managed to strike deals with regional allies during the BJP-led National Democratic Alliance Government in New Delhi headed by Atal Behari Vajpayee (1998–99 & 1999–2004). Notable among these secular allies of BJP were Samata Party/Janata Dal (United) in Bihar, Biju Janata Dal in Orissa, Trinamool Congress in West Bengal, DMK and AIADMK alternately in Tamil Nadu, Telugu Desam Party in Andhra Pradesh, Loktantrik Congress Party in (UP), and National Conference in Jammu & Kashmir. The Sikh Right Akali Dal in Punjab also followed suit.

The BJP is said to have oscillated between moderation and militancy (*a la* Christophe Jaffrelot)[28] in the Janata Party/BJP phase which really started right from the time of the Jana Sangh's merger with the Janata Party in 1977. During the earlier phase, the strategy of stigmatization and emulation of the threatening "other" (*a la* Christophe Jaffrelot) was more determinedly followed by this party family and its hangover continues today.

More recently, Jaffrelot has revisited his earlier theory of the inclusion of Hindu nationalist parties in India's democratic process to make it more nuanced and elaborate. The process has not moved in a linear way. Whether the Hindu nationalist parties opted the radical or moderate grooves respecting the values of the Constitution of India has mainly depended on their relation with their mentor organization, the RSS, the perception of Muslims that prevails at a particular time in India, the attitude of other parties towards secularism, and an interaction among all these factors and their correlation with the most effective electoral strategy at a given moment. In Jaffrelot's hypothesis, this process can be broadly sketched into phases such as (i) Jana Sangh's sectarianism (1951–1967); (ii) Jana Sangha's incomplete moderation [1968–1979; BJP as a moderate party (1980–1989)]; (iii) The radical phase of BJP (1989–1998): elections against democracy or polarization of the Indian voters along religious lines; (iv) The relative moderation of a coalition leader: BJP (1998–2004); and

(iv) BJP in opposition, searching for a strategy [(2004–2014); in 2014, BJP under Narendra Modi won a de facto one-party majority at the head of the National Democratic Alliance, and got re-elected in 2019].[29]

The Sangh Parivar has followed the strategy of semitization of the Hindu religious identity which has historically been not a religious phenomenon in the sense of Islam and Christianity but a civilizational phenomenon of Indic or Indological vintage. The word 'Hindu' is not found in the *Amarkosh* supposed to be compiled by one Amar Singh, a princeling during the Gupta period. The word 'Sindhu' is there, but not 'Hindu'.

There was an attempt at the creation of an expanded business class/ industrialists supportive of BJP via privatization during the NDA regime by the Ministry of Disinvestment headed by Arun Shourie. The Disinvestment Commission formed during the United Front regimes earlier was disbanded during the NDA rule. It was not revived during the Congress–led United Progressive Alliance Governments that followed nor by the BJP-led NDA governments headed by Narendra Modi elected in 2014 and again in 2019.

BJP's rise to coalitional power through political moderation in the late 1990s and its quest to expand its social and geographical base beyond the north and the west raised the inevitable question about its mainstreaming in Indian politics, liberalization and constitutionalization.[30]

Pratap Bhanu Mehta's reading of this phenomenon is that "there is some indication that BJP may manage to ride out the tension between maintaining a distinctive profile and enhancing its incorporation capabilities. And it has shown a remarkable capacity for incorporating new groups within its fold. It would appear at this juncture that the obstacles to the expansion of the BJP are no longer ideological. Its ideology has proven to be suppler than observers have acknowledged." Christophe Jaffrelot and Thomas Blom Hansen[31] call it the BJP's "compulsions of politics in India". Partha Ghose argues that BJP's secular allies in the NDA make compulsions for it as well as offer an opportunity to penetrate into social segments that remain blocked to it—because of its ideology. These segments can be won over for the BJP-led coalition by its allies and the coalition can go on for more time. In Ghose's words: "it would not be surprising if it becomes the 'NDA system' of the 'Congress system' vintage which Rajni Kothari theorized years ago and yet has not outlived its utility. It would be, therefore, possible to visualize Indian polity essentially in a two-party bi-coalitional framework—one consisting of Congress and its allies and the other BJP and its allies.[32]

Since 2014 general elections, the BJP led by Modi has emerged as a majority party after three decades during which no party was able to get a majority in the Lok Sabha. The BJP was also voted to power in most of the States of the Indian Union either as a majority party government or at the head of coalition governments. This is reminiscent of the one-party dominant system under the aegis of the Indian National Congress most of the time from 1950s to 1980s. Nevertheless, a set of regional parties in some states of the South and

East have continued to hold the ground and in some recent Assembly elections in Punjab, Madhya Pradesh, Chhattisgarh, Rajasthan, the Congress party has been voted back to power. The BJP has also taken care to keep the NDA coalition intact in face of a number of regional parties and the Indian National Congress that remain largely disunited in a coalitional front.

Janata *Parivar* Parties

The genesis of the Janata Dal family goes back to the JP Movement and the Emergency jails. Merger of four or five parties on the eve of hurriedly called 1977 Lok Sabha elections gave rise to the confederal Janata Party mainly by non-Congress and non-Communist parties active in the JP movement. The electoral turnover of 1977 was followed in quick succession by the Janata Party government headed by Morarji Desai (1977–79), Janata Dal–led National Front/United Front governments (1989–1991 & 1996–98). The process of merger in the Janata Party/Dal since 1988 in the run-up to the ensuing Lok Sabha elections with the merger of V.P. Singh's Jan Morcha—could never be brought to its logical conclusion and its pre-merger constituents continued to function practically as separate parties or strong regional units of the Janata Party/Dal. It was only a matter of time when this plural and confederal party fragmented into regional splinters of Rashtriya Janata Dal in Bihar led by Laloo Prasad Yadav; Samata Party led by Nitish Kumar in Bihar, which subsequently became Janata Dal (United); Samajwadi Party in UP led by Mulayam Singh Yadav; Biju Janata Dal in Orissa, now Odisha, led by Navin Patnaik; Janata Dal (Secular) in Karnataka led by H.D. Devegowda and J.H. Patel, and Lok Shakti of Ramakrishna Hegde.

Two notable features of the Janata Dal as a sociological and organizational phenomenon may here be sketched. Sociologically, it was a party of middle castes/OBCs/'bullock capitalists'. Organizationally, as already mentioned, it was a confederal party with minimal central direction and control. Personality clashes and peasant feuding culture put its confederal organizational style under extreme pressure/tension, resulting in the hopeless fragmentation of the Janata Party/Dal, which in 1977 was seen as a historic centrist alternative to the Indian National Congress. That was not to be, however.

Bahujan Samaj Party

Bahujan Samaj Party (BSP) is a party of scheduled caste 'reservation aristocracy' that has made a mark in the major state of north India, Uttar Pradesh (UP). Historically, on an all-India level we see a gap in the rise of scheduled caste or dalit political consciousness between Maharashtra and north Indian States. Bahujan social reform movement led by Jotiba Phule and later Dalit parties like Scheduled Castes Federation of India and subsequently Republican Party of India led by B.R. Ambedkar (both Maharashtrians) pioneered the process of politicization of Dalit identity and political organization in the country in the colonial and early post-Independence period. Such developments in north India are largely a post-Independence, especially a post-1970s phenomenon. In the earlier decades, the Scheduled Castes were mainly mobilized into politics by upper-caste-led patron-client networks under the aegis of the Indian National Congress.

Two ideological streams merged into one to propel the politicization of Dalits: (a) reform movements like Satya Shodhak Samaj in Maharashtra, Ad Dharam in Punjab, Balmiki and Rabidasi movements in Hindi-speaking States motivated by sanskritization, and (b) Western liberal and constitutional influences transmitted by Ambedkar and others.

The organizational genesis of the BSP may be traced to the Backward and Minority Communities Employees' Federation (BAMCEF) and Dalit Shoshit Samaj Sangharsh Samiti (DS-4) founded by Kanshi Ram, a shaving Scheduled Caste Sikh from Punjab who worked in a government defence laboratory in Pune in Maharshtra before he plunged into full-fledged political activity. BSP was floated in 1984 by Kanshi Ram and his political lieutenant Kumari Mayawati from UP, where the party has politically made it big. A relatively larger Scheduled Castes population in UP (more than 20 per cent) may have contributed to the greater success of the party there. Yet Punjab, West Bengal, and Himachal Pradesh have higher proportions of Scheduled Castes in their populations but BSP has been a non-starter in those States. Protest politics in Punjab has been led by the Akali Dal and in West Bengal by the Communist parties, thus elbowing out a protest party like BSP. In the Himalayan hill State of Himachal Pradesh, the political temper has been liberal or conservative that finds expression in the Congress or the BJP. The decline of the Congress in UP and greater political and social pluralism presumably facilitated the rise of new parties like the BSP and Samajwadi Party.

We notice a transition from clientelism to autonomous agency politics in the BSP. From Harijan identity to Dalit identity has been a long journey. The party is, however, caught between the new middle class leadership and the landless and poor followers. There is also the anti-'Manuvadi' rhetorics and the rubbing of shoulders with the so-called 'Manuvadi' parties or bourgeois parties: BSP's allies in politics at various points in time have been Samajwadi Party, Congress, BJP, but never the left parties. There were extremely short-lived alliances with the Samajwadi Party or the Rashtriya Janata Dal. These alliances were bedevilled by a fundamental conflict between the Dalits and the OBCs in rural political economy. The politics of defection for power and pelf has also hit the BSP severely below the belt in the Parliament and Assemblies. Particularly debilitating was the loss of 40-odd MLAs to join hands with the Samajwadi Party to form the Mulayam Singh Yadav government in UP in the early 2000s. The party did, however, retain its gait and kept going under Mayawati following the failing health and demise of the indomitable Kanshi Ram.

In the 2007 UP assembly elections, the BSP staged a sort of miracle by gaining one-party majority for the first time in more than a decade and a half by forging a social coalition of Dalits, Brahmins and other upper castes, and Muslims.

Mayawati called this strategy, that actually began earlier during BJP-BSP coalition governments in UP after the failure of the BSP-Samajwadi Party coalition government in the state, as her party's transition from the strategy of Dalit-Bahujan mobilization to Dalit-Sarvajan mobilization.

The rise of BJP to governmental power considerably moderated the political aggressiveness of the party due to the need to forge inter-party coalitional alliances or intra-party social engineering beyond the Dalit community. Sudha Pai, in her comprehensive study of the party, attributes its success to the post-Independence democratization of the polity and society and the reservation policy of the state. Democratization has made the BSP, unlike the earlier Dalit parties like Scheduled Castes Federation and the Republican Party of India founded by Ambedkar or his followers, a more politically effective organizational entity based upon a strong Dalit identity and a leadership which cannot be co-opted by the mainstream parties. Reservation policy has facilitated the emergence of a Dalit middle class mobilized by aggressive leaders like Kanshi Ram and Mayawati.

Yet the well-considered conclusion of Sudha Pai is that "the BSP is not a party of the poor, committed to revolutionary transformation of the social order but of the better off sections of the lower castes. Its emergence from a middle-class, government employees' organization—the BAMCEF—has made it elitist and conservative and is also responsible for its preoccupation with state power to introduce social change."[33]

In previous two Lok Sabha elections, BSP has lost its previous salience. In 2014, it was the third largest party in the House having vote share (4.2 per cent nationally) without, however, winning a single seat. As a part of BSP-SP-RLD *mahagathbandh* (Great Alliance), BSP's vote won 10 seats, all in Uttar Pradesh, with 3.63 per cent of votes nationally. This resurrection also allowed it to send the largest number of MPs to the Lok Sabha after the BJP. The SP-BSP has together managed to win 15 seats. In the 2017 Uttar Pradesh Assembly elections, BSP won 19 seats with 22.2 per cent of votes.

Leftwing/Vampaksha Parties

Communism in India has travelled a long way from Communist International to national organization of Communist Party of India (CPI) in the early 1920s to the regionalist CPI(M) in West-Bengal, Kerala, and Tripura. The CPI(M) in West Bengal combines the class and culture of the Bengali *Bhadralok.*

Communism in India tended to get transformed into parliamentary communism in the Nehru era. By 1958, Amritsar Congress of the CPI adopted the idea or tactics of parliamentary road to communism. T.J. Nossiter was later to note that Communism in India was gradually patriated home and 'democratized'[34]. He, however, considers it more of a tactical change rather than a genuine ideological conversion. For, Indian Communism has never formally abandoned the creeds of revolutionary transformation and the dictatorship of the proletariat as a transitional prelude to communism, as the Euro-communist parties have formally done it. For this reason, according to Nossiter, Indian communism has only a *practice* of democracy, not a *theory* of it.

The 1964 split in the CPI, giving birth to the CPI(M), was a result of the division in the world communist movement and the domestic factors in the Indian Communist movement in the form, of class radicalization, and regional differentiations.

The two major Communist parties in India—CPI and CPI(M)—have both "adopted elections as their principle strategy for political power."

Extra electoral mass mobilizational strategies, if at all used, are "carefully dovetailed to suit the electoral prospects of the party".[35] Their trade union wings are also persuaded to abide by this strategy. The CPI and CPM have consistently maintained not an inconsiderable national parliamentary presence with vote share generally below the 10 percentage point, though their regional strengths in West Bengal, Kerala and Tripura are considered higher where they have been in coalitional power continuously since 1977 (West Bengal) or alternately (Kerala) or intermittently (Tripura). Their governments in West Bengal and Kerala have followed redistributive policies short of radical redistribution, especially in land reforms, blaming it to the federal power apparatus under the control of the bourgeois political parties. But this is in reality due to the already extreme fragmentation of land holding due to the heavy population pressure. Their success in promoting industrial development has been unimpressive, despite belated though limited adoption of neo-liberal capitalist reforms. They have also mobilized and organized grassroots democracy via Panchayat Raj to deepen their support base as well as to put pressure on the center from the state and local levels of politics.[36] A notable point about the CPI(M) is its regional basis in three states and its relevance for Indian federal politics from that perspective. Besides, the mobilization of the peasants and workers, the party has also immensely benefitted from its identification with the forces of sub-nationalism in those states. Harihar Bhattacharya has observed: "In every region that experienced some historical development of the Communist movement in India, Communism was connected with sub-national or ethnic searches for identity".[37]

Long and continuous left front rule in West Bengal has tended to turn panchayats into party-dominated or captured bodies, though the situation is more competitive in Kerala where the Left Democratic Front and the United Democratic Front have alternated in power. The Communist parties have suffered heavy electoral reverses in the 2009 parliamentary elections, and the trend of decline appears likely to continue in the forthcoming assembly elections in 2011, in which the Trinamool Congress-INC alliance may well capture power.

The two major Communist parties and their smaller leftist allies initially supported federal coalition governments in New Delhi led by the Janata Dal and the Congress from the parliamentary floor at different points in time. CPI briefly joined Janata Dal-led United Front government holding the portfolio of the union home ministry but CPI(M) always resisted this temptation arguing that it would not join a coalition government unless it was in a position to dominate it. Its leader Jyoti Basu was offered the Prime Ministership in the Janata Dal-led United Front government in 1996 but the collective party leadership did not accept it. Jyoti Basu himself called it a "historic blunder." The left parties with a considerably increased parliamentary strength following the 2004 parliamentary elections also supported the Congress-led UPA government from the parliamentary floor for about nearly two and a half years. The Left Front put considerable pressure on the government to slow the pace of neo-liberal economic reforms and delayed the finalization of the Indo-US Civilian Nuclear Deal. Finally, the UPA proceeded to finalize the deal regardless and the left parties parted company with the government on this issue. The government survived the confidence vote in the Parliament with the floor crossing support of the Samajwadi Party led by Mulayam Singh Yadav. In the 2009 elections that followed, the Left parties suffered a precipitous decline in their parliamentary presence.

The ultra-left or Naxalite divide since 1967–69 has marked the communist movement in India as a residue of leftwing radicalism in parts of the country. Thirty-odd such organizations are active today, mainly in the hinterland or inland tribal belt stretching from Indo-Nepal border down to the Deccan spanning the States of Jharkhand, Orissa, West Bengal, Madhya Pradesh, Chhattisgarh, and Andhra Pradesh, including parts of Bihar. Inequities resulting from control over land and forests and habitats, industrialization and construction contracts cause the occurrence of Naxalism.

In 2004 two major naxalite factions, Peoples War Group and the Maoist Communist Center merged to form the Communist Party of India (Maoist). Since then, there has been a sharp rise in Maoist violence in Andhra Pradesh, Maharashtra, West Bengal and Chattisgarh. Joint police forces from the Central Reserve Police Force and police forces from these states were pressed into action in the so-called Operation Green Hunt in 2010. The Operation has been largely successful in Andhra Pradesh and Maharashtra where the State Governments had created special police units trained to deal with naxalite violence and the central and state police forces and their intelligence agencies mounted a well-coordinated offensive. The Operation Green Hunt was initially less successful in West Bengal and Chhattisgarh, especially in the West Bengal, where the two orders of governments often differed in their approaches and blamed each other for lack of coordination and cooperation. After some tragic ambushes in the latter two states in which the police forces suffered heavy casualities at the hands of the Maoists, some serious rethinking about combining developmental initiatives and concerted action to deal with the problem was in evidence.

The 2014 and 2019 election results showed that both Communist Party of India and Communist Party of India (Marxist) registered their worst poll performance in over six decades. They were literally wiped out in these elections. In 2014, CPI contested 67 seats and won only 1 seat, its overall vote percentage was just 0.52 per cent. The CPI(M) had contested 93 Lok Sabha seats and managed to win only 9, with a vote share of only 2.16 per cent. In 2019 elections, the CPI contested 49 seats, and won only 2, whereas the CPI(M) contested 69 seats and won 3. Their performance was so poor that both of them together could manage to win no more than 5 per cent of seats in 2019. In Assembly elections in West Bengal the CPM-led Left Front lost power to All India Trinamool Congress led by Mamata Banerjee in 2011. In Tripura too the CPM yielded power to the BJP in the 2018 Assembly elections in that state. The CPM-led Left United Front still survives in power in Kerala at this writing (November 2020).

Regional Parties

There are three geographical zones in India of varying intensity of regionalism: (a) areas of *strong* regional identity and cultures, e.g. Deep South, Northwest; and Northeast; (b) areas of *intermediate* regionalism, e.g. Bengal, Andhra Pradesh, Assam, Maharashtra; (c) areas of *moderate* regionalism which had been the centers of sub-continental or nearly sub-continental States in Indian history. These areas have been more nationalistic than regionalistic in present times, e.g. Hindi-speaking States, Gujarat, Orissa, Maharashtra, Karnataka. The oldest regional parties have sprung from areas of strong regional identities (e.g. J&K National Conference (NC), Shiromani Akali Dal, Dravida parties, some Northeastern parties). More recent regional party formations have been witnessed in the areas of intermediate regionalism (e.g. TDP, AGP, etc.). Areas of moderate regionalism are the locus of fragments of erstwhile national parties (e.g. Janata Dal splinters).

By the end of the 1980s, major national parties like the Indian National Congress and the Janata Dal suffered continued decline, while neither the BJP nor the left-wing could continue their rise beyond a plateau. This gave the regional parties a tremendous boost and a wide opening so much so that after the 1989 Lok Sabha elections, regional parties became not only indispensable but in certain cases even decisive factors in formation of federal coalition governments. It was not only the inability of national parties to give adequate representation to newly emergent socio-economic forces in the major states and regions of India that provided unprecedented space to regional parties in state and national politics. Rise of capitalist farming and the regional bourgeoisie also contributed to the growing political clout to the regional political forces, old and new. Akali Dal, Telugu Desam and the major Tamil parties are all strongly backed by the capitalist farmers and regional commercial and industrial interests.

In a perceptive study of the role of regional capitalists and political parties, Sanjay Baru[38] has provided some evidence on how the post-independence trends in agrarian modernization and growth have contributed to the gradual entry of the agricultural capitalist class into agro-based industries, small-medium-large industries in some states like Punjab, Haryana, Western UP, Maharashtra, Gujarat, Tamil Nadu, Andhra Pradesh, and Karnataka. He goes on to argue that the policies followed by individual state governments supportive of regional capitalist class led to industrial growth in their respective states. This kind of support to private enterprise was less effective in the eastern part of India where the indigenous capitalist class is weak. To quote Baru: "It is not surprising that regional political parties have been most active in states where regional business groups have been more dynamic and assertive. The link between the emergence of regional capitalism and regional parties is too stark to be ignored."[39]

Baru is right in his argument so far as it goes, but what is overlooked here is that regional parties have also flourished even without the rise of the regional bourgeoisie in some states where the main impetus for their rise has been factors like caste and regional identities. BSP in UP and Janata Dal splinters led by Nitish Kumar and Laloo Prasad Yadav separately, Mulayam Singh, and Biju Patnaik in Bihar, UP and Orissa respectively are the cases in point.

Political programmes that the regional parties have most commonly espoused are typically the following: assertion of regional identity and demand for statehood, greater autonomy and regional development. However, the advent of the multi-party system and federal coalition governments has added a pragmatic electoral and power-sharing vested interest to the politics of regionalism. This has resulted in extreme fragmentation of the party system initially produced by the decline of the national parties like the Congress and the Janata Dal and the failure of the BJP to continue its rise beyond a certain point.

Since the rise of the BJP under Narendra Modi as the single national party with a majority in the Lok Sabha in the 2014 and then again in 2019, which no party after the Indian National Congress under Rajiv Gandhi in 1984 had been able to do, India has been moving towards the kind of one-party dominant system under the aegis of the Indian National Congress under Jawaharlal Nehru, Indira Gandhi, and Rajiv Gandhi during much of the period between the 1950s to the 1980s. A considerable number of State governments have also come to be formed by the BJP. The Congress party, the second national party, has lately been going through a period of precipitous decline. There are some powerful regional parties in the South, East, Northwest, and Northeast. However, these regional parties are tending to operate in a state of splendid isolation. No oppositional coalitional fronts are in existence or in the making, going by the current reckoning. This may make formation and maintenance of governments at the Center in case the BJP falters in the years ahead. The Assembly elections Punjab in 2017; in Madhya Pradesh, Chhattisgarh, Rajasthan, and Telangana, and Karnataka in 2018, and in Andhra Pradesh, Maharashtra and Haryana in 2019 have not been going well for the BJP. These are favourable to the Congress party or a group of regional parties. Despite the electoral revival of the Congress, its national organizational state of affairs is in a doldrums due to dynastic and undemocratic control of the party. Given the foregoing trends, India may be heading towards the Belgian scenario in which the challenge of formation of a government itself after an election becomes a federal democratic quicksand for the political system to cross.

Ideological Spectrum of the Party System

The cynical view of Indian politics is that ideology has no place in it. It is supposed to be motivated largely by issueless factionalism and opportunism. Yet, this view does not fit well with the fact that political parties spend so much on manifestos and other publicity material and on campaigning which is publicly coached in programmatic terms. The reality obviously lies somewhere in between. Indian politics is perhaps neither entirely doctrinaire nor entirely pragmatic.

Deep down the flickering images and issues in particular elections, certain issues, interests and identities have endured ever since India first went to the polls in 1951–1952 on the basis of universal adult franchise. Some enduring policy issues and cultural cleavages may be synoptically subsumed by the binaries of nationalism and regionalism, State and market, secularism and communalism, caste and class, etc. Political parties in India have taken different views on these issues. The two major national parties today—Bharatiya Janata Party (BJP) and Indian National Congress (INC)—can each be characterized in terms of their respective position on these issues. INC has conventionally been identified with nationalism, statism, secularism and a multi-class, multi-caste, multi-cultural, multi-regional orientation. BJP has tended to be associated with *Hindutva* which it prefers to call "cultural nationalism" (*Hindu Rashtravad*). It has also been more oriented towards subordination of individual and parts to collectivity and society which it calls "Integral Humanism."[40] It has also advocated an economy in which market is largely free from State regulation. The party has also been dominated largely by an upper caste/middle class/ Brahmin–Bania elite, although, of late, it has tried to cultivate wider social base in urban and rural areas.

It is additionally possible to characterize Indian parties in terms of centrist, rightist, leftist orientations, although these demarcations are often blurred, especially in more recent times, on account of major shifts in the area of economic policies. The major centrist parties of Indian politics have been the INC and Janata Dal, now fragmented into several splinters like Rashtriya Janata Dal (RJD) in Bihar, Samajwadi Party (SP) in UP, Biju Janata Dal (BJD) in Orissa (now Odisha), Janata Dal (Secular) in Karnataka, and Janata Dal (United) in Bihar. The Janata *parivar* (family) parties, by and large, have their roots either in the Janata Party formed in 1977 (which became Janata Dal in 1988 following the merger of V.P. Singh's Jan Morcha with it) and the INC. The Janata Party represented the merger of Congress (Organization) led by Morarji Desai, Bharatiya Lok Dal led by Charan Singh, Bharatiya Jana Sangh led by Atal Behari Vajpayee and Lalkrishna Advani, Socialists led by Raj Narain, George Fernandes, Madhu Limaye, and Congress for Democracy led by Jagjeevan Ram, H.N. Bahuguna and others. It was an assortment of those subscribing to free enterprise in business and agriculture as well as socialists with a broad anti-Congress platform supported largely by peasants and traders. As a national party, it seemed to be a surrogate Congress backed by leaders and interest groups who deserted the Congress. It was also joined by the Bharatiya Jana Sangh which had until then remained a "political untouchable" on account of its identification with Hindu communalism. It is for these reasons that only the Congress and Janata Party/Dal may be regarded as the centrist parties in Indian politics.

The Congress Party of the past was considered left-of-the center due to its heritage of Nehruvian "Socialism" and Indira Gandhi's pro-poor "populism". Since 1991 when its minority government headed by P.V. Narasimha Rao introduced the comprehensive package of neo-liberal economic reforms, it has shifted to the right at least on economic issues. However, electoral reverses due to its identification with economic reforms have acted as a check on its right-wing shift. When it came back to power in 2004, and was re-elected in 2009, after about a decade in political wilderness, it self-consciously tried to identify itself with the masses by its electoral slogan of *Congress Ka Haath Aam Aadmi Ke Saath* (Congress' hand with the common man). The Janata Dal always retained a left-of-the center orientation on economic issues. It also retained a pro-peasant and rural bias.

The major right-wing parties in Indian politics are the BJP and the Akali Dal, the former being a national party and the latter being a regional one. These parties are largely status quoist on social and economic issues which is understandable in view of the upper caste/middle class leadership of the BJP and the Sikh Jat/farmer and peasant and trader leadership of the Akali Dal. The neo-liberal economic policy shift has not left these parties untouched. During their stint in power in the NDA coalition government at the Center, the BJP has compromised a bit on Swadeshi and favoured globalization.

As a party predominantly of agriculturists, the Akali Dal also hoped to gain some benefits for its supporters who stand to gain from capitalist developments in agriculture and globalization.

The BJP has also undergone some change in its position on cultural issues. As the Bharatiya Jana Sangh, it had stood for "Hindu-Hindi-Hindustan". When it merged with the Janata Party in 1977, it joined the ideological mainstream of Indian politics. Rajni Kothari argued that this experience liberalized the Hindu communalists in the same way as the communists were liberalized who backed or even joined the Congress in the Nehru era.[41] After the collapse of the

Janata Party government in 1979, the Jana Sangh elements in it left it in 1980 to establish the Bhartiya Janata Party. The BJP ever since has come a long way meandering through the zigzags of militant Hindutva and a more secularized orientation resulting from the experience of the coalition government with secular allies. As a part of the National Democratic Alliance (NDA), the BJP removed the contentious issues of Ram Mandir, uniform civil code, and Article 370 in the Constitution from the Common Minimum Programme. As the leading party in the NDA governments led by BJP's Atal Bihari Vajpayee and later by Narendra Modi, it also deftly distanced itself from the more Hindu-oriented organizations like VHP and Bajrang Dal, though it continued to pay guarded obeisance to the RSS. After the loss of power in 2004, the party went through an identity crisis. During the decade-long Congress-led UPA rule, it reinvented itself as a party deftly combining the planks of economic development as well as Hindutva. Modi led it to two consecutive electoral victories in the 2014 and 2019 general elections in the trail of UPA's second term marked by endemic corruption and scams and policy paralysis.

The BSP, a party of SC 'reservation aristocracy', is somewhat difficult to be classified in terms of right and left. For, it takes a position leaning on the left on social issues (e.g. its critique of the "Manuwadi" parties). However, it is overtly opposed to the left parties on economic issues. On these issues it is, if anything, centrist in orientation. It has never aligned with the left parties. All its alliances so far have been with the Congress, Samajwadi Party, and BJP. Its honeymoon with the Samajwadi Party was most short-lived. These contradictory traits of the party can be explained in terms of its SC middle class leadership and the support base among poor SCs in urban and rural areas. It may also be pointed out that even though it is a National party according to the Election Commission criterion (i.e., put simply, a party which polls 6 per cent of votes in any four or more States and wins at least 4 Lok Sabha seats in the previous Lok Sabha elections), for all practical purposes, it is a regional political force largely based in UP.

However, the BSP's success in UP has been remarkable and needs explanation. There are three other States—West Bengal, Punjab and Himachal Pradesh—which have a higher concentration of SC population than UP. Then, why only in UP has the BSP made a significant political advance? One explanation could be that sizeable SC population in the State is coupled with a fairly fragmented caste and community arithmetic in UP. Another explanation could be that political space in West Bengal is ideologically dominated by Marxism or social democracy, and by religious mobilization of the Akali Dal in Punjab, both bridging over caste divisions. Himachal Pradesh continues to be relatively backward and less politicized, where both secular mobilization by the Congress and Hindutva mobilization by the BJP in recent years have formed the Government and opposition alternately. In an interesting theoretical and empirical study of the BSP and some other ethnic parties, it is suggested that in a type of electoral democracies which can be categorized as "patronage democracies", voting behaviour is determined by competition among parties that campaign on ethnic head counts rather than policy or developmental performance of parties in power. Such electoral competition among ethnic communities is also functional for democracy inasmuch as it leads to democratic competition rather than ethnic confrontation and extremism.[42]

We have already discussed BSP's performance in the recent elections in a preceding section above in this chapter.

The Left-wing in Indian politics today includes the CPI(M), CPI, Revolutionary Socialist Party (RSP), Forward Bloc, and CPI(ML). The 1964 split in the parent CPI was related to the split in the International Communist Movement between Moscow and Beijing. The CPI(M) identified itself with the Chinese Communist Party. The CPI(ML) proclaims its adherence to Marxism-Leninism-Maoism which verges on radical class violence often called Naxalism.

The ideological differences between the CPI, the CPI(M) and the CPI (ML) or Naxalite factions also hinge on their characterization of the bourgeoisie in India. CPI makes a distinction between a monopoly or big bourgeoisie which collaborates with imperialism and the national bourgeoisie which is opposed to imperialism. CPI(M) treats the bourgeoisie as a monolith and national in character and theorizes that this class both collaborates with and opposes imperialism. CPI(ML) factions consider the bourgeoisie as nothing but collaborationist or comprador and believes that it can never be relied upon to defend India's independence.[43]

The CPI has a larger spread and the CPI(M) is regionally concentrated in West Bengal, Kerala and Tripura. The CPI(ML) is not much of an electoral force, though in the last few elections, it has tended to field a large number of candidates in several States and secured some votes. It is a protest party campaigning against the established Communist parties which have become embourgeoised.

The CPI(M)-led Left Front has continuously ruled in West Bengal since 1977. This phenomenal electoral success is attributable to a combination of Marxism with Bengali cultural regionalism. The CPI (M)-led Left Democratic Front in Kerala has regularly alternated in power with the Congress-led United Democratic Front.

The CPI and CPI(M) have also shared power at the center in the Janata Dal led United Front and the Congress-led UPA coalition Governments. The CPI was part of the United Front Cabinet whereas the CPM extended support to it from the parliamentary floor. In the UPA–I coalition, both extended outside support to the Government. In these Governments, the Left has played a pragmatic role in partly accepting the neo-liberal economic reforms and partly using their influence in the Government for slowing the pace of privatization and globalization of the economy. In the 2004 Lok Sabha elections, the Left parties were returned with their largest ever parliamentary presence with 62 Lok Sabha members. In 2009 their parliamentary presence was considerably reduced.

There are two kinds of regional parties in India. First, there are the long-standing regional parties owing their origins to deep cultural divisions of the Indian society, e.g. the Tamil parties whose origins go back to the period around the First World War, the Akali Dal that originated in the Sikh Gurudwara movement of the 1920s, and the National Conference that can be traced back to the Muslim Conference founded in the late 1930s. These old regional parties are a feature of areas with strong religious or linguistic regional identities, even going to the extent of being ambivalent to separatism. Second, there are relatively new regional parties in the States where previously the Congress or Janata Party/Dal held sway in the past. These regional parties emerged in the 1980s and the '90s with the growing politicization of the mass public and the diminishing capability of the Congress to absorb and satisfy regional or ethnic identities. The Telugu Desam, Asom Gana Parishad, the various Janata Dal and Congress splinters in different States are cases in point. A characteristic common to these new parties is their by and large centrist orientation in economic terms. Had they not been regional parties, they could have very well merged with the Congress or the JD. The factors that have contributed to the growth of these parties are the growing salience of the caste, community and local factors in politics. To an extent, they are also related to some personalities with regionalized support base identifiable in terms of regional and caste/tribe factors. The decline of national parties and the advent of coalition governments at the Union level has enormously increased the role, relevance and leverage of regional parties. They play a balancing role in competing coalitions and make or mar the prospect of a coalition government.

The trajectory of regional parties in general is associated with the demands for a separate States within the Indian Union and in some cases, espousing even separatism. Such State autonomy demands after Independence were responsible for the rise of several regional parties in Assam that subsequently was divided into six other units. Most of these regional parties have their bases in tribal regional identities. However, these parties are marked by a great degree of volatility and splits and mergers. Except for a few such tribal political formations such as the Mizo National Front (MNF), they generally tend to coalesce with the national party or party coalition in power in New Delhi.

The proliferation of regional parties in recent decades is attributable in political terms to the decline of the Congress both in terms of its internal accommodative capability and erosion of its electoral base on the one hand, and the inability of non-Congress national parties like the BJP, communist parties and Janata Dal to replicate the political formula of the old Congress as an umbrella party.

In their ideological positions, regional parties base themselves on a broad spectrum of regionalist platforms. The issues espoused by them include demands relating to language, religion, caste and community, sub-State regional economic backwardness, etc. Several of these factors enter into complex combinations in specific cases of political regionalism. Suhas Palshikar perceptively observes:

> Many times regional parties cover non-regionalist ideological ground. While the Akalis tend to define regional identity in terms of religion, the Shiv Sena uses the two ideologies of regionalism and religious communalism according to the exigencies of electoral politics. Regional parties also rely on castes for their ideological formulations. Thus, the DMK originally combined Dravidian identity with non-Brahminism. By employing anti-caste ideological resources, the DMK strengthened its claims pertaining to a separate Dravida identity vis-à-vis the Aryans. More recently, the PMK in Tamil Nadu has also combined the regional rhetoric with an anti-caste social position on behalf of the Other Backward Castes (OBCs). Such ideological formulations should not be seen cynically only as marriages of convenience.[44]

Nevertheless, regional parties can, to an extent, be said to be a moderating influence on ideological or doctrinaire tendencies in politics. It is notable, for example, that regional parties have readily coalesced with left-of-the-center as well as the right-of-the-center coalition governments more freely than national parties. The TDP was a regional kingpin in the JD-led United Front as well as the BJP-led NDA. The Tamil regional parties have easily shifted from Janata Dal-led coalitions to BJP-led and Congress-led coalitions in power in New Delhi.

Political implications of the rise of regional parties with variegated localized power bases are evident in several ways in the contemporary dynamics of federal politics in India today. For one thing, regional parties have "tended to limit the political space for national alternatives to the Congress Party. For instance, the BJP has been competitive in those State assemblies where regional parties are weak or non-existent"[45] For another, inability of the regional fragments of the Janata Dal has scuttled the possibility of that party to provide a national alternative to the Congress. Thirdly, the failure of the Communist parties to extend their electoral bases beyond West Bengal, Kerala and Tripura has meant that regional identities in States outside their sphere of influence cannot be easily aggregated into a broader national framework within their leadership. The net effect is that the current regionalist thrust in Indian politics appears unlikely to be "nationalized" within a broad national party in India today. This is an indicator of the continuing importance of regional parties in State politics and federal coalitions. However, the failure of the regional parties to form a viable third front between the two largest national parties—INC and BJP—is also quite evident. From available indicators, the United Front led by the Janata Dal (JD) was the heyday of the Third Front which is over. The three major components of the Third Front were the Janata Dal, regional parties and the Communist parties. The Janata Dal (United)—despite its name—is a divided house. And the Communist parties for a time between 2004 and 2009 joined the Congress–led United Progressive Alliance (UPA) Government at the Center. If the BJP-led NDA and Congress-led UPA endure, it may well portend that the sunshine days of regional parties are more in the past than in the future. The flagship of the communist movement is a 'national' party by the Election Commission classification. And despite the regionalist existence of communism in India, its motivation is, deep down, nationalist today.

Yet the number of regional parties is still considerable and they have endured in some states in the South and the East, despite the rising tide of BJP and NDA at this writing (November 2020). But there is lack of any serious attempt at unity among them for national power challenging NDA and UPA, or rising from their regional status to the status of national parties.

Electoral democracy coupled with federalization of the polity has largely succeeded in containing separatism. Regional parties of all varieties are today interested in greater State autonomy within the federation. Participation in various federal coalitions by some major regional parties has further moderated or "constitutionalized" and "nationalized" them to some extent as they have become co-sharers in federal power along with ruling at the State level without the fear of being toppled by the Center.

A new political formation, Aam Aadmi Party (AAP), was born out of a civil society anti-corruption movement, India against Corruption, under the overall leadership of Anna Hazare coinciding with the so-called Arab Democratic Spring in 2011. It soon joined the electoral politics under the leadership of Arvind Kejriwal, separating from Hazare's India Against Corruption, which wished to keep it a non-party civil society movement; it claimed to float a 'party with a difference', heralding an alternative politics different from the High Command brand of the run of the mill parties in India. Its electoral symbol broom (*jhadu*) professes to symbolize the mission of wiping out corruption and bad governance. It drew a large number of the youth, public intellectuals, and celebrities in various walks of life. Its political planks include *Swaraj* (self-rule), and enactment of a Jan Lokpal legislation, among others. AAP made its debut in the Union Territory Assembly elections in Delhi in 2013 and emerged as the second largest party winning 28 out of 70 seats with a vote share of 29.49, and BJP won the plurality as the first party and the three term-ruling party, Congress, got relegated to the third place. AAP formed a minority government with outside support of Congress. AAP resigned after 49 days in government, when its government, after moving a Lokpal bill in the Assembly, fell on account of withdrawal of support by Congress. It was mauled by BJP in the Lok Sabha elections in the Delhi UT in 2014. But then, in the Delhi Assembly elections that followed in 2015, AAP won 67 out of 70 seats and formed the government again. BJP got only three seats, and Congress none at all. AAP has, however, been unsuccessful so far in its efforts to other States and at national level. With Congress in precipitous decline, AAP gets looked at as an alternate national party after BJP, both for its national capital location as well its plank of offering an alternative politics and reformist agenda and zeal of its leaders.

ADAPTATION OF PARTY SYSTEM TO SOCIETY

In course of its evolution, the party system has gradually adapted itself more closely to the Indian society. What was theorized as the 'Congress System' by Rajni Kothari[46] (1964, 1970, and 1974) was a party system unique to India yet it was essentially an upper-class and upper-caste phenomenon with an urban bias. It was internally democratic and externally open to public participation and the principal institution that legitimized the new democratic institutions in postcolonial India. In a thoughtful critique of the Congress System, Yogendra Yadav and Suhas Palshikar[47] make the following points. First, the Congress System fabricated a consensus which was based on the elites who came from a common social background but even though they were democratic, they relied on patron-client networks of support. Second, it was forged at a time when politicization was rather limited and political competition circumscribed. Third, Congress party's 'catch-all' and consensual character was driven by charismatic leadership supported by the masses belonging to the various social backgrounds. They conclude that the Congress System "did allow for incubation of democratic politics for a safe experiment with social change, yet it could not have been the political form for a full-fledged engagement of competitive politics with social transformation."[48] A fuller competitive and transformative politics was to come later with the rise of the Left Front governments in states like West Bengal, Kerala, and Tripura, and 'Mandalization', 'Dalitization' as well as 'Hinduization' of Indian politics. This is what Yogendra Yadav has called on various occasions as the 'second democratic upsurge' after the first upsurge in the Congress system of the 1950s and 1960s and Indira Gandhi's populist politics in the 1970s.

Our theme of party system adaptation to the society may also be illustrated by the narrative of the rise of lower castes and marginalized groups in Indian politics offered by Christophe Jaffrelot. During the Congress system period in the 1950s and 1960s, more than 55 per cent of MPs in the north-Indian states came from the upper castes. This remained unchanged even during the populist politics of Prime Minister Indira Gandhi in the 1970s when the ruling Congress in fact became more Brahamanized. Things began to change after the Congress Party lost power in 1977 to the Janata Party in the post-Emergency general election. The proportion of upper caste MPs from north Indian states for the first time fell below 50 per cent and those from intermediate castes and Other Backward Classes (OBCs) increased to almost 20 per cent as compared to 5.5 per cent in 1952. What Jaffrelot calls the 'Silent Revolution' heralding the advent of subaltern castes and classes moved ahead with the Jat leader Charan Singh's mobilization of the peasants (kisans), Mandal Commission's OBCs and Bahujan Samaj Party's (Bahujans). To quote Jaffrelot "India is probably the first country [in the developing world] in which a formal, institutional democracy has been gaining social substance through a *quiet* transfer of power. In most other societies, such a shift has implied a revolutionary and violent phase: the people have gained power by rising up against the ruling traditional elite. In India, democracy had already been granted to the country by the elite, but the earlier entrenched elite had monopolized power for decades. The revolution is now passing through the polling booth: it is by voting that the subalterns have been rising to power because they are large in numbers and have stopped supporting local notables."[49]

Jaffrelot also draws attention to a contrast between the foregoing political process in the north on one hand and the western and southern India on the other hand. In Maharashtra and the south, the rise of the lower castes had started much earlier during the British Raj itself due to social reform movements led by Jotiba Phule and Periyar and subsequently deepened by B.R. Ambedkar and the leaders of the Justice Party in Madras which had won the 1920 Assembly elections. The reservations for the lower castes had been thus initiated in the 1920s and 1930s which had to wait until post-Independence period for the Scheduled Castes and Scheduled Tribes and until 1990s for the OBCs in the north. Yet Jaffrelot points out that the early advance of the backward classes in western and southern India has reached a plateau with the rise to power of the Marathas in Maharashtra, Reddis and Kammas in Andhra Pradesh, and Lingayats and Vokkaligas in Karnataka. The lower castes further down the ladder are still largely un-empowered there, whereas in the north empowerment of lower castes has dug deeper.

Nevertheless, Jaffrelot sounds a cautionary note that the so-called Silent Revolution has tended to subsequently face new hurdles that blunt their cutting edge. To quote him, "the subalterns are gaining power in the elective Assemblies and through quotas in the bureaucracy, but these institutions do not matter as much [now] as before. The decision-making process ignores the Parliament more and more, as is evident from the economic reforms, which have been imposed by a clique of technocrats and have not been properly debated by the MPs. The state apparatus is shrinking, whereas the private sector is flourishing—so much so that the lower castes may well have quotas in bodies which are becoming empty shells."[50]

STATE PARTY SYSTEMS

From the 1950s to the 1970s, the party system in India at the national and state levels was largely convergent in the sense that the Congress Party was hegemonic and dominant throughout the country. The trend of differentiation between the national and state party systems began in a significant way during the 1980s. By the end of the decade, one could not talk meaningfully at all about the national party system being an aggregation of the state party systems as different sets of parties emerged in the states and gradually came to dominate the scene. The phase of an integrated one-party dominant system subsuming the Union and State levels under the aegis of the Congress passed away and a new phase of rather disaggregated National and State party systems came into existence. The emergent state party systems have been classified into three basic types by Yogendra Yadav and Suhas Palshikar[51]: (1) Two-party/bi-polar competition, (2) two-plus competition, and (3) multi-party competition. The first category is exemplified by the United Democratic Front (UDF) led by the Congress and the Left Democratic Front (LDF) led by the CPI(M) in Kerala since 1980. Another example is DMK-AIADMK competition in Tamil Nadu where the two major parties alternately in alliance with Congress-led coalitions with smaller parties in the state.[52] The second type, two-plus competition, is illustrated by Punjab where the Akali Dal and the Congress are the major competitors for power and the BJP has played a secondary role in alliance with the Akali Dal. This competition is not triangular as a third party cannot offer competition all over the state and among all sections of the society. During the 1990s, this form of competition has also tended to develop in the states of Karnataka, Andhra Pradesh, and Orissa with the entry of the BJP into the state politics. The third class of state party systems, multi-party competition, is in existence in the states like Uttar Pradesh since 1991 with parties like BSP, Samajwadi Party, Congress, BJP; and Bihar in the 1990s before the creation of Jharkhand, Assam since 1985, and Kerala in the 1960s and '70s. This syndrome is also found in smaller states like Goa, Haryana, or the north-eastern states.

IMPACT OF PARTY SYSTEM ON DEMOCRACY

This party system was regarded as the most crucial political institution in the early post-Independence decades that contributed to political stability and consolidation of democracy in India. Although, the party system has become fragmented, unstable, and adversely affected by the rise of dynastic politics (in most national and regional parties), political corruption and criminalization on a wide scale, yet it continues to be the principal power- sharing mechanism in India's democracy.

M.V. Rajeev Gowda and E. Sridharan[53] seek to attempt an evaluation of the impact of the present party system on the quality of democracy in the country applying Larry Diamond and Leonardo Morlino's eight dimensions of democratic quality—freedom, participation, competition, horizontal accountability, rule of law, equality, vertical accountability, and responsiveness. They come to a mixed conclusion. On the one hand, the decline of one-party dominance and emergence of a multi-party system have increased electoral freedom of choice, political participation, and competitiveness. On the other hand, the emergence of the large national multi-party coalitions have weakened the federal executive, diluted parliamentary control of the government by stretching collective responsibility to extra-parliamentary centers of power and provided freer play to politically corrupt and criminal operators and lawless political fund-raising. On the balance, they conclude: "...the fragmentation of the party system from Congress dominance to multi-party coalitions in India's regionalized and 'ethnicized' party system has not undermined the basic power-sharing character of the system and has thus helped to consolidate democracy [if not always rule of law and constitutionalism]."[54]

Political parties in any democratic polity are supposed to be vital links between the state and the civil society. Parties in India have failed to perform the basic functions of Government and Opposition on account of a number of reasons. As already pointed out earlier, very few parties take their own constitutions seriously. For this reason they have come under personalized and dynastic dominations. Another dimension of illegality of Indian parties is evident from the Writ petition No. 24 of 1995 to the Supreme Court by the Common Cause, a registered society headed by H.D. Shourie. The public interest case arose out of the alleged violation of the provisions of Section 13A of the Income Tax Act and Section 293A of the Companies Act by political parties with regard to their income and expenditure. The Common Cause argued that these laws "clearly indicate the legislative scheme, the object of which is to ensure that there should be transparency in the matter of sources of funds of the political parties and the manner in which the funds are spent."[55] The laws put "all political parties...under mandatory obligation to maintain accounts, issue receipts for voluntary contributions above the prescribed limit, and of getting their accounts annually audited."[56] Of the major fifteen parties approached for confirmation, none could claim that the legal requirements were complied with (barring the Janata Party, a rump of its namesake of the yore and a pocket organization of Subramaniam Swamy). The responses from the Government department concerned confirmed the contention of the Common Cause (1995: 13; Responses of the Department of Revenue, Ministry of Finance, Government of India, attached to the petition).[57] The Supreme Court's ruling on this petition was: "if a political party deliberately chooses to violate or circumvent these mandatory provisions of law and goes through the election process with the help of black and unaccounted money, the said party ordinarily, cannot be permitted to say that it has incurred or authorized expenditure in connection with the election of its candidates in terms of Explanation to Section 77 of the Representation of People Act (Para 19)."[58] The Parliament subsequently circumvented the judgement by `suitable' statutory amendments.

Another aspect of the degeneration of the party-political processes in the country is what has commonly come to be known as criminalization of politics. There is probably no political party today that does not harbour a number of criminals holding party and even legislative/ministerial posts, the figure in some parties running into double digits as revealed by press reports. In the 1990s, economic scams and political scandals have reached the proportions of an unending deluge. The octopus-like hold of politics and economy by business-politics-administration-crime nexus has reached a stage where even Joint Parliamentary Committee investigations have proved to be utterly ineffective, fruitless and farcical exercises. In July 1993, the Government of India established a committee at the administrative level headed by the then Home Secretary, N.N. Vohra "to take stock of all available information about the activities of crime-syndicate/mafia organizations which had developed links with and were being protected by Government functionaries and political personalities."[59] The Report submitted in October 1993 made the following sinister submissions, among others: "Central Bureau of Investigation has reported that all over India crime syndicates have become a law unto themselves... The nexus between the criminal gangs, police, bureaucracy and politicians has come out clearly in various parts of the country. The existing criminal justice system which was essentially designed to deal with the individual offences/crimes, is unable to deal in the activities of the mafia ..."[60] There is evidently little follow-up action on the Report, notwithstanding the Supreme Court directive to the Government to report what steps had been taken to implement its recommendations.

Another dimension of political corruption is the so-called politics of defection, which since 1967 has turned the legislatures and ministries into licensed casinos for political opportunists and defectors. Huge sums of money change hands and plane-loads of legislators are flown to five-star tourist facilities, often outside the State, to insulate them from temptations offered by other parties. Formerly known to have taken place only in State capitals, a similar vice for the first time surfaced at the national level in the notorious JMM bribery case adjudicated by the Supreme Court in 1998. The Supreme Court ruling in this case was:

1. An MP is a public servant under the provisions of the Prevention of Corruption Act, 1988; since there is no competent authority under the provisions of the Act to remove an MP from his office, the Court can take cognizance of his offence without seeking sanction from any other authority.
2. However, the prosecuting agencies need to seek sanctions for proceeding in the framing of charges from the Speaker of the Lok Sabha or the Chairman of the Rajya Sabha.
3. MPs charged with taking bribe for voting against a no-confidence motion enjoy immunity from courts under Article 105 of the Constitution relating to the parliamentary privileges.
4. Bribe-givers enjoy no such immunity.
5. It is for the competent parliamentary authority to take proper action against offending MPs.[61]

Under the Tenth Schedule of the Constitution introduced in 1985 and amended subsequently (the Ninety-First Amendment Act, 2003), a party member of a House is liable to be expelled from a legislative body unless at least one-thirds of members of the legislative party desert it to form a new party or merge with another party. To reduce temptations for defection, the size of a Council of Ministers is fixed at 10 per cent of the total membership of the popular chamber of the legislature by this Amendment.

Another murky area in this context is funding of political parties for elections. Scattered and skimpy regulations in this regard in the Companies Act as amended in 1985 (Section 293 A), etc. were followed more in breach than in observance. The bulk of the corporate companies' donations to political parties were made via the black money route as following the law divulges the party preference of the companies and resultant problems with the shareholders and the governments.[62]

The BJP-led NDA government notified an electoral funding reform called Electoral Bond Scheme 2018 in January, claiming that it was an alternative to cash donations by corporate companies to parties and ensure transparency in political funding. The opposition parties and academic critics, however, decried its provision of non-disclosure of the names of the donors as a bane for Indian democracy on account of departure from transparency for the public and the opposition parties and transparency only for the government and possible mischief. The Supreme court on 12 April 2019, refused to invalidate the electoral bonds, but directed all political parties to submit receipts of the amounts of money received in a sealed envelope to the Election Commission of India by 30 May as an interim arrangement as a check to ensure that the balance was not tilted in favour of one political party. Eligibility of receiving Electoral Bonds were limited to only the political parties registered under Section 29A of the Representation of the People Act, 1951, and getting no less than one per cent of votes in the last Lok Sabha elections. The electoral Accounts were issuable by the State bank of India and could be purchased by the corporate companies in the months of January, April, July, and October. Verified accounts were issuable to political parties by the Election commission of India. A systematic empirical study of how this scheme worked in the 2019 general elections is not yet available.

A great area of darkness in the study of political parties and party systems after the 1950s and 1960s in case of all major parties, and after the late 1980s and 1990s in case of BJP and RSS, has been the absence of research in party organizations and intra-party democracy. Except of the BJP and communist parties, all political parties in India have no concern for organization-building and organizational elections and empowering of lower party organizational units. Indian psephologists have turned into journalists with interest limited to voting statistics focussed on party preferences of castes, communities and regions.[63] Even Kanchan Chandra, does not go beyond barefoot behavioral empiricism to embrace New Institutionalism concerned with democratic norms and procedures and organizations.

No democracy can do without democratic political parties. Absence of a democratic party system is proving to be the Achilles' heel of Indian democracy. India needs the kind of party system reforms ushered in Canada and America during the Progressive Era in the first two decades of the twentieth century, when the primary elections in parties, empowerment of constituency party associations, national conventions of parties to nominate candidates for top elective offices, etc. were instituted.

PROSPECTS

A notable development of the 1990s is the emergence of the Election Commission of India as an activist federal agency. The Commission under the Chief Election Commissioner T.N. Seshan and his successors appears to have brought about a sea change so far as the conduct of elections is concerned. In the elections in the 1990s and after, there has been a visible impact of the Commission in curbing electoral abuses by the ruling and opposition parties, e.g. obliging the parties to adhere to a moral code of conduct formulated by the Commission in consultation with political parties but followed more in breach than in adherence in the past, reduction of election expenses by a more rigorous rendering of accounts, control over noisy, communal, and polluting campaigns, filing of affidavits regarding non-involvement in criminal convictions and activities, and so on. The Commission has also considerably checked mass transfer of government officers with ulterior electoral purposes, misuse of government machinery by the party in power and announcement and inauguration of schemes for particular sections of the population too close to the electoral schedule to influence voting, and so on. Moreover, the Commission also seems to be presenting more comprehensive and bolder proposals for electoral and party reforms to the Government, but legislation and executive action has been lacking.

The recent proposals of the Election Commission to the government broadly cover a wide range of issues concerning delimitation of constituencies, conduct and administration of elections, and political parties and candidates. In view of the fact that decay of parties and criminalization of politics have assumed alarming proportions in more recent times, we review here mainly proposals relating to these problems. To begin with registration of political parties with the Commission, the Commission recommends measures to discourage frivolous party formations and deregistration of non-serious and defunct parties. Presently, parties are registered with the Commission under the provisions of Section 29A of the Representation of the People Act, 1951.

The number of parties contesting elections in India has varied from 36 in 1980 to 209 in 1996, 176 in 1998, and 169 in 1999.[64] The Election Commission of India revised its classification of political parties in December 2000 into "National" and "State" parties, besides the "Registered (Unrecognized)" parties. The last category includes the largest number of parties that are merely registered but not recognized as either a national or a State party (numbering 461). National parties are those that (i) secure not less than six per cent of the total valid votes in four or more States in the previous Lok Sabha or Vidhan Sabha election AND (ii) return at least four MPs in the last general election "from any State or States" OR the parties that (i) win at least two per cent of the Lok Sabha seats AND. (ii) whose MPs are elected from not less than three States. In 2009, the list of seven national parties that contested included the Indian National Congress, BJP, CPI, CPI(M), NCP and BSP. A State party is a party that (i) secures not less than six per cent of the total valid votes in the State where it is so recognized AND (ii) returns at least two members to the Vidhan Sabha in the previous Assembly election OR wins at least three per cent of the total number of seats in the Vidhan Sabha or at least three seats, whichever is more.[65] The list of major State parties in 2009 included: TDP (Andhra Pradesh), AGP (Assam), RJD (Bihar), INLD (Haryana), JKNC, JKNPP and JKPDP (Jammu & Kashmir), JD(U) and JMM (Jharkhand), JD(S) and JD(U) (Karnataka), Shiv Sena (Maharashtra), BJD (Orissa), SAD and SAD(M) (Punjab), AIADMK, DMK, MDMK and PMK (Tamil Nadu), SP and RLD (Uttar Pradesh), and AITC (West Bengal).

By way of other reforms, the Commission could think in terms of devising more stringent requirements relating to their organizational structure. Indeed, the Commission requires parties to submit copies of their Constitutions and election manifestoes to it. Until T.N. Seshan's incumbency as the CEC, this was a fairly ritualistic affair. Moreover, the Commission has since then started insisting on adherence to their own Constitution by parties in constituting party organs and holding regular organizational elections. The state of affairs at the Nirvachan Sadan are again getting back to the old rut. The Commission could also begin requiring parties to structure themselves democratically, develop grassroots and constituency organizations.

On the important issue of donation by companies to political parties, the Commission is inclined to go along with the current law whereby a company in existence for more than three years may contribute an amount to party funds not exceeding five per cent of its average net profit. The Commission is against a total ban on company donations on the ground that political parties do need funds coming through certain channels for legitimate political activities. Besides, as trade unions and other organizations are allowed under the law of the land to contribute funds to parties, a ban on company donations would appear to be unjustified in the Commission's view. All that the Commission requires is that "such contributions should be limited to a reasonable level and all transactions in this regard must be made in a completely transparent manner."[66] Moreover, the Commission also recommends to the Government that parties must be required to maintain their accounts and get them audited by agencies specified by it.

Further, the Election Commission also recommends that it be empowered to fix ceiling on election expenses before every general election and that expenditure incurred by a political party and other organizations be included in the election expenses of a candidate for purposes of ceiling on election expenses. Besides, the Commission is also in favour of some sort of State-funding of elections to a certain extent. The Commission has indeed already worked out a scheme of allocation of free-time to parties on equitable basis on the State-owned electronic mass media. But it covers a rather small fraction of the expenses involved.

One other serious problem with which the Election Commission has recently been seized with is the difficulty to define a criminal and to prevent his entry in politics:

> The Commission is conscious of the fact in the eye of law a person is presumed to be innocent unless proved guilty... In the Commission's considered opinion, a person who is facing trial in a serious offence, if kept out of the electoral fray till he is exonerated of the charge, should not have a legitimate grievance, as such restriction on his right to contest election would be a reasonable restriction in the greater public interest and for bringing sanctity to the august Houses which are the supreme law making bodies of the country.[67]

Pending Government action on this proposal, the Commission has already initiated some steps in this direction. In August 1997, it invoked Article 324 of the Constitution to oblige all candidates then contesting to file affidavits along with their nominations about their convictions in cases covered by Section 8 of the Representation of the People Act, 1951, which disqualifies persons convicted of those specified offences. Challenged politically, the Commission got legal backing from the Supreme Court.

The issue of party reforms has also received a serious attention in the National Commission for Review of the Working of the Constitution (NCRWC) Report 2002. It is interesting to compare the approach to political parties on the part of the founding fathers of the Republic in the Constituent Assembly and that of this eleven-member Constitution Review Commission. The Constituent Assembly did not consider the issue of party system necessary to be addressed on the legal and constitutional plane. It was apparently hoped that as parties had grown without a legal intervention on the basis of civil society initiative and constitutional convention as in Western liberal democracies, India also could do so. Fifty years later when this fond hope was belied, the NCRWC recommended a comprehensive legislation on political parties providing for "compulsory registration for every political party or pre-poll alliance". The registration rules should require (a) allegiance to the basic constitutional values, (b) open door to all citizens irrespective of any distinctions of caste and community, (c) reservation/representation of at least 30 per cent of organizational positions and legislative seats for women, (d) compulsory maintenance of accounts and audit of funds, and (e) mandatory declaration of assets and liabilities at the time of filing nomination by members for election to the Parliament/State Legislatures.[68] This legislation, to our mind, is a vital precondition for survival of democracy in India. An early action by the government would appear to be an imperative that cannot be dodged to save democracy in India.

AN EXAMPLE INDIA MAY EMULATE

The Election Commission of India and many prominent citizens and jurists like Jayaprakash Narayan and Justice (Rtd.) V.R. Krishna Iyer have been advocating electoral and party reforms over the years.[69] At least two parliamentary committees were appointed to examine and recommend reforms in this area. In view of the seriousness of the malady, it appears imperative now to entrust the task of considering comprehensive electoral and party reforms to a full-scale constitutional commission like the Sarkaria Panel on the Center-State Relations. It may be interesting to draw attention here to the valuable work done in this respect by the Royal Commission on Electoral Reform and Party Financing appointed by the Government of Canada in November 1989. This Commission sponsored a score of academic studies on the problem as well as it held nation-wide hearings itself and submitted its recommendations in four volumes in 1991–1993.[70]

Some of the recommendations of this Commission as well as some Canadian practices in this regard in vogue since the early years of this century may also be considered for adoption in India. Volume 3 of the Report, which is presented in the form of a model legislation, has some interesting ideas about political parties, constituency associations, and party foundations. The proposed legislation lays down detailed legal requirements for registration of parties, their constituency associations, and party foundations under this parliamentary law. Each of these organizations is supposed to be registered under Section 24 of the model Act on the condition that they must have a Constitution that shall

(a) Promote democratic values and practices in a manner consistent with the spirit and intent of the Canadian Charter of Rights and Freedoms;
(b) Provide clear and consistent rules on the selection of candidates, leaders, delegates, if any, and officers;
(c) Provide that members of the party who select the party's candidates, select delegates to a leadership convention or select a party leader must be voters....[71]

The proposed legislation goes on to provide other legal requirements to facilitate smooth functioning of these organizations and procedures for settlement of disputes, which need not necessarily detain us here.

A party foundation may be registered under this Act by a recognized party as "a distinct and permanent institution"

(i) To develop and promote public policy options,
(ii) To educate party members on matters of public policy, and
(iii) To provide the party with research and advise on policy.[72]

The Canadian Royal Commission believes in full disclosure of the size and source of contributions to parties and candidates to forestall any undue influence on elected officials by contributors of large amounts. It recommends submission of interim unaudited report of all contributions by registered parties and their ancillary organizations for the first six months of the year and a "full audited return on their financial activities for the entire year."[73]

The Canada Elections Act neither bans nor limits the fund a person, corporation, or trade union can donate to a federal party or candidate. However, all donations over $100 must be disclosed and 75 per cent tax benefit to the donor can be claimed on only the first $100. Moreover, in June 1999, the Federal Government forbade federal Crown corporations from making contributions to political parties. Bill C-2 proposed most comprehensive amendments to the Canada Election Act since 1974, with a view to rectify 'some of the well-known problems with the regulation of party and candidate financing', though 'some of the most important were ignored'.

The combination of parliamentary and federal systems of Government in Canada has forced the Canadians to depart from the practice of electing party leaders by the parliamentary organizations (elected MPs). The Canadian parties early in the 20th century, gave up the practice of electing party leaders by the parliamentary caucuses in favour of a national leadership convention composed by provincial party delegates voting as individuals rather than as State delegations en bloc as in the American national party conventions organized every four years for nominating Presidential candidates. This device of electing the party leader introduces an overarching national element over the State/province-based national parties in the USA and Canada. The adoption of the party convention system in Canada was done to make the leadership selection process more representative and federal.

In view of the increasing fragmentation of the Indian party system, the adoption of the Canadian system of party leadership convention here would introduce an element of federal aggregation of political forces in the country. This reform is particularly necessary now that the growing regionalization of parties in India has rendered the process of formation and maintenance of stable parliamentary Government at the Center a highly problematic proposition.

Some people believe that the mere configuration of parties in India is more chaotic than systematic. In any case, these reforms will hopefully make this configuration more of a system attuned to the parliamentary federal constitution of the country.

REFERENCES

1. Joseph La Palombara and Myron Weiner (Eds.), *Political Parties and Political Development,* Princeton University Press, Princeton, 1966, p. 3.
2. Seymour Martin Lipset, "The Indispensability of Political Parties", *Journal of Democracy*, Vol. II, No. 1, January 2000.
3. M.P. Singh and Rekha Saxena, *India at the Polls*: *Parliamentary Elections in the Federal Phase,* Orient Longman, New Delhi, 2003, p. 268, backnote 1.

4. See specially the chapters on Great Britain and the old Commonwealth in Segmund Neumann (Ed.), *Modern Political Parties: Approaches to Comparative Politics,* University of Chicago Press, Chicago and London, 1956.
5. This pre-history of modern Indian parties is yet to come under the scan of historians and social scientists.
6. Rajni Kothari, *Politics in India,* Orient Longman, New Delhi, 1970, Ch. 5.
7. Bipan Chandra, *In the Name of Democracy: JP Movement and the Emergency,* Penguin Books, New Delhi, 2003; and Sherlock Stephen, *Indian Railways Strike of 1974: A Study of Power and Organized Labour,* Rupa, New Delhi, 2002.
8. Himanshu Roy, "Party Systems and Coalition Politics in Indian States" in M.P. Singh and Anil Mishra (Eds.), *Coalition Politics in India: Problems and Prospects,* Manohar, New Delhi, 2004.
9. Rekha Saxena, "Party System Transition and Electoral Turning Points in India", *Trends in Social Science Research,* Vol. 5, No. **1**, 1998, pp. 7–47; M.P. Singh and Rekha Saxena, "India Independent: The First Half Century of Political Development and Political Decay", *The Indian Historical Review*, Vol. XXVI, July 1999; M.P. Singh and Rekha Saxena, *India at the Polls: Parliamentary Elections in the Federal Phase,* Orient Longman, New Delhi, 2003, Chs. 1 and 9; Douglas V. Verney, "From Quasi-Federation to Quasi-Confederacy? The Transformation of India's Party System", *Publius: The Journal of Federalism*, Vol. 33, No. **4**, Fall 2003.
10. M.P. Singh, "Political Mobilization and Integration in British India", *Political Science Review,* Vol. XX, No. **1**, January–March 1981.
11. Rajni Kothari, "The Congress System in India", *Asian Survey,* Vol. 12, No. **12**, December 1964; "Congress System Revisited: A Decennial Review", *Asian Survey,* Vol. 14, No. **12**, December 1974; "Opposition in a Consensual Polity" in Robert A. Dahl (Ed.), *Regimes and Oppositions,* Yale University Press, New Haven, 1973.
12. M.P. Singh, *Split in a Predominant Party: The Indian National Congress in 1969*, Abhinav, New Delhi, 1981.
13. Stanley A. Kochanek, "Mrs. Gandhi's Pyramid: The New Congress" in Zoya Hasan (Ed.), *Parties And Party Politics in India*, Oxford University Press, New Delhi, 2002, p. 78.
14. Bipan Chandra, *In the Name of Democracy, op. cit.;* and Sherlock Stephen, *Indian Railways Strike of 1974, op. cit.*
15. For a detailed historical study, see Bipan Chandra, *In the Name of Democracy, op. cit.* Chandra concludes that while the Emergency

"was out of step with the Indian people's interests and traditions", the JP movement too "was not the answer to the problems that the Indian people were facing during 1974–75" due to "its undefined goal, inadequate forms of struggle, gross ideological confusion, absence of an autonomous organization and dependence on the RSS cadres for mass mobilization", p. 294.

16. C.P. Bhambhri, *The Janata Party: A Profile,* National Publishing House, New Delhi, 1980. Also Kumar Rajesh, *The Two Janata Experiments and Beyond* (Delhi: Manak, 2008).

17. Oliver Heath, "Anatomy of BJP's Rise to Power: Social, Regional and Political Expansion in 1990s", *Economic and Political Weekly*, Vol. XXXIV, Nos. **34** and **35**, August 21–27/28, 3 September 1999. The quote is from page 2516.

18. M.P. Singh and Rekha Saxena "Lok Sabha Elections 2004: Change with Continuity," *Think India*, Vol. 8, No. 1, January–March, 2005. Also see Lawrence Saez and Rekha Saxena, "Mandate 2004", *Mainstrem,* Annual No., January 2005.

19. United Progressive Alliance, *Common Minimum Programme of the United Progressive Alliance,* New Delhi, 2004, p. 2.

20. Yogendra Yadav, "The Elusive Mandate of 2004", *Economic and Political Weekly,* Vol. XXXIX, No. **51**, 18–24 December 2004, pp. 5393–5394.

21. M.K. Venu, "Upstaging Theories", *The Indian Express,* New Delhi, April 30, 2010, p. 10.

22. Shreya Sardesai, Pranav Gupta, "Religious Fault Line in the 2014 Elections" in Ashutosh Kumar and Yatindra Singh Sisodia (Eds.), *How India Votes: A State by State Look*,. Orient Blackswan Private Limited, Hyderabad, 2019.

23. Harish Khare, "The Indian National Congress: Problems of Survival and Reinvention" in Subrata K. Mitra *et al.* (Eds.), *Political Parties in South Asia,* New York, Praeger, 2004, pp. 31–54.

24. *Ibid.*, pp. 42–45.

25. Rekha Saxena, "The Indian National Congress: Coping with Challenges of Deepening Democracy, Federalism and Neoliberal Capitalism" in Ashutosh Kumar and Yatindra Singh Sisodia (Eds.), How India Votes: A State-by-State Look. Hyderabad, Orient Blackswan, 2018.

26. V.D. Savarkar, *Hindutva*, Bombay: Veer Savarkar Prakashan, 1969, 1st published, 1924.

27. Pratap Bhanu Mehta, "Introduction to the Omnibus" *in Hindu Nationalism and Indian Politics*, New Delhi: Oxford University Press, 2004, p. xi.

28. Christophe Jaffrelot, *The Hindu Nationalist Movement in India,* Part I & II, Penguin India, New Delhi, 1996. See also Pralay Kanungo, *RSS' Tryst with Politics: From Hedgewar to Sudarshan,* Manohar, New Delhi, 2002.

29. Christophe Jaffrelot, 'Rethinking the "Moderation Thesis" Regarding "Radical Parties": The Jana Sangh and the BJP between Hindu Nationalism and Coalition Politics in India,' Paris: Center d'etudes et de recherches internationals Sciences Po, 2010.

30. Pratap Bhanu Mehta, *op. cit.,* pp. xx.

31. Christopher Jaffrelot and Thomas Blom Hansen (Eds.), The *BJP and the Compulsions of Politics in India*, New Delhi, Oxford University Press, 1998.

32. Partha Ghose, "The Bhartiya Janata Party: Hindu Nationalism and the Compulsions of Pluralism" in Subrata K. Mitra *et. al.* (Eds.), *op. cit.*, p. 73.

33. Sudha Pai, *Dalit Assertion And The Unfinished Democratic Revolution: The Bahujan Samaj Party in Uttar Pradesh*, New Delhi, Sage Publications, 2002.

34. T.J. Nossiter, *Marxist State Governments in India: Politics, Economics and Society,* Pinter Publishers, London and New York, 1988, Chs. 1 and 2.

35. Valerian Rodrigues, "Communist Parties in India" in Peter Ronald de Souza and E. Sridharan (Eds.), *India's Political Parties*, New Delhi, Sage Publications, 2006, p. 240.

36. Amrita Basu, "Parliamentary Communism as a Historical Phenomenon: The CPI(M) in West Bengal" in Zoya Hasan (Ed.), *Parties and Party Politics in India*, New Delhi: Oxford University Press, 2002, pp. 317–350; Valerian Rodrigues in Peter Ronald de Souza and Sridharan, *op. cit.*

37. Harihar Bhattacharya, "Communist Party of India (Marxist): From Rebellion to Governance in Subrata K. Mitra (Ed.), *op. cit.*, p. 88.

38. Sanjaya Baru, "Economic Policy and the Development of Capitalism in India: The Role of Regional Capitalists and Political Parties" in Francine Frankel *et. al.* (Eds.), *Transforming India: Social and Political Dynamics of Democracy*, New Delhi, Oxford University Press, 2000, pp. 207–230.

39. *Ibid.*, p. 226.

40. The term is attributed to Deen Dayal Upadhyaya, a former President of Bharatiya Jan Sangh, who discourse on this theme is published as a booklet by the BJP office, New Delhi.

41. Rajni Kothari, "The Call of the Eighties", *Seminar,* No. **25**, January 1980.

42. Kanchan Chandra, *Why Ethnic Parties Succeed?: Patronages and Ethnic Head Counts in India,* Cambridge University Press, Cambridge, 2004.

43. Javeed Alam, "Communist Politics in Search of Hegemony" in Zoya Hasan (Ed.), *Parties and Party Politics in India*, New Delhi: Oxford University Press, 2002, pp. 314–315.

44. Suhas Palshikar, "The Regional Parties and Democracy: Romantic Rendezvous or Localized Legitimation?" in Ajay K. Mehra, D.D. Khanna, and Gert W. Kueck (Eds.), *Political Parties and Party Systems,* New Delhi, Sage, 2003.

45. Lawrence Saez, *Federalism Without A Centre: The Impact of Political and Economic Reform on India's Federal System,* Sage, New Delhi, 2002, p. 58.

46. Rajni Kothari, "The Congress 'System' in India", *Asian Survey*, Vol. 4, No. **12**, December 1964; his *Politics in India*, New Delhi, Orient Longman, 1970; and his "The Congress 'System' in India Revisited", *Asian Survey*, Vol. 4, No. **12**, December 1974.

47. Yogendra Yadav and Suhas Palshikar, "Party System and Electoral Politics in Indian States, 1952–2002: From Hegemony to Convergence" in Peter Ronald de Souza and E. Sridharan (Eds.), *India's Political Parties*, New Delhi, Sage Publications, 2006, pp. 79–81.

48. *Ibid.*, p. 81.

49. Christophe Jaffrelot, "Caste and the Rise of the Marginalized Groups" in Sumit Ganguly, Lary Diamond, and Marc F. Plattner (Eds.), *The State of India's Democracy*, Baltimore: The Johns Hopkins University Press, 2007, p. 81.

50. *Ibid.*, p. 82.

51. Yogendra Yadav and Suhas Palshikar, *op. cit*, pp. 83–85.

52. For a recent study of the party system change in Tamil Nadu, see Andrew Wyatt, *Party System Change in South India: Political Entrepreneurs, patterns and processes*, London: Routledge, 2010.

53. M.V. Rajeev Gowda and E. Sridharan, "Parties and the Party System, 1947–2006" in Sumit Ganguly, Larry Diamond and Marc Plattner, *op. cit.*, pp. 19–22.

54. *Ibid.*, pp. 21–22.

55. Common Cause, *In the Supreme Court of India, Civil Extra-Ordinary Jurisdiction, Writ Petition No. 24 of 1995,* p. 12, H.D. Shourie, Director, Common Cause.

56. *Ibid.*, p. 13.

57. *Ibid.*

58. *Common Cause (A registered society)* v. *Union of India and others*, Supreme Court, 1996.

59. Government of India, *Vohra Committee Report*, Ministry of Home Affairs (Chair N.N. Vohra, Home Secretary), p. 1.

60. *Ibid.*

61. *P.V. Narasimha Rao* v. *the State (CPI/SPE),* (JMM Bribery case), Supreme Court, 1998.

62. E. Sridharan, "*Parties, the Party System and Collective Action for State Funding of Elections: A Comparative Perspective on Possible Options*" in Peter Ronald de Souza and E. Sridharan, *op. cit.*, p. 320.

63. Kanchan Chandra, (Ed.), *Democratic Dynasties: State, Party, and Family in Contemporary Indian Politics,* Cambridge University Press, 2016.

64. Douglas V. Verney, "From Quasi-Federation to Quasi-Confederacy? The Transformation of India's Party System", *Publius: The Journal of Federalism*, Vol. 33, No. 4, Fall 2003, p. 157.

65. Ascertained from the Election Commission of India by Professor Douglas V. Verney, New Delhi, Spring 2005.

66. Election Commission of India, *Electoral Reforms (Views and Proposals)*, New Delhi, Nirvachan Sadan, n.d. but apparently 1998, p. 7.

67. *Ibid.*, pp. 24–25.

68. *NCRWC Report*, 2002, para 4.30.1 to 4.30.6.

69. M.P. Singh, 'Electoral Politics and Phases of Politicization in India', *Trends in Social Science Research*, Vol. 3, No. 2, December 1996 and "The Party Factor in 'Dirty' Economy", *Denouement*, Special No. on Democracy, Development and 'Dirty' Economy: A Retrospect of India's Fifty Years of Independence, April 1998. Rekha Saxena, "Need for Reforms", *The Pioneer,* New Delhi, 18 September 1998; and her "Political Reforms", *The Pioneer,* New Delhi, 28 October 1998.

70. Government of Canada, *Royal Commission on Electoral Reform and Party Financing, Report,* 4 Vols., Minister of Supply and Services, Ottawa, Canada, 1991–1993.

71. *Ibid.*, 1991.

72. *Ibid.*

73. *Ibid.*

Chapter 13

Civil Society
Going through the Process of 'Civilianization'?

INTRODUCTION

The terms 'society' and 'civil society', commonly used interchangeably, have acquired some degree of conceptual differentiation.[1] While this is analytically useful, it is often unhelpful in comprehensive empirical analysis of entangled and enmeshed realities of life in politics and history. This is especially so in making sense of politics in a diverse and complex country like India. In the emerging conceptual conventions in social sciences, civil society is often conceived as activities, but mostly as associations, that: (a) interconnect individuals and families; (b) straddle the family, on the one hand, and the State, on the other; (c) are autonomous from the State; (d) are organized in associations that cater to cultural, social, economic and political needs of members; and (e) are modern and voluntaristic rather than ascriptive and traditional[2]. Few organizations in the real world meet all the stipulated definitional traits above; most often they are missed, if not formally, at least informally. Some are missed even formally, e.g. a group or party open to only coreligionists and operating in modern arenas of politics. Such organizations are deficient in point (e) listed above.

The idea of civil society in early modern Western political thought in the nineteenth century in both Hegel and Marx arose in the context of the transition of the feudal society into the bourgeois or civil society. Whereas feudalism had kept individuals enclosed within rigid and localized enclaves of corporatist estates, like nobility, clergy, and commons, capitalism destroyed the medieval structures and made the individual freer and mobile. Yet, this new-found individualism was abstract and empty. Hegel was later to hand over his individual to the State, and Marx, to the class, especially the proletariat or the industrial working class, out of which they had no independent or separate existence and meaning. When Weber turned his analytical focus on the new transition, he highlighted the emergent structures of neo-corporatist capitalism (as distinguished from feudal corporate classes) and bureaucracy (modern legal-rational one rather than the feudal patrimonial one of the pre-modern past). The strand of liberal democracy—democracy premised on universalist majoritarianism and liberalism on individual and minority rights and Rule of Law—took its inspiration from Rousseau and Locke, respectively, who conceptualized the 'civil society' or civil Government, as distinguished from natural society or the State of Nature, in their notions of foundational political contracts or constitutional engineering.

One finds a more composite and suitably complex understanding of the state and the civil society and their enmeshed relationships in Gramsci, who observes that though the narrow construction of the term 'state' is often synonymous with government, in its wider extension, the state is inclusive of elements of civil society. Gramsci and Althusser in their neo-Marxist vein argue that the hegemony of the state is organized in civil society persuasively, but the hegemony of the dominant class is fortified by the coercive rather than ideological state apparatus. This formulation makes the democratic or constitutional dimension of the state relatively more ethical than the developmental dimension of capitalism in a bourgeois democracy.

The recent resurgence of interest in civil society emanates from five interrelated contexts: (a) the collapse of statist communism in the Soviet Union and Eastern Europe and China's move to opt for what it calls "market socialism"; (b) the abandonment of political liberalism of welfare State in favour of business liberalism in the advanced capitalist democracies of the West; (c) the breakdown of the family, individual atomization, and the decline of the communitarian ethos in the West; (d) disenchantment with the distortions in the democratic state and disillusionment with the state in India, especially since the 1970s; and (e) rampant authoritarianism and corruption in other Third World societies in the period since World War II.

The renewed scholarly and policy interest in civil society still lacks theoretical elaboration and strategic policy integration. Yet, the growing importance of civil society in political analysis and policy paradigm is evident in the emphasis on voluntary associations, nongovernmental organizations (NGOs), new social movements, and the supplemental crucial role of social and cultural capital in economic and political development.

CONCEPTUAL OMNIBUS OF CIVIL SOCIETY

In political theory, the term, civil society was first used as a general term, meaning political society or state (e.g. in John Locke), but in its more contemporary usage it connotes social and economic institutions as distinguished from the state. Some writers stipulate that the civil society is based on secondary associations and organizations formed volitionally as distinguished from the primordial groups or communities based on birth. However, others reject this dichotomy as rather artificial and lacking in theoretical fruitfulness and empirical validity. Yet others define civil society as the non-state sphere of our collective life.

It is a measure of the early overwhelming legitimacy of the democratic State in India and its strategy of social transformation and economic development that its successes as well as failures are often contradictorily attributed to a same source—the nature of the civil society. The triumph of the movement of national liberation from colonial rule is justly said to be a function of the vigour and vitality of the civil society in its encounter with the alien domination. India's post-Independence reconstruction and political stability are also credited to its relatively developed civil society, mass media, and pressure group and party systems. However, after the initial democratic and developmental thrusts began to falter, analysts began to point accusing fingers to weak state of health of the civil society and its undemocratic and inegalitarian temperament. Since the 1970s, the valorization of the State in Indian political science literature has been gradually giving way to the imperative of building the civil society, as a bulwark against authoritarian tendencies in the State, corruption and criminalization of politics. And attention and emphasis have gradually shifted to economic development under the auspices of the private sector, earlier stunted by the dominant public sector and bureaucratically regulated mechanism of the State.

The putative civil society invoked above is obviously conceptually slippery and imprecise. This problem is aptly but briefly grappled with by Partha Chatterjee[3] by a suggestive distinction between the associative civil society and the "demographic or population society". Chatterji suggests that it was the latter which became the target of policy and political action by both the colonial state and the nationalist elites in turn as subjects and citizens. However, it is the former meaning of the civil society that has some explanatory import.

The competitive mobilization of the population mentioned above was done by the colonial state administration as well as by nationalist politics. The state was demographically enumerating the population by census and reaching out to it for resource extraction and administration wherever and however the people were. The colonial state and nationalists were largely limited to urban centers. But both had strong motivations for expansive penetration into the peripheries. The colonial and national logics left little choice to the colonialists and nationalists to choose between the modern and the traditional. "Nationalist politics", writes Chatterjee, "had to find an adequate strategic response if it were not to remain immobilized within the confines of `properly constituted' civil society of the urban elites."[4] As it happened, this led to the dilemma of choosing between civic nationalism and cultural nationalism. A correct choice could have averted the disastrous partition of India in 1947 on the eve of British withdrawal. The dilemma is not yet over. Hence, the legacies of forms of political relations in India were "very different from the well-structured, principled and constitutionally sanctioned relations between the state and individual members of civil society."[5]

Exploring and probing into ways of mediations between the civil society and the state, Chatterjee formulates a notion of political society that emerges through this interface or interaction. He says that civil society denotes those characteristic institutions of modern associational life originating in Western societies which are based on ideas of equality and liberty, contract, deliberative discourses and decision-making. But, in a country like India, such a notion of civil society is part of the experience of only a small section of its citizens. The major instrumental forms here are the mediations of a developmental state which seeks to relate to different sections of the population through governmental functions of welfare policies and governance. This major mobilization takes place in the domain of what may be called political society whose indicators generally are political parties and movements, etc. which channel and order the popular or the developmental state we generally call democracy. However, the formal institutional forms of this emergent political society are still largely unclear (Partha chatterjee, *Lineages of Political Society: Studies in Postcolonial Democracy*, Columbia University Press, New York, 2011).

Chatterjee suggestively puts forward the following three "theses" for further probing in this regard:

1. The most significant site of transformation in the colonial period is that of civil society; the most significant transformations occurring in the post-colonial period are in political society.
2. The question that frames the debate over social transformation in the colonial period is that of modernity. In political society of the post-colonial period, the framing question is that of democracy.
3. In the context of the latest phase of the globalization of capital, we may well be witnessing an emerging opposition between modernity and democracy, i.e. between civil society and political society."[6]

Even though intuitively understandable, the three theses above are suitably vague and tendentious. For, while the post-colonial period has certainly seen a great expansion of electoral democracy in the political society, it smacks of an Orientalist bias to assert that colonialism in India saw a greater flowering or even beginning of civil society and modernity. Colonial modernity and a corresponding civil society made their beginnings in the British Raj all right but so also began the vicious communalization due to colonial policy of divide and rule; and both civil society and modernity have made tremendous headway after Independence, impediments and distortions notwithstanding. Similarly, the central conflicts of globalization may well be between nationalism, globalism, and regionalism and between labour and capital rather than those between modernity and democracy or between civil society and political society.

Indeed, the sharp contrasts between 'civil society' and 'political society' and between 'modernity' and 'democracy' are academic in the sense that they lack precise empirical import. Most recent and prolific discussions on the civil society in India today are unduly influenced by Western, especially Gramscian, notions of civil society as an arena of contestation between class forces struggling for political hegemony outside the State, to begin with (e.g. Neera Chandhoke, 1996).[7] This is questionable in the Indian context where both during the freedom struggle and post-Independence periods contestations in electoral and mass movement spheres are fought between complex array of social and political forces based on multiple and overlapping identities and interests grounded on caste, class, tribe, religion, language, and region. There are no basic or fundamental bipolarities of classes or groups here typical of industrial or preindustrial Europe. More perceptive Indian as well as foreign observers of civil society in India, therefore, employ a suitably complex and open-ended approach to the problem. Rajni Kothari and Andre Beteille, for example, have both cognized the democratic potentiality of caste and other such supposedly pre-modern groups, without obliterating the distinction between more inclusive civic groups and ethnic groups, and between caste and class (in Lipsettian, if not in Marxist terms).[8] Kothari's notion of civil society is left vaguely omnibus, while Beteille links civil society with citizenship (ironically a reversal of roles between India's leading political scientist and sociologist!). Yet, at the end of the day, both lean on a communitarian rather than liberal individual perspective of rights, Kothari more than Beteille. Civil society is seen as a bulwark against the unresponsive and authoritarian State.[9]

As a perceptive interpreter of the "modernity" of India's "tradition", the Rudolphs[10] were one of earliest foreign observers of Indian politics to explain the democratic incarnation of caste as a political, as distinguished from a sociological factor. In a more recent piece, they offer a deeply insightful analysis of the metaphors of the "coffee house" and the Gandhian "ashram" as powerful instruments of the civil society in the newly emergent public sphere in India. Both created more inclusive, ideally universal, spaces in a society traditionally marked by hierarchy, segmentation and segregation, and other-worldly orientations.[11] A day before his assassination in 1948, it is well known that Mahatma Gandhi gave a call for the dissolution of the Indian National Congress, an instrument of mass politics nurtured by himself, on the plea that, with Independence attained, it should be transformed into a Lok Sevak Sangh. The Rudolphs interpret this apparently baffling advice (which the Congress elites ignored) in the following terms:

> Parties are amphibious creatures in the associational arena. Opposition parties resemble civil society in that they stand in tension with the Government of the day. At the same time, in the role of the 'shadow Cabinet' and as officially recognized participants in the parliamentary arena, they exhibit an identification with the State. As governing parties, they appropriate and run the State. As a man of civil society, Gandhi targeted the statist face of party.[12]

Gandhi, thus, could not, perhaps did not like to, write off the mass movement as an instrument of civil society, even though it was obviously a double-edged sword that could be exploited by socially authoritarian and statist forces alike. That is where the idea of morally trained *satyagrahis* and the Gandhian ashram as a public sphere of ethically propelled political action comes in—as training academy for non-violent cadres and as exemplar of imagined society. The Rudolphs then elaborate on the coffee house as "the public sphere of literate, educated, middle class political persons". The ashram, on the other hand, "sought to draw uneducated urban and rural, working and farming people into a public sphere in the context of mass politics."[13]

In fact, India shares a semi-revolutionary populist streak in its political culture with democracies founded on the basis of wars or bourgeois revolutions, e.g. the USA in 1777, France in 1789, and Switzerland in 1848, in contrast to those having a more or less gradual or evolutionary transition to bourgeois democracy as in the UK, Canada, and Australia. For, even though the transfer of power from the British to Indian hands in 1947 was *legal*, by means of the Independence of India Act, 1947, passed by the British Parliament, this came at the head of a long and widespread mass movement of national liberation, most commonly referred to as the "freedom struggle" by Indians.[14] There was admittedly a bureaucratic and partly representative institutional arena in British India in which the Indian National Congress also operated, but the dominant component of the emergent composite Indian nationalism was more of a mass movement in which extra-legal methods of agitation and direct action were the norm. In his concluding address to the Constituent Assembly, the chairman of its drafting committee, Dr. B.R. Ambedkar, sagely mused and exhorted that the adoption of the Constitution by the Indian nation-state entailed the abandonment of "the bloody method of revolution", of "the method of civil disobedience, non-cooperation and satyagraha". But he hastened to add that (a) Constitutional politics also meant taking to heart John Stuart Mill's caution not "to lay [our] liberties at the feet of even a great man, or to trust him with powers which enable him to subvert [our] institutions", and that (b) "We must make our political democracy a social democracy as well."[15]

And, the Gandhian ideological heritage of satyagraha has continued along with Ambedkar's constitutionalism in pursuit of public and sectional interests against authoritarianism, corruption, and dysfunctionalities of developmentalism causing havoc to society and nature. The examples in this context are the JP Movement, the Narmada Bachao Andolan and Chipko Movement, and the Anna Hazare India Against Corruption Movement, etc.

The populist mass movement strand of Indian political culture registered a second, post-Independence, statement in the Gujarat and Bihar Movements that converged into the wider J.P. Movement (so called after the socialist-turned Gandhian Jayaprakash Narayan) during the 1970s. During the movement, that developed outside the space of the party system and included non-party as well as opposition parties elements, J.P. propounded the doctrine of recall of elected representatives/legislators on mass demand. The Janata Party that was swept to power on the crest of this movement in the post-Emergency Lok Sabha elections of 1977 dismantled the authoritarian 42nd Constitutional Amendment of 1976 put in place by the Emergency regime by the 44th Amendment of 1978, but it did not constitute recall. However, the preamble to the latter amendment provided that "certain changes in the Constitution which would have the effect of impairing its secular or democratic character, abridging or taking away fundamental rights, prejudging or impeding free and fair elections on the basis of adult suffrage and compromising the independence of judiciary, can be made only if they are approved by the people of India by a majority of votes at a referendum in which at least fifty-one per cent of the electorate participate."[16] It may also be added here that in Indian constitutional law, the historic constitutional mandate of the time of the founding of the Indian republic in the trail of the deliberative democratic discourse in the Constituent Assembly is judicially determined to be of greater validity than a transient electoral mandate.[17]

The non-civil or modern authoritarian slippage of mass movements is illustrated by Hindu revivalism since the 1990s. Mark Robinson regards it as "[a]rguably the most important arena of ideological contestation in the public realm in India today [which] concerns the vigorous assertion of Hindutva ideology, centered on the promotion of pan-Hindu identity and nationhood."[18] Robinson's conceptualization of this problem stems from the assumption that (a) the contrast between a *modern* civil society and a *mixed* (traditional/ modern) political society should not be drawn too sharply, and (b) critical referents of political/electoral mobilization like religion and ethnicity should be not dismissed as primordial and thus outside the realm of modern civil society."[19] However, this significant avenue of theorization is not adequately explored by Robinson, and he is mired in superficial stereotypes and polemical characterizations. The alleged quest for Hindu nationhood by the capture of State power misses the point that the politics of Hindu assertion is *symbolic* rather than *substantive*, as the *strategic* political leadership of the Rashtriya Swyamsevak Sangh parivar, especially its political or parliamentary wing, the Bharatiya Janata Party, does not have either a well developed ideological blueprint or a strategy for subversion of the constitutional regime founded on the civic republican nationalism of the federal Indian nation-State. Their target of opposition is what they call "minorityism" or "pseudo-secularism" of the Congress brand practised during their long political predominance. The BJPites reiterate their commitment to what they call "positive secularism."[20] And Atal Bihari Vajpayee as the Prime Minister had gone on record that for him, Bharatiyata and Hindutva meant one and the same thing. It was a valiant attempt by the liberal face of BJP and Sangh Parivar to reconcile Indian constitutional nationalism and Savarkar's *Hindutva* (1923), which stipulates that, irrespective of religious affiliations among the people in India, all are Hindus if they regard the land between the Himalayas and the Oceans as their fatherland (*pitribhumi*) and holy land (*punyabhumi*); Savarkar nowhere says that sacred places of Hindus, Sikhs, Muslims, Christians, Jews, outside the territory of India are not to be identified with. By this stipulation, Savarkar, in his demographic and democratic sweep, redefines *Hindutva* from a narrow ethnicity and expands it into nationalism. Contrast this all-inclusive construction of Hindutva nationalism with the narrow construction of Islamic identity in Pakistan whereby even Ahmadias, Khojas, Bohras, etc. are declared Un-Islamic!

Incidentally, the word sangh in the compound "Sangh parivar" literally means the "federal family." The two stints of the Sangh parivar in federal power in New Delhi in the late 1970s and 1998–2004 were both de facto or de jure coalition governments. They have come to power in States alone as well in coalitions and have regularly and frequently gone through electoral turnover. But this has happened at subnational level under federal tutelage. All these experiences have, if anything, made the Hindutva forces relatively more liberal, moderate, and realistically aware of the problem of governing a complex multi-cultural nation like India. This state-level experience in power has now been replicated for long enough during the National Democratic Alliance governments earlier led by Atal Bihari Vajpayee and now Narendra Modi.

In his Dussehra Address from the RSS headquarters in Nagpur in 2019, when Narendra Modi government has been in power into its second term (2014–2019 and 2019–2024) with a de facto single-party BJP majority (even though at the head of a de jure BJP-led National Democratic Alliance government), 'the RSS Sarsanghchalak Mohan Bhagwat' has clearly echoed the same notion of *Hindutva* nationalism as what Vajpayee has expressed above (Shekhar Gupta, "Cut the Clutter: Reading Between the Lines...", The Print, YouTube. Accessed 10.10.2019).

Frequent communal riots and caste and tribal conflicts are indicators of weakness or breakdown of the civil society. The primary as well as ultimate rationale for the State is its duty to protect the life, liberty, and property of its citizens from internal disorder or external aggression. Political liberalism also enjoins on the State the responsibility for social securities and creating conditions for the realization of the potentialities individuals and groups are capable of. However, no State can succeed in these onerous tasks without an active cooperation of the civil society. In a comparative study of religious-communal conflicts in Aligarh and Calicut, Hyderabad and Lucknow, and the role of the civil society and the State in containing them, Ashutosh Varshney finds convincing evidence for his hypothesis that exogenous shocks, tensions, and rumours lead to serious ethnic violence in cities where civic engagement is largely limited to intra-ethnic relations, whereas in cities in which inter-ethnic civic engagements exist, ethnic peace is more easily maintained or restored. Varshney sums up:

> [T]he civic lives of the two cities are worlds apart. So many Muslims and Hindus are interlocked in associational and neighbourhood relationships in Calicut that peace committees during periods of tension are simply an extension of the pre-existing local networks of engagement. A considerable reservoir of social trust is formed out of the associational and everyday interactions between Muslims and

> Hindus. Routine familiarity facilitates communication between the two communities; rumours are squelched through better communication; and all this helps the local administration keep peace. In Aligarh, however, the average Hindu and Muslim do not meet in those civic settings—economic, social, educational—where mutual trust can be forged. Lacking the support of such networks, even competent police and civil administrators look on helplessly as riots unfold.[21]

Varshney reports "similar processes" from the other pair of cities.

Closely related to the idea of civil society is the idea of "social capital",[22] a new incarnation of the concept of political culture, or, more specifically, "civic culture", or "participant" political culture (as distinguished from "subject" and "parochial" political culture)[23]. Social capital is operationally defined in terms of formal and informal connectivity among individuals and groups in a society that are supportive of or conducive to democracy. In a study of social capital and degrees of democracy in five States in India, Blomkvist finds that measured in terms of (a) formal and (b) informal networks of voluntary associations, and (c) norms of interpersonal trust among the people, Kerala and Gujarat are high in social capital, whereas West Bengal, Orissa, and Uttar Pradesh are low. His measures of Government responsiveness as subjectively perceived by the people and government policy performance (indicated by objective data about income, life expectancy, vaccination, medical facilities, rural water and electricity) showed Kerala, Gujarat, and West Bengal considerably ahead of Orissa and UP.[24]

SOCIAL MOVEMENTS

A political or social movement (often used interchangeably but sometimes distinguished on the basis that political movements strive for state power, whereas social movements seek greater autonomy from state power) may be defined as a form of collective action to bring about change. According to John Wilkinson[25], "A social movement's commitment to change and the *raison d'etre* of its organization are founded upon the conscious volition, normative commitment to the movements' aims or beliefs, and active participation on the part of the followers or members" (emphasis in the source). It is these elements of popular will and commitment that contribute to the embodiment of ideology and organization in social movements.

In the recent literature on social movements a distinction is often made between new and old movements. This distinction is stipulated on the ground that whereas old political movements were generally class-based and concerned with the issues of economic redistribution and state power in industrial societies, new social movements are commonly a feature of post-industrial or "postmodern" societies, they are not narrowly class-based, and they generally raise limited post-material issues of quality of life in terms of newer questions like ecological protection and climate change or hitherto neglected issues of gender, justice, sexuality, identities, etc. But this distinction is neither precise nor universally valid nor free from a historicist fallacy. Consider, for example, the following observation of Andre Gunder Frank and Marta Fuentes[26]:

> Ironically, the 'classical' working class/union movements date mostly only from the last century, and they increasingly appear to be only a passing phenomenon related to the development of industrial capitalism. On the other hand, peasant, localist community, ethnic/nationalist, religious, and even feminist/women's movements have existed for centuries and even millennia in many parts of the world. Yet many of these movements are now commonly new, although European history records countless social movements throughout history.[27]

Frank and Fuentes concede, though, that only the ecological or green movements and the peace movements may be treated as truly new social movements as they are in response to social needs engendered by contemporary world developments.[28]

In the more recent literature on social movements, writers like David Meyer and Sidney Tarrow[29] suggest that many democratic countries are going through the process of gradual institutionalization of social movement politics which heralds the advent of a "social movement society". This development is caused by the fact that protest movements are becoming a regular feature of democratic politics, many diverse constituencies employ them more frequently than ever with ever-widening claims, and such movements are becoming professionalized and institutionalized and part of the conventional politics.

Mary Fainsod, Katzenstein, Smitu Kothari and Uday Singh Mehta[30], argue that this concept of social movement society is empirically relevant to India and that it has strengthened democracy in the country.

To quote them:

> ...it is precisely through the range and dense welter of such movements and organizations that democratic institutions (such as the courts and the bureaucracy) have been able to fine-tune their responses to the fluidity and diversity of India. It is not that these institutions can be (despite their rhetoric) a substitute for the state, but absent the pressures they bring to bear and the issues that they raise at the state and local levels, it is clear that the democratic institutions would not be able, in however inadequate a manner, to meet the challenge of India's diversity and shifting conditions.[31]

PEASANTS/FARMERS' MOVEMENTS AND DALIT MOVEMENTS

Peasants and farmers' movements in India have naturally and structurally been greatly influenced by ethnic identities and class formation in the modern times.

Inevitably, modern class formation in a country of India's size and diversity is marked by sharp regional variations and pre-capitalist residues. The classes of capitalists, middle class professionals, and industrial workers have been more prone to form national federations than the farmers, peasants and agricultural workers. But all these class organizations have been marked by factionalism along regional and party lines. In the event, primordial or ethnic identities bedevil class interests and organizations. The result has been that it was not only the anti-colonial nationalist mobilization and post-colonial "socialistic" reconstruction that the class factor was muted in Indian politics. This pattern continues even in the more recent phase of Indian politics. But the reason this time has less to do with the pull of nationalism and Nehruvian socialism and more with increased regionalization and rise of identity politics with an accent on caste and community and tribe.

On the eve of Independence, the rural society in India was broadly stratified into landowners (*zamindars* and *khudkastkars*), peasants (tenants and sharecroppers) and landless agricultural workers (*khetihar mazdoors*). The major change of the post-Independence period was the rise, by the mid-1960s, of a prosperous peasantry predominantly comprising the "Other Backward Classes/Castes", so called to distinguish them from the Scheduled Castes/Scheduled Tribes (SCs/STs). Economically, they happened to be the major beneficiaries of the land reforms legislations (abolition of zamindari, land ceiling and consolidation of landholdings) and the techno-economic agricultural modernization called the Green Revolution. Their rise to political and economic power gave a fillip to the new reservation policies based on the implementation of the Mungerilal Commission in Bihar in the late 1970s and of the Central Government's Mandal Commission Report in the early 1990s for the OBCs. Such policies favouring the intermediate classes/castes had already been implemented in the South Indian States in the late 1950s/1960s or even earlier.

Peasant politics has found expression in party politics as well as social movements based on the peasantry. Practically all these movements have been led by resourceful but not fabulously rich peasant proprietors dubbed as "bullock capitalists" by the Rudolphs.[32] These peasants were a poorer lot during the Kisan Sabha movements of the pre-Independence period who economically and politically made it good after post 1947 land reforms. Probably even the *Tebhaga* movement of 1946–47 Bengal and Telangana movement of 1946–51 can also be so characterized. Andhra Pradesh did not widely diverge from the above mentioned pattern of peasant leadership.[33] These movements were based on the land-to-the real tiller programme and reforms. However, these movements left the landless agricultural workers out of their fold.

In course of time, the prospering peasants graduated to the status of a new agrarian class, which may be called farmers. Farmer's movements appeared on the Indian agrarian scene partly by the 1970s and mainly by the 1980s. A survey of research on the new phenomenon of farmers' movements observes:

> The movement developed in regions that were largely benefited by the Green Revolution and commercialization of agriculture. Shetkari Sangathana of Maharashtra, Bharatiya Kisan Union of Punjab-Haryana and Uttar Pradesh, its associate Tamil Nadu Vivasyal Sangam, and Karnataka Rajya Ryot Sangha were some of the leading organizations of the farmers' movements.[34]

These movements agitated for agricultural subsidies, State-supported remunerative prices, lower tax/electricity/and water rates, and loans and debt reliefs. The movement also highlighted adverse terms of trade between the urban-industrial and rural sectors and the contradictions between "India" and "Bharat". By these stereotypes, the movement tried to forge a unity of the rural sector, concealing its internal divisions and inequities, vis-à-vis the urban sector.

In 2020, the Modi government enacted three agrarian sector reforms– Farmers' Produce Trade and Commerce (Promotion and Facilitation) Act, Farmers (Empowerment and Protection) Act, Agreement of Price Assurance and Farm Services Act, and Essential Commodities (Amendment) Act. The Modi government claims that these reforms will accelerate growth in the sector through private sector investment in building infrastructure and supply chains for farm produce in national and international markets; allow farmers to sell their produce outside APMC 'mandis' to whoever they want in a more competitive market getting them better prices and cutting cost on transportation; contract farming allows farmers to enter into a contract with agri-business firms or large retailers on pre-agreed prices of their produce; these reforms also remove commodities like cereals, pulses, oilseeds, edible oils, onions and potatoes from the list of essential commodities ending stock-holding limits. Liberal agricultural economists call it the '1991 moment' in agrarian sector. However, farmers' pressure groups and parties in Punjab and Haryana, and Congress state governments are strongly opposing these reforms as favouring the corporate business sector and being anti-farmer.

These trends could not, however, paper over the increasing hiatus between the landowners and the landless, and the OBCs and Harijans/Dalits. This was reflected in the endemic atrocities and violence against Dalits in the countryside from the 1970s to the 1990s, particularly in the North India. This was also expressed in the growing distance between the political parties dominated by OBCs and those by Dalits. Dalit parties like Lok Janshakti Party in Bihar and Bahujan Samaj Party in U.P. are now increasingly also targeting at upper caste, especially Brahman, voters by recruiting party candidates, legislators, and Ministers from the so-called upper castes. The Jotiba Phule and Ambedkar legacies of Dalit organizations and movements also incline them to values of sanskritization and constitutionalism, respectively.

Two patterns of Dalit politics have of late emerged. There are, first, the predominantly politics-driven dalit movements and parties typical of the Hindi-speaking States that are led by the "SC reservation aristocracy" and followed by the Dalit masses in rural and urban areas. Then, there are, secondly, the culturally-cushioned Dalit movements more characteristic of Maharashtra (legacies of Phule and Ambedkar and writers of Dalit *Sahitya*) and Punjab (legacies of Ad Dharam and Arya Samaj and Sikh gurus). The two patterns are now also merging to an extent. The Dalit movements appear to have a greater anti-caste temperament than those of the OBCs. We must hasten to add, however, that no social or political movement in India today can afford to primarily base itself on sectarian ethnic identities. This is due to the compulsions of coalition politics and formation and maintenance of coalition/minority governments.

NAXALITE MOVEMENTS

With political parties, including the two major communist parties—CPI-M and CPI—professing commitment to parliamentary communism and legitimate electoral politics, the Naxalite movements—so called after the Naxalbari area in North Bengal where they first surfaced in the late 1960s—became the notable extra-legal radical class organizations committed to violent class killings in rural areas. They carried forward the demand of redistribution of land and forcible seizure of land even when the communist-State Governments tacitly accepted the fact that any more redistributive land reforms were not possible either because any further fragmentation of landholdings by legislation would be unviable for the political economy of cultivation, or because the relatively rich peasants had captured the party machines, or because of both these reasons. By the 1980s, even the Left Front Government in West Bengal shelved redistributive legislations and concentrated on only *Operation Barga*—registration of *bargadars* (share-croppers)—to prevent their eviction by *jotedars* (cultivators).

The Naxalite movement was more or less contained in West Bengal by the 1980s where it had first made its appearance in the late 1960s. State repression and co-option have forced the movement to adapt to electoral politics more successfully and durably in communist-ruled West Bengal (since 1977 without any break), and in Kerala and Tripura, where communist parties enjoy good competitive edge in elections and governance than elsewhere in India. In Bihar where some Naxalite organizations joined the electoral and legislative politics in and after 1989 through the Indian People's Front winning some seats in Vidhan Sabha and Lok Sabha, this experiment was short-lived. But by the 1990s/2000s the trend was intermittently revived and and in the Assembly elections of 2020 the CPI(ML) performed notably well in Bihar as a part of the RJD/Congress-led Mahagathabandhan forged against the ascendant JD(U)/BJP-led NDA.

The ultra-left divide from the legitimate and established left parties that has more or less continued since 1967–69 has worked through a rather large number of fluid groups. Thirty-odd organizations are reportedly in existence, the more well-known among them being various organizations calling themselves CPI-Marxist or Leninist or Maoist, Marxist Communist Center, and People's War Group. They are now mainly active in the hinterland tribal belt stretching from Indo-Nepal border down to Deccan spanning the States of Jharkhand, Orissa, West Bengal, Madhya Pradesh, Chhattisgarh, and Andhra Pradesh. Parts of Bihar are also affected by these activities, but there the movement has faced reaction from caste-based militias of landholders. This has engendered gangs of criminals from all castes and communities indulging in murders, massacres, and kidnapping for ransom. Radical class and criminal violence is attributable to inequities resulting from scramble for control over land and forest and habitats due to lack of economic development, weak law enforcement, corruption, industrialization and construction of big dams and the resultant displacement of peasants and tribals. There is an inextricable caste-class nexus in the phenomenon of private "caste armies" or militias. A study that leans heavily on caste interpretation remarks: "Caste senas reveal the dynamics of caste as one of the `master narratives' in structuring the engagements between State and society in Bihar. This also shows that construction of an inclusive civil society is hugely painful, tortuous, bound by considerations of social justice and often marred by violent conflicts that are premised on historical perceptions of human communities."[35] Discounting class interpretation of the phenomenon offered by A.R. Desai, D.N. Dhanagare, Pradhan H. Prasad, Utsa Patnaik, and others, the study goes on to comment: "This [class] explanation appears as one-sided and partial at the best. Viewing landowning class as a monolith, this line of reasoning neither takes into account acute power struggles between upper castes and backward castes in the arena of State power nor considers the ideological resilience of caste in contemporary Bihar." However, it is added aptly that "these caste wars are hardly isolated from power struggles in the political and economic arena."[36]

Naxalite organizations have been largely successful in mobilizing dalit and tribal peasants and workers. Tribals in particular are more vulnerable to exploitation by and alienation from society as well as State and industry and contractors. Rajeshwari Deshpande aptly remarks:

> As the tribal society is assumed to be more homogeneous, confrontations in civil society can also be avoided in mobilizing the tribals. Exploitative relations are simplified as existing between tribals and non-tribals. Apart from providing appropriate locale for effective use of strategies of violence, tribal areas provide possibilities of fulfilling the revolutionary dream at a symbolic level. However, its engagement in tribal areas does not permit the movement to wade through the more complicated expressions of relations of exploitation in 'mainstream' civil society. Even among the tribals its success is limited.[37]

Naxalism or Maoism in India and Nepal are, nevertheless, more complex sociological and political phenomena than the foregoing suggests. Its internal and external linkages are deeper and wider as well as multi-faceted. To quote P.V. Ramanna of The Observer Research Foundation:

> In various States in India, the Naxalites have formed purely opportunistic linkages with political leaders belonging to various mainstream political parties. It is mutually beneficial partnership for the two, and is particularly visible at the grassroots level. The Naxalites help the political leaders during elections, as well as act as strongmen for the latter to intimidate or liquidate political rivals. On their part, the political leaders help the Naxalites by arranging the logistics, 'bailing out' arrested Naxalite sympathizers and even influencing Government policies towards the Naxalites. Moreover, even as political expedience is an important factor, the 'fear' of violent retribution from the Naxalites plays a significant role in 'persuading' some political leaders to enter into a 'partnership' with Naxalites.[38]

The annual report of the Ministry of Home Affairs, Government of India (2004–05) put the number of hardcore underground cadres at 9300, holding about 6500 manufactured weapons in addition to the country-made 'cuttas'[39]. In 2004, 1533 violent incidents and 566 deaths were reported in India as a whole, with greatest incidence of violence occurring in Jharkhand, Chhattisgarh, Bihar, and Andhra Pradesh.[40]

These violent attacks on class enemies in the countryside and on the agents and institutions of state continued unabated in the years that followed. Climactic escalation of violence against police and paramilitary forces in the late 2000s in Andhra Pradesh, Maharashtra, and Jharkhand was witnessed and subdued by the state police forces in the first two states mentioned above. The Left Front government in West Bengal and the BJP government in Chhattisgarh found itself with its back to the wall. The Left Front government in West Bengal and the BJP government in Chhattisgarh joined forces with the Congress-led United Progressive Alliance government in New Delhi and mounted the Operation Greenhunt to stem the tide. Simultaneously, the Union Government, in November 2010, is also formulated an action plan for equitable and just economic development in the affected areas, mostly in the mineral and forest rich central tribal belt. Besides an amendment in the mining laws giving a 26 per cent share to the local communities in the mining areas, an ambitious ₹ 13,000 crore Integrated Action Plan for 60 Naxal–affected districts in seven states was launched for governance reforms and devolution of powers to the grassroots for economic and social development over the next three fiscal years from March 2011.[41]

The foregoing narrative and trends have come under a serous challenge since the mid-200s, when the BJP led by Narendra Modi won a single-party majority in 2014 and then again in 2019 with a still greater majority after a gap of three decades since 1984, but the resurgent Hindutva nationalists still maintained the NDA coalition poised against the declining Congress-led UPA and the communist-led Left Front in electoral decimation in West Bengal and Tripura, though not in Kerala.

TRADE UNION MOVEMENTS

The rise of modern Indian working class is a product of decline of feudalism and rise of capitalism. Both these socio-economic transformations were closely connected with the establishment of the British colonial rule in India. Plantations, railway construction, coal field areas, and port cities like Calcutta, Mumbai, and Chennai became the main centers around which colonial as well as Indian bourgeois and working classes flocked. "Calcutta turned out to be the main area of British investment while Bombay developed as the principal center of Indian capital."[42]

The trade union movement during the anti-colonial nationalist movement was muted by the imperatives of putting together a nationalist platform under the leadership of the Indian National Congress and rudimentary working class consciousness. The nation and the community obviously counted for much more than the class. The post-Independence political ambience was more open to party/union and class, yet the compulsions of a backward economy and the ideology of national reconstruction still considerably muffled class consciousness and radicalism. The emergence of a "working class aristocracy" in the organized sector and lack of class consolidation and organizations in the unorganized sector also reinforced the same tendencies and trends.

By the early 1970s, when the dominant Congress Party faced a major split between the factions led by Indira Gandhi and the oldguard leadership, called Syndicate by the press, there were three major federations of trade unions in India: Congress-affiliated Indian National Trade Union Congress (INTUC), Communist-affiliated All India Trade Union Congress (AITUC), and Socialist-affiliated Hind Majdoor Sabha (HMS). More or less around the same time, a fourth federation came to be formed by the Communist Party of India (Marxist) following the split in the Communist Party of India: Center of Indian Trade Union (CITU). The INTUC was the largest trade union movement in the country followed by those led by Communists and Socialists. The Bharatiya Mazdoor Sangh (BMS) affiliated with the Bharatiya Janata Party was a fifth trade union federation then, which by the mid-1980s, superceded the INTUC and became the largest trade union movement and still retains the lead.[43] It may be added here that trade union movements are more effective in West Bengal and Kerala. It is also notable that some recent court rulings have gone against strikes by trade unions and employees' associations.

Since the late 1960s, there also appeared on the scene trade unions aligned with regional parties like DMK, AIADMK, and Shiv Sena. Thus, the trend of party domination of unions came to be replicated at the State or regional levels, particularly in Tamil Nadu and Maharashtra.

The decline of Congress dominance since the late 1970s also witnessed the emergence of independent trade unions without affiliation/domination with political parties. These unions were centered around prominent trade union leaders with Congress as well as leftist background. Datta Samanta, a former medical doctor and Congress legislator, formed a number of such unions in the Bombay–Pune industrial belt, e.g. Association of Engineering Workers, Mumbai General Kamgar Union, Maharashtra Girni Kamgar Union, among others.[44] Samanta also organized a long-drawn-out strike of Bombay textile mills workers in the early 1980s. Other examples of independent trade unions included contract workers in iron-ore mines of Dali Rajhara near Bhilai in Chhattisgarh organized by Shankar Guha Neogi, contract and casual coal-mine workers in the Dhanbad–Jharia belt in Jharkhand set up by A.K. Roy, and women workers in the unorganized sector led by Ela Bhat's Self-Employed Women's Association (SEWA) in Ahmedabad.[45]

The phenomena of independent trade unionism are a feature of two contradictory contexts. First, such unions emerged mostly in unorganized sector where the previously established party-affiliated unions were lukewarm or reluctant to cater to their needs. Second, in traditional industries such as textiles, jute mines, and plantations unions were/are based on industries, whereas in newer industrial sectors—like engineering, information technology and other services that attract more educated and skilled workers—unions are generally based on enterprises instead of industries in general. These newer sectors are also more likely sites for independent trade unionism.[46]

A major turning point in the trade union scene must be attributed to the neo-liberal structural reforms in the economy that gathered momentum by the early 1990s. As C.S. Venkataratnam observes:

> Structural adjustment policies are perceived to result in job losses in the short run whatever the long run consequences. Further, more importantly, job losses are seen to occur more in the East and Northeast while a larger proportion of new jobs may be created in the West, South and North. This may escalate social tensions. In the absence of social insurance and the unemployment benefits, there is widespread concern about the fallout of a thin organized sector employment becoming thinner. The Government has constituted a National Renewal Fund (NRF) with contributions through budget allocations, World Bank grant, allocations from public sector disinvestment proceeds. Though the avowed object of the NRF is to provide for retraining, redeployment and compensation for voluntary separations, but so far the fund has been used mainly to finance voluntary separation [retirement] schemes.[47]

All trade unions, regardless of party affiliations, have strongly opposed the neo-liberal economic reforms as anti-working class. In the last few years almost all unions, including those affiliated with ruling parties, have joined three nationwide *bandhs* in a rare display of class solidarity.[48] But this phenomenon is, by and large, limited to organized unionized sector. However, organized labour force in India accounts for less than 10 per cent of the working population, and the extent of unionization even in the organized sector stands for only 30 per cent of the workers.[49] Multiplicity of unions and manipulative recognition procedures and practices in the tripartite Government-employer-worker legal framework keep the working classes divided and weak. An objective study of the working classes and trade unions in the country would suggest that trade union reforms are as urgently called for as party system and electoral reforms if democracy in India is to survive.

Following labour law reforms by some BJP state governments consistent with the neoliberal economic reforms of 1991, the Modi government at the Centre (BJP-led NDA) capped them by three Central Labour Codes in 2020, dealing with wages, social security and occupational safety, and industrial relations as well as aimed at ensuring ease of business (e.g. allowing business houses to close companies without seeking government permission in enterprises employing 300 workers or less, raising this number from the previous limit of 100 workers or less). The move was opposed by all trade unions, including the largest Bharatiya Mazdoor Union affiliated with the RSS/BJP.

NEW SOCIAL MOVEMENTS

Enormous increase of middle classes and in students population as well as enlargement and differentiations in the elite strata in various sectors of life by the 1970s engendered a new phenomenon variously described as New social movements, middle class and students' activism, women's or feminist movements, and grassroots movements. This new phenomenon differs from the earlier patterns of socio-political movements in a number of ways. Issues that animate the new movements are less concerned with economic production and redistribution than with removal of corruption and authoritarianism, protection of ecology and environment, provision of civic utilities, gender equality and child rights, employment, rights of the most vulnerable and marginalized sections of population like those living in hilly and forested tracts and victims of big dams and construction workers in sites of dams and cities, etc. Good governance and human rights generally are other areas where middle class activism is also much in evidence.

Another feature of New social movements is that they have gradually disengaged from grand narratives of socialism, *Sampoorna Kranti* (*a la* Jayaprakash Narayan), and nationalism, and tended to move into groves of single issues, transient questions, regional and local issues, even sectional and sectarian issues slanted more towards narrow identities than larger objective interests. For this reason, they are often called "micro movements". Since these movements are catching on the long-felt needs of localities and masses at the disempowered grassroots in the top-heavy political and economic systems of India, they are often dubbed as "popular" movements.

The third feature of New social movements in various sectors of social and economic life is their growing proclivity for independence and autonomy from established political parties. This tendency has given rise to dissociation of the emergent civil society groups, organizations, and movements from the preexisting pattern of interest/pressure groups being "colonized" by political parties through affiliation, interlocking leadership, and domination. The earliest evidence for this new trend was evident as much in some new middle class organizations of intelligentsia and men of letters and arts as in some trade unions in Bombay textiles mills led by Datta Samanta and in Dhanbad and Chhattisgarh by A.K. Roy and Shanker Guha Niyogi, respectively. Samanta and Niyogi were incidentally murdered in mysterious circumstances. However, the tendency on the part of interest/pressure groups to nurse the desire for autonomy, often despite party affiliations, has not disappeared.

The fourth feature of New social movements is associated with the phenomenon of privatization of State-dominated economy and globalization. The post-modernist/post-structuralist inclination to give primacy to identities (often pseudo-identities) over interests and "deconstruction" of knowledge (verging on nihilism) has devalued foundationalism and grand narratives of social reconstruction and transformation in the socialist tradition.

Non-Governmental organizations and New social movements on the national as well as global planes have flourished as never before. New social movements can and often do take an oppositional posture against State and industry. However, NGOs, largely dependent on funds from the Government, industry and global national and international funding agencies, are often constrained in taking on oppositional or confrontational roles. Indeed, the nexus between NGOs and social movements often depoliticize the latter and weaken them by co-opting the activists as agents or managers. Nonetheless, the pluralities of groups and movements, and of sources of support in sociological as well as financial terms, do increase the maneuverability of movements and NGOs. And they do sometimes manage to play a creative, critical and constructive role. However, privatization and globalization step in where the State has failed due to distortions of various kinds, but the replacement of welfare liberalism by business liberalism raises new problems of economic and regional disparities. These problems are already causing social tensions and rise in conflict and criminality.

In the spring of 2011, coinciding with the Arab Spring which brought a whiff of democratic upsurge in West Asia, India also witnessed an extra-parliamentary anti-corruption mass movement led by Anna Hazare and an impromptu Team Anna that was put together. It was, by and large, concentrated to the metropolitan Delhi, Mumbai, and Bengaluru, with considerable numbers of famous public intellectuals and middle classes and educated peasantry: The movement stirred the Parliament to take note of itself by passing an empathetic resolution. A committee was composed nominating half of the members from the movement and half from the government and chaired by dual chairpersons from each side—Shanti Bhushan from the movement and Union Minister Pranab Mukherjee from the government. It was tasked with the job of drafting a Lokpal/Lokayukta (Union and State Ombudsman) Bill, which was the flagship demand of the movement. This was the first such drafting exercise ever attempted, but consensus eluded it and finally separately drafted versions were forwarded to a parliamentary select committee. The reconciled version prepared by the parliamentary committee was debated inconclusively in the Parliament and the matter came to a naught. By the autumn of 2012, the Anna Movement ran out of steam. It got split into an younger part of it led by Arvind Kejriwal and his cohorts forming the Aam Aadami Party (AAP) and a part led by seniors like Anna and his associates preferring to stay as a movement in the nature of what Rajni Kothari under the influence of Gandhi and Jayaprakash Narayan calls 'non-party political process'.[50] The movement has receded into the past, and AAP has been contesting in Delhi State Assembly elections and national and state elections in selected areas, but has scored notable success only in Delhi where it is the ruling party at this writing (November 2020).

Shortly before the 2014 general elections, the Congress-led United Progressive Alliance government, at the fag end of its second term in power, finally enacted a Lokpal/Lokayukta Act in December 2013. And, the BJP-led National Democratic Alliance government operationalized the Act in 2019. This was 45 years after such bill was first introduced in pursuance of the first Administrative Reforms Commission (ARC) recommendation (reiterated by the second ARC) and ten failed attempts by the truant political class that India has its first Lokpal in office.

FEMINISM

Today, in India, women's and ecological movements are among the rapidly growing concerns and their ideologies have come to pervade the development discourse as never before. Both are relatively recent developments, by and large, though their origins in modern times may be traced back to the Indian Renaissance in the late 19th and early 20th centuries. Both have come to a head in the 1970s and gathered momentum by the 1980s onwards. Modernization under external, mainly Western, impact appears to have been the catalyst in giving rise to both these concerns in modern times. However, the greatest impact of both feminism and ecologism in India can be seen where they do not challenge the tradition too radically and manoeuvre change incrementally. It is another matter that ideally a much faster rate of change is called for the emancipation of women from male and macho domination of society and for freeing the nature from industrial and sociological assault. Until this objective is achieved, equitable sustainable development would remain an empty rhetoric.

Ecofeminism in the West, rooted in the analogy of woman's and nature's biological, procreative, and maternal role, is echoed in Indian concepts of *Purush/Prakriti* and *Shakti.* The popular metaphorical ecofeminist theme is elaborated by Mies and Shiva (1993) in countering 'the capitalist, patriarchal world system' founded on 'three colonizations'—of women, of colonies and neo-colonies, and of nature.[51]

This new dimension of growing environmental and ecological conflicts among social and regional groups in India has been added to the conflicts over agricultural and industrial production and distribution. Environmental and ecological movements in India are not entirely new as they first surfaced during the British colonial Indian economy and politics. Yet their frequency and intensity has significantly increased in the post-Nehru era in independent India.

Madhav Gadgil and Ramchandra Guha analytically distinguish among *material, political*, and *ideological* aspects of these movements. Struggle over natural resources provide the material context, political action on behalf of or by the victims of 'development' sponsored by the state or the corporate capitalist sector forms the political sociological context, and attempts to forge a broad coalition of ideas and actions transcending party-divided political processes seek to create the ideological framework for extending the meaning and scope of democracy beyond the political to the social, economic, and ecological planes.[52]

All major religious traditions in India in their ancient texts, by and large, accord formal equality of status to women with men in this world, but in social practice since at least the medieval times, women have been subjected to abject male and social domination. Even equal inheritance right and alimony in case of divorce (unilateral summary divorce in Islam) enjoyed by women in the traditional Muslim personal law and reformed Hindu personal law (applicable to Jains, Buddhists, and Sikhs) remain a set of paper rights due to lack of enforcement or compulsions of avoiding unviable fragmentation of parental property. Education and individual employment or self-employment remain the main avenues of empowerment of middle class women and availability of manual work for working class women.

A recent development is the Muslim Women (Protection of Rights on Marriage) Act, 2019, abolishing the conventional 'triple talaq' right of Muslim husbands and crimininalsing it entailing punishment of imprisonment for a term which may extend to three years and also liable to fine.

A uniform civil code for all religious communities is envisaged in the Directive Principles of State Policy in the Constitution, but this constitutional goal remains unrealized. Even positive incremental judicial advance in this direction, e.g. the Supreme Court judgement in the Shah Bano case, is negated by parliamentary legislation by vote-seeking political entrepreneurs out to placate the Muslim communal vote to the chagrin of liberals even among the Muslims.

Development process benefits men and women differentially both in agriculture and industry. Everywhere men outnumber women in work force, in the industrial sector even more overwhelmingly. Almost everywhere women are generally paid less for the same work, are less mobile, and are losing control over physical assets, education, jobs, promotional avenues and technology. And in India in particular, women are a declining gender in number too. Capitalist modernization puts, at least initially, a double burden on working women, adding to the household chores and child-care the new responsibilities of the workplace. Everywhere women generally work longer hours than men, often doing the most arduous parts and still suffering the stigmatization of being absentees and shirkers! A cultural revolution of sorts is needed to alter the biased scales of justice. It is important to recognize that sex is a biological fact but gender inequality is a social construction and hence not only alterable but also desirably so. To quote Kapur and Cossman:[53]

> Although women in India live in an enormous diversity of family norms, we believe that it is nevertheless possible to identify a dominant ideology of family [probably they mean more than patriarchy] that informs the legal regulation of women. Familial ideology constructs the family as the basic and sacred unit in society, and women's role as wives and mothers as natural and immutable. This vision of the family, and women's role therein, appears throughout the law as self-evident, and beyond question. [It] ... continues to limit law's ability to deliver on its promise of equality for women.

Despite the visible participation of women in the freedom struggle in the Gandhi-Nehru phase of the nationalist movement, their representation in the political structures and processes can hardly be said to have gone beyond tokenism even in the 1990s. In 1974, the Committee on the Status of Women in India in its Report *Towards Equality* lamented:

> The difficulties being experienced by women in obtaining adequate representation and spokesmen of their cause in these bodies, and the declining trend in the number of women legislators is the result of the reluctance of political parties to sponsor women candidates. The parties reflect the established values of a male dominated society, which would be difficult to alter without certain structural changes in the socio-political set-up. The parties would continue to pay lip service to the cause of women's progress and the policy of 'tokenism' by having a few women in the legislative and executive wings of Government whose minority and dependent status offer serious obstacles of their acting as spokesmen for women's rights and opportunities.[54]

Yet, the Committee did not recommend reservation for women in the Parliament or State legislatures for the following reasons: (a) women's cause has always been supported by 'all progressive elements, men as well as women'; (b) 'separate constituencies for women would narrow their outlook'; (c) their 'interests as such cannot be isolated from economic, social and political interests of groups, strata and classes in the society'; (d) 'system of special representation may precipitate similar demands from various other interests and communities and threaten national integration'; (e) 'the privilege of reservation once granted, is difficult to withdraw'; (f) women must compete as equals with men as since 1952; and (g) the minority argument is inapplicable to women as they 'are not a community, they are a category'[55]. However, the above committee did recommend '*the establishment of statutory Women's Panchayats at the village level to ensure greater participation, by women in the political process*' (emphasis in the source), not as 'parallel organizations to the Gram Panchayats', but as 'an integral part of the Panchayati Raj structure, with autonomy and resources of their own for the management and administration of welfare and development programmes for women and children'.[56]

The political opinion on the issue of women's reserved representation has since changed significantly. The 1990s have witnessed the 33 per cent reservation for women in Panchayati Raj institutions, women's organizations and political leaders cutting across party lines are up in arms for similar reserved representation in the Parliament and State legislatures.

An amendment bill with this objective was largely supported by the women's movement but the segments of the movement were also worried that (a) "the quotas could form a ceiling rather than a minimum to be improved upon," and (b) "that women candidates might be pliable because of their dependence on male party leaders," and (c) "that reservation will treat women like a homogeneous group, which increases the likelihood that the 'biwi brigade' of the educated, upper class, upper caste women will be elected, particularly because the Bill does not provide for sub-quotas of OBCs."[57]

This bill, in any case, got passed by the Rajya Sabha early this year (2010) by the UPA government, but it has not yet been placed before the Lok Sabha. The government professes to be committed to it and says it is trying to secure consensual support of the opposition, mainly the OBC-led parties Rashtriya Janata Dal (RJD), Samajwadi Party (SP), and Janata Dal (JD)(U) and the Bahujan Samaj Party (BSP), a party of the SC 'reservation aristocracy'.

Women's movements by now have had a long and chequered history. Taking stock of women's movements in relation to the state as the target of demands, Lakshmi Lingam[58] gives a classification and evolutionary profile of women's movements as follows: (1) social reform movements, (2) agrarian struggles and revolts, (3) issue-based campaigns such as traditional roles and values of women, anti-price rise campaigns, campaigns on water, the Chipko movement, etc., and (4) women's liberation movements against patriarchy by "autonomous women's organization not affiliated to any political party. As is evident from the discussion, issues important for women are quite diverse with locations in diverse sites. This naturally diffuses and weakens women's movements, with the possible exception of the anti-patriarchy autonomous movements. This fact is also evident in an earlier study of women's movements by Nivedita Menon.[59] She shows that women's movements are concerned with issues as wide-ranging as development, social violence/violence against women, health, sexuality, work, reservation for women in representative institutions, uniform civil code, etc. Menon also finds that women's movements by themselves are not sufficiently powerful and effective. They face the dilemma that in all broader alliances forged by them with the nationalist movement, left-wing movements and parties, they must subordinate their cause and radicalism to imperatives of the nationalist or class issues lest they are decried as forces divisive of the nationalist campaign or class struggle.

In a more recent analysis of the women's movements, Anupama Roy observes that autonomy became the major objective and feature of the women's movement in the 1970s and 1980s. However, by the 1990s, "there has been a proliferation of autonomous organizations running on funds from government and international bodies".[60] It is baffling how can these organizations be autonomous if they run on funds from governmental and international bodies![61] But she makes sense further down the line when she refers to the observation of Menon[62] who decries the trend of "NGO-ization of the women's movement" pushing them into "rethinking autonomy in their search for radical political alliances and solidarity." Roy herself sensibly attributes this trend to "the liberalization of the economy and the abdication of 'social' responsibilities by the state to NGOs."[63]

Ironically, *India Development Report,* 1997 contains nothing on women's development! In 1970, females per 100 males in primary schools were only 60, while their percentage dropped to 39 in secondary schools. In 1995, as many as 62 per cent of females were illiterate compared to 35 per cent of males. Maternal mortality rate (per 1,00,000 live births) in 1989–95 was as high as 437. Contraceptive prevalence rate in the same period was only 43 per cent.

Beginning with the Sixth Plan (1980–85), there was a separate chapter on the concern for women's development for the first time emphasizing health, education and employment. The Eighth Plan (1992–97) mentioned the concept of empowerment of women and the Tenth Plan elaborated a strategy for this in terms of equal access to basic human services, economic self-reliance and gender justice.[64]

The 73rd and 74th Constitutional Amendments (1992) have recommended the reservation of one-third of seats in urban and rural local government councils for women. Since then 16 states have legally increased it to 50 per cent in Panchayat Raj institutions.

Environmentalism/Ecologism

Classical Indian texts and myths depict ecology as an integral part of man and society. India today has, however, become a byword for environmental and ecological pollution. Originating in the early 1970s, (e.g. the Stockholm conference in 1972) environmentalism as an organized movement made its presence felt in India and abroad by the 1992 Earth Summit in Rio de Janeiro. The Bhopal gas disaster of December 1984 served as a major alarm signal to bring it tragically to mass awareness. The media, NGOs, and agitations against big dams and deforestation have gone ahead of the Government and the industry in bringing the issue of ecological protection to the forefront of public consciousness. In 1980, the Union Government first established the Department of Environment, which was expanded into the new Ministry of Environment and Forests, in 1985. *India Development Report,* 1997 warns:[65]

> Environmental problems have become serious in many parts of the country. The main environmental problems in India relate to air pollution and water pollution, particularly in the metropolitan and industrial zones, degradation of common property resources which affect the poor adversely due to a degeneration of their life support system, threat to biodiversity and inadequate system of solid waste disposal and sanitation with consequent adverse impact on health, infant mortality and birth rate.

India in 1993–94 contained 18 per cent of the world's population and 15 per cent of livestock in only two per cent of the world's total land area, of which only one per cent was under forest cover. Within the country, India's forest area of 64 mha constitute only 19.5 per cent of the total land area. Vehicular pollution load (tonnes per day) in March 1987 in 12 metropolitan cities was a total of 2998, with Delhi topping the list with 872, followed by Mumbai at 549, Bangalore at 254, Calcutta at 245, Ahmedabad at 244, Pune at 213, Chennai at 188, Hyderabad at 169, Jaipur at 75, Kanpur at 72, Lucknow at 70, and Nagpur at 48. The Ganga even in Haridwar looks terribly polluted, to say nothing of the stream further down the plains.

In a poor country like India, environmental protection and upgradation do not get the requisite priority due to other more immediate economic problems. Although affluent nations of the world consume and destroy a greater part of the renewable and non-renewable resources of the planet, the visible pollution and threat to environmental quality is much worse in economically less developed nations. Deliberations at international ecological summits show that neither the rich nor the poor nations are either willing or able to pay for planatory ecological dangers like depletion of the Ozone layer, global warming, acid-rain, etc. or for more immediate threats to regional or national environments. Ecological protection must go beyond rhetorics and industrial and military calculus.

Environmentalism in India is yet to graduate from wild life protection and agitation against some specific developmental and defence projects to a comprehensive debate on sustainable development and alternative life-style. Even the apparent early success of the movement in a few instances is more in terms of media visibility. As Krishna[66] aptly observes:

> The success of popular environmental struggles, such as Chipko,[67] reflect the strength of social movements to counter the hegemony of the State. I have suggested that this 'success' is made possible only because popular environmentalism has an intrinsically conservative political outlook. It is this conservatism that enables the elite to accommodate the new political spaces within their scheme of things. Accommodation is generally a two-way process, which is aided by the environmentalists' predilection for symbolization and rhetorical techniques of persuasion.

She believes it is also true of the Narmada Bachao Andolan (NBA). The Narmada Valley Project the work on which started in the mid-1950s comprises 31 major dams, 135 medium dams, and 3000 minor dams spread over the States of Madhya Pradesh, Gujarat and Maharashtra. Among the largest such projects globally, it has given rise to perhaps the most sustained and controversial movements against ecological and sociological damages caused by such big dams in India since the Silent River Valley Project in Kerala stirred up popular protests in the 1970s. Incidentally, the Bhakara Nangal and Heera Kud dams in Punjab and Orissa in the Nehru era had escaped such social protests presumably because of the first flush of modernist enthusiasm in favour of these "new temples of development" planned by the post-independence Indian State. Popular protests have also marked the completion of the Tehri dam in Uttarakhand that caused displacement of thousands of people from their homes and hearths including the submersion of the entire town of Tehri in the year 2005. Besides social displacement, the dam is also supposed to increase seismic susceptibility of the region to earthquakes.

In October 2010, the NBA, which is often credited with having introduced an alternative development discourse in India, celebrated its 25 years as India's largest organized protest movement against the construction of big dams and the displacement of people. This Gandhian nonviolent movement could not stop the construction of the Sardar Sarovar Dam. But it did force the states concerned—Gujarat, Maharashtra, and Madhya Pradesh—to address the issue of rehabilitation of the displaced more seriously than before. Its campaign also led to the international financial agencies like the World Bank and USAID to withdraw funding for the project. The movement transcended caste and community divisions, mobilized women in large numbers, but the anti-dam protestors were often divided along party lines of Congress and BJP. They failed to stem the tide of Maoist violence among the tribal communities. In answer to the critique that the movement was an anti-dam phenomenon alone, Medha Patkar, the moving spirit of the movement advocates the concept of a 'people's parliament', a platform against globalization and communalism and for ecological democracy and sustained development.[68]

Environmental movements have been more effective when the people are threatened with an immediate dislocation due to submergence of habitat and farm lands as a consequence of construction of big dams and reservoirs. A prospective ecological perception and vision has been lacking. The success stories have been rather unique in their initial conditions and not easily generalizable. And, to get back to the conservative bias of Indian environmentalism, 'Environmental advocacy is wary of movements, such as the Gonds of Adilabad, where the struggles for rights are acutely destabilizing, even while a less threatening peasant movement like Chipko is celebrated'.[69] Bereft of the militancy of the more conventional movements of workers and peasants around the issues of production and distribution, the new social movements centring on the quality of life issues do not evoke the same passions on a common plane. They also lack the resources, scientific expertise, and institutionalized infrastructure to effectively counter the hegemonic scientific knowledge discourses of the Government and the industry. However, judicial activism on ecology and environment in the 1990s is a positive development in this regard. The Calcutta High Court pioneered in setting up a separate environment Bench. It must be complemented by civic action on this front from the civil society as well.

Some other social movements centered on the issue of environmental and ecological protection have occurred on the questions of forest management, inland water and marine resources, and aqua cultural farming. Tribal and non-tribal communities living in and around forests for a long time had exercised some kind of conventional community control or right to use forest resources for their survival. Laws subsequently made by State Governments changed this convention by claiming State control and regulation. An example of social movements protesting against this change is the Banwasi Sewa Ashram Andolan in UP which moved the Court with a PIL under Articles 21 and 32 of the Constitution. The Supreme Court in 1993 ruled that eviction of the claims of these people was not sustainable. However, the Government of UP told the Court that it planned to build the Rihand plant of the National Thermal Power Corporation (NTPC) in the forest areas concerned. The Court revised its earlier order to reconcile the claims of the State as well as the people by ordering the NTPC to offer compensation to the people likely to be displaced by the project.[70]

The social movements opposing over-exploitation of marine resources have also proliferated in several States spearheaded by the fisherfolks and their organizations supported by ecology groups concerned. Several Supreme Court judgements have tried to arbitrate over the claims of these movements and those made by the State Governments and the industries. Besides, the Union and State Governments have also set up several regulatory authorities in the area of aquaculture farming, including the Marine Products Exports Development Authority under the Ministry of Commerce, Government of India. The Chilka Bachao Andolan in Orissa has also been active in this context since 1992. This policy area has to deal with new problems and challenges arising out of globalization and the advent of multinational companies on the scene.[71]

Climate change, supposedly the most serious ecological challenge facing the wider humanity today, has only belatedly been recognized as an agenda for national and global action in the concern about ecological balance. The first major and successful international agreement in this context was the Vienna Convention in 1985 that led to the mechanisms for international cooperation in research into the ozone layer and the effects of ozone depleting chemicals (ODCs). This culminated into the Montreal Protocol on substances that deplete the ozone layer signed by 24 countries and the European Economic Community in September 1987. This protocol stipulates the phasing out of the ODCs (chloroflurocarbons or CFCs, halons, carbon tetrachloride, and methyl chloroform) by 2000 (2005 for methyl chloroform). Production and consumption of these compounds significantly depletes the stratospheric ozone layer that protects the planet from damaging UV-B radiation. Noncompliance to the terms of this agreement entailed trade sanctions. It also offered incentives for new signatories to join the agreement. Negotiations under the United Nations auspices aimed at an international treaty on global climate protection. The outcome was a framework convention on climate change, which was put up for signature at the Earth Summit in Rio de Janeiro in June 1991 at which the Government of India was also represented. The convention took effect from March 1994. It entails some binding obligations for nations such as limiting carbon dioxide and other greenhouse emissions by "addressing anthropogenic emissions by sources and removals through sinks of greenhouse gases". The targets lack specificity and a timetable for reducing greenhouse gases. Only developed country signatories are required to stabilize greenhouse gas emissions at 1990 levels. The convention thus sought to establish "common but differentiated responsibility" for developed and developing countries in accordance with their past and present contributions to pollution. The issue of climate change as it relates to India has the following implications:

(a) Although India is presently free from any obligation under the international convention, we need to be more self-conscious about the problem in futuristic terms,
(b) The Indian research establishment and community needs to undertake ecological research, especially beyond our frontiers, and
(c) India needs to have a comprehensive disaster thought, research and action framework for dealing with floods, droughts, cyclones, Tsunamis and other meteorological hazards.[72]

Two more landmark developments in this area are the Kyoto Protocol and the Copenhagen Climate summit. The former negotiated in December 1997 and enforced with binding effect in February 2005. The industrialized countries agreed to reduce their collective emission of greenhouse gases that cause global warming by 5.2 per cent by 2010 compared to the year 1990. The major polluters agreed to the national targets ranging from 8 per cent for the European Union to 7 per cent for the USA, 6 per cent for Japan, zero per cent for Russia. The developing countries were exempted. The Copenhagen Accord (December 2009) could not come to a binding consensus but industrial nations committed to implementing only voluntarily set reduction of greenhouse gas emission targets by 2020. It also accepted the principle that the polluter pays. It established a multi-billion-dollar-per-year trust fund to finance the attempt of the developing countries to cope with the problem of global warming.

Another major landmark development in this context is the Paris agreement within the United Nations Framework Convention on Climate Change, dealing with greenhouse gas emissions mitigation signed in 2016. In 2017, the US President, Donald Trump announced the United States' withdrawal from it. 197 members have signed the agreement, but 13 remain yet to ratify, including some major emitters. Its central aim is to strengthen the global response to the threat of climate change by keeping the global temperature rise this century well below 2 degrees Celsius above pre-industrial levels and to strive to limit it further to 1.5 degrees Celsius. It requires all parties to come forward to make their 'nationally determined contributions'. There would be five-yearly collective stocktaking of the progress made.

NONGOVERNMENTAL ORGANIZATIONS (NGOs)

India has had a long tradition of collective social activism including at the local level—as distinguished from the state or governments. In ancient India, the Mauryan state represented the strong state tradition, while the Gupta period witnessed a revival of social institutions at a notable scale. In south India, the rise of the Vijayanagara State marked a decline of social and local institutions of the society. The medieval feudal states like those of the Sultans of Delhi and Mughal Badshahs as well as the British Indian colonial state left large areas of life beyond the direct reach of the bureaucratic arm of the state to be taken care of by social and cultural organizations.

In modern India the main spurts in the origin and development of the voluntary, nongovernmental activities and organizations between the family and the state are to be found in the social and religious reform movements of the late nineteenth century, charitable and missionary work initiated by communities, Gandhian work in "constructive politics" since the 1920s, the 1934 Bihar earthquake relief organized by Rajendra Prasad, and draught relief coordinated by Jayaprakash Narayan in north India in the mid-1960s.

The post-colonial state in India established a huge corpus of bureaucratic and managerial cadre manning Government departments and public sector undertakings. Initiation of slow neo-liberal economic reforms since the late 1970s and their acceleration since 1991 have prompted strategies of bureaucratic downsizing and deregulation, generation and regeneration of civil society institutions, modally represented by the associational voluntary sector or nongovernmental organizations (NGOs). NGOs are not a new experiment; what is new is their mushrooming and enormous expansion. They have particularly proliferated in areas where government programmes are ineffective, limited, or non-existent. They enter the field as social activists executing schemes, delivering services, mobilizing opinions, creating awareness, prompting activities.[73]

India today has a large voluntary sector. NGOs are estimated to number approximately one lac, about one-third of which are supposed to be active on the ground.[74] The largest inventory of such organizations was found in the Foreign Contribution (Regulation) Act, 1976, which listed 12,314 NGOs as of 31 December 1989, in addition to 726 NGOs under its prior permission category.[75] According to a survey conducted by Society for Participatory Research in Asia (PRIA), 26.5 per cent of NGOs are involved in religious activities, whereas 21.3 per cent operate in the field of social community and social service. About one in five NGO is engaged in the area of education, 6.6 per cent in the health sector, and 17.9 per cent in sports and culture.[76]

The bulk of NGOs depend on domestic funding by State and private donors. In 1993–94, 10,963 such organizations received foreign aid totalling to ` 18,657 millions[77] Ironically, at least foreign aid was found to be more likely to go to more developed than less developed ones.[78] Although their role is recognized by all Five-Year Plans since the Sixth Five-Year Plan (1980–85), in particular, NGOs have become a strategic organizational alternative to the bureaucratic apparatus of the Indian state.[79] This experience of India may be said to be consistent with the theorization elsewhere that bureaucratization was more a feature of the early stages of rise of the modern state than of the more recent contemporary phases.[80] It is also argued that the global rise of the non-profit voluntary sector may well be as notable development of the late twentieth century as the development of the nation-State of the nineteenth century.[81]

The working of NGOs in India has not been entirely successful. Apart from their inherent weakness in dependence on Government, private and foreign funds and resultant subservience, they are also haunted by 'grantsmanly' flippance and corruption. The Central Social Welfare Board alone had blacklisted as many as 3416 NGOs in various States of the Indian Union for non-submission of accounts, misappropriation of funds, non-compliance of guidelines, etc.[82]

The dominance of the Center in the Indian state, even though changing since the 1990s, still provides the operating framework of NGO-state relations. Neema Kudva delineates three major phases of this evolving relationship as a subset of the changing state-society relationships in independent India. The first phase (1947–1966) coincided with the Nehru era when in the central democratic planning master frame the NGOs played a secondary and silent role in the nationalist reconstruction. The second phase (1966–1988), especially the turbulent 1970s, witnessed a contentious and antagonistic relationship of the NGOs with the state as the electoral contestation became overtly adversarial and the crisis of political deinstitutionalization deepened. The third phase (1989 to the present) is marked by the "active involvement of the state in the rhetoric (and reality) of promoting 'partnership' with the NGO sector, mainly through the increases in state funding for NGOs." Foreign funds have also expanded in the new ideological climate of the so-called Washington consensus of the 1980s in favour of neo-liberal capitalist reforms with increased accent on market and civil society vis-à-vis state. The increased emphasis on political decentralization in the 73rd and 74th constitutional amendments have also reinforced this trend. The NGO sector has under these conditions both mushroomed and become increasingly more professionalized. In the words of Kudva: "NGO responses to the state now cover the range from strongly oppositional to closely collaborative, sometimes reluctant, but pragmatic with the Indian state in its various forms".[83]

The Modi government amended the Foreign Contribution (Regulation) Act (FCRA), 2020, which regulates the acceptance and utilisation of foreign funds by individuals, associations (including NGOs and political parties), and companies. Among others, it stipulates that not more than 20 per cent of the total foreign funds received can be spent on administrative expenses, reducing it from the previous limit of 50 per cent. Earlier (2018), the Modi government had cancelled the licenses of nearly 20,000 NGOs receiving foreign funds under the pre-amended FCRA.

GOVERNMENT'S CRITICAL STANCE TOWORDS NGOs AND SUSPICION OF FOREIGN FUNDS

More recently, political atmosphere has turned inhospitable to the NGO sector on account of changes in both the national and international contexts. Nationally, the rise of the Hindu right to power in 2014 and then again in 2019 general elections and the global fight against money laundering and terrorist activities have contributed to this change. In July 2010, the Financial Action Task Force formed at the initiative of G7 called upon Indian authorities to 'undertake a comprehensive outreach to the NGO sector with a view to protecting the sector from abuse of terrorist financing as well as wider outreach in relation to good governance and accountability'.[84] The Modi government early in its first term cancelled licenses of over 10,000 NGOs—national as well as international. The nationalist drive of the government is also fuelled by the fact of the BJP's proximity to the corporate business sector, which along with the government feels impeded in its industrial and infrastructural developmental drive by the NGOs that fight for people's struggles for their rights to the natural resources (*jal, jungle, jamin*). Moreover, the Rashtriya Swayamsewak Sangh (RSS), the ideological mentor of the slew of the 'Sangh parivar' organizations to which BJP belongs, is itself a huge NGO in a competitive terrain with other NGOs (*Ibid.*).

The Modi government, through the Finance Bill/Act, 2018 brought about an amendment to the Foreign Contribution Regulation Act (FCRA), 2010, which had repealed the FCRA, 1976, that bans overseas corporations from funding political parties. Political parties are also barred from accepting foreign funds under the Representation of People Act, 1951, which lays down rules for elections. Through the Finance Act, 2016, passed earlier, the BJP government had amended the FCRA to allow parties to accept foreign funds. Now, it amended it further to do away with scrutiny of accounts of political parties retrospectively since 1976. This will put the BJP and the Congress off the hook set up by a Delhi High Court judgement, which had held both the parties guilty of violating FCRA.[85] Thus, a net effect of the Modi government has been the weakening of the NGO sector.

A report in The Economic Times indicates that the Modi government's crackdown on foreign funding to non-profit organizations has caused considerable decline of 40 per cent of flow of foreign funds for social development in India during 2014 to 2017–2018. The Union Home Ministry has cancelled the licenses of 13,000 NGOs active in rights-based advocacy. The list includes most well-known advocacy groups, both national and international. Nonetheless, the total private fund raised for the social sector is estimated to have gone up ₹ 70,000 crore in the financial year 2018, up from ₹ 60,000 crore in FY 2015, even though the share of foreign contributions has shrunk. The Indian private corporate sector contributed to the tune of ₹ 13,000 crore by way the mandatory corporate social responsibility (CSR) undertaken by them under the Companies Act, while individual donations amounted to ₹ 43,000 crore.[86]

NEW MARKET ECONOMY

The impact of economic liberalization on the Indian economy is evident in the growing share of private investment in the gross domestic fixed investment (up from $38,567 millions in 1990 to $1,84,605 millions in 1999), a jump in the number of listed domestic companies (from 2435 in 1990 to 5863 in 1998), and a hike in foreign direct investment (FDI) (from $162 millions in 1990 to $2635 in 1997). There was a marginal decline in subsidies and other current transfers as percentage of total Government expenditure (from 43 in 1990 to 40 in 1997). However, value added public (State) sector enterprises as percentage of GDP remained constant at 13.4 between 1990–97.[87] The disinvestment (partial or full privatization) has been accelerated since then by the NDA Government, but under the UPA public sector companies still own assets worth of ₹ 15,54,545 crores versus ₹ 9,74,734 crores worth of assets owned by the private sector companies.[88]

In India's mixed economy, the public sector not only still continues to be huge but has also reformed itself for better performance. In point of fact, "the performance of the public sector has been pretty much on par with private sector companies ... [This former is] ahead ... not only in terms of sales growth but also operating profits." The public sector is now ahead of the private sector by 5.2 percentage points in sales growth, by the same magnitude in operating profits, and by 1 percentage in growth of total assets.[89]

In the era of economic reforms, the role of the State in economy has significantly changed from a direct bureaucratic regulator to an indirect regulatory State performing this role through independent regulatory agencies with autonomous and semi-judicial authority under legislative statutes. In the last few years, such regulatory agencies have been set up under parliamentary statutes in sectors such as the electricity, telecommunications, companies affairs, etc., and more are in the pipeline both at the Center and in States.[90]

India is not a fit case for either a centralized command economy or a *laissez faire* market economy. We would do well to settle for a dualistic or diarchical model of state-market relations. This is important in view of the almost universal conclusion of studies showing adverse or mixed effect of privatization and globalization on segments of Indian society and economy and on public spending on social sectors of health, education, and welfare.[91] It would be undesirable by a society like India, marked by cumulative inequalities, regional disparities, and mass unemployment and illiteracy to allow the State to abandon its regulatory and egalitarian role in any substantial way. It would produce tremendous social and political upheaval disastrous for India's democracy, development and security.

Economic liberalization and political federalization have opened up the Indian economy to internal and external competition, and allowed a certain degree of leeway to autonomy seeking State Governments and institutions of the civil society from the deadweight of an overly centralized Central State in New Delhi. These trends have served a purpose. Carried to the other extreme, the Indian model of development and democracy would run into deeper throes of crisis. We must avoid this by all means.

It is still open to debate whether India has fully arrived as a civil society yet. The question marks in this regard are prompted by the high incidence of violence and corruption—structural and otherwise—in society, polity, and economy, and the enormity of what is called the 'unorganized' or 'informal' sector of the economy. This sector "either lies outside the scope of State regulation, or is officially subject to State regulation, but nevertheless does not operate according to the rules that State regulation officially prescribe."[92] According to one study of State capital, unorganized labours in various corporations amount to between 40 to 85 per cent. Only seven per cent of India's 390 million labour force are workers with regular wages and salaries and only half of them are unionized.[93] Lack of internal democracy and regular organizational structuring in most political parties and absence of gender justice in the bulk of Indian families, especially in rural areas and among the urban poor also, suggest that full social and political civility in India is still a distant dream.

MASS MEDIA

While radio broadcasting was instituted in India in 1930 and television in 1965, India leapt into the radio age only in the 1960s and the television age in the 1980s. By 1991, the All India Radio covered 95 per cent of the population, while Doordarshan (TV) reached out to 75 per cent of the public. The programmes are broadcast in India's two official languages—Hindi and English—and in regional languages that are official media in various States. The linguistic diversity of the country can be gauged from Table 13.1 that pertains to the print media. Following the linguistic reorganization of States in the present century, linguistic regional communities have become the most common criterion of the federal framework of the Indian nation. The linguistic boundaries were accepted for the organizational units of the Indian National Congress as early as the 1920s when most provincial boundaries in British India did not coincide with linguistic regional communities.

TABLE 13.1 Number of Newspapers and Magazines in 1989

No.	*Languages*	*Dailies*	*Other periodicals*	*Total*	*Per cent of grand total*
1.	Hindi	1013	7911	8924	33.0
2.	English	197	3430	4627	17.0
3.	Assamese	8	111	119	0.4
4.	Bengali	63	1822	1885	7.0
5.	Gujarati	53	807	860	3.2
6.	Kannada	148	784	932	3.4
7.	Kashmiri	0	1	1	0
8.	Malayalam	159	978	1037	4.0
9.	Marathi	172	1165	1337	5.0
10.	Oriya	30	375	405	1.5
11.	Punjabi	60	532	592	2.2
12.	Sanskrit	2	33	35	0.1
13.	Sindhi	8	73	81	0.3
14.	Tamil	192	919	1111	4.1
15.	Telugu	65	634	699	2.6
16.	Urdu	269	1526	1795	6.6
17.	Bilingual	37	1836	1875	7.0
18.	Multilingual	9	380	389	1.4
19.	Others	53	297	350	1.3

Note: All the periodicities other than dailies given in the source have been lumped together, and the figures in the last column have been converted into percentages.

Source: Government of India, I&B Ministry (1992: 320).

The mass media technology in itself is not inherently centralizing in its effect. It all depends on its structure of ownership and the contents of the message. The federal Government's exclusive control over the electronic mass media until the 1980s was countervailed by private ownership of major national and regional newspapers and news magazines. The long-standing promise of the Central Government to reorganize radio and television into an autonomous corporation has not yet materialized. The centrally legislated Prasar Bharati Act was legislated in 1997 and a statutory autonomous body Prasar Bharati came into existence in November 1997. Despite the government granting financial and operational autonomy, it is mostly in news for administrative and governmental interference. There have been occasions when some State Chief Ministers felt ruffled by the editing of their national day messages to the people by the officials of the electronic mass media, with some incumbents demanding allocation of a TV channel to the States. A more autonomous corporation can go a long way in removing these irritants.

Politics and mass circulation films have formed a close nexus in some States. This is especially true of the Tamil and Telugu film industry where matinee idols and others associated with films have easily mixed politics and films. They have used popular and mythological films in the service of political mobilization for successful regional parties such as the DMK/AIADMK and the Telugu Desam. The star fan clubs spread over the region engage in party political work in addition to film appreciation. The Hindi mega movie industry with its bases in Bombay, Madras and Calcutta with antecedent roots in Lahore, has been more metropolitan and secular, and in a sense rootless. That may explain why despite several attempts, Hindi film stars have not been successful politically. The Bengali film industry is deeply rooted in its regional culture but has not ventured into electoral politics, presumably due to its artistic and metropolitan propensity. Being the first major outpost of the British rule, Bengal experienced a relatively more thoroughgoing modernization than other regions of India. The new Indian nation in a very real sense was born in Bengal. From Bengal, Bombay, and Madras coastal areas, the national consciousness gradually percolated to the hinterlands. In the Gandhi-Nehru era of the mass nationalist movement against the British Raj and feudal princely rulers, the center of political gravity shifted to the more populous Hindi States and the bands of non Hindi linguistic communities around. The pattern broadly continued until the 1970s. Subsequently, the political configuration has become more widely coalitional and divergent in both the governing and opposition segments of the party system.

New entrants on the communication scene in India, ending the federal government's monopoly on electronic mass media are the CNN and the Hong Kong-based STAR TV, CNN-IBN including the Hindi Zee TV, and others. These communication options, however, are available only on additionally paid cables. A proposed entertainment tax on cable TV by the Bihar Janata Government at par with the entertainment tax payable by film theatres is likely to make them still more expensive. But to those they are available, they have overshadowed the Doordarshan.

The 1990s has witnessed an enormous expansion of the Government-controlled and private TV channels. Competition with private radio and TV channels has forced the official All India Radio and Doordarshan to multiply their bandwidth, channels, and programmes. The Government's promise to make them autonomous public corporation is yet to be made good. As many as 21 private TV channels can be viewed from Delhi and some more—regional ones—from States. Hundreds of private channels are in the pipeline. Most popular private TV channels include the NDTV, Star India/Star Bharat, Zee TV, Aaj Tak, Sahara, Jain, Channel 7, among others. These news channels are managed as private corporations with 74 per cent Indian equity with a maximum of 26 per cent foreign ownership, but managerial and editorial responsibilities resting with the Indian nationals. The Indira Gandhi Emergency regime during 1975–1977 was the only period during which India experienced press censorship. More recently, we hear some talk about informal pressures on the print and electronic media under the Modi regime more recently, but the media is much stronger now than during the 1970s.

From the late 1990s, social media has entered the media sector in India and is continuously expanding. With the ease of internet access, social media users have expanded to 326.1 million in 2018, the most popular among the various platforms being the Facebook, followed in this order by Google, YouTube and Twitter, among others. The power of social media is a double-edged swords of digital democratization and also misinformation. The exploratory steps towards the regulation of social media are taking shape. One issued by the Union Information Technology Ministry requires them, among other things, to proactively detect and delete within 24 hours any content impacting the 'sovereignty and integrity of India' or 'decency or morality'. Moreover, the Telecom Regulatory Authority of India (TRAI) has sought views from industry and public on whether or not the so-called Over The Top (OTT) operators like WhatsApp and others should be regulated.

The Supreme Court has recently (September 2019) expressed its opinion in favour of the need for greater regulation of social media to curb fake news, defamation, and trolling, while protecting users' privacy expeditiously. In India, social media platforms already come under the Information Technology Act and the guidelines issued under it and the Indian Penal code. A debate is underway on the issues raised.

The Government of India issued an Order in November 2020 bringing online news portals and Over The Top (OTT) content providers such as Netflix, Amazon PrimeVideo, and Hotstar under the regulatory purview of the Information and Broadcasting Ministry. From now on, government regulations will also apply to news on social media platforms such as Facebook, Twitter, and Instagram.

In the wake of the de-operationalization of Articles 370 and 35A in relation of Jammu & Kashmir and reorganization of the state into two Union territories, there have come to the fore the issues of state control of media and fundamental rights of Kashmiris and cases filed in constitutional courts which hopefully are a passing phase before normalcy is restored.

REFERENCES

1. Carolyn M. Elliott (Ed.), *Civil Society and Democracy: A Reader* (Themes in Politics Series), Oxford University Press, New Delhi, 2003.
2. Asutosh Varshney, "Ethnic Conflict and Civil Society: India and Beyond" in Carolyn Elliott, *op. cit.*, p. 429. See also Sudipta Kaviraj and Sunil Khilnani (Eds.), *Civil Society: History and Possibilities,* Cambridge University Press, UK, 2001.
3. Partha Chatterjee (2001), "On Civil and Political Society in Post-colonial Democracies" in Sudipta Kaviraj and Sunil Khilnani, *op. cit.*, pp. 174–178.
4. Partha Chatterjee (2002), *Ibid.,* p. 175.
5. *Ibid.*, p. 178.
6. *Ibid.*
7. Neera Chandhoke, *State and Civil Society: Explorations in Political Theory,* Sage Publications, New Delhi, 1995.
8. Lipset, *Political Man: The Social Bases of Politics*, Anchor Books, New York, 1963, Chapter 9.
9. Kothari, Beteille, and Gurpreet Mahajan in Carolyn Elliot, *op. cit.*
10. Lloyd and Susanne Rudolph, *The Modernity of Tradition*, University of Chicago Press, Chicago, 1967. See also Rajni Kothari (Ed.), *Caste and Politics in India.*
11. Rudolphs in Carolyn Elliott, *op. cit.*
12. *Ibid.*, p. 378.
13. *Ibid.*, p. 399.
14. Bipin Chandra, et. al., *India's Struggle for Independence*, New Delhi: Penguin, 2000.
15. *Constituent Assembly Debates*, Book No. 5, Lok Sabha Secretariat, 1999, 3rd reprint, New Delhi, pp. 978–979.
16. M.V. Pylee, *Constitutional Amendments in India* (A Documentary Sourcebook), Universal Law Publishing Co. Pvt. Ltd., Delhi, 2003, p. 206. This part could not become an enacted amendment to the

Constitution for lack of requisite two-thirds majority of the ruling Janata party in the Congress-majority Rajya Sabha as required by Article 368, the amending provision in the Constitution.

17. Supreme Court, *B.R. Kapur* v. *State of Tamil Nadu*, 2001 (the Jayalalitha Chief Ministership case).
18. Mark Robinson, "Civil Society and Ideological Contestation in India", in Carolyn Elliott (Ed.), *op. cit.*, p. 374.
19. *Ibid.*
20. M.P. Singh and Rekha Saxena, "Ideological Spectrum of Indian Party System in 1996" in Singh and Saxena (Eds.), *Ideologies and Institutions in Indian Politics,* Deep & Deep, New Delhi, 1998, pp. 246–250.
21. Ashutosh Varshney in Carolyn M. Elliott, *op. cit.*
22. Robert Putnam, *Making Democracy Work: Civic Traditions in Italy,* Princeton University Press, Princeton, 1993.
23. Hans Blomkvist, "Social Capital, Civil Society and Degrees of Democracy in India" in Carolyn Elliott (Ed.), *op. cit.*
24. The Agora Project in Civil Society and Democracy in India and South Africa from which Blomkvist draws his data set that dates back to 1995.
25. John Wilkinson, *Introduction to Social Movements*, New York: Basic Books, 1973, p. 27.
26. Andre Gunder Frank and Marta Fuentes, "Nine Theses on Social Movement" in Ghanshyam Shah (Ed.), *Social Movements in India*, New Delhi: Sage, 2002, pp 32–55.
27. *Ibid.*, p. 33.
28. *Ibid.*, p. 34.
29. David S. Meyer and Sidney Tarrow, *The Social Movement Society: Contentions Politics for a New Century*, Boulder: Rowman and Little Field, 1999, p. 4.
30. Mary Fainsod, Katzenstein, Smitu Kothari and Uday Singh Mehta, *Social Movement Politics in India: Institutions, Interests, and Identities*, typescript, n.d.
31. *Ibid.*, p. 37.
32. Lloyd and Susanne, Rudolph, *In Pursuit of Lakshmi: The Political Economy of the Indian State,* Orient Longman, Delhi, 1987.
33. Debal K. Singha Roy, *Peasant Movements in Post-Colonial India: Dynamics of Mobilization and Identity,* New Delhi, Sage, 2004.

34. Rajeshwari Deshpande, "Social Movements in Crisis?" in Rajendra Vora and Suhas Palshikar (Eds.), *Indian Democracy: Meanings and Practices*, Sage Publication, New Delhi, 2004, p. 387.

35. Ashwini Kumar, *Community Warriors: State Power, Peasants and Caste Armies in Bihar*, typescript, p. 23, subsequently published by Anthem Press, London.

36. *Ibid.,* pp. 29 and 39.

37. Rajeshwari Deshpande, *op. cit.,* p. 387.

38. P.V. Ramanna, "Internal and International Linkages of Naxalites", *Dialogue*, New Delhi, Vol. 6, No. 4, April–June 2005, p. 65.

39. Quoted by B.B. Kumar, "Editorial Perspective", *Dialogue*, *Ibid.*, Special issue on Naxalism, p. 7.

40. Government of India, Home Ministry, *Annual Report 2004–2005,* tabular data reproduced in *Dialogue*, *Ibid.*, pp. 182–183.

41. *The Economic Times*, New Delhi, November 17, 2010, p. 3.

42. Sukomal Sen, *Working Class of India: History of Emergence and Movement 1830–1990 (with an overview upto 1995),* K.P. Bagchi, Calcutta, 1997, 2nd ed., p. 24.

43. Sarat Bhowmik (2005), "The Trade Union Movements", in Mahendra Prasad Singh, Himanshu Roy (Eds.), *Indian Political System: Structure, Policies, Development,* Manak, 2005, New Delhi, pp. 269–270.

44. *Ibid.,* p. 270.

45. *Ibid.,* pp. 270–71.

46. *Ibid.,* p. 271.

47. C.S. Venkata Ratnam, "Changing Role of Trade Unions in a Period of Transition" in C.S. Venkata Ratnam *et. al., Labour and Unions in a Period of Transition*, Friedrich Ebert Stiftung, New Delhi, 1994, pp. 16–17.

48. Sarath Davala, "New Economic Policy and Trade Union Response" in *Labour and Unions in a Period of Transition*, *Ibid.,* p. 139.

49. C.S. Venkata Ratnam, *op. cit.,* p. 5.

50. Rajni Kothari, "The Non-Party Political Process", *Economic and Political Weekly*, Vol. 19, No. 5, February 4, 1984, pp. 216–224.

51. Sumi Krishna, *Environmental Politics: People's Lives and Development Choices,* Sage, New Delhi, 1996, pp. 269–70.

52. Madhav Gadgil and Ramachandra Guha, "Ecological Conflicts and the Environmental Movement in India" in Mahesh Rangarajan (Ed.), *Environmental Issues in India: A Reader*, Delhi: Pearson/Longman, 2007, pp. 407–410.

53. Ratna Kapur and Brenda Cossman, *Subversive Sites: Feminist Engagements with Law in India,* Sage Publications, New Delhi, 1996, p. 13.
54. Government of India, Ministry of Social and Women's Welfare, New Delhi, *Towards Equality: Report on the Status of Women*, Chapter 7, 7.103(a), p. 302.
55. *Ibid.*, pp. 303–4.
56. *Ibid.*, pp. 304–5.
57. Madhu Kishwar and Nivedita Menon cited in Amrita Basu, "Gender and Governance: Concepts and Contexts" in Martha Nussbaum *et al., Essays on Gender and Governance,* UNDP and Macmillian, New Delhi, 2005, p. 45.
58. Lakshmi Lingam, "Taking Stock: Women's Movement and the State" in Ghanshyam Shah (Eds.), *Social Movements and the State*, New Delhi: Sage, 2002, pp. 310–334.
59. Nivedita Menon (Ed.), "Introduction", *Themes in Indian Politics: Gender and Politics in India*, New Delhi, Oxford University Press, 1999, pp. 1–36.
60. Anupama Roy, "The Women's Movement" in Neerja Gopal Jayal and Pratap Bhanu Mehta (Eds.), *The Oxford Companion to Politics in India*, New Delhi: Oxford University Press, 2010, pp. 409–422 at 413–419.
61. *Ibid.*, p. 418.
62. Nivedita Menon, 'Elusive "Woman": Feminism and Women's Reservation Bill', *Economic and Political Weekly*, XXXV (43 and 44), 2000, p. 3839 cited in Anupama Roy, "The Women's Movement", *op. cit.*
63. Anupama Roy, "The Women's Movement", *op. cit.*, p. 418.
64. Meera Verma, "Women's Movement in India" in *Essays on Indian Government and Politics: A Continuing Review,* Meera Verma *et al.* (Eds.), Jawahar Publishers & Distributors, New Delhi, 2004, pp. 485–486.
65. World Bank, *India Development Report, 1997,* p. 95.
66. Sumi Krishna, *Environmental Politics: People's Lives and Development Choices,* Sage, New Delhi, 1996, pp. 268–269.
67. Chipko movement started in the 1970s' in Uttarakhand region of Uttar Pradesh, now a separate State.
68. Ajoy Ashirwad Mahaprashasta, "Movements: Call of the River", *Frontline,* November 19, 2010, pp. 29–32.
69. Sumi Krishna, *op. cit.,* pp. 269–270.

70. Poonam Kanwal, "Environmental Conflicts, Protests and Movements in India: Question of Survival and Democracy" in Meera Verma *et. al., op. cit.,* pp. 518–520.

71. *Ibid.,* pp. 520–525, See also Satyajit Singh, *Taming the Waters: The Political Economy of Large Dams in India* (1997), OUP, New Delhi.

72. Anand Patwardhan, "Global Warming and India" in Mahesh Rangarajan (Ed.), *Environmental Issues in India: A Reader,* Pearson/Longman, New Delhi, 2007, pp. 552–57.

73. Bidyut Chakrabarty, "Voluntary Associations and Development Imperatives: The Indian Experience", cited in Bidyut Chakrabarty and Mohit Bhattacharya (Eds.), *Public Administration: A Reader,* Oxford University Press, Delhi, 2003, p. 299.

74. R.B. Jain, "Non-State Actors and Authority in the Global System: Responses and Dilemmas of NGOs as the Emerging Third Sector in India" in M.P. Singh and Rekha Saxena (Eds.), *Ideologies and Institutions in Indian Politics,* Deep & Deep, New Delhi, 1998, p. 450.

75. *Ibid.*, pp. 450–451.

76. Asian Development Bank, " Overview of Civil Society Organizations: INDIA", www.adb.org/ Documents/Reports/Civil Society.../CSB-IND. pdf. Accessed on 16 November 2010.

77. *The Week*, 15 September 1996, p. 15.

78. Upasana Mahanta, "Role of NGOs in Childcare: A Case Study Prayas", M.Phil dissertation in Political Science, University of Delhi, 2003, Table 3.2 on pp. 77–78.

79. R.B. Jain, *op. cit.*, pp. 449–450.

80. *Ibid.*

81. Lester M. Salamon and Helmut K. Anheier, *The Civil Society Sector: A New Global Force,* Baltimore: Institute for Policy Studies, Johns Hopkins University, Memeo., March 1995, p. 3.

82. Mahanta, *op. cit.*, pp. 78–79.

83. Neema Kudva, "Uneasy Relations: NGOs and the State in Karnataka, India", paper presented to an international conference in Bangalore organized by ISEC/Cornell University/World Bank, June 10–12, 2005.

84. Bharat Bhushan, "Modi govt crackdown on NGOs: What is driving the repression?", *Catchnews*, 13 February 2017, www.catchnews.com. Accessed 10.10.2019.

85. *The Hindu*, New Delhi, 18 March 2018, www.thehindu.com, Accessed 11.10.2019.

86. *The Economic Times*, 10 March 2019, economictimes.com, Accessed 11.10.2019.

87. *World Development Report, 2000/2001*, pp. 304–307 & 314.

88. *The Economic Times, ET 50, The Changing Face of India Inc.,* March 2002, p. 12.

89. *The Economic Times, ET 500,* March 2002, p. 12.

90. M.P. Singh, "The Impact of Global and Regional Integration on Federal Political Systems: A Case Study of India", presented to the international seminar on the above theme in Ottawa under the auspices of the Institute of Intergovernmental Relations, Queen's University, Kingston, Canada, 8–9 December 2000.

91. Shurmer-Smith, Pamela, *India*: *Globalization and Change,* London: Arnold, co-published in the United States of America by Oxford University Press, New York, 2000.

92. Barbara Harris White, "India's Informal Economy: Facing the Twenty-First Century" in Kaushik Basu (Ed.), *India's Emerging Economy: Performance and Prospects in the 1990's and Beyond,* Oxford University Press, Delhi, 2004, p. 265.

93. *Ibid.*

EPILOGUE

India's Tryst with Democracy, Development and Federal-National State

Democracy today, like socialism of yore, is a hat that has lost its shape because everyone wears it. It means everything to everyone including its total disappearance among some sections in the name of supposed democracy itself! The most common versions of 'democracy' marked by its absence are the 'people's democracy' in the communist world that collapsed in the Soviet Union and Eastern Europe at the end of the Cold War or are undergoing a process of transition to capitalism in China and some other countries. Another such version is populist democracies with majoritarian pretentions in various parts of the world. Indeed, in the early decades of the 21st century, there is a universal trend of the rise of rightwing nationalism and retreat of capitalist globalization. India too has witnessed the rise of the Hindu Right Bharatiya Janata Party and its mentor Rashtriya Swayam Sevak Sangh, especially since 2014 re-elected with more formidable majority in 2019.

Most people in India are naively oblivious of the two compound terms 'liberal-democracy' and 'parliamentary-federal government'. Put simply, democracy is based on majoritarian principle, whereas liberalism is predicated on counter-majoritarian measures in the interest of individual rights, minority rights, weaker sections, and human rights. Similarly, parliamentarism is defined in terms of majoritarian nationalism and centralization of powers in the Parliament, whereas federalism is founded on counter-majoritarian principles and institutions of regional, multicultural, sectional or functional interests and rights, and decentralization of powers. A balance between the two foregoing values and institutions is for preservation of liberty and equality and national unity and stability.

India's democracy has generally received more generous assessment from observers for a much longer time than its developmental track record. Much ado about India's impressive economic growth is hardly a development of the decades since the acceleration of neo-liberal economic reforms in 1991, although India has suffered both an economic slowdown and pressures on the autonomy of democratic institutions and media and civil society organizations in recent years. We have put under analytical scanner in this book India's post-Independence achievements and failures in much detail in the foregoing chapters. We need not recapitulate them here. We do wish to use the space of this concluding chapter to highlight the fact that the 'glory' of Indian democracy lies in its sheer survival through the latter half of the twentieth century and the first two decades of the twenty-first century, and its going reasonably strong at the present juncture under the Prime Minister, Narendra Damodardas Modi. India's 'burden' is its inability to remove mass poverty and illiteracy and to provide a decent humane condition of sheer existence to a large part of humanity. In 2004–05, as much as 37.2 per cent of Indians were still living below the poverty line (25.7 urban and 41.8 per cent rural) according to the expert committee under the chairmanship of economist Suresh Tendulkar appointed by the Planning Commission. By the World Bank estimates over 80 per cent of Indian population lives under the global poverty line of two dollars a day. As per the estimates of the Asian Development Bank, in 2014, 21.9 per cent of India's population still lives below the national poverty line.

Yet in the midst of all this, it is really remarkable that India still continues to simultaneously pursue Project Democracy as well as Project Development. Despite grim apprehensions of a 'fascistic' slide, neither the Democratic State nor the Developmental State has appeared to be on the precipice of a failed state, at least not in the way of some failed or failing states in our neighbourhood inclusive of Afghanistan and probably Pakistan in South Asia, and some states in sub-Sahara Africa and West Asia, in our neighbourhood. This is a matter of some consequence in a hemisphere where failing or failed states have often been grimly debated in the recent literature of comparative politics. Even in the domain of economic development, if South Korea is found to be "galloping ahead" in a comparative study, India is at least rated moderately as "slow but steady": "On the one hand, starting from very little, India now has a substantial and diversified industrial base, considerably more sophisticated than, say, that found in much of Africa, the Middle East, or even parts of Latin America. On the other hand, when compared with a South Korea or a Brazil, the progress of industrialization in India has not been all that rapid, and levels of efficiency have generally been low."[1] And, it needs to be added that the impressive macro-economic growth of nine per cent in India in the not too distant past when India was among the fastest growing economies of the world, displayed a depressing mismatch with equitable human development and sustainable micro-economic growth scenario. Despite the recent economic growth slowdown and democratic and federal setbacks, India cannot be easily dismissed as a lost case.

How do we explain India's continued and considerable democratic and developmental success as political scientists?

SUSTAINABILITY OF INDIAN DEMOCRACY

One positive aspect of Indian social diversities is its distinctive overlapping and cross-cutting ethnic and class cleavages in the macro-national as well as in the micro-subnational/regional contexts. While this crisscrossing social matrix may make, in some sense, collective action difficult to mobilize across the cellular apartments, it also prevents, in another sense, passions and discontents to acquire the proportions of a mass political upheaval, especially in the absence of an overt structural common target like the British colonial state in the wake of the unsettled conditions resulting from the Second World War. Democracy in its robust electoral and federal versions, barring some states and regions of the Northwest and the Northeast, has managed to provide a reliable safety valve and prevented the rigidities and stultifications of permanent political majorities and minorities in Indian politics. This, to our mind, is an important political explanation for the sustainability of the liberal democratic constitutional regime established in 1949/1950.

Another political explanation of India's sustained muddling through the democratic and federal paths without a total breakdown is the gradual transition of an executive-dominated majoritarian parliamentary regime to a counter-majoritarian consensual and federalized political system of formal and informal checks and balances. India is not exactly a US-like formal constitutional separation of powers among legislature, executive, and judiciary and considerably more autonomous state governments in a formal way under a presidential federal Constitution. India formally belongs to the genealogy of the British Commonwealth parliamentary federalism leaning towards parliamentary centralism, if not parliamentary sovereignty in the British mode *a la* Albert Venn Dicey. In practice, however, it has moved closer to an institutionally complex system of deliberative democracy with a variety of formal governmental and informal political institutions in the federal and provincial states, alongside the media, market, and civil society organizations and institutions.[2] A culturally and regionally divided society and a set of divided governments make India a highly complex multicultural and federal political system. Its diversified party systems in the states and the bicameral Parliament throw up multi-partisan coalitional governing dispensations. These have at least some compensations in terms of enhanced legitimacy and national integration, despite some delays, indecisiveness, and roll-backs in policy making and implementation. This complex institutional labyrinth in the political system also makes the takeover of the state, especially the federal state, by authoritarian political tendencies evident in the religious-communal, Marxist-Maoist Left, and dynastic political parties at national and regional levels. Authoritarian forces in religious and political ideologies are themselves also riddled with inherent internal differences and even deeper contradictions. This makes a concerted attack on democracy and federalism difficult to mount or succeed.

SUSTAINABILITY OF INDIAN DEMOCRATIC AND DEVELOPMENTAL STATE

Like democracy, development in India has also miraculously survived in some form or other—socialistic, populist, neo-liberal—for over seventy years. India in the second decade of the 21st century has been, barring its recent economic slowdown, among the fastest growing economies (in GNP terms) of the world. Some degree of bare physical and social sector infrastructure were laid down by the British colonial state largely in its own interest and that of the British capital and empire. Following Independence, the modernizing nationalist elites set out on a state-led strategy of industrialization in pursuit of what may be called the Nehruvian 'socialism'. The Nehru generation of Indian elites successfully laid down the frameworks of the liberal-democratic state, the heavy industrial base, and the core of an industrial working class with organized bargaining power. By the time of Nehru's departure, the system faced the growing challenge of increased electoral participatory pressures from the newly politicized middle and lower castes that could not be easily accommodated by his successors in the "Congress system" (*a la* Rajni Kothari).[3] By the time Indira Gandhi managed to consolidate herself in the driving seat elbowing out her rivals among the Congress hierarchs, she was forced by democratic pressures to reorient Nehru's socialistic model in her own improvised populist model under a new personalized and centralized Congress power pyramid that sought to buy political support by an improvised phase of ad hoc populist planning. This made enormous fiscal demand on the state, public sector of the economy, and nationalized 14 major banks. However, it was successful at least in containing the revolution of rising mass expectations and frustrations for some time. The economy in overall term was also not marked by a downslide; if anything, the first signs of an exit from the so-called "Hindu rate of annual growth" (*a la* economist Raj Krishna) of around 3 per cent since Independence registered a marginal improvement in the Janata phase of resumed systematic economic planning. However, the Janata Party experiment of federal governance under a confederal party—a de facto coalition government as the pre-merger constituent parties continued to function almost independently of each other—proved to be a political failure, resulting in the fall of the government before its five-year mandate was over.

The Congress restoration in 1980 under Indira Gandhi sought to moderately alter the ruralizing and OBC tilt of the Janata Party government's politico-economic policy shift. Her successor Rajiv Gandhi from 1984 to 1989 proved to be more inclined towards liberalizing the economy from government control as well as accommodating strong pressures for federal autonomy in Punjab, Assam, and Mizoram by signing ethnic accords with regional parties and movements to buy peace. These economic and political reorientations reached a greater momentum in the phase of multi-party system with coalition/minority governments in New Delhi since 1989, especially following the

Congress minority government headed by P.V. Narasimha Rao that heralded the introduction of the most comprehensive package of neo-liberal economic policies of bureaucratic deregulation, privatization, and globalization. Since then and until 2014, coalition governments led by Janata Dal (erstwhile Janata Party, until 1988), BJP, and Congress alternated in power with center-right or center-left tilts. However, only the pace of move towards business liberalism became faster or slower under these changing political dispensations. The national and multinational business classes, by and large, were more likely to gain from the BJP-led National Democratic Alliance, and peasants and workers from Janata Dal-led National/United Fronts and Congress-led United Progressive Alliance. The overall tilt towards business liberalism with annual growth rate of 5 to 7 per cent continued to move up. This figure concealed, however, problematic economic and regional disparities.

In the late 1960s and '70s, the tardy rate of economic growth had failed to contain and accommodate the intra-elite conflicts and aspirations within the Congress itself and the larger political class in the opposition parties. The cumulative political pressures worked themselves out in the extra-parliamentary mass movement(s) led by Morarji Desai and later Jayprakash Narayan, the 1974 railway strike led by George Fernandes, the 1975 national emergency, and the 1977 electoral upheavals and the formation of the first-ever non-Congress government in New Delhi under the Janata Party. The Janata Party government phase had also deepened and broadened the federal/regional pressures of Indian politics almost throughout North India that was earlier limited only to Tamil Nadu since 1967 under various factions of the Tamil political parties and mass cultural movement drawing sustenance from a nexus between politics and film.

A crisis of federal power-sharing kept becoming deeper and broader. Throughout the 1980s, it expressed itself broadly in three forms: (a) electoral turnover of Congress regimes in Karnataka, Andhra Pradesh, Haryana, Punjab and Assam, etc.; (b) politics of insurgencies in the Northeastern tribal states that spread to Assamese linguistic community in the wake of the issues of the 'sons of the soil' movement against foreigners and migrants which remained largely unresolved despite the signing of the Assam Accord with the Congress government under Rajiv Gandhi in 1985; and (c) the surfacing of insurgencies and cross-border terrorism in Punjab (in the 1980s) and Jammu and Kashmir (in the 1990s). These trends gathered momentum and deepened *the political* and *economic* crises—the latter manifesting themselves in industrial deceleration, wheat- and later rice-crop Green Revolution failing to extend to other crops and wider areas, increased internal and external borrowing by the Rajiv Gandhi Congress government to revive the economy, and a severe balance of payment crisis towards the end of the 1980s. The euphoria of political and economic recovery under Rajiv Gandhi proved to be both illusory and short-lived. A more credible and sustained recovery—though far from unproblematic—followed after the 1989 general elections which ushered in the era of federal coalition/minority governments. Two paradigmatic shifts occurred around this time, which may be summarily labeled as (a) federalization—of the previously predominantly parliamentary regime—with increased state autonomy and regionalization of the erstwhile nationalized party system under the Congress party's predominance and the nationalized political system in general; and (b) acceleration of neo-liberal policy reorientations in 1991 predicated on economic liberalization, privatization, and globalization. These two broad new trends—new in the sense of greater magnitude and moment of these changes—were flagged by the metaphors of Mandal, Mandir, Market, and Marx. The majoritarian pretentions of Mandal of OBC politics and Mandir-Masjid politics of the Hindu Right were animated by intentions of emulating the parliamentary dominance of Congress vintage, but they really amounted to regional control of some state governments and coalitional power-sharing in federal governments. Market, of course, was the flagship of what is called 'economic reforms' or LPG (economic liberalization, privatization, and globalization). Marx refers to the continued Left Front rule in Kerala, West Bengal, and Tripura then for years until it was ended in West Bengal in 2011 and in Tripura in 2018.

The two terms of Congress-led UPA (2004–2009 and 2009–2014) and the two terms of BJP-led NDA that followed the earlier phase of relatively unstable coalition governments could have been expected to be better because of their greater governmental stability, but these expectations have not been as purposive and productive as hoped for. The former was marked by debilitating duality of leadership between the Congress president, Sonia Gandhi and the then Prime Minister, Manmohan Singh. Its second term was also marked by endemic corruption and policy paralysis. The latter has been marked by the Prime Minister, Narendra Modi's economic and political policy adventurisms, with disdain for experts and autonomy of states and independence of judiciary and non-partisan agencies and regulatory authorities and the media, adversely affecting both democratic governance and economic development. The economic downturn in the wake of Prime Minister Modi's adventurist demonetisation of 86 per cent of India's currency in November 2016 was deepened more disastrously by the outbreak of COVID-19 early in 2020 and its concomitant lockdowns that continued for long. Nevertheless, India as the democratic and developmental state survives and is not beyond repair or recovery.

In a nutshell, both democracy and development in India have survived considerably over a reasonably long time following the end of the World War and the Cold War. India's simultaneous pursuit of democracy *with* development, rather than development *without* democracy, rejected the assumptions of those who believed that developmental progress in cases of delayed industrialization and poorer countries is better achieved by a strong authoritarian state. To an extent not inconsiderable, Indian exceptionalism in this regard has somehow survived and is intriguing as well as admirable for its nobility as well as heroism.

James Manor in his contribution to an interesting volume in the Series of Oxford Studies in Democratization has persuasively emphasized the need for balance between order and conflict, self-interested personalized politics and institutionalization, informal and formal politics of institutions, continuity and innovation, and confidentiality and transparency in regimes in search of democratic developmentalism. He concludes:

> If democratization and the new developmental state are fostered cautiously, realistically, and (crucially) with an awareness of the need for the types of balance examined here, some of the unhelpful ironies that attend both processes can be minimized. So can dissonances between two processes. That can make the simultaneous pursuit of these two goals more likely to meet with some success.[4]

This is obviously a tall demand in the sense that the fine, delicate balance suggested here requires a rare combination of cultural and constitutional configuration of values and institutions, including leadership that few countries in the developing world can manage to provide or improvise. It is our hope, more than a fond one we presume, that India, with its complex cellular multicultural mosaic, mixed constitutional framework, and moderately centrist ideological spectrum may well have a reasonably high probability of success in actualizing the model of democratic developmental state.[5]

The major challenges for Indian democracy that lie ahead on the frontiers of development are: (a) human development, and (b) good governance. India's record in both these areas leaves much to be desired. Table 1 gives data regarding the level of human development in India in the South Asian comparative perspective. The data are statistically compressed and computed into a composite index measuring average achievement in three basic dimensions of human development: a long and healthy life, knowledge, and a decent standard of living. Globally, India ranks 127th with Norway at the top and Niger at the bottom 177th position. More recently In 2020, India's HDI value increased by 50 per cent—from 0.431 to 0.647—which places it above other South Asian countries. For inequality-adjusted HDI value, India ranks 130. Going back to earlier data, in South Asian region India is ahead of the rest of the countries, barring only Sri Lanka at 93 and Maldives at 96. In terms of Human Development Index (HDI), India with a value of 0.602 is below the world average of 0.741. In South Asia again, India is ahead of Bhutan, Pakistan, Nepal and Bangladesh but trails behind Sri Lanka's 0.751 and Maldives 0.745. All South Asian nations are within the global medium HDI level defined in terms of the values 0.500 to 0.799. The global High ranges between 0.800 and above. Within the South Asian region, if we stratify levels of HDI into Highs with a cut-off point at Bhutan's HDI value 0.536, India makes it to the High category, with the rest of the members of South Asian Association for Regional Cooperation (SAARC). This dismal level of human development alone, if nothing else, should prompt the regional warriors to forge swords into ploughshares.

Table 1 presents data regarding governance indicators in South Asia. The index is conceptually and statistically constructed so as to range from the notionally maximum value of +2.5 to –2.5. For interpretative code, the higher the value of the index, the better the record of governance. A multidimensional governance concept is fabricated with six major aspects: voice and accountability, political stability, Government effectiveness, regulatory quality, rule of law, and control of corruption.

TABLE 1 World Bank Indices of Governance in South Asia, 1996–2004

State	*Voice & accountability index*	*Index of political stability*	*Index of government effectiveness*	*Index of regulatory quality*	*Index of rule of law*	*Index of control of corruption*
Bangladesh	−0.69	−1.24	−0.72	−1.15	−0.86	−1.09
India	0.27	−0.81	−0.04	−0.59	−0.09	−0.31
Nepal	−1.00	−1.74	−0.90	−0.60	−0.82	−0.61
Pakistan	−1.31	−1.59	−0.57	−1.03	−0.78	−0.87
Bhutan	−1.18	0.84	−0.14	0.0	0.57	0.69
Maldives	−1.07	0.82	0.47	0.0	−0.57	0.12
Sri Lanka	−0.16	−1.06	−0.27	0.21	−0.03	−0.16

Source: "World Bank Policy Research Working Paper 3630" by Daniel Kaufmann, Aart Kraay, and Massimo Mastruzzi, *Governance Matters IV: Governance Indicators for 1996–2004, Washington: The World Bank,* June 2005.

The accountability index value for India is 0.27, the highest in the region, yet quite low in absolute terms inasmuch as the notional top value is as high as +2.5. Sri Lanka ranks No. 2 in the region with –0.16, and Bangladesh ranks No. 3. Governance in Pakistan is least accountable in the region, with –1.31.

In terms of index of political stability, Bhutan and Maldives are the most stable regimes in the region, and Nepal, Pakistan and Sri Lanka—in this order—are the least stable ones. India's stability figure is still negative but moderately so at –0.81 value. In terms of Government effectiveness, among the larger South Asian political systems India ranks No. 1, but with the moderately negative value of the index at –0.04, Sri Lanka No. 2 with –0.27, Bangladesh No. 3 with –0.72, Pakistan No. 4 with –0.57, and Nepal is least effective with –0.90. Gunnar Myrdal's characterization of South Asian states as "soft" in the early post-colonial decades still lingers on.

The index of regulatory quality is rated low in all of South Asia, with a meager positive value of 0.21 only in Sri Lanka. India at –0.59 is better than the rest in the region. The index of rule of law is also uniformly low across South Asia, but Sri Lanka and India have a somewhat better record though still with negative values of –0.03 and –0.09 respectively. Finally, the index of corruption control is again uniformly negative, excepting only Bhutan and Maldives that have marginally positive values of 0.69 and 0.12. India at –0.31 is considerably better off than others (but behind Sri Lanka) with a negative value of –0.16.

It is important to treat the World Bank data presented above with caution and a pinch of salt. For the measures or indices of good governance used are often trite and trivial if we look at human development with serious social science commitment and philosophically. For example, the index of rule of law is heavily biased in favour of property and authoritarian notions of law and order. For similar reasons, it may appear ironical that Maldives and Bhutan emerge as politically most stable Governments in the region. As it happens, this index is measured solely in terms of the longevity of a Government and undervalues democratic participation and protest. The challenge of capitalist globalization in the global South is more formidable than in the global North. For, both the economic well-being and democratic consolidation are much ahead in the former than in the latter. We in India need to develop our State and civil society to a greater democratic moment to take on the challenges of nation-building and globalization in supranational regional and global theatres. Contrary to the common perceptions, there is nothing in the new economic policy that undercuts the role of the State in any substantive sense in social sectors of education and health and physical and national security infrastructures. Delivering the Prakash Bhandari Memorial Lecture in Jaipur in October 2005, C. Rangarajan, Chairman of the Prime Minister's Economic Advisory Council, wondered in retrospect, however, if the slow and lop-sided development record of India would have been more balanced if in the 1950s and '60s the Indian State had put greater emphasis on agriculture and production of other wage goods instead of on "machines which can make machines". In his view, the "trickle-down" development thesis did not have any significant effect on mass poverty. He cautioned, however, that improved health and education are necessary but not sufficient condition for higher economic growth. "They only create conditions under which growth in the sense of rise in national income can be accelerated. However, enhanced human development expenditures cannot be sustained over a long period unless supported by accelerated economic growth." He sagely cautioned, though that lack of concordance between human development indicators and economic development ones could be a source of social tension.[6]

Rangarajan's caution underlines the fact that the state in India failed to deliver economic growth, and it had to bring the market back in a significant way since 1990s. Nevertheless, the state cannot abdicate to market fundamentalism. In a recent book *The Nation State in Question*[7] with a comparative theoretical perspective the concluding essay by G. John Ikenberry poses the question "*What States Can Do Now*" (emphasis ours)? The paradigmatic changes that he draws attention to as the backdrop of his poser is worth recapitulating:

- Disintegration of communism in Eastern Europe and Eurasia
- Emergence of market states in the developing countries
- Attempt to build rudimentary states in poor and undeveloped countries
- The rise of the geopolitical dominance of the USA
- Doubt about the viability of sovereign territorial states in the age of open market and mobile capital
- Ambivalence between supranational regional continental state and the abolition of the state in Western Europe ''the birth place of the modern, territorial state''

Where do we go from this complex global scenario? Summing up the collegial thought and analysis of the authors of this remarkable book, Ikenberry offers the lowest common denominator of the continuing *raison d'etre* of the state. First, there are no critical, modern institutional alternatives of the state—locally, regionally, transnationally, or globally—''that have the full multidimensional capacities of the state'' to be used in the interest of the all-inclusive national political community. Second, we are in for an age of a new species of the state. "The first half of the twentieth century belonged to strong states that could mobilize their societies for industrialization and war.... states [today] need to be flexible and work efficiently with societal groups." Third, of the four types of state sovereignty classified by Stephen Krasner—domestic, interdependent, international legal, and Westphalian—we have to opt for the most appropriate one for our times and place. Paraphrasing John Campbell, Ikenberry suggestively surmises: "[I]t is precisely because the advanced industrial countries have developed effective state capacities to manage their domestic socio-economic orders that they are willing to open their borders to high levels of international economic flows."[8] However, the same choice is not uniformly available to the states across the globe. Each state must respond to its challenges according to its own context and predicaments. India's national state due to its regional and internal compulsions is gingerly renegotiating the terms of its global and regional economic integration in the post-Cold War world with parameter-altering geopolitical realities.

In typical Western, particularly European understanding, the nation precedes the state and attains a fuller realization in the state. In modern Indian history, the state preceded the nation, which in some ways is still in the making. That is why any observer who is inclined to make a declaration that Indian nationalism has turned the corner on its unity and integrity must look over one's shoulders in agonizing reappraisal. In a way of saying, it seems to be India's destiny , not only in this regard, but many other, to be perennially on the threshold of arrival : about to reach there, but not quite there.[9]

In domestic and regional geopolitical context, the persistence of proxy-war via terrorist infiltration into Jammu & Kashmir has forced India to revoke Article 370 of the Constitution in relation to that state in August 2019. Despite Pakistan and China trying to mobilize international community against this move, most of the countries have looked at it as an internal affair within the domestic jurisdiction of India. China's abrasive rise to power and its growing authoritarianism is a challenge that India and other concerned powers are seeking to deal with strategic alignments sans alliances both regionally and globally.

REFERENCES

1. Atul Kohli, *State-Directed Development: Political Power and Industrialization in the Global Periphery,* Cambridge University Press, Cambridge, 2004, p. 285.
2. Rekha Saxena (Ed.), *Varieties of Federal Governance: Major Contemporary Models*, Foundation Books: Cambridge University Press, New Delhi, 2011. "M.P. Singh, "Federalism", in *Max Planck Encyclopaedia of Comparative Constitution Law*, Oxford University Press, New York, 2017 .
3. Rajni Kothari, "Congress System Revisited: A Decennial Review", *Asian Survey,* Vol. 14, No. 12, December 1974.
4. James Manor, "Democratization and the Developmental: The Search for Balance" in Mark Robinson and Gordan White (Eds.), *The Democratic Developmental State: Political and Institutional Design*, Oxford University Press, Oxford, UK, 1998, pp. 147–148.
5. For an early, seminal argument presaging the theory of democratic developmental State in the Indian context, see Mahendra Prasad Singh, "The Crisis of the Indian State: From Quiet Developmentalism to Noisy Democracy", *Asian Survey,* Vol. XXX, No. 8, August 1990, especially pp. 816–819.
6. *The Hindu*, New Delhi, 5 October 2005, p. 14.
7. T.V. Paul, G. John Ikenberry, and John A. Hall (Eds.) *The Nation-State in question,* Princeton University Press, Princeton & Oxford, 2003.
8. "What States Can Do Now" in *ibid.,* pp. 350–371.
9. Mahendra Prasad Singh, "Multicultural Identity and Democracy in India" in Veena Kukreja and Mahendra Prasad Singh (Eds.), *Democracy, Development and Discontent in South Asia*, Sage Publication, New Delhi, 2008, p. 67.

Name Index

Subject Index